The People's Patriarch

The People's Patriarch

Tikhon Bellavin and the Orthodox Church in North America and Revolutionary Russia

SCOTT M. KENWORTHY

OXFORD
UNIVERSITY PRESS

Oxford University Press is a department of the University of Oxford.
It furthers the University's objective of excellence in research, scholarship,
and education by publishing worldwide. Oxford is a registered trade mark of
Oxford University Press in the UK and in certain other countries.

Published in the United States of America by Oxford University Press
198 Madison Avenue, New York, NY 10016, United States of America.

© Oxford University Press 2025

All rights reserved. No part of this publication may be reproduced, stored in a retrieval system, transmitted, used for text and data mining, or used for training artificial intelligence, in any form or by any means, without the prior permission in writing of Oxford University Press, or as expressly permitted by law, by license or under terms agreed with the appropriate reprographics rights organization. Inquiries concerning reproduction outside the scope of the above should be sent to the Rights Department, Oxford University Press, at the address above.

You must not circulate this work in any other form
and you must impose this same condition on any acquirer.

Library of Congress Cataloging-in-Publication Data
Names: Kenworthy, Scott M. author
Title: The people's patriarch : Tikhon Bellavin and the Orthodox Church in
North America and revolutionary Russia / Scott M. Kenworthy.
Description: 1. | New York, NY, United States of America :
Oxford University Press, [2025] |
Includes bibliographical references and index.
Identifiers: LCCN 2025018508 (print) | LCCN 2025018509 (ebook) |
ISBN 9780197644751 hardback | ISBN 9780197644782 | ISBN 9780197644775 epub
Subjects: LCSH: Tikhon, Patriarch of Moscow and All Russia, 1865–1925 |
Orthodox Eastern Church—Soviet Union—Bishops—Biography |
Russkai︠a︡ pravoslavnai︠a︡ tserkovʹ—Bishops—Biography | Orthodox Eastern
Church—Soviet Union—History | Russkai︠a︡ pravoslavnai︠a︡
tserkovʹ—Soviet Union—History | Orthodox Eastern Church—
North America—History—20th century | Russkai︠a︡ pravoslavnai︠a︡
tserkovʹ—North America—History—20th century | LCGFT: Biographies.
Classification: LCC BX597.T5 K46 2025 (print) | LCC BX597.T5 (ebook) |
DDC 281.9/47—dc23/eng/20250821
LC record available at https://lccn.loc.gov/2025018508
LC ebook record available at https://lccn.loc.gov/2025018509

DOI: 10.1093/9780197644782.001.0001

Printed by Marquis Book Printing, Canada

The manufacturer's authorized representative in the EU for product safety is
Oxford University Press España S.A., Parque Empresarial San Fernando de Henares,
Avenida de Castilla, 2 – 28830 Madrid (www.oup.es/en or product.safety@oup.com).
OUP España S.A. also acts as importer into Spain of products made by the manufacturer.

For Oana and Paul

Contents

List of Figures	ix
Acknowledgments	xi
A Note on Dates, Spelling, and Translation	xv
Introduction	1
1. Beginnings (1865–1898)	11
2. Bishop of the Aleutians (1898–1903)	42
3. Archbishop of North America (1904–1907)	72
4. Yaroslavl-Vilna-Moscow (1907–1917)	104
5. The Patriarch and the October Revolution (1917–1918)	134
6. Neither Red nor White: The Civil War (1918–1920)	165
7. Famine and the Confiscation of Church Valuables (1921–April 1922)	198
8. The Case Against Tikhon (May 1922–June 1923)	228
9. Interlude: Transnational Orthodoxy (1917–1925)	261
10. Rebuilding the Church (1923–1925)	280
Conclusions	314
A Note on Historiography and Sources	329
Abbreviations	337
Notes	341
Bibliography	391
Index	409

Figures

1. Dedication of St. Tikhon's Monastery by Bishops Tikhon, Raphael, and Innokenty, May 30, 1906 — 89
2. Consecration of Reginald Heber Weller ("Fond du Lac Circus"), November 8, 1900 — 92
3. Convention of the Russian American Mutual Aid Society, April 1903 — 97
4. Archbishop Tikhon and Emperor Nicholas II in Yaroslavl, 1913 — 112
5. Archbishop Tikhon at the front with the 70th Riga Regiment — 125
6. Council of the Orthodox Church in Russia — 147
7. Patriarch Tikhon with clergy and parishioners in Golenishchevo — 192
8. Patriarch Tikhon after release from prison, June 27, 1923 — 281
9. Patriarch Tikhon in 1924 — 306
10. Icon of St. Tikhon the Confessor, Patriarch of Moscow and Enlightener of North America — 324

Acknowledgments

This book is about a Church leader who exercised his authority not singularly, but cooperatively. Although writing a book like this is certainly a singular enterprise, at the same time I could not have written it without a great number of people who have given me enormous help along the way. Various people have read the manuscript in whole or in part. I owe a great debt to Nadieszda Kizenko, who read the whole manuscript very carefully and made countless helpful suggestions. Francesca Silano also read the entire manuscript, and Christine Worobec read several chapters, and both provided invaluable feedback. A special thanks also to Aram Sarkisian, who provided fantastic feedback on the American chapters, shared digital copies of crucial resources, and came up with the first part of the title one evening as we were all sitting around for a drink and brainstorming at the conference of the Association for the Study of Eastern Christianity. Page Herrlinger also offered feedback on chapters. The Midwest Historians Workshop read one chapter, and my colleagues from the Havighurst Center, Ben Sutcliffe, Zara Torlone, Venelin Ganev, Brendan Mooney, Steve Norris, and Dan Prior, also commented on early proposals and later chapters. Thanks to Harrison King for inviting me to participate in the Berkeley Kruzhok and to all the participants, especially Victoria Frede and Stephen Bitner, for their feedback on the chapter I circulated. I am grateful to Thomas Bremer for hosting me at the University of Münster during my Humboldt fellowship as well as his feedback on parts of the manuscript; I also benefitted from presenting my material at his Kolloquium and from many conversations with colleagues in Münster, especially Alena Kharko and Rita Zimmerman. Matthew Namee and Monica Cognolato generously shared materials they collected. And to Lina Steiner for many conversations about research while at CEU in Budapest. Catherine Evtuhov also supported the project. Others who helped along the way include Andrej Szabaciuk, Aliksandr Gorny, Darius Staliunas, and Daniel Scarborough.

I am grateful to my nonacademic readers, Lena Zezulin, Jennifer Kassen and Brian Jonson, for their input. Simon Belokowski served as a research assistant at the Kennan Institute. Two students assisted as Miami University Humanities Center apprentices: August Hagemann worked on copies that I made from the YMCA Archive, while Ally Britton-Heitz edited the manuscript and prepared the bibliography. My former student Natasha Netzorg also read and commented on the manuscript. I am also grateful to my students in the Havighurst Colloquium seminar on the Russian Revolution in 2024 who read drafts and offered suggestions, particularly Matthew Reich and Mikhail Svirin.

Many colleagues in Russia provided tremendous help in a variety of ways. Most of all, Father Aleksandr Popov of St. Petersburg gave me photocopies of archival documents from the Russian State Historical archive. I am grateful for help from many Russian colleagues, especially Stanislav Petrov, Aleksandr Mramornov, Boris Kolonitskii, Pavel Rogoznyi, Aleksei Beglov, Sergei Firsov, and those at St. Tikhon's University, Fr. Aleksandr Mazyrin, Andrei Kostriukov, Natalia Krivosheeva, and Fr. Sergii Ivanov for sending me his just-published book so I could make use of it at late stages of my own. I am as always grateful for the archival guidance and friendship of Lenia Vaintraub.

This work could not have been possible without assistance from librarians and archivists at numerous institutions, especially Harry Leich from the Library of Congress (who will be greatly missed), Ed Kasinic, Anatol Shmelev at Hoover, Alex Liberovsky at the OCA Archives, Joe Lenkart and others of the Slavic service at the University of Illinois at Urbana–Champaign, and Matthew Payne of the Fond du Lac Archives for providing me with a copy of Tikhon's correspondence with Bishop Grafton, as well as all those in libraries in Russia, Lithuania, Poland, the United Kingdom, and the United States who helped out along the way.

Finally, this book, many years in the making, would not have been possible without the financial support of many funding agencies and foundations, including the National Endowment for the Humanities, the Alexander von Humboldt Foundation in Germany, the Kennan Institute, and the Summer Research Lab at the University of Illinois Urbana–Champaign. I am grateful to the staff at the Institutes for Advanced Study at the University of Notre Dame and Central European University for providing a great environment for research and writing. Grant and book proposal workshops at Miami University's Humanities Center both led to their desired results. Miami

University also provided support by providing funding for a research leave, a course release, and book subvention.

Above all, my greatest gratitude goes to me wife, Oana, and my son, Paul, who sacrificed many evenings, weekends, and summer months as I was writing the book and who supported me in countless ways. It is to them I dedicate the book.

A Note on Dates, Spelling, and Translation

Before February 1918, Russia followed the Julian calendar that was behind the Gregorian calendar used in the West by twelve days (in the nineteenth century) or thirteen days (in the twentieth). The Soviet government adopted the Gregorian calendar so that January 31, 1918, was followed by February 14, although the Russian Orthodox Church did not change calendars and ecclesiastical documents are frequently dated according to the Julian calendar. Throughout the book, the narrative follows the civil calendar—thus, the Julian calendar in Russia before January 31, 1918, the Gregorian calendar for the chapters when Tikhon was in North America, and the Gregorian calendar after January 1918.

I have used a modified Library of Congress format for transliterating Russian names into English, simplifying the -ii ending with -y and beginnings Ya- instead of Ia- (so Yaroslavsky instead of Iaroslavskii). In cases where individuals are better known by the English versions of their names, I have used these (such as Tsar Nicholas II). However, the standard Library of Congress format is followed in the footnotes. I have simplified place names by omitting the soft sign. Place names follow the official spelling used by the government at the time, so Kiev and Vilna rather than Kyiv and Vilnius.

When "Church" is capitalized, it is a reference to the Russian Orthodox Church.

All translations from the Russian are my own unless explicitly citing from a source already translated into English, especially Tikhon's sermons in America (abbr. *Instructions*) and the memoirs of Metropolitan Evlogy (Georgievsky) (abbr. Evlogy).

Introduction

On March 2, 1917, the seemingly unshakable Russian monarchy collapsed, ushering in the promise of freedom and democracy for the first time. For the Russian Orthodox Church—the state church and Russia's largest religious confession—this presented an unprecedented challenge. Though many Church figures were horrified by the collapse of the monarchy, others welcomed it as an opportunity. The Church had been under heavy-handed state control in imperial Russia. A vibrant renewal movement emerged in the last decades of the old regime that sought to revivify religious life by liberating the Orthodox Church from state tutelage and giving greater voice to rank-and-file clergy and lay believers. With the collapse of the monarchy, the movement for renewal in Russian Orthodoxy had its moment.

Emblematic of the freedom and renewal of the Russian Orthodox Church was the popular election of the archbishop of Moscow in June 1917. The congress of clergy and laity that gathered to elect the archbishop consisted of delegates who had been elected by deanery assemblies, whose delegates in turn had been freely elected by the votes of all adult male and female Orthodox believers in the Moscow diocese. The congress elected Tikhon (Bellavin) to be their new archbishop. Tikhon, who was fifty-two, had served as bishop in extremely diverse settings, including the westernmost part of the Russian Empire in both Poland and Lithuania, in North America for eight years, and in the ancient city of Yaroslavl. Although not one of the most prominent bishops in Russia at the time, he was universally beloved everywhere he had served. Tikhon, at least, was one who saw in the fall of the monarchy an opportunity to rebuild both the Orthodox Church and the Russian state on a new, freer basis.[1]

The debates around the elections for the archbishopric, taking place at a time of political and social polarization, were contentious. A Moscow diocesan paper observed that those who had served under Tikhon in all these different circumstances spoke highly of him. His personal life was marked by humility, and he was "always accessible to each and all. When he made the rounds of his diocese, he was met everywhere not as a boss before whom one had to tremble, but as the best benevolent father." Though kindly and good-natured, he was not weak but could stand up for his principles. Characterizing him as "European-enlightened and educated," the article concluded, "Archbishop Tikhon was consistently distinguished by a progressive orientation, and in church matters always an advocate of allowing local social forces broad independence."[2] Tikhon, in other words, was not a typical bishop of the age; he was tied neither to the autocratic state nor to autocratic ecclesiastical rule, but rather encouraged and gave voice and initiative to the clergy and laity in his dioceses. The periodical of the Moscow Theological Academy asserted that "Vladyka Tikhon was one of those few beacons in an era of gloomy ecclesiastical reaction."[3] Conservatives equally praised Tikhon as one who did not compromise the Church to political agendas of either the left or the right.[4] Tikhon was one of those rare types that both conservatives and progressives could claim as their own.

After the Bolshevik Revolution, Tikhon would lead the Russian Church as patriarch through one of the most profound upheavals in the history of Christianity, on par with the Protestant Reformation and the French Revolution. Just two months after his election as archbishop of Moscow, the monumental Council of the Orthodox Church in Russia convened to implement renewal at every level of the Church. No church council had been held in Russia for over two centuries. One of the first items on the agenda was whether to restore the patriarchate—the ancient and traditional structure of the Orthodox Church that had been abolished by Peter the Great two centuries prior. At the same time, Russia's first experiment in democracy was failing. On October 25, 1917, the most radical of all political forces in Russia—the far-left Marxist-Communist Bolshevik Party, led by Vladimir Lenin—seized power. Two days later, the Church Council voted to restore the patriarchate, and on November 5, Tikhon was chosen to fill that office. Now, however, Tikhon's role was not to be a progressive ecclesiastical leader in a free, democratic society, but to be a defender of Russia's largest religious confession in the face of an aggressively militant atheist regime. That regime was determined to destroy the Orthodox Church as an institution and uproot Orthodoxy as a cultural system that shaped the beliefs and lifeways of citizens to "liberate" them from religious "superstitions" and create the humanity of the future.

In the first months of their rule, the Bolsheviks passed legislation that not only disestablished the Church, but stripped it of juridical status and its right to own property—even the very church buildings themselves. Disestablishment quickly turned into repression. Patriarch Tikhon countered Bolshevik decrees and assaults with a combination of public criticisms against those assaults, efforts to intercede with the government to uphold its own principles of freedom of conscience, and appeals to believers to defend the Church.

The patriarch was immensely popular—far more than the Bolsheviks—and was viewed by tens of millions of Orthodox Christians as their spiritual leader. Because Patriarch Tikhon was a religious leader of international stature, the Bolsheviks could not silence him the way they did other opponents, so instead they sought to either discredit or eliminate him. Soviet propaganda proclaimed Patriarch Tikhon an archenemy of the state and of the people, a reactionary monarchist who devoted himself to overthrowing the regime by anathematizing the Bolsheviks and manipulating the common people with religious rhetoric.[5]

Russian émigrés, who normally assumed positions diametrically opposed to the Soviets, agreed that Patriarch Tikhon vehemently condemned the Bolsheviks. They believed that such a position was fully justified because of the antireligious policies of the Bolsheviks against the Church and overthrow of everything that old Russia represented. In the émigré interpretation, despite years of immense pressure, Patriarch Tikhon stayed true to the Church and became a martyr through the years of suffering inflicted by the Soviet regime.

These conflicting depictions of Patriarch Tikhon portray him in completely contrary ways: the progressive, open, down-to-earth bishop beloved by the people, the arch-counter-revolutionary and enemy of the people who used the Church as a cloak to mask and coordinate his political activities aimed at overthrowing the Soviet regime, or the anticommunist martyr persecuted by the militantly antireligious Soviet regime. Who was the real Patriarch Tikhon? What was the nature of the relationship between the Russian Orthodox Church under his leadership and the Soviet regime? Although more than three decades have passed since the collapse of communism, the revival of the Orthodox Church in Russia, and the opening of the archives, no historians in the West have even attempted to answer these questions. If they bother to mention Patriarch Tikhon at all, one of the old images is repeated uncritically—most often some variant derived from Soviet propaganda. With the opening of access to Soviet archives and the publication of critical documents from the Orthodox Church, the Bolshevik

Party, the Soviet state, and the secret police, it is now possible to tell his story in a way never before possible.

The Persistence of Belief in the Soviet Union

In 1917, when the Bolsheviks seized power, the Russian Orthodox Church was a vast institution, and Orthodox Christianity formed the worldview and value system of the majority of Russian citizens. On the eve of World War I, there were 115 million registered Orthodox Christians—70 percent of the Russian Empire's population, with very high levels of religious observance.[6] The Orthodox Church had an institutional structure that reached from a central administration down to virtually every single village, and its beliefs were profoundly intertwined with the daily life of people of all social classes. But since the Bolsheviks aimed not only to transform Russia's political and economic structure but completely revolutionize the mentalities and values of the population, they inevitably came into conflict with the worldview which they sought to displace and replace. It was not just about the institution of the Orthodox Church, but about transforming the culture and values of every single person in the realm. It was a colossal and brutal effort of social engineering.

Twenty years after the Bolshevik Revolution, in 1937, the Soviet government conducted a census in which they discovered the astounding fact that 56 percent of Soviet citizens still believed in God versus 43 percent who were nonbelievers. Stalin added the question about religion to assess the success of the antireligious campaign. Dismayed at the outcome, he suppressed the results of the census and then embarked on a brutal, all-out reign of terror to exterminate religion and those who represented it. Out of 98 million people over the age of sixteen whose data were collected, over 41 million (42.3 percent of the population and 75 percent of those who claimed to be believers) identified themselves as Orthodox Christians, despite rumors that those identified as believers might suffer consequences.[7] Twenty years of Soviet efforts to eradicate religion and Orthodox Christianity had not succeeded, despite atheist education in the schools, attacks on the institution of the Orthodox Church, and repression against clergy and believers.

The fact that more than half the population dared to tell representatives of the Soviet government of their belief and religious identity after twenty years of the most sustained and brutal antireligious campaign the world had ever seen means that for those 40 million people, faith was not nominal, but rather something deeply held. If that was true twenty years after the Revolution, how much more must that have been the case at the time of the Revolution? There were those who hated the Church with a passion and lashed out at it in revolutionary fervor, and no small number of those who were either nominal believers or indifferent to faith. All the same, if 40 million were still committed Orthodox believers in 1937, that number must have been far higher a generation earlier.

This is an astonishing fact that historians have not even acknowledged, let alone reckoned with its implications. Two questions arise from this discovery: If the overwhelming majority of Russian citizens were Orthodox Christians at the time of the Revolution, holding a worldview that the Bolsheviks believed to be totally incompatible with the future world they were trying to build and which, therefore, had to be eradicated, how is it that Western historians of Russia have almost completely ignored this dimension of the Russian Revolution? Second, how did Orthodoxy survive after twenty years of aggressive antireligious campaigns?

Western Historiography of the Orthodox Church and Revolution

Western historians of Russia have almost completely neglected this crucial dimension of the Russian Revolution. The body of historical literature about the Russian Revolution is vast, yet magisterial works published for the centenary of the Russian Revolution (since 2017) completely ignore Russian Orthodoxy as if it did not matter.[8] This neglect has a history. It stems from a disinterest in religion among secular historians, a bias against the Russian Orthodox Church inherited from the Russian intellectuals that shaped early Russian historiography in the West, and because scholars of the Soviet Union were influenced by the narrative shaped by the Soviets themselves. It had become standard to view the Russian Orthodox Church as a mere prop of the imperial state, which, in turn, was propped up by the old regime—so that, when the latter fell, the Church crumbled alongside it. In such a view, the Church simply ceased to be relevant in the atheist, secular Soviet state, not a subject that warranted research. In fact, the Soviet government expended enormous energy and violence to make it disappear—and ultimately failed, as Orthodoxy outlasted the Soviet experiment itself, reemerging as a powerful force in contemporary Russia.[9]

Even today, the default resource for historians writing about the Orthodox Church and the Bolshevik Revolution remains John Shelton Curtiss's *The Russian Church and the Soviet State, 1917–1950*, published in 1953.[10] Its overarching narrative long prevailed, despite the fact that it was based primarily upon Soviet sources and the general framework established by Soviet propaganda.[11] According to Curtiss's narrative, the Orthodox Church leadership was actively playing a conservative political role after the February Revolution. After the Bolshevik seizure of power, the government passed progressive legislation separating church and state and granting freedom of conscience to create a secular society along Western lines through legal means. The Orthodox Church, fearing the loss of its wealth and privileges, became a counter-revolutionary agent to subvert the Soviet regime. Patriarch Tikhon's messages in 1918 were intended to arouse the populace against the Soviet regime, but the patriarch's policy proved ineffective because the people did not support the Church, so that the Church leadership turned its support to the anti-Bolshevik White Army. Despite the openly hostile attitude of the Church and Patriarch Tikhon, the Bolsheviks allegedly remained conciliatory and did not retaliate, but advocated moderation instead. In this narrative, it was the Church that provoked the Bolsheviks into using repressive measures, which Curtiss attempted to render understandable and even justifiable.[12] Even when admitting that there was insufficient evidence to corroborate Soviet claims, he gave preference to their interpretations over others and lent them credibility.

With the publication of previously inaccessible documents since the collapse of the Soviet Union, including those from the highest level of the Soviet leadership and the secret police, it is now possible to reassess this history (see the Note on Historiography and Sources). Given that the Bolsheviks had no more qualms about using deception to achieve their aims than they did violence,[13] public statements made by Bolshevik leaders and coverage of Soviet newspapers can now be examined in the light of internal and secret reports, memos, directives, and actual policy. At the same time, conflicting views among Bolshevik leaders also shaped how policy developed.

Tikhon's legacy was a complex and contested one throughout the twentieth century. Although Russian émigré literature about the Orthodox Church was largely dismissed by Curtiss and has had little impact on Western historiography of the Soviet Union, it has had a larger impact on shaping perceptions of Patriarch Tikhon, especially among Orthodox believers in the West. Paradoxically, Russian émigré and Soviet approaches converge on one point, namely in depicting Patriarch Tikhon as unfalteringly hostile to the Soviet regime. Although the Russian Orthodox Church Abroad canonized Tikhon as a saint in 1981, it had difficulties in interpreting the patriarch's final years, when he became willing to compromise with the Soviet government. By contrast, the Russian Orthodox Church of the Moscow Patriarchate emphasized his last years precisely as a justification for its subsequent policy of compromise with the Soviet regime.

Although Patriarch Tikhon was looked upon as the spiritual leader by tens of millions of Orthodox believers at the time of his death in 1925, he has been virtually ignored by Western historians.[14] Although there are countless biographies of Rasputin, Nicholas II, Lenin, Trotsky, and Stalin, as well as biographies of many minor figures of the revolutionary era, the only book in English devoted to him is Jane Swan's *Biography of Patriarch Tikhon*, published by the Holy Trinity Monastery in 1964 and based on her dissertation written in 1955.[15] In Russia, there is a large and growing body of specialized studies, but even in Russian there is no adequate scholarly biography which tells the story of his whole life.[16] To understand his role during the Revolution and the legacy of his leadership after the Revolution, it is crucial to understand the kind of Church leader Tikhon had become before 1917—especially the many years he spent in North America. Those experiences had an impact on how he navigated questions of the relationship of the Church to politics and the state.

Orthodox Christianity and Modernity

Returning to the 1937 census, the second crucial question is, How did Orthodoxy survive twenty years of militant atheist propaganda and policy? And how did it outlast the Soviet system? This is an enormous question, one which requires far more research into religion at the grassroots level. This book argues that Patriarch Tikhon's leadership proved decisive. As a Church leader committed to the principle of conciliarity that gave voice to rank-and-file clergy and ordinary believers, he empowered them to make their churches their own, to take control over them and be responsible for them, at a decisive moment in 1918. As a result, even when the Soviets were attacking the Church hierarchy, that was not enough to uproot the faith as guarded by the people.

Second, the patriarch sought a course that would defend and uphold Orthodoxy, while realizing that this would require negotiation and conciliation in the Soviet context. This proved to be of pivotal importance for Orthodoxy's survival as well—though Patriarch Tikhon's successors were less successful in keeping the balance between compromise and protecting the integrity of the Church. In the late Soviet era, the leadership (at the top, though by no means at all levels) of the Russian Orthodox Church was firmly controlled by the regime—a condition that has returned in the Putin era.

Patriarch Tikhon was in a unique position of confronting an entire series of distinctly modern challenges to the Orthodox Church, which renders his story one of enduring significance. In his years in North America, he encountered a secular state with a degree of religious pluralism unknown in Russia. It was an environment where Orthodox Christians were a tiny minority and composed of diverse ethnicities and national Orthodox traditions. Here Tikhon's goal was to maintain an overarching unity of ecclesiastical structure while supporting the maintenance of distinct Orthodox traditions. While assuming the Orthodox Church in America would remain under the jurisdiction of Russia until the time came when it would become a completely independent (autocephalous) Orthodox Church, he advocated broad autonomy for the American Church and sought to act in concert with the home Orthodox Churches where immigrants stemmed from such as the patriarchate of Antioch and the leadership of the Serbian Orthodox Church.

Tikhon observed that American culture, which was pragmatic and materialistic but also religious, was very different from Russian lifeways that were steeped in Orthodoxy. He always encouraged his flock to stay true to the faith of their forebears. At the same time, he did not see American culture as a threat to Orthodoxy. He did not find it a problem that Orthodox children would attend American public schools, believing it was the role of the churches to provide them with religious education, something he placed much emphasis on. He also sought to mobilize the American "congregationalist" spirit, where the laity had so much control over their local church, rather than seeing it as a threat to his authority.

When faced with religious pluralism in America, Tikhon was defensive against those he saw trying to "poach" his flock away from the Orthodox Church, especially Protestant and Catholic missionaries in Alaska.

Otherwise, however, he developed very cordial relations with religious others, especially the Episcopal Church in America, and his efforts led to the establishment of a commission in Russia to develop ecumenical ties with the Episcopal Church. During the 1921 famine in Soviet Russia, Tikhon appealed to world Christian leaders, including the pope and the archbishop of Canterbury, for assistance, and they responded. When Tikhon was under arrest and facing trial in the Soviet Union, the archbishop of Canterbury and the ecumenical patriarch issued strong statements in his defense, and this played an important role in saving his life. Despite subsequent intense pressures by the Soviet government for him to issue statements criticizing these international church leaders, he staunchly refused to comply.

While seeing the differences between American and Russian culture, Tikhon did not interpret the world through the lens of any sort of "clash of civilizations" between some ostensible Russian or Orthodox culture and the West. He understood the complexities of the modern world were greater than a simplistic binary contrast between Russia and the West. Rather, the challenge of modernity was secularization, the loss of faith and rootedness in tradition, because he believed that a life deprived of higher values became impoverished when reduced to selfish materialistic ends. In Tikhon's view of the world, a life centered on the love of God and one's neighbor was infinitely more fulfilling, even if it demanded self-sacrifice, than one centered on the self.

From that vantage point, he understood that Russia was facing the challenges of modernity just as America was, and he sought to prepare his flock for those challenges. In Yaroslavl and Lithuania, he did not find the solutions to Russia's challenges in the realm of politics. He understood that tying the Church to political platforms would only serve to subordinate the Church to those political agendas. His position on that point did not change even after the Bolshevik seizure of power: He consistently argued that the roots of Russia's problems were spiritual, and so the solutions also had to be spiritual. Even though Bolshevism was so contrary to his Christian worldview, he did not oppose it by embracing an opposing political platform, let alone support military action aimed to overthrow the Soviet regime. His criticisms against the Soviet regime never focused on socialism per se, that is, the Bolshevik socioeconomic platform, but rather on their atheism and materialism that denied any higher meaning and value to human life together with their notions of class conflict that served to divide rather than unite people and justified civil war and repression.

As patriarch, Tikhon did not respond to the Bolshevik Revolution in a simplistic, rigid way. Rather, his leadership was constantly adapting, seeking the balance between adherence to principles that must not be compromised and dialogue where compromise was possible. At first, he rejected the 1918 Soviet law on the separation of church and state because it stripped the Orthodox Church of its legal status and right to own property. Subsequently, however, he became the champion of the separation of church and state and the Soviet Constitution's declaration of freedom of conscience, repeatedly arguing with the Soviet leadership that particular policies in fact violated the Soviets' own laws and principles. So long as Lenin was alive, those arguments fell on deaf ears, but after Lenin's death they even succeeded in convincing some Soviet leaders that Tikhon was right. Instead of doggedly condemning the Soviet regime and rejecting any dialogue with it—which probably would have resulted in his martyrdom—he skillfully negotiated, making compromises in exchange for concessions that saved the Church when it was most threatened.

The extreme challenges that Patriarch Tikhon had to confront in the face of a hostile totalitarian state place him alongside other major religious figures generally better known in the West, such as Dietrich Bonhoeffer. Popes John Paul II and Francis also had to face momentous global transformations, from the collapse of communism to climate change and the culture wars, and sought to find ways of balancing adherence to the principles of faith while adapting to the modern world. Such endeavors are never without controversy. Contrary to the mutual suspicion that dominates the relationship of Orthodox Church leaders in the early twenty-first century, however, Patriarch Tikhon consistently sought to unite people rather than divide them, and chose dialogue and reconciliation over confrontation and conflict, all without sacrificing his principles.

1
Beginnings (1865–1898)

Patriarch Tikhon was born on January 19, 1865, in Klin (Toropets district, Pskov province), a remote village deep in northwestern provincial Russia between Moscow and Riga. At his baptism four days later, he was given the name Vasily (Basil), after St. Basil the Great, the fourth-century bishop of Caesarea. His full name was Vasily Ivanovich Bellavin. He always spelled his family name with two *l*'s, although it is frequently misspelled with one *l* (even in Church sources), thanks to an early Soviet mistake.[1] On taking monastic vows decades later, in accordance with Orthodox tradition, he was given a new name: Tikhon.

Background and Historical Context

Patriarch Tikhon's life spanned a period of profound social and political transformation in Russia, culminating in two revolutions in 1917 and the consolidation of the Soviet state in the early 1920s. All of this had a profound impact on the Russian Orthodox Church as well. Given Tikhon's postings in diverse parts of the Russian Empire (including Poland) and his experiences with former Greek Catholics in the Orthodox Church, some context is necessary.

Orthodoxy was the historically dominant form of Christianity in Russia through the centuries. The Eastern Slavs adopted Christianity in 988 from Constantinople. Adopting the Greek rather than Latin form of Christianity had profound consequences, including Slavic liturgical language, eastern liturgical rites, and a married priesthood.[2] After Kyivan Rus was conquered by the Mongols in 1240, the Poles and Lithuanians conquered the western parts of the Rus lands. These different historical trajectories, broadly speaking, led to the eventual emergence of three different peoples—the Russians (or Muscovites), who were subject to the Mongols, and the Ukrainians and Belarusians, who were ruled over by the Poles and Lithuanians. The Orthodox Church had a prominent place in Lithuania in the thirteenth and fourteenth centuries. In 1387, however, Lithuania officially became Roman Catholic, at the same time that Poland and Lithuania began to be ruled by the same monarch.[3] Orthodoxy was tolerated in Poland-Lithuania (after 1569 the Polish-Lithuanian Commonwealth) until after the Reformation in the sixteenth century. At the Union of Brest in 1595–1596, the Orthodox bishops transferred their jurisdiction from Constantinople to Rome and the Orthodox hierarchy was outlawed for several decades to enforce religious unity. The resulting Church, known as Uniate (the term "Uniate" was commonly used as a self-designator in the nineteenth and early twentieth century, though considered pejorative today) or Greek Catholic, remained Eastern in practice (liturgical rite and language, with a married priesthood), but it came under the pope. The Uniate Church became gradually Latinized, however. After the partitions of Poland at the end of the eighteenth century, a significant number of Uniates were brought into the Russian Empire.[4] In 1839, the reverse process happened, by which some Uniate bishops petitioned to reunite with the Orthodox Church so that all the Uniates in Belarusian and Ukrainian territories ruled by the Russian Empire were brought into the Orthodox Church. Significant parts of the future patriarch Tikhon's ecclesiastical career would deal with former Greek Catholics.

In 1448, the Muscovites elected the head of their own church for the first time instead of the patriarch of Constantinople appointing one, in effect declaring the independence of the Russian Church from the Greek. Constantinople formally recognized the autocephaly of the Russian Church and elevated the head of its church to the status of patriarch in 1589. Patriarch Germogen (1606–1612) played a pivotal role in leading the country out of the interregnum known as the "Time of Troubles" before the establishment of the Romanov dynasty. Patriarch Nikon (1652–1666) introduced heavyhanded liturgical reforms that led to the so-called Old Believers schism.

In the early eighteenth century, Tsar Peter the Great (rule 1682/1689–1725) sought to modernize and Europeanize Russia. His reforms affected all aspects of Russian state and society, including the Church. He abolished the patriarchate, which was replaced by a collegial body of prelates named the Most Holy Governing Synod (or simply Holy Synod) in 1721. He also appointed a lay bureaucrat, the chief procurator (*ober-procuror*), to act as a liaison between the crown and the Holy Synod. Peter's reforms prompted the Church to develop its bureaucratic infrastructure. The effect of Peter's reforms has frequently been exaggerated, as if the Orthodox Church became a department of state and the chief procurator the head of the Synod.

In fact, the Church existed as a kind of parallel institution to the state, with the Church headed by the Holy Synod and the state headed by the Senate—though both were ultimately subordinate to the tsar. The Holy Synod was normally presided over by the metropolitan of St. Petersburg, and it included the metropolitans of Moscow and Kiev, as well as other bishops in rotation. According to the initial establishment of the Holy Synod, the chief procurator's role was consultative rather than issuing orders. With time, however, especially in the late nineteenth century, the power of the chief procurators grew so that they ruled the Synod de facto, if not de jure.[5] Moreover, Church and state structures were tightly interwoven. The state's increasing control over the Church in late imperial Russia was resented by many Church leaders and a cause of significant tension between the two.

In the Russian Empire, Orthodoxy was legally defined as the "predominant and preeminent" faith. The overwhelming majority of Russians, Ukrainians, Belarusians, Moldovans, and Georgians were Orthodox. Other ethnic minorities belonged to other religions: Poles and Lithuanians were Roman Catholics; Finns, Germans, and others were Protestant; in addition to Mulsims, Jews, and Buddhists. These religions were broadly tolerated, but Russian Orthodoxy was privileged in that the law allowed people only to convert to, but not away from, it. Jews were subject to legal discrimination and mob violence, but state policy toward the Jews was not shaped primarily by their religious identity.[6]

Contrary to the stereotype, priests in nineteenth-century Russia were not mostly ignorant drunkards. They received an education not inferior to that of many aristocrats. But the lives of provincial parish clergy were far from easy because they were financially dependent upon their typically poor parishioners. The condition of most clergy was paradoxical: Their education was closer to the aristocracy while their income was closer to the peasants. Although frequently looked down upon by the aristocracy and the intelligentsia, the fact that they shared the hardships of their flocks meant that there was far less anticlericalism in Russia than in revolutionary France, for example.

The condition of bishops was very different. Most of the bishops were from clergy families, received a higher education at a Theological Academy (the Church's equivalent of the university), took monastic vows after their studies, and embarked upon a career of educational and administrative positions. Once they became ruling diocesan bishops, they governed vast dioceses and had extensive powers within them. By contrast with the parish clergy, they were regarded—and typically acted—like princes of the Church, forcing terrified parish clergy to grovel before them. When contemporaries described Tikhon as approachable and accessible rather than domineering and condescending, it signaled something quite unusual and noteworthy.

The 1860s and 1870s were a period of tremendous change. Many of the people who would lead during Russia's revolutionary upheaval were born then, including Nikolai Romanov, the future tsar Nicholas II (1868–1918), and Vladimir Ulianov, the future Lenin (1870–1924)—three and five years after Tikhon, respectively. Half a century earlier, Russia defeated Napoleon and emerged as the most powerful nation in Europe, only to suffer a humiliating defeat during the Crimean War (1853–1856). The crisis that followed precipitated the "Great Reforms" of the 1860s–1870s that ended serfdom and liberalized censorship, education, the legal system, and government administration.

By the last decades of the Russian Empire, the institution of the Russian Orthodox Church was subjected to heavy government control. This generated a widespread sense that the Church was in a state of paralysis and in desperate need of renewal. Much older English-language historiography dismissed Russian Orthodoxy as the "handmaiden of the state," so subordinated that it had become a virtual department of state that existed primarily to justify the autocracy. Among ordinary believers, however, lived Orthodoxy was vibrant. Depictions of Russian peasants as being essentially pagan with only a superficial veneer of Christianity are very wide of the mark. A flurry of new scholarship has demonstrated that there was a tremendous religious ferment in the last half century of imperial Russia. That ferment found expression in an upsurge of monasticism and pilgrimage, in charismatic clergy like John of Kronstadt becoming virtually household names, or in deep religious commitment that could be found among all social classes. Sometimes that ferment spilled over beyond the Orthodox Church and found expression in other movements. At the same time, the rise of atheism was driven not so much by the intellectual doubts raised by science and historical-critical scholarship as in the West, but by the political opposition's identification of the Orthodox Church with the tsarist regime they were trying to overthrow.[7] That milieu profoundly shaped the future Bolshevik leaders and their perceptions of the Orthodox Church.

The institutional structures of the Orthodox Church struggled to be responsive to these rapid social and cultural changes. Since the Holy Synod and the Church hierarchy as a body were seen as products of the system, many felt they could not renew the Church. Russian Orthodox thinkers from the Slavophiles onward began to conceptualize "Church" not as a hierarchical institution made up of the clergy, but as the entire organic body of believers. The way to renewal was precisely by giving voice to the whole body of the Church. This was embodied for many in the notion of *sobornost*, or conciliarity: The whole body of the Church could express itself above all through a church council, historically the highest authority in the Orthodox Church, which could address the Church's needs without state dictate.[8]

The modern history of the Russian Orthodox Church has been, in part, a struggle between this hierarchical institutional understanding of Church that has tied itself to the imperial state and its agendas, and a more organic understanding of Church as a community of believers. Even when believers were highly critical of the Church institution and the "paralysis" of its leadership, this did not diminish their attachment to Orthodoxy as a faith, a set of values, traditions, and practices. It was not uncommon to find ordinary people being simultaneously anticlerical—in the sense of critical of the clergy—and committed Orthodox believers.

Family and Childhood

The Bellavin family were servitors of the Church in one capacity or another as far back as can be established. Other than the basic facts about his family, and where he lived and studied, we know almost nothing about the first nineteen years of Vasily Bellavin's life. There is no evidence from contemporary sources that describe his family life or youth. Only memoir sources provide a few tantalizing impressions of his time in the seminary, when he was already a teen. We only have more in-depth portrayals about his experiences and personality from the time he was at the Theological Academy. One glimpse into his childhood is a story of a prophetic dream his father reputedly had in which Vasily's grandmother came to his father and foretold that one of his sons would die young, one would be unfortunate, but that Vasily would "be great." The dream evidently was told by Tikhon himself after he became patriarch—the earliest known version was found in the archives, written in 1918 by the prior of the Trinity-Sergius Lavra after Tikhon's stay there, which differs in significant details from the version passed on in émigré circles later. But no version squares with the facts of the Bellavin family life. The story therefore belongs more to an examination of the veneration of Tikhon as a saint rather than to his biography.[9]

Vasily Bellavin's father, Ioann Bellavin, was priest of the parish church in the village of Klin. Almost nothing is known about Vasily's mother except her name, Anna Gavrilova, and her birthdate, and that she was illiterate; born in 1832, she was sixteen at the time of her marriage and ten years younger than her husband. Given that there are no other records about her family, it is possible she was an orphan. Vasily's father was ordained in October 1847 and in December 1848 received his own parish in the village (*pogost*) of Klin.[10] The village where the future patriarch was born was then, as it is now, very remote, some three hundred kilometers from the provincial capital of Pskov, thirty-five kilometers from Velikie Luki or the same distance, in the opposite direction, to Pushkin's estate in Mikhailovskoe, passing through Mussorgsky's birthplace of Karevo. The land around Klin was uneven and not very fertile, and there were no rivers or lakes nearby. The Church of the Resurrection was a spacious stone church, built in 1733, with a bell tower, which still stands and was restored in the 2000s. The church was dilapidated when Fr. Ioann took over the parish, and he was responsible for fixing it up.[11]

We know something of the family life from a report Fr. Ioann submitted in 1863, two years before Vasily's birth. The parish consisted of Klin itself together with numerous surrounding villages (within a nine-kilometer radius), and in the 1860s there were some nine hundred residents. As a particularly poor parish, income received from parishioners for various services (*treby*), such as house blessings and funerals, was "so insignificant that for the clergy with a family it is not enough to buy decent shoes for the year." Therefore, the clergy received a supplemental income from the state. Each of the clergy families had their own wooden home that they acquired with their own funds. Although in some regions of Russia there existed the tradition of the parishioners providing a fixed support for the clergy (*ruga*), often through payment in kind with agricultural goods, the clergy in Klin did not receive this. Finally, and perhaps most importantly, the clergy families supported themselves through the land that belonged to the parish church for the clergy's use. This land, as was the norm, was thirty-three desiatinas (thirty-six hectares/eighty-nine acres), divided between three clergy families, half going to the priest's family. Fr. Ioann complained that the land was not fertile and was very difficult to work, and even with very thrifty agricultural labor they could not hope to make up the insufficiencies in their monetary income.

In short, the Bellavin family shared in the labor and the poverty of the peasants in whose midst they lived.[12]

After serving the parish in Klin for twenty years, Fr. Ioann Bellavin was transferred on January 22, 1869—three days after Vasily's fourth birthday—to the Church of the Transfiguration in the district city of Toropets. It was here that Vasily would spend the next decade of his boyhood and attend the ecclesiastical elementary school. Life for the Bellavins was certainly much different in Toropets than it was in Klin. Toropets was spared the destruction that afflicted neighboring cities such as Velikie Luki and Rzhev during World War II, and therefore still retains much of the picturesque look and feel that it had at the end of the nineteenth century. The river Toropa runs through the town and connects two large lakes on its edges, where the Bellavin boys no doubt frequently fished. The town was ancient, first mentioned in Russian chronicles in the eleventh and twelfth centuries. Prince Aleksandr Nevsky was married in Toropets, and his bride, according to tradition, donated the Korsun Icon of the Mother of God, the town's most valued sacred object. In the early modern period, it became a significant and wealthy trading center, one expression of which was eighteen stone churches, many of them large and architecturally magnificent, built in the seventeenth and eighteenth centuries. In the nineteenth century, however, the new road (and later the railroad) passed by Toropets, so that it ceased to be an important trading center. There were frequent local religious feasts, many involving the Korsun Icon.[13] According to a friend of Vasily Bellavin's, Toropets was a town with "churches at every step, all ancient and quite beautiful." Life there had largely been untouched by modernity, where the "old ways of Russian life (*byt*)" were still preserved. The influence of this environment, together with that of his family, "expressed itself in the youth" that this friend knew from seminary who was pious and friendly.[14]

Fr. Ioann's new church was the large stone Church of the Transfiguration, constructed in the early eighteenth century. In 1870, the parish's clergy consisted of the priest, a deacon, and two sacristans. The clergy of this church were allotted a small salary. In addition, the clergy received some 400 rubles a year for performing various religious services for the parishioners, which was divided among all four clerics, as well as some other supplemental sources of income. Fr. Ioann made considerably more than in Klin, but it was still insufficient to support his family. Although the church was in the city of Toropets, it still had a small amount of land allotted to it that the family also worked.[15]

The Bellavin family had four children, all boys, all of whom, except Vasily, died as relatively young men. The first three children were born in Klin: Pavel in 1857, Ivan in 1859, and Vasily in 1865. The fourth son, Mikhail, was born in 1873 in Toropets. The Bellavin boys all studied in the Toropets ecclesiastical elementary school. Vasily's two older brothers both became teachers; both died suddenly: Pavel in 1883 at age twenty-six, and Ivan in 1891 at age thirty-two. None of the Bellavin boys married or had children. Vasily's father also died in the mid-1890s.[16]

Later, when he was rector of the Kholm seminary, Tikhon described the upbringing of a priest's son that must have reflected his own experience: As he was growing up, pious parents brought their son to church as often as possible. Even before he could read or write, he participated in the liturgy: bringing the censor to the priest, lighting candles, ringing the bells, and once able to read he did so in church. "This is how a [priest's] boy truly receives his education in the church of God; even his child's games take place near the church, in the church courtyard. And sweeter and dearer his family's church becomes to him." He began his studies at home, using church books, with the idea that it was a great and important task. In addition to studies, he also received "moral life lessons" in how to bear deprivations, which often happens in clergy families—"lessons of being satisfied with little, of tireless labor, of selfless service." All of this was imprinted in his receptive soul so that the qualities necessary for a future pastor were nurtured in him.[17] Though perhaps an idealized portrait of his own childhood, Vasily clearly grew up with a dedication to the church and a love of the liturgy, as well as a way of relating to others with kindness and respect that would follow such an upbringing.

Vasily's Education: Elementary School and Seminary, Toropets and Pskov (1874–1884)

In 1874, at age nine, Vasily Bellavin entered the Toropets school for clergy sons (*dukhovnoe uchilishche*). By the nineteenth century, the Russian Orthodox Church had an elaborate school system for sons of clergy. Church leaders saw the seminary as a way to create a clerical elite, so the model of education was based on the classical grammar school that was the norm in Central Europe at the time. A seminary education became the primary determining factor in a clergyman's career, as bishops sought to place only seminary-educated candidates into parishes. Indeed, by 1880, 97 percent of Russian Orthodox priests had a seminary degree.[18] Because of insufficient financial resources, the Church opened the seminaries only to sons of parish clergy, and since one had to have a seminary degree to become a priest, only sons of clergy became priests—turning the clergy into a veritable caste. Bishops were also expected to have a higher theological education, meaning that most bishops also came from clergy families.

The first four years of the seminary curriculum followed the gymnasium model, centered on classical languages, mathematics, and general humanities subjects. Those who finished the first four years could freely enter the university. Those who wished to enter ecclesiastical service continued to the final two years of the seminary, which focused on theological subjects.[19] The memoirs of Metropolitan Evlogy (Georgievsky, 1868–1946)—a contemporary of Tikhon who would become an important bishop in the emigration after the Revolution—reveal that the atmosphere of schools and seminaries was very dependent upon the personalities of administrators and teachers, many of whom taught by rote learning and administered with strict militaristic discipline.[20]

Vasily Bellavin studied at the Toropets ecclesiastical elementary school for four years from 1874 to 1878. He was no doubt very fortunate that he was able to study at a clerical elementary school located in his hometown and therefore he was able to live at home in the supportive atmosphere of his family until he finished the school at the age of thirteen. All of the Bellavin boys studied at the Toropets ecclesiastical school, which had between 110 and 130 students.[21] Upon entering, pupils would be tested to ensure that they could already read and write Russian; read Church Slavonic (the language of the liturgy), do basic mathematics, and knew basic elements of the faith such as the Creed, the Commandments, and daily prayers, which they had learned at home.[22] The curriculum in the school consisted of "Salvation history of the Old and New Testaments," the longer catechism, an explanation of the Divine Liturgy together with the *typikon*,[23] Russian and Church Slavonic, Latin and Greek, calligraphy (*chistopisanie*), geography, arithmetic, music notation, and liturgical singing. Greek and Latin constituted nearly half the curriculum.[24]

After finishing the Toropets school, Vasily Bellavin entered the Pskov seminary in 1878, where he would spend the next six years.[25] Pskov was one of the oldest Russian cities. It played a key role in the Middle Ages as old Russia's westernmost city, both as a bridge and as a defense. The city flourished in the Middle Ages and developed its own distinctive schools of iconography and church architecture. It declined significantly in importance during the eighteenth and first half of the nineteenth century, though it was the seat of the provincial administration. When Vasily was living there, it was already connected to Warsaw and St. Petersburg by railroad, which led to the development of trade and industry in the region and a growing population (30,000 in 1897).[26] Thus, the city in which Vasily Bellavin spent his youth was a modest-sized city, peaceful, green, where "life flowed evenly and tranquilly, enlivened in the days of fairs and bazaars, promenades, religious processions, secular and religious holidays. The Church played a particularly important role in the life of city inhabitants."[27]

The Pskov seminary was founded in 1725, one of the first in Russia. While Vasily was a student, two deans administered Pskov seminary—neither of whom were Russian. Archimandrite Gerasimos (Iared, 1840–1899) was dean of the Pskov seminary from 1876 to 1881. He was an Arab Orthodox Christian from Syria who came to Russia in 1865 for theological education, where he completed the Moscow seminary and the St. Petersburg Theological Academy (in 1869). Eventually he would become a metropolitan in the Patriarchate of Antioch and be one of the candidates for the patriarchate itself in 1899 shortly before his death.[28] In 1881, Archimandrite Gerasimos exchanged positions with the dean of the seminary in Riga, Archpriest Mikhail Drexler (1838–1885), the son of a Latvian peasant who graduated from the Moscow Theological Academy and joined the seminary in Riga in 1862, becoming its dean in 1870. A leading figure in the development of Orthodoxy in the Baltics, he translated liturgical texts into Latvian, and he taught and preached in Latvian as well as Russian. He was a well-known and respected figure among Latvians and Orthodox in Riga. These early influences demonstrated to the young Bellavin that Orthodoxy was more than Russian, no doubt sensitizing him to differences in language and customs among various Orthodox Churches, elements that would become so critical in his later career, especially in America. Tikhon's connections with both Syrian Orthodox and the Baltics would continue later in life: In America, one of his closest coworkers would be Raphael Hawaweeny, an Arab Christian from Syria with a similar background to Archimandrite Gerasimos, and later Tikhon served in the Baltics when he was appointed archbishop of Vilna.[29]

Vasily studied together with some 180 to 200 fellow students.[30] The education that Vasily received at the seminary was broad: He studied Greek and

Latin as well as French. In addition to general subjects (mathematics, literature, history, and philosophy), he studied scripture for six years, reading through the entire Bible (the New Testament in the original Greek).[31]

Theological subjects, including church history, pedagogy, homiletics, and liturgics, were primarily taken in the final two years of study. Fourth-year students took a course on Apologetic Theology (*Osnovnoe bogoslovie*), which was taught by the dean, Archpriest Drexler. That course explored such contemporary issues as the relationship of natural sciences to the Bible, immortality, and the existence of God, and used, in addition to the standard Russian textbook, books by German and French authors (in Russian translation), in which they explored such subjects as "Natural Religion" and readings about world religions by Max Müller. The course was intended to show how one could confirm Christian truth through understanding the human development of religion and philosophy, while at the same time making a critical analysis of those views and teachings which contradicted Christianity. In the single mention of concrete student work, in the context of discussing the entire seminary curriculum, Fr. Drexler's report singled out Vasily Bellavin (along with two other students) for having written the best papers in Apologetic Theology, suggesting that Bellavin indeed developed a close relationship with Fr. Drexler and that his work stood out.[32]

In the final year, students took moral, dogmatic, and pastoral theology. According to the dean's report, instruction in moral theology attempted to give life to the "dry, abstract" propositions of the textbook with examples from real life. The course also focused on a comparison of different Christian confessions in their approach to moral issues. In homiletics, students in Vasily Bellavin's class read great sermons, especially from early Church Fathers Basil the Great, Gregory the Theologian, and John Chrysostom. In reading model sermons, students were not only to understand what made a sermon great but also how it was to be understood in its historical context, presumably to teach students that they cannot simply imitate fourth-century sermons. Finally, students also put into practice what they learned by composing their own sermons for the class. The Dogmatic Theology class focused on the classic text by Metropolitan Makary (Bulgakov).[33] Although nineteenth-century Russian seminary education was notorious for rote learning, the reforms of 1867 brought in a new spirit of education. Dean Drexler valued his students' ability to assimilate and make their own the subjects they were studying rather than merely learn by rote, and he encouraged the instructors under him not simply to lecture but to raise questions among the students to facilitate their ability to articulate their own understanding of the material.

From Vasily Bellavin's seminary days come the earliest reminiscences by Archpriest Aleksandr Rozhdestvensky (1864–1930), who studied five years together with Vasily in the seminary and two more at the St. Petersburg Theological Academy and after graduating, like Vasily, returned to teach at the Pskov Seminary. According to him, Vasily Bellavin was a "modest" seminarian, who "distinguished himself by [his] religiosity, [and his] affectionate and attractive character." He was tall and fair. The students loved him, "but always united to this love a feeling of respect, explained by his steadfast—though not at all affected—religiosity, his brilliant academic success and his perpetual readiness to help his comrades." His fellow students regularly turned to Bellavin for help in understanding their lessons and with their written assignments. Bellavin "found some sort of pleasure and fun" in this, and though he put on a serious face, helped with "continual jokes, whole hours busying himself with his comrades," one-on-one or in groups, who came to him for help. "It is remarkable that his comrades in the seminary jokingly called him the 'hierarch.'"[34] This combination of seriousness with a light-heartedness, always with a joke on his lips, was a character trait that the patriarch preserved until the end of his life, lightening his interlocutors even in the darkest of times. Upon graduating from the Pskov seminary in 1884, Vasily Bellavin was one of the outstanding students who was sent on for further studies.

St. Petersburg Theological Academy (1884–1888)

While Vasily Bellavin was a seminary student, a fateful event shook Russia: the assassination by revolutionary terrorists in 1881 of Tsar Alexander II, the "tsar liberator" who emancipated the serfs. What followed under Tsar Alexander III was decidedly different. The new tsar, together with his former tutor Konstantin Pobedonostsev, believed that government restructuring during the Great Reforms amounted to an import of Western ideals alien to Russia that in fact threatened Russia's stability. Rather, that stability was to be ensured by returning to the principles enshrined by Nicholas I (1825–1855): the tsar's unlimited autocracy, Russian nationality, and Orthodox Christianity. In 1880, Pobedonostsev became chief procurator, the tsar's lay representative on the Holy Synod, and he sought to implement his ideas and policies directly through the Church.³⁵ This had a direct impact on Bellavin because of the introduction of a new statute of theological schools of 1884, implemented during his first year at the Academy.

After the liberal reforms of theological education in the 1860s, the academies and seminaries were staffed with scholarly, lay, often "liberal" professors, who were products of the more open times. The large degree of autonomy exercised by the seminaries and academies was precisely the type of alien Western ideas that Pobedonostsev found dangerous. The new statute of 1884 greatly strengthened the power of the bishops over the schools. Educational administrators were appointed rather than elected. The power of the dean, who was chosen from the monastic clergy, was strengthened. During Bellavin's time at the Academy, there were internal tensions between a conservative administration, liberal professors, and some radical students, competing for influence over the student body—and with it, the future of the Church's leadership.³⁶

Student life was strictly regulated. The day began with prayer in Church followed by breakfast in the cafeteria and then classes all morning until lunch at 2 p.m. After lunch, from 2 to 4 p.m., they were given free time, for "rest and walks in the garden," when they were allowed to play chess (but not cards). At 4 p.m. they had afternoon tea, and the evenings until 9:30 were devoted to homework. At 9:30 p.m. they had supper in the cafeteria followed by evening prayer in the Church, and by 11 p.m. they were to go to bed. The doors to the dormitories were locked at midnight. Students were generally not permitted to leave campus, aside from authorized trips to the public library for research, except for Sundays and holidays.³⁷

In nineteenth-century Russia, potential bishops were drawn from graduates of the Theological Academies who took monastic vows, and then followed a particular career path that entailed becoming a seminary professor and administrator for some years before being consecrated to the episcopate, and then working their way up the episcopal career track from lesser to more important episcopal sees. Bishops were thus drawn from a special group of "learned monks," those who had received a higher education but never actually lived in a monastery. The monastic clergy were generally more conservative than married clergy. During the more liberal Reform era of the 1860s and 1870s, the Academies had virtually ceased producing "learned monks," which was viewed as a shortcoming by the Church administration.

Chief Procurator Pobedonostsev therefore promoted the recruitment of "learned monks" because he hoped they would be future conservative leaders of the Church. According to some critics within the Church, the authorities sought out those who would take monastic vows as students and, once they graduated, promoted them very quickly through the ranks of Church administration—but in this way, those promoted were indebted and beholden to the chief procurator and passive to state control over the Church. This meant tonsuring many young men who were still in their early twenties and had not time to test their vocation. In monasteries, by contrast, novices were not permitted to take monastic vows before the age of thirty. It also thrust these young and inexperienced men into positions of great authority and responsibility, with negative consequences for both themselves and those under them. This system appealed to "careerists," individuals who were ambitious but not necessarily the best moral exemplars of the Church, fit neither for monasticism nor positions of leadership.[38]

The first cohort which began taking monastic vows again at the Academy in the 1880s, most importantly Mikhail (Gribanovsky, 1856–1898) and Antony (Khrapovitsky, 1863–1936), stayed on as professors and administrators. Khrapovitsky, who would become head of the émigré church after the Revolution, had his own vision of the revival of "learned monasticism" that did not coincide with Pobedonostsev's. Born from an aristocratic family, he was genuinely interested in higher education, which he regarded as necessary for engaging an increasingly literate Russian society. He was young and dynamic, and gathered students around him for evening discussions of burning issues.[39] These issues included the renewal of the Church by reversing the reforms of Peter the Great, particularly his replacement of the patriarchate with the Holy Synod, which Khrapovitsky regarded as having led to the bureaucratization of and state control over the Church. He and Mikhail (Gribanovsky) became the first advocates for the restoration of the patriarchate in the 1880s, which would finally come to fruition in 1917.

Antony (Khrapovitsky) zealously encouraged monasticism among students at the Academy. According to Evlogy, his "fiery monastic spirit infected, enticed, and inflamed hearts. Thanks to him our view of monasticism was raised to the ideal of a united brotherhood, an order, Christ's army, which was to save the Church from the procurators, returning it to its rightful place as an independent instructor and spiritual guide for the Russian people. A grandiose vision was unfolding before our eyes, which included the restoration of the patriarchate."[40] Khrapovitsky succeeded in attracting many to the path of learned monasticism, who would lead the Church in the first half of the twentieth century.

One of the most vivid accounts of Bellavin's years in the Academy was written by a classmate, Petr Bulgakov (1862-1931), uncle of the writer Mikhail Bulgakov, who ended up as a priest in California. His account paints a vivid picture of those years at the Academy. Bulgakov met Vasily Bellavin for the first time at the entrance exams, when they were sitting next to each other in the first row (since their last names both began with "B"). The first students to be examined were nervous, but Bellavin approached the examining professor confidently. He gave thorough answers and returned to his seat. When it was his turn, Bulgakov got confused in his answers and returned to his seat "like a wet chicken" because of his mistake. Bellavin turned to him and whispered, "Don't worry, they gave you high marks." Bulgakov saw this first encounter as encapsulating much of Bellavin's personality and effect on those around him, and that his "Don't worry" became the motto of their turbulent years at the Academy.[41]

The mid-1880s in St. Petersburg were tense. Reactionary forces were ready to pounce on any sign of sedition, while students in all educational institutions—including the Theological Academy—were like a simmering pot ready to boil over. Academy students lived in a semimonastic environment somewhat isolated from the center of the city, but they were still caught up in the intellectual ferment of the age. Leo Tolstoy's religious conversion led to his novel version of Christianity. Tolstoy rejected both the Church and the state, became a radical pacifist and anarchistic; he also advocated vegetarianism, and rejected marriage and sexuality as carnal and selfish. Lithographed copies of Tolstoy's *Confession* (published abroad) circulated among students at the Academy, some of whom became ardent Tolstoians. In the 1880s, Russian radicals also turned to the ideas of the German socialist philosopher Karl Marx, and academy students, like their university counterparts, were ardently reading *Das Kapital*. At the same time, the "monastic propaganda" of Antony (Khrapovitsky) was producing an ultra-Orthodox current among other Academy students. The "collision of Tolstoyanism and Marxism with monastic propaganda" manifested itself in that the upper class in Bellavin's first year at the Academy included both Antony (Khrapovitsky) and Mikhail Novorussky. The latter joined the revolutionary party "The Peoples' Will" and the year after his graduation was involved, together with Lenin's brother Aleksandr Ul'ianov, in a plot to assassinate Alexander III on March 1, 1887. As a consequence of the ensuing scandal, the Academy was nearly shut down by the authorities.[42]

In the midst of these polarizing forces, Vasily Bellavin found a path that was solidly Orthodox which went to neither the extreme of the radicals (the Tolstoyans and the Marxists) nor the ultra-Orthodox. He also had a way of sticking to his principles, even against the pressures from one or the other faction to bend. Bellavin came to his moderate but firmly Orthodox position with the help of the Academy professors, who were the leading theologians and scholars of the Russian Church in that age. The professors, who "lovingly guided the students" according to Bulgakov, gave them the "full possibility to work out the Orthodox truths independently." For example, the students of their class were assigned to write compositions on the latest writings of Tolstoy. Although the ultra-Orthodox elements reproached the professors, Bulgakov asserts that it was precisely the freedom of academic inquiry that allowed for this solidly but moderate Orthodox position of Bellavin and his cohort to emerge.[43] Tikhon would continue to engage Tolstoy's ideas for years after the Academy.

It was during his years at the Academy that Bellavin developed the capacity to act independently in the face of external pressures. In his first year, the Holy Synod prohibited students from attending dissertation defenses, which had previously been public. The students expressed their outrage at the annual Academy celebration in Februrary 1885, when representatives of the Holy Synod were in attendance, by walking out before the ceremonies began. Bellavin, however, did not join the walkout. Although some of the upperclassmen accused him of betraying the students' cause, his classmates defended him by asserting that there could not even be a "shadow of betrayal" with Bellavin, but that he acted on the principle that it was not right to spoil the Academy's celebration to express their protest. Bellavin also defended himself against his critics, who claimed to be defenders of freedom, by countering that they were criticizing him for acting freely. In another instance, on November 17, 1886, university students in St. Petersburg united to commemorate the anniversary of the death of one of the leaders of the radical intelligentsia, Nikolai Dobroliubov (1836–1861), with an Orthodox memorial service at his grave. Bellavin dissuaded the Academy students from participating in the memorial service on the principle that it was wrong to turn a liturgical service into a means of political protest—a principle he would also appeal to decades later during the Civil War. Instead, they participated by laying a wreath at Dobroliubov's grave, which Bellavin supported. Bulgakov observed that there were numerous such instances when Bellavin would not compromise his principles even when he was going against the current, which he saw as expressions of both Bellavin's courage and his perspicacity.⁴⁴ The following year one of Bellavin's classmates was expelled only because he was called as a witness to Novorussky's trial, causing great anxiety among the students. Bellavin's calm and steady character helped his classmates prevent this turmoil from totally disrupting their studies.⁴⁵

Emblematic of these years was the selection of Bellavin as the student librarian. Students wanted to read contemporary literature not available in the Academy library and keep up with what was happening in society, so they kept their own library, built up by their own means, and elected their own librarian. The Statute of 1884 did away with these elections and the librarian was to be appointed by the dean. The new dean, Bishop Antony (Vadkovsky, 1846–1912), knew his students well and was sensitive to their mood, so he appointed Vasily Bellavin. Among the students on both the "right" and on the "left" there was some dissatisfaction: The former wanted the student library to consist only of church fathers and Orthodox spiritual literature, whereas the latter wanted to stock it with Tolstoy and Marx. But Bellavin's moderate yet firmly Orthodox position—which was rooted in the Church but open to engaging secular literature and thought—won the support of the majority of the students.⁴⁶ His role in this capacity was remembered decades later, when he became the first-ever popularly elected bishop of Moscow, symbolizing the characteristics that distinguished him as the right church leader for the new Russia in the summer of 1917.⁴⁷

Both Antony (Vadkovsky) and Antony (Khrapovitsky) acknowledged that Russian society was changing rapidly, that people were being exposed to new challenges, doubts, and ideas. Both believed that Orthodoxy could and should provide the solutions and tried to shape Academy students to be a "light" in the darkness and turmoil in society. Vadkovsky, however, represented a viewpoint that was broader and more open, while Khrapovitsky was more conservative. Vadkovsky, for example, supported the involvement of students in the Society for the Spread of Religious-Moral Enlightenment, which was aimed at the working class in St. Petersburg. He believed that the love of Christ should be combined with service to the world, and that "learned monasticism" was a special vocation—though unlike Khrapovitsky, he did not denigrate marriage or view monasticism as superior to the vocation of married clergy. As Francesca Silano has argued, Tikhon was closer to Vadkovsky than to "fiery" spirit of Khrapovitsky, and perhaps that was a factor in why he did not take monastic vows while at the Academy.⁴⁸

Bellavin won the affection and respect of his fellow students, as expressed in their nickname for him—"the patriarch"—because of his "steady, imperturbably solid disposition and godly frame of mind."[49] Not only was Bellavin the "patriarch," but his classmates made up the "patriarch's entourage." This found expression in moments of daily life in the dormitories when students would return after the evening tea (or on Sundays, a day on the town) to find Bellavin and his roommate already in their room reading or studying. Bellavin rarely went out on the town for secular amusements, usually going into the city center only to visit the public library for research. His usual pose was sitting in the corner on a leather couch. As other students gathered in the room, they would chat, exchanging their impressions of the day. If the conversation degenerated into sarcasm, Bellavin's roommate would remind them that they would have to give an account for "every idle word" on Judgment Day (Matthew 12:36). Bellavin sometimes would then pick up the Gospel and start reading, prefaced by someone assuming the role of Protodeacon[50] calling all to attention with a liturgical "Let us attend." As the reading ended, students would gather from neighboring rooms and perform an impromptu liturgical service. On other occasions the "protodeacon" would intone the phrase "*eis polla eti despota*" ("many years to you, master"), chanted (always in Greek) when a bishop serves, and Bellavin would continue the service in the role of the bishop, though without any sacramental blessings, and other students would assume other roles. Evidently not all the Academy's students—the ultra-Orthodox ones—approved of these activities, which they regarded as somewhat blasphemous. But half the Academy choir was in Bellavin's class for all four years, and singing was very important to most of his classmates. These improvised concerts would sometimes last for hours. They were an "artistic pleasure," which simultaneously helped train students in singing and performance of the services.[51] So important was their singing that, as Tikhon wrote to the Bulgakov, "we even sang the old songs" at their twenty-fifth class reunion in 1914.[52]

At the Academy's annual celebration on February 17, 1889, the professor who read the report of the Academy's activities in the previous year declared that the class which graduated in 1888 was an "exceptional manifestation" according to the students' talent and hard work.[53] Vasily Bellavin graduated from the Petersburg Theological Academy in 1888 fifth in his class (out of fifty-six students). He received the highest mark on half the courses that he took, and the lowest grade he received was 4.25 (on a 5-point scale). In addition to the eighteen required courses, he continued his study of Greek and

French, and for his electives chose the history tract, taking classes on the history of Western confessions, the Russian Church Schism, as well as general and Russian secular history.[54]

Vasily wrote a final thesis on the seventeenth-century French Roman Catholic current known as Jansenism. The original thesis has been lost, but an unpublished article based on the thesis was recently found in the archives. Bellavin was likely interested in the subject because Jansenism was a dissenting movement within Roman Catholicism associated with Gallicanism and opposition to the Jesuits as well as the ultramontane exaltation of papal authority.[55] His advisor evaluated the thesis as solidly researched, but noted that the author was hesitant to assert his own conclusions.[56] Upon graduation, Bellavin received the degree of candidate in theology with the right to advance to the master's level without further oral exams.[57] After he became dean of the seminary in Kholm, he became too busy to pursue his research further in pursuit of a master's degree.[58] However, unlike some of his contemporaries such as Antony (Khrapovitsky), he was not academically inclined and never attempted to write major theological treatises.

Teacher at the Pskov Seminary and Monastic Tonsure (1888–1892)

Although there certainly was encouragement, even pressure, for students still at the Academy to take monastic vows, and two of his roommates did so before graduation, Bellavin did not choose this route. As a stipulation for receiving a scholarship for four years as a student at the Academy, he was obliged to serve in the ecclesiastical-educational domain for six years.[59] Immediately upon graduation in June 1888, Bellavin learned of an opening for a position in theology.

The opening at the Pskov seminary was for a professor of apologetic, dogmatic, and moral theology. Bellavin's closeness to the Academy's dean, Antony (Vadkovsky), is revealed in the latter's recommendation letter to Bishop Germogen (Dobronravin, 1820–1893) of Pskov: "I can recommend with full confidence Mr. Bellavin as the most excellent and solid person. He was not only an excellent student, but he was also outstanding among the students in a serious, churchly way." Such a glowing reference convinced the bishop, who wrote to the Educational Committee of the Holy Synod, that he wished for Bellavin to be appointed.[60] Bellavin also wrote directly to Chief

Procurator Pobedonostsev to apply: "I take the liberty of appealing to Your Excellency with a very humble request to appoint me to the vacant position of teacher of Dogmatic, Moral, and Apologetic Theology at the Pskov Theological Seminary." He also pointed out to Pobedonostsev that Bishop Germogen, "with the support of the Academy Administration, expressed his wish to have me" for the position.[61]

While Tikhon had approached the bishop to apply for the position, another candidate had approached the seminary and won their approval. The Synodal Education Committee therefore had to decide between the two candidates. The Education Committee did not simply follow the bishop's wishes, but examined the two candidates' records. By contrast with Bellavin, the other candidate received lower marks in the subjects to be taught and ranked thirtieth in his class of forty-seven students. Given Vadkovsky's enthusiastic support for Bellavin, together with the fact that Bellavin had "significantly higher grades in the subjects of the vacant position," the Education Committee supported Bishop Germogen's request to appoint him as theology teacher at Pskov seminary.[62]

At the age of twenty-two, Vasily Bellavin returned to the Pskov seminary. He lived humbly, renting the attic from the family of another Pskov priest on a quiet lane next to the Church of St. Nicholas down the road from the seminary. He would teach at the Pskov seminary for nearly four academic years. The seminary had changed significantly since Bellavin had studied there only five years earlier: The curriculum changed with the introduction of the new statute, and only a handful of his former teachers remained.[63]

Bellavin was hired to teach three theology subjects. Apologetics, or the defense of the Christian faith in general and Orthodox Christianity in particular, was taught in the fourth and fifth years. As a teacher, according to the seminary dean's report, Bellavin sought to demonstrate to students that the religious need, or striving for God, was deeply rooted in human nature, which was created in the image of God and therefore aspired after its prototype. Those who suppress their religious needs rejected something basic to human nature. He also sought to show that, although the religious need was innate to human nature, this was not enough for its proper development and expression, and especially as a consequence of the Fall, human beings needed God's help and guidance. Therefore, although there was truth in all religions, others were human strivings toward God, whereas Christianity was God's revelation to human beings. He used not only a range of Russian theologians but also Western authors.[64]

Bellavin taught students dogmatic theology, that is, the core Christian doctrines of the Trinity (the nature of God) and Christology (doctrines concerning Christ) for fifth- and sixth-year students. In teaching, he sought not so much to have the students learn the formal aspects of the doctrines as to "lead the students to an understanding of the spirit, meaning and significance of the doctrines, so that they not only mastered and memorized them, but would also be vividly and deeply penetrated by them, imprint them in their hearts and bring out of their studies completely conscious and rational convictions, which is so necessary and important for pastoral service."[65] He wanted the students to see that the doctrines were not something abstract and far from life, but address the great questions of life which people ask, and were important to resolving these questions correctly by providing the truth about humanity's spiritual nature. To achieve this goal, he acquainted the students with doctrinal treatises from theology texts of various authors as well as from theological journals. Students also had to write compositions on themes such as the "different opinions of the fathers and teachers of the church on the question of the origin of the soul."[66] The dean's description of Bellavin's teaching was in striking contrast to the rote learning that was standard in Russian seminaries. And rather than the dry scholastic textbook of Makary (Bulgakov), Bellavin had the students read the church fathers and articles being written by contemporary theologians. As one of his students recalled after he became patriarch, Tikhon took a broad view of Orthodox theology. When discussing M. M. Tareev, a controversial liberal theologian that some criticized as "unorthodox," Tikhon rejected that characterization. "What's good about Orthodoxy," he responded, "is that it is capable of including a great deal in its deep channels."[67]

In addition to teaching the theology courses he was originally hired for, Vasily Bellavin was also appointed as the French instructor. This brought with it a raise in his salary from 700 to 1,000 rubles per year. In the final year the students were translating theological and philosophical articles from French into Russian as well as Russian short stories into French. In addition to his permanent subjects, Bellavin also had to teach other subjects for extended periods when his colleagues became ill, including Greek and Latin as well as homiletics. On the whole, Bellavin does not seem to have been a very hard grader by comparison with his colleagues who taught Scripture or Church History (the majority of students in Dogmatic and Moral Theology received 4's and 5's).[58]

Vasily Bellavin was a popular and beloved teacher. Fr. Rozhdestvensky recalled that Bellavin's "students vividly remembered the young teacher who sharply stood out among others" by his enthusiasm for his work, for his "friendly attention to the needs of students, and his reliable protection in their conflicts with seminary authorities. The other teachers were cold and formal," regarded the students dismissively as "lowly seminarians," whom they were obliged to teach a set content and otherwise should be invisible. "I have many times encountered V. I. Bellavin's students from the Pskov seminary, and they all preserve the brightest memories of him."[69] Bellavin distinguished himself by having a distinct approach both to teaching and to his students—characteristics that continued to set him apart. Bellavin's life in Pskov was also very sociable, and in later years Tikhon would often recollect fondly his Pskov friends and the many hours of relaxing conversation he had with them.[70]

At the end of 1891, at the age of twenty-six, Bellavin took a major step: He informed his bishop of his wish to take monastic vows. Both Bulgakov and Rozhdestvensky, Bellavin's friends from the Academy, are quite clear that, unlike others who sought to climb the ecclesiastical career ladder quickly, Bellavin did not take monastic vows while still at the Academy because he was not a careerist. When he left the Academy, evidently, he had not yet decided which path he would choose for his life. Metropolitan Evlogy, whose life and experiences have many parallels with Vasily Bellavin in his youth, struggled with the decision of whether to follow the path of the married priesthood or of learned monasticism. Evlogy described how, when he finished the seminary, he dreamed of following in the footsteps of his father and becoming an ordinary married village priest to serve the people. During his studies at the Academy, he encountered the vision of learned monasticism popularized by Antony (Khrapovitsky). By the time Evlogy left the Academy, he was more inclined toward monasticism but still torn; therefore, he left as a layman and taught for several years before coming to the firm decision at about the same age as Bellavin to take monastic vows.[71] Just as Evlogy had a sister of a friend he considered marrying, there is an anecdotal story that Bellavin also considered marrying.[72] At the same time, one of his former students in Pskov related how professor Bellavin had come over for dinner, and after he left, the student's mother and sister were praising him as a fine young man—how intelligent, warm, and good-natured he was. But then the father instructed them not to pay attention to the fact that he was outgoing and cheerful, because the prospects for him as a groom were not good; he informed them that his classmates in the Academy had nicknamed him "patriarch," which indicated that "his road is to become a monk."[73]

Bishop Germogen approved Bellavin's request to be tonsured, and set a date for December 14, 1891, about a month before Bellavin's twenty-seventh birthday. When a monk or nun is tonsured, it is the one performing the tonsure, in this case the bishop, who typically gives the person a new name—the new name signifying a new identity, a new start to life, as it were, and it is given, rather than chosen, as a sign that this new life follows a path of obedience. Vasily Bellavin was given the monastic name Tikhon, after the eighteenth-century saint and spiritual writer Tikhon of Zadonsk. The local newspaper wrote about the event, noting that the seminary chapel, where the tonsure took place, was "overflowing" with those in attendance. The solemn rite, thanks in part to the beautiful singing of the seminary choir, "made a profound impression" on those present.[74] Rozhdestvensky noted that the performance of a tonsure was "so rare in a provincial town, and even more for a person who many knew so well," that this attracted "nearly the whole town." Rozhdestvensky observed that Bellavin "consciously and deliberately entered the new life, considering himself, clearly, not inclined for family obligations and desiring to devote himself exclusively to the service of the Church."[75]

Petr Bulgakov wrote to Tikhon to congratulate him, observing that the news of his tonsure did not surprise him very much. Tikhon replied, "Indeed, when I was at the Academy I did gravitate to monasticism by my inner disposition, but decided not to be tonsured then, because, first, I wanted to test myself; in any event I knew myself less than now. Secondly, if I were tonsured in the Academy, most likely, immediately after graduation they would have appointed me to some administrative post, as with other young monks, despite my absence of experience; in the majority of such cases, it seems, this is accompanied by some harm both for the person and for the work."[76] From these remarks, it is clear that Bellavin was inclined toward monasticism, which was also apparent to those around him, but that he had not made any firm choice. He did not wish to rush into such an important decision, but to be certain of his vocation. At the same time, he showed great maturity for a twenty-two-year-old in realizing that it was better not to begin assuming positions of authority and responsibility at such a young age.

Tikhon wrote to Bulgakov: "It goes without saying that teaching is more peaceful than administration.... I am already serving my fourth year, and by the grace of God I have not had in that time even one serious unpleasantness, but in an administrative post that certainly will happen. The true monk more than anyone needs to arm himself with patience, humility," and not indulge in being soft with himself. "Isn't this the cause of all the failures in our affairs, that we trouble more about ourselves, about our personality, and less about the work? And if this is understandable and forgivable in people who are caught up in worldly affairs, how are we, who have renounced the world, to justify ourselves?"[77] He was quite aware, then, that his step of "renouncing the world" would not lead him to the peace and quietude of traditional monasticism, but rather the cares of ecclesiastical administration. Though he apparently set down that path with some apprehension, he did so because he felt called to serve the Church rather than his own personal aims.

The day after his tonsure, the monk Tikhon was ordained to the deaconate, and a week later, on December 22, 1891, he was ordained to the priesthood. As he anticipated, his call for further Church service was not long in following.[78]

Seminary Rector and Episcopal Consecration: Kholm (1892–1898)

In mid-March, 1892, the Holy Synod appointed hieromonk Tikhon as inspector of the Kholm seminary, which was located in the eastern part of the Kingdom of Poland.[79] Tikhon, taking his younger brother Mikhail with him, traveled first to Warsaw to meet his new bishop, Flavian (Gorodetsky, 1849–1915). Tikhon's first encounter with Flavian was evidently similar to Evlogy's some years later: Flavian "left a very favorable impression upon me, for he was incredibly kind to me."[80] It appeared that Tikhon would not remain long in Kholm, however, for he was appointed as dean of the seminary in Kazan on June 24, 1892. On July 5, Tikhon was elevated to the rank of archimandrite as befitting the dean of a seminary. Within a few weeks, however, the dean of the Kholm seminary received another appointment, so the Synod decided to appoint Tikhon to replace him as dean in Kholm.[81] The seminary in Kholm played an important role in the public life of the city and therefore the dean of the seminary was "an important person."[82] Likely Flavian also had a favorable impression of Tikhon and wanted him to return; the two formed a very close bond and continued to correspond regularly after Flavian left Warsaw until Flavian's death in 1915.

That the young hieromonk Tikhon was sent to Kholm and then appointed dean of the seminary demonstrates the promise that the ecclesiastical authorities in St. Petersburg, including Pobedonostsev and his assistant, Vladimir Sabler (1845–1929), saw in him. Kholm (Chełm in today's Poland) was a unique region, and a uniquely sensitive one in the Russian Empire. It had once been part of Kyivan Rus and, at that time, its inhabitants were Orthodox. The region became part of Poland in the fourteenth century, and the Orthodox population became Uniate after the Union of Brest in 1595–1596. Although notable differences between the Orthodox and Catholic usage were addressed—namely commemorating the pope instead of the patriarch of Constantinople and inserting the filioque in the creed—the Byzantine rite remained unchanged for a century after the Union. As late as the second half of the eighteenth century, at least some priests in the Uniate Chełm diocese were still using Orthodox liturgical books. The seminary was established in Chełm in part to unify liturgical practice, and during the process the ritual was also Latinized. Changes were also made to the churches themselves, such as removing the iconostasis and placing the altar against the wall instead of free-standing, sometimes even introducing organs. Often the adoption of Latin practices and feasts came from the initiative of the people themselves. People of the region became deeply attached to the Latin elements in their worship.[83]

Chełm became part of the Russian Empire as a result of the Congress of Vienna in 1815, remaining part of the relatively autonomous Kingdom of Poland.[84] Just as the 1839 suppression of the Uniates in Belarus and Ukraine was sparked by the Polish uprising of 1830–1831, so the suppression of the Unia in Kholm began as a response to the Polish insurrection of 1863.[85] The administrator of the diocese appointed by the Russian authorities, Markell (Popel, 1825–1903), attempted in 1874 to purify the Uniate rite of all Latin borrowings, which was often resisted by parishioners. The resistance resulted in disturbances—and, in response to the disturbances, the Russian government sent in police and Cossacks to force people to accept the purified ritual, often with the cudgel and the whip.[86] In one instance in 1874, thirteen Uniates were killed by Russian soldiers in the village of Pratulin, who were subsequently canonized by the Catholic Church as the Pratulin Martyrs.

The Russian government aimed to separate the East Slavic Ruthenians (whom they considered "Little Russians") as much as possible from Polish influence, and administrators in St. Petersburg and Warsaw, together with Markell Popel, viewed the purification of Uniate rituals as serving that purpose, at least for the time being. The process of "reunification" began on January 12, 1875, when some 50,000 Uniates who had petitioned to join the Orthodox Church were received en masse, and the process continued swiftly until Popel petitioned St. Petersburg for a complete union of his diocese with the Orthodox Church, which came in May 1875, ending the last Uniate diocese in Russia. In the southern Kholm region (Lublin province), the clergy—led by Popel—united themselves to the Orthodox Church without official pressure from above and with little resistance from below. In the northern region of Podlachia/Podlasie (Siedlce province), however, the governor Stepan Gromeka (1823–1877) sought a swift suppression of the Uniate Church, by force if necessary.[87] Some 260,000 faithful were automatically registered by the Russian government as belonging to the Orthodox Church—which meant that they could only be legally married or have their children baptized in it—regardless of whether they wanted it. Many who did not want to be Orthodox, especially in the north, remained what official sources refer to as "recalcitrants," resisting incorporation into the Orthodox Church for decades.

The Orthodox Church incorporated the former Kholm Uniate diocese into a reorganized diocese that was renamed the "Kholm-Warsaw" diocese and established a vicar bishop of Lublin, who resided in Kholm. The region was a religiously and ethnically mixed one, in which the former Uniate Ruthenians were living amid Jews and Polish Catholics, and there was a significant degree of religious competition over the former Uniates between Catholics and Orthodox, which preoccupied local Orthodox leaders.[88] Flavian (Gorodetsky), who was bishop of Lublin from 1885 until his appointment as the presiding bishop of the diocese in Warsaw in 1891, endeavored to "purify" the ritual from "Uniate remnants." Gedeon (Pokrovsky), who became dean of the Kholm seminary in 1889 and bishop of Lublin in 1892, continued the practice of purifying the rite of Uniate remnants, but he did so in a hasty manner that encountered opposition and eventually led to his dismissal at the end of 1896.[89]

Because of the sensitivity of the region, the Synod sent many of its most promising young monastic clergy there to take leading positions in the seminary or as bishop of Lublin.[90] The Orthodox Church devoted significant missionizing efforts. The Church played a role as imperial agent; in the state's eyes, making the inhabitants of Kholm Orthodox also served to make them more Russian—and ensure they did not become more Polish.

Tikhon expressed his understanding of the link between Russian religious and national identity in his sermon at the funeral of Markell Popel in St. Petersburg in 1903. He asserted that the Kholm land had of old been "inhabited by Russian Orthodox people," but it fell under Polish rule. The Poles, seeking to remake the people "in the Polish manner," knew that "the Russians draw their core strength for the preservation of their national character from the Orthodox faith." They engineered the Unia to undermine the "Russian faith and nationality," which they did by gradually Latinizing the services. Barely a spark of the "Russian faith and nationality" survived, but after the Polish rebellion of 1863, "it was decided" (he stated in passive voice) "to liberate the Russian people from the Polish oppression, to awaken them in Russian self-awareness, to restore the ritual, customs, and language." And this was the work that Markell Popel was recruited to undertake—work he had already been engaged in in his native Galicia.[91] Significantly, Tikhon referred as much to the "Russian faith" as to the "Orthodox faith," and always coupled with "Russian nationality." However, unlike Evlogy, who was intensely involved in the political project of Russifying the region, Tikhon focused his words and activities more on strengthening Orthodoxy and combatting Catholic influences.[92]

The seminary in Kholm was established in 1759 as a Uniate seminary and made Orthodox in 1875. The atmosphere and student body of the Kholm seminary were very different, however, from any other seminary in the Russian Empire. Whereas typical Russian seminaries primarily educated sons of parish clergy, seminarians in Kholm came from a variety of social classes. They were more cultured and better groomed than the typical Russian seminarians, not as given to drunkenness and rowdiness, and not as cut off from the surrounding society and culture. Most also spoke Polish and viewed the Ruthenian language condescendingly as a "peasant" tongue.[93]

Soon after Tikhon arrived, while he was still inspector, an outside reviewer conducted a review of the seminary. According to the report to the chief procurator, Tikhon had not been in his post long enough to be able to judge his performance. But in personal interaction, "he gives the impression of a cautious and restrained person, and at the same time quiet and mild, and in general he wins you over. The dean speaks highly of him as a good colleague and assistant."[94] Overall, however, the report was not overly positive about the educational level of the seminary.[95] Becoming dean immediately after this report was submitted, Tikhon had his work cut out for him. He was able to contribute significantly to the functioning of the seminary educationally, institutionally, and financially in the five years he was dean.

The seminary had 116 students in the 1891–1892 school year when Tikhon joined. By the 1896–1897 school year, that number had risen to 164, a substantial increase.[96] Since the majority of students lived at the seminary, the increase in the number of students resulted in overcrowding in the dormitory. Tikhon resolved this by encouraging the faculty, who had been living in the seminary building as well, to move into town so that their apartments could be converted into student housing.[97] The increase in the number of students also necessitated a new chapel for the seminary, so Tikhon initiated the transformation of the seminary's gymnastics hall into a church.[98] Under Tikhon, the seminary leadership paid particular attention to the development of the seminarians' sense of the "ecclesial spirit" and love for the liturgy. Part of the reason the local population was attracted to the Catholic Church was because of the splendor of its baroque services—so Tikhon wanted to ensure that future Orthodox priests also appreciated the beauty of liturgical services and learned how to conduct them with particular solemnity in the seminary chapel. To that end, Tikhon himself, together with the other leading clergy of the seminary, conducted the daily services together. Moreover, the students all took part (in turns) in reading the Epistle, serving at the altar, attending to candles and incense, and other essential features of the service, as well as singing in the choir. The students were instructed to sing and chant clearly, in an unhurried fashion, so that the readings were comprehensible and so they were attentive to what was happening in the liturgy. However, Tikhon was not only concerned with students' religious formation in the church but also with the development of aesthetic taste. Seminarians were encouraged to engage in painting and music and even to form an orchestra to practice music in their free time.[99]

Among his initiatives as dean, Tikhon also started Sunday afternoon "readings" at the seminary, which were aimed at the public. The afternoon would begin with a concert from the seminary students, and then seminary professors would give lectures that, in the early years of the initiative, were aimed at explaining the differences between Catholicism and Orthodoxy. As it developed, the lectures would focus on topics of interest to educated society; Tikhon, for example, gave a lecture on Tolstoy's story "Master and Man."[100] Tikhon further conducted such sessions for the common people focused on pastoral themes. In addition to all of his activities focused on the seminary itself, Tikhon was actively engaged in the church and educational life of the region more broadly. Thus, he was an active member of the Kholm Orthodox Holy Theotokos Brotherhood, which raised money for the students but also had a broad publishing platform. Tikhon developed and expanded a model elementary school that was attached to the seminary. He was also active on the board of the Church's regional Educational Committee; during this period the number of schools, including schools operated by parishes, expanded significantly.[101]

Tikhon's primary focus as dean of the Kholm seminary was the spiritual formation of the seminarians. As he had endeavored to do as a seminary professor in Pskov, so in Kholm he encouraged the students not to think of Orthodox doctrine as dry formulas detached from real life, but rather as responding to and providing solutions for the most important questions in life. The purpose of Orthodox theology was to guide believers to finding true fulfillment because it provided the deepest answers for what human beings strive for.[102] In a speech to graduating students, he reflected on what it meant to be free: not to be free to do whatever one wants, which ends in slavery to sin. Rather, true freedom meant to define for oneself how one was to act rather than from something external and alien.[103] He instructed another class of graduating students that what stood before them in life above all was to labor. Life and labor, he said, were one and the same—without labor, a person "dies spiritually and physically."[104]

This was the most active writing period in Tikhon's life, as he published short public-facing theological articles for various ecclesiastical periodicals. Among his publications include articles in response to Tolstoy's ideas, in which the great author advocated celibacy and vegetarianism. Unlike many Orthodox writers who vociferously attacked Tolstoy for his rejection of traditional Christian doctrine, Tikhon granted that Tolstoy had articulated problems of the human condition very well. Where Tolstoy fell short, however, was in his unrealistic idealization of human beings (for example, for all to completely give up sexuality), which resulted in Utopian solutions to human and social problems. Orthodoxy, by contrast, realistically takes human beings as they are, in their fallen state, but through Christ and the Church one receives God's grace and, through that, the means of transformation and transcendence.[105] In short, as a teacher and pastoral writer, Tikhon engaged in contemporary issues and problems and presented Orthodoxy as providing the solution to those modern existential problems.[106]

According to Evlogy, Tikhon "had a great deal of practical wisdom with a sense of tactfulness and moderation. In spite of his mildness and good nature he was able to enact useful measures with determination." Tikhon was very popular as dean both among the students and the local population and he frequently was invited to serve liturgy in parishes. "As dean he managed to establish a living and lasting relationship with the people."[107]

Because of his successes and popularity with the people, Archbishop Flavian and the Holy Synod supported consecrating him bishop of Lublin. Following the customary formal process, on October 4, 1897, Pobedonostsev sent to Emperor Nicholas II the Synod's list of three candidates for the vacant post of the bishop of Lublin, ranking Tikhon first; Nicholas II resolved, as normal, that it should "go to the first."[108] Tikhon was still a few months shy of the age of thirty-three, the canonical age for elevation to the episcopate in the Orthodox Church. Tikhon traveled to St. Petersburg for the consecration. The elevation to the episcopate took place in two stages, first the nomination, and on the next day the consecration.

Tikhon's speech at the nomination is a remarkable text, pointing out his level of maturity and indicating the path his episcopal career would take. He first quoted the words of Moses, who expressed his unworthiness to lead the people when God elected him, and Jeremiah, who protested to God that he was still too young. Reflecting on the exalted position of the episcopal rank at the time, he observed: "At one point, in my early youth, episcopal service appeared to me—and not to me alone!—to consist of honor, reverence, power, authority.... Now I understand that the episcopate is first and above all not honor, power, and authority, but work, labor, and spiritual effort [*delo, trud, podvig*]. Indeed, is it easy to be everything to everyone (1 Cor. 9:22)?" He concluded that "the true life of a bishop is continual dying from cares, labors and sorrows."[109] He further reflected on the special challenges of being a bishop in Kholm, where his job would be to defend the flock against those trying to poach them (presumably the Catholics) and bring back the "lost sheep." He also observed that "the burden of the episcopate is being laid on me at a relatively young age." And though youth brought with it energy, it was not "rich with life experience," patience, and sober judgment—the things needed above all for success.[110]

Tikhon would serve as bishop of Lublin for less than a year. In that time, however, he was extremely active, visiting 110 parishes and monasteries where he preached and served liturgy. He continued with even greater energy to establish new schools in the region, organizing 102 in the period that he was chair of the educational committee. When Evlogy arrived to replace him as dean of the seminary, Tikhon received him with an openness that was totally unfamiliar to Evlogy from his previous experience. Evlogy witnessed a "brotherly atmosphere which held not even a shadow of condescending kindness. I realized that I had to cast off any formality in my relationships of the kind to which I was accustomed to . . . and that I would be dealing simply with my superiors with an open heart." In one of his most telling episodes, Evlogy, who later became the bishop of Lublin himself, was making the rounds of the diocese where he would read priest's liturgical chronicles. In one parish, a priest wrote of Tikhon's visit years before and commented: "For the first time I see a human being in a hierarch."[111] Although Evlogy was rather put off by this comment and nearly reported the priest to the chancery, it is nevertheless extremely revealing of how Tikhon as bishop was able to relate to the clergy under him that was very different than they were used to experiencing. As bishop, Tikhon's sphere of activity with the region deepened, and he found a way to defend Orthodoxy tactfully, without being heavy-handed, in a way that endeared him to the local population. "As bishop he deepened and expanded his links with the people even more, and became truly the Kholm Region's own hierarch." On the day of his departure, "the whole of Kholm" gathered at the train station to see off their beloved archpastor.[12]

2
Bishop of the Aleutians (1898–1903)

Bishop Tikhon was thirty-three years old and had been a bishop less than a year when he was appointed bishop for the entirety of North America.[1] He first learned of his new appointment to America unofficially, secondhand through personal contacts—and he did not welcome the news.[2] Things were going well in Khom and he did not want to leave so soon after becoming its bishop. Indeed, he was unhappy enough with the appointment that he considered refusing it, and his senior, Archbishop Ieronim of Warsaw, also sought unsuccessfully to keep Tikhon in Kholm. Candidates could and did, in fact, refuse unwanted appointments from the Synod. Before leaving Kholm, Tikhon met with the assistant chief procurator of the Holy Synod, Vladimir Sabler, who told him that there was a consensus in the Synod regarding his appointment. Informing him about the affairs in America, Sabler also explained that previous bishops sent to America were "nervous" people, and moreover that the current Bishop Nikolai (Ziorov) so ardently desired to leave America that he was even threatening to retire. Though clearly reluctant to go to America, Tikhon decided he would "submit to the will of God and the Authorities."[3] This was a sentiment Tikhon would have to repeat on numerous occasions in his life.

After a visit to his mother in Toropets, Tikhon came to St. Petersburg toward the end of October 1898, and he would spend about three weeks there preparing for his journey. This entailed familiarizing himself with "entire bundles of 'files'" on the Orthodox mission in America, as well as meetings with a variety of people. He felt overwhelmed by the prospect, as he candidly wrote to Archbishop Flavian at the end of October. "It's been almost two months that I am in confusion, anxiety, and in a fog. . . . I am going to America only for the sake of obedience, and only this thought calms me—that this is not something I sought or desired, and if it came about, then it is not without the will of God, and therefore I think that God will not leave me without His help!"[4]

Tikhon departed from St. Petersburg in mid-November 1898. Many people accompanied him to the train station to see him off, including Sabler, several professors of the Theological Academy, and about twenty former students. He traveled to America with Benedict Turkevich, who would become an important priest in America; Nikanor Grivsky, the Pskov seminary choir director; and Tikhon's brother Mikhail, who was to serve as his secretary. Bishop Tikhon traveled across Europe and departed from Le Havre, arriving in New York on December 12.[5]

In his first years in North America, Tikhon traveled extensively across the continent. During these journeys, he came to a clear understanding of the problems, needs, and challenges of the diocese. By the time he made a return trip to Russia in 1903, he developed a plan for how to address the needs of the diocese. By that point he was exhausted by all his efforts and not eager to go back to America, but his sense of duty outweighed his personal frustrations. This chapter looks at several stories that ran in parallel with each other in the years between 1899 and 1903: his missionary journeys to Alaska and Canada, his efforts to further the conversion of Greek Catholics to Orthodoxy, and his intimate involvement in the construction of important new churches in New York and Chicago.

Orthodoxy in North America

Orthodox Christianity in North America began with the Russian expansion in Alaska in the eighteenth century. In 1794, the first missionary team arrived on Kodiak Island. The missionaries found the Native Alaskans, especially on Kodiak and the Aleutian Islands, to be very receptive to the faith and baptized thousands. The mission received new impetus under Father John Veniaminov, who learned local languages and translated scriptural and liturgical texts into them. After becoming bishop with the name Innocent, the seat of the diocese became New Archangel (Sitka).[6] The Alaskan missionaries, who were largely independent of and frequently in conflict with the colonial administration (which was primarily commercial rather than governmental), distinguished between faith and culture and sought to adapt Christianity to Native culture and language. The success of the Alaskan mission can be attributed to this approach. By the 1860s, there were some twelve thousand Alaskan Christians in forty-three communities with nine churches and thirty-five chapels as well as schools and orphanages.[7]

The sale of Alaska to the United States in 1867 dramatically changed the situation of the Russian mission there. The mission suffered from the efforts of the Presbyterian missionary Sheldon Jackson (1834–1909), who was appointed the General Agent of Education from 1885 to 1906. Jackson believed that the Americanization and Christianization of the Natives had to proceed together. To ensure they only spoke English, he established boarding schools for Native children which cut them off from their families—and, for those who were Orthodox, from their churches and clergy. This was intentional, since the eradication of Native culture and "superstitions" included eliminating their Russian Orthodoxy and replacing it with American Protestantism.[8]

The Russian Mission also suffered from poor leadership. After the sale of Alaska, an independent diocese was created for the mission, which now became the diocese of the "Aleutians and Alaska." The diocesan headquarters was moved from Sitka to San Francisco, which established a presence of Orthodoxy on the mainland but meant that there was less oversight in Alaska. Through the 1870s and 1880s, there were long stretches with no bishop, while the bishops who came were beset by personal problems.[9] The situation was only stabilized in the 1890s under Bishop Nikolai (Ziorov, 1851–1915), under whose capable leadership (1891–1898) the Orthodox Church in America began to take root and grow.

Nearly a century after the Orthodox mission to Alaska started, it began to experience a sudden growth in the continental United States through immigration. The first Orthodox parish on the continent was established primarily by Greeks in New Orleans in 1860s. Early Orthodox immigrants came from diverse ethnic backgrounds. Multiethnic Orthodox communities were established in cities such as New York, San Francisco, Seattle, and Chicago and turned to the Russian bishop as the only legitimate episcopal authority in the country: Orthodox congregations need a bishop to supply them with priests and other necessities to function. Since Orthodox episcopal authority was traditionally defined along territorial lines, the presence of the Russian diocesan structure and bishop meant that Orthodox congregations would likely (though not always) turn to that authority for their needs.

The "new immigration" wave from the 1880 to 1920 included many Eastern Christians. The numbers escalated dramatically in the 1890s. The largest group came from the Austro-Hungarian Empire, from what are today Slovakia, Poland, and Ukraine. They constituted diverse groups that do not align well with today's ethnic categories, and they were known as Ruthenians or Rusyns, Carpatho-Rusyns, Uhro-Rusyns, Galicians, and other groups depending on where they hailed from. Russians tended to regard them all as "Little Russians." As Eastern Slavs, their ancestors were Eastern Orthodox Christians, but during the Polish-Lithuanian Commonwealth they became Uniates (Greek Catholics). Some came to North America as Greek Catholics, though some had already become Orthodox in Austro-Hungary.[10]

Bishop Nikolai (Ziorov) did much to build up the diocese. He accepted numerous parishes of Greek Catholics into the Orthodox Church. He also attracted capable missionary priests such as John Kochurov (1871–1917) and Alexander Hotovitzky (1872–1937), who would prove indispensable for Bishop Tikhon. Fr. Alexander Hotovitzky established the periodical of the diocese, *The Russian Orthodox American Messenger* (in Russian, the *Amerikansky Pravoslavnyi Vestnik*), which published news, sermons, directives, and theological articles in both Russian and English. Tikhon was able to accomplish as much as he did in North America not only because of his own energy and abilities, but also because Nikolai had laid such a firm foundation for him to build on.[11]

First Days in America

When the *SS La Champagne* docked in New York on December 12, 1898, Tikhon was met by a large welcoming party that included the Russian Consul in New York as well as clergy and faithful from the Russian and Syro-Arab churches headed by Archimandrite Raphael (Hawaweeny). Bishop Tikhon and his companions went straight to the Russian church, which was a rented building on 2nd Avenue, where Tikhon was greeted by the church's rector, Rev. Alexander Hotovitzky. Tikhon's first speech in America referred to the gradual strengthening of Orthodoxy in the New World, which provided suitable soil on which to take root since Americans had a reputation for being a religious people and America was the land of religious tolerance.[12] On his first day, Tikhon was confronted with some of the complex challenges of his new post: He was facing a country that was totally new and unfamiliar to him, staffed with Russian clergy he did not know, serving far-flung locales he did not understand. He was also met by the Syrian priest, representing completely different communities from entirely different parts of the world that he had no experience with. Then there was the Russian Consul. Because of the Russian Orthodox Church's ties to the Russian state, a Russian bishop abroad was also an official representative of Russia itself. Tikhon would have to serve as something of a diplomat, dealing with government officials from

Russia, the United States—especially Alaska, which was its own unique situation in the American context—and Canada. It was an incredibly tall order for the thirty-three-year-old who had been bishop for only a year.

According to the *New York Herald*, "Bishop Tikhon won the hearts of all present not only by his words, but also by his beautiful simplicity and cordiality of manner." The article noted he was young to be governing the largest Orthodox diocese in the world.[13] Tikhon spent four days in New York, during which he managed to find some time for sightseeing—and was impressed by both the skyscrapers and the bitter cold—as well as to serve liturgy in both the Russian and Syrian churches. En route to San Francisco, Tikhon traveled through Washington to visit the Russian embassy there and then through Pittsburgh and Chicago. On the evening of December 23, 1898, Tikhon arrived in San Francisco; despite the late hour, he set off directly for the cathedral. Nikolai handed Tikhon the staff that was once carried by Innocent, the "enlightener of Alaska," expressing his wish that Tikhon's service in America be as fruitful as Innocent's.[14]

That evening, Bishop Tikhon then delivered his first speech in San Francisco, the first of many full speeches and sermons that would be published in *The Russian Orthodox American Messenger*; in that first speech, he set the tone for how he would relate to his clergy and flock that would characterize his episcopate far beyond America. He began by quoting St. Paul's letter to the Romans, who was citing the Prophet Hosea: "And I will say to them which were not my people, 'Thou art my people,' and to her which was not my beloved, 'Thou art my beloved'" (Romans 9:25, citing Hosea 2:23). St. Paul interpreted Hosea in terms of God choosing the Gentiles. Tikhon drew a parallel to himself: He had been sent to a new land, and a people who were not his people had become his. He had left everything that was dear to him behind—his aging mother and his friends—to come to a place and people foreign to him. But now they were his people. "From this day on, to you and to your welfare I direct my thoughts and my care; my strength and my faculties I dedicate to ministering unto you." He told the flock that he came to them with love, which would be expressed in his service to them, and asked them to accept him in love that would be expressed in "in obeying me, trusting me, co-operating with me."[15]

In the remainder of the sermon, he emphasized the last element. This cooperation (*sodeistvie*), he said, referred, first, to his "co-workers" (*sotrudniki*), the pastors of the church. Tikhon noted that the country was new to him, whereas the clergy had already labored long there and knew it better than he—so he needed their knowledge and experience of the land and people and that they would become "truly my *co-laborers*" (emphasis in the original), offering him their counsel and understanding. Tikhon then asked for *sodeistvie i sotrudnichestvo*, cooperation as fellow-laborers, also from his "entire beloved flock."[16] Drawing on St. Paul's image of the church as a body, he stated that, though not every member of the church had the same function, each was necessary and could not exist without the other. He called upon the faithful, the laity, to work together with him in building up the church and—quoting John Chrysostom—not to put everything on the clergy, "for you yourselves can do much, and you know one another better than we."[17] This was strikingly democratic language for a Russian bishop in the nineteenth century, where the episcopal office was usually exercised only by hierarchy and obedience, not cooperation with clergy and believers who were regarded as equal partners rather than subordinates. Conceptualizing the Church as the body of the people, clergy and laity alike who play essential roles and who could contribute to building up the Church would become the hallmark of the renewal movement in Russia between 1905 and 1917; but for a bishop to be expressing this to his flock in 1898 was far from typical.

The following day, Bishop Nikolai quickly debriefed his successor and handed over to him the property and paperwork of the diocese before departing later that day. Tikhon now assumed charge of his new diocese.

Bishop Tikhon Gets Acquainted with His New Diocese

Bishop Tikhon spent the winter and spring of 1898–1899 in San Francisco getting acquainted with his new cathedral (at 1715 Powell Street) and clergy. Tikhon's initial impression of San Francisco was very positive: He appreciated the beauty, the mild climate, and its calmness compared to New York and Chicago.[18]

Bishops in the prerevolutionary Russian Church were required to submit annual reports on the state of their diocese each year. Tikhon's reports from America recounted his activities and his observations of the diocese that developed significantly from year to year. His first report was a brief one for the year 1898. He provided the basic data about the diocese: It consisted of 27,378 Orthodox parishioners. On the continental United States and Canada (11,144 people), more than half were listed as "Russians" (mostly

Rusyns and Galicians), with the rest being Syrians (3,000), Serbs, Greeks, and a few Americans. The Alaskan mission (16,234 parishioners) was made up, in the categories of the time, of Creoles, Aleuts, Indians, and Eskimos (Yupik). Thus, at the time Tikhon started his service as bishop in America, the number of Orthodox Christians in Alaska was larger than the flock on the mainland. At the end of the report, Tikhon stated that he would refrain from drawing any conclusions because in the short time he was in the diocese he knew it only "theoretically and on paper."[19]

Tikhon left to visit the diocese on the eastern half of the United States on the Tuesday after Easter (May 2, 1899). This became his pattern: setting off after Easter to tour the diocese, traversing North America for months at a time. He made the effort to visit every functional parish (i.e., a community that already had a church building and a priest). Often on visits he would receive delegations from nearby communities that were endeavoring to form their own parishes, consulting with him on purchasing property, building a church, or requesting a priest. Tikhon was virtually always on the move, spending no more than a few nights in any one place, except in the largest cities. New York served as the base for making day trips to nearby locations. In each place he was extremely busy. He always participated in a round of liturgical services (evening vespers or vigil followed by liturgy the following morning), at which he would give a sermon. Liturgy would be followed by a reception, banquet, or festal meal with parishioners. Later he met with the local clergy and inspected parish records. If the parish had a school, he would visit or spend some time with the children, test their knowledge of the faith and prayers, and dole out sweets (which always made him very popular with children). He met with representatives of the brotherhood connected to the parish. Finally, he also met with leading members of the parish to discuss their issues, concerns, and aspirations, including finances and plans for future growth.

Bishop Tikhon's first trip eastward included visits to Minneapolis, Chicago, Cleveland, Pittsburgh, and New York, where he stayed for ten days. He wrote to Flavian from Cleveland: "My diocese is almost boundless: I have inspected all of four parishes, and have already had to travel by railroad more than 5,000 kilometers."[20] On the way back he went through Galveston, returning to San Francisco by June 18. Travel could be adventurous: Their horse-drawn carriage was nearly hit by a train at one point, and later the same day their trip was disrupted by mangled train tracks.[21] After returning to San Francisco, having barely caught up on diocesan paperwork, he departed for

Alaska, and only returned to San Francisco in September. Altogether he was on the road for four months, visited thirty-nine places, and traveled some 25,000 kilometers, 9,600 kilometers of which was by sea—yet he had to leave the furthest points for the following year.[22]

After his first year's travels through his diocese, Tikhon reported to the Holy Synod that "the Aleutian diocese encompasses the whole of North America, though the Orthodox live predominantly in Alaska and in the eastern states. The Bishop's see is located in between and is close neither to one, nor to the other, and because of the long distances not only the flock, but even the pastors can rarely visit San Francisco, and therefore only the bishop's journeys for inspecting the diocese, despite their difficulty (especially in Alaska), are an absolute necessity. For me, having just assumed the administration of the diocese, a personal inspection was all the more necessary."[23] One thing became clear to him in his first year: His diocese was no longer centered in Alaska, but now had two very different poles, the other consisting of new parishes in the eastern part of the United States. That meant that the title of the diocese and the bishop's title—of "the Aleutians and Alaska"—no longer reflected the realities. Therefore, one of the first changes he sought to make was to change the name of the diocese. He proposed (and the Synod approved) changing the name to the diocese of "the Aleutians and North America," retaining the Aleutian Islands for historical reasons since they were the first Orthodox congregations in America, but including North America to reflect reality.[24]

Alaska

Because of the significant presence of Orthodoxy in particular regions of Alaska, it presented unique challenges that Tikhon had to navigate, especially regarding American officials. In 1899, he had an exchange with Sheldon Jackson, then General Agent of Education in Alaska, focused on schools operated by the Orthodox Church. While the exchange was cordial, Tikhon felt the need to defend the Church's schools from charges that they were trying to Russify the Natives. He also argued for the usefulness of their schools, because very often they served communities that did not yet have public schools.[25]

Tikhon went to Alaska each of his first three years as bishop of the diocese (1899, 1900, and 1901). The first two trips were both long, and the second was especially grueling. The Alaska mission was also extremely spread out; it consisted of fourteen parishes with seventeen churches and fifty-three chapels. Many small and remote communities had chapels that were served by a priest at most a few times a year, and they might never have seen a bishop. If they were lucky, they had a reader who conducted lay services without the sacraments on a regular basis. Tikhon sought to visit every single parish and even as many of the chapels as he could. On the first trip, he departed San Francisco in early July 1899, took a steamship from Seattle to Juneau, and then on to Sitka.[26] From there, Tikhon traveled on the SS *Dora*, "the bulldog of the North Pacific," which had the largest mail run in the world. When the ship stopped to deliver mail and provisions to small settlements, the bishop would disembark to visit the villagers and the chapel. Tikhon stayed at Kenai for two weeks and then caught the *Dora* to Kodiak on August 5. He was greeted there by Fr. Tikhon Shalamov (1868–1933, father of the writer Varlam Shalamov) and with him visited the hermitage of Herman (d. 1837) on Spruce Island, the beloved missionary of the early nineteenth century. On August 11, he departed for Unalaska on the SS *Excelsior*—the steamboat that launched the Klondike Gold Rush two years earlier. He returned to San Francisco on September 6.[27]

Bishop Tikhon made a second trip to Alaska in the summer of 1900. He visited the Yukon and Kuskokwim missions, which, because they were the most remote and difficult to reach—so much so that no bishop had ever been there—that they required a separate trip. The Yukon-Kuskokwim Delta—one of the largest deltas in the world (50,000 square miles)—consists mostly of tundra and marshes, and even today has virtually no roads. The Native populations of the region lived in small, relatively isolated communities (typically fewer than three hundred people) and maintained intact traditional cultural systems. But the region was affected by the dramatic influx of thousands of Euro-Americans since gold had been discovered in 1897. By the summer of 1900, a hundred steamers were transporting miners up to the Yukon River gold fields.

Tikhon left San Francisco on May 19, 1900. He traveled alone on a small exploration ship that reached Unalaska two weeks later, from there to Saint Michael, and then up the Yukon River. On June 25, Tikhon arrived at Ikogmute (now known as Russian Mission); the mission there was established by Fr. Iakov Netsvetov (1802–1864) in the 1830s–1840s, but no bishop had made it there before. Therefore, the townspeople were overjoyed at Tikhon's arrival and the mission's priest, Fr. Jacob Korchinsky (1861–1941) expressed the community's gratitude to the bishop for making such an effort to come to them.[28]

From Russian Mission (Ikogmute), however, was when the real ordeal began. The bishop, together with Fr. Korchinsky and Fr. Ioann Orlov, the creole priest from the Kuskokwim mission, departed on June 28, arriving at Pavlovka (today known as Chuathbulak) on July 6. They traveled with two psalmists and five rowers by *baidara*, or umiak, an open skin boat used by the Yupik and Inuit. From the Yukon River, they cut across to the Kuskokwim River on the Yukon-Kuskokwim Portage Trail, where they were likely to meet only wild animals (including bears). When they reached the portages, they had to carry the boats and all their luggage across swampy terrain, which was made more difficult because the heat had dried up many of the streams that normally they could paddle down. As Tikhon wrote to Flavian, "The trip was not the easiest. I succeeded in getting to the Yukon and Kuskokwim, where no bishop has ever been. But that required at times going on foot across the tundra. This is captured in a photograph: dressed in a parka of skins and mosquito nets, making me look like an Armenian catholicos! 12 nights I slept on the ground in a tent; our provisions, as they say here, were 'short,' that is, few. But most of all it was necessary to bear the mosquitos."[29] On July 7, Tikhon served the first-ever hierarchical liturgy at the Kuskokwim mission, with about seventy members of the faithful in attendance, many having come from far away for the occasion. He served liturgy again on Sunday, July 8, and visited all the Natives in their homes, and departed for the return journey across the portage trail with its travails.[30]

At the final portage, when they were ready to stop for the night, someone came from Ikogmute and informed them that everyone in the village had fallen ill, including the priest's family. They decided to push on ahead through the night. The following day, Tikhon served liturgy followed by prayers for the healing of those who were sick, and after the service he visited the dwellings of everyone who was ill. Fr. Korchinsky reported that "Vladyka blessed each sick person and comforted them, taking leave of them with a gentle word, promising to each one that he would pray for their recovery."[31] Tikhon's visit to Alaska coincided with the outbreak of what the Yupik called the "Great Sickness" that devastated Native populations, many of which lost between a quarter and a half of their population. The sickness was brought by the sudden influx of Americans who came as part of the Gold Rush.[32]

On July 14, Tikhon and his traveling companions departed from Russian Mission on a steamer. The captain allowed them to stop at the village of

Andreafsky so Tikhon could visit the chapel and its builder, Peter Andreev, who had fallen ill. In Andreafsky the epidemic was in full force, and again Tikhon visited the ill in their dwellings, undaunted by the contagion, and was able to distribute medicine. The steamer arrived in St. Michael on July 16. Flu and measles were raging there, which hit at the end of June shortly after Tikhon's departure. Tikhon visited the sick here as well. He stayed for a week and arrived in San Francisco on August 4. The entire trip covered 7,300 miles and lasted seventy-eight days.[33]

Tikhon described the devastating effect of the "Great Sickness" in a subsequent report to the Orthodox Missionary Society. Some villages virtually became extinct. He quoted from the report of the Kuskokwim missionary, who stated that three-quarters of the population died, some six hundred people along the Kuskokwim River, including his own wife and daughter, and that the priest himself was ill for a month. Indeed, the number of Orthodox believers in Alaska had been estimated at 16,843, but in 1902, Tikhon stated there were only 11,453. As the missionaries made their rounds to various settlements, they found that people had been buried in collective graves or remained unburied, which the missionaries had to do themselves. The people could not remember anything like it. Tikhon added that "the American government pays almost no attention" to what was befalling the Natives, since it was only interested in exploiting the natural resources: There were no hospitals and few doctors.[34] Elsewhere Tikhon observed the hardships of the Natives, who were becoming poorer instead of richer because of the way the trading companies exploited them.[35]

On the Sunday after his return to San Francisco, Tikhon delivered one of his most powerful sermons. He discussed the Gospel reading about the feeding of the five thousand, noting that Christ cared about the earthly needs and hunger of the people—and that he instructed his disciples to "give them something to eat" (Matthew 14:16). Tikhon told his listeners about his recent journey, and how the Natives had been on the verge of starvation the previous winter only to be decimated by diseases "brought there by white people and from which the natives die quickly."[36] The sermon highlighted the links between poverty, racial inequality, and disease.

Tikhon exhorted his listeners (and readers) to help, just as Christ had instructed his disciples to feed his hungry followers. It should not matter that the Alaskan Natives belonged to another race, Tikhon stated, and then explicitly condemned American indifference toward the fate of the Natives; there were many who spoke of how the Natives were a "weak" people and their decline was inevitable as the whites took over. Tikhon pointed out the paradox that whites consider themselves to be "civilized" compared to brown-skinned peoples and therefore more superior—when in fact, by their actions, they were manifesting the opposite. "It is not civilization at all—which shamefully is preached by some" that the white race should dominate the world or should even "wipe out the other 'colored' races; and if the natives die, it's for the better, so it's not worth taking care of them." On the contrary, Tikhon asserted, "true civilization consists in giving as many people as possible access to the benefits of life." The truly civilized are those who use their privileges to "raise up to their level" those who are less fortunate or developed. Tikhon then explicitly rejected any form of racism: "Since all people originate from one person, all are children of one Heavenly Father; all were redeemed by the most pure blood of Christ, in Whom 'there is neither Jew nor Greek, slave nor free' (Gal. 3:28)." In Christ, racial distinctions have been transcended, all were granted equality. "All are brothers and must love one another," a love which must not only be "in words, but in deeds as well."[37] Tikhon's sermon profoundly critiqued the impact of the colonial domination and racialized politics of the United States toward Native Alaskans.

One of Bishop Tikhon's main concerns in Alaska was the competition coming from other Christian missionaries. In the last decades of the nineteenth century, and especially with the influx of Americans with the Gold Rush, both Protestant and Roman Catholic missionaries were coming in ever-greater numbers. Tikhon was particularly frustrated because, instead of going into territories where Christians had not been before, they targeted Orthodox Christians. "Because it is easier to preach Christ to those who already believe in Him, so they have cast their preaching nets not so much among native pagans as among the Orthodox natives."[38] The Aleuts were so attached to Orthodoxy that foreign missionaries did not have much success with them. But Americans coming because of the Gold Rush married Native women who were Orthodox, and then abandoned them, leaving behind children. Therefore Catholic, Methodist, and Baptist missionaries, who had more financial resources and missionaries than the Orthodox, established orphanages that took children from Orthodox families and raised them in their respective faiths. Therefore, more Orthodox orphanages were needed.[39] At the end of 1900, Tikhon formally proposed the establishment of an orphanage for girls, and the following year it opened on Kodiak, which was met with "great enthusiasm by the local population."[40] He also secured renewed funding for Alaska from the Missionary Society in Russia, which had ended such funding after Alaska's sale to the United States.[41]

Tikhon also wrote to Flavian about the Yukon-Kuskokwim journey in which he expressed his frustrations not just with the hardships of the journey (and the mosquitoes), but with the inability to accomplish more. "Every journey and every 'bite' is no calamity, it's possible to bear it, and no matter where you are it's necessary to labor. But the most difficult part is that all this is spent for nothing and doesn't help, for I myself am left without help, that is, without people and means." The Holy Synod did not provide him with sufficient funds to accomplish what needed to be done, and also missionaries were unwilling to serve in the harsh climate. He was also frustrated that the Synod did not even always reply, even when he did not "ask for any money."[42]

The Conversion of Greek Catholics

Through the course of his first year in North America, it became clear to the young Bishop Tikhon that the center of gravity of his diocese was shifting. The main driver of this change was the conversion of Greek Catholics to Orthodoxy. These Greek Catholics came to North America by the tens of thousands at the turn of the century. They found work in coal mines and factories and were very attached to their church and their traditions, which meant that they were not satisfied going to Roman Catholic parishes.

An instrumental figure in the conversion of Greek Catholics to Orthodoxy was Father Alexis Toth. Toth was a Greek Catholic priest who, when he arrived from present-day Slovakia in 1889, presented himself to the local Roman Catholic Archbishop Patrick Ireland. Ireland thought the Greek Catholics far too exotic for his goal of integrating Catholics into American life. He forbade Toth from serving in a church. Toth and his parishioners then sent a delegation to meet with the Russian bishop and were received into the Orthodox Church in 1892. Thus began a movement that would bring more than one hundred thousand Greek Catholics into the Orthodox Church in the subsequent decades that would dramatically transform the Orthodox mission in America.[43]

A major reason Tikhon was chosen for North America was no doubt his extensive experience with former Uniates in Kholm. Aside from a handful of parishes and the Syro-Arab mission, the rest of the parishes were formed of former Greek Catholics, who numbered more than six thousand people.

Tikhon regarded the movement of Greek Catholics into the Orthodox Church to be very significant. Rusyns were characterized by a high degree of religiosity. Further, it established the presence of Orthodoxy in far more American cities than before, which served a broader missionary purpose by providing opportunities for Americans interested in Orthodoxy to encounter it directly. Finally, the movement was having a profound impact on Greek Catholics in the Austro-Hungarian Empire, where a movement of conversion from Greek Catholicism to Orthodoxy had been inspired by remigrants from America.[44]

The reasons motivating the conversion of Greek Catholics to Orthodoxy were many and complex. As Tikhon heard from many such converts, they never heard of the "Unia" in the home country, and they never understood the history of how these churches that were once Eastern Orthodox later came under Rome. They had always thought of themselves as Orthodox (indeed, prayers for "all Orthodox Christians" in the Orthodox liturgy remained in the Greek Catholic rite) and were surprised to learn otherwise on coming to America. For many, becoming Orthodox was not understood so much as a "conversion" as "becoming what we always were." This was reinforced by their less than welcoming reception by Latin-rite Catholic bishops, who did not want parallel Catholic churches in the same places and refused to recognize their priests because they were married. For a people profoundly attached to their liturgy and rituals, this was unthinkable. Concrete factors might also be involved in a congregation's decision to become Orthodox, such as dissatisfaction with their priest or tensions within a community.[45]

The processes of conversion could be complex, however. For one, Greek Catholic churches often had design features that clashed with Orthodox ritual, or the ritual itself—though very different than the Latin rite—was no longer the same as the Orthodox one. In the beginning, the Russian government was providing financial assistance for churches that converted (along with other Orthodox parishes in the United States)—which led to accusations by Catholics that they were "buying" converts.[46] But in 1896, Sergei Witte, the Russian minister of finance, cut off subsides for the "Austrians" on the basis that they were not Russian citizens. By the time Tikhon was bishop, parishes that wished to convert had to guarantee that they could pay off debts they incurred while building their churches and could pay their priests. This slowed down the process, since many could not afford to do so without assistance; as Tikhon wrote to Flavian, "many are ready to unite, but they cannot support clergy themselves, and we also do not have money."[47] Moreover, some who promised that they would handle their financial obligations on converting failed to do so and had to be bailed out by the diocese.[48] Tikhon therefore was cautious about receiving new parishes, putting the diocese's resources into strengthening those that had already converted. Further complications arose if only part of the entire congregation wished to convert, which led to disputes over the church property—and in some cases, to lawsuits; as a result of a lawsuit in Wilkes-Barre, Pennsylvania, where Toth had relocated, the Orthodox community lost the church to the Greek Catholics and had to build a new one.[49]

Although some Greek Catholics were attracted to Orthodoxy because they already felt themselves already to be Orthodox, they were divided in their attitude toward the Russian Orthodox Church. Some saw themselves as "Rus[s]ky," which ambiguously could describe both Great Russians from Russia but also Rusyns, and therefore saw a natural tie with the Russian Church.[50] But others criticized the subordination of the Russian Church to the tsar, and Catholic critics especially pushed the point that the "head" of the Russian Church was the tsar and that it was not Orthodoxy (*pravoslavie*), but "tsar-doxy" (*tsareslavie*). Tikhon was at pains to point out that this was incorrect, that the tsar was the "protector" of the Orthodox Church but that the "head" of the Church was Christ. Confusion was caused, however, by the fact that the Church continued to pray for the tsar. Tikhon's solution was to ensure that clergy also pray during the liturgy for the president of the United States (or the British monarch if in Canada) alongside the tsar, and that if they were in a mixed parish they could pray for the Greek or Serbian king as well. The clergy should explain to their parishioners that they were not praying for the tsar as for their ruler, but as their benefactor (since many congregations were, in one way or another, supported by Russia financially).[51]

If Tikhon had the sense in 1899 that the process of conversion was slowing down, time would tell a different story. By 1902, he was reporting to the Holy Synod that the mission was growing stronger and spreading across the continental United States: The number of parishioners had doubled from 11,000 in 1898 to 22,000 in 1902, and this came not only from immigration, but through the conversion of more than 3,000 people. Further, the number of parishes had grown (from fourteen to twenty-four), and the number of clergy had doubled to thirty. Parishioners were increasingly able to support their clergy. The mission went much more smoothly, Tikhon reported, when entire parishes converted with their priests; then there would be no contestations over church properties. But the majority of Greek Catholic clergy would not convert because most still intended to return home. If a congregation converted without their priest, then the Russian Mission had to supply them with one—and this was no easy matter. Priests coming from Russia often knew nothing about the history of the Unia, nor were they familiar with their language.[52]

At the end of 1902, the parish of St. John the Baptist in Mayfield, Pennsylvania, converted, which was the high point of all of Tikhon's labors regarding Greek Catholic conversions. It was the ideal scenario: A large congregation (more than one thousand people) converted entirely, led by their priest, Father John Olshevsky, and a massive and beautiful church building. Though the parish had been inclined toward Orthodoxy for a while, it also felt no urgent need to convert until the Roman Catholic bishop tried to force the congregation to sign over the parish to his name. They informed Tikhon that they wanted to become Orthodox but only under certain conditions: that they would not have to have a special ceremony rejecting the union with Rome, since they did not recognize any union with Rome; that Tikhon not demand that they put the church in his name; and that he allow them to continue singing and serving the way they always had (in the "little Russian" manner). Tikhon accepted these conditions. The parish was brought in on November 3, 1902. The following May, Tikhon visited the parish and gave a sermon during liturgy congratulating the parishioners on their entry into the Orthodox Church. Tikhon declared: "With your joining the Orthodox Church you have filled our heart abundantly with jubilation and joy"—and from Tikhon's own letters and reports, this was a genuine statement, for this was clearly one of the high points in his first five years in North America.[53]

Canada

In 1901, Tikhon accomplished another first: He became the first Orthodox bishop to visit Canada. In 1896, the Liberals won federal elections in Canada and the new Minister of Interior, Clifford Sifton (1861–1929), initiated a concerted policy to encourage immigration that would settle the prairies in the western part of the country. Sifton thought Eastern European minorities— the "stalwart peasant in a sheepskin coat, born of the soil"—would make successful farmers. Some of these were ethnic minorities from the Austro-Hungarian Empire, such as Greek Catholics from Galicia and Orthodox Christians from Bucovina. They were offered 160-acre homesteads and the

Canadian government helped relocate them. These people were generally very poor and arrived in their new homeland with next to nothing. But come they did, to the Canadian provinces of Manitoba, Saskatchewan, and Alberta, by the tens of thousands—by 1914, nearly a quarter million Ukrainians and some fifteen thousand Romanians had emigrated.[54]

The Greek Catholic Galicians who came to Canada encountered the same misunderstanding and lack of support as their co-religionists south of the border from the (primarily French) Roman Catholic bishops. By 1900, Tikhon reported, there were nearly two thousand Orthodox believers in Alberta: nine hundred former Greek Catholic Galicians who had converted to Orthodoxy and another one thousand Orthodox Bucovinians. Therefore, he established a separate Canadian mission (previously it had just been attached to the Seattle mission). Tikhon appointed Father Jacob Korchinsky, with whom he had just traveled the hard road of the Yukon and Kuskokwim mission and one he knew he could rely on, as the first priest for the new Canadian mission. Fr. Korchinsky was from Ukraine, and the people were grateful that the bishop assigned a priest who could speak their language.[55]

Tikhon made his first trip to Alberta in September 1901. He went to the farm of a Galician Rusyn, where a pavilion was set up for holding services and Rusyns came from all around (whether Orthodox or Uniate). Tikhon also met with representatives of local government, a lawyer, and an immigration agent, to discuss matters of establishing and registering the church and ministering to the new immigrants.[56]

On September 6, Tikhon and Fr. Korchinsky were traveling to Beaver Creek to consecrate a chapel on an open horse-drawn peasant cart, when something broke on the harness and the horses galloped away, dragging the cart along behind them over bumps, potholes, and ditches until Tikhon was thrown out of the cart, bruising and scratching his hands and landing hard on one leg while the other was under the wheel. "It could have been far worse," he wrote to Flavian, "but somehow I managed to pull my leg out of the boot which was under the wheel. By the way, this didn't prevent me from serving liturgy right after."[57] The boot, however, was completely destroyed. The injury was serious enough to cause him to limp for weeks afterward.[58] Tikhon consecrated the first Orthodox Church in Canada, the Holy Trinity Church in Wostok, on September 8; this was the first community to convert to Orthodoxy already in 1897.[59] The following day he consecrated a second church, dedicated to St. Nicholas, in the colony of Bucowina.[60]

Before his trip to Canada ended, Bishop Tikhon went to Edmonton, where he met with a Canadian parliamentarian who promised to help the Orthodox Church, as the government was providing plots of land for churches to be built. He wrote to Flavian after the trip, "I had to travel [in Canada] more than two hundred kilometers on horseback along nasty roads, far inferior even to Toropets country paths. Unfortunately sometimes the rains came down and completely soaked us."[61]

Bishop Tikhon made a second trip to Canada in the winter of 1903. The trip was unplanned and had to be squeezed in between planned travels. He made the trip to respond to a specific crisis. The influx of immigrants was particularly rapid at the turn of the century, and finding ways of ministering to them was even more challenging since they were dispersed across large territories rather than concentrated in cities. As elsewhere, there was a shortage of priests and lack of financial resources. The Church and state in Russia provided no stipends for Canada. And though virtually all Orthodox communities in North America were poor, the ones in Canada were among the poorest at this early stage, and they struggled to build churches and support clergy. Even when funds could be found, it was extremely difficult to find missionaries for Canada. The Orthodox Church had certain standards: They would only ordain candidates who had a seminary education, which meant that virtually all had to come from Russia. But few Russians had any interest in going to the Western Canadian prairies. Missionaries to North America viewed an assignment to Western Canada as akin to Siberian exile: With a sparse population and harsh climate, it was even less attractive than Alaska, which at least held a certain romantic appeal for Russians (and came with a guaranteed income).[62] Even Fr. Korchinsky did not last long; he was replaced by Mikhail Skibinsky, a graduate of the Kholm seminary, whom Tikhon ordained in Wostok in 1902.[63]

By the beginning of 1903, there was still only one Orthodox priest in Canada. Then an unexpected challenger appeared on the scene. Serafim (Stefan Ustvolsky, 1858–?) had been ordained a priest in Russia and later became a monk. He appeared in North America at the end of 1902, falsely claiming that he was sent by the eastern patriarchs to be a missionary bishop in North America. He went to Winnipeg and declared himself to be the metropolitan of all America.[64] Serafim was able to play on the resistance of some Galicians (both Orthodox and Greek Catholic) to being under the Russian Orthodox Church through his claim that he represented a truer former of Orthodoxy because he was sent by the Greek patriarchs. Unlike Tikhon, who ordained those who finished seminary, Serafim ordained any whom communities put forward.[65]

It was this threat from Serafim that precipitated Tikhon's unplanned trip to Manitoba and Assiniboia (Saskatchewan) in March 1903. After a fourteen-hour train ride to Yorkton from Winnipeg, he traveled twenty-eight miles by sleigh to a colony of Bucovinians at Crooked Lake. It was bitterly cold, especially for Tikhon, who had just come from California and did not have suitable clothing. As he wrote to Flavian, "we had to freeze not a little: the winter there now is cold, with a lot of snow. More than once it was necessary to run behind the sleigh to warm up, which is not so comfortable in a long cassock."[66] The Bucovinians at Crooked Lake were Romanian. On learning that there were some five hundred Bucovina farming families around Yorkton, Tikhon suggested they pool their resources to be able to support a priest. At one farm, he and the priest traveling with him heard nearly a hundred confessions and baptized or chrismated a group of children.[67] Tikhon wrote the metropolitan of Bucovina to send them a priest who could serve in Romanian. After the metropolitan of Bucovina replied that he had no priests to spare, Tikhon appointed a Ukrainian priest from Kishinev (Chisinau) who also spoke Romanian. Tikhon was able to keep most of the Orthodox Bucovinians away from Serafim, who was, nevertheless, quite successful in attracting a large number of Greek Catholics.[68]

Tikhon found he still had to battle against the Serafimite movement on his third trip to Canada in 1904.[69] Tikhon made another trip to Winnipeg in September 1905 and visited fifteen settlements. By that time, there were some five thousand Orthodox Bucovinians, who had built four churches and eleven chapels, but still only had one permanent priest in Wostok alongside a priest who visited from Minneapolis. Tikhon continued to try to recruit priests, especially from Kishinev.[70] In sum, Tikhon expended no little energy trying to build up the church in Canada, where there was a growing number of Orthodox Christians. And though those Orthodox believers were building churches and chapels and eager to have priests, Tikhon's greatest challenge was in recruiting suitable clergy for them.

New Churches in New York and Chicago

The situation looked quite different in the burgeoning cities in the United States. Orthodoxy developed gradually in the two major American cities of New York and Chicago; in New York, it had a presence and a chapel in the 1870s that disappeared for a decade until a community was established in 1895 in a rented house on Second Avenue. Slavs founded the parish of St. Vladimir's in Chicago in 1892. Both Chicago and New York had energetic priests when Tikhon arrived: Fathers Alexander Hotovitzky and Ilia Zotikov in New York and John Kochurov in Chicago.[71] Tikhon immediately saw the need to erect Orthodox Churches in these two cities. As he wrote in his first annual report, the churches in New York and Chicago "were extremely cramped, far from accommodating all the worshipers, and located in rented living spaces, not distinguished from them at all, which causes more than a little embarrassment for the Orthodox and elicits criticism even from the non-Orthodox. There is an urgent need to build new churches in these places."[72] Although many congregations were building new churches during Tikhon's first five years, these two—in two of the most important American cities—received his special attention and direct participation. All of this demanded no little time and energy, and he made repeated trips to both cities expressly for that purpose.

Tikhon began requesting funds from Russia to purchase the land for the cathedral in New York shortly after his arrival in America.[73] Purchasing land in New York was an enormous challenge, given the high cost of property. On his first trip east, he came to New York in May 1899 and went with members of the building commission to inspect various plots, trying to find something that met their needs. They decided on a 97th Street plot close to Central Park; although it was not on the corner—and the church would have to be between two other buildings—it was the best they could find that was large enough, affordable, and in a good location.[74] The commission purchased the land for $36,000 in September 1899. They made the purchase without the final approval of either Tikhon (who was in Alaska and out of reach) or the Holy Synod, which necessitated Tikhon writing a long letter of explanation to Chief Procurator Pobedonostsev.[75] The Holy Synod finally approved a collection to raise money in Russia for the construction of the church; the collection was approved by Tsar Nicholas II himself, who also made the first donation of 5,000 rubles.[76]

Tikhon made a special trip to New York at the end of 1899—his second across the continent that year—"to clarify several questions connected to the construction" of the new church.[77] They wanted it to be a "worthy exponent of the greatness of the Orthodox faith and the glory" of Russia and that it be immediately recognizable as a Russian church.[78] Spending over two weeks in

New York, his "entire time was busy, aside from services, with determining the plans and estimates for the future church [and] ... everything was sent to Petersburg. The church will be in the Russian style, and a little home attached to it—but with an American layout of rooms. In it will be two–three rooms also for the hierarch, so that I can, without cramping anyone, live for two months in the winter."[79] Tikhon chaired meetings of the building committee and examined architectural plans. In the end, Tikhon and the committee chose the plan by John Bergesen, who was born in Finland and knew Russian church architecture (and later designed other Orthodox churches in America as well).[80]

Bishop Tikhon appointed Father Hotovitzky to travel to Russia to make the collection. One of the first to donate—and to give a special blessing for the collection—was the famous pastor Father John of Kronstadt; Hotovitzky reported that this helped the process, and he succeeded in raising 60,000 rubles in the months he spent traveling through Russia.[81] The cornerstone ceremony on May 22, 1901, was a major event that was covered in the *New York Times*.[82]

Bishop Tikhon returned to New York to consecrate the church on November 23, 1902. He described that "there was a massive number of people—both Orthodox and Americans. The ambassador was there with his entire staff, the mayor of the city, the Anglican (high church) bishop Grafton. Almost all of our clergy (with the exception of those furthest away) were also there. After the consecration I had a reception for Americans, and then a luncheon for the embassy and clergy. The church is magnificent and beautiful."[83] The *New York Times* described how the city's mayor sat next to the Russian ambassador, who described to him the meaning of the ritual.[84] Tikhon gave a sermon recalling how the community began humbly but now had a temple worthy of the Russian people and the greatness of the Orthodox faith in the great American city. The new church signaled to the audience that Orthodox Christians were not a temporary presence in the New World but were there to stay—and therefore the church could serve a missionary purpose to witness to Americans.[85]

The second important church construction project was the Holy Trinity Church in Chicago. Here, too, Tikhon was intimately involved in the entire process. On his first journey through the diocese, he spent time in Chicago in May 1899 and helped choose the plot of land. The community suffered a major setback when the church warden made off with the money the parish had saved. This also caused a split in the parish over who was to blame.

Tikhon came again in December, reconciled the parish, and encouraged them to continue, also securing assistance from the Russian consul.[86]

In November 1900, Tikhon made a special trip to Chicago. He came to negotiate with the architect the community had found: the famous Louis Sullivan (1856–1924), sometimes called the "father of skyscrapers" and the "father of modernism," mentor to Frank Lloyd Wright. Sullivan was brought in on the project by the wealthy Chicago industrialist Charles R. Crane (1858–1939), who was a Russophile and sympathetic to Russian Orthodoxy. Crane gave substantial financial support to the construction of the churches in both Chicago and New York, so much so that Tikhon requested that the Holy Synod give special recognition to Crane for his substantial donation to the Chicago church and other support for the mission in America.[87] This was late in Sullivan's career and he needed work. Although designing a Russian church was very different from his previous work, Sullivan based his model on pictures of Siberian churches he had seen and came up with a plan that was in the Russian style yet affordable for the congregation. Tikhon went over the plans with Sullivan and indicated changes he wanted made, and he also discussed estimates for the cost of the building.[88]

This time Fr. Kochurov made a trip to Russia to raise money. Again, the emperor donated 5,000 rubles (and at the end another 3,000 rubles), and Fr. John of Kronstadt made a donation and a public declaration in support of the collection. Tikhon visited Chicago in February 1902, spending days meeting with Sullivan to finalize the plans and resolve pressing questions so construction could begin, and returned two months later for the ceremony of laying the cornerstone. Tikhon came to consecrate the church on March 29, 1903. The consecration of the Holy Trinity Church in Chicago was the crown of four years of efforts accomplished shortly before his return to Russia.[89]

The First Five Years

By 1903, Tikhon had completed five years as bishop in North America. During those years, he had spent an enormous amount of time traveling. After his first tour of the diocese in 1899, he understood, given the far-flung nature of the diocese, that he would have to travel much: "It is necessary to be on the road, and here it is unavoidable: the closest priest (and only one at that) is located two days away by railroad. In a word, here for a very understandable reason the priests do not trouble the hierarch with their personal visits, and therefore it falls on him to trouble and to be troubled."[90] In the first years of his appointment, the young bishop devoted his energies to learning his new diocese and flock, its needs and issues, and solving concrete problems. He also took advantage of the possibilities that the expanding presence of Orthodoxy presented to the Russian Church to expand its mission to Americans, from a mission to Native Alaskans and Greek Catholics to increased interaction with American Christians such as Episcopalians. Tikhon had to balance this sense of mission in terms of outreach with the role of the Church in serving immigrants.[91]

One of Tikhon's persistent concerns was that his flock, which consisted of religious and ethnic minority immigrants in a land very foreign to their homelands, not lose their identity and become assimilated into the American "melting pot." Tikhon was concerned that Orthodox Christians be lured away by two temptations in America: either by other Christian confessions or by material concerns that left them indifferent to their faith. He was aware that migrants came to America seeking a better material life—and instructed his clergy to seek out those who may have forgotten the spiritual, especially in places where there had been no priests or churches for a long time.[92] He also exhorted his listeners not to stray away from the Church. He lamented that some "in this country of many faiths and many nationalities little by little do lose the Orthodox Faith! They begin their departure with things that in their opinion are insignificant," things considered outdated, such as wearing a cross or praying before meals, and from there stop observing the fasts or go to church less frequently. Moreover, thinking that they were somehow superior, they mocked those who still observed the old traditions—which Tikhon considered a more serious sin. Rather, Tikhon asserted, Orthodoxy was the true faith, and the true Orthodox believers should not merely adhere to the faith themselves but also share it—which was not just the faith of a particular group of people but a universal faith. This responsibility belonged not just to missionaries but to every member of the Church in their own way.[93] He advocated a "spiritual conservatism," encouraging his flock to adhere to the unchanging Orthodox faith and not succumb to the attraction of those who criticize it for being stagnant and lifeless. Russians, he told the faithful in the New York church, were distinguished by their dedication to the faith, and this was true when they were abroad; and, indeed, it was through the church that they also best preserved their national identity. Therefore, though living among foreigners with foreign faiths that would like to "enlighten" them, they should remain firm in the "faith of their fathers."[94] In a sermon to a

Serbian church, he similarly encouraged his audience them to maintain their national identities; however, he also stressed that national identity had only a temporal significance, whereas maintaining Orthodoxy was more important, and that transcended national differences.[95]

Tikhon was not only concerned with the spiritual challenges of his immigrant flock but also their material difficulties and their economic exploitation. In an open letter to the paper *Svit* concerning a strike of coal miners, Tikhon sympathized with the strikers who, without work, were growing poorer. He noted that, even if an agreement were reached this time, it would only be temporary because "life will become more expensive, supplies and goods will increase in price, while wages will remain the same and therefore be insufficient. This means, with the way things are around here, it will again become necessary to resort to a strike, and suffer again, and continue to live in poverty." Tikhon was writing not only to lament the situation, however, but to propose a course of action: "in these circumstances it is necessary to come to help the needy." He proposed establishing "a special fund specifically for the purpose of helping during the strikes." In the immediate case, those working in factories that were not striking should help those who were. Brotherhoods could do this, or the Orthodox Mutual Aid Society could set up a special fund for that purpose—and to that end, Tikhon himself donated the first hundred dollars to establish the fund.[96]

After five years, Tikhon identified what he considered to be the greatest challenges to administering the diocese. One remained the lack of financial resources. Orthodox immigrants in America were poor. Tikhon constantly wrote the Holy Synod and the chief procurator for financial assistance for particular projects or aspects of the mission, with mixed success. He convinced the Missionary Society in Russia to return to supporting the church in Alaska, which helped relieve some of the pressures there, but as a consequence the Holy Synod rejected his proposal to establish an American Missionary Society that could raise funds in Russia for the entire diocese.[97]

A second intractable problem was finding qualified and willing missionaries to fill the constantly growing need.[98] When possible, he recruited people that he knew personally or family members of clergy already in America. Otherwise, he recruited people based on references from others. Tikhon wrote to Sabler about his desperation for people: "I need someone, and in this regard I experience great difficulties: people are needed, but I do not know them [or] where to get them from?"[99] Tikhon was frustrated that he had to "put up with all sorts of rubbish" in the process. It frequently happened that even those who came wanted to return to Russia after a short time: "the Russian-American 'birdies' annoy not a little with their frequent flights back and forth."[100]

The third challenge was the sheer size of the diocese. Tikhon reported to the Synod on his visitations of the diocese in 1900 that he chose to visit six parishes in Alaska and three in the states that were the farthest away, which necessitated traveling 25,000 kilometers and being away from San Francisco for four months. "Such lengthy absences have an unfavorable effect in the affairs of diocesan administration. In the parishes on the Continent church life for still some time to come will demand *the constant and closest supervision* from the side of the diocesan *hierarch*. And, moreover, there is the necessity of visiting at times the parishes in Alaska, where there is not only no telegraph, but even the mail is sent only once a month and takes almost a month to get there." And when he was in Alaska, he was unable to respond to issues in the Lower forty-eight that needed quick resolution.[101]

Returning home after having been away from San Francisco from mid-May to the end of October 1901, he wrote to Flavian: "having returned back home, instead of rest I found a mass of all sorts of paperwork and business." This, he told Flavian, convinced him that he needed an assistant bishop for Alaska. He therefore wrote Pobedonostsev with this request. "Of course no few objections and difficulties will be found, of which the main one is money; but I wrote that I am ready to remain with three thousand gold rubles and cede two thousand to the vicar; it will be sufficient for both. The ruling [bishop] will stay in the states, and the vicar in Sitka, where everything is ready for him: a cathedral, an episcopal residence with a church, clergy, a school."[102] The two parts of the diocese—Alaska and the east coast of the states—were so different from one another and so far apart that it was no longer feasible for one person to administer both properly.

While Bishop Tikhon had plans to improve the diocese, he was also exhausted. He wrote to Flavian in 1901 that he was "being torn from all sides" and that the American diocese "will distress its primate for some time to come!"[103] He observed to another correspondent: "by the grace of God, we are developing and becoming firmly established in the States, but at the same time it is very difficult here for the bishop, and I pine not a little for the Kholm vicariate."[104] Although many of his labors were coming to fruition toward the end of 1902, his patience was running out. In the system of the imperial Russian Church, bishops were transferred frequently, and these transfers were a recurrent point of discussion in Tikhon's correspondence with Flavian—who already had been transferred twice—so Tikhon was also thinking that "it's time already to ask about being recalled."[105]

Then on December 6, 1902, while in Old Forge, Pennsylvania, Tikhon received a telegram informing him of his younger brother Mikhail's sudden death in San Francisco. Tikhon was devastated. He stayed in Old Forge for a week and served a requiem liturgy every day.[106] He had had enough, and he wanted to go home. He wrote to Flavian that "a heavy sorrow has befallen me: while I was traveling about the neighboring parishes . . . my brother died unexpectedly in San Francisco. . . . I didn't even succeed in making it for the funeral, and I directed that they should place his body in the cellar, because I want to send it to Russia. And I myself am planning to go there in the spring and thinking not to return to America. There will be more sacrifice and forbearance!"[107]

In early 1903, Tikhon submitted a request to the Holy Synod that it would be useful for him personally to address certain vital questions of the American mission to the Synod, as well as the need to put his brother's affairs in order and to tend to his mother. He therefore requested a three-month sabbatical to return to Russia.[108] He also wrote to the metropolitan of St. Petersburg that he wished to be replaced. As he wrote to Flavian, "no matter how much you live here, all the same you can't accomplish everything, there is more than enough work" for several subsequent bishops.[109] His desire to return to Russia was not simply personal, however, but also to resolve crucial affairs of the American mission. Tikhon had developed a plan for how the American mission could be substantially improved, but he also recognized that the Holy Synod would drag its feet unless he was there to push matters. There had been issues about which Tikhon wrote to the Synod or to Pobedonostsev that would not be answered even in a year, which was not helpful when matters were developing so quickly.[110] The Synod granted his sabbatical and was not opposed to transferring him, but it had difficulty in finding a replacement.[111]

If Tikhon had run out of patience with the challenges of being bishop in America, his flock felt the opposite about their pastor. An article devoted to the anniversary of Tikhon's fifth year as bishop noted that the diocese had flourished under him, doubling in size on the mainland both in the number of parishioners and parishes. The article recollected many small details about his service: how, in the absence of the priest in a parish he was visiting, he would serve all the sacraments and liturgical needs of the flock. During his travels across the country, it befell him to go hungry and sleep "on the bare floor in an unheated room." He bore these difficulties without ever expressing frustration with those around him. "It is not surprising, therefore, that the entire diocese... awaits his return with impatience!"[112]

On May 27, 1903, on the eve of Ascension, Tikhon served Vigil in the Russian Church in New York. Father Hotovitzky delivered an address on behalf of the diocese's clergy: "on the thorny path of missionary service—over the course of five years—we have had in your person a guardian angel." He had been their leader bearing the burdens of service "not only in word, but also in deed.... The Aleutian Islands had awaited their new Innocent, who disregarded the dangers for the glory of God, and we all perceive the prelate who resurrected for Orthodox Rus beyond the oceans the early centuries of Christianity, when the pastor personally knew his sheep and could call them by name. Each bunch of Orthodox believers, spread out across the entirety of North America, had the happiness to see you—and more than once a year—as their own father, for whom all his flock is dear."[113]

Tikhon, in his final address to the clergy, recalled how he was terrified upon learning of his appointment to America and thought of refusing the appointment, but decided to rely upon God's mercy—and his hopes were not disappointed. He recalled Ezekiel's scroll, on which was written "lamentation and mourning and woe," but after Ezekiel swallowed it, it was sweet as honey (Ezekiel 2:10, 3:3). "In the course of five years... I have borne no little grief in America, and often and deeply I grieved in my soul over the ailments of my flock. But God also rewarded me with spiritual joys of a father rejoicing in his flock. I recall, for example, the recent unification of the Mayfielders! And it turned out that my sorrows were not in vain in the eyes of God, but brought me spiritual sweetness. And you, father-missionaries, have so attached me to America with your love, that it is difficult for me to go on leave."[114]

The Alaska Vicariate

On the feast of the Ascension, May 28, 1903, Bishop Tikhon departed from New York for Europe. Tikhon's first destination in Russia was Toropets to see his mother, who was now alone, her husband and her other sons having passed away. He spent about two weeks at home, and during that time also met with friends and acquaintances and served in local churches as something of a local celebrity.[115]

Securing an assistant bishop for Alaska became the linchpin for all of Tikhon's reforms in the diocese: Only when Alaska was properly cared for could the ruling hierarch attend to the ever-increasing demands on the mainland and in Canada. Tikhon anticipated that the Synod would be reluctant to grant his request. "The main thing is to secure a hierarch for Alaska, in whose service I am ready to sacrifice part of my salary. If there occurs any hitch in this, then without any further discussion I will refuse to return to America, even though my clergy and the Chief Procurator really don't want this. K. Petrovich [Pobedonostsev] asks with horror: 'who will we replace [you with] and who will we send?'"[116] Though Tikhon has often been viewed, even by contemporaries, as gentle and mild, these letters make it clear that when important matters were at stake, he could be very adamant and resolute—even as a young bishop in the face of the mighty chief procurator and the Holy Synod.

On his arrival in St. Petersburg on June 16, 1903, Tikhon was in for a surprise: He was assigned to serve on the Holy Synod. The metropolitan of St. Petersburg, Antony (Vadkovsky), was leaving for Sarov for the canonization of St. Serafim, and two other members were unwell and not attending regularly. Tikhon was added to the Synod during his leave "until they find me a see, although they are already throwing words about my return to America."[117] What was intended as a sabbatical in Russia for much-needed rest turned into a working stay for Tikhon—and not three months as originally planned, but for the remainder of 1903. He sat on the Synod for the entirety of that time—which helped him to see through crucial matters for the American Mission.[118] He made trips home and found some time to spend with friends, and he kept busy with the paperwork that he continued to receive from America on top of Synodal business.[119]

Making the case for appointing an assistant bishop for Alaska clearly did not come quickly, however. He finally presented his plan for a vicar bishop for Sitka to the Synod only three months later in August.[120] He made the case that establishing the vicariate would be a restoration of what existed before, when Innocent was appointed bishop of Siberia and a vicar bishop was appointed for Alaska. That situation lasted until the establishment of the independent diocese in 1870. The see was relocated to San Francisco for reasons of travel to Alaska and to establish the presence of Orthodoxy in America where there was growing interest. Those reasons, Tikhon argued, were no longer compelling.[121]

Tikhon asserted that Sitka was already set up for a bishop to come. The North American diocese was not large in the number of parishioners (43,500) and parishes (forty) by comparison with dioceses in Russia. But, he argued, a single parish there often demanded the expense of energy and attention that was consumed by dozens of parishes in Russia. In Alaska, challenging travel meant that the bishop was cut off from the rest of the diocese for extended periods. Given the rising demands of the mainland, it would be increasingly difficult for a bishop to be able to have time to visit the more difficult-to-reach parts of Alaska. At the same time, Alaska still needed the attention and supervision of a bishop.[122]

Tikhon proposed that the vicar in Alaska would have a greater range of rights and authority than assistant bishops in Russia to appoint, transfer, and retire clergy. He would also deal directly with the American civil authorities in Alaska and with the Russian Missionary Society. Tikhon concluded by proposing Archimandrite Innokenty (Pustynsky, 1868–1937) as a candidate. Innokenty studied at the Kiev Theological Academy and served for three years in America, including in the diocesan administration, when he was tonsured a monk and ordained by Bishop Nikolai.[123]

The Synod took time to deliberate Tikhon's proposal and make various inquiries such as with the Ministry of Foreign Affairs. Finally in November the Synod asked him to return to America for at least two more years until the "seedlings ripen"—that is, until potential replacements were ready. But they agreed to grant him a vicar and 7,200 rubles per year of support total. As Tikhon wrote to Flavian, "I, by the way, said that I would like to see the resolution of this question myself (so as not to be left empty handed afterwards)."[124] Tikhon was not content with promises of being granted a vicar, but wanted to ensure his vicar was chosen and consecrated, ready to come. The day the Synod was to finally issue a resolution on establishing the Alaska vicariate, November 12, 1903, St. Petersburg was flooded—Tikhon was barely able to make it by cab to the Synod, but the decision went in his favor.[125] In the end, though absent from his diocese longer than planned, he had accomplished what it needed for its long-term development.

On December 4, the Holy Synod issued the resolution to Tikhon, noting that on November 29, the Emperor had approved the establishment of the vicariate with the title "Bishop of Alaska."[126] On December 12, he participated in his last Synodal session, at which Innokenty (Pustynsky) was nominated as bishop of Alaska. Innokenty was consecrated bishop two days later. Tikhon noted in his sermon for the occasion that Innokenty was being consecrated in the same church, the Kazan Cathedral in St. Petersburg, almost the same day, and for the same mission to Alaska, as his namesake Metropolitan Innocent (Innokenty Veniaminov). He would have to defend his flock from the oppression and exploitation of trading companies. Being bishop in America was not the honor of a high position; it was "hard work and not luxury," and it was fatherly care and not dominating authority. Finally, he instructed Innokenty that his pastoral staff symbolized both the wanderer's staff, because he would have to take long, arduous journeys, and also a staff to defend his flock from predators, namely those missionaries who love to "build their house on somebody else's foundation."[127]

Securing the vicariate for Alaska was the cornerstone of plans that Bishop Tikhon had devised for the further development of the American Orthodox diocese. The day after Innokenty's consecration, on December 15, 1903, Tikhon had an audience with Emperor Nicholas II. A week later he traveled to Toropets to spend Christmas with his mother, and departed on December 28, 1903.[128]

3
Archbishop of North America (1904–1907)

Tikhon returned to New York on January 25, 1904, a week before his thirty-ninth birthday.[1] He stayed in New York for Easter before traveling across the country to San Francisco. Tikhon told his flock there that his return reminded him of the first time he entered that church five years earlier: Then everything was unknown and lay in the future, whereas now they all knew one another well, and though there was still much to do, much had already been accomplished.[2] Two weeks later, Tikhon learned that his mother had passed away at the age of seventy-two. "My return to America dispirited her. Now I am completely alone—I don't even have cousins."[3] The obituary for her in the *Russian Orthodox American Messenger* acknowledged how Tikhon had left his mother in the care of those close to him, knowing that she was ill and probably would not live much longer, because he had again "drawn the lot of apostolic service in America."[4]

Tikhon continued to keep an eye on episcopal appointments and transfers in Russia. In the spring of 1904, he noted that, if they elevate him to archbishop, it would be more difficult to transfer him because they would have to transfer him to a more prestigious see—and it would also be more difficult to replace him with another archbishop.[5] He was also aware that he himself made it more difficult for them to replace him because he kept initiating new projects and then had to see them through to completion—only to then begin more. But those accomplishments would make the job easier for the next person.[6] As he had anticipated, Tikhon was elevated by the Holy Synod to the rank of archbishop in May 1905 for his "outstandingly zealous service and his special labors."[7]

Tikhon continued to travel extensively. He stayed in California for three months before departing on August 3, 1904, for his inspection of the diocese, including a month-long trip in Canada (both Alberta and Manitoba) with its usual challenges, arriving in New York in October.[8] On the return journey, Tikhon spent about a week in St. Louis, where he consecrated a new church (in Madison, Illinois) and visited the World's Fair. While there, he found many people he knew, including Aleuts manning the Alaska exhibit and Syrians operating the Jerusalem exhibit. The Westinghouse exhibit included an authentic Russian *izba* (cottage) set up for Russian tea with a samovar, which was later bought by Charles Crane. The highlight for Tikhon of the entire fair was the Grunwaldt collection of Russian painting.[9] He spent the winter in San Francisco and traveled again extensively in the summer of 1905, visiting new places such as Colorado, where new parishes were being opened.

During his first five years in America, as Tikhon laid out in a report to the Holy Synod in 1905, he came to understand the key challenges to the rapidly changing diocese. The influx of Greek Catholic converts shifted the pole of the diocese from Alaska to the eastern part of the United States and demanded the bishop's constant attention, which he was now able to concentrate on since establishing the vicariate in Alaska. He set out to accomplish the remaining parts of his plan. This included creating separate missions for Syrian and Serbian Orthodox Christians and transferring the bishop's residence to New York to be closer to the majority of parishes, which was made possible by the construction of the new church in New York. The constant shortage of clergy necessitated establishing a seminary in North America.[10] Tikhon implemented these and other ambitious plans, including founding the first monastery and convening the first Council, in the three years that he was in America before his departure in 1907.

The Russo-Japanese War and the 1905 Revolution

On February 8–9, 1904, two weeks after Tikhon returned to America, Japan launched a surprise attack on the Russian navy at Port Arthur and Chemulpo Bay. Two of the ships sunk, the *Retvizan* and the *Variag*, were built in Philadelphia. Tikhon had visited both and even conducted a prayer service on the *Retvizan*; its crew had been a great support for the fledgling church in Philadelphia and formed the choir that sang at the cornerstone-laying ceremony in New York.[11] After some months of collecting donations for the Red Cross, Tikhon sent them with a letter to Emperor Nicholas II, saying that though the contributions were modest, all the Orthodox in America of various ethnicities supported Russia.[12] The diocese in particular helped Russian prisoners of war through the Orthodox Church in Japan.

The American press was sympathetic to Japan, and anti-Russian sentiment increased. Tikhon had originally planned to come to St. Louis for the opening of the Russian division at the World's Fair, but in February he was worried that Russia would not even be allowed to participate. He complained to Flavian that it was "not easy" for Russians in America at that moment.[13] In response to the anti-Russian sentiments, Tikhon gave a sermon on the tsar's birthday on May 19, 1904. As he had done before during the Boxer Rebellion, so now Tikhon presented Nicholas II as "our Most Peace-Loving Tsar" and said the war with Japan was "forced" upon him.[14] His depiction was rather romanticized, given that Russia provoked the war through its incautiously aggressive policy in the Far East.[15] Speaking to an audience of immigrants in America, Tikhon was trying to defend Russia from the American mistrust and perceptions that the Russian people and government were backward.[16]

Russia's losses in the war throughout 1904 exacerbated social tensions in Russia that erupted after troops fired upon peaceful demonstrators, led by the priest Georgy Gapon, killing many innocent people. What followed was over two years of mass political and social unrest known as the 1905 Revolution. Tikhon, from far-away America, was very troubled by what was taking place and dismayed by what he read in American newspapers, as he expressed in personal letters. In an Easter greeting to his friend Fr. Petr Bulgakov, who was in Vladivostok, he quoted from an Easter hymn (from Psalm 68): "Let God arise, and let His enemies be scattered," adding "and those [enemies] of the Holy Church and Orthodox Rus. And they are many in these last times, especially domestic ones! God only knows what's happening in our fatherland, especially if one believes all the foreign reports." He even suggested that order might need to be restored by "Peter the Great's club," and only then would reforms be possible.[17] Later in the year, however, he laid blame equally on the ruling classes, who seemed to have "lost their heads." As for the peasants, he suggested inviting some of their representatives for a fraternal meal to talk matters over to bring them to their senses.[18]

The American public's critical sentiments regarding the Russian government, which began during the Russo-Japanese war, intensified during the Revolution of 1905. As a semiofficial representative of Russia, Tikhon felt it important to clarify the Russian perspective to Americans as well as to Orthodox Christians subject to the influence of the American attitudes. Tikhon defended autocracy in a sermon in May 1905 against its American critics—and "homegrown politicians" who agreed with them—who asserted that Russia would "remain a colossus with clay feet until it introduces in its land a Western-style constitution, order based on law, and a constituent assembly." Tikhon countered that the autocratic tsar was able to stand above the interests of any particular segment of society and thereby rule more fairly. The autocracy meant that the tsar could rule without being limited by the interests of the rich and powerful and defend the vulnerable. Tikhon also asserted that democracy had its problems. In a democracy, it was not the people who ruled directly, but rather their elected representatives. And since they were elected by a particular party, "they express the will not of all the people but only their party . . . and care only for the well-being and interests of their own party" and contrary to the interests of the opposing party. He concluded by suggesting that no political system was perfect, and that some were better suited for certain peoples—democracy had deep roots in America and was the best system for it, but that did not mean it should be transplanted onto a totally different soil where it had no roots, as in Russia. Therefore, it was better for Russia to improve and fix the shortcomings of its own system rather than abandon it for something completely alien.[19] Tikhon idealized the autocracy in defending it, and the idea that Western institutions were "alien" to Russia was a staple for Russian conservatives such as Pobedonostsev. His assessment of American democracy, at the same time, bears similarities with Alexis de Tocqueville's arguments about the "tyranny of the majority." Significantly, Tikhon added a footnote to the printed version of his sermon, noting that churchmen had argued in defense of autocracy as the best government order for Russia and regarded it as most appropriate; nevertheless, the Church would always instruct people to obey any government, even a republican or people's government, for "authority is from God" (citing Romans 13:1).[20] This point would become an especially acute question after the Bolshevik seizure of power.

The revolutionary turmoil forced the tsar to grant concessions, including a decree on religious tolerance on April 17, 1905, and in October an elected Duma or parliament. Tens of thousands of those who had felt compelled to be Orthodox apostatized from the Orthodox Church. The toleration decree came unexpectedly and caught the leadership of the Orthodox Church unprepared. Church leaders felt threatened and demoralized, and it was a watershed moment in Church–state relations. The Orthodox Church's social contract with the imperial state had meant that the Church was subject to significant state control, but in exchange had been given a privileged position that restricted competing religious groups. With the decree, the restrictions on other groups were removed without removing government control over the Orthodox Church, so that Church leaders felt as though they were now at a disadvantage. This resulted in increasing calls for Church reform, the convocation of a Church Council—one had not been convened since before Peter the Great—and the restoration of the patriarchate to give the Church an independent voice vis-à-vis the state. Pobedonostsev believed that the bishops would not support wide-sweeping reform; to that end, he had them submit responses to questionnaires about questions of reform. It turned out, however, that the Orthodox episcopate was well-aware of the need for fundamental reform, as evidenced by the "Replies" that they submitted—as a consequence of which Pobedonostsev retired as chief procurator.[21]

Tikhon was particularly disturbed by the impact the toleration decree had on Kholm, where many of the "recalcitrants" took the opportunity to leave the Orthodox Church and become Catholics.[22] He was also cautious about Church reform. He wrote to Flavian in April that he did not think it "completely correct" to abolish the office of the chief procurator and govern the Church completely free of the state, because the Orthodox Church would remain the predominant confession in Russia—"otherwise Rus will fall apart," he added parenthetically—and therefore the government would never agree to leave the Church without some control. Rather, it would be better for civil and ecclesiastical officials to cooperate on ecclesiastical reform.[23] He acknowledged to Petr Bulgakov in July that reform was necessary, but that it should not be rushed, especially when society was in the midst of turmoil. Rather than descend into disagreement with each other, the unrest called for unity within the Church, and when things settled down, reform could be conducted properly.[24]

In his "Reply" in November to questions of Church reform and a forthcoming council, Tikhon advocated fairly extensive reforms in the Russian Orthodox Church. He advocated the restoration of the patriarchate because it would both "reflect the significance and grandeur of the Russian Church" as well as be more canonically correct. Since authority in the Church was far too centralized in the Holy Synod, he proposed dividing it into metropolitan districts in which bishops would answer to the metropolitan as a kind of intermediate authority. Certain regions of the empire, such as the Caucasus, had their own special circumstances and needed a degree of autonomy to deal best with those.[25] He also advocated reforming the rigidly formal diocesan consistories so that they also contain those elected by other clergymen. On elections to ecclesiastical offices in general, Tikhon took a moderate position, suggesting that it was not appropriate in all circumstances, but that it could be beneficial in others. Electing the heads of deaneries, for example, was appropriate because it would render them representatives of the clergy (and laity) and their needs to the bishop rather than agents of the bishop's authority over them.

Tikhon also made a noteworthy proposal that divorce—which, like marriage, was entirely in the control of the Orthodox Church (or other religious institutions for adherents of other faiths)—should be transferred to civil courts. Divorce cases, which all had to be decided by both diocesan bishops and the Synod, were increasingly overwhelming the ecclesiastical administration by this point. Tikhon also suggested that diocesan congresses—which were only permitted to deal with financial issues—should have a much more expanded purview and include lay participation.[26] Tikhon proposed substantive reform that would give parish councils and elected officers authority to manage parish funds and property, and he gave the positive example of how the parish worked in America, advocating as a model the role of brotherhoods as well. He proposed that the current school system for clergy sons be fundamentally transformed to allow more choice for sons of clergy and attract potential clergy from all social classes.[27] Tikhon argued that it was appropriate for clergy to serve on the Duma so that they could represent the interests of the Church and provide a Christian influence on politics.[28]

Tikhon ended his "Reply" by addressing questions of liturgical reform. He advocated reforming the Slavonic liturgical books, which needed updating and correction, rather than using modern Russian. Further, he favored the Council enacting other liturgical reforms: The issue of the calendar needed to be addressed, the repetitive petitions could be curtailed, and some of the priest's silent prayers could be read aloud. He concluded by noting that many of these issues concerned not only the Orthodox Church in Russia, but all the Orthodox Churches, and that their representatives should also be present.[29] In his "Reply," therefore, Tikhon not only expressed a significant vision for Orthodoxy in America but also advocated extensive reforms to revitalize the Orthodox Church in Russia, at the same time emphasizing that reform must not be rushed and must be worked out in a conciliar fashion.

Tikhon's Vision for American Orthodoxy

When Bishop Tikhon had arrived in America for the very first time, on December 12, 1898, among those who welcomed him was the Syrian

Orthodox priest-monk, Archimandrite Raphael (Hawaweeny). He addressed Tikhon on behalf of thousands of Syro-Arab Orthodox Christians in North America, asking that the new bishop support them, promising in return their obedience to Tikhon as their bishop. Tikhon replied that all members of the Orthodox flock were dear to him, that he would be "well-disposed in equal measure to all the Orthodox, no matter which nationality they belong to. Orthodoxy is catholic," he explained, and though this was not always felt in Russia, in America—where there were Russians, Greeks, Arabs and others—"the understanding of the catholicity of Orthodoxy is for us fully palpable."[30] From the first day Tikhon was in America, he recognized the multiethnic nature of Orthodoxy and sought to support that diversity rather than give preferential treatment to Russians or impose any sort of uniformity.

Tikhon's flock was very diverse at the time of his arrival and continued to grow more so. Raphael's promise to obey Tikhon as their bishop if he supported them was significant. It was not a given that other Orthodox Christians would accept the episcopal authority of the Russian bishop, even though the Russian bishop and diocese were the only ones established in North America at the time. There were tensions within the Syrian, Greek, and Serbian communities about whether to consider themselves part of the Russian diocese or whether they were still under their bishops back in their home country, in which case they would turn to them for their needs, such as sending priests. Although the Syrian and Serbian communities recognized the authority of the Russian bishop in Tikhon's time, most of the Greek communities did not.[31] Securing the allegiance of the Syrians and Serbs necessitated meeting their needs—supporting and consecrating new churches, supplying them with priests, providing them with elements necessary for the sacraments (myrrh and the antimins, an altar cloth signed by a bishop which must be placed on the altar table for the Eucharist to be valid). It also meant being sensitive to the fact that there were some in those communities who feared their interests would be subordinated to imperialistic Russian priorities.

In a later sermon, Tikhon said that, just as the Corinthian church in St. Paul's time had been divided into parties (1 Corinthians 1: 10–12), so also in American Orthodoxy the church was divided into "parties" according to nationality. But there should be no place for division or stiving for power in the Church, for in Christ the faith was one and transcended national distinctions.[32]

In the twenty-first century, Orthodox Christianity in North America is divided into overlapping parallel dioceses defined not along geographical lines, as is traditional for Orthodox Christianity, but along ethnic lines: Greek, Antiochian (Arab), Russian, Serbian, Romanian, and so on. But that situation only emerged after the crisis in the Russian Orthodox Church resulting from the Russian Revolution in 1917. What the future of Orthodoxy in America would or should look like in Tikhon's time, given the ever-increasingly diverse immigration, was far from clear.[33] The realities on the ground were often ambiguous: Sometimes Russian bishops assumed every parish, no matter the ethnicity, would acknowledge their authority, but in other situations they did not object when priests came from Serbia or Lebanon and did not subordinate themselves to the Russian diocese. Even when a Serbian or Syrian clergyman did recognize the authority of the Russian bishop in North America, there remained a degree of ambiguity as to whether they then became part of the Russian Church or remained under their home bishop.

In this situation of unclarity, Archbishop Tikhon articulated a vision for the Orthodox Church in America. In his 1905 "Reply" on church reform, Tikhon laid out a plan for a single multiethnic Orthodox Church for America. He proposed that the North American diocese be transformed into an Exarchate (something higher than an ordinary diocese or even metropolitanate, with greater powers for autonomous administration). He observed that the composition of the diocese included not just different ethnicities, but different national Orthodox Churches, which were unified in faith, but each with its own particularities in canonical order, liturgical rite, and parish life. These particularities "are dear to them and are quite tolerable from the common Orthodox point of view. Therefore, we do not believe we have the right to encroach upon the national character of local Churches. On the contrary, we are trying to preserve it in them, giving them an opportunity to be under the direct authority of a superior of their very own nationality." In other words, there would be bishops of each nationality, who would administer subdioceses defined along national lines. "In one word, an entire exarchate of Orthodox national Churches might form in North America, with their own bishops headed by an Exarch—a Russian archbishop. Each of them would be independent in his own area but matters common for the entire American Church would be dealt with by way of a sobor [council] under the chairmanship of the Russian archbishop." Although the Exarch could remain subordinate to the Russian Church, Tikhon also stressed that the local church in America should have the right to respond to local particularities that only it understood—in other words, not be subordinated to Russian interests. "Therefore a greater degree of autonomy (autocephaly) should be granted to the American Church."[34] It was bold to envision already in 1905 that the Orthodox Church in America could and should become an autocephalous (fully independent) local Orthodox Church, rather than being conceived as merely a "mission" or a land of temporary Orthodox diaspora that needed to remain under the mother church of the home country. He evidently understood that this independence was necessary, because so long as the Church in America remained under the Russians, other national groups would fear being subordinated to Russian interests and resist the creation of a unified church. Indeed, in the decades after his departure, competing interests would take Orthodoxy in America in a different direction.

Raphael (Hawaweeny) and the Arab Orthodox Christians

By the time Tikhon articulated his vision in the 1905 "Reply," he had already begun to implement his plans regarding the Syrians and the Serbs. Arabs were one of the largest groups of Orthodox Christians in North America at the time of Tikhon's arrival. Referred to as "Syro-Arabs" in the documents of the time, they came mostly from the province of Greater Syria in the Ottoman Empire, a territory that today includes Syria, Lebanon, Palestine, and Transjordan. In 1895, the community in New York asked Archimandrite Raphael (Hawaweeny) to come serve in America. Raphael was from Syria and studied in Constantinople and Russia.[35] After meeting Bishop Nikolai (Ziorov), who was in Russia at the time, Raphael accompanied him back to America. Shortly after arriving, Raphael established St. Nicholas Church for the Syrian Orthodox Christians in New York.[36]

Bishop Tikhon and Archimandrite Raphael grew to be very close coworkers and regularly served together. Tikhon corresponded with the patriarchate of Antioch to receive clergy for the mission, and he ordained clergy for the Syrian mission himself. Raphael traversed the continent, visiting and ministering to Syrian Christians and helping them to establish churches.[37] Tikhon respected the wishes of both Raphael and his flock and fought to keep him in America when the patriarch of Antioch wanted him to return to elevate him to the episcopate in Syria in 1900 and again in 1901, when the Antiochian patriarchate appointed Raphael bishop of Zahle (in Lebanon) to replace Gerasimos (Iared), Tikhon's former teacher in Pskov, who had passed away.[38]

Raphael's flock wanted him to remain because he had done much for them, and Tikhon supported him in these endeavors and fought to keep him. After years of renting a room in Manhattan, the Syrian community was able to purchase (with financial assistance that Tikhon secured from Russia) a Protestant church on Pacific Street in Brooklyn, where many Arab Christians lived. On November 9, shortly before the consecration of the Russian church in New York, Tikhon and Raphael consecrated this church. It was a major event in the life of the Syrian community.[39] Tikhon delivered a sermon at the consecration of the church in which he congratulated the community for having been faithful and worked hard so that, from the humble beginnings of the rented room, they were able now to have their own church. It was also a joyous moment for the Russians, since they were brothers in the faith and even the tsar himself had helped with the purchase of this church.[40]

With the diocese growing so fast and becoming so complex, Tikhon sought for ways to make the mission more manageable and more successful. As a vicariate, Alaska became virtually independent under its own bishop. The next step was to grant similar autonomy to the Syrians by turning their mission into a vicariate as well. Tikhon petitioned the Holy Synod to elevate Raphael to the episcopate on December 28, 1903, noting the challenges of the mission in which Syrian Christians were spread out in small groups throughout North America. In elevating Raphael to the episcopate, all the Syrian parishes would be placed under him. The Holy Synod sent a decree to Tikhon approving his request in February 1904.[41]

Once Tikhon received the approval, he consecrated Raphael while Bishop Innokenty was still in New York. On the March 13, 1904, Bishops Tikhon and Innokenty consecrated Raphael to the episcopate in the Syrian church in Brooklyn—the first Orthodox episcopal consecration in America. Tikhon invested Raphael with the episcopal staff, symbolic of the shepherd who must gather his scattered sheep, because the Syrians were scattered across the land like sheep without their shepherd.[42]

Patriarch Meletius II (Doumani, 1839–1906) of Antioch thanked Tikhon for consecrating Raphael, stating that he also considered Raphael "as a member of our body, since he comes from our midst, and we number him as one of us in faith and in virtue of his responsibilities over our Syrian children, dispersed in North America."[43] Tikhon replied that Raphael "has never interrupted the closest spiritual tie with his mother-Church of Antioch . . .

even though the Lord determined for him to succeed in the feats of apostolic service ... not in his homeland, but among the workers of another great and glorious branch of the true vineyard of Christ, the Russian Church." Tikhon emphasized that the American church is made up "of all Orthodox nations." Both Tikhon and Raphael were laboring to realize "the pledge of that blessed unity which alone can lead the work of all Orthodox nations and Churches to the desired end, bypassing the differences in tongues and nations."[44] This exchange is noteworthy because it expressed the sense that the Orthodox Church was one, and that Raphael could simultaneously belong canonically to the Russian Church, but still retain his bond with the patriarchate of Antioch. The creation of the vicariate for the Syrian Orthodox proved to be the most successful of Tikhon's efforts to create a multinational Orthodox Church in America.

Sebastian Dabovich and the Serbs

Tikhon sought to establish the same kind of structure for Serbian migrants as he had for the Syrians. Serbian immigration from the Ottoman and Austro-Hungarian Empires increased rapidly in the 1890s. Though the number of purely Serbian parishes was few, Tikhon reported that Serbs had formed many brotherhoods and were building churches, so that more could be expected in the near future; therefore, they needed their own church structure.[45]

The person Tikhon appointed to head the Serbian mission was Sebastian (Dabovich, 1863–1940).[46] Born in San Francisco in 1863, his parents were some of the earliest Serbian immigrants. Sebastian was the first Orthodox priest born in the continental United States. He studied in American public schools, which made him important and unique among the mission's clergy because he was the only native English speaker. Dabovich was tonsured a monk and ordained to the diaconate in December 1888.[47] After studying in Russia, he returned to San Francisco and was ordained to the priesthood by Bishop Nikolai (Ziorov) in 1892. Fr. Sebastian served mostly as an itinerant missionary in the western United States.

Tikhon oversaw the foundation of all the Serbian parishes established in North America during his time there, and indeed he consecrated most of them, sometimes expending great effort to do so, such as traveling all the way from New York to Montana in December to consecrate a church.[48] He noted that it was still "difficult for the Serbs to start their own Serbian diocese here"—indicating he did not exclude that possibility—but he supposed there was not an "urgent need." He believed that the Serbs "will be completely satisfied if a Serbian vicariate is formed here" on the model of the Arabs, placing all the Serbian parishes under their own Serbian bishop.[49]

As a first step, Tikhon formed a special Serbian Mission. In June 1905, he reported to the Holy Synod that "there are now more than 30 thousand Orthodox Serbs" dispersed in different cities and noted the "revitalization" of their religious life. New parishes were being formed, and they were waiting for clergy. It was necessary to form a special mission for the Serbs, he claimed, to support the further development of their ecclesial life in America. In August, the Holy Synod approved the plan.[50] The center of the mission was to be Chicago, a city with a large concentration of Serbs.

Tikhon went to Chicago on October 1, 1905, to officially open the Serbian Mission and elevate Hegumen Sebastian as an archimandrite. The event was attended by many Americans, including the Episcopal theologian Francis Hall, who had corresponded with Sebastian.[51] Tikhon intended next to establish the Serbian vicariate and consecrate Sebastian as a vicar bishop. What should have been the crowning moment in Sebastian's missionary career turned out to be the beginning of its most difficult phase.

For Tikhon, creating the Serbian, Syrian, and Alaskan vicariates constituted stages of his plan to create an Exarchate, which would serve as the first steps to an independent national Church. Since the Serbian Church was unable to provide for the Serbs in America, Tikhon's efforts were therefore intended to support the development of Serbian Orthodoxy in America by providing it with a stable structure and authority to provide for its needs. Tikhon consecrated Serbian parishes and supplied them with priests when he was able. Other parishes wrote to their bishops in the old country to send them priests. In those cases, their Serbian bishops allowed them to stay temporarily in America and remain under their authority, but if they were to remain longer, then they had to come under Tikhon.[52]

Tikhon sought the approval of Serbian ecclesiastical authorities to consecrate Sebastian as he had received from the patriarch of Antioch in consecrating Raphael. This, however, proved to be the decisive stumbling block. The Serbian Orthodox Church was itself divided between the Patriarchate of Karlovci in the Austro-Hungarian Empire, the metropolitanate of Belgrade in the Kingdom of Serbia, and the metropolitanate of Cetinje in Montenegro (which united in 1920 to form the Serbian Orthodox

Church). Since there was no single Serbian Church authority, it was not clear who would authorize Tikhon's proposal. The Patriarchate of Karlovci, under pressure from the Austro-Hungarian authorities, would not grant anything that would strengthen the Russian influence.[53] Opposition also came from American Serbian parishes. They had been happy to be under Tikhon so long as it could be viewed as a temporary situation. The plans for the establishment of a Serbian vicariate as part of an Exarchate of the Russian Church in North America presented a totally different prospect—one that would have permanently placed the Serbian churches under Russian jurisdiction, which some opposed as "Russian usurpation" and a scheme to take over their church properties.[54] Although Archbishop Tikhon's plans to create a Serbian vicariate failed, all but one of the Serbian priests officially belonged to the North American archdiocese under Tikhon at the time he left.[55] Sebastian was saddened by Tikhon's departure and wrote a letter expressing his devotion to him and what an honor it was to serve with him.[56]

Transferring the Episcopal See to New York

An important part of Tikhon's broader plan to transform the diocese entailed transferring the bishop's see from San Francisco to New York. Tikhon's proposal to the Synod in 1904 explained the reasons for the transfer: The bishop could visit the majority of parishes much more easily from New York, often by making day trips. Living in New York, the bishop could meet all the missionaries arriving from Russia, to instruct them on the conditions of the mission in America in general and the place of their assignment in particular, which he had not been able to do from San Francisco. In New York the bishop would be much closer to the "movement" of Greek Catholics converting to Orthodoxy and could guide it. And finally, from New York the bishop would be much closer to Russia, which would make written communication twice as quick (six days instead of twelve), which would greatly facilitate quicker resolution of issues necessary for America.[57]

Since civil and ecclesiastical authorities in Russia viewed the cathedral as an official Russian institution (unlike any other parish), the Synod first had to secure approval from the Ministry of Foreign Affairs and the emperor, which took an entire year. Tikhon looked forward to having the move completed, because it would make his life much easier.[58] The emperor gave his approval in May 1905, and the Synod issued its approval in June. On receiving the decree, Tikhon set the date for the transfer on September 14.[59]

Moving everything, including the Church's chancellery and archive, was not an easy process.[60] Tikhon arrived in New York on October 3, 1905. His arrival now as archbishop of New York was a festive occasion, and Bishop Raphael greeted Tikhon with a speech congratulating him for the move and his elevation as archbishop, both of which were a sign that the diocese was really growing. Five days later, Tikhon delivered his first sermon as archbishop of New York. He said that it was right that the Orthodox see was in New York, since "your city is second in the world and first in this country," one in which every nationality and every church was represented, and its Orthodox church was the most splendid in the diocese. "It is befitting also for the Russian hierarch to live precisely at this parish, which among all parishes is the most Russian." He encouraged the parish to be first among American parishes in its devotion to God and the Orthodox faith and in "care for those who are poor or without work."[61] After the transfer, Tikhon did not have to spend so many consecutive months traveling.

Shortly after the San Francisco cathedral was sold, and while the clergy were still in the process of moving things out, the great earthquake struck San Francisco on April 18, 1906, which also caused a fire that engulfed the city and destroyed the building, the clergy themselves barely escaping.[62]

Religious Education and Establishing a Seminary

By contrast with Russia, American schools were secular and provided no religious education. Unlike Roman Catholics, who felt that American public schools were permeated by a Protestant anti-Catholic ethos and therefore created a parallel system of their own parochial schools, Tikhon did not question that students would attend public schools and saw the secular nature of the schools as neutral. It was only in Alaska that schools operated by the Church provided general education—often in remote areas where public schools had not yet been established. But in the States, church schools taught children after school, on Saturdays, or over the summer. When Bishop Tikhon arrived in North America, there were fifty-five schools in the diocese, in which participated eight hundred children. By 1905, the numbers had risen to eighty schools with twenty-one hundred students.[63]

In addition, three missionary schools existed in the diocese in Unalaska, Sitka, and Minneapolis. These schools had dormitories for students to live in and pupils studied full time rather than going to the public schools, and therefore the program included both religious and secular subjects. The end goal was to prepare those who could become psalmists and teachers. The best students were sent to Russia to study in seminary with the intention that they would return to America as clergy.[64]

The arrangement with the missionary schools was deficient because the pupils who studied there were prepared only for church work, but on graduation they were still too young. Some were sent to Russia for seminary, but they had to spend eight years there to graduate, and much of the Russian seminary program was not relevant for America. Being sent away from their families and homes at such a young age to live in Russia often proved to be traumatic. Others grew accustomed to Russia and did not want to return to America.[65]

The American Orthodox mission continued to rely primarily upon priests from Russia, and the issue grew more urgent as the number of new parishes increased rapidly. For Tikhon, finding reliable candidates from Russia was a constant difficulty. Those who volunteered to come to America did not all come just to serve the Church. Tikhon explained that many who came did not last long, even if they were suitable: They found it difficult to adjust to the culture and style of life or were homesick. Some came and became disenchanted with America; other times their parishes "became disenchanted with them." Moreover, the American flock, mainly parishes of former Greek Catholic Rusyns, found the Russian priests to be very different—they were "Muscovites" who did not speak their language or know their traditions and customs. In short, Tikhon concluded, it would be far better to have candidates for the priesthood who came from America, who knew their own people and the situation of the church. Tikhon therefore concluded that the only solution was to establish a seminary in America and established a commission to work out the details.[66]

By the end of 1904, Tikhon had developed a plan: The seminary would be located in Minneapolis, which already had some teachers, a dormitory, and space for the school. The seminary would be established gradually, with a first class consisting of the graduates from the Minneapolis missionary school and so on until all the current classes at the Minneapolis school had matriculated into the seminary. Likewise, the curriculum would be developed over time, through trial and error, rather than being predetermined from the outset.[67] He simultaneously launched a new school in Cleveland that replaced the missionary school as preparation for the seminary, though students still studied in regular American public schools alongside it.[68] The seminary opened in September 1905. As rector, Tikhon recruited Fr. Leonid Turkevich, who had graduated from the Kazan Theology Academy and whose brother, Fr. Benedict Turkevich, was a trusted priest in America.[69] Already by the end of the first year, three graduates were ordained to the priesthood, and in the long run the seminary became one of the most important contributions Tikhon made to the diocese.

Founding St. Tikhon's Monastery

When Archbishop Tikhon consecrated the first monastery in North America in May 1906, he observed that the Church in America had grown tremendously with the establishment of new parishes, brotherhoods, schools, and even a seminary—but had been missing one of the key institutions that had always been central to Orthodoxy.[70] Monasticism has been a crucially important expression of religious life throughout the history of Orthodoxy. Monasteries served as centers of worship and retreat for ordinary believers as well as missionary, educational, and philanthropic centers.[71] It was, therefore, natural that the leaders of the Orthodox Mission in America would consider it important to establish one. At the same time, it was an enormous challenge to establish something so traditional and so deeply rooted in Orthodox culture in a completely new and not particularly hospitable environment.

In his early years in the diocese, Bishop Tikhon primarily considered the possibility of establishing a small missionary monastery in Alaska. The priest-monks could travel to various surrounding settlements to minister to the faithful that lived far from a church. Monastic missionaries were more mobile (and less costly) than married priests. However, nothing much came of the idea. He also had the idea that a monastery could be a benefit in the lower forty-eight for itinerant priest-monks, but he was uncertain that such a monastery would not be corrupted by the American lifestyle.[72]

The initiative for establishing the monastery came from Hieromonk Arseny (Chagovtsov, 1866–1945). Arseny was a widowed priest from Kharkov who took monastic vows and then wished to become a missionary; he arrived in America in January 1903.[73] Already in his first year in America, Arseny published articles in the *Russian Orthodox American Messenger* making the case for opening a monastery in America.[74] In 1904, Arseny was appointed to the parish in Mayfield, and by 1905 he had several Orthodox farmers in the region supporting his idea of establishing a monastery and even willing to donate land for it. In May 1905, the Convention of the Orthodox Mutual Aid Society decided to establish an orphanage, and Arseny suggested establishing the orphanage and monastery simultaneously, so that the monastery could support the orphanage. In June, Tikhon came out to inspect proposed sites, and the most suitable one was chosen. Tikhon clearly had confidence in both Arseny and the idea of the monastery, and that same month he appointed Arseny to be the overseer of the new monastery. The farm was purchased for $2,600 later in June, and Tikhon personally donated an additional $1,000 for the monastery and the orphanage. The first clergy decided to dedicate the monastery to St. Tikhon of Zadonsk, Archbishop Tikhon's patron saint. Tikhon visited the monastery for the first time in October 1905.[75]

Having laid the foundations, Tikhon requested permission from the Synod to establish the monastery in November 1905. He noted that he had encountered numerous people in America who were attracted to the monastic life. Even though Americans prioritize "business," nevertheless there were those who sought something transcendent, and the Catholics (and even Episcopalians) had monasteries. Moreover, several of the missionaries in America were monks serving parishes, and a monastery could be a place of retreat for them to periodically refresh their spiritual life. Rusyns love the majestic monastic services and would visit the monastery. Finally, Tikhon argued, the monastery could serve a philanthropic purpose. Tikhon informed the Synod that the first steps had already been taken, noting that there were already twelve orphans and, in addition to Hieromonk Arseny, another hieromonk and three novices. Archbishop Tikhon also sought permission to elevate Hieromonk Arseny to Hegumen, noting that he was distinguished by the great energy he put into founding the monastery.[76] The approval process got dragged out, however, just as the transfer of the bishop's see, which was a source of frustration for Tikhon.[77]

As the new monastery building was completed, the consecration and formal opening ceremonies took place on May 30, 1906 (Figure 1). It was planned for Memorial Day so people could come without it interfering either with Sunday parish worship or work, which began a regular tradition at the monastery. A special train brought in the faithful, and people walked

Figure 1. Dedication of St. Tikhon's Monastery by Bishops Tikhon, Raphael, and Innokenty, May 30, 1906

in procession from the station to the monastery.[78] In his sermon for the consecration, Tikhon said it was not a vain effort to establish a monastery in America, even if the contemplative way of life might not seem natural in "a land whose inhabitants are known throughout the world for their practical needs, external efficiency and a lifestyle of worldly comforts." Even in America there were those who thirst for a "true, unworldly life." He hoped the Orthodox Slavs would make their own deposit to the spiritual treasury of the American people through their "hunger for the spiritual, a passion for the heavenly, a longing for universal brotherhood, concern for others, humility, feelings of repentance, and patience."[79] The Holy Synod finally approved the establishment of the monastery after it was already opened.[80]

In the summer of 1906, Tikhon took a retreat at the monastery himself, spending forty days in the monastery in July and August. He arrived in a simple buggy and once there shared in the life of the monastery.[81] He frequently helped the brothers in the physical tasks of the monastery, attended all the services, and always ate the same food as, and together with, the brothers. But he also brought with him diocesan paperwork that needed attending to, and he was often up very early in the morning, or sometimes late at night, attending to this work. A particularly festive occasion was the feast of St. Tikhon of Zadonsk on August 13, which was both the monastery's patronal feast and the archbishop's name's day. Some two hundred faithful came to celebrate the occasion, and Arseny spoke of how much the monks were touched to have Tikhon with them. Tikhon tonsured the first two novices as monks for the monastery. After his departure, Arseny wrote about how they were anxious about his stay, about what he would eat and how he would adjust to their poverty, simple life, and complete lack of comfort. But they need not have worried: "You are a monk, a simple person who is cloaked with the position of a Bishop. You are a merciful father, who cares for us and our needs more than we ourselves. Even more—You are a true, sincere friend of humble monks. With your simplicity You won over all of us; with your unexacting nature You humbled us, with your prayers you comforted our hearts."[82]

Relations with the Episcopal and Other Churches

Although there were tensions between Catholic and Protestant missionaries in Alaska and the Orthodox Church, as well as with Greek Catholics over the conversions, Tikhon developed cordial relations with the Protestant Episcopal Church. The Episcopal Church was internally divided between those who identified more strongly with Protestantism and those who sought to bring out its Catholic dimensions. At the end of the nineteenth century, one of the foremost leaders of the latter was Charles Chapman Grafton (1830–1912), bishop of Fond du Lac in Wisconsin. Grafton, like many Anglo-Catholics, subscribed to the "branch" theory of the Church, according to which the Anglican, Roman Catholic, and Orthodox Churches were all "branches" of the "one, holy, catholic, and apostolic Church" confessed in the creed, all sharing an episcopal structure and apostolic succession. They viewed the Orthodox Church as containing elements of the traditional church that the Anglican Church had lost under the influence of the Protestant Reformation, but at the same time they did not want to "become" Orthodox, but rather to have the Orthodox Church recognize them as a valid sister Church with an equal claim to the catholic and apostolic tradition. However, relations with the Orthodox Church were complicated by its remoteness both culturally and geographically. Therefore, the presence of the Russian Orthodox Church in North America allowed opportunities for High Church Episcopalians that Anglicans never had.[83]

Bishop Grafton used the consecration of his coadjutor (assistant) bishop, Reginald Weller (1857–1935), on November 8, 1900, as an opportunity to strengthen the bonds between the Protestant Episcopal and Orthodox Churches. Grafton invited two special guests: Bishop Tikhon and the Polish Old Catholic Bishop Antoni Kozlowski. Though nothing like this had ever happened before, Tikhon readily accepted, showing striking initiative. He traveled to Fond du Lac accompanied by Fr. John Kochurov and Hegumen Sebastian (Dabovich). Wearing the mantle (*mantiya*), the outerwear a bishop wears during ceremonial entrances into the church and for certain services (but not the vestments worn during liturgy), Tikhon occupied the bishop's throne in the sanctuary during the consecration, though he observed rather than participated in the ceremony.[84]

During the meal afterward, Tikhon stated that he hoped his visit would bear fruit in the matter of church unification. He commented that the division of Christians is "unpleasant to Christ" and weakens Christianity, so that "we must ourselves make every effort and labor for this holy undertaking" of working toward the reunification of Christians, even if it were just sowing seeds that would bear fruit in the future. To work toward unity, they should study one another's churches and get to know one another better, which was now possible as never before.[85] The event initiated a warm friendship between Grafton and Tikhon and led to further engagement between the two churches. There was, however, criticism from some Orthodox and a backlash in the Episcopalian Church, especially after the publication of a photograph of the occasion, which critics labeled as the "Fond du Lac Circus" (Figure 2).[86] Others, however, praised the event. The Rev. Dr. Francis J. Hall, a leading High Church theologian, called the service "the most important event which had taken place since the reformation" because of Tikhon's presence.[87] Though America presented many challenges for Tikhon and the Orthodox Church, it also presented unique opportunities.

On his return to San Francisco, Tikhon wrote a warm letter to Grafton expressing his gratitude and sent him a collection of liturgical texts that had just been translated into English, together with some incense. The correspondence between the two lasted several years.[88] Tikhon also invited Grafton to the consecration of the churches both in Chicago and New York, as well as the consecration of Raphael (Hawaweeny) to the episcopate in 1904.

Figure 2. Consecration of Reginald Heber Weller ("Fond du Lac Circus"), November 8, 1900

When Tikhon returned to Russia in 1903, Grafton sent a lengthy letter with him for Metropolitan Antony (Vadkovsky) of St. Petersburg, explaining his theological position. Tikhon explained to the Synod that American interest in Orthodoxy was growing, and sympathy was particularly shown by Episcopalians like Grafton. He asked for clarification as to how the Orthodox Church should view the Episcopalian Church, as well as also what to do in case an entire parish wished to become Orthodox: How should they receive the clergy, and what of Episcopal liturgy and canon law could be retained if a whole parish converted? These questions were beyond the competence of a diocesan bishop, Tikhon believed, and he suggested that the Synod appoint a commission to investigate these issues, which it did.[89] Then Grafton himself made a trip to Russia, and though Tikhon thought it premature, it was a success.[90]

In October 1904, the Holy Synod sent Tikhon a resolution explaining the responses of the commission on Anglicanism to his questions. If an entire parish were to convert to Orthodoxy, in that case it could continue to use a Western-rite liturgy based on the *Book of Common Prayer*, though the contents of the latter would have to be corrected in accordance with Orthodoxy in a few places. As regards the question of Anglican clergy who wished to convert to Orthodoxy, the Holy Synod concluded that this was a question that needed to be addressed by the entire Orthodox Church—since it was a question that went beyond just one national Orthodox Church but pertained to the relations between Orthodoxy as a whole and another confession. It therefore decreed that until such a decision come, Anglican clergy should be reordained.[91]

Exchanges with Episcopalians became more frequent.[92] When Tikhon consecrated the side altar of St. Nicholas Church in New York in the fall of 1904, over twenty Episcopal priests were in attendance and were given a special place in the church so they could observe every aspect of the rite. After the service, Fr. Hotovitzky addressed them in English, expressing his joy at seeing such a large number of clergy from the "friendly Western branch of the Church." They were no doubt gratified at the validation of having an Orthodox representative refer to their church as a "branch of the Church."[93] Nashotah House Seminary even bestowed an honorary doctorate upon Tikhon in 1905.[94]

Although relations had developed in a positive way both between the churches and personally between Tikhon and Grafton, the relationship would be ruptured in 1905 over Tikhon's ordination of Ingram N. W. Irvine (1849–1921).[95] Irvine was an Episcopal priest defrocked by his bishop over a disagreement regarding how to treat one of Ingram's parishioners, with Irvine taking the rigorist position. Five years later Irvine wanted to convert to Orthodoxy. Through the mediation of Archimandrite Sebastian (Dabovich), Tikhon decided to ordain him an Orthodox priest. As he wrote to Pobedonostsev, Irvine could be very helpful in the task of acquainting Americans more deeply with Orthodoxy and translating services into English. "In such a way, in order to open up our mission among them, after a long and fitting probation, I am planning to receive and re-ordain Irvine...; he suffered unjustly from his bishop, which even many Episcopalians acknowledge; he may be very useful for us in publishing English supplements to our *Messenger*, in preaching in the Engl. lang., etc. In general, if we are to have a mission among Americans, then it is hard to do without the assistance of a person of their language, upbringing and way of thinking."[96]

Before the ordination, Tikhon wrote to the presiding bishop of the Episcopal Church, Daniel Tuttle, explaining why he was ordaining Irvine and hoping to avoid any misunderstanding.⁹⁷ News of the ordination quickly reached Bishop Grafton, leading to a flurry of telegraph correspondence between the two in the days before the ordination, in which Grafton desperately appealed to Tikhon to postpone until they had had more time to discuss the matter in order to avoid a rupture in relations. Grafton also sent a telegram to the Russian ambassador, appealing for his intervention, and Bishop Tuttle also sent a letter of protest to the Holy Synod in Russia.⁹⁸ Tikhon responded to Grafton, trying to mitigate the damage, stating that the decision did not imply anything about the Orthodox Church's view of Episcopalian orders in principle, but also clearly not willing to delay Irvine's ordination. Grafton wrote in a personal letter to another person that day about his efforts "to stop Bishop Tikhon from ordaining Dr. Irvine to the priesthood. . . . He is a good gentle pious Christian bishop who has been imposed upon. . . . The Arcbp has made a big bad blunder."⁹⁹ Tikhon went ahead and received Irvine into the Orthodox Church on November 4 and ordained him to the priesthood the following day. Given bitter outcry from the Episcopalians, Tikhon wrote a lengthy letter to Grafton explaining his theological justifications for his actions on the basis that Irvine had converted to Orthodoxy, that he was not interfering in internal Episcopalian matters, and, moreover, since Irvine had been defrocked, he was no longer a priest and was not being reordained.¹⁰⁰

The two exchanged another pair of letters trying to address the misunderstanding, but by the end of 1905 the correspondence ended, and evidently their friendship. It also resulted in a broader rupture in the Episcopal-Orthodox dialogue. The response of the Episcopal press was damning, and especially the non-High Church press attacked Tikhon as merely a "Russian bureaucrat" and lackey of Pobedonostsev, which they also used to discredit the High Church dialogues with the Orthodox.¹⁰¹ Although clearly Tikhon had high hopes for what Irvine could do as an Orthodox American missionary (exaggerated, as it turned out), and believed his actions were justified, it is not clear why he would not even delay in Irvine's ordination to avoid the negative fallout.

Despite the fallout, a fragment of a personal letter from Grafton (written in 1906) asserted that Tikhon did not reject the validity of Anglican orders, and Grafton thought "it possible that good may come out of the Irvine case and lead the Russian Synod to acknowledge our orders. The Emperor has granted the Church the privilege of holding a Council. It will meet sometime this year. I think the ancient patriarchate (of Moscow) will be revived."[102] Even though Tikhon's relationship with Grafton went sour, some in the Episcopal Church credited him with initiating a "remarkable movement" that led to the establishment of the Holy Synod's commission on Orthodox–Anglican relations, which in turn resulted in its positive commentary on the *Book of Common Prayer*.[103]

One of Archbishop Tikhon's most fruitful cooperations with Episcopalians was with Isabel Hapgood (1858–1928), a devout Episcopalian who was also a translator of Russian and French literature and personally knew Leo Tolstoy, among others. Hapgood produced a major translation of Orthodox liturgical services into English. She had begun the translation in the time of Tikhon's predecessor, but Tikhon fully supported her work and saw it through to completion and publication. Over the years, they corresponded numerous times, with Hapgood asking Tikhon for advice on translation matters.[104] Tikhon envisioned the service book as serving a missionary purpose, since increasing numbers of Americans were interested in Orthodoxy and attending their services, and such a book would at least provide them with the possibility of following along. It would also be helpful for Orthodox clergymen to conduct services in English. The major obstacle was finding money to have it published.[105]

While in Russia in 1903, Tikhon secured 2,000 rubles for publishing Hapgood's translation. Moreover, Sergei Witte, who came to the United States in 1905 to negotiate the Treaty of Portsmouth, gave an additional $2,000. As it turned out, however, the publication cost twice what they originally expected, more than $4,000—so in 1907 Tikhon had to appeal to the Holy Synod yet again for additional funds. When it was finally published, Tikhon personally sent a copy to the emperor, who in turn thanked him through the chief procurator.[106] Hapgood's translation was important because it was a more complete translation of the Orthodox service book including not only the liturgy but also Vespers and Matins, as well as other services such as marriage, baptism, and funerals. In 1922, Hapgood saw to a second edition of the book, even securing a preface from Tikhon—by then patriarch of the Russian Church—and sent him a copy after it was published.[107] It remained in use for a long time, and it is still used for some services today. For Tikhon, having English-language services was crucial both for missionary purposes, to reach Americans who were not from Orthodox backgrounds, and for the future as Orthodoxy took root in America.

The First American Church Council

In his first sermon in San Francisco, Bishop Tikhon addressed the clergy and believers as his "coworkers" and called on them to cooperate with him in the work of the diocese. These were not mere words, moreover, but were borne out in the way Tikhon actually administered the diocese during his years in North America. Although the structures did not change, his way of relating to his clergy and parishioners was different. When visiting parishes, he met with parish leaders to discuss their plans, giving advice without dictating—and the laity enthusiastically responded to his efforts. He also consulted the clergy in all major decisions of the diocese. Some of his accomplishments for the diocese were his initiative, while others were initiatives of others that he supported and saw through to completion.

In administering the diocese, Tikhon practiced sobornost in a very concrete way not only through his reliance upon the input from his clergy but also from direct cooperation with the laity. The most important interface between the laity and their bishop were the brotherhoods (and sisterhoods), which were formed in each parish. Brotherhoods were important in the western, especially former Uniate, portions of the Russian Empire, and Tikhon already had experience of involvement with them in Kholm. In America, however, they were especially important. The brotherhoods were not under the control of the clergy, but elected their own officers. Tikhon explained that the brotherhoods served two primary functions: to provide financial assistance to fellow immigrants who were injured, ill, or unemployed, and to support the church. The means of supporting the church and the parish were diverse: They could raise money to purchase land or build the church, or to help beautify the church and pay for its upkeep; they also helped support the clergy and the parish schools.[108] Especially in these latter areas, Tikhon found it critical to encourage the brotherhoods, to both guide and listen to them, and to cooperate with them in supporting the church and the clergy. Therefore, meeting with brotherhood members was a vital part of his visitations through the diocese. Local brotherhoods were also a visible manifestation of Orthodoxy, marching in parade and wearing uniforms, to greet Tikhon when he arrived at the train station and accompanying him to the church.

All the brotherhoods in the country were united in the national Russian Orthodox Catholic Mutual Aid Society, which undertook nationwide projects such as publishing the newspaper *Svit* and supporting the orphanage at St. Tikhon's Monastery. Each brotherhood sent delegates to the Mutual Aid Society's Convention, which took place every other year, for which Tikhon served as honorary chairman (Figure 3). As an extension of the brotherhoods, Tikhon also proposed the establishment of temperance societies to provide more wholesome pastimes for parishioners. The number of brotherhoods and their membership continually rose during Tikhon's time in America; by 1905, there were eighty of them with 2,600 members. It was important for Tikhon that mutual aid was organized precisely along religious, not national or professional, lines to strengthen the role of faith in local life. The ideal of greater lay participation advocated by many in Russia was not only a reality in America, but a necessity—and an experience that would be vital for Tikhon later on.[109]

Tikhon's conception of the bishop's role is most clearly articulated in his sermons at the consecration of other bishops. He told Bishop Innokenty that he should not think of the episcopacy in terms of honor for a high position, because in America the episcopacy was "labor, not splendor, responsible service, not irresponsible domination, fatherly care, not overpowering

Figure 3. Convention of the Russian American Mutual Aid Society, April 1903

despotism."[110] Similarly, he instructed Raphael Hawaweeny by reminding him of the words of Christ in the Gospel of Matthew that among the Gentiles one exercised authority through domination, but among Christ's followers, those who led did so by ministering to others: "whoever will be great among you must be your servant" (Matthew 20: 26 RSV). So the spiritual authority of a bishop was also exercised in service to others.[111] Tikhon viewed the role of the bishop not as one who exercises power over others, enjoying the benefits of an exalted position, but rather as the chief of servants who must sacrifice himself in his untiring labor for others.

The language of sobornost, of conciliarism or synodality, according to which the Church was understood as an organic body that included the laity as well as hierarchy and clergy, had developed in the nineteenth century under Slavophile influence. However, it was during the 1905 Revolution in Russia that the language became central to urgent calls for Church reform. Demands to convoke a Church Council, which had not been held during the entire Synodal period (since 1689), were increasingly insistent.

Very quickly these discussions in Russia found reverberations in America. At a clergy meeting in Cleveland on June 2, 1905, Archbishop Tikhon himself raised the idea of convoking a Council in America because the "life of the mission and activities of our diocese grow more complex every year and demand particular care and special attentiveness on behalf of those workers" responsible for the mission. If in Russia many expressed the necessity of a council for a multifaceted reexamination of church matters, then in America "such a necessity is clearly acknowledged by us all," because in America it was evident that, for the success of church affairs, the "active collective work of the Head of the Mission—the hierarch—[and] his coworkers, the clergy and the laity," was necessary. Tikhon proposed to the clergy meeting that it needed to discuss the question of organizing such a Council and drawing the participation of the laity in it as well as in general the work of the mission.[112]

The clergy at the meeting received Tikhon's call with gratitude. Though in Russia, reform discussions had become contentious, the American clergy trusted that their archbishop would guarantee a peaceful, brotherly cooperation for the good of the church.[113] A special commission was set up to prepare for the Council; as Fr. Hotovitzky stated, Tikhon "proposed to us complete freedom of voice and deliberations."[114] Tikhon, for his part, wrote to Bishop Nikolai of Japan—who had already convened councils of clergy and laity—for advice.[115] The conviction that a council should include the participation of the laity was not universally accepted in Russia itself at the time and was a bold step.

The announcement of the Council generated much discussion in the periodicals of the diocese. In Russia, American clergy observed, the administration of the Church had "almost completely" fallen into the hands of the state, contrary to the canons of the church; from the living body of Christ—a gathering of believers—the Church had become an administrative governing institution. In America, where the government had no role in religion, sobornost became the basic principle of ecclesial life of its own accord. All the major decisions were made by the community with their pastors in accord with the people's needs.[116] In Russia, the bishops had become like dignitaries and the clergy like subordinates and servants. Convening regular Councils would be a way for the bishops to be in open dialogue with their clergy so that they could understand better the real needs of the Church, to could heal its divisions and weaknesses.[117]

Some clergy and laity in the diocese did not see the need for the Council. After all, some said, "Russian formalism has been curtailed to a minimum by our Vladyka, the personal initiative of the priests is given wide scope." Everything the Russians were fighting for—greater voice for the parish clergy and greater lay participation—was already a reality in the American Church. But others responded that these positive developments were an "excellent initiative of an excellent person. And only a person of the very broadest views of highly humane feelings, can give to the priests such freedom in the interest of the common cause. But will all our bishop's successors be like him? His successor may look on such freedom as laxity and a limitation of episcopal power and eliminate it."[118] Thus, although there was a broad sense that, under Archbishop Tikhon, the ideal of sobornost was already a reality in the American Church, there was also a recognition that that was dependent upon Tikhon's person. They therefore intended the forthcoming Council—called by Tikhon himself—to give structure and make permanent the transformed model of ecclesiastical leadership that Tikhon embodied.[119]

The suspicion that another bishop might not give them the freedom that Tikhon did was not without foundation. Bishop Innokenty (Pustynsky), Tikhon's vicar in Alaska, was highly critical precisely of the freedom that Archbishop Tikhon granted to the clergy in the diocese, especially the leading clergy who made up the ecclesiastical administration. As he wrote in a biting personal letter back to Russia in 1906, using diminutives for Alexander Hotovitzky and Benedict Turkevich in a sarcastic way: "Judge for yourself: the advisors of our bishop consist of 'Shurochka' Hotovitzky, who gets carried away by every wind . . ., our friend 'Venechka' Turkevich, the fanatic Hegumen Arseny [Chagovtsov], the fool-for-Christ Fr. Nemolovsky. . . . What sort of authority, what sort of Administration (*Pravlenie*) can there be in the presence of such people?" By contrast, Tikhon's predecessor, Bishop Nikolai, had a "stout hand" and knew how to put order in clergy meetings by literally banging his fist on the table. Under Tikhon, Innokenty complained, there was an air of informality: "It's not that way at all now: Shurochka and Venechka come to meetings in their jackets. . . . The clergy in the States do whatever they want, the parishioners also. And everything is hidden in plain sight under the gracious wing of Vladyka!"[120] Innokenty was happy when Tikhon was transferred, though feared that affairs in the diocese were beyond fixing.[121] Tikhon's style of leadership, which encouraged active participation of the clergy and the laity, was acknowledged by all; but it went against the grain of the episcopal culture of the Russian Church and was viewed critically by some of his peers.

In the summer of 1905, there was hope that the Council in Russia would take place soon and that the one in America could take place later that year. The American Council was delayed for logistical reasons until 1907. The logistical issues were solved by holding the Council at the same time as the Convention of the Mutual Aid Society, when clergy and laity from across the diocese would already be gathering. Because the Russian Church Council was then anticipated to take place in the summer of 1907, Tikhon called the Mutual Aid Society Convention earlier than usual, so that the American Church could have its Local Council before the convening of the Council in Russia so that he could go for that.[122] It is noteworthy that the terminology for the American Council was the same as for the entire Church of Russia (*pomestnyi sobor*), not merely an assembly or congress of clergy as happened in dioceses in Russia in 1917.[123] The date was set for March 3, 1907. That the Council was to take place in conjunction with the Mutual Aid Society Convention helped with the finances and logistics—but also limited the scope of the Council, since the Mutual Aid Society consisted of Rusyns. In other words, the Council was not broadly representative of the entire diocese of the Orthodox Church in America—it did not include representatives from either the Serbian or Syrian missions or from Alaska.

On February 7, the Holy Synod resolved to transfer Tikhon back to Russia to become archbishop of Yaroslavl.[124] The news only reached New York less than a week before the Council was set to begin.[125] It was a devastating blow to the Council: with his transfer, Tikhon was formally no longer the ruling bishop of the diocese and therefore could not confirm any of its decisions, in effect undermining the Council's real possibility of accomplishing anything meaningful before it even began. The Council was nearly aborted, but they decided to go ahead with it, with Tikhon guiding the Council de facto if not de jure.

The Convention of the Mutual Aid Society began on March 3, 1907, in Mayfield, Pennsylvania, and the Council opened on March 5. The original plan was that the Convention would last the first half of the week and the Council the second half. The work of the Convention consumed much more time than planned, however, further eroding the work of the Council. In the end, the Council was reduced to four sessions, mostly in the evenings after the delegates had spent their full days with the sessions of the Convention, for a total of only seven hours.

Tikhon opened the Council and put forward its guiding parameters. The goal of the Council was "how to expand the Mission." Although it would not have much time to deliberate, he encouraged participants that it could still be important. The vital thing was for the participants to put the collective benefit first, above any personal interests.[126] One of the major issues discussed was how the mission could become financially self-sustaining. A second issue was the name for the Church in English, which was the only issue decisively resolved. This was an issue Tikhon had raised already in 1902, soliciting input from all the clergy rather than either turning to the Holy Synod for an answer or just deciding it on his own.[127] The name finally given at the Council was the "Russian Orthodox Greek Catholic Church in North America." This was intended, among other things, to serve as a means by which the Church would continue to attract Uniates by declaring, in effect, that this was the "true" Greek Catholic Church.[128]

Although the principle of sobornost empowered the clergy and laity, the Council did not challenge episcopal authority. In the council chairman's closing speech, Fr. Leonid Turkevich spoke of how the strength in the Church was their bishop. Tikhon had supported all of them, cast throughout America and having little chance to see one another. "On him alone lay the burden of caring for regulating and unifying all the members of our Church. To him above all we owe the increase in our numbers and our spiritual growth. In a word, at this Council it was once again brought before everyone and in all clarity that the bishop in our church is the head, might, wisdom and future."[129] A reciprocal relationship had developed between Tikhon, his clergy, and his flock, whereby he granted them great authority and responsibility in the affairs of the diocese, and they, in turn, recognized the key role he played in holding all of their individual efforts into one collective whole.

At the closing of the Council and the Convention of the Mutual Aid Society on March 7, Tikhon gave a speech in which he thanked the clergy and laity at the meeting for their collective work over his years in North America. "We acted and labored jointly. In some matters I gave you the initiative, inspired you, and you went to work and brought my thoughts to life; in other instances, on the contrary, you suggested the thought to me—I am not embarrassed to acknowledge this—and I sought the means and opportunity to practically realize your idea." He reminded them how he called them to cooperative work in his first address in San Francisco. "If something was done here, then not by me alone, but jointly with you." He recalled how he had been troubled on learning of his appointment to America, because he felt unprepared for such a task, with which he was so unfamiliar. But now he had come to believe that his appointment had been providential because of all they had built up with God's help. "From the very beginning I proposed broad initiative to my coworkers. So long as the work got done, it did not seem important to me whether that emanated from me or from others. And the consequences of this quickly became evident: the number of parishes started increasing, new churches were built, the number of parishioners grew, new institutions appeared." He knew there were some who were critical that he "allowed too much" of his clergy. Perhaps he had been too patient in allowing initiatives to continue that were not developing, instead of cutting them short. Perhaps, he concluded, his usefulness in America had run its course and it was time for someone else to develop it further.[130]

Although the first American Council was not as productive as its planners originally hoped, the very fact that it happened was significant. By contrast, in Russia, the tsar refused to allow the Church Council to convene, and although preparations continued, the Council itself had to wait until the fall of the monarchy.

Tikhon's Farewell

When Tikhon arrived in North America at the end of 1898, the diocese consisted of some 27,000 parishioners, 11,000 of whom were in the continental United States and Canada. There were twenty-nine parishes, half of which were in Alaska, and thirty-four priests. By 1905, the number of parishioners, parishes and priests had more than doubled (sixty parishes, seventy-two priests, and 55,000 parishioners); while the number of parishioners in Alaska had declined, those in the continental United States and Canada had nearly quadrupled.[131] In just seven years, the diocese had more than doubled in size and continued to grow very fast.

On Forgiveness Sunday (March 17, 1907), the Sunday before the beginning of Great Lent, the brotherhoods in the New York area put on a special event in anticipation of Tikhon's departure. Representatives of different brotherhoods and the local sisterhood gave speeches expressing their deep gratitude to Tikhon for all that he had done and their sadness at being parted from him. Tikhon concluded by asking forgiveness for the ways in which he had fallen short of the ideal of the bishop as supreme pastor of the flock.[132]

The following week Tikhon delivered a sermon for the Sunday of Orthodoxy on March 24, 1907. He observed that just a dozen years earlier, outside Alaska there were few churches, only some few hundreds of Orthodox Christians spread throughout the country, and no priests. "And now? . . . We have a multitude of clergy, and tens of thousands of faithful. . . . Schools are opened, brotherhoods are established. Even strangers acknowledge the success of Orthodoxy here. So how can we ourselves not celebrate the 'Triumph of Orthodoxy,' and not thank the Lord who helps His Church!" But this was not enough: The people must not only faithfully preserve Orthodoxy, "everyone must also take care to spread it among the non-Orthodox. The light of the Orthodox Faith has not been lit to shine only for a small circle of people. No, the Orthodox Church is *catholic*." And this was a task not just for special missionaries or for the clergy, but everyone had to do his or her part.[133] His flock was very sad to have their beloved bishop leave, but at least Tikhon felt like he was leaving them a strong foundation upon which to build.

On March 26, 1907, at 1 p.m., Archbishop Tikhon was accompanied by the leading clergy of the diocese as well as the Consul Lodyzhensky to the harbor, from which he departed from America back to Russia.[134]

4
Yaroslavl-Vilna-Moscow (1907–1917)

The decade between Tikhon's return to Russia and his elevation to the patriarchate spanned the era between the revolutions of 1905 and 1917. He became archbishop first in Yaroslavl, then Vilna, then Moscow—in each case in very complex circumstances. Although the situation in Yaroslavl was tense when he arrived, it proved to be a relatively peaceful time for him.[1] That would all change after his transfer from Yaroslavl, however, with the outbreak of World War I in 1914 followed by the collapse of the monarchy in 1917.

The Russia Tikhon returned to in spring 1907 was profoundly different than the Russia he left at the end of 1898, or even 1903. The 1905 Revolution profoundly destabilized Russian government and society. Despite the concession of the October Manifesto, widespread violence continued in the countryside and order was restored only through repression. The Revolution of 1905 and the introduction of the Duma resulted in the emergence of legal political parties, election campaigns, and a dramatic intensification of social and political polarization. The tsar's unwillingness to relinquish the autocracy, however, undermined moderates who advocated gradual change and resulted in the political field becoming dominated by the extremes. On the one hand, there was the radical right—monarchists who were also Russian nationalists and usually virulently antisemitic; on the other, the radical left—revolutionaries who wanted to completely overturn Russia's political and social system, overthrow the monarchy, expropriate the aristocracy's land for the peasantry, and abolish the market economy. The impact was directly felt in Yaroslavl. In February 1907, the Constitutional Democratic (Cadet) Party and other left-wing parties won Duma elections in the province. Moreover, a Socialist Revolutionary terrorist had attempted to assassinate governor Aleksandr Rimsky-Korsakov (1849–1922, governor 1905–1909).

The turmoil directly impacted church life in Yaroslavl. As in other dioceses, there was a rebellion in the seminary as students went on strike, protesting substandard conditions.[2] The Yaroslavl seminarians protested one particular faculty member who recently came to the seminary, the young hieromonk Iliodor (Sergei Trufanov, 1880–1952). Iliodor would later rise to prominence first as friend, and then bitter enemy, of Grigory Rasputin, and cause much grief for the Orthodox Church because of his large following and refusal to obey ecclesiastical authorities.³ In Yaroslavl, Iliodor gave fiery speeches for the Union of Russian People (URP), a radical right nationalist and monarchist political movement. The seminarians, who mostly sympathized with the liberation movement, boycotted Fr. Iliodor's classes. The archbishop of Yaroslavl, Iakov (Piatnitsky, 1844–1922), did not support Iliodor's political activities, and the Holy Synod transferred Iliodor to another diocese. Governor Rimsky-Korsakov and Ivan N. Katsaurov (1855–1914), head of the Yaroslavl URP, complained to ecclesiastical officials and even to the emperor about Iliodor's transfer. The URP was very influential in government and court circles and could force their will on the Church. As a result, Archbishop Iakov was transferred to another diocese in January 1907.⁴ Tikhon was entering a fraught and politically charged environment.

Archbishop of Yaroslavl, 1907–1913

Tikhon arrived in Yaroslavl on April 11, 1907. In his first speech in the cathedral, he said that he "heard many good things about Yaroslavl and its inhabitants," about their love of the Church and the faith, especially as expressed in the grandeur of its churches. He said that the distinguishing characteristic of Russians among the nations was their love for the Church and the faith, and he encouraged them to continue this rather than striving to emulate foreign ways.⁵ The centrality of Orthodoxy for traditional Russian customs and values was being challenged in the Russia he returned to in 1907. New radical ideas advocated overthrowing all that was old to build a new Russia. Peasants were leaving the villages to work in factories, which uprooted them from their traditional way of life. Tikhon believed that Orthodoxy provided the answers to the challenges of modern life and the best path for Russia was for its people to strengthen their rootedness in the faith.⁶ He ended his first words to his new flock the same way he did in North America: He called on the clergy to work with him for "cooperative pastoral labors," and he appealed to the faithful "that by our common efforts and endeavors we work in the field of God."⁷ His collaborative and synergistic approach to ecclesiastical leadership was not reserved just for America, with its congregationalist atmosphere, but remained his approach even after his return to Russia.

Yaroslavl was an ancient and central diocese with some of Russia's most beautiful churches. It included Rostov the Great with its remarkable kremlin, which in earlier centuries had been an important city in its own right. In the early twentieth century, the diocese had over 1 million Orthodox believers and a thousand priests serving some 880 parishes.[8] He wrote to Metropolitan Flavian simply: "Of course it's easier and better here than in America." The bishop's residence was the large and spacious complex of the Spassky (or Holy Transfiguration) Monastery in the center of Yaroslavl, where the bishop typically served on Sundays rather than the cathedral.[9]

In his first annual report on the state of the diocese, Tikhon waxed poetic: "after the simplicity of the American churches," which had only the bare minimum of accoutrements inside and out, "I was very astounded by the grandeur, beautification, [and] special characteristics of the churches, the originality and the extraordinary variety of the architecture, the grandiose dimensions of the structures of monastery buildings, city cathedrals and village churches, brilliant from the outside and radiant from the inside with gold of iconstases and decorations from valuable stones on the covers of icons."[10] For someone who loved all aspects of serving in church—liturgy, architecture, iconography, the entire setting—Tikhon could hardly have found a more congenial place than Yaroslavl and Rostov the Great.

Soon after his arrival, Tikhon issued instructions that expressed his manner of relating to subordinates. The archbishop requested "that he not be sent anonymous denunciations, for these will not only not be given any significance, he will not even read them"; and further that when clergy present themselves to the archbishop, they "do not make a full prostration before him."[11] It was common practice when greeting a bishop that clergy had to prostrate themselves to the ground before him to emphasize the distance between the hierarch and other clergy, but this was not Tikhon's style. To make himself accessible to anyone who wanted to speak with him, Tikhon announced in the diocesan journal his receiving hours: "His Eminence receives petitioners and persons who have need of him on official business every day, except Sunday and holidays, between 10 am and 1 pm."[12] Petitioners who were accustomed to approach the bishop in fear found Tikhon much more amiable.[13]

Tikhon traveled through his diocese, and by the end of 1907, he had made eight trips in which he visited all twenty monasteries in the diocese, all the city churches, and eleven village churches. In contrast with America, where he had to travel for months at a time, in Yaroslavl he could make trips lasting four to five days to visit a series of churches and monasteries and return home. Except for when he was away serving on the Synod, he made an average of one trip per month each year.[14] When making announced visits, village school children lined the path to the church with flowers. But sometimes he liked to arrive unannounced so that he could see how things really were. Tikhon endeared himself to the clergy and flock of Yaroslavl by the way he treated people during such visits.[15]

Archbishop Tikhon was a conscientious administrator, paying close attention to the decisions governing the diocese. Such matters centered on the clergy: appointments, retirements, pensions for priests' widows, conflicts between the priest and lower clergy, complaints about drunkenness, and the like. There were also matters concerning the laity, above all questions of marriage and divorce. Tikhon conscientiously read through all the paperwork of the Diocesan Consistory and gave his input on cases more than the average bishop.[16]

Tikhon was always concerned with education, in particular the diocesan school for clergy daughters. His annual salary as archbishop of Yaroslavl was far less than he received in America (1,500 rubles as opposed to 5,000),[17] and over the course of his seven years as archbishop of Yaroslavl, he donated everything he earned to this Diocesan Women's School.[18] His donations facilitated constructing a new building for it. After blessing the new building in 1910, he spoke to the students that the Church constructed this new building for them—but the Church itself received its means from the people, which meant that the students were indebted to the people and obliged to serve them in return. "Most of you will become teachers of the common people; this is where you can benefit the people by conscientiously fulfilling your teaching duties."[19] Just as he envisioned an important role for the laity in ecclesial life, so also women such as clergy daughters had distinctive contributions to make. Tikhon's vision of the Church as a steward of the people's resources, which it received from them but then returned to them through services not only in the strictly religious sense but also through education and philanthropy, would clash with the Bolsheviks after 1917; the latter drew a sharp distinction between the Church and the people when it stripped the former of its property—including schools—on the justification that the Church only took from the people but did not give back.

Tikhon's focus was not only on the education of future priests and teachers but also on popular education. He praised the impact of education and literacy, asserting that the faithful now knew their prayers, the creed, and catechism better than before, and they also understood their faith more deeply and were less prone to be tempted away from Orthodoxy by sectarians.[20]

Each year, Tikhon reported on the state of his flock to the Synod. His assessment was based on both his own observations as well as the detailed reports he received from each deanery about each parish.[21] "Debauchery" was a growing problem among those who left the supportive environment of home and village to work in factories where they had no beneficial moral influence and easily succumbed to riotous living. He believed that factory administrators needed to create better conditions to address these problems.[22] He also observed a growing indifference or even hostility to the Church and religion among the urban intelligentsia and youth.[23]

Overall, however, he concluded that "despite contemporary anti-religious propaganda and atheistic teachings," there had not been a significant decline of faith and piety in Yaroslavl.[24] Moreover, non-Orthodox faiths had a small presence and were not drawing Orthodox believers away from the Church. Although there was competition from "schismatics and sectarians," Tikhon did not think they posed much of a threat.[25] Rather, parishioners were distinguished by their faithfulness to Orthodoxy, cared for their churches, and donated not only for their upkeep but also for philanthropic and educational activities. He praised the diocese's clergy for being conscious of their service responsibilities and for striving to serve the people in the face of the increasing complexities of a modernizing society.[26]

Archbishop Tikhon served as a member of the Holy Synod during the winter session in 1909–1910 and again the winter of 1910–1911, when he was also appointed to various committees and commissions.[27] He chaired a commission on questions of ecumenical dialogue with Anglicans and Old Catholics, part of which had come about because of his dialogue with Episcopalians in 1903.[28] His experiences on the Synod and its various commissions deepened and broadened his understanding of the needs and challenges of the whole Church, not just his particular diocese, at a time when broader changes in society were threatening the prestige of the Church.

Archbishop Tikhon and Late Imperial Politics

Archbishop Tikhon's relationship to right-wing politics and movements such as the Union of Russian People has always been a question. Tikhon's sudden transfer to Vilna in 1913, which could appear as a kind of demotion, was interpreted by some contemporaries as a result of his having run afoul of the governor of Yaroslavl Province on account of his lack of participation in monarchist organizations.[29] By contrast, the Soviets always referred to Tikhon as a "black hundred," a collective term for the radical right in prerevolutionary Russia. Everything from the *Big Soviet Encyclopedia* to the *Jewish Encyclopedia* to a nationalist encyclopedia of *Black Hundreds* falsely state that Tikhon headed the Yaroslavl branch of the Union of Russian People or was its honorary chairman.[30]

Tikhon rarely spoke directly about politics. The Orthodox Church presented itself as nonpartisan, or rather "supra-partisan"—standing above party politics, though some clergy supported right-wing political movements. Tikhon placed the Church first, and what limited connections he had with right-wing organizations stemmed from their promise to defend the Church. There is no evidence that he supported their radical nationalist and antisemitic ideology, which contradicted his universalist vision of Orthodoxy and his peaceable character. He also opposed their meddling in the affairs of the Church. But Tikhon was tactful and cautious enough not to provoke a confrontation as his predecessor had done. He was discerning enough to realize that all political movements were fraught and divisive. Therefore, he understood that tying the Church to any such political movement was more likely to be harmful than beneficial in the end. As a result, both progressives and conservatives could claim him as "theirs," without Tikhon identifying himself with either.

Before 1917, Tikhon was clearly a supporter of the monarchy. But in of itself, that says little. After 1905, there were many variations of monarchism.[31] Under interrogation by the Soviet authorities in 1923, Tikhon stated that he was an honorary member of the URP from 1907.[32] But neither does that tell us much: Rightist organizations frequently made clergymen honorary members, without those clergymen becoming active supporters.[33] One thing is certain: Tikhon had no leadership role in the Yaroslavl branch of the URP. In letters to Flavian, Tikhon mentioned personal conversations with its head, Katsaurov, indicating Tikhon was on friendly terms with him. For his part, Katsaurov, shortly after Tikhon came to Yaroslavl, believed that Tikhon was "sympathetic" to their cause.[34] Katsaurov was especially devoted to the Church and argued that "the faith is everything," that if the URP did not cleave closer to the Church it could lose "everything," including the tsar.[35] Tikhon evidently went to "bless the banners" of the Union shortly after he arrived.[36] It is possible that, when Tikhon arrived in Yaroslavl, he was sympathetic to the movement: Leftist parties elected to the first and second Duma sought to pass legislation that threatened the Church's interests. Some leaders of rightist organizations such as Katsaurov placed Orthodoxy at the center of their political platform and sought to defend the interests of the Church, and in that way won initial sympathy from churchmen such as Tikhon.[37]

There is, however, no evidence that Tikhon played an active role in the URP. The records of the national URP meeting, which took place in Yaroslavl in March 1909, contain no mention of Tikhon even attending as a participant.[38] There is only one record of him having been present at a meeting of the local URP branch, in 1912. When the meeting opened, Tikhon addressed it briefly, wishing them success in doing good deeds. A longer speech was given by his vicar bishop Silvester, who praised the activities of the local branch on the grounds that, in the past year, those activities had been devoid of any extremes.[39] Tikhon also blessed a cooperative effort by some clergy and URP members to hold educational meetings among factory workers that focused on patriotic historical as well as moral and religious lessons.[40] His only other expression of support for monarchist organizations were telegram greetings to the Congress of Russian People in Moscow in 1909 and again in 1913.[41] Tikhon did not, therefore, refuse any cooperation with monarchist organizations. At the same time, he cannot be numbered among those Church leaders who took an active role in them, engaged in any organizational measures, or promoted either their cause or ideas.[42]

Tikhon quickly came to realize that, while the right-wing organizations may tout Orthodoxy as part of their platform, in actual practice, rather than defending the interests of the Church, they were trying to manipulate the Church to serve their interests—and would meddle directly in Church affairs to achieve their agenda. This meddling affected him directly: In 1908, the URP supported an ambitious Rostov archimandrite, Anatoly (Iunger, 1861–1912), in his campaign to establish a second vicariate in the diocese for Rostov—a position Anatoly wanted for himself. Anatoly was also friends with the religious publicist Nikolai N. Durnovo (1842–1919), who published newspaper articles criticizing Tikhon for not supporting the establishment of the vicariate. Tikhon did not oppose the establishment of a second vicariate or having a bishop in Rostov—but he was certain he did not want Archimandrite Anatoly for the position. However, he could not ignore the pressure that Durnovo was even putting on the Synod. The Rostov URP was threatening to send a telegram to the tsar about it, something "one can expect from them based on past examples—they need somehow to make a statement about themselves," as Tikhon wrote to Flavian.[43] Tikhon therefore had to handle the issue carefully, endeavoring not to bow to their pressure but also not to invite further interference by ignoring their demands.[44]

The whole affair took nearly a year to conclude. Tikhon found a compromise solution: He established a vicariate but chose a different candidate.[45] Evidently the URP was satisfied with this solution.[46] His new vicar organized the important celebration of the two-hundredth anniversary since the death of St. Dimitry of Rostov (October 1909).[47]

Perhaps most revealing, Tikhon made it clear, in a private letter to Flavian, that the Church should not draw too close to the URP. There were rumors that the composition of the Holy Synod would be staffed with more members sympathetic to the movement. Tikhon did not think this was a good idea; he objected to the URP's attacks against Metropolitan Antony (Vadkovsky). Further, he saw that the URP, which was undergoing its own schism, was a divisive movement, and support for it was a divisive issue among the clergy.[48] In short, Tikhon's support for the URP was at best restrained: He welcomed it if it were going to defend the interests of the Church, but not if it would interfere in the Church's internal affairs or threatened to be divisive for the Church.

In the last years of the old regime, government officials and even the tsar himself interfered in ecclesiastical affairs to an unprecedented degree. The tsar reversed a Synodal decision in the notorious case of the fanatical monk Iliodor (Trufanov). After he left Yaroslavl, Iliodor continued to attract attention and a following with his fiery sermons but also his unwillingness to submit to ecclesiastical authority. Because of his refusal to obey, the Holy Synod resolved in 1911 to strip Iliodor of any position and incarcerate him in a monastery. Tikhon hoped that would be an end to the troubles. The decision aroused protests from Iliodor's supporters that reached the tsar himself, who overrode the Synod's decision. Tikhon was particularly disappointed: "our decision on Iliodor's case was sensible and inoffensive, and he shouldn't be allowed to stay in Tsaritsyn *now*. After that how can ecclesial discipline not falter?"[49] The Iliodor affair and the tsar's interference eroded respect for the authority of the Church's leadership.

Archbishop Tikhon was also under pressure from the governor, Dmitry Tatishchev (1867–1919, governor 1909–1915), to exert his influence on the clergy in the diocese as the 1912 Duma elections approached. The governor's office sent Tikhon lists of clergy in the diocese, labeling some as "reliable" (meaning that they would support conservative political parties), some as "unreliable," and others as those whose political orientation was unknown. The archival file has no trace of how, or even if, Tikhon responded to the governor's request, however.[50]

One of the most important public events during Tikhon's period as archbishop of Yaroslavl was the three hundredth anniversary of the founding of the Romanov dynasty in 1913.[51] The royal family made a journey through central Russian cities that retraced the route of the first Romanov tsar, Mikhail, from Kostroma to Moscow. They arrived in Yaroslavl by boat on May 21, 1913, and proceeded to the Dormition Cathedral, where Archbishop Tikhon awaited them. Tikhon gave a short speech recalling the events in Yaroslavl three centuries prior. From there the royal family and others made their way toward the Spassky Monastery (Figure 4). The next morning, they traveled to Rostov, where they spent the day visiting historic and sacred sites, and Tikhon gave another short speech recalling historical events in Rostov.[52]

In later years, there were persistent rumors that Archbishop Tikhon had a falling-out with the Yaroslavl governor Tatishchev during these events or that the emperor was somehow displeased.[53] Subsequent events make that seem unlikely. In fact, the emperor had already bestowed on Tikhon the order of St. Alexandr Nevsky, an honorary award bestowed by the emperor, on May

Figure 4. Archbishop Tikhon and Emperor Nicholas II in Yaroslavl, 1913

6, 1913, in recognition of his archpastoral service expressed in his "love for his flock, his labors for well-ordered parish life and fervent guardianship for ecclesiastical splendor, liturgical harmony, the religious and moral education of the people."[54] Later the emperor sent a telegram to Archbishop Tikhon expressing his and the empress's gratitude for the visit: "with sincere joy we recollect our visit with you" to the Tolgsky Monastery.[55] Tikhon was relieved, but hardly effusive, that the visit was successful.[56]

Transfer to Vilna

Archbishop Tikhon was happy in Yaroslavl, and Yaroslavl was happy with him. Then in late December 1913, he received a letter from Metropolitan Flavian informing him that he was going to be transferred to Vilna. Tikhon replied: "I think that my candidacy for Vilna was put forward by you. Of course, life has been good to me in Yaroslavl: mutual satisfaction with the flock, relative calm, decent provisions, a good city and the rest. But if the authorities find the transfer to Vilna beneficial, then I am ready to obey."[57] On January 2, 1914, the Holy Synod sent a decree to Archbishop Tikhon, informing him that he and Archbishop Agafangel (Preobrazhensky, 1854–1928) of Vilna and Lithuania were exchanging sees.[58] Tikhon clearly was not happy with the news. He wrote to Bulgakov about the twenty-fifth academy class reunion that "I was not even able to completely give myself over to our academy celebration, because at the holidays I unexpectedly received my transfer to Vilna, where affairs are apparently at a standstill and they swapped Archbishop Agafangel and I."[59]

Yaroslavl was equally unhappy to lose him. Vicar Bishop Silvester planned a farewell event for Tikhon on January 19, the day before his departure.[60] The church at the Spassky Monastery was so full for liturgy that many of the pilgrims were unable to get in. Tikhon addressed those gathered, noting that it was his forty-ninth birthday. "A native of the north," he was always drawn to a place like Yaroslavl, "but by the will of God and the authorities," he had always had to serve in the West—so he rejoiced when he had received the appointment in Yaroslavl. As the diocesan periodical paraphrased his speech (in third person): "In Yaroslavl, Vladyka found the center of Orthodoxy: an abundance and splendor of the churches, a religious and believing people. About seven years passed. Vladyka had succeeded in settling in during that time, of thriving with the diocese, and then suddenly this new, unexpected appointment." At the end of his speech, Tikhon dropped to his knees and bowed down to all the clergy and people, and then afterward blessed each person.[61]

At a festal banquet afterward, governor Count Dimitry Tatishchev spoke about how Tikhon "showed an extraordinary receptivity to all public initiatives and undertakings in response to the diverse needs of contemporary life." Those who approached him felt his "broad Christian goodwill toward people of all positions, ranks, and situations." He had grown connected to the region and devoted his energies to its spiritual successes. It was therefore bitter for them to part with their archbishop. There were 180 signatures from prominent citizens of Yaroslavl on the address delivered by the governor, testifying that the sentiments were widely shared.[62]

On the day of his departure, the "whole city" came out to see him off. City bells rang and the streets were lined with people as he made his way to the train station. Thousands more were at the station waiting. He blessed the people as the train departed, and the people remained on the platform until the train was out of sight.[63]

A few days later, the Yaroslavl City Duma unanimously accepted a proposal to award Tikhon with the title of honorary citizen of the city of Yaroslavl. The proposal noted how the events of January 19 and 20 demonstrated "what love and what respect [Tikhon] enjoyed among the population of Yaroslavl," which he gained "for his responsiveness to everyone and for his loving heart. The Archbishop always did much good work."[64] This was a unique occurrence in which a city bestowed on a bishop such an honorary title. Tikhon shared his grief over his separation from the Yaroslavl flock when he arrived in Vilna. The archpastor looks upon his flock not only as people who attend liturgical services, but as "an assembly of believers, united by one idea, one thought, one love, which makes of them one body, one organism with their Archpastor. And therefore when this spiritual connection ... is broken, then a heavy sorrow occurs" that weighs on the heart of both the flock and the bishop.[65]

It has long been a puzzle why Tikhon was transferred to Vilna. Soviet investigators sought to understand the puzzle, presumably because of rumors that the transfer was connected to the Union of Russian People: The file on the transfer in the chief procurator's archive is missing, with a note in the archival register that it was "taken on 19 April 1921 to Moscow" by a Cheka officer.[66] The URP played a decisive role in the transfer, as people speculated—but not in Yaroslavl, but rather in Vilna. Archbishop Agafangel had a conflict with them because they wanted to use a religious procession for political purposes which he opposed. The URP then pressured authorities in St. Petersburg to have him removed.⁶⁷ One newspaper observed that even conservatives now believed that URP meddling served to diminish the Church's spiritual authority.⁶⁸ Archbishop Arseny (Stadnitsky, 1862–1936) of Novgorod, after speaking to Agafangel, was also outraged that political interference led to the transfer of a bishop and was outraged at chief procurator Vladimir Sabler, "who disposes of hierarchs like checker pieces. This can't go any further! It is becoming simply dreadful. When will this despotism of the secular government stop? When will this lawlessness stop? A Council (*Sobor*) is needed, is urgently necessary, which would say to such Sablers: 'Hands off! It is time for the Lord to act!' "⁶⁹ Arseny's diary is a witness to the deep frustration held by many leading churchmen with URP and government control over the Church, which contributed to a growing estrangement between the two.

Agafangel protested that he had held the banner of Orthodoxy high, "bowing it neither before the non-Orthodox nor before the 'Unionists' who tried to drag the Church into politics and put their flags not simply next to, but in front of the Church's banners."⁷⁰ Agafangel declared that "one does not need to do the Russian work in the borderlands with the cry 'We are the bosses here!', but with a life according to the divine commandments..., with truth and with love toward those around us."⁷¹ Although Tikhon never made such explicit statements, his actions suggest that he was in complete agreement with Agafangel. The "castling" move of swapping two bishops—which was highly unusual—was not a demotion. The Synod needed someone who could navigate pressures from Russian conservatives in a multiconfessional and multiethnic region.

Archbishop of Vilna and Lithuania

Archbishop Tikhon was greeted on arriving in Vilna on January 24, 1914, by local dignitaries and the vicar bishop, Elevfery (Bogoiavlensky) of Kovno (Kaunas). A representative of the Russian social organizations presented him with an elaborate wooden plate inscribed with a list of the city's Russian social, patriotic, and monarchist organizations—which would later be used by the Soviets as the only material evidence he was a "black hundred."⁷² All the bells of the Orthodox churches were ringing as he made his way through the city. His first stop was the Holy Spirit Monastery, which had been founded in the sixteenth century and was a key force for Orthodoxy in the region. The abbot of the monastery greeted him with a speech about the history of the monastery and its significance, asking the spiritual assistance of the Lithuanian martyrs—three brothers who were put to death by a pagan prince of Lithuania in the fourteenth century—for his "new, difficult, and responsible post. Receive us into your heart as you received the Yaroslavl flock," the abbot concluded.[73]

The new archbishop then led a grand procession from the monastery to the St. Nicholas Cathedral, the bishop's seat in Vilna. Tikhon noted that he hoped he could share with his new flock the "reserves" he stocked up from the richness of ecclesial life in Yaroslavl. "I am aware of all the difficulties of the prelate's service in this region of varied confessions and varied nationalities." He repeated sentiments that echoed his first words in San Francisco, inviting the clergy to be his coworkers and the laity, as an essential part of the body of the Church, to participate as well.[74]

The Lithuania diocese of the Russian Orthodox Church posed unique challenges, located in a region where both the Orthodox and Russians were a minority, replete with the tensions of a multiconfessional and multiethnic imperial borderland. By the early seventeenth century, all the Orthodox churches of Vilna, with the exception of the Holy Spirit monastery church, had been given to the Greek Catholics. The majority of the territories of the Grand Duchy of Lithuania were annexed by the Russian Empire in 1795. Until the 1830s, there remained very few Orthodox in Vilna and its province. The Orthodox diocese of Lithuania was created after the union of the Greek Catholic Church with Orthodoxy in 1839. The important Catholic Church of St. Kazimir was handed over to the Orthodox and reconsecrated as the St. Nicholas Cathedral. More Catholic churches were made Orthodox after the Polish uprising of 1863–1864.[75]

The Lithuanian diocese in January 1914 encompassed two provinces of the Russian Empire, that of Vilna in the south and Kovno in the north, where a vicar bishop administered the Orthodox Church. The two provinces were considerably different from one another: The imperial province of Vilna consisted of a region that today is divided between Lithuania and Belarus. According to the 1897 census of the Russian Empire, the Vilna province was predominantly Belorussian (over 60 percent), especially in the countryside, with decreasing percentages of Lithuanians, Jews, Poles, and Russians. The city of Vilna, by contrast, was primarily Jewish (40 percent) and Polish

(30 percent), with a substantial number of Russians (20 percent), but very small numbers of Belarussians and Lithuanians. In the Vilna province, there were nearly a million Catholics and 420,000 Orthodox believers (in 1902). The Kovno province had a majority of Roman Catholic Lithuanians (66 percent). The Orthodox Church was seen by many—among the local population (Russian and non-Russian alike), officials in the Russian government, and sometimes the Church itself—as an agent of the Russian Empire that served not only to further the cause of Orthodox Christianity but also imperial rule and Russian national identity in the borderlands.[76]

After the Polish Uprising of 1863–1864, Russian imperial authorities coercively "reunited" 75,000 Roman Catholic Belarusians to the Orthodox Church in the northwest provinces. The Orthodox Church in Vilna province received 18,775 new believers between 1863 and 1867. The majority of these "converts" did not consider themselves to be Orthodox even though legally they were forced to be, and 16,286 converted back to Catholicism in 1905 after the decree of religious tolerance, leaving the Orthodox Church in the region feeling embattled and threatened by Catholic "propaganda" and "fanaticism."[77] Tensions between the two confessions persisted, especially as many villages had mixed populations.

Vilna in Peacetime

One of those present on the day of Tikhon's arrival was Aleksandr Zhirkevich (1857–1927), an aristocrat, former military lawyer, Russian cultural activist (who knew and corresponded with leading writers and artists of the day), and philanthropist in Vilna. An avid diarist, Zhirkevich wrote about his encounters with Archbishop Tikhon. After the first encounter, he described Tikhon as a provincial and not very handsome elderly man, lively and quick-moving, unlike Agafangel who had an aristocratic bearing. When Tikhon entered the Holy Spirit monastery church the first time, he avoided the small eagle rugs—Byzantine trappings that added to the bishop's pomp—that the monks had laid out for him, instead just going to venerate the icons. "Evidently they will not quickly get used to him in Vilna."[78] A few weeks later the archbishop came to visit Zhirkevich, who now described him as "a person not yet old, happy, lively, good-natured, simple and good." Tikhon was quick at making decisions and explained himself "not without humor." He still believed that Vilna was used to seeing grand and magnificent prelates, but Tikhon "strives for simplicity and the absence of superfluous pomp." "There is no sort of worldliness in him, but a lively relationship to those around him."[79]

Some weeks later Zhirkevich repaid the visit. "How everything has changed in the episcopal residence, in the reception room, in the bishop's rooms, and the manner of reception! Not even a trace of the aristocratic décor, cultivated by Agafangel, remained: everything is simple, as Tikhon himself is simple." Tikhon received visitors and petitioners so long as he was not traveling; even when out on walks he would bring a pencil, and people would often approach him with a petition, on which he would write his resolution. For Tikhon, Vilna was not difficult because the diocese was not large and the number of petitioners he received was far fewer than in Yaroslavl.[80]

Tikhon embarked on inspections of his diocese, and by the end of the year he had visited all the city churches and made five trips outside Vilna. "In all of the places I visited I was met with masses of people headed by the representatives of the local administration who would present the bread and salt; such attention toward the prelate was also observed by the Jews, who in several places sent their own delegation." During his inspections of churches in these towns, parishioners usually welcomed him with a ceremonial arch covered with flowers.[81]

One of the major anxieties for the Russian Church in borderland regions was its minority status. In his annual reports to the Synod, Tikhon observed that competition became intense after the 1905 law on religious toleration when it became permitted for Orthodox Christians to convert to Catholicism. But he was not particularly anxious about it anymore and observed that there was no apostasy from Orthodoxy to Catholicism, and the intensity of the competition lessened each year. The majority of conversions in either direction (Orthodox to Catholic or vice versa) was primarily the result of mixed marriages.[82] During Archbishop Tikhon's first week in his new position, he summoned a meeting of the diocese's clergy to discuss a range of questions concerning the diocese. These questions pertained to the population as a whole, such as increasing the number of "medical service points" in villages. He also proposed introducing Lithuanian language instruction in the Vilna seminary.[83]

Tikhon's relationship to Russian patriotic, nationalist, and monarchist organizations in Vilna was similar to that in Yaroslavl. He arrived in the wake of the row over Archbishop Agafangel. He discussed the situation with Zhirkevich, who also believed that Agafangel "fell victim to rightist organizations."⁸⁴ Such organizations played a particular role in a borderland region like Vilna, where they were oriented toward defending Russian nationality where they felt they faced serious competition from other nationalities. This was particularly true in the cities, where the Russians were a minority and faced what they perceived to be a Polish cultural hegemony and a Jewish economic hegemony. There was, however, a great diversity of such organizations in the region that embraced a spectrum of goals. The more radical political organizations were local branches of the Union of Russian People, which sought to defend the monarchy, the Orthodox Church, and the dominance of Russians as pillars of the empire. In the Vilna diocese, however, more moderate monarchist and nationalist organizations dominated, which were focused on cultural and educational, rather than political, activities, especially around the time Tikhon arrived.⁸⁵

Shortly after his arrival, Tikhon received a delegation from a URP local chapter, held a thirty-minute discussion with them, and wished them success in "defending the sacred principles" inscribed on their banner for the "Faith, Tsar, and Fatherland."⁸⁶ Clearly they were seeking Tikhon's support for their efforts, and in general were sending the message that they regarded the local prelate not only as the head of the Orthodox community but also as a key player in imperial policies. There is no further evidence, however, that Tikhon played an active role. Avoiding Agafangel's confrontational approach, he tactfully remained on friendly terms with these "patriots" without allowing them to pull him or the Church into overt political action. A priest of the diocese later wrote that Tikhon "immediately calmed the political passions that played a special role in the Northwest Territory and showed the clergy a fruitful path of work on cooperatives, agriculture, and the organization of public lectures for the benefit of the people without distinction of faith and nationality."⁸⁷

Vilna on the Front Lines: August 1914 to August 1915

At the end of the summer of 1914, Europe entered the catastrophic war that engulfed much of the world. Vilna was of critical strategic importance because the railway ran through it to the front. For the first year of the war, the city was a bustling hub of troops and war materiel moving to the front, and wounded soldiers and refugees moving away from it. Nicholas II stopped in Vilna on September 25, 1914, on the way back from the front. The tsar's first stop was the Holy Spirit Monastery, where Archbishop Tikhon greeted him. The prelate declared that Russia was strong with its tsar: "Russia defends the Tsar, and the Tsar defends Russia."[88] The tsar's visit was unexpected, with Tikhon learning about it the day before; his previous experience in receiving the tsar came in handy, and he was relieved that everything went well.[89]

Virtually overnight, Archbishop Tikhon's diocese and his ministry were fundamentally altered. The churches prayed for victory and blessed soldiers headed to the front. Tikhon attended the first meeting of the Vilna Ladies Committee of the Red Cross, which was raising money and establishing an infirmary. The meeting was attended by leading civic and church figures as well the head of the Catholic diocese, and representatives of Russian, Polish, and Jewish social organizations. Tikhon said that in serving the wounded they were serving Christ.[90] The Church provided the seminary's buildings for the Red Cross to establish another infirmary, relocating the seminary initially in his own residence. Tikhon himself visited infirmaries, talking with soldiers and distributing donations.[91]

Tikhon observed that the religious mood of the people was in a heightened state after the outbreak of the war. This was due in part, he believed, to the prohibition against the sale of alcohol, in part in response to the horrors that accompanied war, as a consequence of which peasants attended church with more zeal, "seeking comfort in faith and prayer."[92] A year later, Tikhon stated that the war had muted nationalist discord and tensions between Catholics and Orthodox, whose clergy were even cooperating.[93] In his sermons, Tikhon generally interpreted the war as a trial from God that he hoped would lead those who had strayed back to a godly path. He counseled his listeners to rely more than ever on prayer and faith during the difficulties they were experiencing. In one sermon, he said that the Western emphasis on developing rationality and technological progress led to the neglect of spiritual values—which, he believed, was at the root of immoral actions allegedly committed by the German army—which he contrasted with Russia's continued emphasis on spiritual values.[94]

Later, however, Tikhon noted that the war was taking its toll on a population that was so close to the front.[95] By the middle of 1915, as the war dragged on, Vilna clergy's work, under the direction and inspiration of their archbishop, intensified. They supported the patriotic efforts of the war among soldiers and their parishioners; they served the war wounded; and they contributed to philanthropic efforts devoted to families of soldiers and refugees. By the middle of 1915, there were twenty-seven infirmaries in

Vilna, with priests appointed to each one. Tikhon directed clergy work and brought them together as often as possible to share their impressions and best practices.[96] Clergy conducted liturgical services in the infirmaries and heard confessions. Tikhon himself served the Paschal liturgy in the infirmary of the Ladies' Committee. All the wounded and medical staff gathered in the largest ward. Tikhon spoke afterward with all the wounded soldiers.[97]

For many months, only the north of Kovno province that bordered Prussia was under direct threat. In the middle of 1915, a German offensive broke through. After the fall of the Kovno fortress, the Germans approached Vilna. On June 21, 1915, the governor of Vilna ordered the evacuation of various institutions belonging to the Church, which was soon followed by an evacuation of clergy families.[98] According to one contemporary, Tikhon did not want to leave Vilna but would obey the governor's order, "but in any event, I will be the last to leave."[99]

The Diocesan Consistory retreated to the Danilov Monastery in Moscow, while the seminary relocated to Riazan.[100] There were reports of German soldiers desecrating Orthodox churches, so Tikhon sent away the most valuable and sacred objects, including their bells and the relics of the Lithuanian martyrs. In the midst of all this, Tikhon found time to comfort Zhirkevich in the last days before they evacuated.[101]

Tikhon served his last liturgies in Vilna in the Holy Spirit Monastery on August 28–29 and the final liturgy in the St. Nicholas cathedral on August 30. During these last services, they could hear the German planes and zeppelins flying overhead. It became clear that it was time to leave, but by that point all the trains were tied up by the military evacuation. On September 4, Tikhon was able to take one of the last trains. The Germans took the city the following day. The train took a very circuitous route, traveling for five days "with various adventures" and only black bread and tea for provisions, and he did not arrive in Moscow until September 15, as Tikhon wrote the following day in his last letter to Flavian before the latter's death.[102]

Refugee Archbishop

From the time he left Vilna in September 1915 until he was elected to the see of Moscow, Archbishop Tikhon was a bishop in exile. His time was divided between the Belarusian portions of his diocese that remained unoccupied, Moscow and Riazan to attend to affairs of the consistory and the seminary, and Petrograd (as St. Petersburg was renamed). At the end of October, Tikhon was appointed to serve on the winter session of the Synod, which he served on until June 1916.[103]

In December 1915, he was given a particularly sensitive task regarding the canonization of Ioann Maksimovich (1651–1715) of Tobolsk. The bishop of Tobolsk, Varnava (Nakropin, 1861–1924), was a peasant who had no theological education and only became a bishop through the influence on the emperor of Rasputin—the Siberian peasant faith healer who was taken into the confidence of the royal family—contrary to the recommendation of the Holy Synod. As Tikhon critically observed to Metropolitan Flavian when Varnava was appointed in 1913, "the *starets* [elder, i.e., Rasputin] has completely become the chief procurator, and Vladimir Karlovich [Sabler] has returned to his 'first position' as assistant to the chief procurator!"[104] Varnava then pushed for the canonization of Ioann Maksimovich, an early eighteenth-century missionary bishop in Siberia who was widely venerated; his canonization would certainly also play to Varnava's glory. The Synod and Sabler did not oppose Ioann's canonization but were in no hurry to satisfy Varnava's vanity, responding that the case needed more investigation and the ceremony should not be undertaken in a time of war.[105]

Varnava went around the Synod, received some approval by telegram from the tsar, and in August 1915, conducted a service before the coffin of Ioann Maksimovich that was interpreted as his canonization. Such an act, without the approval of the Holy Synod, was unprecedented and caused an enormous scandal that threatened the legitimacy of the Synod and placed it at odds with the emperor. In June 1915, Chief Procurator Sabler—who was much reviled in church circles because of his despotic control over the Synod—was replaced by Aleksandr Samarin (1868–1932), who was devoted to the Church and well-respected in society but also refused to bow to Rasputin's meddling. Samarin, together with the metropolitan of St. Petersburg, Vladimir (Bogoiavlensky, 1848–1918), who presided over the Holy Synod, condemned Varnava's actions and the Synod resolved to remove Varnava from his post. Once again, the tsar intervened, and Samarin was sacked (after holding the post only a few months), and Vladimir was transferred to the see of Kiev (after Flavian's death) and replaced in Petrograd by another protégé of Rasputin, Pitirim (Oknov). The entire complex of events was enormously damaging for the Synod and its authority, which was undermined by both Rasputin and the tsar. Lev Tikhomirov, the revolutionary turned conservative monarchist thinker, commented in his diary that the tsar, "by supporting these Rasputins and Varnavas, is driving even the nobility and the clergy away from him. I don't know how the war will end, but after it a revolution seems to be utterly unavoidable."[106]

The Holy Synod decided to throw the resolution of this highly complex and sensitive situation onto Tikhon by sending him to Tobolsk in December 1915.[107] The task was no easy one: He had to avoid antagonizing the tsar, avoid scandalizing the faithful by denying Ioann's sainthood, and save the Synod's reputation after it was flagrantly disregarded. Tikhon thoroughly investigated the case for the canonization, including the extensive records that the canonization commission had collected. He reported back to the Synod on December 31 that Varnava had beatified (*velichanie*) Ioann for local veneration and had not conducted a full canonization (*proslavlenie*), which the Synod had not yet authorized. At the same time, Tikhon concluded that the case for canonization was solid and that the Holy Synod should proceed with authorizing it—indeed, that delaying it would bring no benefit to the Church.[108] The Holy Synod followed Tikhon's suggestion and approved the canonization in January 1916; Tikhon returned to participate in the canonization in June.

After Easter, in April 1916, Tikhon made a quick trip to Moscow and Riazan and then to what remained of his diocese.[109] He stayed in Disna (today Dzisna in Belarus), a part of his diocese that was not taken by the Germans. A town of about seven thousand people, the civil administration evacuated there. His trip was cut short when he had to return to Petrograd because the tsar was bestowing upon him a diamond cross to wear on his *klobuk*. The tsar's message spoke of Tikhon's zeal for the welfare of the Church and improvement of parish life, his concern for the welfare of his flock, and the Christian benevolence he showed toward both his clergy.[110] Presumably the tsar bestowed this award on Tikhon at this time to express his gratitude for the way Tikhon handled the Tobolsk affair.

After finishing the winter session of the Synod, Tikhon visited Moscow again before proceeding to Disna at the end of June, where he would remain until the end of October. He liked Disna in summer, which he described as "beautiful, healthy and peaceful."[111] One of Tikhon's enduring concerns was the financial hardships suffered by the clergy during wartime, including those who remained in the occupied territories, when they were unable to receive normal support from their parishioners and had to support their families who had evacuated. Tikhon appealed to the Holy Synod for additional financial support, and after that was granted, he was involved in distributing assistance to clergy in need.[112] During those months, he traveled to over sixty parishes of his diocese that were not under German occupation, visiting some remote places where no one in the village remembered having been visited by a bishop. As he had in America, he supported the work of Orthodox brotherhoods. In a speech at one brotherhood meeting, he said that "the war has given the impetus to an intensified discussion of the issue of reviving parish life and its activities.... And in this case, the first and best guide can only be the brotherhood: this is the nucleus where the revival, reform, and transformation of the parish must be born and mature." He told the faithful that they should do as much as they can because it was more evident to them what was needed, and each could contribute what they were able, be it for education, philanthropy, or other areas.[113]

The Orthodox faithful were much comforted in having their archpastor visit them in such difficult times. But in his visits, he interacted not only with the Orthodox. In the village of Prozorki, after a prayer service for victory, Roman Catholics as well as Orthodox believers approached to receive his blessing. As he was leaving, representatives of the Jewish community brought him bread and salt. Tikhon got out of his carriage and addressed them: "We have a different faith than you, but are children of one heavenly father and children of one earthly father—the Emperor," and as citizens of the Russian Empire, should strive toward a common goal of victory over the enemy and being good citizens. "The God of Abraham, Isaac, and Jacob bless you and send you peace and quiet."[114]

Tikhon also visited army infirmaries as well as soldiers at the front, even in the trenches 150 steps from the Germans (Figure 5). Not only the front, but even some of the villages he visited were under constant threat of being bombed or shelled; in one case, a village was bombed shortly after he left.[115] "With his fearlessness, friendliness, accessibility, and archpastoral care for people," Tikhon "charmed everyone from the senior general to the lower ranks during his tour of our front."[116] The emperor recognized Tikhon's labors toward both wounded and active soldiers, and he was awarded an insignia of the Red Cross from the Red Cross Society and the military insignia of swords to add to his Order of Saint Alexander Nevsky.[117]

After months in the Belarusian territories, he returned to Petrograd at the end of October 1916, having been summoned again to serve on the Synod. The Synod was planning to send him to Astrakhan during the first week of March to prepare for the canonization of Jospeh of Astrakhan, a seventeenth-century bishop who was killed in an uprising of the townspeople.[118]

Figure 5. Archbishop Tikhon at the front with the 70th Riga Regiment

February Revolution

The increasing strains on Russian society caused by World War I, combined with the government's decreasing competence, resulted in a revolutionary situation by the beginning of 1917. Support for the monarchy eroded even among those who should have been its most natural supporters. Demonstrations began on February 23 and gained momentum each day. When the soldiers refused to repress the demonstrations on February 25, the situation was clearly serious.

On February 26, the deputy chief procurator proposed to Metropolitan Vladimir of Kiev, the presiding member of the Synod, to issue an appeal to the people in support of the monarchy and call for an end to the demonstrations, but he declined. A similar proposal to the entire Synod, including Tikhon, also had no result. The Holy Synod, long considered a bastion of the autocracy, refused to come to its support in its final hour. Even conservative hierarchs had grown frustrated over the meddling of Rasputin, the chief procurators, and even the tsar in matters such as episcopal appointments and canonizations.[119] Though some historians have blamed the Church for the fall of the monarchy because of this lack of support at such a critical moment, it is more likely the Synod did not anticipate how precarious the situation was, and that its response was driven by resentment over meddling government interference.[120]

Nicholas II abdicated the throne on March 2, 1917, not only for himself but for also his son Alexei, in favor of Grand Duke Mikhail. But Mikhail refused the crown, transferring authority to a Provisional Government. More suddenly than anyone anticipated, the centuries-old and seemingly unshakable autocracy simply crumbled. Eleven Duma deputies, handpicked by Paul Miliukov (1859–1943), declared themselves the Provisional Government and that all government authority resided in it (not the elected Duma). The government was to convene a Constituent Assembly, an elected national body that would form Russia's new constitution—though kept delaying it.

The collapse of the monarchy would bring radical changes to the Russian Orthodox Church as it would to the entire country. Many, not only among the laity and rank-and-file clergy, but even many bishops welcomed the change as a promise of true freedom; others wondered how the Church—and Russia itself—could exist without the monarchy.[121] The Church leadership began to plan immediately for the convocation of the long-awaited Church Council. The Provisional Government appointed Vladimir Lvov (1872–1930) as chief procurator of the Synod. The Synod, on Lvov's urging, issued two statements regarding the fall of the monarchy. The first, issued on March 6, was simply an acknowledgment of Nicholas's abdication and Mikhail's refusal, stating that these should be read out in the churches. The second, on March 9, was an encyclical to the faithful. It began: "God's will has been done. Russia has embarked on the path of a new governmental life." The encyclical, which was intended to calm and reassure the population in a moment of uncertainty, stated that the Synod blessed the Provisional Government in its efforts and initiatives, and that people should trust it and unite around it. Both of these were signed by all members of the Synod, including Tikhon as well as Metropolitans Vladimir (Bogoiavlensky) and Makary (Nevsky, 1835–1926). The Synod also issued a decree changing the petitions in the liturgy from praying for the dynasty to praying for the "God-preserved Russian state and the Faithful Provisional Government."[122] Tikhon directed the Lithuanian diocesan consistory that all these were to be carried out "immediately."[123]

Lvov initially promised the Synod that the Church would be free from the kind of despotism that chief procurators had wielded before him.

Within days, however, Lvov announced to the Synod that the Provisional Government retained all the powers and authority vis-à-vis the Church that the imperial government had and that he, as chief procurator, was endowed with the authority to reform the Church. The Synod protested that he was acting with no less despotism than the tsarist procurators.[124] In first order, Lvov pressured those who were thought to be "Rasputinites" to resign—especially the Metropolitans of Petrograd and Moscow, Pitirim (Oknov, 1858–1920) and Makary (Nevsky).

During the Synod's Easter recess, only three members remained in Petrograd: Archbishops Tikhon, Sergy (Stragorodsky, 1867–1944) and Protopresbyter Georgy Shavelsky (1871–1951). Lvov seized the opportunity to transfer the Synod's periodical, the *All-Russian Ecclesial-Social Herald* (*Vserossiiskii Tserkovno-obshchestvennyi vestnik*), to the editorship of the liberal professor of the St. Petersburg Theological Academy, Boris Titlinov (1879–1944), without a full Synod in session to oppose it. This would make one of the foremost printed organs of the Church a vessel for his reformist ideas. Lvov succeeded in securing the signatures of Sergy and Shavelsky, but Tikhon refused to sign. Tikhon expressed his dissent in the Synod's logbook that this was an issue which demanded the discussion of the entire Synod. Lvov went ahead and transferred the periodical anyway. This was the first instance in which Tikhon stood firm against government pressure to compromise when Sergy did not, foreshadowing a difference in approach that would become much starker in later years. On April 14, 1917, the Synod held its first session after the Easter holidays and expressed its opposition to the illegitimate transfer of its periodical out of its control.[125]

In response, Lvov secured a Provisional Government decree dismissing all members of the Synod except Sergy (Stragorodsky) and appointing new members. When the members of the Synod assembled on April 15, Lvov read out this decree to them. In response, the members of the disbanded Synod issued two documents protesting the transfer of the journal and the means of forming the new Synod. Lvov's actions cast a shadow over the legitimacy of the new Synod until the Church Council finally replaced it.[126]

The February Revolution impacted the Russian Orthodox Church not only from above, with the loss of the protection and sponsorship of the monarchy and through the heavy-handed tactics of chief procurator Lvov, but also from below. Congresses of clergy and laity across the country voted whether to keep their current bishops—and in several cases voted to oust their bishops in a form of "church revolution."[127] By the summer of 1917, lower clergy were rebelling against their priests, who were also being ousted by parish councils. There were also rising instances of anticlerical actions, not only robberies of churches or desecration of sacred items but widespread cases of peasants seizing lands belonging to churches and monasteries.[128] None of these issues played out in the Lithuania diocese, however, still suffering from the pressures of the war. The diocesan congress which it held in Disna in mid-May focused especially on the financial hardships of the clergy.[129]

Tikhon's speech in opening the congress in Disna reveals his thinking about both Church and state after the February Revolution. He recalled how he had appealed to them for their cooperation in his very first address on assuming the see of the Lithuanian diocese—and that such cooperation included not just the priests but also the common laypeople. He again recalled St. Paul's teaching that the Church was a body, and that every member had a vital role to play. Now there was even broader possibilities for such participation than ever before. "With the change of government that has now taken place, you are called upon not only to organize" local parish life, but contribute to national questions concerning the transformation of both the Church and the state with the upcoming Church Council and the Constituent Assembly. In one line, which was later crossed out, he was even more explicit in laying upon his audience the responsibility for organizing "everything ecclesiastical and even governmental." In other words, Tikhon's vision of sobornost—the cooperation of all clergy and laity in building up the Church—had suddenly been transformed from a focus on their participation in building up their local parish to their participation in reconstructing both the Church and the state.

Tikhon also reminded his audience that, for believers and the Church, the eternal questions were more important than the earthly, the spiritual than the secular. Guided by eternal values when evaluating temporal problems, they had a special role to play at that critical moment. "In support of the new people's government, take care of the true welfare of the people, and be not only 'with the people,' but also ahead of them, lead them along the path of realizing the truly cultural and Christian principles of brotherhood, equality, and freedom."[130] Although Tikhon had explicitly defended the monarchy in 1905, and always assumed that a Russian patriot had to be loyal to the tsar, the fall of the monarchy opened up for him the idea that, just as he had always had confidence in the ordinary laity to cooperate in building up the Church, now that confidence could be extended to their democratic participation in building up a new state order as well. The Church in its practice of sobornost could become a laboratory for democracy. He believed that Orthodox believers, rooted in eternal values, should play an active and indeed leading role in the renewal of Russian social and political life, for whom the revolutionary ideals of brotherhood, equality, and freedom were rooted in the absolute value of each human person. After the Bolshevik seizure of power, Tikhon would find himself defending those values against the Bolshevik vision of class conflict, class enemies, and dictatorship of the proletariat that conflicted with universal notions of brotherhood, equality, and freedom for all.

Election to the See of Moscow

Since the metropolitans of Petrograd and Moscow had been ousted, chief procurator Lvov allowed the two capitals to choose their bishops democratically.[131] In Petrograd, the popular Veniamin (Kazansky, 1873–1922) was elected. The case of Moscow was particularly complex and contested, especially because Metropolitan Makary (Nevsky) refused to step down. A longtime and respected missionary in the Altai region, he was appointed on the tsar's insistence to the see of Moscow, despite his advanced age and lack of higher education—thanks, it was believed, to Rasputin's influence. He was not well received by the clergy and flock in Moscow.[132] First Lvov pressured him to retire, and later a delegation of leading laymen from Moscow and the other members of the Holy Synod did the same. Makary agreed, but later changed his mind, and subsequently continued to assert that he was still the rightful bishop of Moscow and casting doubt on his successor's legitimacy.[133]

The clergy and laity of Moscow held a series of meetings in March 1917, some of which were very polarized, that decided on how to proceed with selecting a new bishop. A group of influential clergy and laity in Moscow, led by the former chief procurator Aleksandr Samarin and including leading intellectuals such as Evgeny Trubetskoi (1863–1920) and Sergei Bulgakov (1871–1944), demanded a fundamental break with the old imperial ecclesiastical system. The meetings decided that candidates for the new Moscow prelate need not be monks or bishops or even clergy, but any individual so long as they were at least single or widowed (the celibate status of bishops was firmly entrenched in Orthodox canon law). The selection of delegates for the congress to choose the prelate began with a democratic vote in each parish of the Moscow diocese, in which every adult male and female parishioner cast their vote for lay delegates. An equal number of clergy and laity were elected.[134]

The Extraordinary Congress of Clergy and Laity of the Moscow Diocese to elect the metropolitan opened on June 19, 1917. Candidates included Archbishops Tikhon (Bellavin), Sergy (Stragorodsky), Platon (Rozhdestvensky, 1866–1934), and, unusually, the layman Aleksandr Samarin, a widower. Intense debates ensued on June 19 and 20, with discussions spilling after the sessions late into the night. It soon became clear that there were two favored candidates who stood out over the others: Tikhon and Samarin. Samarin, who had been ousted as chief procurator mainly because of the Tobolsk affair, was deeply respected as a man of principle who would not compromise in defending the interests of the Church. Though the debates were about the respective candidates, they were more about what each represented than about their personalities per se. No one attempted to discredit the other camp's candidate, as both were regarded as worthy—it was more about which principle should be followed. Those who supported Samarin wanted a radical break with the old regime's hierarchy, whom they blamed for the Church's crisis, as the only path to renewing ecclesial life. Although no one had anything to say against Tikhon, some delegates simply refused to vote for a monk or anyone who was a part of the old hierarchy. They sought a radical reshaping of the entire internal and external makeup of the episcopate which had been compromised in the last years of the old regime.[135]

Those who advocated for Tikhon did not, in principle, disagree with these positions. But they sought a solution that would not break so radically from tradition. As the chairman of the congress, Father Nikolai Bogoliubsky (1856–1926)—no conservative—stated in his opening speech, the candidacy of a layman could scandalize ordinary Orthodox believers and therefore it was better to follow tradition and choose a bishop.[136] For this camp, Tikhon was the ideal candidate—a bishop who was not tainted by compromises with Rasputin or the old regime. Moreover, although Samarin's candidacy represented a radical break with the past in ecclesiastical terms, Samarin himself was a nobleman and a conservative monarchist. Nothing was less in keeping with the spirit of the February Revolution than to elect as head of the diocese an aristocratic monarchist. Samarin had asserted a dominant control over the congresses in March so that some feared he, as the Moscow primate, would only continue the "episcopal autocracy," whereas Tikhon was well-known as someone who embodied the principle of conciliar ecclesiastical leadership. Therefore, as one contemporary observer put it, "the struggle of these two candidates—archbishop Tikhon and A. D. Samarin—in essence, was the struggle between the progressive ecclesiastical current and the conservative-reactionary."[137] Tikhon was, paradoxically, simultaneously the more traditional and yet the more progressive option.

On the first day of voting, Samarin and Tikhon received the same number of votes (297). Samarin, however, said that his candidacy should be removed because he lacked the proper experience and office. The next morning, June 21, began with religious services at the Church of Christ the Savior, where the voting also took place. The ancient Vladimir icon of the Theotokos was brought in to oversee the elections. Before the voting began, Agafangel, the Synod's representative, spoke of the magnitude of the people being freely able to elect their archpastor. "Now the will of God must be expressed by your voices. Not without reason is it said that the voice of the people is the voice of God!"[138] Preceding the vote by liturgy as opposed to heated debates created a different atmosphere and mood among the delegates, who were also aware that entire diocese would be affected by their decision. Tikhon received 481 votes and Samarin 303. The result was taken to the bishops in the altar, who prepared an official Act as the church doors were opened for the public to enter the Church. The bishops came out onto the solea and the Act was read out that, with the blessing of the Holy Synod, the representatives of the clergy and laity of the Moscow diocese elected Archbishop Tikhon. Archbishop Agafangel declared: "Axios!" "He is worthy!" and all those gathered sang out: "Axios! Axios! Axios!," a traditional response indicating that the believers affirm the selection of a clerical candidate.[139] On June 23, 1917, the Holy Synod issued a decree confirming the election of Tikhon to the see of Moscow retaining the rank of archbishop.[140] John Mott (1865–1955), leader of the Young Men's Christian Association (YMCA) who was in Russia as part of a diplomatic mission sent by President Woodrow Wilson, was present during the election and observed that Tikhon's election "met with general approval."[141]

Periodicals of very different political and ecclesiastical orientations praised Tikhon's election. The journal of the Moscow Theological Academy celebrated the fact that, for the first time in the six-hundred-year history of the Moscow see, the Orthodox people of Moscow "entered into the fullness of their rights in the organization of church life." With this historic act, the church of Moscow "decisively broke with the old deadened bureaucratic foundations of diocesan life" and began a new life on the basis of early Christian ecclesial freedom. In the last decade of the painful apogee of tsarism and arbitrary episcopal rule in the Church, all the initiatives for the renewal of church life were stifled. There were only a few bishops to whom advocates of ecclesial renewal could look to for support. "Vladyka Tikhon was one of those few beacons in an era of gloomy ecclesiastical reaction, and those on whom the lot fell to actively fight for ecclesial truth and freedom are unable to forget the unfailing support and sincere participation which they encountered in Archbishop Tikhon." Moreover, "the progressiveness of his attitude and views has been characteristic of Vladyka since the student's bench"—recalling his role as student librarian. His long service in America left a "very deep imprint of democracy both in the political and in the ecclesial-social outlook of Vladyka and on the character of his relationship to those around him." A European-enlightened archbishop, in each place of his service he conducted himself as an "independent actor of high honesty, strong energy and, at the same time, great tact." At such a crucial moment for the future of the Moscow Church, "the bright name of Archbishop Tikhon— as a noble bearer of progressive ecclesial ideals and experienced ecclesial and social actor—by itself, without any organized biased agitation, by the power of its internal significance alone, the overwhelming majority of the progressive current were brought together and given decisive victory."[142]

The conservative *Moskovskie vedomosti*, which was hardly going to praise Tikhon as a progressive, equally lauded the congress for choosing such a worthy candidate as Tikhon. Like the other articles, it praised Tikhon as a "broadly enlightened hierarch," and beloved by his flock everywhere he served. "He is a person of broad Christian love, kind and tactful." At the same time, he was not compromised to any forces outside the Church, "such as Rasputin," for he had bowed down neither to the last tsarist chief procurator who was Rasputin's protégé nor to Lvov, the revolutionary chief procurator. "With its election of archbishop Tikhon, the Moscow congress as it were signed on to the protest of the Russian bishops in defense of the Church's true freedom" from any government interreference. Rather than emphasizing that Tikhon was not part of the "ecclesiastical reaction," this article focused on his independence from all political pressures.[143]

As this article indicates, one of the reasons Tikhon was so respected as a candidate was because he was someone who had neither compromised under the old regime from the pressures of Rasputin and the old corrupt system nor to the equally intense pressures coming from the Provisional Government in the person of Lvov. Historian Simon Dixon's assertion that Tikhon was elected to the see of Moscow because a conservative political shift in church circles favored him as a "patron of the radical Right" is wide of the mark.[144] In fact, politics were marginal to the debates. Rather, it was primarily ecclesiastical considerations that dominated.[145] Tikhon was chosen in part because, as a monk and a bishop, he would not cause a rift with either the Holy Synod or the mass of believers, but also because his lifelong conciliar ecclesiastical leadership was in keeping with the spirit of the post-February political and ecclesiastical ethos.

On June 21, the day of the election, Archbishop Tikhon was not even present at the congress that elected him, but in Petrograd working on the preconciliar commission preparing for the Church Council, chairing its session on ecclesiastical courts.[146] A friend came to inform and congratulate him on his election but Tikhon "did not display particular joy on account of his new and still higher position." When discussing who would replace him in Vilna, Tikhon stated that his vicar there was already more important to the diocese than he because "'I am more democratic,' Metropolitan Tikhon said, smiling, sitting in his favorite pose, leaning on the sofa cushion: 'my stay in America contributed a lot to my democraticness.'"[147]

On June 28 at noon, Tikhon arrived in Moscow. He spoke to those awaiting him at the station of his joy in coming to Moscow, which had been so welcoming to him and other refugees from Lithuania. The following day, June 29, he participated in the ceremonial accession to the Moscow see in the Kremlin Dormition cathedral. He said to the congregation: "Not without trepidation do I ascend to this cathedra.... But the thought that I am your choice encourages and strengthens me." As before, he called clergy and laity to work together with him.[148]

Tikhon was immediately thrown into intensive work. He served liturgies nearly every day. He supported the conciliar work of a congress of clergy and laity, emphasizing that "the voice of the laity is very important for expressing the needs of the Church."[149] Most importantly, he had to prepare his diocese for hosting the monumental Church Council that was scheduled to convene in a mere six weeks.[150]

5
The Patriarch and the October Revolution (1917–1918)

The year between the autumns of 1917 and 1918 proved one of the most eventful, and most fateful, for Tikhon, the Orthodox Church, and for Russia. The Council of the Orthodox Church in Russia—the first in over two centuries and planned since 1905 but prevented by the tsar—was finally convened in August to discuss a wide range of administrative and religious issues. By November, the Council resolved to restore the office of the patriarchate, abolished two centuries earlier by Peter the Great, and elected Tikhon to fill that office. At virtually the same moment, the Bolsheviks seized power; within months, the newly enthroned Patriarch Tikhon found himself having to defend the Church against the Bolshevik's radical program of militant atheism. Throughout his career, Tikhon had embodied a conciliar model of ecclesiastical leadership, actively mobilizing the participation of all clergy and laity in his dioceses to support the Church. Then suddenly elected head of the Church by the Church Council—where both the Council and the patriarchate were ancient institutions reinvented for very modern conditions—he found himself leading the entire Church as a conciliar head. He quickly found that leading the Church in a conciliar fashion was not simply an ecclesiological ideal, however, but a necessity: The Church would only survive Bolshevik assaults if he succeeded in mobilizing believers to defend it.

As the Russian Orthodox Church prepared for its Council, Russia's experiment in democracy became unstable. While the Church acted quickly to call its Council, the Provisional Government—which itself was unelected—kept postponing its equivalent, the Constituent Assembly, which was to determine the shape of the Russian government and resolve pressing national questions. By September, the Provisional Government had lost virtually all credibility, and the country became increasingly unstable precisely as the Church Council was getting underway.

The Church Council

The Council of the Orthodox Church in Russia convened on August 15, 1917. On the eve of the Council's opening, August 13, the Holy Synod elevated Archbishop Tikhon and two other archbishops to the rank of metropolitan.[1] The Council opened on the feast of the Dormition of the Mother of God with a liturgy in the Kremlin's Dormition Cathedral. After liturgy was served in all the parishes and monasteries across Moscow, people processed toward the Kremlin, filling the entirety of Red Square with Orthodox faithful. Bells rang in all the churches of Moscow all day long.[2]

The composition of the Council consisted of bishops, rank-and-file clergy, and laity, with each having the same voting rights. The role of the laity was contentious during the preparation for the Council and giving them full voting rights was an unprecedented step. In the summer, elections were held across Russia for delegates. At the parish level, every adult member (male and female) voted for delegates from their parish to be represented at the deanery level. Each deanery assembly then elected its lay and clergy representatives for a diocesan assembly, which in turn elected five representatives for the Council, three laymen and two clergy. More than 560 delegates were elected to the Council, including 91 bishops, 20 monks, 170 parish clergy of various ranks, and 288 laymen.[3] All social classes, including a substantial number of peasants, were represented. Since the Constituent Assembly would only last one day, the Russian Church Council was arguably the most democratic national body in the country in 1917–1918. When the Council and Tikhon claimed to speak on behalf of all Orthodox people of Russia, their claims were not entirely unfounded.

The work of the Council was conducted first in commissions which brought forth reports and resolutions to be debated and voted upon in the General Assembly. Twenty-two commissions discussed higher ecclesiastical administration, diocesan administration, parishes, canon law, liturgy and preaching, church discipline, missionary activities, monasticism, education, finances, the legal standing of the Church, the role of women, and other issues.

As the bishop of the host diocese, Metropolitan Tikhon greeted delegates on the first working day of the Council. For a long time, he said, the clergy and faithful of Moscow had longed for the day when a Council would be called to renew the conciliar life of the Church. Now, more than just renewing the Church, the faithful were hoping the Council would play a role in Russia's troubled civil life. Recalling the seventeenth-century Time of Troubles, when the Riurik dynasty ended and the Russian state collapsed, Tikhon stated that in the past the Church had "actively participated in the formation of the Russian state. Now the motherland was in collapse and danger, on the verge of downfall. How to save it—that is the question."[4] The sense that the Church Council was not only to have an impact on the Church, but affect broader Russian civic life at a time of crisis, was widespread in the Council.[5] Its delegates tried to walk a fine line between asserting its vision of Russian society as a whole, driven by the hope of renewing Russia guided by the Orthodox faith rather than secular ideas, but without engaging in "party politics," since the Church envisioned itself representing the whole nation, not just particular interest groups.

On August 18, the Council elected Metropolitan Tikhon to be chairman of the Council by a vote of 407 to 33 because he was the presiding bishop of the diocese.[6] Archbishop Arseny (Stadnitsky) observed in his diaries that the very qualities that made Tikhon beloved—his kindness, calmness, humility, and lenience toward others—were not the best qualities for managing the frequently boisterous sessions of the Council. After he was elected patriarch, he turned over the chairmanship entirely to Arseny.[7]

At the end of September, after some soldiers profaned synagogues, the Petrograd State Rabbi requested that the Council issue an encyclical in defense of Jewish sacred sites. On behalf of the Council, Tikhon formally asked the commander-in-chief to take "all measures in his power" to prevent such acts. Tikhon added that the Council was ordering all military chaplains to explain to soldiers "the criminality . . . of any taunt and mockery of other beliefs, no matter which religion they belong to."[8] Thus, Metropolitan Tikhon and the Church Council sought to defend not only the Orthodox Church from acts of profanation and desecration by radicalized soldiers but also to defend the Jews from antisemitic attacks.

The commission on the higher ecclesiastical administration presented its resolutions on the restoration of the patriarchate at the Council beginning October 11, 1917. While restoring the patriarchate was a central feature of discussions for church reform after 1905 and was favored by earlier Preconciliar Commissions, after the February Revolution, the idea of concentrating power in the hands of one person appeared to impose on the Church what society had liberated itself from in the political sphere. The Council itself embodied sobornost, in which the voice of all Orthodox believers was represented. The patriarchate appeared contrary to sobornost.[9]

By October, when the commission presented its report to the General Assembly of the Council, the mood of the Council had shifted in favor of the patriarchate. Those who opposed it were in a clear minority. The commission on higher ecclesiastical administration argued that Peter the Great's reforms, which had abolished the patriarchate, had also marginalized the Church from its role in guiding Russian society—which, in turn, was the root of Russia's current problems. Restoring the patriarchate was part of an effort to regain the Church's role in society. Proponents were looking to the patriarch not simply as an administrative ecclesiastical head but as the spiritual leader of the nation.[10] Archbishop Anastasy (Gribanovsky, 1873–1956) of Kishinev stated that "the peasants, when they elected their representatives to the Council ... told us one thing: give us a father, give us a shepherd who will gather those who have been scattered."[11] In an influential speech, Archimandrite Ilarion (Troitsky, 1886–1929) argued that restoring the patriarchate was necessary because it was the canonical form of ecclesiastical administration—but that the form had changed over the centuries and the Council was free to determine what the patriarchate would look like in the twentieth century.[12] The Council was, in effect, balancing tradition with innovative adaptation to new circumstances.

The commission's proposal declared the Council to be the supreme authority within the Church. The patriarch would preside over the ecclesiastical administration. The patriarch was "first among equals" with his fellow bishops: He was to lead the Church, but not dominate over it. He and the administration answered to the Council. In effect, the Council was to play the primary legislative role, whereas the patriarch with the administration was to have an executive function, administering the Church on a day-to-day basis, especially when the Council was not in session.[13] The commission believed that, in this way, patriarchal leadership would work in harmony with the principle of sobornost.

While these discussions were ongoing, the Bolsheviks arrested the Provisional Government in Petrograd on the night of October 25–26. Although there was widespread frustration with the Provisional Government and broad support for a democratic coalition of socialist parties taking power, the Bolshevik's antidemocratic seizure of power enabled them to marginalize all other political parties and establish a monopoly on power. Delegates at the Council in Moscow, like most other Russians, did not understand clearly what was transpiring, and it seemed to them, for weeks, that there was no government at all.[14]

The next General Assembly of the Church Council met on Saturday, October 28. Tikhon led the Council in a prayer for peace in Russia. The Council needed to ensure that their work bore fruit to bring the peace that reigned in the Council to all Russia. Tikhon read out a proposal that the debate on the restoration of the patriarchate cease and the Council proceed to voting on the restoration of the patriarchate.[15] The resolution passed and the Council proceeded to vote "by an overwhelming majority" to reinstate the patriarchate.[16]

Tikhon's Election and Enthronement

The question of whether to proceed right away with electing the patriarch proved more contentious than that of reinstating the patriarchate itself. During the battle for Moscow, many delegates were unable even to make it to the Council. Once, when Tikhon himself had set out to serve liturgy, he was unable to make it because his carriage was nearly struck by a shell, and he was forced to return.[17]

The violence prompted some to advocate waiting until things calmed down. Others, however, felt the urgency of holding the elections, uncertain if the Council itself might be prevented from meeting. The latter position won (141 in favor, 112 against).[18] Fr. Leonid Turkevich, who represented the Church in America, wrote in his diary that day that the vote about proceeding with the elections "was taken at exactly 12 o'clock. At that very same time in Moscow was heard, as it were, as a salute: the shots in the direction of the Kremlin or somewhere near the Strastnyi Monastery quickened. Terrible circumstances for great actions!"[19] The Council then debated how to elect the patriarch, since there was no precedent that was entirely fitting the present circumstances. It drew on earlier practices in Russia and other Orthodox patriarchates, especially Alexandria. The solution chosen was to have all the delegates vote, with the patriarch chosen by lot from among three candidates who received the most votes. The October 30 session closed by choosing the list of candidates.[20]

The voting took place the following day, October 31. Tikhon opened the voting by reminding the delegates of the sacred nature of their undertaking: In selecting the patriarch, they were not just electing a functionary to an office, but a "spiritual father of fathers." Personal inclinations, sympathies, and antipathies should not guide them; rather, they should be guided by the thought of choosing a person who would benefit the Church.[21]

The elections proceeded in three rounds, each time delegates writing three names, and each time taking the candidate who received an absolute majority of votes (out of 309 delegates present). In the first round, Archbishop Antony (Khrapovitsky) received the most votes (159) and an absolute majority, but not an overwhelming one: The next candidate, Arseny (Stadnitsky), received only 11 fewer votes; Tikhon was third with 125 votes. In the second round, Arseny received the absolute majority with 199 votes (62 more than Tikhon). In the third round, out of 291 ballots cast, Tikhon received 162 votes (88 more than the next candidate).[22] It was therefore clear that the Council preferred these three candidates above all others. At the same time, the Council was sharply divided between the top two candidates. Archbishop Antony, who had long been the strongest advocate for restoring the patriarchate and many believed would become patriarch, remained a popular but also polarizing figure, supported by only a slim majority and strongly opposed by many.[23]

The fighting over Moscow centered on the Kremlin, which was held by forces loyal to the Provisional Government and which the Bolsheviks bombed. On November 3, Metropolitan Tikhon and Archbishop Anastasy (Gribanovsky) visited the Kremlin as soon as the fighting ended to inspect damage to the churches. An artillery shell had fallen through a dome of the Dormition Cathedral, landing, symbolically, between the tsar's and the patriarch's thrones. Although the windows were broken and everything was covered with dust, the most revered icons were not damaged. The Church of the Twelve Apostles had suffered more. Tikhon witnessed the pools of blood mixed with brains from the Junkers killed. As they exited the monastery, the colonel who was defending the Kremlin was brought out, beaten, and then shot close to Tikhon and his companions.[24]

The date for choosing the patriarch was set for November 5. According to subsequent memoir accounts, Arseny was terrified of the prospect, Antony hankered after it, and Tikhon "entrusted everything to the will of God."[25] Archbishop Anastasy observed that Tikhon "was the calmest of all in awaiting the decision of his fate. His characteristic equanimity did not change him even for one minute." On the morning of November 5, as Anastasy was leaving for the Council, Tikhon said to him: "Do your work there, I will serve here, have lunch and lie down for a rest." Anastasy commented that "these words were not only a joke: they expressed his actual mental state.

No one pursued power less than he, but authority itself sought him by special judgment from above."[26] In these later accounts, Tikhon was depicted in ways that echoed Orthodox ideals of saintliness—someone who was humble and gentle, who did not seek power. Yet Tikhon's contemporaries largely portrayed him in the same way even before he was elected patriarch, noting how those qualities sharply distinguished him from other bishops—even when they were not sure such qualities were the most suited for leadership of the entire Church.

According to Arseny's diaries, he and Tikhon spent the evening of November 4 together, walking about the Trinity Metochion (the representation church complex of the Trinity-St. Sergius Lavra in Moscow), his residence, and talking. Arseny was extremely anxious, and even Tikhon lost his usual calmness with agitation by what the next day would bring. As they talked, "We sincerely expressed our innermost thoughts, that this lot fall on Archbishop Antony, not because he was the most perfectly suited for it, but because the whole time he was the ideologist of the patriarchate, which has been the vital question for him for a long time already. Aside from that, I completely sincerely pointed to Metropolitan Tikhon as the most worthy candidate, above all according to practical considerations and his character." From the practical standpoint, it would be simplest for Tikhon to become patriarch since he was already metropolitan of Moscow. "And by his character—he is good-natured and calm—that is very important. . . . In this way we conversed until midnight. I came back to my cell to write these lines so as to distract myself from prospect of the patriarchate. Lord! Deliver me from this high honor."[27]

On November 5, the entire Council, except for the three candidates, gathered at the Christ the Savior Cathedral for Divine Liturgy and the selection of the patriarch. The cathedral, which had a capacity of 12,000 people, was completely full.[28] Before the liturgy began, Metropolitan Vladimir (Bogoiavlensky) wrote the names of the three candidates on separate pieces of paper, in the presence of witnesses, put a ring around each and placed them in a small chest, shook them around, and sealed it. He then placed the chest on a small table in front of the iconostasis. During Liturgy, the Vladimir icon of the Theotokos was brought from the Kremlin and placed on the table with the chest, providing a kind of special blessing. Bishop Mitrofan gave a sermon that expressed the hopes and expectations of many: that the patriarch would be a leader who could inspire the people, who would lead them back to faith and out of the new Time of Troubles.[29]

After the liturgy, a special prayer service was conducted with all the Council's bishops gathered before the iconostasis. Metropolitan Vladimir took the chest and carried it up the ambo, where he held it up for all to see that it was still sealed. The elder priest-monk Aleksy (Soloviev, 1846–1928), who was revered as a living holy elder and enjoyed great popularity and respect at the Council, approached.[30] Metropolitan Vladimir then cut the ties around the reliquary chest, opened it, and held it out to Aleksy, who, making the sign of the cross three times, selected one of the lots from the reliquary chest and handed it to Metropolitan Vladimir. The latter then took the ring off the slip of paper and unrolled it, showed it to all the witnesses gathered around him, and then proclaimed to the entire gathering the name of the person chosen to be patriarch: Metropolitan of Moscow Tikhon. Then the senior witness took the two unchosen lots out of the chest, opened them, and showed the rest of the witnesses that they contained the other candidates' names. The entire gathering sang, "Axios, axios, axios!" in honor of Tikhon as the newly elected patriarch, followed by a hymn of thanksgiving to God.[31]

After Tikhon's name was pronounced, from all sides could be heard, "Such is the will of God" and "There is the one chosen by the Mother of God." "The feeling of inner satisfaction which appeared on everyone's faces," Anastasy thought, "demonstrated that the people obtained for themselves a Patriarch according to their heart." Antony was respected for his deep mind and broad education, and Arseny as a model of strong will and decisiveness; but "the one chosen turned out to be the one that everyone loved for his extraordinary simplicity, accessibility, and amiability, who himself was full of love and good feeling toward everyone around him. The selection of Metropolitan Tikhon somehow immediately reconciled all those who had earlier disagreed. On the way home, most members reflected on how, during these hours of collective disquiet, division, and upheaval, just such a person was needed, one who could relate to everyone equally benevolently, who could reconcile all. This was recognized even by the passionate supporters of Antony and Arseny."[32] Though some passionately wanted (or opposed) Antony or Arseny, Tikhon was a candidate that virtually all could accept and therefore served to reconcile and unite the Council—especially since the selection by lot was understood as meaning that he was divinely chosen.

A delegation from the Council went to the Trinity Metochion to announce the news. Arseny related how, after liturgy, he had tea with Tikhon and then returned to his room like one awaiting condemnation. They heard carriages approaching at 1:30 p.m., and "my heart froze," he recounted. But then Tikhon's attendant ran in and announced: "Ours has been chosen!"[33] Metropolitan Vladimir approached Tikhon and proclaimed that the Church Council had chosen him as patriarch. Tikhon replied first with a formulaic response that, because the Holy Council had chosen "me, the unworthy, to such a service, I am grateful, I accept, and I have nothing to say against it." After the delegates sang "Many Years" to him, Tikhon thanked God and the members of the Council for the great honor. "Considering it from the human perspective, however, I can say much against my election. The news about my election as Patriarch appears to me as the scroll on which was written: 'lamentation, and mourning, and woe,' which the prophet Ezekiel was supposed to eat (Ez. 2:10, 3:1). And how many tears and groans will I have to swallow in my impending patriarchal service, particularly in this present difficult time!" Recollecting Moses' words (Numbers 11:11–14), Tikhon declared himself unworthy and unable to carry the burden of the whole people. "From now on the care for all the churches of Russia are laid upon me and there stands before me a dying for them each day. And who can be glad at this, yea, even they that are mightier than I! But God's will be done! I find support in the fact that I did not seek this election, and that it came by divine lot, apart from me and apart even from humans." He believed that God would help him bear the burden that He laid upon him. He also considered it especially significant that both his selection as archbishop of Moscow and as patriarch took place before the Vladimir icon of the Theotokos, and he believed himself to be under her special protection.[34]

Tikhon sensed that his service as patriarch would not consist of honor, but of a great burden filled with suffering. His speech echoes many recurrent themes: He mentioned the continual dying for the flock when he was first consecrated bishop, recollected Ezekiel's scroll with reference to his placement in America, and repeatedly had been assigned roles not according to his wishes, but always accepted them as the will of God. The process of choosing the patriarch by lot was also important for Tikhon in reconciling himself to accepting a post that he had not sought and did not desire.

At 3:00 p.m. other bishops arrived, and Archbishop Antony (Khrapovitsky) addressed Tikhon. Congratulating him, Antony declared that his election was "above all the work of Divine Providence, for it was unconsciously predicted by the friends of your youth, your comrades in the Academy.... [who] called you 'Patriarch' when you were still a layman and when neither they, nor you yourself could even imagine the actual realization of such a title." This was not only a great event for Tikhon personally, but for the whole Russian Church which had been waiting two hundred years for a patriarch. The time of the Church's "bitter widowhood and sad slavery," when it had been little more than an appendage to the state was, Antony believed, coming to an end, and the "dawn of her freedom, her independent life," was breaking. Tikhon was chosen by God because he had never sought hierarchical elevations, "but fulfilled your duty according to your pastoral conscience." Antony had dreamed of the restoration of the patriarchate since he was nine years old, and on behalf of himself and all the bishops of the Council, he greeted Tikhon with a full prostration, who responded with the same gesture. Rising, Antony kissed Tikhon's hand, which Tikhon also reciprocated.[35]

Tikhon replied in "an agitated voice and with tears in his eyes," recalling the days at the Academy when Antony was a young professor and kindled in students' hearts the idea of the restoration of the patriarchate. Not only were the events of the day the fulfilment of what Antony himself had dreamed of since his boyhood, but if it was taking place at all, it was the fruit of Antony's own efforts, the energy which he poured into defending the idea. In conclusion, Tikhon turned to all his brother bishops and appealed to them for help and cooperation because bearing the burden "of the whole people" would be too much for one person, and he could succeed only with their cooperation. With that, Tikhon made a full prostration to all the bishops, who then sang the traditional Greek hymn for a bishop, "eis polla eti despota."[36]

Arseny observed that "the Patriarch was as before simple, good-natured and happy: the patriarchate almost hasn't changed him, and I am confident—it will not change him.... Many are happy with this choice, around whom the majority can unite."[37] Arseny, however, did not think Tikhon a very extraordinary or imposing personality—though that was in fact what was needed. Indeed, before the elections Tikhon himself had said the same thing—that the first patriarch should be an "unexceptional" person. If an outstanding personality like Antony (Khrapovitsky) were elected, he might well overpower the accomplishments of sobornost and be more likely to impose his will on the Church; Antony had a reputation for opposing lay involvement in the Council. Later, however, Arseny wondered whether Tikhon's natural humility, kindness, and accessibility were enough in a revolutionary context.[38]

After his election, Tikhon prepared himself for the enthronement by prayer and meditation at the famed monastery, the Trinity-St. Sergius Lavra. Tikhon proposed that the monks conduct a special prayer service because Russia was beset by a powerful external enemy (the Germans) and internal strife, civil conflict, food shortages, and "the absence of stable government."[39] On November 18, an armed brigade appeared at the monastery, claiming to be revolutionary authorities. They searched the monastery and inventoried property. Tikhon questioned according to what authority they were acting; when they presented papers from the local Revolutionary Committee, Tikhon replied, "Well if that's the case, I have nothing against it—search away."[40] The soldiers refused to address Tikhon by his ecclesiastical title but addressed him instead as "comrade." According to Arseny, "it was surprising with what calmness and even humor the Patriarch told this story about the adventure and in general about his new 'comrades.'"[41] However, the revolutionary threats to the church had taken their toll, as another contemporary observed: "There was a noticeable change in him: he became still more concentrated, relating with equanimity to all unpleasantness that arose for him personally, but sensitively alert to any talk or news about the afflictions of the people, about the sorrows that our Church is undergoing right now."[42]

The Council authorized a delegation that met regularly with the Moscow Revolutionary Committee (and later with the Moscow Soviet) to negotiate a variety of issues. Most importantly, the Council members wanted to enthrone the patriarch in the Kremlin's Dormition Cathedral. They were not granted all they wanted: No permission for massive processions converging on Red Square, as at the opening of the Council; though they were permitted use of the cathedral, only a limited number of people would be given tickets and admitted to the Kremlin, preventing large numbers of pilgrims. Archbishop Anastasy visited the Commandant of the Kremlin and later learned that he came from a religious peasant family. Anastasy concluded that "the revolutionary poison had not yet succeeded in deeply poisoning the organism of the people, and many of those who attached themselves to the communists did so unconsciously, remaining in their hearts believing Orthodox Russian people."[43] This observation would guide the patriarch's encyclicals to the faithful. Although the Council had no contact with the Bolsheviks in Petrograd, its relations with the revolutionary leadership in Moscow were cordial enough that it avoided passing any kind of broader judgment on the Revolution.[44]

The Council's first sitting further elaborated resolutions on the higher ecclesiastical administration. Councils (*sobory*) had supreme authority in the Church and should be convoked periodically. The patriarch had certain moral rights: sending pastoral letters to the entire church, the right to pardon, and the right to intercede with civil authorities—an important role patriarchs had played in the past and a responsibility Patriarch Tikhon felt he had before the Soviet government. He represented the Russian Church in relation to other autocephalous Orthodox churches and had certain disciplinary powers over other bishops. The ongoing governance of the Church in between councils belonged to the patriarch together with the Holy Synod and the Higher Church Council (*soviet*). The patriarch presided over both of those bodies. The Synod, consisting of bishops, had authority over matters of faith and morals. The Higher Church Council, which also included lower clergy and laity, oversaw matters such as finances and education.[45]

The enthronement of Tikhon as Patriarch took place in the Kremlin on November 21, 1917. A special commission composed the ceremony, deliberately appropriating older traditions in a creative way that ultimately resulted in something new.[46] Although it was supposed to be a day of great celebration, there was a gloomy atmosphere in the Kremlin.[47] Bishops were not allowed to enter with their carriages but had to enter on foot through a narrow passageway surrounded by hostile soldiers, and even a threatening shot was heard. The patriarch himself entered through the Spassky gates, from which the tsar used to enter. Anxiety was visible on everyone's faces. Only Tikhon "did not show the least agitation and seemed to be deeply concentrated." One Council participant, Sergei Rudnov, later observed that "he had evidently grown older, and most important—the usual kind tenderness of his blue eyes and the pure smile at the corner of his mouth—so characteristic of him—had disappeared. Now we saw before us as it were a different, stricter, even severe elder, full of majestic calmness and determination."[48] At the most solemn moment of the ceremony, during the singing of "Holy God," Metropolitans Vladimir and Platon led Tikhon by the arms to the patriarch's throne at the center of the apse of the church's sanctuary right behind the altar and seated him in ritual fashion. Then the metropolitans with the deacons vested Tikhon in patriarchal vestments: The sakkos belonged to Patriarch Pitirim (d. 1673), the omophor to Patriarch Adrian (1638–1700), the panagia to patriarchs Job (d. 1607) and Hermogen (1530–1612), and the mitre to Patriarch Nikon (1605–1681).[49] Although participants had seen these items before in the museum, it made a profound impression to "see it all on a living person."[50]

The sermon and speeches given by Archbishop Anastasy, Metropolitan Vladimir, and Patriarch Tikhon recalled the history of Russia's Church leaders and patriarchs, including Metropolitan Filipp (1507–1569), who had confronted political power (Ivan the Terrible) on behalf of the people at the cost of his own life. At the end of the liturgy, Metropolitan Vladimir handed the new patriarch the staff of Metropolitan Peter (1260–1326), the first head of the Church who began to reside in Moscow. Tikhon referred to the staff as symbolizing the shepherd who must find the lost and stolen sheep, to admonish them to repent and return to the Church. Tikhon was not thinking of Russia as "us" versus "them," but all—even the "lost" sheep of the revolutionaries—as part of his flock.

At 1:52 p.m., Tikhon left through the Trinity Gate to process through Red Square in a carriage, going to each end of Red Square for short prayer services, blessing the city of Moscow in all four directions. Although the authorities had not permitted the processions, pilgrims gathered in some areas of Red Square. When Tikhon stopped to pray at the Iverskaia Chapel, a great crowd of people came for his blessing and ran alongside the carriage as he continued. They came upon a group of Bolshevik workers and soldiers, carrying revolutionary flags and banners, headed to the graves of those who had fallen in the battle. Many of the soldiers turned their backs to the patriarch and began to sing the revolutionary anthem the Marseillaise, but others broke away and approached the patriarch to be blessed and sprinkled with holy water.[51] Arseny wrote in his diary: "The talk dubbed this a meeting of two worlds: Russia's old historical past meets by the Moscow Kremlin with the terrifying present and the hidden future." Archbishop Anastasy later put it, "It was a deeply dramatic moment. The resurrected old Rus', the symbol of which was the Patriarch, meets for the first time face to face with the new Revolutionary Russia."[52]

The day after the enthronement, November 22, Tikhon made his first appearance at the Church Council as patriarch. Archbishop Arseny greeted Tikhon on behalf of the entire Church of Russia, which the Council was elected to represent. "Before us is the Patriarch as a symbol of unity, as the center of conciliar solidarity, as an older brother and father." The restoration of the patriarchate, though a joy for the Church and the Council, would be a cross for the one occupying the position—especially in the current circumstances, "under the roar of deadly weapons, machine guns and rifle shots." As state and society were disintegrating, the Church needed to become the center of spiritual unity and source of regeneration, concentrating its conciliar unity around the person of the patriarch (Figure 6).[53]

Tikhon addressed the body. In the current circumstances, he said, the joy of restoring the patriarchate was mixed with sorrow about Russia's instability. He tried to reassure those who opposed the patriarchate that under him, and

Figure 6. Council of the Orthodox Church in Russia

he hoped under his successors, it would not be a threat to sobornost. The patriarchate was not domination over the Church, but rather service to it. "That good is created by the common work of all, by cooperation. As in every living organism, each member must be in its place and contribute to the overall work of the whole organism, so it is in Church life." Having been chosen by the Council, he would act in agreement with it.[54] Tikhon's first Epistle as patriarch, which was drafted by Sergei Bulgakov (with editorial assistance from Viacheslav Ivanov) indicated a recurrent theme of his patriarchate: Russia was not only experiencing war and civil conflict but also a spiritual crisis.[55]

The first sitting of the Church Council held its final session on December 9, 1917. Patriarch Tikhon expressed his hope for everyone's return for the second sitting, which was set to begin January 20. The Council had tackled major issues, foremost among them being the restoration of the patriarchate. But much work remained to be completed.[56]

Tikhon's Anathema Encyclical

After October, the political factions were not just left versus right, "Red" versus "White," socialist versus monarchist, with the Church allying itself with the latter. Virtually every political group refused to recognize the

Bolshevik seizure of power as legitimate, including other socialists. On October 27, the Bolsheviks formed the Council of People's Commissars (Sovnarkom), which was to serve as a "provisional workers' and peasants' government" until the convocation of the Constituent Assembly. Everyone (except for Lenin and Trotsky) understood the new Bolshevik-Soviet government as "provisional," to cede power to the Constituent Assembly. The Constituent Assembly alone would have a universally recognized legitimacy to form a new, democratic government for Russia and shape its new laws. For non-Bolshevik parties, "the Revolution" meant February, which had promised a free, democratic Russia. But Lenin and Trotsky seized the mantle of revolution and immediately presented themselves as the sole legitimate authority—and cast anyone who opposed or even criticized them as counter-revolutionary. Everyone—critics and Bolsheviks alike—knew that the Bolsheviks could establish a monopoly on power only by means of civil war and terror.[57] Given that the term was a value-laden label that asserted the legitimacy of those defining the terms and used to justify repression, characterizing the Patriarch Tikhon and the Orthodox Church as "counter-revolutionary" was part of Bolshevik propaganda. Patriarch Tikhon's encyclical of January 19, 1918, has long been interpreted by historians as proof that he "anathematized" the Bolsheviks and condemned the Revolution. A careful analysis of the text in its context, however, reveals a more nuanced picture. Events between the Bolshevik seizure of power and the patriarch's first official response to the Revolution must be considered for the text itself, and Tikhon's position, to be properly understood.

In the six weeks after they seized power, while the Council was still in session, the Bolsheviks did little that directly affected the Church, so that the Council largely ignored them.[58] After the Council completed its first sitting on December 9, 1917, however, the Bolsheviks passed decrees that affected the Church and its social role. Bolshevik decrees excluded the legal role for the Church regarding marriage and divorce as well as registering births and deaths. Another decree transferred all educational institutions belonging to the Department of the Orthodox Confession, even those designed to prepare clergy, to the Commissariat of Enlightenment.[59] On December 31, the Bolsheviks published a draft law on the Separation of Church and State that went far beyond just disestablishing the Church, but would deprive it of the right to own any kind of property and any juridical status as an institution.[60] On top of all this, the lawyer Ivan Shpitsberg was giving antireligious lectures in which he stated that the regime would close down all churches and prohibit the sacraments. Even still, the Church leadership did not react, since all these matters were considered provisional before the Constituent Assembly. The Bolsheviks, after all, received less than a quarter of the votes in elections for that body, so their program was not widely supported.

When the Bolsheviks forcibly closed the Constituent Assembly on January 5, 1918, after just one day, everything changed. No longer was there going to be a democracy, by which the majority could modify the Bolsheviks' radical policies. Instead, the Bolsheviks were going to impose a dictatorship in the name of the industrial proletariat (a miniscule percentage of the Russian population), which was in fact a dictatorship of the Bolshevik Party.[61] On January 10, Metropolitan Veniamin of Petrograd wrote a letter to Sovnarkom objecting to elements of the proposed law but received no reply.[62]

The direct confrontation between the new regime and the Church began on January 13, 1918. Alexandra Kollontai, the commissar for social welfare, announced the confiscation of one of the Church's foremost institutions in Petrograd, the Alexander-Nevsky Lavra, to house crippled soldiers. Metropolitan Veniamin's attempts to negotiate a compromise were rebuffed. On January 19, a unit of Red Army soldiers and sailors arrived to seize the monastery and expel all the monks and the metropolitan. The bells were rung, and many pilgrims flooded the monastery. The soldiers fired and killed a priest but were overwhelmed and had to withdraw. Thanks to the popular support for the monastery, the Bolsheviks retreated.[63]

During the winter of 1917–1918, Russia descended into anarchy and mob violence. Radicalized soldiers and workers would assault generals and officers, aristocrats, and clergy in public places. On January 7, a band of sailors brutally murdered two former ministers of the Provisional Government, A. I. Shingarev (1869–1918) and F. F. Kokoshkin (1871–1918), in their hospital beds. These cruel murders were profoundly shocking. Cases of mob violence against "class enemies" became routine. Sometimes such acts were done in the name of the Revolution or by armed groups claiming revolutionary authority; often they were simply acts of robbery and vengeance. The Bolsheviks did little to curb such actions; indeed, they permitted or even encouraged the "looting of the looters."[64]

Patriarch Tikhon received numerous reports of such instances of violence that winter. Peasants or groups of soldiers (or simply "armed men") robbed monasteries and churches, while in some places priests were attacked or murdered.[65] The details of these episodes are important because they help understand the patriarch's "anathema." In one instance, a priest narrowly escaped with his life after being attacked by a group of villagers who, curiously, were in the church during service before the attack and even kissed the icons on entering the church, with the would-be murderer lighting a candle before an icon. The attacker said he did not have anything personal against the priest, who was very popular in the village, but that he had been bribed to do it.[66] Often villages were divided regarding the Church, with anticlerical hostility stemming especially from soldiers who had returned from the front. There was a sense that, with the lack of order and under harmful influences, people who used to be ordinary churchgoers had lost their moral compass and were swept up into acts against the Church.

Patriarch Tikhon's most well-known, or perhaps infamous, encyclical, issued on January 19, 1918, was in response to all these developments. That day, the assault on the Alexander-Nevsky Lavra took place; it also happened to be the patriarch's fifty-third birthday. Arseny wrote in his diary on January 18 that Protopresbyter Nikolai Liubimov (1858–1924), chair of the Council's Executive Committee, drafted the initial text, and the Executive Committee (including Tikhon and Arseny) debated and edited it to produce the final version. The Committee feared that the patriarch would be arrested as a result, but Tikhon merely responded that no one was guaranteed against that possibility.[67] Thus, Tikhon did not compose the encyclical, which was more bombastic in tone than was his style, himself; nevertheless, he agreed to issue it under his name.

The encyclical was addressed to "archpastors, pastors, and all the faithful flock" of the Orthodox Church. The Orthodox Church was living through a heavy time of persecution, the text began, by those who sowed seeds of enmity, hatred, and civil strife. Every day the patriarch received news of "brutal slaughter of those not guilty of anything and even people laying on their sick bed, guilty only of honestly fulfilling their duty to the Motherland"— a reference to Shingarev and Kokoshkin. Acts of barbarity were being committed all over Russia, in broad daylight, and the culprits were getting away with it in violation of any law and order. Therefore, the patriarch was issuing a pastoral rebuke to those who committed such heinous acts—whom he labeled "monsters of the human race." "Come to your senses, madmen, stop your bloody reprisals." He declared that they were committing not only savage deeds, but satanic ones that would result in eternal damnation. He therefore excommunicated and anathematized such people, even if they only bore Christian names and belonged to the Orthodox Church by birth. Moreover, he warned faithful believers not to have anything to do with such people.[68]

Patriarch Tikhon did not anathematize the Bolsheviks, though the encyclical has almost universally been interpreted to mean that. The first part of the encyclical does not refer to actions committed by the Soviet authorities, but rather to spontaneous local acts of class violence, and the harshest condemnation ("monsters of the human race") and ecclesiastical judgment (excommunication and anathema) were reserved for them. Excommunication is imposed on a person who commits a grievous sin (such as murder or adultery), but the person is still assumed to be a member of the Church and can return through repentance; an anathema is an extreme religious sanction of last resort, usually applied to heretics but later to enemies of the Russian state like Stepan Razin (1630–1671), Ivan Mazepa (1639–1709), and Emelian Pugachev (1742–1775), that expels the person from the Church altogether.[69] They were intended as an exhortation to repentance, not a blanket condemnation. The authors of this encyclical understood that the Bolsheviks were atheists, that many did not come from Orthodox backgrounds—so such ecclesiastical action could hardly be intended for them. But the local stories that Tikhon was hearing told complicated tales. In the attempted murder of the priest in the Moscow region, for example, the perpetrator had attended the church with this same priest for twenty years. For such a person, the threat of complete exclusion from the Church, of eternal damnation, and ostracization by his fellow villagers might indeed have brought him to his senses.

The next part of the encyclical, by contrast, was clearly directed specifically at the Bolsheviks and their recent actions and decrees that affected the Church and its social role—which amounted to "the most severe persecution." The encyclical criticized Bolshevik decrees secularizing marriage and the registration of births as rendering the sacraments as "unnecessary [and] superfluous." The encyclical also criticized the bombing of the Moscow Kremlin churches and the seizure "by the godless rulers of this dark age" of revered monasteries such as Alexander-Nevsky. The property of monasteries and churches was "being confiscated under the pretext that it is the people's property, but without any right and without even the desire to reckon with the legitimate will of the people themselves." The Church's schools were being confiscated and turned into "schools of unbelief." The criticisms ended by asserting that "the government which promised to establish rights and truth in Rus, to ensure freedom and order, everywhere shows only the most unbridled highhandedness against everyone and, in particular, over the holy Orthodox Church."[70] The encyclical thus criticized the Bolshevik regime for its despotic rule and especially for its attacks on the Church, but refrained from condemning the Revolution or Bolshevism per se.

Since the encyclical was directed to believers, and not the Bolsheviks, the crux of the matter came at the end: What should the faithful do? The encyclical called on them to "stand in defense" of the Church. While their opponents seized power over the Church and its property using death-dealing weapons, believers "must oppose them with the power of your faith, of your commanding nationwide cry, which will stop the madmen and demonstrate to them that they do not have the right to call themselves champions of the good of the people, the builders of a new life at the behest the people's mind, for they act directly against the people's conscience."[71] The encyclical summoned believers to demonstrate their support for the Church in the belief that, since they called themselves the "people's government" and claimed to rule on their behalf, the Bolsheviks would be compelled to listen to the voice of such a large proportion of the population and change course. The encyclical also adjured believers to be ready to suffer for Christ. Clergy should summon their flock to defend the rights of the Church by means of forming "spiritual unions" to oppose external force with the strength of their "holy inspiration."

The encyclical's call to defend the Church was interpreted by the Soviets (and some later historians) as a call to overthrow the Bolsheviks by force, and therefore an act of counter-revolution—though the encyclical makes it clear that believers were to defend the Church by opposing force only with the power of faith and be prepared to endure, not inflict, harm. The aim of the encyclical was not to encourage the overthrow of the Bolsheviks, but to summon popular support for the Church so that the Bolsheviks would change course. In hindsight, the Bolsheviks had no qualms about using violence against nonviolent resistance; but after the successful resistance at the Alexander Nevsky Lavra, it seemed a realistic approach.

The authors of the encyclical, of course, had no sympathy for the atheist Bolshevik ideology that summoned people to class conflict—and as both sides understood, they stood for opposing values. The encyclical, however, did not criticize Bolshevik ideology per se, but rather criticized the Bolsheviks for claiming to rule on behalf of the people while ignoring the people's will. To be sure, it also criticized in no uncertain terms concrete Bolshevik actions and policies against the Church. But the harshest condemnation and anathema was directed not at them specifically, but rather at the lawlessness and brutality that was sweeping the country, especially when it was committed by baptized Orthodox Christians.⁷² Those close to the patriarch understood the message in this way. As one contemporary wrote: "The first half of the encyclical refers specifically to mob lynchings and addresses reckless murderers, subjecting them to excommunication from the Church and anathema. The second part speaks about force carried out mainly against the Church by representatives of the government." Soviet charges that the patriarch "anathematized the revolutionary government" were false because "the Patriarch anathematized not the government, but street murderers."⁷³ In the heat of the times, however, such nuances were lost on most commentators: The Bolsheviks and even many churchmen interpreted it as an anathema against the government and the October Revolution. Perhaps for that reason, it was one of only three statements Tikhon would later admit were "anti-Soviet."⁷⁴

The Church Council began its second sitting on the following day. Tikhon tasked the Council with developing a response to the attacks on the Church. The session was devoted to discussing Tikhon's encyclical and what was happening in various parts of Russia. Delegates asked Tikhon why he issued the encyclical under his own name, rather than waiting for the Council to issue it. He replied that he did not want to place the Council in danger and preferred to take the consequences on himself alone.⁷⁵ Delegates responded positively to Tikhon's encyclical, but they understood it in different ways, and for some it even caused confusion. Some called for Kollontai and other concrete representatives of the government to be excommunicated. Fr. Aleksandr Hotovitzky, the former priest of the New York cathedral and now the dean of the Christ the Savior Cathedral in Moscow, praised the patriarch for speaking boldly. At the same time, he was confused; he understood the encyclical's call to believers to break relations with evildoers as meaning that they should have not have any dealings with the government—which he found personally challenging, since even his own church's security guards were civil employees.⁷⁶ It was not clear even to him that the reference to eschewing contact did not refer to the government. Although there was consensus in criticizing the new regime, the extreme condemnations expressed by a minority were not shared by the majority.⁷⁷ At its next session, on January 22, the Council accepted a proposed statement that the Council was in agreement with the patriarch's encyclical and was ready—and called on the entire Church to be ready—to obey its summons to defend the Church.⁷⁸

Perhaps because of the confusion, the patriarch attempted to clarify his message in an interview in the newspaper *The Lantern* (*Fonar'*) on January

23, 1918. Tikhon stressed that the proclamation was not political, but "only moral." Excommunication meant that the Church was casting out murderers and robbers or those who defiled churches. When the interviewer asked about whether people would be expelled from the Church for associating with representatives of the government, Tikhon replied: "We are not summoning to rebellion . . . against the government, but only to struggle against its deformed and criminal fruits. The government can be monarchist or republican, constitutional democratic or Bolshevik, but it should not arouse with impunity such unparalleled upheavals and disintegration of moral principles."[79] The patriarch clearly articulated his position, which would remain consistent in the coming years, that he was not calling for the overthrow of the Bolsheviks, but claimed the right to defend the Church and criticize harmful government policies.

The Church Council passed a resolution on January 24 that the encyclical should be distributed as widely as possible and ordered the Synodal office, diocesan bishops, and clergy to spread it among the people, announce it in churches, and spread it among monasteries and brotherhoods. It was sent to all the dioceses for distribution.[80] The encyclical was also sent to all the newspapers.[81] The full text was published in *Morning of Russia* (*Utro Rossii*) as well as *Church Bulletin* (*Tserkovnye vedomosti*), and many other papers commented on it. Socialist newspapers were critical of it, as well as of the Bolsheviks, for provoking hostility with the Church. Independent newspapers wrote supportively of the encyclical as a turning point in which the Church was taking a strong stand amid revolutionary turmoil. Dmitry Merezhkovsky (1865–1941), the famous writer and thinker, commented sympathetically on what he understood as an anathema of the Bolsheviks, calling it an act of great heroism.[82]

The Bolshevik Vladimir Bonch-Bruevich (1873–1955), who headed a commission to battle counter-revolution in Petrograd, heard about a declaration plastered throughout the city that cursed the Soviet government and called on believers to take "all measures" against this diabolical government and "under no circumstances obey it." After reading Tikhon's encyclical, Bonch-Bruevich admitted he "even liked" it: "At least I saw that this person was not among the cowardly and did not send anonymous letters, as many other organizations had done, but said what he thought and not only put his signature, but even indicated his address." Bonch-Bruevich sent one of his deputies to eliminate "patriarch Tikhon's conspiratorial headquarters" in Petrograd, where they arrested everyone and confiscated all the materials.[83]

Bonch-Bruevich showed Lenin Tikhon's "proclamation" and asked what they should do with Tikhon himself. "Nothing," Lenin answered. "Inform him that the Soviet government is not inclined to place on his head the crown of martyrdom, but all those who will spread his works will immediately be arrested and severely prosecuted." Bonch-Bruevich intended to warn Metropolitan Veniamin that he would be held responsible for any anti-Soviet propaganda in the churches. Lenin responded approvingly: "it is always necessary to lay the responsibility on the highest people of the Orthodox church, remembering well that the lower clergy and especially the flock are weapons in their hands and often not completely responsible for what the higher ecclesiastical administration and its ringleaders do."[84] Lenin's strategy of not making a martyr of Tikhon, but of getting at him by repressing those under and around him, in fact became one of the main strategies that the Bolsheviks applied toward the patriarch in the coming years.

In Moscow and Petrograd, the Bolsheviks conducted themselves with caution, mainly countering the Church with their own propaganda and preventing the publication of Tikhon's encyclical. In the provinces, however, many clergy were arrested for reading or distributing Tikhon's encyclical.[85] This put priests in a very difficult position—they were obligated by the Church hierarchy to proclaim the patriarch's encyclical, but in doing so they faced arrest. Apparently, many chose not to read it—even in Moscow itself.[86]

The Decree of Separation of Church and State

The Bolsheviks answered Patriarch Tikhon's anathema encyclical by immediately issuing the Decree of Separation of Church from the State and the School from the Church. Lenin himself edited the decree, crossing out the first line of the draft, which read "Religion is the private affair of every citizen," and replaced it with "the Church is separated from the state." In one stroke, Lenin transformed the decree from one that guaranteed a basic human right (the freedom of conscience) into a political act. At the same time, this was the only line in the decree that even acknowledged the existence of the Orthodox Church as such.[87] The Decree, issued on January 23, 1918, declared that the government would not establish any preferences based on religion and no public functions would be accompanied by religious rites; that every citizen may profess any religious belief or none at all; and that free performance of religious rites was "permissible as long as it does not disturb public order." The Church objected not so much to those, but to three further clauses: Religious instruction was prohibited in any school where "general instruction is given," even private schools. "No church or religious associations have the right to own property. They do not possess the rights of juridical persons." The last article read: "The property of all ecclesiastical and religious associations in Russia is pronounced the property of the People. Buildings and objects especially used for the purposes of worship shall be let, free of charge, to the respective religious associations, by resolution of the local or Central state authorities."[88] The Russian Orthodox Church lost the ownership of all property, not just landed estates but even church buildings themselves with the contents necessary for conducting services. Even more consequential, the Church ceased to exist in the eyes of the law, which meant it had no rights or any possibility to defend itself legally.

Soviet propaganda portrayed this decree as progressive modern secular legislation, similar to laws in the United States or France, and some historians agreed that it primarily secularized society but did not contradict the freedom of conscience.[89] But key clauses of the law went much further in the areas of education, property, and legal status. The French law of 1905, which was intended to undercut the political power of the Catholic Church, transferred church property to *associations culturelles*, bodies made up of parishioners, to end the hierarchy's domination over the laity. Pope Pius X believed that the law would undermine the Church's hierarchical basis and therefore forbade these lay religious associations in France, as a consequence of which the church had no legal right to its own property (until 1924)—and during the intervening time much property was converted to other uses such as museums. The intent, however, was not for the government to expropriate ecclesiastical property, as was the case with the Bolsheviks.[90] That Tikhon responded differently than the pope proved decisively important for the future of the Russian Orthodox Church.

On January 25, the Church Council issued a statement declaring that the decree was duplicitous hypocrisy: Declaring the freedom of religion, it nullified it. The Council declared that it welcomed any authentic broadening of the freedom of conscience, but that the decree was tantamount to making the Church's very existence impossible. This might appear to be an over-reaction; but later application of the law would demonstrate that the Council was correct to interpret the law as not guaranteeing the freedom of conscience it proclaimed.

In his interview with *The Lantern*, Tikhon observed that separating church and state was "easier to carry out on paper than in the heart," especially because it was unknown how many of the hundred million Orthodox Christians supported it. The Bolsheviks wanted to take away the Church's property—but, the patriarch countered, it effectively was already the property of the people, who had donated it to the Church over the centuries. "We are always ready to part with it, if only it were known into whose hands it will fall." The patriarch also noted that the prohibition of religious education contradicted the proclamation of the freedom of conscience. Tikhon observed that in America, religion was not taught in public school, but there was no hindrance to teaching religion in a private context. From his American experience, Tikhon understood what the separation of church and state was supposed to look like. According to the interviewer, Tikhon was critical of the Bolsheviks but not in a state of panic: "It is not as easy to overthrow the Heavenly King as it is the earthly tsar."[91]

Believers responded to the patriarch's summons with a massive show of support for the Church. On January 21, an enormous procession in Petrograd up Nevsky Prospect ended at the Alexander-Nevsky Lavra. Newspapers estimated the crowds numbered several hundred thousand.[92] The Council organized a similar procession in Moscow on January 28 which was even more colossal—observers noted an entire ocean of people converged on Red Square, filling it down to the river and all the surrounding streets. This was precisely the kind of show of support for the Church that the patriarch called for in the encyclical—and people responded in unprecedented numbers. Patriarch Tikhon hoped that showing the so-called People's Government that the people stood with the Church, and did not support policies that restricted it, would cause them to rethink their policies.

Indeed, the heart of the battle between the Church and the Bolsheviks was precisely over—and ultimately for—"the people," which both sides appealed to in rather abstract terms. The Bolsheviks declared that they stood for "the laboring people," though in reality they had little sympathy for most of the laboring people (the peasantry) and in any event assumed they knew better than the people themselves what was best for them. The patriarch and the Church Council claimed the majority of Russia's population—115 million people—were Orthodox believers and supported them. As time went on, however, some Council delegates began to admit they had no idea how many of those people really stood with the Church.[93] To be sure, there were no shortage of radicalized soldiers and workers and even peasants who were willing to carry out Bolshevik policies against the Church. Likely there were even more who were simply indifferent. But if there were 40 million still willing to declare their adherence to the Orthodox Church to Soviet census takers in 1937, the number was surely far higher in 1918. Indeed, believers demonstrated such massive support for the Church in the first half of 1918 that the Bolsheviks backed off from an aggressive policy against the Church, just as the patriarch hoped. That turned out, however, to be a temporary retreat.[94]

Spring–Summer 1918

After the massive processions in Petrograd and Moscow, mass processions followed in provincial cities—though many of these were fired upon by troops, clergy were arrested, and clashes took place between supporters of the Church and of the regime. On January 30, in response to a letter from a priest who had suffered from the hands of revolutionaries, Patriarch Tikhon wrote an open letter warning clergy to prepare for persecution. But he also instructed the clergy to begin to gather the faithful laity, read the scriptures with them, instruct them, and prepare them—in other words, they should not take for granted that the people stood behind them. In particular, he instructed them "not to neglect discussions with pious women, who often restrain their husbands and brothers from lawless acts and defend the Church of God." Clergy should form brotherhoods, unions, and councils out of right-minded laity to defend the Church—and defend themselves.[95] Tikhon thus not only wanted the clergy to mobilize the laity in general to defend the Church, but specifically singled out women—who indeed would play a critical role in the Church's survival during the Revolution.[96]

In response to Patriarch Tikhon's summons, believers across Russia formed brotherhoods and unions to defend their churches. The patriarch and the Council received a flood of letters from parishes and reports from diocesan bishops expressing support for the January 19 encyclical, about processions, about forming unions, and about their petitions to the Soviet government to overturn the Decree of Separation.[97] A particularly important grassroots organization was the Council of United Parishes of Moscow under the chairmanship of Aleksandr Samarin. Among its activities, the group organized a regular bodyguard for the patriarch. Although the patriarch himself dismissed the need and refused it, nevertheless the Council of United

Parishes decided to convene a rotating guard of volunteers on patrol outside his residence.[98] Taking up the patriarch's encouragement for women's participation, a group of women, headed by Samarin's sister Sofia, established the Union of Orthodox Women in June 1918. This union had a wide range of activities both philanthropic and educational. Patriarch Tikhon valued one role in particular—namely, that members of the women's union visited clergy who were imprisoned, assisting them with food and other needs. The patriarch particularly tasked them with compiling a list of all the clergy who were imprisoned in Moscow; members of the women's union reported to Tikhon in April 1919 with a list of those imprisoned and how the union had assisted them—for which the patriarch was very grateful.[99]

On February 28,[100] Patriarch Tikhon and the Holy Synod issued important instructions for the clergy and faithful. They instructed pastors to welcome initiatives from believers—this proved pivotal. The instructions also directed the laity to form unions or collectives connected to every church, and that these unions should have stated educational and philanthropic goals and names; since religious organizations were deprived of legal rights by the new decree, such organizations needed to appear under a different guise. These could be chaired by laity, which thereby extended significant control over churches to the laity, even over church property.[101] If someone came to steal or confiscate church property (and it was often difficult to distinguish between the two), someone should ring the church bells to summon the people to the church's defense. The instructions also directed parents and teachers to work together to defend religious education from state incursion, which was the element of the Decree of Separation that believers most vigorously objected to. These instructions were directed more against the uncontrolled and unregulated actions of local authorities (and defending the Church against simple banditry, which was a pervasive threat) than at the Decree of Separation itself.[102] The instructions issued by the patriarch and the Synod therefore placed the defense—and ultimately the future itself—of the local church and religious life in the hands of the laity. The patriarch acknowledged that the Church would not survive if not defended by the people. He drew upon his lifetime experience of working with brotherhoods, especially in America, to encourage their universal foundation now.[103]

There were some in the Church and in the Council who believed that the patriarch should take a much more active role in the country's politics and were critical that he was not doing more. They hoped the patriarch would be a new Patriarch Hermogen, who appealed to the Russian people to expel the intruders in Moscow and restore stability during the seventeenth-century Time of Troubles.[104] In an interview, Tikhon defended the Church against criticisms that it was not acting decisively enough; even processions had become dangerous because people's safety could not be guaranteed. Other than the proclamations that he and the Council issued, Tikhon did not think it was appropriate for churchmen to do more in the political arena. The correspondent was clearly disappointed, believing that the religious upsurge in Moscow could allow the Church to mobilize the people to eradicate "the abominations in human affairs."[105] Nor was he alone in criticizing the patriarch for not doing more to lead Russia out of its Time of Troubles. Patriarch Tikhon was in a very difficult position because of the contending ideas among Orthodox believers about how he should lead.[106]

The upsurge in religiosity noted by the journalist was witnessed everywhere that the patriarch served. When he presided, churches were overflowing, even the largest churches, especially once Great Lent began on March 17, 1918.[107] It was announced in advance where the patriarch would serve, so that word spread and drew crowds.[108] Observers concluded from this that support for the Church was stronger than ever. Indeed, there seemed to be a major reversal from just the previous year: In 1917, there were many popular expressions of anticlericalism and frustration with the institutional Church, but in 1918, once the government began persecuting the Church, people who might have been critical of the old imperial Church came to its defense.

The rise in public displays of Orthodox religiosity that came after the massive processions in Petrograd, Moscow, and other cities, did not dissipate in the spring. For the May 1 socialist festivities, which were intended to be a celebration of the Revolution (but in the end were poorly attended), a banner that read "Long live the international" was placed over the icon of St. Nicholas above the Kremlin's Nicholas Gate. By the end of the day, the banner was torn—which believers interpreted as a miracle that drew large crowds to pray before the icon.[109] A grassroots movement in Moscow parishes culminated in the organization of a city-wide procession on the spring feast of St. Nicholas (May 22). Patriarch Tikhon blessed the procession and summoned people to gather at their parish churches and process together with them but also urged that the day not be "darkened" by any human passions, that people gather not in the spirit of hostility and violence but rather in prayer.[110] Several hundred thousand people, of all social classes, converged on Red Square. One journalist noted that while the Bolsheviks had promised that by May 1 they would be celebrating the victory of worldwide revolution, the "miracle" of the international failed to appear, but another "miracle" had taken place—which was that the spirit of the people was turning away from the revolution and back toward the foundations of Russian culture, including Orthodoxy. In an interview, Patriarch Tikhon himself believed that people would unite around the Church for Russia's renewal.[111]

Patriarch Tikhon made a long-awaited journey to Petrograd in June 1918. Although Petrograd was the "cradle of the revolution," Tikhon encountered massive crowds eager to see him everywhere he went.[112] On June 13, Tikhon visited the Petrograd Brotherhood of Parish Councils. Brotherhood representatives praised the Church Council for granting the laity a far more significant place in the life of the Church—for now the laity could organize at that crucial moment to defend the Church and sustain it through the trials coming from the Soviet government. Patriarch Tikhon, for his part, affirmed that he had always been a supporter of lay involvement in Church life and knew from experience in America how vital it was to building up the Church—and that it would be decisive for the very survival of the Church, given the current circumstances. In response to a comment that the brotherhood was preparing people for potential martyrdom in defense of their churches, Tikhon replied: "the Russian person knows how to die—but he does not know how to live. The task of the Brotherhood is not only to inspire people to martyrdom and death, but to exhort them how they need to live.... Our hope—this is life, not death and the grave."[113]

The patriarch's experiences in Petrograd and Moscow gave him some sense of hope that people were returning to Church, including those who had been alienated from it before the Revolution. Although there was still persecution and priests were paying with their lives, he believed that this was coming not from the Russian people as a whole, but only from some "obstinate circles."[114] He also observed that workers, who had cooled to religion under the influence of political events, were taking new interest in it—something that particularly struck him in his visits to Petrograd and Kronstadt—and were doing so consciously and deliberately, whereas previously religion had been for them only a formality.[115]

In addition to expressions of religious upswing and Tikhon's encouragement of popular support for the Church, he also commented on the developing political situation. In the spring of 1918, he issued encyclicals which discussed the renewed hostilities with the Germans that coincided with new conflicts between the Bolsheviks and their opponents. In early March, he issued an encyclical in which he rebuked soldiers for retreating from the front, where they were defending the country against the Germans, only to turn their weapons against one another in civil war. The encyclical exhorted the people to cease reprisals and internecine strife, to set aside mutual hatred but rather to love one another across class divides.[116]

On March 18, 1918, Patriarch Tikhon issued his most political proclamation criticizing the Bolshevik Treaty of Brest-Litovsk with the Germans. Signed on March 3, the Soviet government renounced claims to territories containing a third of imperial Russia's population, arable land, and factories. The patriarch wrote that the Church always prayed for peace, which the people longed for, but this was a shameful peace. It surrendered entire regions inhabited by Orthodox people to an enemy "who is alien by faith." He especially lamented that Ukraine and Kiev, the "mother of Russian cities," was torn from the Russian state. Moreover, Russia's treaty with Germany had not brought peace, but only an intensification of the civil conflict.[117] Most of the patriarch's fellow countrymen, even many Bolsheviks, also condemned the Brest-Litovsk treaty. But this encyclical more than any other criticized a Soviet political decision that was not directly about defending the Church, and on an issue where the Bolsheviks' legitimacy was especially at stake. This proclamation he would later retract.[118]

Patriarch Tikhon also condemned the execution of Nicholas II. The former tsar, together with his wife, five children, and their servants, was executed by local Bolsheviks in Ekaterinburg in the Urals on the night of July 16–17, 1918, though only Nicholas II's execution was announced. On July 19, Tikhon opened the third sitting of the Church Council by leading a memorial service for Nicholas.[119] On Sunday July 21, Patriarch Tikhon gave an emotional sermon at the Kazan cathedral next to the Kremlin, condemning the fact that the former tsar was shot somewhere in the depths of Russia by a small group of people who decided the former tsar's fate without a trial; this was only approved by the central government after the fact because they were afraid that the tsar would be captured by the opposing forces. Tikhon stated his conscience necessitated him to condemn the act, even if doing so led to his own imprisonment or execution.[120]

Initially there was no direct dialogue between the central Bolshevik government in Petrograd and the Church Council. Shortly after the government's move to Moscow in March 1918, the patriarch with the Holy Synod sent a delegation to negotiate with Sovnarkom about the Decree of Separation of Church and State.[121] At first, the talks indicated that a compromise was possible so long as the talks were headed by Bonch-Bruevich, a Bolshevik who had a deeper understanding of religion than most. But then in May 1918, the Soviet government established the eighth, or "liquidation," department of the Commissariat of Justice to handle policy toward the Church. Petr Krasikov (1870–1939), a longtime friend of Lenin's who declared that the Orthodox Church was an enemy that "needed to be fought," was appointed its head. Any possibility of compromise disappeared, and Soviet efforts to dismantle the Church became systematic state policy.[122] The intent of the Liquidation Department in stripping the Church of legal status was precisely to deprive it of the possibility of existing as an organization.[123]

The relationship between the Russian Orthodox Church and the Soviet state took a decisive turn in late summer. Krasikov's Liquidation Department issued Instructions for the implementation of the Decree of Separation of Church and State on August 30. The Instructions gave a harsh interpretation of the Decree of Separation, specifically regarding the contentious issues of juridical personhood, the confiscation of property, and the prohibition against religious education. All types of religious organizations were stripped of corporate personhood, including societies that had philanthropic or educational purposes but were associated with religion—thus undermining the Church's ability to engage in any kind of philanthropy. All property belonging to the Orthodox Church was to be transferred to the management of the local Soviets of Workers' and Peasants' Deputies. After making an inventory, any property that had an explicitly religious purpose (the church building and its contents) could be let out to local inhabitants if a group of twenty people signed a contract for its use. All other forms of property (land, candle factories, printing presses, and bank accounts) were to be confiscated by local authorities. Finally, all types of religious education, except for theological courses for adults, were prohibited, and any type of religious procession or rite that took place outside a church building had to receive authorization. The only legal interface between the Soviet regime and the Russian Orthodox Church, therefore, became the local bodies of parishioners who signed contracts to use the buildings.[124] After the publication of these Instructions, the Soviet campaign to confiscate property belonging to the Orthodox Church became much more systematic and aggressive.[125]

Patriarch Tikhon and the Church Council vehemently protested the August Instructions and issued their own instructions to believers as a practical response. Initially, the Council aimed to boycott the Instructions and members of the Church were forbidden from any kind of participation in the implementation of the decree, including signing contracts with the Soviet government. In the end, delegates realized that if parish communities refused to cooperate, the authorities could simply close all churches. Therefore, the Council called on believers to defend their churches from desecration, but instructed them to enter into agreement with the authorities and take over the use of the churches.[126] Unlike the pope, who forbade lay associations from assuming control of Catholic Church properties in France after the 1905 law, the Church Council's decision to instruct the faithful to take control over their parish churches, and the patriarch's support for the laity's role, proved to be of decisive importance for the very survival of the Orthodox Church in the Soviet Union.

The Church Council, no longer able to function because of Bolshevik requisitioning of funds and buildings, held its last session on September 20, 1918. One of the last issues the Council discussed was the role of women in the Church, and it was broadly supportive of substantially increasing that role, including permitting women to serve on parish and diocesan councils, as well as church wardens and cantors. The Council also supported restoring the office of the deaconess, which existed in the first millennium of the Church but had fallen into disuse, but the Council closed just as it was set to decide on the issue.[127] In closing the final session, Patriarch Tikhon spoke of the brotherly love and cooperation that worked as "spiritual cement" bringing together the disparate participants into a unified body. Its act of restoring the patriarchate would serve as a rock to anchor the Church in the future—but only if all worked together collectively with the patriarch. He ended by appealing for continued support with their prayer, advice, guidance, experience, and cooperation.[128] The patriarch's last words to the Council were not only a practical appeal but also encapsulated the significance of the Council itself: It provided the Church with the continuing leadership of the patriarch, who in turn vowed to keep the Council's spirit of conciliarity alive in preserving the Church in the new, hostile environment.

6

Neither Red nor White

The Civil War (1918–1920)

> The people flock to church more than ever they did before, and this applies not only to the peasants and factory hands but also to the bourgeoisie, who it was thought were growing indifferent to religion.... I will... content myself with quoting the words of a Moscow workman... whom I met... in November, 1920. "There is only one man in the whole of Russia," said this workman, "whom the Bolsheviks fear from the bottom of their hearts, and that is Tihon, the Patriarch of the Russian Church."
> —Paul Dukes, British intelligence officer[1]

The new harsh line of the Soviet regime toward the Orthodox Church coincided with the hardening of divisions between the Bolsheviks and all their political opponents, which erupted into brutal Civil War that lasted through 1920. Patriarch Tikhon had to defend the Orthodox Church when its clergy became targets of the Red Terror and criticized the revolutionary regime for its abuses of human rights. Asserting that criticism did not make him a counter-revolutionary, he claimed he had the right to point out the regime's abuses without calling for its overthrow. He never lent his support to the Whites and even made a declaration of the Church's political neutrality, though this did not protect him from being arrested. The regime, despite claims that it granted religious freedom and sought to avoid offending religious believers, embarked on an assault on popular piety. In this context, Patriarch Tikhon sought to defend Orthodoxy based on the Soviets' own laws.

Red Terror

Much of the violence and terror in the first months of the revolution had been spontaneous, from below, fueled by Bolshevik rhetoric but not by its dictate.

Violence against clergy had been sporadic in the first eight months of the Revolution. It was primarily local, made up of spontaneous instances of mob "justice" committed especially by soldiers without any orders from above, such as the shooting of Patriarch Tikhon's close coworker in America, Fr. John Kochurov, by Red Guards on October 31, 1917, or that of Metropolitan Vladimir (Bogoiavlensky) on January 25, 1918.[2] But from the summer of 1918, clergy were included in repression of "counter-revolutionary" elements. More individual clergymen were killed, including bishops such as Germogen (Dolganov, 1858–1918) and Andronik (Nikolsky, 1870–1918), who were brutally murdered in June 1918. Lenin himself directed "merciless mass terror" against clergy among other elements after an uprising in Penza in August 1918.[3]

Then on August 30, Moisei Uritsky (1873–1918), head of the Petrograd Cheka, was assassinated, and on the same day Fanny Kaplan (1890–1918) attempted to assassinate Lenin. In response, the Soviet government pronounced the Red Terror on September 5. Terror was intended to eliminate both actual and potential enemies, and guarantee submission to state power. By placing the blame on "class enemies" such as the aristocracy and the bourgeoisie, Bolshevik rhetoric linked all opposition to "international capital," masking that opposition came from other socialists, and thereby monopolized the claim to revolution for themselves, rendering everyone else "counter-revolutionaries."[4]

Now mass terror turned into a centrally justified, determined, and asserted policy. In response to the assassination of Uritsky and the attempt on Lenin, hundreds of people associated with the opposition were arrested and executed not because of any direct association with the assassination plots but simply as retribution, to "atone for the blood" of Lenin and Uritsky. In the initial period of the Red Terror, at least 10,000 people were shot, while thousands more were taken hostage by the regime or sent to concentration camps; the total number of victims is conservatively estimated at least 100,000 for the Civil War. Although the Red Terror as an official policy came to an end in November 1918, terror was widely used as a tactic, and in many regions the secret police, the All-Russian Extraordinary Commission or Cheka established in December 1917, was completely unchecked. Since many were summary executions in zones of the conflict, establishing the number of victims is nearly impossible; recent research estimates 15,000 clergy and believers were repressed during the Revolution and Civil War, of which 13,000 were shot.[5]

The first prominent Moscow clergyman to be executed was Archpriest Ioann Vostorgov. Fr. Vostorgov had been arrested in June 1918 after preaching a fiery sermon during the massive May 22 procession led by Patriarch Tikhon to the icon of St. Nicholas on the Kremlin tower. The Cheka caught Vostorgov in a "sting" operation over the sale of a house that was intended to compromise not only Vostorgov but also the patriarch. Fr. Vostorgov and a bishop were shot on September 5, the day the Red Terror was decreed, two of its first victims.[6] As the number of clergy arrested rose, the patriarch frequently appealed to his right of *pechalovanie*, a historical right of patriarchs to intercede for mercy before the ruler on behalf of the condemned (which had not been exercised since the death of the previous patriarch in 1700).[7] Patriarch Tikhon interceded not only for the Orthodox clergy and believers but also Roman Catholic priests taken as hostages during the Soviet-Polish conflict.[8]

The patriarch himself came under scrutiny and the threat of arrest in late summer 1918 in connection with the so-called Lockhart Plot. The plot involved the British agent Robert Bruce Lockhart, together with the French and American ambassadors, who devised a scheme that was to combine foreign troops with Russian opposition to overthrow the Bolsheviks. After it was uncovered, Soviet newspapers alleged that Patriarch Tikhon supported the conspiracy. According to the Soviet newspaper *Izvestiia*, the patriarch promised that, if the plot succeeded in overthrowing the Bolsheviks, he would serve an "all-Russian moleben" and issue a special word to the people to accept foreign intervention.[9] Apparently the British were indeed hoping that the patriarch would support them and discussed setting aside substantial funds to give the patriarch in exchange.[10]

As soon as this news broke in the Soviet press, Patriarch Tikhon explained to the Church Council that the allegations were baseless. The Council issued a statement to the government to that effect. Metropolitan Arseny also proposed that the guard around the patriarch be increased for the coming night.[11] In a sermon in March the following year, the patriarch made clear that he did not know Lockhart and that he would not bless any foreign intervention into Russia's affairs to solve its internal disorders, because Russia's salvation could not come from outside but only through a change from within Russia itself.[12] The Soviet authorities found no incriminating evidence against him. The Vostorgov and Lockhart cases were the first of many attempts by the Bolsheviks to find something with which to implicate the patriarch to justify some action against him.

Patriarch Tikhon Addresses the Bolshevik Leadership

On the first anniversary of the Bolshevik Revolution, November 7, 1918, Patriarch Tikhon sent an exhortation to the Council of People's Commissars. In what historian Richard Pipes labeled "the most daring challenge to the new regime that any public figure had had the courage to issue," Tikhon addressed the Bolshevik leadership directly for the first time.[13] The patriarch said later that he intended it as a letter for the Bolshevik leadership only and not for the public; however, it was printed and widely distributed—tens of thousands of copies were sent around Moscow and 5 million copies outside Soviet territory—and created a sensation.[14] The letter was a critical assessment of the Bolsheviks' first year in power, not intended as a condemnation so much as an exhortation to change. In the context of Red Terror and intensifying Civil War, Tikhon contrasted what the Bolsheviks had promised with what they were delivering. They promised, first, to bring peace, that is, to end Russia's involvement in World War I "without annexations and indemnities." Instead, they concluded a shameful peace with humiliating conditions that resulted in the dismemberment of Russia. The Soviet government had not brought peace, but instead ended the war against the external enemy so that they could direct the military against internal enemies in civil conflict, which Tikhon consistently labeled as "fratricide."[15]

Further, the patriarch continued, people in Russia did not feel safe, for everyone lived under constant fear of being robbed, searched, arrested, or shot. Hundreds of people had been arrested and spent months in jail. Many had been executed, without investigation or trial, not for their own personal guilt, but taken hostage and then killed in retaliation for acts committed by people with whom they had no direct connection. Moreover, bishops, priests, monks, and nuns had been put to death on the grounds of some vague accusation of "counter-revolution." The patriarch found it ironic that the Bolsheviks, who claimed to be carrying out a revolution for the benefit of humanity, were engaging in such purposeless cruelty.[16]

The Bolsheviks promised freedom but, the patriarch asked, "Is it freedom when no one can openly express their opinion without the danger of falling under the accusation of counter-revolution? Where is the freedom of speech and the press?" Open public discussion was silenced, and the non-Bolshevik press had been completely stifled. The Bolsheviks had promised freedom of conscience and the freedom of "religious propaganda," but in fact it was not permitted, and some preachers had already paid for that with their lives.[17]

The patriarch concluded his letter to the Soviet leaders by observing that "we know that our exhortation will arouse in you only animosity and indignation and that you will search for a pretext of accusing us of opposing the government." But, he concluded, it was not his business to judge earthly power, and any government would receive his blessing so long as it was truly good for its people. Therefore, he exhorted the Soviet leadership to turn from using their power for persecution and rather to celebrate their anniversary "by freeing prisoners and ceasing bloodshed, violence, ruin, and oppressing the faith; turn not to destruction, but to the establishment of order and legality, grant people the desired and deserved rest from internecine strife."[18] Although Maxim Gorky had criticized the Bolsheviks along similar terms in 1917, Patriarch Tikhon was perhaps the only person who, one year into the revolution, was in a position to openly criticize the Bolsheviks to an audience that could reach all Russians (in both Soviet and White territories) and not immediately become a victim of the Red Terror.[19] After this biting message, the Bolsheviks became more determined than ever to crush him and the Church leadership.

First Arrest

The criticisms leveled by the patriarch in his anniversary letter stung hard because the Bolsheviks were keenly aware of the patriarch's massive influence in Russian society, and for over a year they tried to get him to recant his words and to undermine his social influence and authority. In response to Tikhon's letter, the Soviets accused the patriarch of counter-revolution, just as he predicted they would. On the night of November 24–25, 1918, the Cheka placed the patriarch under house arrest and searched his residence.[20] Nikolai Kuznetsov, the lawyer who represented the Church in negotiations with the government throughout 1918, petitioned for the patriarch's release. In addition to hampering the Church administration from doing its work, he argued, the patriarch's arrest was upsetting to the Orthodox population of Moscow that was expecting the patriarch to be conducting services in their parishes, and in this way only fueling people's dissatisfaction with the regime—both within Soviet-controlled territories and in those that the Soviets were trying to claim.[21] The Holy Synod and Higher Church Administration informed believers in Moscow of the patriarch's detainment and sent in their own appeal for his release.[22] The Cheka nonetheless refused to release him, declaring that the seriousness of the accusations "demanded thorough investigation."[23]

On December 6, Patriarch Tikhon sent a declaration to the Council of People's Commissars (Sovnarkom) that he had signed no proclamation calling for the overthrow of the Soviet government as they alleged. He stated directly: "I do not sympathize with and cannot sympathize with many of the measures of the people's government . . . which I do not hide and openly wrote about in my letter in address to the People's Commissars before the celebration of the first anniversary of the October Revolution, but I just as openly declared that it is not our affair to judge earthly power that has been allowed by God and all the more to take actions directed at its overthrow. Our duty is only to point out human deviations from Christ's great commandments of love, freedom, and brotherhood, to call out actions based on violence and hatred, and to call everyone to Christ."[24] His declarations, however, were not considered sufficient for his release.[25]

Although appeals from the Church administration had little effect, the government responded to appeals from believers with huge numbers of signatures. All such appeals were directed to Vladimir Bonch-Bruevich as administrator of the affairs of Sovnarkom. The central government had not been involved in the patriarch's arrest and was not aware of its terms. Having received popular petitions, Bonch-Bruevich wrote to the head of the Justice Commissariat, who in turn wrote the Cheka.[26] The patriarch was finally released from house arrest on Christmas eve, January 6, 1919, and that evening and the following morning he led services for the holiday. The patriarch preached on Christmas, explicating the hymn "Glory to God in the highest, and on earth peace, goodwill toward men" and the lack of peace in Russia. He told his listeners that God offered salvation to humanity, but cannot save without people's willing participation. "We are dying not so much from cold and hunger as from hostility, enmity and hatred." Only if Christ be embodied in people's lives and deeds could there truly be peace and goodwill among people.[27] Even after being unjustly detained for over some six weeks, the patriarch's central message was not one of placing the blame on others for their misdeeds, but rather asking his listeners what they could do to change themselves and make things better.

Patriarch Tikhon, the Orthodox Church, and the Civil War

The military conflict of the Civil War escalated in the fall of 1918. The Church leadership unabashedly supported the Whites in the regions controlled by them. In both Siberia under Admiral Alexander Kolchak (1874–1920) and the south under Generals Anton Denikin (1872–1947) and Pyotr Wrangel (1878–1928), the Church leadership created Higher Temporary Church Administrations, justified by their inability to communicate effectively with the patriarch, which were to be terminated once normal communications were reestablished. Church leaders participated in propaganda efforts through sermons and leaflets that condemned Bolshevism and supported the White movement. Given what the Bolsheviks were doing to the Church, such support for the White movement was hardly surprising. On the ground, however, the situation was far more complex. Rank-and-file clergy had varying political sympathies or were indifferent to politics, wanting simply to be left alone to care for their flock. As for the Orthodox Church in Soviet-controlled territories, there is scant evidence that it supported the White cause.[28]

Given the alien worldview of Bolshevik ideology and the hostility of the regime toward the Orthodox Church, one can only assume that Patriarch Tikhon did not wish the Bolsheviks to be victorious. Nevertheless, he never supported efforts to overthrow them. This was true not only of his public statements but even his private ones. Grigory Trubetskoi (1873–1930), for example, reported that he went to the patriarch before his departure for the south and asked him "for permission to give his blessings to one of the eminent leaders of the White movement on the condition that the whole thing would be kept secret."[29] The patriarch, however, "told me that he did not consider it possible to do this because, remaining in Russia, he wanted not only outwardly, but even in essence to avoid reproach for any sort of interference of the Church in politics."[30] Metropolitan Veniamin (Fedchenkov, 1880–1961) wrote of one princess who sought the patriarch's blessing for Wrangel, and Tikhon refused—telling her he had done the same when someone came for a blessing for Kolchak. In Veniamin's interpretation, Tikhon refused because "it would have been disloyal in relation to the Soviet government and threatened the patriarch with execution. . . . Did he sympathize in his heart with Kolchak, Denikin, and Wrangel? I don't know. Probably he sympathized. We were all then on the side of the Whites, the 'believing' government, and not on the side of the atheists."[31] Evidently the patriarch was motivated by a mixture of principle and prudence in not supporting the Whites: He opposed the Church's interference but also did not want to give them justification for their accusations against the clergy.

Anton Kartashev (1875–1960), the last minister of confessions under the Provisional Government (and later eminent church historian in Paris), was involved in a conspiratorial anti-Bolshevik group that met with the patriarch to receive his feedback on their plan for a new government. In September 1918, the patriarch received them at his residence and after listening intently, "he suddenly laughed indulgently at our 'fine words' like a wise elder laughs at idealistic dreams of a youth. 'Good! It's all really good! But only when will all this be? Not now of course.'" In Kartashev's understanding, the patriarch, as a "son of the people," instinctively felt the strength and endurance of the people's attraction to the Bolsheviks and did not believe in the quick victory of the White movement, and therefore could not agree with their political calculations. Kartashev also understood that Tikhon wished to avoid tying the Church to any political movement.[32] Although Tikhon did nothing more than meet with these people, that would later factor into the indictment against him as evidence that he supported counter-revolution.[33]

Tikhon developed his ideas in a series of sermons in spring 1919 that were public but not published (the Church had little possibility of publishing anything) so therefore limited in their audience and largely unknown until recently.[34] In a sermon on Forgiveness Sunday before the beginning of Great Lent on March 2, the patriarch quoted one of the hymns to St. Germogen (commemorated that day) which claimed that "the salvation of Rus is from the Orthodox Church."

Those hostile to the Church claimed that it sought to save the nation through restoring the monarchy, and accused clergy of counter-revolution. The patriarch countered that

> The establishment of one or another form of government is not the business of the Church, but of the people themselves. Be it a Tsar, be it a constitution, be it a president of the Russian republic—the people themselves decide; the Church does not tie itself for the ages to a particular form of government because they have only relative historical significance. The Church bears a different service: it is and should be the conscience of the government. Obeying the government in worldly matters, the Church says to it that power is established by God to serve the people, to care for its good, to defend its interests, and it [the Church] can bless only such an

authority—and such an order—that brings people peace and truth, and not violence, resentment, and class animosity.³⁵

The patriarch also asserted that foreign intervention would not save Russia. "The main evil that the motherland is suffering from is internecine conflict." Russians got a taste for violence during World War I, but instead of completing the war against the external enemy, began destroying one another: "White Guards and Red Army men, the South makes war against the North, the East against the West." "In its brutal reprisals, destruction and devastation, this domestic war is not not lesser than foreign wars." Therefore, the voice of the Church pleaded with its flock—by which he meant all Russians, Red and White—to "stop the blood-spilling carnage [and] insane self-destruction . . . and try peacefully to come to an agreement with each other."³⁶

In every soul, the patriarch continued, there was a "struggle of two persons": one was earthly, without God, filled with self-love, while the other was spiritual and guided by conscience. When the weight in society was on the former, people divided into groups to struggle for their class interests; when spiritual development was supported in society, then there was a "predominance of the high requirements of conscience, truth, and love." Therefore, the Church and its message were critical to the salvation not only of the individual, but of the nation, because its primary task was to cultivate the spiritual side of a person; by implication, the Bolsheviks, with their materialism, could only encourage self-interest and class interest that were inevitably divisive. Society could only be healed if people were called to labor for the good of their neighbor and the whole and not be concerned only with class and self-interest. Finally, the patriarch asserted that the destructive currents in Russia that were bringing the country to ruin could not be stopped by external material force. Because the root cause was primarily a moral crisis, only spiritual strength could put an end to the cycle of violence by inspiring love of one's neighbor and "respect for the human person as the image and likeness of God"—ideals that the Church alone bore.³⁷ In another sermon, the patriarch emphasized that what made a government good was not the high ideals it proclaimed, but its ability to bring benefit to everyone, not just one class or party.³⁸

In this way, the patriarch was presenting a counter to Bolshevism on ideological, not political grounds. Although Soviet ideology encouraged self-sacrifice for the greater good, the patriarch implied that a materialistic worldview, which placed all of its emphasis on class interest, was inherently incapable of motivating society as a whole to self-sacrifice. If there was nothing else than this material existence, the majority would fail to see a motivation to sacrifice themselves, but rather be motivated to better their own material conditions—even at the expense of others.

The patriarch's critique of Soviet ideology was, however, hardly supportive of the White cause. In asserting that the Church was not tied to any particular form of government, he was undermining the position taken by the Whites who sought the restoration of the monarchy. Moreover, every time the patriarch spoke of the Civil War, he consistently spoke of it as fratricide. Although the Whites claimed to support the Church, their rhetoric was just as dehumanizing of their enemies as Bolshevik rhetoric. The patriarch understood that the majority of those fighting on both sides had been baptized Orthodox Christians, and therefore he considered them all his flock and could not accept any grounds for either side killing their opponents. Though war could be justified if it was in defense of the nation against a foreign enemy, he rejected any justification for Civil War.

At the same time as the Civil War was intensifying in the summer of 1919, there was an attempt on the patriarch's life. On July 12, he served liturgy for the feast of Saints Peter and Paul with a host of clergy and thousands of worshippers in the Christ the Savior cathedral. As he was exiting the cathedral, surrounded by a huge crowd as he was blessing people, a woman suddenly approached and stabbed him in the right side. Her knife was unable to penetrate deeply thanks to many layers of his vestments, and he was not mortally injured. In a bizarre twist of fate, the perpetrator was Pelageia Guseva, the sister of Khionia Guseva who had attacked Rasputin in the same way, on the same day, five years earlier. During her interrogation and trial, Guseva explained her motives with a strange mixture of religious and revolutionary language. She claimed that she had seen visions of Christ and the Mother of God, and that she had been commanded by God to kill the patriarch—in doing so she was killing the Antichrist. She also said she attacked him because he was "going against the people, as are all the clergy." The court found her not guilty by reason of insanity; Petr Krasikov, who closed the case for the prosecution, claimed she had "delusions of grandeur of a religious nature." The trial and its conclusion in the People's Court were intriguing: Soviet antireligious propaganda frequently characterized actions in defense of one's faith (such as defending churches from being ransacked by Soviet authorities) as "religious fanaticism" and held people engaged in such actions as accountable and therefore prosecutable. Yet here the court regarded Guseva's "religious fanaticism" as symptomatic of insanity that rendered her not responsible for her actions, though still subject to criminal investigation and trial—unlike the countless numbers of Red Army men, Cheka agents, and simple bandits that killed clergy as "class enemies." In the end, she was sent to an insane asylum.[39]

After the patriarch recovered, the Church held a festive liturgy in the Christ the Savior cathedral on July 27 followed by a special prayer of thanksgiving that the patriarch avoided mortal injury. The massive church was packed with worshippers, and the patriarch's path was strewn with flowers. After the service, Metropolitan Arseny (Stadnitsky) spoke of how Tikhon had not desired the patriarchate, but rather God desired him to bear the cross of leading the Russian Church—and therefore God preserved his life for the good of the Church. In his reply, Patriarch Tikhon said, perhaps with the characteristic smile on his face, that "the hand that was directed against me with a knife was not for amusement, of course." He asked that "the Lord preserve me so long as my life is needed for the Church. Obedient to the will of God, I remain calm and accept my fate.... [I]f it is my fate to live few days and die from a knife, or be shot, or some other untimely death ... let God's will be done." He only wished that his death would serve as a purification of his own sins and would be accepted by God as a "fragrant sacrifice for the people."[40] Even in the face of death, the patriarch accepted whatever God had in store for him.

Patriarch Tikhon Condemns the Pogroms

The Civil War reached a peak of ferocity in the summer of 1919, with both sides inflicting brutal reprisals against opponents. Pogroms against Jewish communities also intensified. Although the Red Army engaged in pogroms, since they frequently viewed Jews as "bourgeois," the main perpetrators were partisan groups in Ukraine and the White Armies. White Army propaganda was frequently interlaced with antisemitic tropes that identified Jews with Bolsheviks and the Bolshevik Revolution as part of a Jewish conspiracy against Russia and Orthodoxy.[41] Patriarch Tikhon issued an encyclical that was directed more at the Whites than at the Reds in condemning reprisals and pogroms on July 21, 1919.[42]

The patriarch's encyclical argued that the persecution that the Church was undergoing was a test of its faith. Though outsiders consider it weakness that Christians bear persecution without retaliation, the Christian must not deviate from the path of the Cross, for in that lay their salvation. If Christians were to turn to the path of retaliation, this would reduce them to the same level as their persecutors. It was difficult, the patriarch acknowledged, to forgive one's enemy when the enemy was defeated and the one oppressed found himself in judgment over his former oppressor. All Russia had become a battlefield. The fire of settling scores was spreading; it was no longer just a matter of warfare, but of hatred for one's fellow human beings. A source of even greater horror, the encyclical stated, were the pogroms against Jews, in which an entire people was attacked without regard to age, gender, beliefs, or personal guilt. Those who had themselves suffered looked for someone to blame and, "blinded by the thirst for revenge," they struck out at the party or group blamed for their misfortunes, and in doing so inflicted their revenge on innocent people. "Remember: pogroms are a dishonor for you and a dishonor for the Holy Church!" Christ did not draw the sword in his defense, but rather prayed for his enemies. Not only would vengeance result in new retributions, but Christians who engaged in retaliation betrayed Christ and lost whatever they had gained by their previous suffering.[43]

As he had done earlier, the patriarch condemned the Soviet practice of repressing people based on their class identity:

> We shudder with horror and pain when, after the attempts on the [lives of] representatives of our current government in Petrograd and Moscow . . . to atone for the guilt of the attackers, whole mounds were erected from the corpses of persons who were completely uninvolved in these attempts, and these insane sacrifices were greeted with triumph by the ones who should have put a stop to such atrocities. We shuddered—but after all, these actions took place . . . where religion is considered the opium of the people, where Christian ideals are a harmful vestige, where the extermination of one class by another and internecine strife are openly and cynically elevated to the most urgent task.[44]

In the Christian view, one was responsible for one's actions which were objectively right or wrong according to God's law, by contrast with the Soviet view that judged people primarily based on their class identity.

Reminding his audience of the horrors of the Red Terror, the patriarch applied the same criteria to atrocities, reprisals, and pogroms committed by the Whites. By engaging in reprisals and pogroms, Christians betrayed their own salvation. "Only on this rock—the healing of evil with good—will the indestructible glory and greatness of our Holy Orthodoxy Church in the Russian land be built."[45] The patriarch reiterated that the salvation of Russia would not come through military victories, but by overcoming hatred and enmity.

Although this encyclical was mostly directed at the Whites, it is not clear whether they heard the message. By this point the Church had very limited capabilities for printing and distributing anything, and getting messages to White-controlled territories presented even greater challenges. A copy was sent to each priest in Moscow to proclaim; it was also distributed in the provinces, not by the clergy but by some "unknown lay elements." But clergy were afraid of being repressed by the Soviet authorities for discussing anything political in Church (as many had been arrested for reading the patriarch's earlier encyclicals) and therefore did not read it aloud. Nevertheless, it was spread secretly among the public. The encyclical was, however, not widely distributed outside the Soviet territories—in other words, precisely where the pogroms were occurring and it was most needed.[46]

Patriarch Tikhon's encyclical stands in stark contrast to Soviet propaganda which alleged that the Russian Orthodox Church was inherently antisemitic and helped instigate pogroms. A July 30 article in *Izvestiia* alleged that clergy in Moscow churches "conduct the most unrestrained antisemitic and white-guardist agitation and propaganda," which they could do because of the "complete non-interference of the government in the affairs of religion"—and the article proceeded to justify further government intervention into the Church to stop such "propaganda." Tikhon refuted the article's slanderous claims in a letter to Sovnarkom—all the more since his encyclical was read out in Moscow churches just the prior week. "It is not our fault," he wrote, "that, deprived of the means of publishing our appeal to the people, its distribution is limited as also the benefit" it could bring to society at such a critical moment.[47] The patriarch received no response, and *Izvestiia* published no correction.

Patriarch Tikhon, the Executive Committee on Clergy Affairs, and Political Neutrality

During the Red Terror, the primary tactic in dealing with the clergy was terror and repression. As the Civil War progressed in 1919 and 1920, the Cheka's Secret Department (sometimes Secret-Operational Department) broadened its operations from repression to efforts to gather information, develop contacts with clergy, infiltrate Church circles, and target clergy who could be turned into collaborators. A key figure in this development was the notorious Chekist Martin Latsis (1888–1938), a leading ideologue of the Red Terror justifying mass violence in fall 1918, who headed the Secret Department from September 1919 to September 1920.[48] Another central actor was Aleksei Filippov (1869–1936), who informed for and collaborated with the Cheka but was not a Bolshevik; he believed that both the Church, with its critical statements against the Bolsheviks, and the regime and its policies were responsible for the hostility between the two.[49] Filippov established the Executive Committee for Clergy Affairs, known in Russian as *Ispolkomdukh*, in August 1919. It consisted of laymen and clergy of various confessions. Filippov later claimed that he was pursuing the general aims of the Cheka and the Party, but that Ispolkomdukh acted as an independent body. The stated tasks of the Committee—which, based on its actual activities, seems to reflect genuine intentions—were to help the clergy to adapt to Soviet conditions and defend them from unjust political repression.[50]

In September 1919, Filippov sought Patriarch Tikhon's support for Ispolkomdukh. The patriarch agreed with the need for a body that could soften tensions and clear up confusion between the clergy and the Soviet government and met with Filippov on September 21. The Committee subsequently asked Patriarch Tikhon to send a circular ordering the Orthodox clergy not to engage in political agitation.[51]

Filippov succeeded in convincing Patriarch Tikhon to issue an encyclical on October 8, 1919. Before the patriarch issued the encyclical, Filippov provided detailed commentary on the draft to ensure that the encyclical did not appear polemical against the Soviet government. Filippov claimed the text was epoch-making at a decisive moment—when Denikin was marching on Moscow—because it meant a fundamental change in the Church's relationship to the state, which he believed would be better both for the Church and for Russia. Filippov's editorial suggestions were mostly followed, including issuing the encyclical from the Trinity-St. Sergius Lavra on St. Sergius's feast day for added symbolic significance.⁵²

Though the patriarch composed the encyclical on Filippov's prompting, its argument reflected ideas developed in his earlier sermons—namely that the Church did not tie itself to any particular form of government, that choosing the government was the business of the people not the Church, and that the Church did not support foreign intervention because Russians had to solve their problems themselves. He also contended that clergy had welcomed the Whites with bells and thanksgiving services (which were central to Soviet accusations against them) not on their own initiative—rather, they were conducting such services because the people wanted them to. The main thrust of the encyclical was to call the clergy not to take sides in the Civil War. By their clerical ordination, they "should stand above and beyond any political interests, they must remember the canonical rules of the Holy Church, which forbids its servants from interfering in the political life of the country, to belong to any parties, and even more to make liturgical rites and sacred ceremonies into an instrument of political demonstrations." Clergy should avoid those who create strife and division (Romans 16:17) and obey human authorities in worldly affairs (1 Peter 2:13). It was particularly important for them not to do anything that justified the Soviet government's suspicions; they should also obey its decrees "so long as they do not contradict faith and piety."⁵³

The patriarch's main purpose in issuing the encyclical was to protect the clergy and ensure they did not commit acts that would bring suspicion— and therefore repression—upon themselves.⁵⁴ Filippov wanted the patriarch to give more explicit instructions that the clergy were to obey the Soviet government—but this he refused to do, since the encyclical was also directed to clergy who at that moment were under White rather than Soviet rule.⁵⁵ Filippov feared that the encyclical was still not strong enough to assuage Soviet suspicions and improve relations.⁵⁶ The patriarch together with the Higher Church Administration decreed that the October 8 encyclical should be sent to all diocesan bishops. In the Moscow diocese, deans were instructed to send it to clergy in their deanery. However, Filippov later reported that the encyclical was sent to the dioceses only after it was finally printed in March 1920, and then only in one copy for the bishop—in other words, it did not receive wide distribution.⁵⁷

Filippov expended great efforts to control how the Soviet leadership perceived the patriarch's encyclical. He submitted a report to the Cheka the day before Tikhon issued his encyclical in which he asserted that though the patriarch's previous encyclicals had been anti-Soviet, the new one represented a radical change. He claimed that the patriarch finally accepted the principle of the separation of church and state, and that he now instructed the clergy to obey the Soviet government.[58] Evidently Latsis was convinced by Filippov's arguments: The Cheka instructed its local agents to encourage clergy to read and explain the encyclical to their congregations. "Drastic measures should be taken" against clergy if they "reduced the significance" of the encyclical and undermined "the authority of the highest church authorities, which in this case are not acting contrary to the Soviet government."[59] This was a stunning reversal: Instead of trying to undermine the patriarch's authority, which it had long been at pains to do, now the Cheka would repress clergy for minimizing it. Filippov also wrote to Lev Kamenev (1883–1936) as the chair of the Moscow Soviet for permission to print the encyclical—25,000 copies without commentary and another 100,000 copies with Filippov's commentary. He requested such a large number so that it could be distributed in White-controlled territories because of its important propaganda value.[60]

Since all printing was in the hands of the state, the Organizational Bureau of the Party's Central Committee and the Politburo deliberated whether it was appropriate for the patriarch's encyclical to be printed.[61] Krasikov of the Liquidation Department vigorously objected, declaring it entirely inappropriate for the Soviet state to print anything from a religious body. He believed that the patriarch issued this proclamation only as a tactical move, a sign of weakness because the Whites were failing (when Krasikov was writing at the end of October, it was clearer that the Whites would be repelled from the center than it was when the patriarch issued the encyclical). The Church was desperately trying to adapt once it perceived that the White cause would fail, Krasikov maintained, but the Soviet government should only allow the process of collapse to continue, which he was confident would happen soon. Significantly, Krasikov feared that the distribution of the encyclical would negatively affect Red Army soldiers. "Regarding the impression that this proclamation could have on the average rank-and-file peasant or worker, on those of them who still have faith in the authority of the Church, it must be concluded that it will weaken their desire to take up arms in what, in the language of the patriarch, is called a feud," since Tikhon interpreted the Civil War as unjustifiable fratricide. Krasikov feared that this would have a detrimental effect upon a substantial contingent of Red Army soldiers for whom the patriarch's voice was still authoritative and undermine their resolve to fight.[62]

On October 28, Latsis presented the case for publishing the patriarch's encyclical to Sovnarkom headed by Lenin. Though the archives do not tell us more than that the issue was discussed, evidently Latsis, supporting Filippov's position, convinced the party leadership over Krasikov's objections.[63] Ispolkomdukh printed 50,000 copies of a pamphlet that included the patriarch's encyclical in full followed by Filippov's commentary interpreting it in a way that emphasized the Church's necessity to accept the Soviet government, but at the same time tried to protect the clergy from the blanket accusation of being inherently counter-revolutionary. His commentary also emphasized that Patriarch Tikhon sincerely intended the encyclical's message, that he had not capitulated to Soviet pressure to issue it.[64]

The encyclical had a very mixed reception among the Whites. Grigory Trubetskoi recounted that the encyclical grieved "those [of us] who stood round the Volunteer Army," because it appeared to undercut the legitimacy of their efforts. Only later did Trubetskoi come to see its wisdom because clergy who had conducted prayer services for the victory of the White Army were forced to flee with the Whites and thereby abandon their flocks, "to the great detriment of the Church's cause."[65] Bishop Veniamin (Fedchenkov), who was part of the Temporary Higher Church Administration in South-East Russia, recounted that they received the encyclical "already in the time of Wrangel" (spring 1920). "We read it at one of the sessions of the Synod" and resolved to put it in the desk drawer, "without announcing it to the people, so as not to cause our movement embarrassment. In our justification, we decided that this decree applied to those areas where the Soviet government exists, and cannot be extended to areas where the Whites rule." If the Church was not actively supporting the Whites, he claimed, it would be interpreted as disagreement with them and even sympathy for the Reds. They believed that the White movement corresponded to the interests of the Church. Veniamin wrote that he himself was a bit disturbed by their disobedience to the patriarch. Although he believed that the patriarch must have understood it would be impossible for the clergy in White territories to fulfill it, in fact the patriarch intended it for everyone and that affected how he worded the encyclical.[66]

Arrest and Interrogation

Although in October 1919 Latsis supported the publication of Patriarch Tikhon's October encyclical, by the end of December the Cheka's attitude toward him reversed again. On December 23, he was placed under house arrest, this time for far longer than the first time. It is not clear what brought about this shift—perhaps because the threat of the Whites was no longer so pressing and the Soviet authorities felt less need to be conciliatory. In addition to Tikhon, Metropolitans Arseny (Stadnitsky) and Kirill (Smirnov, 1863–1937) were also arrested, effectively crippling the top leadership of the Holy Synod. The higher ecclesiastical administration and groups of believers sent repeated appeals to the government for the patriarch's release, and both the administration and groups of believers appealed to Bonch-Bruevich for their release. As before, Bonch-Bruevich wrote to the Commissariat of Justice, which turned to the Cheka for an explanation.[67] Latsis explained that Tikhon was under arrest because he was suspected of "counter-revolutionary agitation" and provided a secret report explaining the reasons.[68]

The main reason for the patriarch's arrest, according to the secret report, was his criticisms of the regime in his 1918 declarations, especially his letter on the first anniversary of the Revolution, which, in the Cheka's estimation, had made an enormous impression on the Russian masses. The Cheka believed that the patriarch's proclamations shaped an atmosphere of distrust toward the Soviet government and provided ideological justification for the Whites. "It is enough to look at the collection of posters and printed sheets in various formats of Tikhon's famous appeal to the Council of People's Commissars... to understand to what extent the attention and interest of the Russian public was riveted by this appeal and the denunciations contained in it." Tikhon's influence on the masses was so significant and his criticisms so harmful to the new government, according to the report, that the question of whether Tikhon supported the Whites could significantly impact the outcome of the Civil War. Therefore, the Cheka felt it had to act.[69]

The report admitted that the secret police were unable to find incriminating evidence against the patriarch: No agents had successfully infiltrated the clergy, nor had its spies been able to establish any direct links between the patriarch and the Whites. The arrest finally came after a White newspaper claimed that Tikhon had sent favorable greetings through Nestor, the bishop of Kamchatka, to Admiral Kolchak as the White's "Supreme Ruler" with a blessing for his victory, news that allegedly caused a sensation and reenergized White supporters. This news story provided the secret police the evidence it had been waiting for.[70]

Latsis interrogated Tikhon for two hours on December 23, 1919. Two accounts of the interrogation survive, one from the Cheka and one prepared by Protopresbyter Nikolai Liubimov, a member of the Higher Church Administration, who accompanied the patriarch to Lubianka, the Cheka headquarters.[71] During the interrogation, according to the Cheka account, Tikhon dismissed the idea that he sent Nestor to bless Kolchak on the grounds that Nestor had left Moscow before Kolchak had even emerged as leader of the Whites. As to why he did not refute the story in the Soviet press, Tikhon replied that the Soviet press always distorted his words to cast them in the worst possible light. Accepting that explanation, Latsis asserted that the patriarch's failure to disavow the story at least in a letter to the government or even just his fellow bishops was an indication of his tacit support for the Whites.[72]

The questioning focused in turn on the patriarch's four encyclicals, two from 1918 and two from 1919. Latsis included Tikhon's letter on the first anniversary of the Bolshevik regime, since its enormous influence made the patriarch the "head of counter-revolutionary agitation" in his eyes.[73] Tikhon responded that it had not been an encyclical addressed to the people, but rather was his own personal letter to the Bolshevik leaders which he had not intended for distribution. Latsis told the patriarch that his criticisms of the regime were clearly false because even the patriarch himself was now willing to negotiate with the government. Latsis interpreted Tikhon's criticism as a complete rejection of the Soviet government and his declaration of political neutrality in October 1919 a reversal of that position, and therefore expected him to retract his earlier criticisms.

According to Liubimov's account, Tikhon countered that his previous views had not changed: His criticisms of the regime were still valid, but he did not reject the new government per se. In the interrogation, he stated that his relationship with the regime would change "if and when it changed its relationship to the church and the faith of Christ. But this does not mean that he [the patriarch] ignores the decrees of the government." Tikhon had never instructed anyone not to obey the Soviet government in earthly matters, but in matters of faith one had to obey only God. Tikhon asked Latsis what he meant by "counter-revolution," and Latsis answered: "Efforts to overthrow the Soviet government." Tikhon responded directly: "This we do not do."[74]

There was a fundamental difference in perspective—for Latsis, criticism meant denial of legitimacy and therefore amounted to counter-revolution, whereas Tikhon asserted that criticizing the regime did not mean he refused to recognize it or called for its overthrow. This fundamental difference even shaped how the interrogation itself was reported. Regarding Patriarch Tikhon's current attitude toward the Soviet government, the Cheka account summed up the interrogation tersely: The patriarch "could not give an explanation of how he regards the Soviet government."[75]

According to Liubimov's account, however, the patriarch gave a definite yet nuanced account of his political views. Tikhon's response mobilized the language of democracy and civil rights to assert everyone's right to personal political convictions which, in his case, were distinct from his public role as head of the Church. Tikhon explained his political identity as "nonpartisan." On being asked whether he was still a monarchist, Tikhon replied: "I ask that you don't pose me such questions, and I will not avoid answering them. I was, of course, a monarchist before, as we all were who lived in a monarchist country, but what sort of political convictions I now hold is none of your business: I will reveal them when I cast my vote for this or that form of government during the general popular elections."[76] Tikhon asserted that his political convictions were his own private affair, which he had the right to, but that he would not use his position as patriarch for political purposes. He categorically asserted that he had not conducted any kind of agitation for or against any form of government in Russia, "and in no case would he violate (*nasilovat'*) or impose on anyone's conscience in the matter of the general popular election."[77]

Tikhon's answers constitute an implicit rebuke of the Bolsheviks by appealing to the democratic discourse of the February Revolution that all parties had subscribed to in 1917, but once in power the Bolsheviks destroyed by establishing a one-party state. In that light, it was actually the Bolsheviks who were "counter-revolutionary," because their reestablishment of an authoritarian state overthrew the democracy that resulted from the February Revolution. Significantly, he also clarified his primary criticism of the Soviet regime, which did not have to do with socialism, restoring the monarchy, or any of the reasons that the Soviets assumed—but because of Soviet policy against the Church. As he stated directly, his attitude toward the government would change when the government stopped attacking the Church.

Latsis ended the interrogation by stating that "I do not want to say '*do svidaniia*' (literally 'until the meeting'), because I think that this meeting does not bring you particular pleasure."[78] Tikhon remained his usual calm, cheerful self and treated Latsis with the same evenness he did everyone else, which made a good impression on "the formidable Chekist."[79] Afterward, Patriarch Tikhon sent out a letter to the bishops distancing himself from the alleged story of his blessing to the Whites through Bishop Nestor, but all the same there was no change in the Soviet government's relationship to the Church and the patriarch remained under house arrest.[80]

The Cheka allowed Tikhon to participate in the meetings of the church administration and receive visitors, go for walks in the garden, and serve liturgy in the residence chapel. The Cheka ordered the house arrest in order to gather materials on the patriarch's connections, since they believed he received large sums from foreign sources for the needs of counter-revolution inside Russia.[81] Visitors had to leave their name and reason for the visit in a log that the Cheka checked.

By the spring, Tikhon occasionally received permission to serve liturgy in Moscow churches. On March 26, Filippov wrote to Sovnarkom that, because the patriarch was under house arrest, "it is necessary for him to ask permission every single time to serve liturgy" outside his residence. Believers were very unhappy with the patriarch's detainment. Ispolkomdukh appealed to the Soviet government to release the patriarch from house arrest for Holy Week so that he could lead believers in prayer, which would significantly improve relations between the believing masses and the Soviet government.[82] The request was denied, however, and the patriarch served Holy Week and Easter services at his residence.[83] Appeals from believers kept coming in to the central government throughout 1920, usually to the chair of Central Executive Committee (the supreme governing body), Mikhail Kalinin (1875–1946), asking that the patriarch at least be allowed to serve liturgy in Moscow churches. In August, V. V. Fortunatov of the Secret Department of the Cheka agreed to allow Tikhon to serve liturgy at the Novodevichy Monastery, on condition that this be regarded as an exception and not grounds for further permissions, and that the patriarch promise not to give any sermons or speeches on political themes. Fortunatov, a former deacon, attended the service dressed as a priest so that he could observe.[84] Exceptions were made—the patriarch served about a dozen times in Moscow churches in the entirety of 1920—but they were rare.[85]

The Antirelic Campaign

Throughout the Civil War, official Soviet policy toward religion was implemented by the Liquidation Department of the Commissariat of Justice. Its head, Petr Krasikov, and his coworkers such as the lawyer Ivan Shpitsberg and Mikhail Galkin (Gorev, 1885–1948) were guided by their militant atheism in shaping policy. Galkin was a reformist priest who participated in drafting the Decree of Separation of Church and State; he subsequently abandoned the Church and became one of the most vehement antireligious activists.[86] After the August 1918 Instructions on the Implementation of Decree of Separation of Church and State, the Liquidation Department systematically and aggressively "nationalized" (i.e., confiscated) church properties. State authorities signed contracts with believers for their local parish churches, which the government mostly left alone. But other Church institutions—including more than half of the monasteries—were closed and their property confiscated.[87]

The Soviet Constitution guaranteed the freedom of conscience and even the "freedom of religious propaganda." In November 1918, Lenin warned in a speech that the Soviets needed to be careful "in fighting religious prejudice" to avoid offending people's religious feelings.[88] Many historians take these declarations at face value and assume that the Bolshevik leadership tolerated religious belief and practice in the early years.[89] But the reality was more complicated. The March 1919 Communist Party Program stated explicitly that the Party's goal was to ensure the "disappearance of religious prejudices," that is, belief and practice. The separation of church and state was something that belonged to "bourgeois democracies" and did not go far enough. The Party aimed to "destroy the ties between the exploiting classes and the organization of religious propaganda, at the same time helping the toiling masses actually to liberate their minds from religious superstitions." The aim was to destroy the ties between believers and their Church and uproot their faith. This was supposed to be carried out without "offending the religious sensibilities of believers."[90] In practice, some government officials (such as Bonch-Bruevich and Kalinin) sought to avoid offending believers, but the Liquidation Department—which actually implemented policy—prioritized destroying the power of the Orthodoxy. Its antireligious policies were intentionally offensive to desacralize what believers held to be holy as a means to "liberate their minds from religious superstitions."

At the height of the Civil War, the Soviets embarked on a campaign against the Orthodox veneration of saints, which was deeply rooted in popular piety, by targeting their relics. The campaign began when local Soviet operatives falsely claimed they found a "wax doll" instead of the body of St. Aleksandr Svirsky (1448–1533), which was seized upon by the local press and became a sensation.[91] The Liquidation Department seized upon the idea that the Church's veneration of relics was a scam and turned the exposure of relics into a nationwide campaign aiming to discredit the clergy as perpetrators of fraud, and thereby also deal a mortal blow to popular belief.[92] It was commonly believed by the faithful that the relics of saints were incorrupt—that is, they did not decompose—and though it was not Church doctrine, the Church did little to dispel popular notions. The Soviets approached relics as if they had to be, by definition, incorrupt. In its propaganda, the Liquidation Department asserted that the campaign was only aimed at exposing the "fraud" of the clergy and not an attack on religious belief as such, though in internal documents Bolshevik leaders—including Lenin—expressed their hopes that in fact the campaign would also destroy popular belief.[93]

Patriarch Tikhon's first response was to try to avoid further scandal. On February 17, 1919, he sent a confidential directive to diocesan bishops that they should have churches and monasteries with relics conduct their own inspections of reliquaries. The patriarch explained that relics that had been preserved as bones were, out of piety, placed in elaborate shrines and sometimes also frames or covered with vestments in such a way that gave the likeness of a human body. This, he wrote, gave rise to the accusation that the Church was deceiving people through the appearance of an incorrupt body when there was only a skeleton. He therefore instructed that bishops should "eliminate all reasons for temptation"—in other words, to remove any objects in the reliquaries other than the bones and the vestments that covered them.[94] The patriarch's directive later became part of the indictment against him on the grounds that it was an effort to "conceal traces of the crime" and an act of opposition to the Soviet government in its efforts to expose the Church's fraud.[95]

The Relics of Saint Sergius of Radonezh

The episode of the campaign that particularly concerned Patriarch Tikhon was the exposure of the relics of St. Sergius of Radonezh (1314–1392), one of Russia's most beloved saints, and the closure of the monastery he founded and one of Orthodoxy's holiest sites, the Trinity-St. Sergius Lavra.[96] At the end of March 1919, local authorities in Sergiev Posad announced their plan to exhume the relics of St. Sergius. Patriarch Tikhon wrote to Lenin on April 2, 1919, asking him to prevent this, asserting that such an action would "deeply offend the religious feelings" of believers and might cause such indignation that they would stand in defense of what they held sacred.[97] The patriarch's letter was ignored, and the relics were exposed on April 11, 1919. What they found, as in most cases, was neither an incorrupt body nor a falsification, but a human skeleton. A massive antireligious propaganda campaign, including a film showing the exhumation of the relics, followed.[98] The exhumation of the relics failed to achieve its goal: It was viewed as an offense against the saint and resulted in an upsurge of pilgrimage to the monastery.[99]

To undermine continued veneration of the saint, the monastery was closed in November 1919. When the authorities planned to remove the relics altogether from the monastery, Patriarch Tikhon, as he had done when the monastery was closed, wrote another letter to Lenin on March 24, 1920, protesting the latest offense against believers. He did not understand why this was necessary when the country was in the midst of Civil War and looming famine—and in need of unity. Therefore, in the name of the freedom of conscience and for the good of the people, the patriarch requested Lenin to stop the relics' removal.[100] The removal of St. Sergius's relics from the monastery was considered at the highest level of the Soviet government, the Soviet of People's Commissars (Sovnarkom) on April 9, 1920. It resolved not to remove the relics but to turn the monastery into a museum and use that as a pretext to close the churches. The patriarch protested again to Lenin.[101]

Bonch-Bruevich passed on Tikhon's protest to Lenin for investigation by the Bureau of Complaints, a division of the Workers' and Peasants' Inspection (Rabkrin), which was established so that any citizen could file a complaint against a government official to give the people a voice in their government. The lead investigator, the former Tsarist lawyer P. N. Molver, conducted his work assiduously, interviewing the patriarch himself and not only reading reports from the Church, but reviewing secret correspondence of Soviet agencies. The investigation concluded that closing the churches and removing the relics was a violation of the separation of the church and state and constituted state interference in the inner matters of the Church—and therefore the patriarch's complaint was justified and required satisfaction.[102] Krasikov outright rejected Molver's report. He and Galkin took the issue to the "small Sovnarkom," headed by Lenin, which decided on August 27 that the patriarch's appeals and complaints should remain unanswered, St. Sergius's relics should be removed to a museum, and, moreover, a court case should be opened against Molver.[103] That investigation continued into 1921, and a central feature of the accusation against Molver was that he met with the patriarch, which was interpreted conspiratorially. In the end, Molver was sentenced to ten years in prison (later commuted to five years in a concentration camp).[104] Internal Soviet records therefore demonstrate that the Soviet leadership at the highest level knowingly and deliberately violated the freedom of conscience and separation of Church and state, repressing even their own functionaries who dared to point this out.

Throughout 1919–1920, therefore, Patriarch Tikhon appealed privately through letters to the government to alter its course of action that was so offensive to Orthodox believers. After receiving word that his complaint was rejected and that Sovnarkom approved the relics' removal on September 2, 1920,[105] Patriarch Tikhon made a public protest in an encyclical of September 10, 1920; addressing the faithful, he recounted the entire history of the saga over the relics of St. Sergius and the monastery. He informed the faithful how the authorities believed that, by exposing the relics of St. Sergius in 1919, people would stop making pilgrimage to the monastery and would lose their faith in their spiritual leaders, but that no deception was revealed and, contrary to their expectation, the offense against the relics of the saint elicited a great religious upsurge. In response, the authorities expelled the monks who served the reliquary and then closed the monastery's churches despite the contract signed between believers and the authorities. Now, the patriarch continued, the authorities planned to remove the relics altogether. He requested to speak with Lenin about this but was told that Lenin was too busy with "important matters" to meet him, so he appealed to Lenin in written form, declaring that the closure of the Lavra's churches and decision to remove the relics was a government intrusion in the Church's inner life and therefore a violation of the Decree of Separation of Church and State. Not only the patriarch appealed to Lenin, but the believers of Sergiev Posad, Moscow, and other cities submitted petitions. Finally, Tikhon explained, he received an answer that his complaint would not be satisfied but rather the government authorized the "liquidation" of the relics of St. Sergius.[106]

The patriarch ended the encyclical by quoting the famous historian Vasily Kliuchevsky (1841–1911), who, in an 1892 speech, spoke of how, for five centuries, the Russian people drew spiritual strength from the shrine of St.

Sergius and that its gates would be closed only "when we have lost without a trace all the spiritual and moral reserves" bequeathed by the saint. The patriarch wondered whether they had indeed exhausted all their spiritual and moral reserves and that nothing remained for the Russian people but "cold and hunger." "We are alive in name only, but in reality we are already dead," the patriarch concluded, and the only thing left to do before the approaching dread times was to repent and pray that St. Sergius not abandon his flock entirely.[107] In the end, however, the relics were not removed from the monastery, though its churches were closed and access to venerate them was barred.

Despite Soviet proclamations about not wishing to offend the religious sensibilities of believers, the antireligious activists of the Commissariat of Justice—with the full support of Lenin and the Soviet of People's Commisars—doggedly pursued an extremely offensive campaign in the vain hope that it would turn ordinary believers against the Church and destroy their faith. The antirelic campaign eventually petered out because local officials evaded complying with the center's directives to avoid popular discontent.

The Vilnius Martyrs and Charges of "Speculation"

To push the antirelic campaign to completion, the Commissariat of Justice issued a circular on August 25, 1920, which stipulated that clergy guilty of "falsifying" relics to "exploit the ignorance of believers" should be prosecuted.[108] Such cases against clergy involved dubious legal categories, criminalizing traditional Orthodox practices. But such trials were not so much legal processes as ideological exercises to undermine religious belief.[109]

One relic exhumation led to a criminal court case in 1920 that involved Patriarch Tikhon—and led to new accusations against him. The relics of the three Vilnius martyrs had been evacuated to Moscow by Tikhon as the Germans took over Vilnius during World War I and were housed in the Donskoi Monastery (see Chapter 4). A clergy inspection found the relics to be remarkably undecayed, which left the Soviets scrambling to invent various "scientific" explanations when they found the same.[110]

Based on traditional Orthodox practices regarding the veneration of saints' relics, the Soviet authorities opened a case against a hieromonk, who was the relics' caretaker, and an abbess from Smolensk. The Soviet authorities convicted both of "using the cult of mummified corpses in the centuries-old deception . . . of the laboring masses," "counter-revolutionary activity," and "blackmail."[111] During the trial against them in the People's Court in July 1920, Tikhon was called to testify as a witness. The interrogator asked Tikhon whether he had given his blessing to consecrate an icon with a fragment of the relics. The patriarch stated that, "since this is not forbidden by the Soviet government, I permitted it." The judge retorted that this was a "question of faith, and not at all of the Soviet government"—a very ironic comment, given the context of the trial.[112] Ivan Shpitsberg served as both prosecutor and expert witness in the trial. When the patriarch was on the stand, Shpitsberg began to question him about a totally unrelated issue, namely the income that the patriarch received from the Iversk chapel on Red Square. This chapel held a revered icon of the Theotokos, and every pious Orthodox Christian who visited Red Square lit a candle before this icon—hence the chapel's income was substantial. After the Soviet government stripped the Church of all of its financial resources, part of the chapel's income went to the patriarch to support the central Church administration's work. Aleksei Filippov commented on what a "strange, pathetic figure the patriarch was in his silk cassock before these judges of the common people, their ragged jackets and simple boots, who were asking him what sort of income he receives."[113] On learning that the patriarch received 40,000 rubles a month from this chapel (or 600,000 rubles in 1919), Shpitsberg declared he was going to open a case against the patriarch for "speculation."[114]

By that point, Tikhon had been under house arrest since the end of 1919 with no charge. It had become clear there was no credible case against him; hence, there was no justification for depriving him of his freedom. But now they could accuse him of "speculation." In fact, according to Filippov, the Liquidation Department concocted the entire case regarding the Vilnius martyrs precisely to target the patriarch.[115]

The accusation of "speculation" (and an added one of "blackmail") was immediately used to justify the patriarch's detainment. In September, a group of workers petitioned for the patriarch to be allowed to serve liturgy in their parish, which Mikhail Kalinin permitted. Felix Dzerzhinsky (1877–1926), head of the Cheka, and the new head of its Secret Department, T. P. Samsonov (1838–1955), responded to Kalinin in a "top secret" letter. Dzerzhinsky reminded Kalinin that the patriarch was under house arrest and that the Liquidation Department was investigating the "accusation of speculation," which would be passed on to the People's Court soon. Tikhon's house arrest, as well as the investigation and the impending trial, was the result of policies conducted by the Cheka and the Commissariat of Justice that were aimed at "discrediting the clergy and depriving them of the opportunity to hold festive liturgies that attract masses of pilgrims and serve as hotbeds of religious—and to some extent political anti-Soviet—agitation." They stated that the house arrest, investigation, and impending trial were designed to provide them with a pretext to refuse requests "to allow the patriarch to serve" in parishes.[116]

As this letter reveals, the Cheka kept the patriarch under house arrest not because of any putative "counter-revolutionary" activity, but rather to prevent him from conducting religious services because every time he did, massive numbers of believers attended and he greatly uplifted their religious spirit (Figure 7). Indeed, the accusations were after-the-fact justifications for depriving him of his freedom, and they had little legal substance but, it was hoped, would serve to justify the house arrest and further to discredit the patriarch or tarnish him in the eyes of the people. All this reveals how great the patriarch's influence continued to be throughout 1920, even when the people were barely able to see him—and how much the Bolsheviks were threatened by this continued influence.

Although Kalinin's permission to serve was not retracted in that instance, the patriarch would serve in only two other Moscow parishes for the remainder of 1920. The requests, nevertheless, continued to come in. When

Figure 7. Patriarch Tikhon with clergy and parishioners in Golenishchevo

Kalinin granted one in December from the town of Pavlov Posad in the Moscow province, Krasikov wrote to the Cheka for their support in continuing to constrain Tikhon's freedom and especially blocking him from serving outside the city of Moscow. The Cheka also secured the support of the Moscow Soviet. The Pavlov Posad communists also opposed the patriarch's visit—and urged the hastening of the trial against the patriarch.[117]

The threat of being put on trial and potentially unable to lead the Church altogether evidently prompted the patriarch and the Higher Church Administration to issue instructions for that possibility. As it was, the Civil War had made it nearly impossible for the patriarch to communicate with large swaths of his Church, especially those in territories not under Soviet control—regions under the control of the Whites or the Germans, or those ending up in new states such as Poland and the Baltics. On November 20, 1920, they issued Decree No. 362, which instructed bishops in dioceses unable to communicate with the patriarch or the higher ecclesiastical administration either because the latter ceased their activities for some reason, or because of the front shifting or a change in state borders. In such cases, bishops were to organize with bishops of neighboring dioceses and form temporary regional ecclesiastical administrations (much as had been done in the White-controlled south and Siberia, though those administrations had already ceased their operations by this point), and if they were unable to do that, then they should administer their own diocese autonomously. Their autonomy was to last last until they reestablished the connection with the administration in Moscow.[118] Although the patriarch was not brought to trial at this point, this resolution would become important after his arrest in May 1922. It would subsequently play a crucial role for both the Church Abroad and the catacomb churches in the Soviet Union, which viewed the resolution as providing canonical justification for their operating independently of the Moscow ecclesiastical authorities.

In the end, Tikhon was not brought to trial for "speculation." Since 1918, the Soviet authorities had tried throwing various accusations at the patriarch but failed to present a credible case. In January 1921, Kalinin, after receiving more petitions from believers, wrote to Dzerzhinsky about whether it was possible to free Tikhon from house arrest.[119] Ultimately, Kalinin granted the patriarch permission to serve in various parishes with increasing frequency in 1921—he served more in January and February 1921 alone than he had in all of 1920. There were significant differences among Soviet leaders about how to handle the patriarch and the Church; the hard line was typically assumed by the Cheka and the Liquidation Department, with government officials such as Kalinin taking a more conciliatory position, especially in response to the demands of the people.

Patriarch Tikhon Challenges Soviet Policy

At the culmination of the antirelic campaign and the new accusations leveled against him, Tikhon wrote his most detailed objection to Soviet leaders on August 9, 1920. The patriarch made his case on a thoroughgoing appeal to Soviet law to demonstrate that the campaign against relics and the trials of clergy were in fact violating the Soviet constitution, laws, and stated principles. The letter reiterated that both the Constitution and the Decree of Separation of Church and State guaranteed freedom of conscience, including the "freedom of religious propaganda" (according to the Constitution) and the freedom of religious practice and ritual. The patriarch asserted that the veneration of saints and their relics, together with bringing an offering in the form of candles, was an ancient practice related directly to worship. The Liquidation Department engaged in the antirelic campaign based on the incorrect assertion that relics were, by definition, incorrupt, and even when exposed relics turned out to be incorrupt (as in the case of the Vilnius martyrs), a court case was initiated against clergy based on some claim that the Church incorrectly canonized the saints. Quoting Soviet resolutions and statements by Lenin, the patriarch asserted that the Liquidation Department was violating Soviet law, which guaranteed free fulfillment of religious rites. The antirelic campaign was illegitimate according to Soviet law and therefore amounted to religious persecution—and by the twentieth century, based upon historical examples from the Roman emperors to the Inquisition, the patriarch asserted that it should be obvious to everyone that religious persecution never succeeded in coercing anyone to change their ideas.

The patriarch refuted the accusation of "speculation," when lighting a candle was a voluntary offering and the believer was free to purchase it wherever they chose. The accusation of "blackmail" meant he had to be coercing people. Perhaps in imperial Russia, Tikhon argued, when people were legally registered with a particular confession, such an argument could be made—but not in Soviet Russia when everyone was free to confess any faith they wanted to. It cannot be blackmail if believers voluntarily follow what the Church had always taught. If the government had a say in internal Church matters in imperial Russia, that was no longer the case since the Decree of Separation, which by its very nature precluded the state from legitimately interfering in the internal affairs of the Church's faith and practice.[120]

Tikhon's letter therefore treated Soviet law as granting greater freedom, both to believers and to the Church, than had been the case in imperial Russia. The problem, he stated, was that the very Soviet institution intended to implement the laws—the Commissariat of Justice—was violating the principles that lay at the heart of the laws themselves. The patriarch's letter was ignored. The Bolshevik leadership again refused to listen to reason or to compromise.

A month later, after the Commissariat of Justice issued its August 25 circular on the "liquidation" of relics, the patriarch followed up with a second letter of protest to Kalinin (September 10, 1920). Building on the arguments of the previous letter, he began with a historical example: The Roman emperors claimed they had to persecute Christianity because it was "superstition" and ostensibly opposed by "the people," and those two elements became the leitmotif for all subsequent religious persecutions. But whenever persecutors "threw the entire weight of state power against believers," then first Christians and later nonbelievers "opposed fire and iron with the principle of a free conscience and toleration for religious convictions. The Edict of Milan, the Reformation, and the Declaration of the Rights of Man are colossal monuments to the victory of the human spirit over the coercion of the human person."[121] By persecuting religion on the basis that it was "superstition," the Soviet government was abandoning the path of progress and returning to obsolete antiquated practices of religious persecution.[122]

Tikhon further asserted that Orthodox believers were ready to obey the government—St. Paul taught Christians to submit even to the Roman government that was persecuting them—but only so long as obeying the state did not go against the faith. The patriarch argued that the Soviets were pushing Orthodox believers into opposing the government because of antireligious policies that contradicted the Soviets' own declared principles. He therefore asked the Soviet leadership to "observe your own laws laid out in the constitution on religious tolerance and the freedom of conscience, and remember that we live in the 20th century, not in the dark period of the Middle Ages, and thus it is necessary to leave behind any compulsion in matters of faith.... Do not overstep the lines of what is forbidden for a Christian, do not make persecutors of yourselves and do not make martyrs of us."[123] It was central to the Bolshevik project to present themselves as progressive and whatever opposed them as backward; in this letter, the patriarch turned these notions on their head by arguing that the initial Soviet laws were progressive, but by embarking on antireligious campaigns they were returning to obsolete premodern practices of religious persecution and compulsion.

Kalinin replied to the patriarch, informing him that if he believed that specific officials had violated Soviet decrees, then he had the right "like any citizen of the Soviet republic to bring to justice . . . those whose illegal actions you can demonstrate, regardless of their official position."[124] But of course the patriarch knew well from his recent experience with Molver and the Bureau of Complaints what the result of such official complaints would be—even if the case turned out favorable for him, the decision would be overturned. It was impossible to "demonstrate" such a case when the top Soviet leadership refused to question their own policies. At the same time, Kalinin wrote to Krasikov that he thought it necessary to replace Shpitsberg in prosecuting the case against Tikhon (which they were still planning) for practical and political reasons, with a parenthetical note that "the audience in the court will, most likely, be majority Orthodox"—in other words, Shpitsberg was too offensive to prosecute a public trial against the patriarch, which would end up making the Soviets look bad rather than the patriarch. Kalinin also asserted that "you agree with me that the agitational goal will be achieved to a greater extent the weaker the punitive side and the stronger the unmasking."[125] The main goal of a trial against the patriarch was, therefore, to try to discredit him in order to damage his reputation and authority. Kalinin, at least, was against any harsh punishments that would make a martyr of the patriarch.

In November 1920, the patriarch sent out his final encyclical for the year to mark the third anniversary of his enthronement as patriarch. He began by acknowledging that, when he was enthroned, many had high hopes and expectations that he would lead the Church and the nation out of its troubles. Russia was still, however, beset by war and internecine strife, devastation, hunger, and disorder. But if the hopes for salvation were placed on the Church and on him, the means of salvation must be sought instead within each believer. The believer should not search for the salvation of the nation in one or another form of government or anything earthly. It must be sought in the realm of the spirit: faith in the providence of God, in consciousness of one's own sinfulness, repentance, love for one's neighbor, an end to strife, and a readiness to sacrifice for the motherland. These themes—repentance, faith, love rather than enmity, forgiveness rather than vengeance—were the consistent themes of his sermons and encyclicals during the Civil War. He called again for reconciliation, for an agreement of all from various classes to work together to save the motherland. He called for reform not through violence but through gradual moral influence and individual enlightenment and reeducating society on Christian principles. "Only on these foundations is the salvation of the state possible."[126] Despite spending the year under house arrest and enduring attacks against Orthodoxy, Tikhon reiterated his most important message: Russia could only be healed through each person examining their own wrongs and repenting of them, and rather than class or ideological conflict, people coming together through reconciliation and cooperation.

Unlike the previous year, Patriarch Tikhon was able to serve for Christmas on January 7, 1921. The number of worshippers, according to an eyewitness, was exceptionally great. This observer also noted how the patriarch looked grand during the service in his mitre and vestments, but after the service, he slipped out of the church looking like an ordinary priest and stepped into a simple sledge, drawing no attention to himself, and drove away.[127]

7
Famine and the Confiscation of Church Valuables (1921–April 1922)

By the beginning of 1921, the Soviet regime emerged victorious from the Civil War. But the country was on the verge of economic collapse. The peasantry, who tolerated the Bolsheviks as a lesser evil than the Whites, had had enough of Soviet forced grain requisitioning that took place during the Civil War. At the Tenth Party Congress in March 1921, Lenin pushed through the New Economic Policy (NEP), which ended War Communism and granted major economic concessions to the peasantry and restored a market economy in agriculture. At the same time, there were no corresponding concessions in the political sphere, but a determination to eliminate all dissent. The Tenth Party Congress not only consolidated one-party rule but even banned factions within the Bolshevik Party.

In 1921, a massive famine erupted in Soviet Russia that would claim millions of lives. By early 1922, the Soviet government passed a decree that launched a campaign to seize all the valuables and precious objects from all churches. They claimed this was necessitated for famine relief, because the government had run out of funds. The forced seizure was justified because, they claimed, the Orthodox Church was not doing enough to assist voluntarily in famine relief. When Patriarch Tikhon issued an encyclical labeling as "sacrilege" the forced seizure of consecrated vessels used in the sacraments, the Soviets launched an all-out propaganda campaign that painted him as caring more about the Church's wealth than the suffering of millions of starving people. Clashes ensued between Soviet authorities and believers who tried to protect their churches, which not only resulted in bloodshed but then ended in trials against clergy and believers for opposing the Soviet confiscation decree. What resulted was the most intense assault on the Orthodox Church by the Soviet government to that point. Until the opening of the archives after the Soviet Union collapsed, it was impossible to know the truth about all this history. Western historians such as John Shelton Curtiss accepted the narrative that the Church was not doing enough and that the confiscations were necessary for famine relief. Even since the opening of the archives, some historians continue to maintain that the confiscations were necessitated by the famine and that Patriarch Tikhon's uncompromising position was partly responsible for the consequent clash.[1] This chapter reexamines Patriarch Tikhon's relationship to the anti-Soviet Church Abroad, his response to the famine in 1921, the genesis of the campaign to confiscate church valuables, and the Bolshevik assault on the Orthodox Church in spring 1922 on the basis of newly available evidence.[2]

The Secret Police and the Patriarch

The policy toward the Russian Orthodox Church after the end of the Civil War paralleled broader developments. Aggressive campaigns such as that against relics ended. It was recognized that the mass of the population—especially the peasantry—were still deeply religious; policy had to change so as not to alienate them. In April 1921, Lenin instructed that, in relation to May Day and Easter celebrations, the Soviet government and press should avoid "any sort of offense to religion," and this time evidently he meant it.[3] The Plenum of the Central Committee in July 1921 directed that all party and press organs should not emphasize antireligious agitation, to facilitate the accord with the peasantry, which "is still full of religious prejudices."[4] At the same time, the Cheka asserted that, having lost the Civil War, counter-revolutionaries, including clergy, would strive to overthrow the Soviet government from within—and therefore vigilance was more important than ever.[5] In 1920–1921, the Cheka, supported by Commissar of Enlightenment Anatoly Lunacharsky (1875–1933), explored schemes to undercut the authority and influence of Patriarch Tikhon by creating parallel ecclesiastical structures to split the Church from within. The Liquidation Department under Krasikov, however, opposed the creation of a "Soviet Church" and schemes that involved Soviet support for any religious leaders. Lenin sided with Krasikov, and for the moment none of these ventures came to fruition.[6]

Although the Cheka remained anxious about Patriarch Tikhon's continued influence, throughout 1921 they exercised restraint toward the Church leadership.[7] The Trinity Metochion, where the patriarch lived under house arrest, was a relatively large compound with a church, several buildings, and a park with gardens. The patriarch and his staff occupied a two-story building that overlooked the park and contained a house church within.

Other buildings belonging to the complex had already been confiscated. The chancellery and staff were located downstairs, and the patriarch, with his attendant and secretary, along with the metropolitan of Krutitsky (who administered the Moscow diocese), lived upstairs. The Cheka sought ways to spy on the patriarch because it suspected that he was communicating with émigré circles to orchestrate counter-revolution in Russia. Several rooms of the chancellery were sealed off, and later the housing department ostensibly settled a couple into those rooms. The husband was in fact a Cheka agent sent to spy on the patriarch. The remaining room of the chancellery was adjacent to their apartment, and more than once they searched it, but never found anything incriminating in part because the patriarch's staff suspected they worked for the Cheka.[8]

In spring 1921, the Cheka also tried to plant someone in close personal proximity to the patriarch to gain intelligence. Ivan Shpitsberg, now working for the Cheka, recruited a monk, Nikita Iudin, who worked at the patriarch's residence. Iudin was doing menial tasks in the residence and rarely had the opportunity to listen in on conversations or examine the patriarch's papers. Shpitsberg schemed to arrest Iakov Polozov (1879–1924), the patriarch's trusted *keleinik*, or cell attendant. Bishops customarily had a *keleinik*, an assistant like an army officer's orderly, who served as a traveling companion and assisted with preparing for official duties and liturgical services. Polozov had been Tikhon's trusted assistant since his time in America. Polozov remained a layman and married when they returned to Russia. He was devoted to Tikhon like a son and always remained by his side. Polozov's arrest was extremely distressing for the patriarch.[9]

On March 19, 1921, Dzerzhinsky himself signed the order for Polozov's arrest. Even though the security services had no incriminating evidence against him, the arrest was for "tactical" purposes to pressure Tikhon. The patriarch wrote to Shpitsberg and pleaded with him to release Polozov because his wife was just about to give birth to their first child and she was distraught, not knowing what was happening to her husband. Polozov was not released; his wife fell ill and lost the baby a week after giving birth. Only in July did Shpitsberg's replacement make an accusation—namely that Polozov was the lever around which revolved the entire machine of the patriarch's control over the clergy for his counter-revolutionary purposes. Because there was intelligence that the patriarch, "since Polozov is isolated from him, [is] overwhelmed by anxiety and sometimes by helplessness, I therefore find it necessary to isolate him from Tikhon, who is harmful to Soviet power."

Since there was no credible case, however, Polozov was finally released in November.[10] While Polozov was under arrest, Iudin took his place as cell attendant, which made it possible for him to listen to conversations and steal documents from the chancellery. However, between Tikhon's caution and Iudin's lack of abilities as an agent, he failed to gather any useful intelligence.[11]

By the end of summer 1921, there was some relaxation in the conditions of Tikhon's house arrest. With permission, he was routinely serving in parishes all over Moscow and even outside it, so much so that the patriarch, in his simple carriage and clad with his white *klobuk*, was a familiar sight to all Moscow.[12] Therefore, a Moscow Cheka agent observed, the house arrest had become meaningless, but rather granted him and those who respected him "the right and basis to consider Tikhon as a sufferer, as oppressed for the Orthodox faith." The agent proposed that Tikhon be formally notified that he was no longer under arrest. The central Cheka considered it best that his arrest be ended de facto, but not to make it official.[13] The patriarch used his new freedom to return to leading the Holy Synod and to consecrate new bishops. But the new toleration was always precarious, and by the end of the year, the patriarch's chancellery and access to its archive were closed.[14]

The Church Abroad

Patriarch Tikhon not only faced challenges in administering the Orthodox Church in Soviet Russia but also the transnational Russian Orthodox Church beyond its bounds. In addition to regions that were now outside the Russian Empire, such as the Baltics and parts of Poland (see Chapter 9), after the Civil War there were many Russian Orthodox refugees and émigrés living dispersed in Europe and Asia. The Russian Orthodox Church Abroad established itself there, but its relations with the patriarch were complicated because of difficulties in communication. When the Whites were defeated in Crimea in November 1920, bishops of the Temporary Higher Church Administration in South-Eastern Russia fled with the White armies. On November 19, 1920, on a steamer in the port of Constantinople, a group of bishops headed by Metropolitan Antony (Khrapovitsky) resolved to transform their administration into the Higher Church Administration Abroad (or "outside Russia", *za granitsei*) in order to serve the religious life of Russian refugees and armies in all countries that refugees found themselves in.[15] Since they were in Constantinople, they appealed to the Ecumenical

Patriarch to clarify their canonical status. On December 2, the Ecumenical Patriarchate gave permission to form a "temporary ecclesiastical commission" under his authority to minister to Russian refugees. The rights granted to this temporary commission were limited, with administrative functions to be undertaken by the Ecumenical Patriarchate or by the Churches of whatever Orthodox country the refugees found themselves in—there was no mention of authorizing the Russian bishops to establish an ecclesiastical administration.[16]

In January 1921, the Higher Church Administration Abroad relocated to Sremski, Serbia, on the invitation of the Serbian patriarch. Metropolitan Antony, as head of the church administration, attempted to contact Patriarch Tikhon to receive his approval, though some of his letters never made it.[17] He was anxious to receive Tikhon's validation of their administration, since their canonical status was irregular, given that they were organizing in territories where other Orthodox Church hierarchies already existed. Later the Church Abroad cited the patriarch's decree No. 362 of November 1920, instructing dioceses to become temporarily independent if cut off from the patriarch, although the decree was not directed at the situation of the Church Abroad and they only learned of that decree after the establishment of their administration (in January 1922).[18] It was an momentous step, in Orthodox ecclesiological terms, to establish a supraterritorial ecclesiastical administration, especially when the jurisdiction they claimed overlapped with other Orthodox Churches.

In January 1921, the Higher Church Administration declared itself the ecclesiastical authority for Russian churches abroad and appointed Archbishop Evlogy to administer the parishes of Western Europe.[19] This news reached the patriarch, who on March 21, 1921, confirmed the appointment of Evlogy over the parishes of Western Europe—temporarily, until the reestablishment of normal relations between those parishes and Russia.[20] This would be virtually the only official confirmation that the Church Abroad would receive from the patriarch recognizing their administration. Patriarch Tikhon later explained that he affirmed the Church Abroad administration because Antony informed him that its existence had already been confirmed by the patriarch of Constantinople.[21]

On receiving that resolution, the bishops of the Church Abroad wrote to Tikhon in July 1921 asking him to confirm the scope of their administration's authority. They proposed that it administer all parts of the Russian Church outside of Soviet Russia—not just the parishes of Russian refugees in Europe and Asia but also the Russian Church in countries that gained independence after the Russian Revolution (Poland, Finland, and the Baltic States), as well as in North America, Japan, and China. In short, they wanted to assume the patriarch's authority everywhere outside of Soviet Russia. They therefore proposed that the head of the administration bear the title of "Deputy of the Russian Patriarch Abroad." Claiming they were not intending to extend their authority where it did not belong or where it was not welcomed, they promised to obediently fulfill whatever instructions the patriarch gave. Finally, Metropolitan Antony also asked for the patriarch's blessing for an assembly (*sobranie*) of the Church that they were planning to hold in the fall.[22] In a subsequent letter to Tikhon, Metropolitan Antony asserted: "Do not think that we are striving to expand our power—I will not make claims if they will not be approved" by the patriarch.[23]

In response, the patriarch with the Holy Synod and Higher Church Council issued a decree on October 13, 1921. They viewed the Higher Church Administration Abroad as overreaching by trying to extend its authority over all Russian churches outside of Russia. The decree stated that the Church Abroad should remain "with its previous authorization, without spreading its sphere of activity to the Orthodox churches in Poland, Finland, Estonia, Latvia, and Lithuania, which preserve their existing form of church administration." The decree further rejected the title of "Deputy of the Patriarch Abroad" as unnecessary. The news of the planned "council of Russian Orthodox churches abroad" was "taken into account," in effect granting their permission and blessing.[24] The patriarch and his higher church administration viewed the Church Abroad's sphere to be Russian refugees, and that only—rejecting its global claims to administer the Russian Church everywhere outside Soviet Russia. Indeed, in a September 1921 letter to Archbishop Georgy (Yaroshevsky) in Poland, over which the Church Abroad attempted to assert its authority, Patriarch Tikhon expressed his skepticism about the purpose of the Church Abroad's administration: "the administration Abroad is good in the sense of an episcopal conference, but in the sense of an administrative organ it has nothing to administer" because the churches in Europe were already under Archbishop Evlogy.[25] After the end of the Civil War, Tikhon had managed to reestablish some semblance of communication with the Baltics and Poland, and also attempted himself to direct ecclesiastical affairs in North America and Asia until his arrest.[26] Evidently Patriarch Tikhon, like the Ecumenical Patriarch, did not see the possibility for a Russian ecclesiastical administration to exist in parallel with the church structures in Orthodox countries like Serbia, even if there were a substantial number of Russian refugees there.

Patriarch Tikhon sent the October 13 decree back to Antony through the same diplomatic channels he had received Antony's letter. Mysteriously, this crucially important decree, which could have changed the course of the Russian Church outside Russia during the twentieth century, apparently never reached its destination. It remained unknown until the publication of the patriarch's secret police file in 2000.[27] It does, however, clarify the patriarch's position on the Church Abroad that is critical for understanding subsequent developments.

The Council of the Russian Church Abroad took place in Sremski-Karlovci from November 21 to December 3, 1921. Partway through, this "assembly" (*sobranie*) elevated itself to the status of a Council (*Sobor*). Lay delegates outnumbered the clergy. The Council in Russia in 1917–1918 was broadly representative of the laity and clergy in Russia; by contrast, the Karlovci Council was not, but rather was dominated by invited delegates from monarchist organizations, so that it was shaped by delegates representing one strand of Russian Orthodoxy that pushed the council in a particular political direction. All of the Council's decisions were declared to be "with the blessing of Patriarch Tikhon," though in fact he only learned of its decisions weeks or months later.[28]

The Karlovci Council issued a political appeal to its flock that supported the restoration of the monarchy and specifically the Romanov dynasty. Archbishop Evlogy argued that such a declaration was untimely—nothing would come of it, and they were only "aggravating the situation" and making matters more difficult for the patriarch. Bishop Veniamin (Fedchenkov) also opposed the declaration. He reminded the Council of the patriarch's October 1919 encyclical, in which Tikhon had instructed the clergy to stand outside politics—and with good reason: The spiritual rebirth of Russia could only come about by spiritual, not political, means. On behalf of the majority of the clergy, Veniamin declared that he was defending the ecclesial nature (*tserkovnost'*) of the assembly, "for the Church should not become a weapon of politics." The leading monarchist Nikolai Markov (1866–1945) countered that they were declaring what Russia was waiting to hear and what the Church in Russia wanted to say but was unable to. Metropolitan Antony (Khrapovitsky) also defended the declaration, arguing that the issue of the monarchy and the dynasty were "purely ecclesiastical questions." In the end, the bishops were split over the issue, the majority of clergy were against it, but since the number of laymen from political organizations outnumbered the clergy, the motion passed. The declaration to the "Flock of the Russian Orthodox Church in the Diaspora and in Exile" calling for the restoration of the Romanov dynasty was issued on behalf of the Council.[29]

The attitude of Patriarch Tikhon and his administration toward the political role of the Church could not have been more different. Tikhon's position was clearly expressed by his closest coworker in the ecclesiastical administration, Metropolitan Evsevy (Nikolsky, 1860–1922), in a letter published in a paper in the Far East (outside Soviet control). In the October 1921 letter to an unnamed recipient, Evsevy wrote that "we here do not meddle in politics, but we carry on a struggle, within our powers, against atheism. . . . But I repeat: we do fight against not the government. . . . Therefore, from our point of view, you are standing on the right path, not meddling in and not siding with any political parties, but carrying on the struggle only with atheism and exclusively by spiritual means, sermons, lectures, conversations, and publishing pamphlets and brochures."[30] There were members of the Karlovci Council who reminded participants of the patriarch's instructions regarding political action and also those who understood how such statements would only lead to the increase of repression against the patriarch and the Church in Russia.

In Russia, the reaction to the Karlovci Council and its political declaration made little initial impact. Patriarch Tikhon learned of it secondhand, through rumor, newspaper articles, and letters from Evlogy—but he did not initially see any documents from the council itself.[31] The news caused fear among his associates. On hearing about the Karlovci Council's declaration in support for the restoration of the monarchy, those in the patriarchal administration were afraid that it would result in "suspicion by the government" that the clergy in Russia were also engaged in "reactionary politicking," and "that would bring on the worst repressions."[32] Initially, however, the news apparently did not reach the Soviet authorities.

International Appeal for Famine Relief

In the summer of 1921, a catastrophic famine was looming in Soviet Russia. As Patriarch Tikhon described the situation in his appeal to America for help, "a great part of her population is doomed to a hunger death." The crops in many provinces, "formerly the country's granary, is now burned by drought. The famine breeds epidemics.... The people are dying, the future is dying, because the population is deserting homes, lands, fields, farms, and is fleeing eastward, crying for bread."[33] The patriarch was not exaggerating. At its worst in the winter of 1921–1922, tens of millions of people were reduced to eating whatever they could find—bark, grass, weeds, straw from their thatched roofs—evidently even other human beings. Diseases consumed people already weakened by hunger. In all, an estimated 5 million people perished.

Although the approaching famine was apparent in the winter of 1920–1921, a consequence of years of war and grain requisitioning, the Soviet authorities refused even to admit there was a problem. The situation finally forced Lenin to abandon War Communism and adopt NEP in March 1921, which served to incentivize the peasantry to grow grain for profit—but this came far too late to avert disaster, especially when drought hit. The Soviet government had few resources to address the famine on its own and refused to appeal to the "capitalist" and "imperialist" countries of the West that they routinely disparaged in their propaganda. That would be to admit the failure of the Soviet project.

The initiative for famine relief was taken up by non-Bolshevik former civic activists who had been involved in famine relief in 1891–1892. The group united around the writer Maxim Gorky (1868–1936), who, given his ties to the Bolshevik leadership, succeeded in securing Lenin's support to make an international appeal that the government itself would not make. Someone had to make the appeal who would elicit international trust and response. Lenin evidently suggested to Gorky that both he and Patriarch Tikhon should make the appeal: Gorky, as Russia's most famous living writer of international stature (he visited the United States in 1906 on Mark Twain's invitation), and Patriarch Tikhon, as head of the world's largest Orthodox Church.[34]

Gorky asked the patriarch to write an appeal to world religious leaders. When they met, Gorky was uncertain how to address the patriarch: Saying "your holiness" and asking for a blessing would be insincere for Gorky the confirmed atheist, but to address him as "Comrade" and hold out his hand to shake the patriarch's hand would be equally inappropriate. The patriarch sensed Gorky's confusion, smiled amiably, and held out his hand to shake the writer's.[35] The patriarch readily agreed with Gorky's proposal, and the two stayed up late writing the appeals together.[36] Gorky sent the patriarch's appeal to the Ukrainian writer and humanitarian Vladimir Korolenko

(1853–1921) in order to enlist his aid, commenting that Tikhon "is a very intelligent and honest-minded person, he knows well the sad shortcomings of the great Russian tribe."[37] Clearly the patriarch made an impression on the writer, who was no lover of the Church.

The issue of how to distribute the patriarch's appeal was discussed by the Politburo—the top leadership of the Communist Party that was functionally its highest decision-making authority and dictated policies and decisions to all government organs. On July 7, it allowed the patriarch's appeal to be broadcast on the radio; it could be mentioned in Soviet newspapers but not published in its entirety.[38] When the patriarch's appeal was mentioned in *Izvestiia*, however, it was framed with deprecating remarks that it was "about time."[39] The Soviet leadership felt compelled to rely on the patriarch to appeal to Europe and America for help, knowing that this would elicit a response—but they could not have been comfortable with allowing him to play such a prominent role and sought to denigrate its significance at home. The appeals of Gorky and Patriarch Tikhon were sent out together, on opposite sides of the same sheet, to foreign radio and newspapers as well as through diplomatic channels. As Gorky observed, "Patriarch Tikhon and your servant put out these appeals, which have already been broadcast on the radio in Chicago, New York, London, Paris, Madrid, Berlin, Prague, etc."[40]

The patriarch issued appeals to the Episcopal Bishop of New York and the archbishop of Canterbury. The *New York Times* reported on July 17 on "the widespread radio appeals of Maxim Gorky and the Most Rev. Dr. Tikhon, Patriarch of all Russia."[41] Two days later the paper mentioned the patriarch's "frantic wireless appeal," and then on July 31 the *New York Times* published the appeals of both Gorky and Patriarch Tikhon in their entirety on the front page. In the appeal, the patriarch asked the bishop of New York and, through him, the American people, to cast aside "all other considerations" and "send immediately bread and medicines."[42] He also sent an appeal to Pope Benedict XV (1854–1922)—the first time the head of the Russian Orthodox Church had ever written directly to the pope. He stated that he hoped the pope's response would not only alleviate the suffering of the Russian people, but also that "the Almighty Lord would strengthen the love between our Churches."[43] A month later, he sent a second appeal to the pope as well as to the Eastern patriarchs.[44] Georgy Chicherin (1872–1936), the Soviet Commissar for Foreign Affairs, admitted in internal correspondence that the appeal was "having a positive influence."[45]

The archbishop of Canterbury, Randall Davidson (1848–1930), was slow to respond in part because the Russian Trade Delegation, a body primarily engaged in Soviet propaganda in Britain, downplayed the famine.[46] Pope Benedict XV responded more readily, immediately sending money and appealing to the League of Nations to help. The Catholic Church organized a relief mission under the American Jesuit Edmund Walsh (1885–1956), but that did not come into effect for another year.[47]

The one person who heard (or read) the appeals of Gorky and the patriarch and responded immediately was Herbert Hoover (1874–1864), head of the American Relief Administration (ARA), which aided in Europe after World War I. Understanding that Gorky was closer to the centers of power than the patriarch, Hoover telegraphed the writer on July 23 with an offer and conditions—which the Soviets accepted. An agreement was signed on August 21, 1921. Hoover offered aid on a massive scale, and by the winter of 1921–1922, the ARA was feeding over 10 million people a day, and by the end of the famine saved that many lives.[48]

Ecclesiastical Committee for Famine Relief

Gorky and the civic activists established the All-Russian Committee for the Relief of the Starving, a nongovernmental organization that the Soviet government confirmed on July 21, 1921, with broad rights of operation for collecting and distributing aid. The head of the Moscow Soviet, Lev Kamenev, was made chair, but most of the committee consisted of people that the Bolsheviks considered political enemies. The Committee's leadership appealed to Patriarch Tikhon for cooperation because they understood his authority at home and abroad. Moreover, according to one of their members, Ekaterina Kuskova (1869–1958), they, as members of the intelligentsia, could successfully put together a relief organization in the urban centers, but they did not have the proper networks and connections with famine-struck regions. A centralized organization with a network that was embedded in the provinces was needed, and they knew of the Orthodox Church's successful contributions to the famine relief in 1891–1892. The government itself admitted that it had "not yet mastered" the countryside, and neither schools nor doctors could do it—only the Church had a central command and with an established network into the deepest parts of provincial Russia.[49]

Two members of the Committee visited the patriarch, who listened attentively to their proposal. He asked about the details, including about the Committee's relationship to the government, and after thinking it over carefully, told them that "this needs to be done," that he blessed their activities and would cooperate with them. Treating them to tea with Linden honey, the patriarch conversed with them for a considerable time. The following day he sent them an appeal directed to Russian Orthodox believers and asked the committee to print 100,000 copies. He also informed them that he was organizing an Ecclesiastical Committee for Famine Relief that would work in conjunction with their committee and, finally, that he had designated August 18 to be a nationwide day of prayer and that, on that day, he would launch the Church's relief committee and collection effort at Christ the Savior cathedral (the permission for which he asked them to secure).[50]

The patriarch's plans and requests were discussed by the Committee that day. Although Kamenev was not pleased at cooperating with "forces of counter-revolution," he promised to fulfill all the requests. After reading Tikhon's appeal and discussing it with other Bolshevik leaders, however, Kamenev phoned the Committee and told them that they could not print it because they objected to its "mystical nonsense" and asked that the patriarch change the wording. The Committee insisted to Kamenev that they could not censor the patriarch and did not recommend the Soviets try to do so either, since "everyone has their own language." Although angry at this response, Kamenev allowed them to publish 100,000 copies of the patriarch's appeal.[51]

The patriarch also sent the Committee a letter that outlined his plans and conditions for establishing an Ecclesiastical Committee for famine relief. The Church, he wrote, always responded in times of the people's hardship, and he considered it his duty to appeal to all believers to show mercy by actively assisting. He was certain that every diocese, every parish committee, would respond. For the Church to succeed in famine relief, however, the clergy must be able to make appeals to its people through printed addresses, preaching, and holding events such as spiritual concerts; the Church's committee must have the right to organize relief, to be distributed without distinction to confession, class, or nationality, in the form of soup kitchens, orphanages, and points for the distribution of food and medicine. The patriarch insisted that all money and provisions collected by the committee be secured from "confiscation or requisition" by the government. Members of the Church's committee must have the right to meet (free association was restricted under Soviet law), and its activities not subject to government inspection. At the same time, he promised full cooperation and coordination between the Church's committee for relief and the civic Committee.[52] At its meeting on August 17, the Committee responded affirmatively to the patriarch's letter. On the same day, the patriarch wrote to the Soviet Central Executive Committee (VTsIK) to receive permission for the Church's relief committee under those conditions.[53] Given that he himself was still under house arrest, that the Church's involvement in public charitable activities was rendered impossible by Soviet law, and that public activity by the clergy could lead to arrest, the patriarch could not act without Soviet approval of his initiatives. Patriarch Tikhon was offering to mobilize Russian Orthodox believers—still the majority of the population—throughout the country to collect relief from areas not affected by the famine and deliver it to those in need which, without doubt, could have significantly altered the situation. The prospect of the Church mobilizing the entire nation more effectively than the government, however, was far more threatening to the Bolsheviks than that of millions of people starving to death.

For the National Day of Prayer on August 18, the patriarch served liturgy at the Christ the Savior cathedral. The event drew believers and unbelievers alike. When Ekaterina Kuskova arrived at 5 p.m., the entire area around the church was flooded with people. She made it to the church itself with great difficulty and could barely get inside because the massive church was so packed. Around the building were church servitors with plates containing the patriarch's appeal; people would take a copy of his appeal in exchange for a donation. Ten million rubles were collected just that day. Although Kuskova was not a regular churchgoer and was unfamiliar with patriarchal services, she was particularly struck when the patriarch, "terribly pale in his light blue patriarchal robe," together with all the clergy and the choir, would pause for long moments of silence, when the only sound were sobs from the worshippers. During the service, the patriarch preached in a "quiet, weak voice," calling the people to show mercy in a collective manifestation of unity. After the service, he gave a speech about the famine and the need for everyone's service to the suffering. Afterward, people approached the patriarch for his blessing—first all those in the cathedral, followed by those gathered outside, which took several hours until Tikhon was "completely exhausted." Kuskova concluded that four years after the October Revolution "the mysticism of Orthodoxy was still in full, undiminished power."[54] The patriarch's appeal was subsequently read in all the churches in Moscow, and donations flowed in.[55]

Once the Soviet regime succeeded in securing relief from the ARA, it no longer needed the civic Committee for famine relief, whose members were suspected of plotting to overthrow the government. The government disbanded the Committee on August 27, 1921, a week after the agreement was signed with the ARA, and had all its members arrested (except Gorky).[56] Kuskova later mused whether the patriarch "ever suspected that by developing such powerful energy and rousing all believing Russia and [those abroad] to the cause of saving [the hungry], he dealt a mortal blow to the very cause" of social forces such as the civic Committee and the Church. "Indeed, in the eyes of the Bolsheviks, the manifestation of his and our energy was only the organization of counter-revolution."[57]

On disbanding the civic Committee, the Soviet leadership replaced it with a government relief organization under the Central Executive Committee for famine relief (abbreviated with the same acronym as the previous committee, Pomgol). After the civic Committee was disbanded, the patriarch wrote the Central Executive Committee asking for a second time whether the government would confirm the status of the Church's famine relief committee.[58] He received no answer. It was on the VTsIK Presidium's agenda for September 12, but that discussion did not take place.[59] The government confiscated all the donations that the Church had collected until that point. The Church had previously been prohibited from raising money for anything beyond the upkeep of individual parishes; because the Church's relief committee had no control over or knowledge of how its collections would be used, the donations from believers dried up. Since the government did not authorize the Church's participation, believers concluded that the government did not need their help.[60]

During the winter of 1921-1922, the famine reached its most catastrophic phase. Millions more went hungry. The Politburo finally decided to allow help from religious communities on December 5, 1921, after a Muslim appeal to Stalin in November. The government resolution was not published but sent out just to the Mufti and Patriarch Tikhon. It instructed Pomgol to enter into agreement with religious communities about collecting and distributing donations.[61]

Patriarch Tikhon's August requests for government permission for the Church's participation in famine relief were finally answered after four months of precious time was lost. By the end of December, Pomgol worked out the details of its cooperation with religious communities.[62] By February 1, representatives of Pomgol and the patriarch agreed on regulations for the Church's cooperation in famine relief that gave a public role for the patriarch and the Church.[63] The significance of this agreement had implications for the Church far beyond the famine relief. Since Pomgol was under the Central Executive Committee and therefore an official Soviet body, these regulations signified a legal recognition of the Church's role. It would have been the first such recognition of the Church hierarchy by a Soviet government body. It also granted the right of the patriarch to communicate with his flock and to bolster the ranks of the Higher Church Administration—something the government had been preventing.

A significant number of donations from abroad were addressed to Tikhon that were delivered through the ARA. After consulting the patriarch, the ARA would deliver the donations wherever he indicated they should go. Donations were addressed to him from Orthodox and Episcopal parishes in the United States throughout the fall of 1921 and the first half of 1922, which he sent on to various bishops in the famine areas for local distribution. This also afforded the patriarch with the opportunity to interact with ARA workers such as Ethan Colton (1872–1970), the YMCA's liaison to the ARA, who also then served as couriers for him to communicate with bishops abroad.[64] On YMCA chief John Mott's suggestion, Colton set aside $5,000 at his disposal expressly for the patriarch to distribute to those he knew would be in need. Colton sometimes came to church services as a discreet way of meeting with the patriarch.[65] Tikhon even received a letter in November 1921 from the head of the ARA's London mission inviting him to become the Church's representative to the ARA, though Tikhon replied that this was "hardly feasible given the current situation of the Orthodox Church in Russia."[66]

In short, in the summer of 1921 the patriarch responded immediately to the famine, and his stature as Church leader meant he was able to mobilize substantial international and domestic relief. The Bolshevik leadership was happy to receive the international support. However, it was troubled by the Church's ability to organize and the recognition the patriarch would receive for saving the population better than they. It stymied his efforts to organize famine relief until the situation was entirely desperate. At just the moment when the Soviet government could have normalized relations with the Russian Orthodox Church and reaped benefits for the population through its relief efforts, the Bolsheviks completely reversed course.

The Fate of Church Valuables

Although the Soviet regime's assault on the Orthodox Church began within months of its seizure of power, it reached a new level of intensity in 1922, when it embarked on an all-out assault on the Orthodox Church at every level, from the patriarch down to every individual parish. The assault erupted over the government's campaign to seize valuables from all parish churches, which it justified for famine relief. Patriarch Tikhon's resistance to the forcible confiscations was portrayed as evidence of his greed and callousness toward those whose were starving—concealing the fact that the patriarch had tried for six months to get permission to engage in famine relief, which the government refused to permit. Clashes that erupted as parishioners resisted the plundering of their beloved churches was portrayed as an orchestrated counter-revolution led by Patriarch Tikhon, thereby justifying the patriarch's arrest and prosecution. Jonathan Daly, who demonstrated the falsehood of the Soviet narrative, suggests this was a decisive moment in the development of a modern state's deliberate use of mass propaganda in peacetime to carry out a campaign against a popular rival institution under false pretenses.[67]

The plan to seize church valuables was devised by Lev Trotsky (1879–1940). In November 1921, Trotsky was put in charge of gathering all the treasures that the government had already confiscated from the aristocracy, closed monasteries, and other sources, to fund the Red Army (of which he was head) as well as the government, which was broke.[68] The decision to seize church valuables was about filling the state treasury from the beginning—it had nothing to do with famine relief. When Trotsky began to plan to seize valuables from functioning churches, he knew he would need a convincing propaganda campaign to justify such an enormously unpopular move. It was at that point that Trotsky and his team tied the seizure of church valuables to famine relief—that is, exclusively for propaganda purposes.[69] Newspaper pieces, ostensibly from ordinary people, right on cue, demanded that the Orthodox Church surrender up its valuables for famine relief while pointing the finger specifically at Patriarch Tikhon and alleging that he received "many millions" in income that he was unwilling to part with—so that the government should take it by force.[70] The Bolsheviks routinely prepared for the implementation of unpopular policies by claiming they were only responding to popular demand.

The Soviet leadership was playing a double game: At the very same time it was planning to seize valuables by force in the first months of 1922,

Pomgol was negotiating with the patriarch on the Church's voluntary participation. The Pomgol representative, Aleksandr Vinokurov (1869–1944), asked the patriarch to authorize the voluntary donation of valuables from churches because monetary donations would be insufficient, but he did not push for consecrated vessels that were used for sacramental purposes (such as chalices), since that was prohibited by the canons, as Tikhon's representative Archpriest Nikolai Tsvetkov (1862–1942) explained. Their agreement was spelled out in a specific point (number 11) in the instructions prepared by Vinokurov and Tsvetkov regarding the voluntary donation of precious decorations.[71]

Vinokurov also pressured Patriarch Tikhon to issue another appeal to believers, which would relaunch the Church's relief campaign and specifically encourage believers to donate precious objects from churches. Knowing this would be unpopular, this was a major concession on the patriarch's part, considering that, for six months, the government had not authorized the Church to collect either monetary or food donations. His appeal, issued on February 6, 1922, stated that "we are permitting the possibility of clergy and parish councils, with agreement of the community of believers in whose charge lies the property belonging to the church [building], to use precious things that do not have a liturgical function . . . for famine relief," specifying examples of what could be donated.[72] On February 9, the Politburo approved the publication of the patriarch's appeal, followed by Pomgol's approval on February 11.[73] The patriarch's appeal was published as a leaflet and also in *Izvestiia* on February 15, though in the newspapers it was followed by comments that believers would not likely give up the valuables voluntarily and would have to be forcibly seized.[74]

Again, the patriarch devoted a special service at Christ the Savior cathedral to famine relief. Unlike his appeal from the previous year, the patriarch's February 6, 1922, appeal for giving up precious objects from churches was not well received by believers. According to the informants of Irish journalist Francis McCullagh (1874–1956), some criticized the patriarch for "weakness and excessive subservience." Believers considered that precious objects donated to the church were given to God and therefore inalienable. "No confidence was placed in the promise of the Government that it would utilize the money obtained from the sale of the Church valuables exclusively for the purchase of corn for food and for sowing. . . . There seemed no doubt that the Soviet government would utilize the valuables which it seized for ends having nothing to do with famine relief; [but]. . . would be used to cover the endless current needs of the Government."[75] A key feature of the agreed-upon Instructions allowed for clergy and believers to participate not only in the collection but also in the distribution of donations that came from churches—otherwise believers would not have confidence in how their donations were going to be used. But suddenly—without informing the patriarch—Pomgol issued the instructions omitting the point about the valuables being voluntary donations.[76]

In the first half of February, in parallel with these developments, Trotsky was preparing for the forced confiscation of church valuables. Trotsky instructed that the decree on the seizures be issued by the Central Executive Committee, which oversaw Pomgol, to reinforce the illusion that the confiscations were for famine relief. Trotsky's team, including Krasikov and Vinokurov, drafted the decree in the second week of February when Trotsky himself was ill and away from Moscow. The decree was finalized without the approval of either Trotsky or the Politburo. The Central Executive Committee passed the Decree on the Seizure of Church Valuables on February 16, 1922 (dated February 23), the day after the patriarch's appeal was published in *Izvestiia*. The decree instructed local authorities to seize from active churches "all valuable objects of gold, silver, and stones, the seizure of which does not essentially affect the interests of the cult." What was "essential" for the interests of the cult was to be determined by the Soviet authorities conducting the confiscations. The decree declared that the confiscated property was to be used "exclusively for the needs of helping the starving."[77]

On February 24, 1922, *Izvestiia* published a short notice announcing the decree.[78] Patriarch Tikhon was thunderstruck. He had done everything he could to compromise, even to a degree that opened him up to criticism from believers, and while doing so been given assurances from Vinokurov that his concessions would be satisfactory—and all the while the regime was preparing the forceful seizure anyway. The decree came like a stab in the back. He had presented the situation to believers that he had been negotiating with the government and they had reached an agreement on the participation of clergy and believers in the process of donating church valuables—and then the government announced it was planning something entirely different.

The following day, the patriarch shot off an indignant letter to Kalinin who, as chair of the Central Executive Committee, had signed the Decree. He reminded Kalinin of his previous efforts that had been thwarted by the government, asserting that, if the government had given its permission for the Church to engage in famine relief when the patriarch originally asked, the situation would not have become so catastrophic. When the government finally came around to negotiating the Church's involvement, the patriarch was ready to do everything it asked. He recounted Vinokurov's assurances that valuables would not include consecrated vessels and could be given voluntarily. And precisely when he had given his agreement, the press began to attack him with accusations that were absurd, since the clergy did not personally enjoy the wealth of these treasures but only preserved them for future generations. Tikhon trusted that Pomgol was negotiating in good faith—and, he told Kalinin, he "was deceived." As a result, the patriarch himself (like Gorky and Korolenko earlier) appeared to be deceiving his people, as a provocateur. Tikhon ended his letter to Kalinin by imploring him to return to the voluntary participation of the Church that they agreed on, because the seizure of valuables by force would cause unrest among believers.[79]

Kalinin was away from Moscow, and when he returned, he sent Tikhon's letter to Vinokurov. Vinokurov's response was both dismissive and arrogant. He acknowledged he pressured the patriarch to agree to giving up church valuables voluntarily for "agitational" purposes—to get the patriarch first to voice the need for giving them up to prepare the ground for their seizure. He stated to Kalinin that there could be no "negotiations" between the Soviet government and the Orthodox Church, since the church valuables were already government property and believers were only conditionally allowed to use them—therefore, the government had the right to change the conditions. He was—naively as it turned out—unconcerned about the possible reaction by believers.[80]

Patriarch Tikhon was pressured by Archbishop Nikandr (Fenomenov, 1872–1933), recently appointed administrator of the Moscow diocese, to issue a sharp protest immediately.[81] Patriarch Tikhon waited three days, and receiving no response from Kalinin, he issued one of his most consequential encyclicals on February 28, 1922. In it, he recounted all he had done for famine relief in 1921 until the government prevented the Church from doing more. And though he had been willing to permit the donation of some valuables, he declared that the seizure of consecrated vessels used in the sacraments was "sacrilege." "We cannot approve the seizure from churches, even as if by voluntary donation, of sacred objects because their use for non-liturgical goals is forbidden by the canons of the Ecumenical Church." Those who participated in their seizure would be excommunicated or defrocked. The encyclical did not, however, instruct believers how they should respond.[82]

The patriarch's encyclical was sent by "reliable means" to bishops throughout the country. More than any other to this point, this encyclical was critically received within the Church. Some thought he was too lenient, others that he was not giving clear enough directions, yet others that he had given a legalistic interpretation to the canons. At stake was whether the canons he cited, which prohibited the use of consecrated vessels for profane purposes, prohibited their donation for charitable purposes. Some, such as Metropolitan Arseny (Stadnitsky), sought to avoid clashes and therefore did not have the encyclical read out in churches. Other bishops distributed it to their deans.[83] A meeting of Moscow deans resolved to read the patriarch's appeal in all the parishes. They made it clear that they did not intend to oppose the government with force but to show parishes what they assumed was a legal means of expressing their opposition to the Confiscation Decree. Nikandr drew up a model petition for parishes to send to the government protesting the decree which stated explicitly that "we are not summoning either to rebellion or to disturbances," but to legally protest the decree that was so profoundly disturbing to them.[84]

In the last days of February 1922, Tikhon faced the greatest dilemma thus far in his life: He had to give some indication of how the Orthodox faithful should respond and how bishops should instruct their clergy regarding the Soviet decree on the seizure of church valuables, something that intimately touched every single parish. If he advocated cooperating with the government in implementing the decree, after all the negotiations and compromise, it would mean complete submission to the Soviet government and abandoning his own authority; he would also leave the churches completely undefended against the government's plunder. If he followed Nikandr's suggestion of issuing an encyclical with a stern protest of the regime, it could lead to clashes that would result in the government's repression of clergy and believers. Given that the government had played a double game, he also no doubt suspected that something else was at work than famine relief. The patriarch felt compelled, therefore, to take a stand in defense of the Church, but one that was not worded as harshly as Nikandr advocated.[85] The patriarch expressed his own uncertainties about exactly how to handle the situation and how to word his encyclical. Ultimately, as he later stated repeatedly under interrogation, his goal was to encourage believers to appeal to the government, express their opposition to the decree, and come to a compromise agreement.[86] Since the Soviet regime had ceased its more repressive measures since the announcement of NEP a year earlier, that seemed a realistic possibility.

March 1922: The Confiscation Campaign

The patriarch daring to defy the Soviet government and calling on believers to resist—and resist they did—was more than the Bolshevik leadership could tolerate. The top Party leadership, especially Lenin and Trotsky, reacted to the Church's bold opposition with ruthlessness aimed to crush the Church into absolute submission. The Russian Orthodox Church was the only organization left in Soviet Russia that matched the reach of the government and commanded greater allegiance of the country's majority (especially the peasantry) than the communists did. Although Patriarch Tikhon had made a concerted effort to ensure the Church was politically neutral, that was not enough. The Bolsheviks could not allow something on the scale of the Orthodox Church to exist independently, outside of Soviet control. As James Ryan has argued, given the Bolsheviks' absolutist worldview, they viewed anyone who was not pro-Soviet as inherently hostile and counter-revolutionary.[87]

Some historians argue that the Confiscation Decree was intended deliberately to provoke a conflict with the Church.[88] In fact, there is no evidence of that—those who drafted the Confiscation Decree were minor functionaries who were apparently unaware of the reaction it would cause. The only person who was involved both in drafting the decree and in negotiating with the patriarch on voluntary donations was Vinokurov, who had previously served as Commissar of Social Security (1918–1921).[89] Neither Trotsky nor Lenin was in Moscow, as both were ill. The publication of the decree caught even Trotsky by surprise, and he was furious that it had been passed and made public before there had been more preparation for it—he was aware of the Church's likely opposition and called it a "blank shot." But he also believed the matter could be "fixed" if it occupied the center of the Party's attention—and he presented his plan of how to make it work for their benefit.[90]

Trotsky created a network of secret commissions to handle the valuables for sale abroad to fund the government. These secret commissions shadowed Pomgol so that it appeared that the confiscated valuables were going to famine relief.[91] Trotsky and those working with him were, apparently, expecting resistance—and prepared to use repression before the campaign even began, but primarily sought to prepare the campaign through propaganda to avoid conflict.[92]

Trotsky was also aware that there were some progressive priests that were dissatisfied with the patriarch's leadership. The Cheka had been cultivating clergy who could be turned against the patriarch since the end of the Civil War. Though Patriarch Tikhon strongly opposed the forced seizure of church valuables, there were clergy who were ready to support the campaign.[93] Though at first Trotsky was interested in these dissenting priests because they could provide propaganda support for the confiscations, in time he seized upon the idea that the dissident clergy could be united into an opposition that would split the Church.[94] He planned (with Politburo approval) to provoke schism among the clergy that entailed a Soviet propaganda narrative sympathetic to priests who supported the confiscations and attacked the "princes of the Church," above all the patriarch, who opposed the confiscations because they were heartless.[95]

As the campaign began, the Church tried to find alternatives. The patriarch sent a delegation to Ethan Colton and proposed that a foreign loan be secured to purchase food with the church valuables serving as security—but the ARA thought this too dangerous political territory for it to tread.[96] Believers also tried to find ways to compromise, for example by offering the amount of food and bread or money or personal valuables equal in value to the precious objects in their churches. One delegation came to Patriarch Tikhon to receive permission for such a proposal; he blessed them and sent them to Kalinin. Kalinin's deputy, Petr Smidovich (1874–1935), told them that what was needed was "not bread, but gold"—which contributed to suspicions that the siezures were not actually about helping the starving.[97] In some cases, local authorities agreed to these compromises to avoid conflict, but later the Party and state leadership directed that any failure to seize all the valuables would be regarded as "negligence."[98]

Initially, the situation was fluid enough that on March 15, *Izvestiia* published an interview with Patriarch Tikhon. The patriarch did not criticize the Confiscation Decree directly. The Church, he said, could not remain indifferent to the great suffering of the starving, which was why he had issued his February 6 appeal. From believers across the country, he knew they were ready to sacrifice for the starving and were voluntarily and generously ready to hand over valuables that were not for sacramental purposes. He also cautioned that "there is not such a great quantity of precious gems and gold in the churches that on their liquidation some sort of monstrous sums could be gained." He feared that too much was being made of church valuables and that expectations would be disappointed. He also hoped the commissions taking the valuables would be careful with objects that may not have great monetary value but did have artistic and historical significance.[99]

Ten days later, an article appeared in *Izvestiia* recounting the visit of several peasants from famine regions (who had been brought by the GPU) to Patriarch Tikhon. The peasants only repeat the Soviet propaganda narrative that the government had done all it could for famine relief and the Church, by giving up its valuables, could save millions of lives. All the patriarch's attempts to explain the situation fell on deaf ears, and the article was constructed in such a way that Tikhon comes out looking indifferent to the suffering of the starving, culminating in one of the peasants saying that the choice before the patriarch was either saving the lives of people—or saving the valuables and letting the people die. All the same, Tikhon's answers were direct—and accurately captured the situation. He explained that he had tried to do more, but that the government excluded the Church and clergy from participating in famine relief, wanting to control everything. Further, it was not he, the patriarch, that refused to give up the valuables, for the believers held control over them and did not want to give them up. "They do not believe that they will end up where they are supposed to go, but will go the army, not to the starving. Do you know where Trotsky is?" asked the patriarch. Tikhon and ordinary believers divined the truth— that Trotsky was responsible for the confiscations and that the valuables were intended to fund the army; remarkably, these suspicions were printed in *Izvestiia*. The patriarch explained one other crucial point: that there was enough bread, "only they are not able to distribute it."[100] In fact, Colonel William Haskell, the director of ARA operations in Russia, observed that the ARA already had more aid at the ports and on the way than the Soviet infrastructure could handle—which led Haskell himself to conclude that the seizure of valuables was not intended for famine relief.[101] Given Tikhon's ARA contacts, he evidently knew this. Mikhail Galkin, who was part of Trotsky's team, understood how much of the hidden truth was contained in the patriarch's words and wrote to Trotsky that the *Izvestiia* article needed to be reworked and could not be published as it was—but apparently his note to did not reach Trotsky before the article went to print.[102]

The bloodiest clash over the confiscations took place on March 15 in the textile town of Shuia. Thousands of people from the city and surrounding villages gathered around the church to obstruct the authorities from carrying out the confiscations. The soldiers accompanying the commission were surrounded and disarmed, so trucks came with machine guns and opened fire on the unarmed crowd, killing several people and wounding more. In protest, factories went on strike. Disorders broke out independently in other places such as Smolensk.[103]

When the Bolshevik Party Central Committee received reports on the events in Shuia, it ordered on March 19 that the confiscation of church valuables should halt, that more preparatory agitational work was needed to avoid clashes. Neither the Politburo, the Central Committee, the GPU (the State Political Administration, the new name for the secret police after February 1922), or even Trotsky appeared eager for bloodshed; though ready to crack down on resisters, they still sought to avoid disorders.[104]

In response to this retreat, Lenin wrote a top-secret but now infamous letter to Politburo members on March 19, 1922. On reading the reports about Shuia and other cases of resistance and the patriarch's encyclical of February 28, Lenin concluded that it was "crystal clear that the Black Hundred clergy headed by its leader is quite deliberately implementing the plan to engage us in a decisive battle precisely at this moment."[105] Lenin interpreted the resistance not as what it actually was—spontaneous acts by local populations against the plundering of their beloved churches—but as a conspiracy headed by Patriarch Tikhon to overthrow the government. Lenin, who came to power after a lifetime of conspiratorial revolutionary strategizing, was incapable of not seeing conspiracies everywhere and assuming that others were acting as he would have.

Lenin considered the moment was "exceptionally favorable" to wage war on the Church, indeed the "only moment" when they could "smash the enemy and secure ourselves an indispensable position for many decades to come." The famine provided a unique opportunity because people would either welcome the confiscations as bringing them aid or at least be too weak to resist. Lenin thought that the government could secure for itself "a fund of several hundred million gold rubles," or "perhaps even several billion," which would make it possible for the government to function. The famine, for Lenin, was only a cynical opportunity to destroy the Church and fund the government at its expense. He further insisted that this was the moment that the regime "must give battle to the Black Hundred clergy in the most decisive and merciless manner and crush its resistance with such brutality that it will not forget it for decades to come."[106]

Lenin directed that there be no halt to the confiscation campaign. Moreover, as many as possible should be arrested in Shuia and "a very large number" should be executed after a show trial. Lenin believed it "expedient for us not to touch Patriarch Tikhon himself, although he is undoubtedly heading this entire rebellion of slaveholders." Rather, he instructed the GPU to watch him vigilantly, and that Dzerzhinsky and Iosif Unshlikht (1879–1938), deputy head of the GPU, should "report weekly on this to the Politburo." The confiscation of valuables "should be conducted with merciless determination, unconditionally stopping at nothing." Provoking disturbances should not deter the authorities from carrying out confiscations, quite the contrary— more disturbances gave the opportunity for greater repression. "The greater number of representatives of the reactionary clergy and reactionary bourgeoisie we succeed in executing for this reason, the better." That would "teach these people" a lesson not to "dare even to think of any resistance."[107] Lenin's goal was to crush the one independent organization left in Soviet Russia and bring it into complete submission to Bolshevism. His instructions effectively gave the green light to Trotsky to implement the scheme he had already drawn up, but now with greater haste and ruthlessness.

The next day, the GPU reported to the Politburo that there were clergy who would support the confiscation campaign but were constrained by the patriarch. With the patriarch's arrest, some clergy proposed, this "would present them with the possibility of arranging a council at which they could elect to the patriarchal throne and the synod people of a more loyal attitude to the Soviet Government." The GPU believed it had sufficient evidence to arrest the patriarch, and it was an opportune time to carry out such a plan.[108] Trotsky agreed with the plan but believed it needed to be prepared for with a vigorous propaganda campaign, and he instructed the press accordingly.[109]

The campaign had transformed from being primarily about the valuables into an all-out assault on the Church that sought to provoke conflict, and it was a campaign not only directed against the Church hierarchy but against every single Orthodox parish community, even poor remote rural ones. The confiscations were carried out with the assistance of the army and the GPU, and resisters were mercilessly repressed.[110] The confiscations plundered ordinary parish churches throughout the country of sacred objects that had remained in local communities for decades or centuries. The campaign resulted in fifty-five show trials, many of which ended in executions. According to recent research, some 16,000 clergy and believers suffered repression during the campaign, with approximately five hundred executions; some executions were directed specifically by the Politburo. At the same time, based on an exhaustive examination of what became of the valuables seized from churches, historian Sergy Ivanov concludes that there was no sale of these valuables abroad that went for purchasing bread for the starving, as Soviet propaganda had promised—that the seizure of church valuables played no role in alleviating the famine in 1922. Colonel Haskell, who followed the affair closely, came to the same conclusion at the time.[111] The effect on Patriarch Tikhon and on the Orthodox Church, however, was devastating.

The Interrogations Begin (March 27–May 3)

On March 22, 1922, Metropolitan Nikandr (Fenomenov), the administrator of the Moscow diocese, was arrested along with other key figures in the patriarch's inner circle, including Bishop Ilarion (Troitsky) and lay assistant Iakov Polozov (again).[112] On March 28, Patriarch Tikhon received a summons "inviting" him to come to Lubianka, to give testimony in the case against them.[113] The patriarch was interrogated about two matters which formed the central elements of his interrogations until his arrest in May—namely his encyclical of February 28, 1922, and the opposition to confiscation of church valuables, and his relationship to the Church Abroad and their political stance.[114]

Until late March, the Bolshevik leadership and secret police had been focused on the patriarch's resistance to the seizure of church valuables. The Soviet government did not react to the Karlovci Council's declaration on the restoration of the Romanov dynasty at the time, if they were even aware of it. But that situation changed dramatically when the Church Abroad issued an appeal to the Genoa Conference published in the émigré newspaper *Novoe Vremia* (Belgrade) on March 14, 1922. The Genoa Conference (April 10–May 19, 1922) was organized by British Prime Minister Lloyd George to establish economic ties with Soviet Russia (and Germany). Though ambivalent about relations with the capitalist countries, the Soviet government desperately needed economic recovery. The Church Abroad's appeal rejected the right of the Soviet government to represent the Russian people and argued that Bolshevism was a scourge on humanity that could spread beyond the bounds of Russia. Rather than assist the Soviet government by establishing trade relations and sending famine aid, the appeal asserted that it would be better for Western governments to support the true, honest Russians (i.e., the émigrés) and arm them so they could return and overthrow the Bolsheviks—who were especially vulnerable because of the famine.[115] Given that the timing coincided with the clashes over confiscations, Tikhon's relationship to the Church Abroad stood alongside his resistance to the confiscation of church valuables in GPU accusations and interrogations from that point forward.

In the March 28 interrogation, Timofei Samsonov (1888–1955), the head of the Secret Department of the GPU after Latsis, questioned Tikhon on his relationship with the Church Abroad—specifically whether it was ecclesiastically subordinate to him, in which case he bore responsibility for its statements in the name of the whole Russian Church. Moreover, they would be bound to obey him if he censured them and ordered them to disavow their political statements. Tikhon answered that every churchman had a right to his own political convictions, but he condemned their political declarations because it was not right to make their positions as churchmen a platform for political advocacy.[116] The patriarch thus readily censured the Church Abroad's political proclamations from the beginning.

The GPU gave the patriarch a written ultimatum consisting of two demands. They asserted that the patriarch was responsible for the clashes in Shuia and elsewhere because of his encyclical of February 28 and demanded that he take immediate measures to stop opposition to the Confiscation Decree by a new directive to the clergy—or otherwise the GPU would bring measures against the Church hierarchy for their responsibility. Second, he must publicly declare his position on the political activities of the Church Abroad. Samsonov expected an answer in three days.[117]

On March 30, the patriarch received a second subpoena to appear at Lubianka the following day at 3:00 p.m. The patriarch responded that he was unable to come in person because he would be getting ready for a church service that evening, but he would answer in writing.[118] In his letter to the GPU of March 31, he defended himself against the accusation that his encyclical was responsible for provoking the tragic events in Shuia, which he doubted even made it there by that time. The patriarch asserted that, because the Soviet government had declared church property to be public property and transferred it to the control of believers for appropriate religious use, it was up to those religious groups and their parish councils to control the property and decide what was to be donated for the needs of the hungry. "We earnestly ask both the representatives of the authorities and believers themselves not to permit violent actions leading to beatings and bloodshed—there is no place for anger and enmity." Although the Soviet authorities placed all the blame on the clergy and believers for excesses, the patriarch was reminding them that government agents actually caused the bloodshed. As for the Church Abroad, he stated that he condemned their political manifestations, but he could not do more because he only knew of their activities secondhand.[119]

Patriarch Tikhon was interrogated again during the first week of April by Petr Krasikov. In response to Krasikov's demand that the patriarch make an appeal to the flock to stop the bloodshed that resulted from opposition to the confiscations, Tikhon retorted, "Is it we who are shedding blood?" When Krasikov demanded that it was necessary to hand over all the valuables without exception, the patriarch replied: "All—never." To the demand that he issue a statement justifying the seizure of church valuables, Tikhon replied: "Why did you prohibit the formation of a church committee for famine relief?" Finally, Krasikov pushed Tikhon to take measures against clergy who engaged in "counter-revolutionary" work—that is, those who resisted the confiscations—as well as issue a public statement about the legality of the Confiscation Decree and necessity to obey it. Tikhon retorted: "I protest. We came to an agreement with the representatives of the government, and the latter, behind our backs, decreed the seizure of everything."[120] Tikhon boldly and categorically refused to be blamed for the conflict over church valuables because the Soviet government had turned away from the agreement they had negotiated and turned instead to the use of force.

As a follow up to the demand to make a public statement about the confiscation of church valuables, Patriarch Tikhon wrote an encyclical addressed to all the faithful and sent it to Kalinin on April 4. In it, the patriarch called on people to give generously to famine relief, to avoid bloodshed over the confiscations, but at the same time asserted that they had the right to demand that authorities not desecrate sacred objects.[121] Such a message was hardly satisfactory to the Soviet leadership and was not printed. Tikhon prepared a second one on April 9 addressed to diocesan bishops. This one decried violence and said that some people may, in their zeal for the Church, have acted incorrectly in their opposition to government representatives. Any act that led to violence was contrary to the Christian faith. The bishops should instruct the clergy under them and their flock to avoid any undesirable manifestations—and those who disobeyed their bishop's directives should be brought to account. This message was not published but was sent to bishops.[122]

Although the patriarch was critical of the political statements of the Church Abroad, he resisted the GPU's pressure to censure them publicly because he had not actually seen their declaration on the restoration of the monarchy or the appeal to the Genoa Conference.[123] In early April, before he received these documents, he still assumed the continued existence of the Church Abroad's administration, as witnessed by a conversation he had with the American Ethan Colton on April 6.[124] But after receiving the Church Abroad's political proclamations, Tikhon sent copies to the members of the Holy Synod and Higher Church Administration on April 10 with a proposal. The patriarch stated that he regarded their declarations as acts of a political character that disobeyed his encyclical of October 1919. "I consider the Karlovci Council of the Russian clergy and laity abroad to have no canonical significance, and its encyclical about the restoration of the Romanov dynasty and the appeal to the Genoa conference as not expressing the official voice of the Russian Orthodox Church." Since the Russian Church Administration Abroad was digressing into political declarations, and the Russian parishes in Europe had already been entrusted to Metropolitan Evlogy, Tikhon proposed that the administration be dissolved. Finally, the Holy Synod would have to engage in disciplinary actions against those who made political statements in the Church's name.[125] Having met the GPU's initial demands, interrogations of the patriarch were paused for the rest of the month.

Having seen for himself its political declarations, Tikhon concluded that it was necessary to abolish the Church Abroad administration, as he wrote to Metropolitan Mikhail (Ermakov) on April 16.[126] Father Theodore Pashkovsky (1874–1950), a priest from America, visited the patriarch on May 3, 1922, just before he was to leave for America. Given that so many Moscow clergymen had been arrested, he visited the patriarch in disguise. Tikhon informed him that he "directed and ordered that the so-called Russian Supreme Church Administration Abroad... be dissolved," and he asked Pashkovsky to communicate this to both metropolitans Evlogy and Platon, "who thereupon became sole rulers" of the Russian Orthodox Church "in Western Europe and North America, respectively."[127] The patriarch instructed Pashkovsky to return May 5 and he would give this to him in writing—but when he came that day, the patriarch's residence was surrounded by soldiers "and I was told if I would go, I would be arrested by the Cheka."[128] Pashkovsky's inability to receive this documentation allowed for doubts about both Tikhon's actual intentions toward the Church Abroad and about his appointment of Metropolitan Platon.

Patriarch Tikhon was put in the position of having to pronounce on the Church Abroad, given that he had given his blessing for the Karlovci Council to convene—which he later admitted was a mistake—which made him responsible for its statements.[129] An appeal that threatened to subvert the establishment of desperately needed economic ties with Western Europe was something the Soviet government could not ignore. The timing was also explosive: The Church Abroad's appeal was published the day before the Shuia incident. At the very moment the Church leadership abroad was calling for an armed intervention to overthrow the Soviet government, violent resistance broke out across Russia to the seizure of church valuables—so that Bolshevik leaders concluded that a vast conspiracy was at work both inside and outside Soviet Russia, centered on the Orthodox Church and orchestrated by Patriarch Tikhon, to overthrow the Soviet regime. Given that the Soviet leadership was prone to fantastic conspiracy theories (they themselves had come to power through a scarcely believable conspiracy, after all) and were already ramping up repression against the patriarch and the Church leadership in Russia, the declarations of the Church Abroad could not have been more ill-timed. Although he was under immense pressure from the GPU, Patriarch Tikhon did not simply give in to its demands, as the early April interrogation record attests. His position on the Church Abroad cannot be explained away as him giving in to pressure: Unlike the resistance to the confiscation of church valuables, which was a necessary defense of the Church from an unjustified assault, the Church Abroad's anti-Soviet statements directly contravened the patriarch's orders to clergy to remain politically neutral and only served to intensify the persecution of the Church in Russia.

8
The Case Against Tikhon
(May 1922–June 1923)

Having provoked a conflict with the Church, the Bolshevik leadership seized the opportunity to destroy it—and to finally rid themselves of Patriarch Tikhon. Although Lenin believed Tikhon headed a conspiracy to overthrow the Soviet regime, he also suggested that they not "touch Patriarch Tikhon himself" yet. A credible case would have to be made against him to convince the public. The Bolsheviks had been trying to find a way to rid themselves of the patriarch since 1918, but they had not been able to build a convincing case. With the Church Abroad's clear counter-revolutionary statements, Tikhon's resistance to the decree of seizing church valuables, and the violent opposition that erupted over the seizures, the top Bolshevik leadership was convinced they could unquestionably accuse the patriarch of "counter-revolution." Although Lenin provided the impetus for destroying the Church, the plan for doing so was worked out and directed by Trotsky— which entailed a "divide and conquer" strategy of orchestrating schism within the ranks of the Orthodox Church that would assist in overthrowing the Church's old leadership and replacing it with a pro-Soviet one. For the next year, the Bolsheviks pursued the two— fomenting schism in the Church and preparing the case against Tikhon—in parallel. Neither, however, would work out as Lenin and Trotsky planned.

Trials, Interrogations, Detainment

On April 26, 1922, the Soviets launched a trial against fifty-four Moscow clergy and laity accused of counter-revolutionary activity and anti-Soviet agitation by distributing the patriarch's February 28 encyclical and other acts in opposition to the confiscation decree. The trial sought to show that Tikhon's encyclical misapplied the canons because the patriarch's citation of them was not genuine, but only a cover for what was a political—not religious—opposition to the Soviet decree.[1] On May 4, the Politburo directed the Moscow Tribunal to summon the patriarch to the trial "immediately" and to "apply capital punishment" to the clergy on trial.[2] Tikhon was called to the stand and testified from 11:00 p.m. on May 4 until 1:00 a.m. on May 5.[3] On taking the stand, the patriarch, dressed in a simple cassock, blessed the crowd, and the overwhelming majority of people in the audience stood up to receive his blessing. Even the Soviet newspapers reported that he held himself with dignity, spoke with confidence, even joked in his usual manner, and answered very clearly and deliberately.[4] When, however, the prosecutor was rude to him, it created such an uproar that the trial was forced to take a break and part of the audience was expelled.[5]

Testifying on the stand, Tikhon reiterated the history of his efforts for famine relief and that the government issued its confiscation decree just after they had reached an agreement on the Church's voluntary participation. He explained that he hoped his February 28 encyclical would lead to believers' legal protests that might cause the government to reconsider.[6] In response to the prosecutor's question of whether it was more important to preserve valuables or save starving people, Tikhon rejected the premise of the question—replying that up until the eve of the confiscation campaign, Soviet newspapers had downplayed the severity of the famine and insisted that the government had it under control.[7] When asked how he defined "counter-revolution," the patriarch stated simply: actions directed at the overthrow of the Soviet government (the answer Latsis gave him in 1919). When the prosecutor restated: "that means any action directed against the Soviet government," the patriarch corrected him—no, only actions directed to its overthrow, which petitions against the confiscations were not.[8] The Soviet government, the patriarch insisted, was not infallible, just as the head of the Church was not infallible, and opposition was legitimate if it was intended to correct a mistaken direction. To make this point, he also insisted that the clergy had the right to disagree with him and discuss issues of ecclesiastical policy.[9]

When the trial of the Moscow clergy and believers ended on May 8 (resulting in five death sentences), the Revolutionary Tribunal declared that the Decree of Separation of Church and State (January 1918) recognized the legal existence only of individual parish communities; no other religious organization had the right to operate as if it had authority over them. The court therefore stated that the patriarchal administration, in claiming to have canonical, administrative, and economic rights over parishes, was itself illegal—all the more since the "organization known as the Orthodox hierarchy" pursued political goals under the cover of a religious organization.[10] Until this moment, the Decree of Separation of Church and State had been interpreted to mean that the Church hierarchy was not recognized as having any legal status or rights. Now the Tribunal was declaring that the very existence of the Church hierarchy as such, as a structure, was intrinsically *illegal*. The illegal nature of the Church hierarchy became a central part of the accusation against Patriarch Tikhon.[11]

Immediately after he finished hours of grueling questioning at the trial at 1:00 a.m. on May 5, Tikhon was taken to Lubianka for further interrogation. The GPU demanded that the patriarch publicly condemn the Church Abroad, summon them to judgment, and that he declare that all church property belonged to the Soviet government even if it was abroad.[12]

Later that day, May 5, the patriarch called an urgent meeting of the Higher Church Administration to discuss his proposal judging the Karlovci Council. The Synod agreed with the patriarch's overall assessment and issued Decree No. 348, which confirmed Tikhon's judgment on the political declarations of the Church Abroad. The final decree differed from the patriarch's earlier proposal in declaring the Karlovci Council's political proclamations, not the Council as a whole, as having no ecclesial or canonical significance; it also declared that its political statements did not express the official voice of the Russian Orthodox Church. The second point agreed with the patriarch's statement that the Higher Church Authority Abroad should be dissolved because it made such political statements, especially since Russian émigré parishes were already under Metropolitan Evlogy and there was no territory over which the administration would exercise its authority. Finally, the Synod stated that, to judge the "ecclesiastical responsibility" of the clergy abroad for their political declarations on behalf of the Church, it must obtain the materials pertaining to their actions. Since some were bishops, any judgment would have to await the resumption of normal activities of the Holy Synod with a full number of members.[13]

A second interrogation took place the same day at 7:00 p.m., when Samsonov followed up on the demands given the patriarch in the middle of the night. Samsonov asked the patriarch about what they had done regarding the Church Abroad and whether they would depose, defrock, or excommunicate them. The patriarch explained the Higher Church Administration's decision—and explained that any ecclesiastical judgment or punishment would have to be carried out by an ecclesiastical court of twelve bishops.

Samsonov then wanted to know whether the patriarch had given a directive to the Church Abroad to immediately hand over all Church property to representatives of the Soviet government. Here, too, the patriarch stonewalled by stating that he could make no decisions on Church property by himself, but that it would have to be discussed by the Higher Church Administration.[14] Since most members of the Synod and Higher Church Council were under arrest or in exile, by making those qualifications the patriarch was effectively either refusing to give in to the GPU demands, or countering that he could do what they wished—if and when they restored the Church administration.

Leaders of the Church Abroad, and its historians since, argued that the patriarch dissolved their administration only because he was forced to, and therefore that Decree No. 348 could be followed in the letter but not the spirit (see Chapter 9).[15] Although clearly the GPU was pressuring the patriarch to censure the Church Abroad, the evidence indicates that the patriarch only viewed the Church Abroad administration as having jurisdiction over Russian émigrés in Europe (as articulated in the October 13, 1921 decree), which was redundant since those parishes were under Evlogy (or on territories of other Orthodox Churches). Once he became acquainted firsthand with the political declarations of the Church Abroad and concluded that it repeatedly violated his 1919 encyclical on political neutrality, he abolished its administration—but resisted the Soviet pressure to take ecclesiastical action against its leaders.

The same day, May 5, 1922, the Moscow Revolutionary Tribunal announced that it was bringing Patriarch Tikhon to trial.[16] Although it was framed as though the Moscow trial had brought forward testimony from the accused and witnesses that incriminated the patriarch, in fact, the trial itself had been planned that way for propaganda purposes, to begin with lesser figures to build up the case against the patriarch in an attempt to prepare the public for it and justify bringing the patriarch to trial. On May 9, 1922, Patriarch Tikhon was interrogated one last time that spring.[17] Although he was not officially placed under arrest, he was placed under armed guard and unable to leave his residence or receive visitors.

The Renovationist Coup

A major part of Trotsky's scheme to destroy the Orthodox Church entailed supporting a revolution within the Church by clergy who declared themselves loyal to the Soviet government, thus pursuing a "divide and conquer" strategy. The clergy who seized the Church Administration in May 1922 referred to themselves at the time as "progressive" clergy. They not only declared their loyalty to the Soviet government and support for socialist revolution, but they also sought to enact sweeping reforms to renew and modernize the religious life of the Orthodox Church. From their stated goal of renewal or renovation of what they regarded as obsolete church practices, the general movement has been labeled as "Renovationism" (*obnovlenchestvo*).[18]

The GPU had long sought ways of exploiting divisions within the Church to undermine Patriarch Tikhon, but such schemes, which would entail government support for one faction against another, never received support from Lenin. In January 1922, in the planning stages, Trotsky and his team schemed to recruit individual clergymen to help them justify the confiscation campaign. After the confiscation campaign was in full swing, on March 30, Trotsky elaborated an entire plan, based on a Marxist view of history, that entailed promoting a "bourgeois reformation" in the Orthodox Church to break the power of the old Church, to be followed by crushing the "fellow-travelers" (the Renovationists) among the clergy. Trotsky asserted that the confiscation campaign was "extremely advantageous" for this plan because clergy were divided over it. The old hierarchy could be arrested for their opposition to the confiscations, and the "progressive" clergy could convene their own church council to secure their control over the Church and replace the current ecclesiastical leadership.[19]

Key members of the Petrograd progressive clergy arrived in Moscow on May 9, headed by Fr. Aleksandr Vvedensky (1889–1946). They met with a Moscow group on May 10 and produced a draft declaration that followed the main points as dictated by the GPU, blaming the Church hierarchy for the conflict with the Soviet state and for indifference to people suffering from the famine. The Politburo approved the message.[20] A commission under Trotsky instructed a delegation of Renovationist priests to go to Patriarch Tikhon, lay the blame on him for all the violence during the confiscation of church valuables, and demand his abdication—all of which was to be recorded by a GPU agent for later publication.[21]

Late on the night of May 12–13, the reformist clergy together with Evgeny Tuchkov (1892–1957) visited the patriarch at the Trinity Metochion, waking him up. Tuchkov, a thirty-year-old GPU agent with an elementary education, had become head of the sixth division of the GPU Secret Department in charge of the clergy; he served the patriarch's main "handler" from this time until his death. The clergy told Tikhon that, since he was going to be put on trial, he would be unable to administer the Church and should transfer its administration to someone else. The patriarch flatly refused their proposal to appoint the Bishop Antonin (Granovsky, 1865–1927), whom the patriarch had suspended from serving because of his liturgical innovations. They also told him that, if he cooperated, the eleven people sentenced to death in the Moscow trial would be pardoned—an incredible tool to try to manipulate the patriarch. Although he did not agree to all their demands, Tikhon must have realized that indeed it would be impossible for him to administer the Church if he was about to be tried.[22] According to Fr. Aleksandr Vvedensky, Tikhon said that he had "always looked upon the patriarchate as a cross" and would be grateful to be freed from it.[23] He wrote a statement to Kalinin that, given the situation, "I consider it beneficial, for the good of the Church, temporarily until the convocation of a Council, to place at the head of the church administration either Metropolitan Agafangel of Yaroslavl or Metropolitan Veniamin of Petrograd." Four priests verified that this declaration was authentically signed by the patriarch: Aleksandr Vvedensky, Vladimir Krasnitsky (1881–1936), Evgeny Belkov (1882–1930), and Sergei Kalinovsky (1884–?).[24] The account that was given in the Soviet newspapers and later by the Renovationists themselves was strikingly different—namely that the priests rebuked the patriarch for having caused the crisis, and in response the patriarchate abdicated. In reality, the patriarch refused to abdicate; he agreed only to allow someone else of his choosing to administer the ecclesiastical administration temporarily while he was unable to.[25]

On May 14, 1922, *Izvestiia* and *Pravda* published the Renovationist proclamation condemning the Church leadership.[26] The Renovationist leaders visited the patriarch for a second time on May 16, informing him of Kalinin's decision to allow Metropolitan Agafangel to assume the ecclesiastical leadership. They also assured the patriarch that the government would permit a Council, which the patriarch welcomed, since the Council of 1917–1918 stipulated that one should be convened every three years. The patriarch wrote to Metropolitan Agafangel, appointing him as his deputy and instructing him to come to Moscow as soon as possible. Agafangel was ready to come.[27]

Vvedensky, Belkov, and Kalinovsky returned to the patriarch a third time on May 18. Since the patriarch had transferred leadership to another hierarch, the Church was without any administration; they assured him that the government authorities would permit them to open the patriarchal chancellery and asked his blessing for them to conduct affairs of the Church until Agafangel arrived. The patriarch did not sign their ambiguously worded request, but rather gave them his own statement that he was entrusting the three priests to "receive and pass on to Metropolitan Agafangel upon his arrival in Moscow" the Synodal chancellery, and similarly made provisions for the Moscow diocesan administration.[28] It is also clear from this note that the Trinity Metochion would remain the location of the ecclesiastical administration—which meant that the patriarch himself had to move.

Tikhon could not have foreseen the catastrophe that was about to befall the Church. There was no way for him to know about the secret negotiations the priests were conducting behind the scenes with the GPU and Galkin (who was serving as Trotsky's assistant). The Renovationist leaders had been cautious up to that point; they had not openly attacked or defied the patriarch and when they visited him expressed their "filial" obedience. They only criticized him openly with their May 14 declaration, which Tikhon would not have known about since he was being detained. It is likely the patriarch did not trust them entirely—hence the documents he gave them were very carefully worded. He evidently concluded that, if he could use them as intermediaries, he could secure the transition of ecclesiastical authority to the person he had designated, with the government's approval. In his final instructions, he only permitted them to open the chancellery (which the Soviets had sealed off) in preparation for Agafangel's arrival. Contrary to later claims by the Renovationists and in the Soviet press, Patriarch Tikhon did not authorize the establishment of the Renovationist Higher Church Administration.[29]

Given that Patriarch Tikhon was handing over the administration to Agafangel, on May 19, he left the Trinity Metochion for the latter to occupy so the administration would remain in the same place. Because he had already been confined for ten days, many contemporaries believed he was under arrest; however, the authorities did not formally place him under arrest until the summer.[30] He stopped in the Iversk chapel on Red Square to pray. He wrote to the GPU that day to inform them that he had relocated to the Donskoi Monastery on the outskirts of the city of Moscow.[31] After he arrived at the Donskoi Monastery, guards were placed at all the exits and entrances, and he was not permitted to leave his quarters.[32] From that moment he would remain cut off from the Church for over a year.

The Church Revolution

The Renovationist leaders declared themselves in charge of the ecclesiastical administration as soon as Patriarch Tikhon vacated the Trinity Metochion. Already on May 20, *Pravda* and *Izvestiia* published an interview with Kalinovsky in which he falsely claimed that they had reached an agreement with the patriarch allowing them to form a new ecclesiastical administration.[33] That same day, the new administration moved into the Trinity Metochion and set to work asserting its control over the Church.

A movement for renewing the Church began among progressive parish clergy a generation earlier, especially in St. Petersburg in 1905. Scholars have debated the extent of the continuities and discontinuities between the earlier renewal movement and that of the 1920s. The degree to which the leaders of the movement in 1922 were motivated by reform or power, as well as how widespread was their support, are also contentious issues. What is clear is that the 1920s Renovationists were more politically active than the liberal clergy in 1905 had been, and they welcomed not only the February Revolution but also the Bolsheviks. Having taken over the higher church administration, the Renovationists set out, with the assistance of the GPU, to take control over the entire Russian Orthodox Church.

Metropolitan Agafangel publicly opposed the Renovationists from the beginning and therefore the GPU prevented him from leaving Yaroslavl so he could not assume the administration.[34] Metropolitan Veniamin of Petrograd also opposed the Renovationist takeover of the administration and was arrested on June 1; although Veniamin had succeeded in negotiating over the confiscation of church valuables with local authorities and avoiding conflict, he was subjected to a show trial, along with other clergy, sentenced to death, and executed on August 13, 1922, on orders from the Politburo.[35] The Renovationist church leadership received legitimation, however, when three other authoritative bishops—Metropolitan Sergy (Stragorodsky) of Vladimir, Archbishop Evdokim (Meshchersky, 1869–1935) of Nizhny Novgorod, and Archbishop Serafim (Meshcheriakov, 1860–1933) of Kostroma, issued a declaration (known as the "Memorandum of Three") on June 16, recognizing their Higher Church Administration as the canonical ecclesiastical authority. This declaration played a significant role in convincing other bishops and clergy to accept the Renovationist administration.[36] On June 18, Agafangel responded by issuing an encyclical refuting the legitimacy of the Renovationist administration and instructing bishops to govern their dioceses independently until the legitimate administration was restored. Ten days later he was arrested and transferred to the GPU prison in Moscow and by the end of the year sent to exile in Siberia for three years.[37]

The Renovationists justified their movement by asserting in a series of publications that the Church was in crisis because its leadership, headed by the patriarch, opposed the Soviet government and supported counter-revolution. The Renovationists opposed the old monastic hierarchy and the very institution of the patriarchate, seeking to empower the parish clergy. The Renovationists also advocated wide-sweeping reform to modernize religious life such as a Russian language rather than Church Slavonic liturgy; they criticized traditional practices such as monasticism and the veneration of saints' relics.[38] After the Church Council ended in 1918 without being able to consider questions of liturgical reform, many of the progressive clergy engaged in liturgical innovation. Patriarch Tikhon's position regarding liturgical reform was characteristic: He did not rigidly insist that liturgical practice never changed. At the same time, he was very cautious about such change. In November 1921, he issued an appeal to the bishops to prevent any liturgical innovations or experimentation. Some of the issues under consideration—such as abbreviating some parts of the services and saying the priest's prayers aloud—he himself had advocated in 1905. He had not changed his position; rather, he was opposed to changes that were introduced arbitrarily by individual priests, and he also believed that liturgy should not just change with the "demands of the times." He feared that such experimentation would cause division, especially at a moment when the Church was already in danger. Perhaps most importantly, he believed that only a Church Council had the authority to reform the liturgy.[39] Some of the progressive clergy, however, felt oppressed by the patriarch's prohibition.[40]

Prisoner in Donskoi Monastery

Initially the patriarch was not strictly isolated at the Donskoi Monastery. He was able to receive letters and packages, and he was still directing packages and relief sent through the American Relief Administration. A GPU informant reported that he had even succeeded in passing out a note in the dirty laundry, and notes were handed to him with the jam. The Red Army soldiers were kind to him and came to receive his blessing—some would even remain with him after their shifts ended.[41] Although he could not leave the rooms he was confined to, he could take walks along the wall. In anticipation, people would gather beneath to see the patriarch and receive his blessing, and sometimes exchange a few words with him. His main concern was what was happening with the Church, and whether Metropolitan Agafangel had arrived to assume leadership.[42]

Later in the summer, the GPU began guarding and supervising the patriarch much more strictly. He was assigned agents from the GPU who kept him under constant supervision. These agents did not permit the patriarch to interact with anyone, keeping him in complete isolation; notes inside care packages were confiscated. No more conversations through windows or over the wall were allowed, though he was still allowed to walk along the wall and bless people who gathered—and people would gather, in large numbers, especially after liturgy. The patriarch tossed down apples and sweets to children below.[43] He was permitted to receive telegrams or notes (which sometimes were simply prayer requests), which were screened by the GPU, but his responses were handed to Tuchkov, who decided whether to send them. The case against him did not move forward all summer until the formal order for his arrest was issued in mid-August 1922.[44] The patriarch's situation was then regularized and would remain constant until his release at the end of June 1923.

The GPU agents assigned to him that fall were two young women, Maria Semenova and Nadezhda Sidneva. Sidneva came from an aristocratic background, and Semenova spent idle hours of her watch reading poetry. Semenova was recruited from the communist youth league, the Komsomol. The young women were on duty rotation, each serving for twenty-four hours. According to the memoir account that she later wrote, Semenova was surprised at her new assignment, asking her superior how she should address the patriarch—"Citizen Patriarch? Comrade Tikhon? Your Eminence?" Her superior replied, "The devil knows!" When Tikhon entered the room, he lightly slapped him on the shoulder and asked, "How's life, señor?" to which the patriarch responded with a friendly greeting.[45]

The patriarch lived in a chamber-tower attached to the monastery wall next to the northern gate. The narrow stone staircase of two flights led to the tower, which was the only entrance. The tower-chamber had four rooms located on the top floor: three adjacent rooms for the patriarch and a fourth one for his guards, either Semenova or Sidneva plus a Red Army soldier. Sentries were posted outside. The stairs and the walkway along the top of the wall were accessed through their room. Each of the patriarch's rooms had two small windows, and the first two rooms had furniture "corresponding to the age" of the building (sixteenth–seventeenth century), but the back room, where the patriarch actually lived, had newer and more comfortable furniture with a bed, a marble washbasin, and a solid desk. Out through the dark hallway was the loo, which Semenova described "as in the 16th century." One time Semenova's superior came and, in a panic, asked, "Where is the old man?" The soldier replied that he was "sitting 'in the sixteenth century,'" which confused the GPU agent. After Semenova explained it to him, he chuckled at first, but then yelled at them because it was "not allowed"—the patriarch was only allowed to "use a bucket," despite the protestations of the sentries that they were very watchful and careful.[46]

The patriarch was not permitted to see anyone or talk to anyone except the cook, guards, and GPU agents. This condition lasted for nearly a year. A constant stream of people brought Tikhon gifts, mostly of food, firewood, darned socks, candles, and so on. Semenova would pass on any messages to Tikhon and give his reply.[47]

The patriarch maintained a strict schedule; imposing discipline upon himself physically, mentally, and spiritually was a way to stay "fit" through a year of isolation. He woke at 6 a.m., started the day with gymnastics, washed, and prayed until breakfast at 9 a.m. He spent the rest of the morning writing—though what he wrote, and what happened to it, is unknown. An hour before lunch he would walk along the wall, to the tower and back. His guards watched him from the window. During that time, believers would wait below for him to bless them, though only in silence since he was forbidden to speak with anyone. At 1:00 p.m. he would eat and then rest until 3 p.m. At 4 p.m. he would take his tea and then sit down at his table to work some more, reading or writing. At 5 p.m., his guards would light the furnaces, and Tikhon would walk around with his poker and stir the fires. Sometimes the three of them—the soldier, Semenova, and the patriarch—would sit in front of the stove on the landing and bake potatoes and eat them together while having a friendly chat. At 7 p.m. he would have dinner, and after that he would not come out of his room until morning, though the sentries could see through the window that he remained on his knees in prayer for a long time, sometimes all night long.[48]

Semenova was amazed at the patriarch's tact—he talked to them freely and easily but without touching on forbidden topics. Once the soldier asked, addressing the patriarch in the familiar, "Tell me, father, does God exist?" to which the patriarch gave an extended answer. It was also known that many of the soldiers were still believers and were respectful to the patriarch, who interacted with them in his usual cheerful and joking manner.[49] Tikhon always took an interest in whatever Semenova was reading, especially the journals, and would always ask her to let him take a look. In turn, he managed to convince her to read the *Lives of the Saints*.

Though she understood that the patriarch was supposed to be a class enemy, and a very dangerous one at that, Semenova could not see him that way. "He interacted with us in an ideal way. He was always attentive, gentle, even. I did not see him irritated or capricious." Her colleague explained to her that the patriarch lived according to the Gospel and "forgave his enemies." Understanding that the patriarch's daily life was in their hands, the female agents sought to lighten his burden as much as they could, even if that meant not always following the rules of what was "permitted."

The patriarch was not allowed to serve in or attend church for the entire time of his confinement, which was a particular hardship for him. He was, however, able to receive communion on Sundays and feast days. A priest would walk over from the church with the chalice, followed by a sentry with a gun. The patriarch was not allowed to be with the priest alone.[50]

For someone who had always been very sociable, it must have been incredibly difficult for Tikhon to be completely isolated. When Semenova's duty was at an end, he gave her a gift of an embroidered cloth for her "care and attention." She resisted at first—surely it was not allowed to receive gifts from prisoners—but he said that it had no material value, but was "a symbol, a memory of the days in Donskoi."[51] Tikhon's kind human relations even with the nonbeliever GPU agent assigned to guard him left enough of an impression on her that she wrote about it decades later.

The Anti-Religious Commission

During the campaign to confiscate church valuables in 1922, the assault on the Church was managed by the same secret commissions that Trotsky originally created for the concentration of valuables.[52] In the fall of 1922, Bolshevik Party organs that were under Stalin's control created a new commission that would manage both antireligious propaganda and policy, and would be directly subordinate to the Politburo—and thus marginalized Trotsky from his leading role in religious policy. Officially entitled the "Commission for the Implementation of the Separation of Church and State," it was usually referred to as the Anti-Religious Commission (ARK). The GPU (through Tuchkov) implemented ARK's policies. It operated in complete secrecy—its very existence was unknown until the collapse of the Soviet Union.[53]

In its first year, ARK focused primarily on supporting the Renovationist movement and battling against the "Tikhonites," as those loyal to the patriarch and traditional Orthodoxy became known. ARK and the GPU exiled Tikhonite bishops and priests and replaced them with Renovationists, and then purged parish councils of laity loyal to the patriarch. With GPU help, the Renovationist administration gained control of the majority of the Russian Orthodox Church by the end of 1922. Many clergy submitted out of conviction, opportunism, fear of repression, or confusion due to the Renovationist propaganda that the patriarch had authorized them.[54]

Preparation for the Trial

After Tikhon was formally placed under arrest in August 1922, he was interrogated by Tuchkov. Then there was little movement on the case against him, and he was not interrogated again, until mid-December. On December 15, 1922, Iakov Agranov (born Yankel Sorenson, 1893–1938) became the specially authorized investigator to proceed with the case and conducted all subsequent interrogations.[55] In August, the patriarch himself wrote out his replies to Tuchkov's questions, but Agranov's records consist of his written summaries of multiple interrogations. The language is distinctly different from earlier interrogations, and it is difficult to assess how trustworthy they are; one, in particular, employs the Soviet characterization of events (going back to the Church Council of 1917–1918) and has the patriarch even ostensibly admitting that his early encyclicals were "counter-revolutionary"— things he admitted at no other time.[56] From the end of December 1922 until the middle of March 1923, Patriarch Tikhon was routinely interrogated. Although Tikhon denied he was ever tortured, Semenova observed that over a period he was taken to Lubyanka for interrogations every day, and each time the patriarch would return to Donskoi extremely exhausted.[57]

According to the picture that emerges from these interrogation records, in this period Patriarch Tikhon came to acknowledge that some of proclamations were "anti-Soviet." In particular, he admitted his "guilt" for issuing the February 28, 1922, encyclical that labeled the seizure of consecrated vessels as "sacrilege." He explained that he issued this message because the

Soviets had betrayed the agreement they had just reached; he did not intend to summon the population to violence against the Soviet government, but rather hoped believers, by expressing legal opposition, could reach an agreement with the state. He did, however, accept some responsibility for the violence that ensued. He also acknowledged that even consecrated vessels could be used for charitable purposes—when the Church (or believers) voluntarily gave them for that purpose. He asserted that he offered no support for the Whites, and that he blessed the convocation of the Karlovci Council without anticipating that they would issue political statements.[58]

In the first months of 1923, ARK labored to put together a convincing case against the patriarch.[59] Central to the accusation was Tikhon's opposition to the seizure of church valuables—and that he misused the canons in alleging that the confiscations amounted to sacrilege. But they also sought—though without success—to establish that he supported and blessed counterrevolutionary plots at home and abroad. In February, the Politburo created a commission to oversee Tikhon's trial that consisted of Alexei Rykov (1881–1938), deputy chairman to Lenin on the Soviet of People's Commissars and member of the Politburo; Nikolai Krylenko (1885–1938), deputy commissar of justice and assistant prosecutor general of Soviet Russia; and Kalinin, chairman of the Central Executive Committee.[60] Such high-profile figures indicate that the Party leadership held the trial of Patriarch Tikhon as of the highest importance. ARK also directed the propaganda campaign in preparation for the trial, from which observers within the Church attempted to divine what the charges would be.[61] In March, ARK asked the Politburo "to give precise directives to the court on the measure of punishment."[62] Although the death penalty was a likely outcome, ARK did not want to take responsibility for such a decision, and it later informed the Politburo that it explicitly opposed the death sentence.[63] Everything from the press coverage to the outcomes of trials was directed by ARK and the Politburo; neither the press nor the court was independent in an important case such as this.

On March 6, the GPU handed the case over to the Supreme Court.[64] Agranov, who stayed on the case, prepared the indictment that explained which articles from the new criminal code (ratified in June 1922) Tikhon was alleged to have broken. The indictment claimed that Tikhon supported the bourgeoisie in its struggle against the workers and peasants and their government. He exploited the superstition of the masses to organize opposition to the Soviet regime in the name of religion. He exploited the famine, when the government was vulnerable, to arouse opposition to the government over its efforts to provide famine relief through church valuables. When given a chance to respond to the accusations, the patriarch admitted that his encyclicals called believers to oppose Soviet measures—but not with the goal of overthrowing the Soviet regime.[65] Though willing to admit some "guilt" in opposing the Soviet government, perhaps to take responsibility on himself rather than others who were to be tried with him, he denied guilt for any accusations that would have carried the death penalty.

Patriarch Tikhon petitioned the Supreme Court to allow him to celebrate the liturgy for Pascha, stating that for ten months he was prohibited from attending liturgy even in the Donskoi Monastery, which was especially painful, as the most important holiday of the Christian year was approaching. The court denied his request. The GPU even denied his right to receive communion for Pascha.[66]

The trial was set to begin in March—but then kept getting postponed for reasons that are not entirely clear. At the same time as preparing the impending trial against the patriarch, the Soviet authorities arrested a group of leading Roman Catholic clergy and prepared to put them on trial, perhaps as a kind of "dress rehearsal" for Tikhon's trial, which attracted negative international attention.[67] The archbishop of Canterbury, Randall Davidson, gave a speech before the British Parliament in which he defended Patriarch Tikhon as one who had actively engaged in famine relief and was being unjustly accused of opposing the Soviet government.[68] The trial of the Catholic clergy at the end of March ended with death sentences for Archbishop Jan Cieplak (1857–1926) and his assistant, Monsignor Constantine Budkiewicz (Konstantin Butkevich, 1867–1923), which created a huge international outcry.[69] That cry dramatically intensified after Budkiewicz was executed on Catholic Easter (the night of March 31–April 1).

All the same, the Party leadership forged ahead with planning Tikhon's trial in the first half of April. The only piece of material evidence that they were able to produce was a decorative wooden plate given to Tikhon by nationalist and monarchist organizations in Vilna in 1914. The trial was set for April 17. Emilian Yaroslavsky, the head of ARK, prepared centralized control over the press coverage. The charges continued to be in flux—it proved to be difficult to define the patriarch's alleged crimes in legal terms.[70] By April 10, 1923, the trial was fully prepared and ready to start, and tickets for the spectators were issued before being delayed another week. Meanwhile, Yaroslavsky was to hold secret meetings with regional Party leaders at the XII Party Congress (April 17–25, 1923) and instruct them on the Party's policy toward the Church.[71] As one contemporary Orthodox observer wryly commented, there seemed to be no movement on the trial and "therefore it was completely unexpected for us when, on Good Friday, it was published in the papers that the trial was set for the Wednesday of Bright Week. It was also unexpected for the court itself, because even the indictment itself was not yet completed on that day." The tickets, moreover, were distributed mostly to committed communists—and since their number was limited, they became a hot commodity and could fetch a high price.[72]

In mid-April, Andrei Vyshinsky (1883–1954) completed a new eighty-eight-page indictment of the patriarch and his co-defendants.[73] In composing it, Vyshinsky honed his skills in fabricating conspiracy theories, selectively choosing and distorting facts to fit a predetermined narrative, that he would deploy later in the famous show trials of the 1930s. The team assembled to prosecute Patriarch Tikhon—Agranov, Krylenko, and Vyshinsky—would all play leading roles in the key cases at the height of Stalin's Terror in the 1930s (which also claimed the lives of the first two).

The indictment composed by Vyshinsky "demonstrated" the patriarch's guilt, first of all, by painting a picture of a vast and intricate conspiracy that tied together the entire Orthodox Church in Soviet Russia, from the patriarch down to the parish, the Russian Orthodox Church among the Whites during the Civil War and in the emigration after, the White generals, and foreign powers, all aiming in concert to overthrow the "worker-peasant government" to reestablish monarchy and the bourgeoisie. Tikhon's every attempt to defend the Orthodox Church from Soviet assaults was interpreted as the Church seizing opportunities to undermine the Soviet regime, to use religion to turn people against the Soviets.

The patriarch's appeal to believers to defend their churches in the revolutionary turmoil of 1918 was interpreted as a call "for rebellion and murder" (even though such appeals explicitly instructed believers not to resist with force or weapons).[74] Tikhon's correspondence with churchmen abroad about ecclesiastical matters was evidence of "criminal exchanges." The patriarch's instructions to remove extraneous objects from reliquaries to avoid scandal amounted to "concealing traces of a crime." The political pronouncements of the Church Abroad figured prominently, especially since it claimed to be acting in obedience to and with the blessing of Tikhon. The indictment further asserted that Tikhon "maintained contact" with White Generals and assisted them against the Soviet government through his influence on the masses and blessing their activities.[75] None of these claims were supported by any concrete evidence or substantiated in even the most circumstantial way during the investigation. All the same, the indictment became the foundation for how later Soviet authors interpreted the early history of the relationship between the Orthodox Church and the Bolshevik Revolution, and even John Shelton Curtiss granted it credibility.[76]

Foreign and Domestic Reaction

The Soviet Union's Foreign Affairs Commissariat and representatives abroad were growing increasingly nervous about Tikhon's case in the wake of the international backlash against Budkiewicz's execution. Even British leftists were critical of the Soviet persecution of religious figures, and Leonid Krasin (1870–1926), the Soviet representative in London, asked for propaganda materials.[77] The *New York Times* and other major international newspapers reported routinely on Patriarch Tikhon's impending trial in ways that were not sympathetic to the Soviet Union.[78] Soviet foreign representatives stated that the clergy trials and executions were undermining the position of those in Europe who sought to establish friendlier ties with the Soviet Union and were threatening a rupture in relations between Britain and Soviet Russia.[79]

Because of the negative international coverage, Georgy Chicherin, the Commissar of Foreign Affairs, wrote a lengthy memo to the Politburo on April 10, 1923. He proposed that the Politburo preemptively exclude the death penalty for Tikhon because of the enormous harm done by the execution of Budkiewicz. Efforts of groups in Britain and the United States who sought to normalize relations with the Soviet Union were put on hold after that execution. "In every respect our position has gotten much worse as a result of this affair." Aware of the weakness of the case against Tikhon, Chicherin wrote that "every other country will see in such a verdict nothing other than naked religious persecution." The Anglo-Saxon world was interested in Orthodoxy and would be paying particular attention to Tikhon's case. "In a word, pronouncing a death sentence in the case of Tikhon will worsen far more our international position in every respect." And to pass a death sentence, Chicherin concluded, but not carry it out because of international pressure, would be extremely disadvantageous; it was much better just to take the death penalty off the table before the trial began.[80]

The Politburo rejected Chicherin's proposal. It resolved instead to intensify the propaganda campaign, both within Russia and internationally, using all available materials in the campaign, making claims that were even more absurdly grandiose, such as that "Tikhon stood not only at the head of the ecclesiastical counter-revolution, but also the counter-revolution of the aristocratic landowners, i.e. against transferring the land to the peasants"—in an attempt to create a vilified image of the patriarch not even reflected in the investigation.[81] Rather than heeding Chicherin's proposal for measure, the Politburo resolved the opposite in a super-secret decision tasking Stalin with issuing a verbal directive to the Supreme Tribunal to "conduct Tikhon's case with all severity, in accordance with the scale of the colossal faults committed by Tikhon."[82]

Chicherin then sent out instructions to foreign representatives on how to conduct the propaganda campaign against the patriarch. The lengthy memo was filled with a litany of distortions and falsehoods. Chicherin instructed them to assert that the patriarch had been the chairman of the Union of Russian People in Yaroslavl, that he was the "spiritual leader of counter-revolution" who maintained "intimate ties" with foreign interventionists during the Civil War, "rendered support to Denikin and Kolchak in every possible way," was in constant contact with the "counter-revolutionary clergy" abroad and blessed their Council which sought to exploit the famine for a new invasion of Russia. Foreign representatives were to claim that Tikhon used the church apparatus as a counter-revolutionary weapon to prepare for the overthrow of the Soviet government, that he never lost an opportunity in the struggle against it. For example, the exhumation of relics served as a "pretext for Tikhon's furious campaign against the Soviet government."[83] These accusations were repeated almost verbatim in *Russian Information and Review* published by the Russian Trade delegation in London.[84] It is a measure of this propaganda's staying power that Western historians later relied on *Russian Information and Review* as if it were a trustworthy source of information.[85]

Contemporary foreign journalists were more attuned to Soviet propaganda, and skeptical about it, than later historians. Canadian journalist F. A. MacKenzie (1869–1931) noted that the international outrage against the execution of Budkiewicz was cast by the Soviets as an unjust campaign to inflame hatred against them. This, MacKenzie astutely observed, was a familiar practice to those covering the Soviets, which "transfers the blame from the people who do wrong to the papers that report it."[86] Similarly, the propaganda mechanism depicting the patriarch's efforts to defend what was held sacred by millions of believers as a "pretext" for him assaulting the Soviet regime placed the blame on the victims and their defenders.[87]

Representatives of various international religious groups also protested what was perceived as an attack on religion in the person of Patriarch Tikhon. In early April, the chief rabbi in Britain informed the archbishop of Canterbury that he was ready to cooperate with the heads of Christian churches to defend religion in the face of Soviet persecution. On April 13, 1923, Archbishop Randall Davidson, together with the Archbishop of York, a Catholic cardinal, leaders of Congregationalist, Baptist, Presbyterian, Wesleyan, United Methodist churches, and the Chief Rabbi Joseph Hertz (1872–1946), issued a powerfully worded statement against the Soviet assault on religion in general, its mockery of religious holidays and practices, and its persecution of representatives of religion. As one of Davidson's biographers put it, "the effect was electric."[88]

Karl Radek, a leader of the communist international with a penchant for bombastic attacks, published a lengthy, sarcasm-laden response, in which he recounted moments of religious persecution in medieval England, concluded that England therefore had no right to criticize the Soviets for persecuting religion.[89] The practice of deflecting criticism for human rights abuses by labeling the critic a hypocrite or transferring the blame to critic or victim has had a long history in Russia even beyond the Soviet period.

The domestic reaction to the impending trial of the patriarch, especially in Moscow, did not look any better. GPU agents observed that "the main theme of all conversations recently is the trial of Tikhon," whom people regarded with sympathy. Rumors circulated that the trial had been postponed out of fear for disturbances or pogroms; that Tikhon would be sentenced to death but not executed because of the international outcry; and that the trial was artificially staged. "In all public places, bazaars, pubs, and churches, rumors stubbornly spread about possible disorders and the inflamed mood of the workers" that might even lead to demonstrations in factories. The GPU sent two summary reports to the Party leadership on April 17.[90] The news could hardly have been comforting.

Trial Postponed

With the approval of the Politburo, Patriarch Tikhon was transferred from the Donskoi Monastery to the internal GPU prison at Lubianka Square on

April 19, 1923, to await the beginning of the trial.[91] One of his lawyers visited him there and "found the Patriarch in a large bright room furnished like a good room in a hotel." He met with the patriarch alone, but he did not know whether the room was bugged. "The Patriarch was cheerful, good-humored, and did not show any signs of agitation or dispiritedness."[92]

On April 21, in the midst of the XII Party Congress and with the trial set to begin three days later, Dzerzhinsky, the head of the secret police, scratched out a short handwritten note to members of the Politburo which read: "I propose that it is necessary to postpone Tikhon's trial because the agitation abroad (the Budkiewicz case) is at its height and it is necessary to prepare for the trial more thoroughly."[93] The GPU was reading the foreign press as avidly as the Foreign Affairs Commissariat, so Dzerzhinsky was surely aware of all the negative press that Chicherin was receiving—as well, no doubt, of the archbishop of Canterbury's statement the previous week.[94] In the midst of the Party Congress, the Politburo tallied votes directly on Dzerzhinsky's note. Grigory Zinoviev (1883–1936), Lev Kamenev, Mikhail Tomsky (1880–1936), and Kalinin agreed with the proposal; Trotsky and Stalin stated that Dzerzhinsky was "absolutely right." Only Rykov, who chaired the commission to prepare the trial, opposed it.[95] The trial was postponed.

On April 24, the day the trial was set to begin, Fritjof Nansen (1860–1930), the Norwegian explorer, diplomat, and humanitarian who led the international Red Cross famine relief effort in Soviet Russia in 1921, wrote a letter to Trotsky about the impending trial. For Soviet Russia's own interests, he pleaded with Trotsky to "use your personal influence in order to save the life of Patriarch Tikhon." "Public opinion of the entire world... is deeply agitated," and he feared that if the patriarch were shot, then those public organizations working to restore relations with Russia would be "seriously compromised" and it would become impossible to count on public help for the continuation of work they were doing in the interests of Russia. He insisted on his "absolute certainty" that if the patriarch were to be sentenced to death, the consequences would be very harmful, but if the Soviet government could show in this case its "well-known benevolence," it would result in positive consequences for Russia in international relations.[96]

As the Party Congress continued, Yaroslavsky submitted a memorandum to the Party leadership protesting the decision of "members of the Politburo," in the midst of the Congress, to delay Tikhon's trial. Although he could accept some delay in the beginning of the patriarch's trial, he opposed any delay to the Renovationist council, which was supposed follow the patriarch's trial. He proposed that the council not be postponed, and that it should condemn the "counter-revolutionary activity of Tikhon," with the trial following in the second-half of May after more propaganda abroad. At the same time, Yaroslavsky stated that ARK considered an "intense agitation in the countryside" around Tikhon's trial "undesirable." Evidently, he feared that such a campaign against Tikhon would backfire and more likely serve to antagonize the peasantry—overwhelmingly sympathetic to the patriarch—against the Soviet regime.[97]

The Renovationist Council

Although the Politburo ignored Yaroslavsky's proposal regarding the timing of Tikhon's trial, it accepted his recommendation that the Renovationist church council proceed. The council had figured from the beginning as a central part of the Bolshevik plan to undermine Tikhon's authority and destroy the "Tikhonite" church. Although the trial had been planned to precede the council, now the Party leadership came to believe that it would be better to reverse the order—so that they would not be trying the patriarch of the Russian Orthodox Church, but rather just a layman already denounced and defrocked by the Church itself. In the spring of 1923, ARK and the GPU discussed how to ensure that the council resulted in a victory for the Renovationists over the Tikhonites. The GPU was therefore involved in the selection of delegates to ensure that it consisted of those who would advocate the defrocking of Tikhon.[98]

The Council took place between April 29 and May 9.[99] It was attended by 476 delegates, the majority of whom were from the different Renovationist factions. The most important decisions were made on May 3, beginning with an expression of a political ideology that the Church should be united with the Soviet government in the struggle against the evil of capitalist exploitation. It proceeded to judge Patriarch Tikhon in terms that echoed the Supreme Court's indictment. Fr Aleksandr Vvedensky delivered a speech that was in effect Tikhon's ecclesiastical "prosecution." The Renovationist council issued a resolution stating that the patriarch continued the reactionary line of the 1917–1918 Council and led the church into a counter-revolutionary struggle against the Soviet government. The council therefore declared him "an apostate from the authentic commandments of Christ" who had betrayed the Church. "On the basis of the church canons," it concluded, the council defrocked him, stripping him from not only his rank as patriarch and clergyman but even his monasticism, so that he was returned to the status of a layman. "From now on patriarch Tikhon—is the layman Vasily Belavin."[100] No evidence was presented, and the patriarch himself was not present as required according to church canons.

The council went on to declare that the Soviet government did not persecute the Church but rather guaranteed freedom of conscience. It abolished the patriarchate on the grounds that its restoration had been a counter-revolutionary act. Finally, the council made a declaration in support of the Soviet decree of separation of church and state. The council's decision to defrock the patriarch was taken by a conference of bishops which met for that purpose—ostensibly unanimous in their decision, though only fifty-four of the sixty-six bishops of the whole council were present for that vote.[101]

The Renovationist council made other important decisions, such as permitting the consecration of married bishops and allowing the remarriage of priests, both of which were significant departures from traditional Orthodox practice. While not rejecting the veneration of relics altogether, it condemned their "falsification," in effect justifying the Soviet campaign against them. Finally, the council also adopted the Gregorian calendar. All the major decisions followed what ARK had laid out, and the GPU had its fingers in the entire council. It would be wrong to conclude that the participants were merely puppets of the GPU, however—clearly a substantial number of churchmen were willing to participate in the process and collaborate with the government. The Renovationist movement appeared to secure its victory, having removed Patriarch Tikhon and legitimated itself through a church council.

After defrocking Tikhon, the Presidium of the Renovationist Council asked permission to visit and announce their decision to Tikhon who was still in the GPU prison awaiting his trial.[102] On May 8, the secretary of the Judicial Collegium and Tuchkov went with Patriarch Tikhon from Lubianka to the Donskoi Monastery. At 2:40 p.m., a delegation from the Renovationist Council, headed by Metropolitan Petr Blinov (1893–1938), came to the patriarch. Blinov informed Tikhon of the council's decision to defrock him. A member of the delegation read the resolution of the council of bishops. Tikhon wanted to know who refrained from voting in favor of the council's decision. On inspecting the resolution of the council of bishops, he observed that more than half of the bishops were unknown to him—meaning that they had been consecrated by the Renovationists. They asked him to sign the document, and he agreed to sign that he read it, but stated that he did not accept the decision because it was uncanonical, given that they had tried him in absentia, contrary to the canons for ecclesiastical courts. He asked whether someone had even suggested that he be summoned to appear, and when he learned that no one had, he asked: "What sort of canonists are they?"[103]

The remainder of the meeting was taken up with various members of the Renovationist delegation cajoling and threatening the patriarch that he had to take off his clerical clothing since the council had declared him to be a layman. Tikhon flatly refused, no matter how much they pressured him. Asked whether he would still wear his clerical clothing during his Supreme Court trial, he replied that he would—which particularly upset the Renovationists. No doubt they realized this would not serve the Soviet plan of trying the layman Vasily Bellavin rather than the patriarch Tikhon, who would thus be a more formidable foe in the courtroom. When one Renovationist "categorically protested" Tikhon wearing his clerical clothing during the trial, Tikhon responded that he protested their resolution defrocking him. At 3:05 p.m., the delegation left, and Tikhon remained at the Donskoi Monastery.[104] The council's decision had little effect on believers. One contemporary observed that the Renovationist council's decisions appeared to believers as obviously "rigged." "Deposing and defrocking only raised the authority of the Patriarch and sympathy for him.... As before the Donskoi monastery is full of visitors, crowds awaiting the appearance of the Patriarch on the monastery wall and his blessing, as before they bring him offerings, as before he sends notes with blessings and signed Patriarch Tikhon."[105]

Foreign Pressure and the Curzon Ultimatum

The Bolshevik leadership had high hopes for the success of the Renovationist council: They believed it would result in a decisive defeat of the "Tikhonite" church, secure the regime-friendly Renovationist control over the entire ecclesiastical apparatus, and make it so that their own trial of Tikhon would be more palatable, since he had already been condemned by his fellow churchmen. They also naively hoped that it would answer the negative foreign reaction to the clergy trials. As Chicherin wrote to a Soviet representative in Germany, they could use it to claim there was no persecution of religion in the Soviet Union. Rather, it was supposed to demonstrate the "strong movement of church renewal" as well as the Church's own rejection of the position pursued under Tikhon. Chicherin optimistically believed that American correspondents, particularly Walter Duranty (1884–1957), were sending their newspapers "very bright accounts" about the council.[106] Believers in the patriarch's circle worried that the Renovationist council would indeed undermine international support for Tikhon.[107]

Chicherin was, however, jumping the gun. To be sure, the Associated Press's initial reporting was relatively neutral, with a front-page story reporting the council's claims that there was no religious persecution in Soviet Russia, recounting Vvedensky's speech condemning Patriarch Tikhon, and quoting the enthusiastic support of the American Methodist bishop Edgar Blake (1869–1943) for the Renovationists and their council.[108] Subsequent articles, however, were less glowing. One perceptive article observed that moderates had replaced the "imperialist reactionaries" in the Church after the February Revolution, and now the radicals were displacing the moderates—as had happened in the political arena. Despite its problems, "there was a living force in the old Russian Church. It received an immense impetus between the first and second revolutions, and ... it has been strengthened by the subsequent persecutions. It is true that you cannot kill an idea, but sometimes you can attain the same end by killing all the people who hold it."[109] Walter Duranty was also skeptical about the council, which was as convincing to him as mediocre theater. Duranty perceptively stated that the question was whether the "peasant masses" would accept the results of the council, because with them "rests the final verdict" of the church.[110]

Neither the Renovationist council nor Soviet propaganda succeeded in lessening the threat of a rupture in relations with Britain, in particular the Anglo-Soviet Trade Treaty of 1921. In spring of 1923, relations between the Soviet Union and Britain were at a low point. Britain had a whole series of complaints against the Soviet government, from the mistreatment of British subjects to anti-British agitation in Asia. Soviet persecution of religion was one of those issues, and relations were nearly ruptured after an exchange over the arrested Catholic clergy between Robert Hodgson (1874–1956), the British representative in Moscow, and his Soviet counterparts.[111] By mid-April, representatives in the Foreign Office thought a rupture in relations with the Soviet Union was premature and would not be accepted by the Liberal and Labour parties. If, however, the trial of Patriarch Tikhon "ends in the Patriarch's execution, surely the result will be that unanimous explosion of indignation in England which would surely facilitate action on our part" to break relations.[112] Though a rather cynical way to achieve foreign policy ends, the note makes clear how intensely the British population would respond to the patriarch's execution.

Rather than wait for the Soviets to execute Tikhon and then break relations, the British foreign secretary, the Marquess Curzon of Kedleston (1859–1925), decided to forewarn them so that the rupture in relations would be knowingly brought on. He issued an ultimatum to the Soviet government threatening to break off relations if a series of issues were not addressed in a satisfactory way. The "Curzon ultimatum" was discussed in the Cabinet and sent on May 2 and delivered to the Soviet government on May 8, 1923. It recounted the trials and executions beginning in 1922, including that of Metropolitan Veniamin and Budkiewicz, and brought forth the issue of Patriarch Tikhon. Although, Curzon said, the British government refrained from expressing its opinion on the validity of the charges brought against the clergy, he asserted that "no attempt, however, is made in Russia itself to deny that these prosecutions and executions are part of a deliberate campaign undertaken by the Soviet Government, with the definite object of destroying all religion in Russia, and enthroning the image of godlessness in its place. As such they have excited the profound consternation and have provoked the indignant remonstrance of the civilised world."[113] Though of course the Soviet government tried to deny that the trials were part of a broader antireligious campaign, what was really happening was transparent enough. The danger of breaking trade relations between Britain and the Soviet Union was acute.

Publicly, the Soviet response was dismissive and defensive. Leonid Krasin, the Soviet trade delegation representative to Britain, had been in Moscow and rushed back to London to negotiate. By mid-June, the Soviets capitulated on the key issues to avoid a rupture.[114] Although the Soviets did not mention Patriarch Tikhon (at least as reflected in any documents) and made no explicit promises regarding his fate, it must have become abundantly clear to the Bolshevik leadership that his execution would have serious consequences. The central importance of the Curzon ultimatum as it affected Patriarch Tikhon's fate is borne out by how frequently the Soviets tried to find a way to "answer" the British even long after.[115]

Since the Anti-Religious Commission had invested much time in preparing for Tikhon's trial, Yaroslavsky followed up on his unanswered note to the Politburo of April 24. He apparently believed that the Renovationist condemnation of the patriarch put the government in a good place to pursue the trial and proposed that it begin the third week of May. The Politburo resolution on May 10 was one word: "postpone."[116]

Therefore, although the Politburo rejected Chicherin's suggestion to modify the trial of the patriarch on April 12, 1923, because of the international pressure, after the statement issued by the archbishop of Canterbury and other British religious leaders on April 13, the Politburo accepted Dzerzhinsky's proposal for the same reason on April 21. That decision was merely to postpone the trial for more propaganda. But after receiving the Curzon ultimatum on May 8, the Politburo postponed the trial again on May 10—but this time indefinitely, with no discussion of setting a new date. It would not therefore, be unfair to say that Britain saved Patriarch Tikhon's life. This was understood in Orthodox circles in Moscow. Someone in the patriarch's circle commented in early June that if the Soviets come to an agreement with England after the Curzon ultimatum, "then perhaps [the trial] won't happen at all, but if there is a rupture and war, they will most likely shoot the patriarch so as to take out their anger on someone."[117]

A Compromise Solution

It became clear that putting Patriarch Tikhon on trial and executing him would be too explosive and have too many negative consequences at home and abroad. For the next month, Yaroslavsky sought a solution by which the Soviets could save face and perhaps win some benefits.[118] One June 6, Tikhon fell ill and fainted after eating some bad fish. According to Robert Hodgson, this provided a pretext for the GPU to relocate the patriarch from Donskoi Monastery to Lubianka two days later, despite Tikhon's protestations. Hodgson noted that Tikhon, even in his isolation, enjoyed "great popularity" among the people and as he was departing Donskoi, he "was allowed to give his blessing to all persons who were present."[119] Because of his illness, rumors spread in Moscow that Tikhon had died.[120] Once in Lubianka, Tuchkov had "conversations" with the patriarch to see if a compromise could be reached.

These conversations evidently yielded some results, and Yaroslavsky submitted a bold proposal to the Politburo of a compromise with the patriarch on June 11.[121] He proposed that the Tikhon's case be conducted "without a time limit." Further, Tikhon could be released if he were to agree to a set of conditions: make a declaration of loyalty to the Soviet government and "repent" of his "crimes" against it; acknowledge the justness of the case against him; dissociate himself from any sort of counter-revolutionary organization; express a negative relationship to the Karlovci Council; and that

Tikhon agree to some ecclesiastical reforms such as adopting the new calendar. Finally, Yaroslavsky proposed that Tikhon criticize the "machinations" of the pope, the archbishop of Canterbury, and the Ecumenical Patriarch of Constantinople; like the Randall Davidson, both Pope Pius XI (1857–1939) and Patriarch Meletius (Metaxakis, 1871–1935) had interceded for Patriarch Tikhon's release. If Tikhon agreed to those conditions, then they could "release him and transfer him to the Valaam metochion, without prohibiting him from church activities."[122]

Yaroslavsky submitted a second note to the Politburo explaining his motivation for the proposal. He stated that they needed some sort of justification of their deferment of Tikhon's case, or otherwise it would be too evident that they were doing it because they were afraid of the international backlash. From conversations with the patriarch, it became clear that "with some pressure and some promises," he would accept the proposals. If he agreed, his statements would have great political significance because it would confuse the émigrés that had looked up to Tikhon as a figure of opposition to the Soviet government and serve as a blow to organizations that were oriented around him. "His personal influence will be compromised by his connection with the GPU and his confessions; Tikhon's declarations against the bishop of Canterbury, Meletius, Antony [Khrapovitsky], and the pope, will be a slap in the face above all to the English government and deprive England's declaration in defense of Tikhon of any significance in the eyes of European circles." Finally, if Tikhon would agree to some church reforms such as the introduction of the new (Gregorian) calendar, this would make him an innovator in the eyes of Church conservatives. Yaroslavsky concluded that the Renovationist church administration would "retain its former position with a significant decrease in influence."[123] The Politburo confirmed Yaroslavsky's proposal on June 14.[124]

Patriarch Tikhon agreed to Yaroslavsky's conditions. He produced a petition to the Supreme Court on June 16, which stated that he was brought up in a monarchist society and until his arrest was under the influence of anti-Soviet persons, that he "really was hostile to the Soviet government," and that hostility at times went from being passive to an active hostility such as in his appeal concerning the Brest peace treaty, the "anathematization of the government," and finally his encyclical against the decree on the confiscation of church valuables. "All my anti-Soviet actions, with a few inaccuracies, are set out in the indictment from the Supreme Court. Recognizing the correctness of the decision of the court to bring me to justice under the articles of the

Criminal Code on anti-Soviet activities indicated in the indictment, I repent of these offenses against the government order and ask the Supreme Court to change the form of my detention, that is, to release me from custody. At the same time, I declare to the Supreme Court that I am no longer an enemy of the Soviet government." The petition ended with the statement that he definitively dissociated himself from both foreign and domestic monarchist counter-revolutionary organizations. The petition was signed: "Patriarch Tikhon (Vasily Bellavin)." The text was written in his own hand.[125]

In this first declaration, Patriarch Tikhon more-or-less met several of the conditions in Yaroslavsky's ultimatum. The patriarch "repented"—though repented not of "crimes" (*prestupleniia*) but of "misdeeds" (*prostupki*) against the government (which certainly carry different legal weight). He expressed not his "loyalty" to the Soviet government, but rather that he was not its enemy, and disassociated himself from counter-revolutionary organizations. The latter two points were in fact nothing new. Up until his arrest in 1922, however, he had always maintained the right to criticize the Soviet government for its treatment of the Church while at the same time declaring that he was not calling for the government's overthrow. Therefore, his admission of "anti-Soviet actions," and labeling his earlier statements as such, was a significant shift—especially accepting, "with a few inaccuracies," the absurd indictment concocted against him.[126]

In addition to his petition to the Supreme Court, Patriarch Tikhon submitted a draft of his address to believers that would be issued after his release. The two texts were considered by ARK on June 19, which sent his Supreme Court petition to all the members of the Politburo to familiarize themselves with it. The second text needed some corrections, and they demanded a third text as well. With all that, ARK considered that it could release the patriarch.[127] That day, Yaroslavsky sent two messages to the Politburo, asking that it decide on Tikhon's case and submitting a draft Politburo directive to the Supreme Court on Tikhon's release, though without ending the investigation against him.[128]

In a top-secret meeting on June 21, the Politburo approved of ARK's proposal to release the patriarch, directing that Tikhon's trial should not be carried out yet.[129] At its next session on June 26, ARK resolved to release Tikhon the following day and to publish the patriarch's petition and encyclical in the papers and distribute them as separate leaflets. The GPU was instructed to close the cases connected with the confiscation of church valuables, and those "Tikhonites" who express their own "repentance" publicly were also to be freed from punishment. Repression should be continued against those churchmen who refused to repent for their crimes the way Tikhon did. Finally, in the next three months the GPU should reexamine all the cases of those churchmen sent into administrative exile and amnesty those who were "less harmful."[130] As far as ARK was concerned, Patriarch Tikhon's compromise not only brought about his own release, but also signaled a profound shift in policy toward the Orthodox Church in general and opened the way for ending repression on a broader scale.

Yaroslavsky, in his proposal to the Politburo, mentioned that "with pressure and some promises" the patriarch would accept their "proposals."[131] We know something of the pressure from Tuchkov's report to GPU deputy-director Viacheslav Menzhinsky (1874–1934). Tuchkov stated that "the entire white emigration and in general the whole black-hundred [i.e., capitalist] world writes and speaks about him with one voice," that Tikhon was standing firm for the faith of Christ and, they believed, would never come to terms with the Bolsheviks and was enduring all sorts of torments. Therefore, the GPU sought a way to destroy his reputation and authority. "Before us stood the task of working over Tikhon, so that he not only apologized to the Soviet government but also repented of his crimes" in such a way that made fools of the monarchists. "It is true, it must be said, that here the work with Tikhon was extremely great, he perfectly understood that the business would not be limited to the repentance alone, but that after that it would be necessary to obey and follow the instructions of the GPU, which weighed on him most of all, but thanks to the situation and conditions where he was kept under guard, and also the correct approach made to him, we managed to convince Tikhon to write a repentance in his own hand."[132] Tuchkov further noted that he had "deliberately left out [of the report] the details of the methods of our work" on Tikhon but only discussed the results, because these methods were "familiar" to Menzhinsky and because "they are so diverse that to describe them would require writing an entire book."[133]

Not having the knowledge of the deputy director of the GPU, we are left guessing what those "methods" were. But it is clear from Tuchkov's report that he expended great efforts "working over" Patriarch Tikhon with a vast array of methods to pressure him to issue the petition to the Supreme Court. Even after all that, the patriarch did not completely follow their dictates, changing the wording in crucial places. Moreover, as Yaroslavsky noted, it took not only "pressure" to get Tikhon to agree but also "promises"—in other words, the Soviets had to make concessions as well. They did not simply release Tikhon; they also gave him what mattered most: the ability to resume his leadership of the Church. Tikhon's petition was not dictated to him that he was forced to sign, as some believed; Tuchkov noted that Tikhon himself wrote it, and ultimately it was the result of a compromise for both sides.

Conciliation Under "Religious NEP"

Why the Bolshevik Party leadership decided against prosecuting and executing the patriarch, as originally planned, and why Tikhon agreed to issue statements "repenting" of his former "anti-Soviet" stance are major questions in Patriarch Tikhon's biography.

Multiple factors were at play on the Soviet side.[134] A key factor were the changes in Party leadership: Lenin and Trotsky were primarily responsible for the assault on the Church in spring 1922. After Lenin's first stroke in May 1922, a power struggle began behind the scenes, and he was completely incapacitated after his third stroke in March 1923. By that point, Trotsky had also been marginalized from religious policy with the creation of the Anti-Religious Commission. Although the changes in leadership did not immediately result in a change in course, after Lenin and Trotsky were no longer directing religious policy, a different direction became possible; within two months of Lenin's final stroke, the Politburo abandoned the effort to put Tikhon on trial. Since the confiscation campaign was associated with Trotsky, shifting to a more tolerant policy could potentially benefit Stalin and Kamenev. The GPU and Soviet leadership were also aware of how much opposition to the patriarch's trial there was not only among the peasantry but even in Moscow among the workers, which also could have caused them to pause. However, it was the international pressure—and ultimately the Curzon ultimatum and the threat of severing trade ties with Britain—that proved decisive. The patriarch's fate continued to concern the British—all the way up to King George himself—until his release.[135] Robert Hodgson understood this clearly; as he wrote to Curzon after Tikhon's release, "the liberation of the Patriarch may, in my belief, be justly attributed to the British memorandum which has induced a very salutary change in the attitude of the Soviet Government towards the religious question."[136]

The Party leadership did not, however, merely drop the case against the patriarch, release and, say, exile him as they had done with the intellectuals on the "philosophers' steamship" the year before. They made an even greater compromise by allowing him to return to ecclesiastical leadership. Earlier policy had been aimed at eliminating the patriarch and destroying the "Tikhonite" Church; allowing him to serve as patriarch and strengthen his support was therefore a radical shift in policy.

If the motivation is clear for why the Soviets released the patriarch, the second key question is why Patriarch Tikhon agreed to the conditions that the Party demanded of him in exchange for his release. Why, when he had denied the charge of being anti-Soviet for so long, did he change his position?[137]

Initially some of those closest to the patriarch were devastated on reading his "confession," which they viewed as "terrible" because the patriarch admitted validity to absurd and unsubstantiated charges against him. No matter the motivation, it was hard for them to imagine that any good for the Church could come from it. "In the beginning we didn't know what to do, and we felt only cold and hopeless grief. It seemed that after such statements everyone would turn away from the patriarch, and the void that would form around him would be filled by the Soviet Church. But in reality, the opposite happened." Tikhon explained that he decided to accept this humiliation in order to receive his liberation to battle against the Renovationists who had by that point taken control of all the dioceses and almost all the parishes because he feared that the reforming of the Church would eventually lead to the "complete separation of the Russian Church from the Eastern" Orthodox communion.[138] There was no other person around whom the Church could unify, and the threat of it fragmenting was real. Therefore, he sacrificed the purity of his uncompromising image. As he said to those who were scandalized by his compromise: "Let my name perish in history, if only it would benefit the Church." He also said that though he would "gladly accept a martyr's death," he was responsible for the fate of the Church.[139]

By contrast with those who were initially troubled by Tikhon's "confession," ordinary believers "greeted the Patriarch with enthusiasm beyond description" that did not diminish even months later. "In Russia in general it is impossible to live without compromises," and therefore ordinary believers accepted Tikhon's "confession" as a necessary compromise to save the Church and therefore did not regard his words as having any great significance.[140]

Hodgson, who had played such an important role informing Curzon of all the developments in Moscow surrounding the patriarch and the Church, understood all this clearly. As he wrote to Curzon, the patriarch's appeal to the Supreme Court

> shocked those Russians who expected of the Patriarch marvels of spiritual fortitude; they deny the authenticity of the document or maintain that it was signed under duress. So far I have no ground for believing the appeal was signed otherwise than voluntarily; nor would it be, I think, surprising if Tikhon after his long period of confinement and complete seclusion from the outside world should have put his signature to a statement of which the terms can hardly satisfy his more exacting sympathisers. Yet it is quite possible that his action was inspired in reality by the desire to save the Orthodox Church—that he saw in subscribing to a document, the contents of which could not but be profoundly distasteful to him, the only means of preserving the Church organization from disruption.[141]

The contents of Hodgson's communication were also passed on to the Archbishop of Canterbury, who thus understood the significance of the patriarch's "confession."[142]

From the distance and safety of their exile, many Russian émigrés were scandalized by the patriarch's Supreme Court petition and believed that it must have been a forgery or that he was coerced. Metropolitan Antony (Khrapovitsky), however, wrote an insightful article in response entitled "Do Not Be Disconcerted." He pointed out that Patriarch Tikhon, by acknowledging he was not an enemy of the Soviet government, had not actually said anything new. Antony cited the same scriptural passage Tikhon would later quote in his "deathbed testament," namely Romans 13:1 ("there is no authority except from God"). Tikhon's petition, according to Antony, would save the Orthodox Church from the Renovationists and lead to the release of clergy from prison. Some may criticize the patriarch for not taking an uncompromising stand against the atheist government and courageously suffering martyrdom for it—but that would have condemned other clergy and believers to martyrdom as well. Christians living in the pagan Roman Empire did not fight against the state but were obedient citizens, only becoming martyrs if the state tried to force them to renounce Christ. In reconciling himself externally with the Soviet government, Patriarch Tikhon, "from a purely ecclesiastical point of view, did not commit an offense either

260 THE PEOPLE'S PATRIARCH

against the faith or against the people." Antony concluded by stating that after the patriarch's petition to the Supreme Court, it would be easier for the Church and believers to live in Russia than it had been in previous years.[143]

On June 27, 1923, Patriarch Tikhon was released from the inner GPU prison. Now more or less a free man, he returned to the same rooms of the Donskoi Monastery he had occupied during his house arrest.

9

Interlude

Transnational Orthodoxy (1917–1925)

Under normal circumstances, Patriarch Tikhon, as head of the largest Orthodox Church in the world, would have been a leading figure of world Orthodoxy. In the conditions of Revolutionary Russia, the difficulties of communicating with the outside world made that virtually impossible. Indeed, it was dangerous for the patriarch to correspond with foreign churchmen, and such correspondence became fodder for Soviet accusations against him.[1] This situation complicated Tikhon's leadership of the Orthodox Church of the Russian Empire as parts of his Church ended up in newly independent countries. Tikhon nevertheless corresponded with the heads of other autocephalous churches as well as he was able. As he wrote to Patriarch Dimitry of Serbia, he considered the unity of different Orthodox Churches necessary because only through their mutual support and communication could they find strength to oppose disbelief, atheism, and other ideas harmful to the Church.[2] Unfortunately, however, Tikhon did not receive consistent support from the leading Church of the Orthodox world, the Ecumenical Patriarchate of Constantinople.

Relations with the Ecumenical Patriarchate

Just as the Russian Church was persecuted by the Soviet state, so the Ecumenical Patriarchate was under enormous pressure from the newly established secular Turkish state. The representative of Patriarch Germanus V of Constantinople in Moscow formally congratulated Tikhon at his enthronement as patriarch. In April 1918, Tikhon sent a communication to Patriarch Germanus (1835–1920) as well as other patriarchs and heads of autocephalous Orthodox Churches informing them of the 1917 Church Council, the restoration of the patriarchate, and his election. Tikhon presented the restoration of the patriarchate in Russia precisely as that—its restoration on the same canonical basis as affirmed by the patriarchate of Constantinople on its foundation—and not a new establishment in need of confirmation. Given World War I and both global and domestic challenges for all Orthodox Churches, Tikhon expressed his hope that a "new time is coming for strengthening, expanding, and building up a close, living and vital intercommunication" of the Russian Church with the Church of Constantinople, which held a primacy of honor among autocephalous Orthodox Churches.[3] Patriarch Germanus V, as well as the patriarchs of Antioch and Alexandria, replied to Tikhon's communication and congratulated him on becoming patriarch.[4]

In May 1918, Tikhon sent another letter to Patriarch Germanus recounting how the Soviet government had begun assaulting the Church and how believers were standing up in its defense.[5] After Germanus was forced to resign in October, the patriarchal throne was vacant during the Greek-Turkish wars that followed World War I until the election of the controversial Meletius (Metaxakis) at the end of 1921. Meletius held that position until fall 1923 when the Greeks were defeated, the allied occupation of Constantinople ended, and the Republic of Turkey was established. In 1923, there was a population exchange in which over a million Orthodox Christians left Turkey for Greece, leaving a very diminished Orthodox community in Turkey.[6] Precisely when his patriarchate was losing its historic role, Patriarch Meletius sought to expand its global reach by claiming that all Orthodox Christians outside historic Orthodox homelands should be under his jurisdiction.

After Patriarch Tikhon's arrest and the beginning of the Renovationist schism, the representative of the Ecumenical Patriarchate in Moscow, Archimandrite Iakov (Dimopoulos, 1855–1924), attended the Renovationist congress in August 1922 and expressed the possibility of the patriarch coming to Russia (for a price) to help resolve the schism to their benefit. In April 1924, however, in response to an appeal from the Church Abroad, Patriarch Meletius declared that he would not send a delegation to the upcoming Renovationist council and that he looked upon Tikhon as the Church's legitimate head. Meletius convened a Pan-Orthodox Congress in Constantinople in May–June 1923, just after the Renovationist council in Moscow had defrocked Tikhon. The Congress considered similar issues as the Renovationists, including adopting the new calendar and questions regarding the marriage of clergy. The participants in the Constantinople Congress included archbishops from the Church Abroad residing in

Constantinople, Anastasy (Gribanovsky) and Alexander (Nemolovsky, 1876-1960), who supported Tikhon. On June 6, 1923, Patriarch Meletius issued a strongly worded defense of Tikhon that had broad international resonance. It declared that Tikhon was undergoing martyrdom with the unjust treatment he received at the Renovationist council, and also appealed to the entire Christian world to press for Tikhon's release, proposing that all the Orthodox Churches consult about ways to help Russian Orthodox believers who were being tested in their faith.[7] A month later, however, Patriarch Meletius acted against the interests of the Moscow patriarchate by bringing the Finnish and Estonian Churches under Constantinople's jurisdiction.

The situation changed under Patriarch Gregory VII (1850-1924), who was patriarch from December 1923 until his death in November 1924. The new representative of the Ecumenical Patriarch in Moscow, Basil (Dimopoulos, 1867-1934), extended the policies of his predecessor (and uncle) of currying favor with the Renovationists and the Soviet government. In May 1924, responding to an appeal from the Renovationists (which likely misrepresented the ecclesiastical position in Russia) to intervene, the Holy Synod in Constantinople resolved to send a commission of bishops to Russia to resolve the schism. Patriarch Gregory VII called on Patriarch Tikhon to abdicate voluntarily, to sacrifice himself for the sake of unity and agree to the temporary abolition of the patriarchate.[8] Patriarch Tikhon wrote a sharp letter to Gregory, declaring that he was the legitimate head of the Russian Church and that Gregory should have contacted him first before making such declarations. Moreover, though the Ecumenical Patriarch enjoyed the primacy of honor in the Orthodox world, he had no right to interfere in the internal affairs of the Russian Church, which would not bring peace and unity, but only serve those causing schism. "The people are not with the schismatics, but only with their legitimate and Orthodox patriarch," Tikhon stated, and moreover a conference of bishops asked him to resume his leadership of the Church—in other words, both the bishops and the faithful affirmed his legitimacy.[9]

Perhaps as a consequence of Tikhon's letter, no commission from Constantinople was ever sent to Russia. At the same time, the episode effectively ended communication between the two patriarchs. Basil (Dimopoulos) continued to cultivate relations with the Renovationists, which the latter utilized for their propaganda purposes. Supported by the Soviet press, the Renovationists claimed that the patriarch of Constantinople recognized their church administration rather than Tikhon as the legitimate head of the Russian Church. Although many scholars have taken this claim as true, in fact Constantinople never took that position.[10] When questioned by Archbishop of Canterbury Randall Davidson why he supported the Renovationists, Gregory replied that he did not, that he recognized Tikhon as head of the Russian Church, and the commission he had planned to send to Moscow was intended to seek Tikhon's views on the ecclesiastical situation.[11]

In practice, the actions of the patriarchate of Constantinople and especially its representatives in Moscow were highly ambiguous, communicating as much or more with the Renovationists as with Tikhon. They hoped at least in part to use the Soviet government as leverage with the Turkish government.[12] Some of the other eastern patriarchs were more categorical. In the summer of 1924, a special commission of twelve representatives from different Orthodox patriarchates traveled throughout Soviet Russia and Ukraine, visiting various churches. They declared unequivocally that Tikhon was the legitimate head of the Russian Church and that he was a "passion-bearer in persecution for the faith of Christ," while the Renovationists were heretics.[13] All the same, patterns of mutual suspicion that emerged during these fraught historical circumstances between Moscow and Constantinople have lasted to our day.

The Autocephaly Question

All the Orthodox churches in the Russian Empire had been under the Holy Synod in St. Petersburg, regardless of ethnicity or history. The Russian Orthodox Church also had a global reach beyond the bounds of the empire that included dioceses in North America and Japan. The Russian Church, like the patriarchate of Constantinople in the Byzantine (or later Ottoman) Empire, had a universalist or imperial orientation that transcended ethnic differences. In the nineteenth century, as Orthodox communities in the Ottoman Empire established independent states, they also established independent or autocephalous national churches (Greek, Serbian, Romanian, Bulgarian). Paradoxically, both the Russian Church and the patriarchate of Constantinople continued to assert their universalist authority while at the same time becoming more "nationalized" themselves, imposing Greek or Russian hierarchy, language, and customs on Orthodox Christians of other nationalities.

The Russian Empire, and with it the Russian Orthodox Church, stretched into many territories that became independent nations after the empire's collapse: Lithuania, Latvia, Estonia, Finland, Poland, and initially Ukraine and Georgia. Ukraine and Georgia were Orthodox-majority countries, but ethnically distinct from Russia; in the others, Orthodox Christians were a minority. New governments wanted to establish their independence from Russia, which also entailed pressuring the Orthodox Church on their territories to sever its ties with Moscow. Some non-Russian Orthodox activists themselves wanted a greater role in leadership and for national expressions of their faith in areas such as liturgical language. The hierarchy consisted mostly of ethnic Russians bishops who resisted these changes and sought to maintain close ties with Moscow. Tikhon's efforts to steer a path between canonicity and responsiveness to local concerns are emblematic of his other attempts to find a golden mean.[14]

Georgia

The Georgian case was a special one, since the Georgian Orthodox Church was ancient and had been autocephalous with its own catholicos (patriarch) for centuries. When Georgia was incorporated into the Russian Empire, the Russian government stripped the Georgian Orthodox Church of its autocephaly and eliminated the office of catholicos, subordinating the Church to the Holy Synod in St. Petersburg in 1811. The Russian ecclesiastical authorities gradually "Russified" the Georgian Church. All but one of the bishops who headed the exarchate were Russians unfamiliar with the Georgian language. Russian began to replace Georgian in the ecclesiastical administration and the Tblisi seminary. This Russification led to a Georgian reaction and demands for the restoration of Georgian autocephaly after the 1905 Revolution. The Georgian case was unusual by comparison with other cases of autocephaly (such as the Balkans) because the Church sought autocephaly even though Georgia was not an independent state.[15] In May 1908, the Russian exarch in Georgia, Archbishop Nikon (Sofiisky, 1861–1906), was murdered by Georgian nationalists. This tragedy touched Tikhon personally: Nikon was his roommate at the Academy, and Tikhon heard rumors that he might be sent to replace Nikon.[16]

After the monarchy fell in 1917, a Georgian Church Council declared the restoration of their autocephaly, which the Council of the Russian Church judged harshly as illegitimate; the Council's decision shaped Tikhon's response to the Georgian bishops on December 29, 1917.[17] He asserted that the question could only be canonically resolved at the Council and that it was in the competence of the Mother Church to grant autocephaly, as Constantinople had done for Greece, Romania, and Serbia, and not for the church seeking autocephaly to declare it unilaterally.[18] Initially, the Georgians expressed to Patriarch Tikhon their desire to reconcile with the Russian Church (while denying that they were the source of the problem). Later, Georgian Catholicos Leonid (1861–1921) argued to Tikhon that it was not Georgian autocephaly that was uncanonical, but rather the Russian government's act of stripping it of autocephaly a century earlier. No resolution was found, and communion between the churches was broken for decades.[19]

Ukraine

During the centuries in which Ukraine was part of Poland and the Polish-Lithuanian Commonwealth, the Orthodox Church was a metropolia—meaning that the metropolitan of Kiev had authority over all Ukrainian dioceses—under the patriarchate of Constantinople. After Left Bank (eastern) Ukraine was annexed by the Russian Empire in the seventeenth century, the metropolitan of Kiev was subordinated to the Moscow patriarchate (in 1686), and his status was reduced to that of an ordinary diocesan bishop; all the other dioceses in Ukraine were subordinated directly to Moscow (and later the Holy Synod in St. Petersburg). There was a process of Russification of the Church, and in the early twentieth century virtually all the bishops in Ukraine were Russians who had little understanding of or sympathy for Ukrainian national aspirations.[20]

Several currents emerged in Ukraine in 1917. Some advocated complete separation from the Russian Church; Russian bishops in Ukraine opposed all "separatism" as a threat to Orthodoxy; many rank-and-file clergy and believers favored a gradual Ukrainization of services and traditions, together with ecclesiastical autonomy, but not complete separation from the Moscow patriarchate. On November 23, 1917—two days after Tikhon's enthronement as patriarch—the Ukrainophiles formed the All-Ukrainian Orthodox Ecclesiastical Rada (Council) and declared it the highest authority of the Orthodox Church in Ukraine, with the intent to summon a

Ukrainian Church Council (*Sobor*).²¹ The issue of Ukraine had factored into the debates on the restoration of the patriarchate, namely whether it would serve as a unifying factor or the opposite.²² Tikhon gave his blessing to a delegation from the Rada to summon a Council in Ukraine. The higher ecclesiastical authorities in Russia, he said, were eager to support conditions for the flourishing of religious life and "would never go against the just demands of the Orthodox inhabitants of Ukraine."²³ In December, he stated that it would be appropriate to grant the Church in Ukraine broad autonomy, though not complete autocephaly, thus preserving its canonical dependence on the Moscow patriarchate.²⁴

The Ukrainian Council opened in January 1918, but the first sitting was short-lived before the Bolsheviks briefly seized control of Kiev in February. Ukraine was ruled for most of 1918 by the conservative Hetmanate under Pavlo Skoropadsky (1873–1945), who advocated autonomy for the Ukrainian Church. In May, a congress of Kiev clergy and laity elected Antony (Khrapovitsky), a known opponent of the Ukrainization of the Church, as their metropolitan. The Skoropadsky government requested that Patriarch Tikhon not confirm the election on the grounds that, for an autonomous Ukrainian Church, the metropolitan should be elected by the Council of the whole Ukrainian Church, not a diocesan congress. Tikhon responded that there was no reason to delay the confirmation of "such a worthy and highly authoritative hierarch."²⁵ He was unlikely to go against the congress's election (similar to his own in the Moscow diocese) or to deny confirmation for Antony, who, after all, had received more votes than he for the patriarchate.

By excluding members of the Ecclesiastical Rada, opponents of autocephaly dominated the second sitting of the Ukrainian Council in June–July 1918. The Ukrainian government was not entirely happy with its draft statute for an autonomous Ukrainian Church that preserved its subordination to the Moscow patriarchate and asked Tikhon not to confirm certain points of it. But Tikhon replied that for him not to confirm it would constitute an improper assertion of patriarchal authority over that of the Council and thus undermine its authority.²⁶ The statute stated that the Ukrainian dioceses formed a special region of the all-Russian Church with privileges of autonomy that extended over all local ecclesiastical affairs. The Ukrainian Church would exist in parallel with the Russian Church, each functionally autonomous with their own Holy Synod, tied together through their subordination to the patriarch. The Church Council in Moscow, however, modified the statute to limit the Ukrainian Church's autonomy.²⁷ The third sitting of the Ukrainian Council (October–December 1918) rejected not only autocephaly but also Ukrainization.[28]

After Ukraine's new government (the Directorate) arrested Antony (Khrapovitsky), Bishop Nazary (Blinov, 1852–1930), one of the vicar bishops, assumed the administration of the Kiev diocese (1919–1921). After the Bolsheviks took power in Kiev in February 1919, pro-Ukrainian clergy took advantage of the Bolshevik law that placed individual parishes in the hands of the laity to assume control of three parishes in Kiev and use the Ukrainian language in services without the bishop's permission, who in turn suspended them. Archbishop Parfeny (Levitsky, 1858–1922), appointed by Tikhon to administer the Poltava diocese in March 1920, was one of the few Ukrainians among the bishops in Ukraine. Hoping to retain the pro-Ukrainian priests within the canonical Church, he allowed them to serve in Ukrainian and ordained several priests for them, including priests who served in other dioceses, which led to conflict with his fellow bishops.[29]

Tikhon did not receive Parfeny's letter in which he justified his actions by saying that he was trying to prevent schism, but only knew of what was happening from Nazary's hostile report. Tikhon therefore reminded Parfeny in September 1920 that, according to the Church's canons, he had no right to oversee clergy in another diocese.[30] In December, Parfeny asserted that there was nothing uncanonical in what the pro-Ukrainian priests were doing and they were even generating religious enthusiasm. Moreover, he explained that the Russian bishops had flip-flopped between allowing them to serve in Ukrainian and then forbidding them, giving them parishes and then taking them away, and in general alienating the pro-Ukrainian priests. While pleading with the patriarch for a sympathetic bishop to oversee the Ukrainian movement, Parfeny obeyed the patriarch's instructions nonetheless.[31]

By the end of 1920, Patriarch Tikhon approved a degree of Ukrainization of the liturgy. But he was skeptical of the leaders of the pro-Ukrainian movement, as their insistence on autocephaly was frequently combined with negative comments about the authority of the patriarch and about episcopal authority altogether. They still needed some episcopal oversight for legitimacy and therefore sought approval from the liberal Bishop Antonin (Granovsky), a Ukrainian sympathizer who was living in retirement in Moscow and who later became a leader of the Renovationist movement. At that time, however, Antonin consulted with the patriarch, and both saw the contradiction of the autocephalist position in disparaging episcopal authority while seeking its approval. He warned Antonin that they wanted to use him only to provide a stamp of legitimacy. Tikhon perceived the autocephalists to be a minority group of radicals lacking widespread support and rejected autocephaly on the grounds that Ukraine was not politically independent.[32]

In February 1921, a Synod of bishops in Kiev granted permission for serving liturgy in Church Slavonic with Ukrainian pronunciation as well as reading the Gospel and the sermon in Ukrainian. It also authorized a special commission to translate liturgical books and the Bible into Ukrainian. In May the Synod permitted serving liturgy in Ukrainian language so long as two-thirds of the parishioners were in favor. Patriarch Tikhon blessed all of these initiatives as "in agreement with the spirit" of Orthodoxy: "Before the Lord all are equal, and the name of God is glorified in all languages of the world."[33] At the same time, the Synod defrocked two of the autocephalist leaders.[34] In response, the autocephalists held meetings in March and May 1921, proposing radical reforms and choosing their own episcopal candidates—but, as there were no bishops among their supporters, they could not consecrate them.[35]

For Patriarch Tikhon, guiding the Church in Ukraine was a problem not only because communication was so difficult during the Civil War, but also because the metropolitan's see was empty and the vicar bishops bore less authority. It was not in Tikhon's power to replace Antony (Khrapovitsky), who still bore the title of Metropolitan of Kiev. The statute of the Ukrainian Church stipulated that a Ukrainian Church Council must appoint the metropolitan of Kiev (with only Tikhon's approval to follow), yet under the Bolsheviks no such council could be summoned. In the summer of 1921, a council of Kiev bishops appealed to Tikhon to send them an authoritative senior bishop to establish order in the diocese. When Tikhon appointed Mikhail (Ermakov, 1862–1929) as his exarch to Ukraine (who retained the title of metropolitan of his diocese of Grodno), he also sent an encyclical to the Ukrainian flock in which he censured those who convened meetings without their bishops' approval and adopted uncanonical resolutions. He also urged the flock to preserve unity and peace in the Church and to receive Metropolitan Mikhail in that spirit.[36] Mikhail unsuccessfully attempted to dialogue with the autocephalists, and his request to Soviet authorities for permission to convene a Church Council to address the concerns of all sides in conciliar fashion was denied.[37]

In October, however, government authorities allowed the autocephalist movement's leaders to hold an "all-Ukrainian Council." Declaring the

Ukrainian Church autocephalous, the council took the radical step of having all council participants—without a single bishop, contrary to Orthodox canon law—lay hands on the priest Vasyl Lipkivsky (1864–1937) and consecrate him as metropolitan of Kiev and all Ukraine. The autocephalists had previously made arguments about the mutability of Orthodox canons, and the council also passed other noncanonical resolutions such as consecrating married men to the episcopate. About one-third of the participants, including half the priests, protested these decisions and left the council. At this moment, the Ukrainian Autocephalous Orthodox Church was born, but one that would not be recognized as canonical by any other Orthodox Church.[38]

Patriarch Tikhon rejected this council in no uncertain terms. He regarded the autocephalist leaders as schismatics who scorned the age-old canonical regulations of the Orthodox Church, and their efforts as dividing—and therefore weakening—the Church.[39] The Soviet authorities had given them tacit support for precisely that reason. After the Renovationist schism, Orthodoxy in Ukraine was deeply fragmented between the patriarchal exarchate, the Autocephalous Church, and the Renovationists who, despite their similarities with the Ukrainian Autocephalous Church, refused to recognize them.[40]

Belarus

In Belarus the situation was very different. After the collapse of the Russian Empire, the short-lived Belarusian People's Republic was declared (in March 1918). After the Riga Peace Treaty in March 1921 ending the Soviet-Polish War, the territory of Belarus was carved up by other states, especially Poland and Soviet Russia. The government of the Belarusian People's Republic in exile petitioned Patriarch Tikhon already in January 1921, outlining Belarusian history and culture in detail. The politicians argued that, since the Belarusian people were divided among different states, the only way to ensure their survival was through language. They accordingly beseeched Tikhon to support the use of the Belarusian language in Church. Patriarch Tikhon considered the issue important enough to bring it before the Holy Synod and Higher Church Council. Because the patriarch's chancellery was subsequently sealed off by the Cheka, he was unable to complete the task for a year. He replied on February 14, 1922, even though he was facing the brewing conflict over church valuables at that moment. Although clergy had not been permitted to use the Belarusian language before 1917, even for sermons, Patriarch Tikhon resolved that, when desired by the majority of parishioners, the Belarusian language could be used for services (aside from Divine Liturgy), sermons, catechism, and the like. Moreover, he encouraged bishops to publish the New Testament, prayers, and other religious literature in Belarusian. Finally, he indicated that in the future he would name Belarusian candidates to the episcopate in Belarusian dioceses when possible.[41]

After Patriarch Tikhon's arrest in 1922, a Minsk diocesan council declared the Belarusian Church an autonomous metropolitanate based on the patriarch's decree in November 1920. After Tikhon's release, the metropolitan of Minsk, Melkhisedek (Paevsky, 1879–1931), submitted a report to the patriarch about the Belarusian situation. In December 1923, Patriarch Tikhon with the Synod considered Melkhisedek's request to confirm the autonomy of the Belarusian metropolitanate; Tikhon did not reject its ecclesiastical autonomy but delayed a decision until he could hear from the other bishops of the metropolitanate. Two of the three bishops were in exile and the third had gone over to the Renovationists, so Patriarch Tikhon was unable to rule on Belarusian autonomy before his death.[42]

The Orthodox Church in Poland

During this same period, Patriarch Tikhon was navigating a drive for autocephaly in the Orthodox Church in Poland.[43] After the Treaty of Riga, the enlarged Poland included large territories of Western Ukraine and Belarus as well as southern Lithuania (including Vilnius) containing some 4 million Orthodox Christians in five dioceses. The laity were predominantly Ukrainians and Belarusians, while the hierarchy was primarily Russian. These groups had different, sometimes conflicting, aspirations for the Church. To complicate matters, the Polish state regarded such a large number of Orthodox believers to be so dangerous to its sovereignty that it demanded control over their Church.[44]

A Polish representative met with Tikhon in September 1921 to express his government's desire to see the Orthodox Church in Poland granted autocephaly. Tikhon replied that the authority to grant autocephaly was not his prerogative but that of a Church Council. Understanding that an independent Polish Orthodox Church would not be canonical without Moscow's consent, the Polish government continued negotiations. It hoped that Tikhon would come around with enough pressure.[45]

Given Poland's special circumstances, Tikhon (with the Synod) was prepared to make the Church in Poland a metropolitan district which would administer all the dioceses in Poland and was willing to negotiate even further privileges for the Polish Church as long as they were canonical.[46] Polish representatives indicated they did not support Serafim (Chichagov, 1856–1937), who had been appointed metropolitan of Warsaw in September 1918 but never allowed into the country, since he was unlikely to be compliant with their interests. They preferred Georgy (Yaroshevsky, 1872–1923), former bishop of Minsk—whose diocese included regions that had become part of Poland—then residing in Italy. Polish government representatives negotiated directly with Georgy, and he proved receptive to their conditions; he arrived in Warsaw in August 1921.[47]

Given that Serafim was under arrest, Tikhon agreed to temporarily appoint Georgy. Writing to Tikhon from Warsaw, Georgy explained the challenges of the Polish situation, including the attempts by the Ukrainian Synod and the Church Abroad to claim prerogatives over its dioceses. The Polish Orthodox Church, he argued, needed its own Higher Church Administration or Synod, which could defend the Orthodox Church's interests more effectively. In a second letter, he noted the Polish government's readiness to give full support to the Orthodox Church but only if it enjoyed autocephalous status. Tikhon responded by confirming the Polish government's appointment of Georgy as administrator of the Warsaw diocese and named him exarch of Poland. He added that he had already given "broad autonomy" to the Polish Church, which, "in our current dealings differs little from autocephaly. I ask you to explain all this to the Polish Government and not insist on autocephaly *right now*. We will protect you from the encroachments of the Ukrainian Synod and the Church Administration Abroad."[48] In subsequent conversations with Polish diplomats Tikhon suggested that creating an exarchate was but a temporary stop on the road to later autocephaly.[49]

In appointing Georgy as interim head of the Polish Church, Tikhon was not only navigating ecclesiastical and international politics but also personalities. A member of a minor noble family and nine years older than Tikhon, Serafim (Chichagov) was one of the senior bishops of the Church and known to be proud and sensitive. Reluctant to simply reassign him, Tikhon encouraged Polish government officials to visit him (in prison) and convince him to voluntarily give up his position as archbishop of

Warsaw. After they failed to convince him, Tikhon did it himself in January 1922 after Serafim was released from prison (and indeed offended him in doing so).[50]

Later that month, a council of Orthodox bishops in Poland considered a set of regulations for Church–state relations that granted the Polish government extensive rights of interference in the Orthodox Church and set it on a path to autocephaly. Refusing to sign the document, two bishops sent their objections secretly to Patriarch Tikhon with hieromonk Tikhon (Sharapov, 1886–1937), who traveled to Moscow incognito.[51] In turn, Patriarch Tikhon dispatched a statute crafted by the Higher Church Administration in Moscow to be approved by the Polish government (which did not happen). The statute's stipulation that the patriarch had to approve all subsequent episcopal nominations was likely designed to prevent Georgy from consecrating more bishops who favored autocephaly, since at the time the majority opposed it.[52]

After hearing Tikhon (Sharapov)'s critical assessment of the activities of the bishops who were cooperating with the Polish government, Patriarch Tikhon issued the following resolution:

> The Holy canons of our Church provide for the autocephaly for separate independent peoples. If the Polish people, who have received independence, were Orthodox and asked for their autocephaly, we would not refuse them, but neither common sense nor the holy canons allow us to grant autocephaly to various ethnicities of Orthodox Christians (*raznoplemennykh pravoslavnykh*) who live within the boundaries of the Polish state as national and religious minorities. That which is possible we have already granted the Orthodox in Poland—broad national-ecclesial autonomy.[53]

Tikhon understood that the majority of the bishops in Poland did not favor breaking the bond with the Moscow patriarchate and that autocephaly was being pushed by the Polish government not for the Orthodox Church's benefit.[54] He had no access to information about what the rank-and-file clergy and believers—especially the Ukrainian majority of Orthodox in Poland—may have wanted. After Patriarch Tikhon was arrested in 1922, bishops opposed to autocephaly in Poland were removed from their posts, and Bishop Elevfery of Vilna was even arrested. An opponent of autocephaly murdered Metropolitan Georgy (Yaroshevsky) in February 1923.

A council of bishops in Warsaw elected Dionisy (Valedinsky) as Metropolitan Georgy's replacement and, in lieu of Patriarch Tikhon (who was under arrest), Patriarch Meletius of Constantinople confirmed Dionisy's election in March 1923 with the authority bestowed upon the metropolitan of Warsaw "by our brother in Christ, Patriarch Tikhon in Moscow." Polish officials had been conducting negotiations with the patriarchate of Constantinople for some time and hoped Meletius might give them what they sought. Meletius's correspondence, however, was very cautiously worded and did not claim that the Polish Church was now under Constantinople's jurisdiction, though it was interpreted that way in Poland.[55]

After Patriarch Tikhon's release, the situation in Poland was perhaps the sole instance of overlapping interests between the patriarch and the Soviet authorities. On his release they wanted him to criticize the Polish government, which also happened to fit his agenda since the Polish government was closing Orthodox churches. Although the Anti-Religious Commission supported Tikhon's general policy toward the Orthodox Church in Poland as "expedient," they did not permit his request to send there his chosen delegate, Archbishop Ilarion (Troitsky), in early 1924. Similarly, ARK wanted Tikhon to depose Metropolian Dionisy and appoint in his place Archbishop Vladimir (Tikhonitsky, 1873–1959), who had been removed from his diocese by the Polish authorities because of his opposition to autocephaly—but Tikhon did not follow these instructions.[56]

Dionisy wrote Patriarch Tikhon and presented the situation to him as though the Polish Church had transferred jurisdiction to Constantinople and been granted independence (*nezavasimost'*). Tikhon responded in June 1924, expressing his confusion over what canonical grounds Constantinople had become involved in part of the Russian Church and asking for clarification about the situation in Poland.[57] For his part, Dionisi wanted to dispatch a delegation to Moscow to give Tikhon all the details to persuade him to grant autocephaly. Seeing no prospect of Tikhon's acquiescing to autocephaly, the Polish government refused to support such a delegation. It turned instead to Patriarch Gregory VII of Constantinople, who, on the basis that these dioceses had been illegitimately transferred from Constantinople to Moscow in 1686 (when the metropolitanate of Kiev was subordinated to Moscow), issued the tomos of autocephaly to the Polish Orthodox Church in November 1924 that was officially proclaimed in Poland in September 1925. In response to the tomos, Tikhon elevated Tikhon (Sharapov) to the episcopate to be the bishop for those in Poland still loyal to the Moscow patriarchate.[58]

The Baltics and Finland

The situations of the minority Orthodox Church in Finland and the Baltic states followed similar trajectories to one another. A significant number of Latvians and Estonians had converted to Orthodoxy in the nineteenth century. In Finland, Orthodox Christians were composed mostly of Finnish-speaking Karelians and some Russians, while in Lithuania the Orthodox were Slavs who constituted a very small minority. Finland declared its independence in December 1917. After periods of German and Soviet occupation in 1918–1919, Lithuania, Latvia, and Estonia were able to assert their independence and signed treaties with Soviet Russia in 1920. During all this turmoil, communication with the patriarch in Moscow proved difficult. The drive for ecclesiastical independence came both from the states and from non-Russian Orthodox activists.

Finland and Lithuania had their own bishops, Serafim (Lukianov, 1879–1959) and Elevfery (Bogoiavlensky), who provided some stability in 1918–1919. Without a ruling bishop, the Orthodox Church in Latvia plunged into disarray. The Orthodox Church in Estonia had been subordinate to the Riga diocese, a situation that changed at the end of 1917 when Patriarch Tikhon established a vicariate of the Riga diocese for Tallinn and appointed as bishop the Estonian Platon (Kulbusch, 1869–1919), who had already been elected by a congress of clergy and laity in August. Platon actively built up the diocese during the German occupation, only to be murdered by the Bolsheviks in Tartu in January 1919.[59]

The peace treaties between the Baltic states and Soviet Russia and the end of Russia's Civil War finally allowed Patriarch Tikhon to address the ecclesiastical situation in each of the new countries. An Estonian Diocesan Council requested that an independent diocese be established for Estonia in March 1919, which Tikhon approved on December 9. After an Estonian representative came to Moscow to meet with Patriarch Tikhon in June 1920, Tikhon, together with the Higher Church Administration, granted the Estonian Church autonomy since, "located in the boundaries of an independent state, in practice [it] already enjoys independence in all ecclesiastical economic, administrative, educational and civil affairs."[60] Tikhon further explained that because the Estonian Church had only just become an independent diocese, autocephaly was premature, especially as the Orthodox constituted but a minority in the country.[61] The Estonians chose Aleksandr Paulus (1872–1953) as their bishop, which Tikhon approved; they also invited the patriarch to

Tallinn for Paulus's consecration, but the Cheka prevented Tikhon from doing so. Paulus was finally consecrated in December 1921, after nearly two years of Estonia having had no bishop.[62]

In 1920, a diocesan council in Latvia elected Janis Pommers (Ioann Pommer, 1876–1934), a Latvian who was serving as archbishop of Penza, to be their bishop. In mid-1921, Patriarch Tikhon transferred Janis to Riga and granted the Orthodox Church in Latvia complete autonomy within the Moscow patriarchate on June 21, 1921.[63]

The patriarch likewise awarded the Church in Finland autonomy in February 1921. Finland was the one region of the Russian Empire that followed the Gregorian calendar rather than the Julian, and after Finland's independence, some Orthodox parishes wished to change calendars. At the end of 1917, Patriarch Tikhon and the Holy Synod, keeping in mind the minority status of the Orthodox Christians, decreed that parishes could use the new calendar "according to necessity" so long as two-thirds of the parishioners voted in its favor. In June 1921, an Extraordinary Council of the Orthodox Church of Finland resolved to shift to the new calendar completely. When Archbishop Serafim asked his blessing for this, Patriarch Tikhon responded that was not for him or the Russian Orthodox Church to resolve such questions, for it was a sensitive issue that concerned the entire Orthodox communion. Nevertheless, the Finnish government approved the Council's decision, and the Orthodox Church in Finland adopted the new calendar in October 1921 in its entirety, including setting the date for Easter (the only Orthodox Church to do so). The calendrical change caused bitter disputes especially at the Valaam Monastery on Lake Ladoga (which consisted primarily of Russian monks, though ended up on Finnish territory), even after Patriarch Tikhon gave his blessing for the calendar's implementation at the monastery in 1923.[64] The patriarch with the Synod also granted permission for parishes in the Estonian Church that wished to adopt the calendrical reform in June 1920.[65]

The governments of Finland, Estonia, and Latvia put intense pressure on the now-autonomous Orthodox Churches to become autocephalous so that they would not be dependent on Moscow. Tikhon responded that autocephaly needed to wait for the next Council of the entire Russian Church, which was scheduled for 1921. When that Council did not take place—and especially after Tikhon was arrested and the Renovationists began taking over the ecclesiastical administration in Russia and beyond—the Finnish and Estonian Churches, like the Polish, sought complete autocephaly. In early

July 1923, Patriarch Meletius IV received Finish and Estonian delegations (as arranged by the Finnish government) and agreed to take both the Finnish and the Estonian Church under his jurisdiction. He granted them autonomy but ruled that full autocephaly had to await approval of the Pan-Orthodox Council planned for 1925. Akin to Tikhon's understanding of calendrical reform, Meletius's ruling regarding autocephaly required the deliberation and consensus of all Orthodox Churches together in conciliar fashion. His justification for intervening was Patriarch Tikhon's arrest and the Renovationist takeover, though by the time Constantinople actually received the Estonian and Finnish Churches under its jurisdiction, Patriarch Tikhon had just been released.[66] The Estonian bishop Aleksandr later explained that he had turned to Constantinople when the situation of the Estonian Church had become dire in 1923 because of internal disagreements and lack of normal relations with the Russian Church.[67] Ethnic Russians in Estonia, however, refused to accept the authority of Constantinople, dividing the Orthodox Church there.

Archbishop Serafim (Lukianov) of Finland protested the government-initiated move to autocephaly but found himself removed from office by the Finnish government. In fall 1923, Patriarch Tikhon—referring to the Patriarch of Constantinople's decision as temporary given his imprisonment—instructed the Finnish Church to return to his jurisdiction now that he was free and had resumed leadership of the Church. He did not, however, formally break communion when the Finnish Church chose to stay with Constantinople.[68] Similarly, Archbishop Alexander (Paulus) of Estonia reported all the circumstances of the move to Constantinople's jurisdiction to Patriarch Tikhon in late 1923, but never received a response. As far as Archbishop Alexander was concerned, there had never been a rupture with the Moscow patriarchate.[69]

When the Latvian government refused to legally recognize the Orthodox Church unless it broke with Moscow, Archbishop Janis (Pommers) countered that, because the patriarch had already granted them autonomy, the Latvian Church did not need to seek autocephaly. Refusing to compromise, the archbishop was able to win legal recognition for the Orthodox Church after he himself was elected to parliament in 1925. In this way, Janis was able to keep the Orthodox Latvians and Russians together, in contrast to what had occurred in Estonia.[70]

The Lithuanian situation was decidedly distinct. In 1921, Tikhon named Elevfery, who had been administering the diocese since Tikhon left in 1917, as archbishop of Vilnius and Lithuania. He resided in Vilnius, then part of Poland. When he refused to support Polish autocephaly, he was arrested. In January 1923, he was released, thanks to pressure from the Lithuanian government, which recognized him as the archbishop of the Orthodox Church in Lithuania. He moved his residence to Kaunas, although he insisted that Vilnius was still part of his diocese. Given his anti-Polish stance, the Lithuanian government did not pressure him regarding the Church's autocephaly.[71]

The pattern in Georgia, Ukraine, Poland, the Baltics, and Finland was similar to that of the Balkans, when the nations of Greece, Serbia, Romania, and Bulgaria became independent of the Ottoman Empire in the nineteenth century. Autocephaly was pushed especially by the new governments, but the patriarch of Constantinople was generally slow in recognizing autocephaly. Much like the Ecumenical Patriarchate, Tikhon viewed the Orthodox Church of the Russian Empire as supranational and transnational. He readily granted autonomy but generally thought autocephaly for the Churches in the new nations was premature.

The Russian Orthodox leadership was not homogenous and bishops held varied opinions. Some were Great Russian chauvinists who, much like the leaders of the White armies, completely opposed the aspirations of national minorities in the Russian Empire. Others, like Arseny (Stadnitsky), acknowledged the "national, everyday, religious and social particularities" shaping their aspirations which "up to now the Great Russians have not only not given any attention, but even persecuted."[72] Tikhon, who was far more cosmopolitan than the Great Russian chauvinists, appears to have occupied a similarly moderate position as Arseny. He opposed Ukrainian autocephaly before Ukraine even had a stable independent state, and autocephaly in Poland, Finland, and the Baltics where the Orthodox constituted a minority. Most importantly, he asserted that autocephaly was not his to grant but was the prerogative of a Council of the All-Russian Church.

In February 1921, informing Archbishop of Finland Serafim that the request for autonomy would be approved, Tikhon also assured Serafim that the aspiration for autonomy was not harmful. "The Lord is instructing us"—in other words, Tikhon's own views were evolving with the emerging situation. But Tikhon also stated that "it seems to me that those who are strenuously seeking autocephaly are falling into our previous mistake, mixing the divine and eternal with the human, temporal, earthly." "Our previous mistake" was evidently the Russian Orthodox Church's identification with the Russian

Empire, which the ecclesiastical leadership had viewed as inseparable from the Church. But each Church's striving for independence, he believed, "is not what is needed now—it is precisely in unity, harmonious action and brotherly love that there is strength."[73] Tikhon resisted the centrifugal impulse to fragment Orthodoxy at precisely the moment when the Church was under assault from the Soviet state and pressure from newly independent governments. He believed the Church would find greater strength in unity, including in the independent states, where autocephalous Churches would be more vulnerable to their governments if they had no higher court of appeal.

Archbishop Janis (Pommers), for one, believed that autonomy was ideal for the Latvian Church under current circumstances. By being functionally independent, but at the same time maintaining the canonical tie with the patriarch, the Latvian Church avoided the tensions and schisms that afflicted other churches. Moreover, it allowed the Church the luxury of not having to yield to unwanted pressures stemming from the Soviet Union, as he explained to Archbishop Elevfery of Lithuania after Metropolitan Sergy (Stragorodsky) demanded loyalty to the Soviet government even of clergy living in other states in 1927. Tikhon, in granting autonomy, "has ensured for the Latvian Church the possibility to peacefully realize on its territory the exalted tasks of the Orthodox Church independently of whether or not ecclesiastical affairs proceed peacefully outside of Latvia." Janis believed that Tikhon, though himself able to resist the Soviet government's demands, envisioned the possibility when the Church might not be able to do so. Consequently, he understood Tikhon to have granted those churches located in new national borders virtual ecclesiastical independence for their own protection. Doing so "in no way" lessened the Moscow patriarchate's dignity, and for the Latvian Church this situation had an "indescribably great and exceptionally positive significance."[74]

10
Rebuilding the Church (1923–1925)

> According to the teaching of the Orthodox Church, the guardian of the purity of the faith and the traditions of the Fathers is not only the head of the Church and not only the Church hierarchy as a whole, but the entire body of the Church, and consequently, also the believing people, to whom belong certain rights and a voice in ecclesiastical affairs. The primate of an individual Orthodox Church, and the Russian Patriarch in particular, is not the pope of Rome who enjoys unlimited and boundless power; he cannot rule the people of God tyrannically without asking their agreement and without regard to their religious conscience, their beliefs, customs, and habits.
> —Patriarch Tikhon, 1924[1]

When Patriarch Tikhon was freed from prison on Wednesday, June 27, 1923, his regular carriage driver was waiting for him. At noon, the patriarch emerged from Lubianka, wearing his patriarchal kukol (headgear), a silk cassock, and the panagia on his neck. Although he held himself tall and straight, his hands were shaking and his face was very pale—signs of his long incarceration. The carriage headed to the Donskoi Monastery, where believers were already amassed. A photographer from the magazine *Ogonek* was on hand to capture the scene (Figure 8). Patriarch Tikhon entered the monastery cathedral to pray before the Donskoi icon of the Theotokos—the first time he had prayed inside a church in over a year. There he was greeted by his former secretary, Archimandrite Anempodist (Alekseev, 1869–1935), and his old cell attendant, Yakov Polozov, both of whom were also released.[2] A GPU informant reported the comment of one of the believers who had approached the patriarch for his blessing: "What a cheerful *batiushka* he is."[3]

In the last two years of his life, Patriarch Tikhon faced an enormous challenge of rebuilding the Orthodox Church after the full-on assault of the Soviet regime over the confiscation of church valuables and the Renovationist schism that tore the Church apart. The conditions of his release allowed him

REBUILDING THE CHURCH (1923–1925)   281

Figure 8. Patriarch Tikhon after release from prison, June 27, 1923

to resume leadership of the Church, but the Anti-Religious Commission (ARK) and the secret police exerted intense pressure to control his efforts and force subsequent compromises. Those compromises included further censuring the Church Abroad, introducing the new calendar, and reconciling with Renovationist leaders. Evgeny Tuchkov, head of the secret police department in charge of dealing with religious organizations, pressured the patriarch with a combination of threats to prosecute him if he failed to cooperate, and arrests of those around him when he failed to do so. Yet Tikhon succeeded in adhering to his principles. Unlike the period before 1922, when he felt he had the right to criticize publicly the Soviet regime for its abuses of human rights and especially its assaults on the Church, after his release he remained steadfastly apolitical in his public voice (though not always in private correspondence with Soviet officials). He was willing to make compromises on religious matters so long as they did not violate the dogmas and canons of the Orthodox Church. He made certain compromises in the hopes of securing the legalization of his Church and its administration to guarantee it a secure future, which he came close to accomplishing. And as the opening quote indicates, he continued to lead the Church in conciliar fashion, listening to and even relying on the voice of the people. When the Soviet pressures proved too much, Tikhon could rely on the resistance of the people as a means of protecting the Church from unacceptable compromises.

First Proclamations

To secure his release, Patriarch Tikhon had to meet the conditions that Yaroslavsky set on June 11. He met half of those demands by his appeal to the Supreme Court. To meet the other demands, the patriarch prepared an encyclical to believers that was approved by ARK before his release. In this and other public statements, he cleverly framed Yaroslavsky's demands in such a way as to serve his own purposes.

The encyclical was issued the day after his release, on June 28, 1923, in an authorized leaflet of 5,000 copies ahead of its newspaper publication.[4] Mounting a defense against the Renovationist Church Council's act of defrocking him in the encyclical, Tikhon first denied its legitimacy on procedural grounds by not summoning him to appear at his trial. He rejected the Council's condemnation of him for using his ecclesiastical and moral authority for counter-revolutionary purposes. "I, of course, do not pretend," he claimed, "to be an admirer of the Soviet government as the church renovators declare themselves to be, but at the same time I am far from such an enemy as they would make me out to be." Admitting to sharply criticizing the regime in its early years because of his "upbringing" and the prevailing orientation within the Church Council, he noted that by 1919, as circumstances changed, he called on the clergy not to interfere in politics. Moreover, the Renovationist council was not truly conciliar or representative because it was composed predominantly of their supporters. Of all the council's decisions, the only one the patriarch indicated he could bless was the introduction of the new calendar. He ended the encyclical by reiterating his "guilt" for speaking against the Soviet government, which, he said, he had been encouraged to do by others—but now he rejected all attacks against the Soviet government.[5] In fulfilling Yaroslavsky's remaining demands through skillfully crafted language, Patriarch Tikhon was able not only to thwart the Soviet authorities' intention of weakening his hold on believers by having him incriminate himself as a compromiser with the regime but also to reassert his authority over the Church and undercut the Renovationists' power grab less than two months after their Council had defrocked him.

Before his release, on June 19, ARK demanded that, in addition to his first two statements (appeal to the Supreme Court and the first encyclical), he write a third. Rather than focusing on the Renovationists, this one should repeat Tikhon's admission of crimes against the Soviet government and laboring people, condemn Antony (Khrapovitsky) and the pope, and state that Patriarch Meletius was an English stooge. It should also criticize the Polish government as well as Russian and foreign "White Guardists" that had pushed him to make declarations against the Soviet government, and finally applaud the introduction of the new orthography for church use. ARK instructed Tuchkov to work with the patriarch on such a proclamation.[6]

Accordingly, on July 1, Tikhon wove ARK's demands into a message to clergy and believers about the importance of Church unity. Instead of a broad critique directed at the pope and the Polish government, Tikhon focused on a matter close to his heart by censuring the Catholic Church for assaulting the Orthodox Church in the Kholm region, where massive church closures were occurring.[7] Further, he "mourned all the victims" of opposition to the Soviet confiscation of church valuables (a sentiment which was undoubtedly sincere). He declared that the Church "is apolitical and from now on desires to be 'neither a red nor a white' church," as the Renovationists and the émigrés, respectively, wanted, but the "one, catholic, and apostolic church."[8]

The patriarch therefore framed his first proclamations to the faithful after his release from prison in such a way that, though they fulfilled several Soviet demands, were subsumed under his assault on the Renovationists and reassertion of his authority over the Church. Although Tikhon was willing to meet many Soviet demands in exchange for his release, some he refused to do—clearly there was a difference between those he was willing to fulfill and those he was not. None of his statements criticized the "intrigues" (that is, criticism of Soviet religious persecution) of the archbishop of Canterbury or Patriarch Meletius of Constantinople, as ARK had demanded. The Soviets were still trying to "answer" the British intervention—the lead editorial in *Pravda* on June 27, by the editor-in-chief Nikolai Bukharin (1888–1938), even attempted to use the words of both Patriarch Tikhon and the Renovationists as a rebuttal to the archbishop of Canterbury and the Curzon ultimatum.[9] Given that both Randall Davidson and Patriarch Meletius had issued strong defenses of him at a critical moment, Tikhon was unwilling to betray their support or poison ecumenical relations, despite immense pressure that the Soviet authorities put on him.

Gathering the Scattered Flock

On a Sunday evening after his release, Patriarch Tikhon invited to his apartments about twenty women who had tended to his needs during his period of house arrest at the Donskoi Monastery by bringing him produce, cooking for him, and washing his linens. They also kept watch in case the patriarch was taken away by the political police in secret. The patriarch announced that it was his turn to serve them. "Sit down and do not stand! You have served me so much this last period, when everyone else abandoned me; you did not for a single day forsake your care for me—who was forgotten and abandoned by everyone. And now I want to serve you a little myself, so that I can thank you a little for everything."[10] Turning toward them with hands in supplication, he asked God to save them all and made a deep bow before them. The women became flustered—they were not used to the patriarch of all Russia bowing before them; some began to cry. The tea party lasted two hours. All the while the patriarch poured and served the tea, "regaled them with jam" and *pirogi* with rice or sweets. He spoke individually with each one, for each one had an "affectionate or joking word," granting them all his considerate attention.[11] While Patriarch Tikhon was disappointed that so many of the clergy had abandoned him at the most difficult moment by going over to the Renovationists, he was profoundly appreciative of the women who remained steadfast and faithful—much as Christ's male disciples fled when he was arrested, and it was the female disciples who were present during his crucifixion and came to his tomb.

With his detainment still on his mind, he stated in an interview with the Russian Telegraph Agency that he had not been tortured as had been reported in the foreign press and that his conditions were good except that he had been denied participation in the liturgy. When the correspondent asked him what he would do now, he answered that as a free man he intended to serve the liturgy again at the Donskoi Monastery and anywhere believers invited him. "If I find a sufficient number of followers, then our ecclesiastical association will take on some sort of organized form."[12] With the Renovationists in charge of most of the Church, there was no guarantee the patriarch had a Church to lead. Through this invitation to the laity in the Soviet press, Patriarch Tikhon signaled his intention of reuniting his scattered flock. Whether he would continue to exercise authority depended upon whether the people wanted him to lead. On the first Sunday after his release, July 1, he served liturgy at the Donskoi Monastery and preached about "all-conquering love," which was the primary task of the Church—a sermon reported on in *Izvestiia*.[13] So many people came to the liturgy that the patriarch stayed until 5 p.m., blessing all who came forward.[14]

In response to his appeal, parishes across Moscow began inviting him to serve. Patriarch Tikhon's embrace of the principle of sobornost had empowered believers to take initiative in their parishes, and their control over the parish was also granted by Soviet law. Ultimately, it was up to believers whether they chose the patriarchal Church or the Renovationist. The Soviets themselves had run up against this reality the previous year when supporting the Renovationist takeover of the Orthodox Church. Having empowered the people in the Church as a means of undercutting the power of the patriarch in 1918, Soviet authorities found parish councils very difficult to control. To undermine the effect of their own law, they frequently resorted to arresting and exiling parish council members who remained loyal to Tikhon. Now, after Tikhon's release, one Moscow parish after another drove out the Renovationist priests and invited the patriarch. Patriarch Tikhon served almost every day, sometimes twice a day, in different churches in the city—some fifty services in July and August 1923. Before he served, Bishop Ilarion (Troitsky), one of the patriarch's closest assistants in this period, would reconsecrate the altar, implying that the Renovationists had defiled it through their usage. Tikhon characterized the Renovationists as a "caste" movement that attracted clergy because it spoke to their interests—but not those of the laity.[15]

The patriarch remained long after these services to bless worshipers. The GPU had informants everywhere the patriarch went, recording details of what happened. After one such service, the GPU informant noted that the church was filled mostly with workers who supported Tikhon. The details are sometimes minute; after one service, the patriarch went with other clergy to a hat shop for lunch, during which alcohol was served, and Tikhon reportedly "had a shot." On numerous occasions two to three thousand people would attend the liturgies—so many that all the people could not fit in the churches (and sometimes neither could the GPU informants). At many of these services, the patriarch consecrated new bishops in elaborate rituals to replenish the ranks of the Orthodox episcopate; perhaps not knowing how long he might be free, Patriarch Tikhon worked hurriedly to rebuild the Church while he was able.[16]

Footage of these resplendent liturgical services was shot, and in the middle of July a film was released in several Moscow theaters entitled "Tikhon after Repentance." Although the intent of making the film may have been to demonstrate to the West that Tikhon was truly free, it was a huge hit among Muscovites—so much so that tickets cost as much as a concert featuring the famous opera singer Fedor Shaliapin (1873–1938). Even *Pravda* admitted that the film would have "success in the proletarian districts" of Moscow. It is unclear who released the film, because ARK was taken by surprise. It resolved to investigate its release and removed the film from screening after only three days.[17]

When Patriarch Tikhon was not serving in churches, he welcomed people at the Donskoi Monastery. His door was open to almost all: A sign on the door requested that those with "counter-revolutionary and anti-Soviet proposals" not seek an audience with the patriarch.[18] Hundreds came to meet with him: bishops, clergy, and ordinary believers. Receiving about fifty people a day, he was unable meet with anyone for long. The GPU had planted agents within the monastery, listening in on the patriarch's interviews with visitors.[19]

The patriarch issued a second encyclical against the Renovationists on July 15, 1923. Unlike his two previous declarations, which had to meet ARK's demands, this encyclical was entirely of the patriarch's own making. It focused exclusively on the nature of the Renovationist schism and the need to restore unity in the Church. Tikhon explained that he had not abdicated, nor had he authorized the Renovationist clerics to place themselves at the head of the Church, but that he had designated Agafangel to lead in his absence.

The Renovationists' claim to the contrary amounted to "a lie and a deception." Detailing how they had violated ecclesiastical canons, sown division in the Church, and gained power by force rather than through the conciliar voice of believers, he declared their resolutions null and void and their sacraments devoid of grace. In resuming his exercise of patriarchal authority in the Church, the patriarch called on those who had remained faithful to him to advise and work with him to restore peace and unity to the Church, and those who had been tempted to recognize the illegitimate ecclesiastical authority to return, by means of repentance, to the "one Universal Church."[20]

Since his previous two proclamations were published by the Soviet press, Tikhon handed this one over to the press as well. The main censorship organ, Glavlit, approved it and printed leaflets, but found itself in a dispute with ARK, which blocked its distribution.[21] Assistant director of Glavlit Nikolai Speransky (1886–1951) responded, noting that he did not see any substantiative difference between this latest encyclical and the previously published patriarchal documents. Moreover, if the Soviet press gave preferential treatment to the Renovationists by publishing their attacks on the patriarch without letting the patriarch respond, that action was tantamount to making the Renovationists "an officially recognized 'Soviet' church." Either they should allow both sides to air their grievances in print—or neither. After ARK received the letter, someone wrote across the top: "Top Secret. Inform Comrade Speransky by telephone that the anti-religious commission does everything with the sanction of the Politburo."[22] ARK did not respond to the substance of Speransky's reasoning but only appealed to its authority stemming from the Politburo—though that was too sensitive to put in writing. ARK further informed Glavlit that all religious literature should be sent to them for approval and that the confiscation of the patriarch's appeal had been appropriate.[23] The printed copies, which had already been delivered to the patriarch, were confiscated from him by the GPU.[24]

Patriarch Tikhon, rather than submit to ARK's censorship, had the text distributed as an early form of *samizdat* through internal church channels at home and abroad, though the Soviet authorities threatened to prosecute those caught distributing or proclaiming the text.[25]

On August 5, ARK favorably assessed the impact of the patriarch's release. In their estimation, his release brought "confusion" to the "ranks of the monarchists and the White Guards." It was able to identify "the most prominent Black Hundreds" in those who broke with the patriarch because of his compromise with the Soviet government. The increased antagonism between the Tikhonites and Renovationists was causing scandal among believers and, the commission believed, the irreconcilability of the two factions was leading to the Church's disintegration. Finally, ARK remained satisfied with its decision not to put the patriarch on trial to avoid endowing him with the "aura of a martyr."[26] The Politburo and ARK decided to postpone the patriarch's trial indefinitely in favor of "prolonging the investigation" against him so that the "threat of a trial" would continue to hang over him and they could extract further compromises. Such compromises, they believed, would deal a blow to those who had looked upon Tikhon as incorruptible and further broaden schism within the Church.[27]

The Church Abroad

Part of ARK's demands for Patriarch Tikhon's release was that he condemn the Church Abroad for its anti-Soviet statements. In the first encyclical after his release (June 28), Tikhon countered the Renovationists' charge that he was a counter-revolutionary by explaining that he abolished the Church Administration Abroad for their political declarations—thus reaffirming his decree of May 5, 1922.[28] The second encyclical that Patriarch Tikhon issued on his release, on July 1, asserted that, if they had ceased their political activities after his censure in spring 1922, that would have been the end of it. The bishops of the Karlovci Council did not cease their anti-Soviet declarations, however, but were "further plunging the Orthodox Church into the political struggle." If they did not stop and repent from using the Church as a political tool, Tikhon would have to summon them to an ecclesiastical court in Moscow.[29]

Patriarch Tikhon's decree No. 348 abolishing the administration of the Church Abroad on May 5, 1922, was received by Metropolitans Evlogy and Antony in mid-June. It immediately caused a crisis. Evlogy, on whom the patriarch had laid responsibility for taking over the administration of parishes in Europe, reacted with hesitation. Antony, by contrast, was initially ready to fulfill the patriarch's decree and retire to Mount Athos. They kept the patriarch's decree secret rather than announce it publicly. By the time the Higher Church Administration held a meeting in September, when they made the patriarch's decree public, their positions had reversed: Evlogy advocated fulfilling the patriarch's decree but Antony did not. Through the course of debate, the majority opposed fulfilling the decree. The key positions were put forward by two influential laymen who raised questions about the authenticity of the patriarch's decree or claimed it must have been issued under Soviet pressure. They also argued that the decree censured the Church Abroad for not fulfilling the patriarch's October 8, 1919, encyclical on political neutrality which, they claimed, only applied to those inside the Soviet Union. They continued to defend their right to condemn the Soviet government.

The strongest argument in favor of obeying the patriarch's decree came from Bishop Veniamin (Fedchenkov), who dismissed questions about its authenticity and asserted that the question of whether it was issued under Soviet pressure made no difference because the decree was consistent with the patriarch's overall position about political neutrality—which should also be adopted by the Church Abroad so as not to harm the Church in Russia. The bishops, meeting in conference, came to a compromise solution, namely that the letter of the patriarch's decree was followed but not the spirit: It abolished the Church Abroad's Higher Church Administration and replaced it with a Temporary Holy Synod of Bishops that consisted of the same members and held the same prerogatives.[30]

The Church Abroad was similarly divided on how to respond to Patriarch Tikhon's encyclicals on his release in 1923. Many claimed that the patriarch's statements must have either been falsified or issued under extreme pressure from the Soviet authorities and therefore did not express his true intent. The Synod Abroad made a secret resolution that, if the patriarch again issued similar instructions concerning the Church Abroad, they would not obey them on the grounds that they were not an expression of his will.[31] In November 1923, the patriarch and Higher Church Administration in Moscow issued another resolution declaring that they "have no relationship" to all the political declarations of the Church Abroad and censured them, and that they would inquire of Metropolitan Evlogy, whom they had tasked with establishing a new ecclesiastical administration abroad, what sort of administration was the new Synod of Bishops Abroad. The resolution declared that Antony (Khrapovitsky) had no right to speak on behalf of the whole Russian Church and Russian people.[32] The Constantinople Holy Synod under Patriarch Gregory VII effectively took the same position as Patriarch Tikhon when, on April 30, 1924, it instructed the clergy of the Church Abroad to refrain from "any interference in questions alien to a churchly character"—in other words, to stop their attacks against the Soviet government. The resolutions also declared that the patriarchate of Constantinople had never blessed the activities of the Synod of Bishops of the Church Abroad to serve as an ecclesiastical administration in regions where other Orthodox Churches were already established and that it should be terminated "in accord with a similar decision . . . announced long ago" by Patriarch Tikhon.[33] Archbishop Anastasy (Gribanovsky) of the Church Abroad, who had been residing in Constantinople, rejected the prohibition against political declarations as tantamount to a defense of the atheist Soviet regime and left the city.[34]

The patriarch's November resolution was used by some émigrés to argue against the Church Abroad's legitimacy. One part of the Church Abroad was ready to obey the patriarch because they understood that its political declarations caused harm for the Church in Russia. Indeed, Archbishop Serafim (Lukianov) of Finland, who had closer contact with the patriarch as well as bishops abroad, explained to Metropolitan Antony that "in Russia they are very dissatisfied with the political declarations of the Karlovci Council, and believe that now the bishops should disassociate themselves from any political activities because all of that is blamed on the Patriarch."[35] Others, however, were ready to break with the patriarch altogether and declare the Church Abroad the legitimate Russian Church authority. A Council of Bishops in October 1924 passed a compromise resolution that if any of the patriarch's instructions "troubled the conscience of the bishops and contradicted the interests" of the Church Abroad, the Synod of Bishops would decide whether to obey those particular instructions, while still preserving faithfulness to the patriarch. This status quo was maintained until the patriarch's death.[36] After Tikhon's death, the Synod of Bishops Abroad declared itself ready to declare Metropolitan Antony (Khrapovitsky) the "patriarch's deputy" who was head of the entire Russian Orthodox Church—not just outside, but even within Russia.[37]

Of particular concern to Patriarch Tikhon was the situation in America. The diocese fell into disarray after the Russian Revolution because of lack of financial support from Russia, lack of recognized episcopal leadership, and divisions among various non-Russian ethnic groups who sought to separate from the Russian archdiocese. In January 1922, Tikhon wrote to the patriarch of Antioch with his concern about divisions that had arisen among Arab Orthodox Christians as to whether to remain under the Russian archdiocese or go under the jurisdiction of the Antiochian patriarchate. The latter was exploring that possibility, and in his letter, Tikhon indicated that he was not opposed to such a solution if it would help solve the problems for the Arab Christians.[38]

An American Council elected Bishop of Canada Alexander (Nemolovsky) to head the diocese in 1919, and in September 1920 it confirmed him as archbishop of North America. Problems, especially financial, continued to mount and Alexander became unpopular. Platon (Rozhdestvensky), who had succeeded Tikhon in 1907, returned to America in 1921 and resumed the administration of the Church, which Tikhon approved orally before his arrest in 1922 and confirmed after his release on September 29, 1923. The Renovationists consecrated as bishop the American Orthodox priest John Kedrovsky (1879–1934) and sent him in November 1923 to America to claim leadership of the Church and its properties. Kedrovsky complained to his handlers that Platon was making his work difficult. In response, the Soviet authorities and GPU agent Tuchkov put intense pressure on the patriarch to remove Platon. Tuchkov even attended the session of the Synod on January 16, 1924, which issued a decree removing Platon because of his political statements. The decree, however, stated that it would be delivered to Platon by an appointed replacement—yet Tikhon never appointed a replacement and the decree was never sent. It was published in *Izvestiia*, but there were doubts in America regarding its authenticity since they never received the original. With the Renovationists threatening to take over the diocese, the Fourth All-American Council in April 1924 declared the American Church self-governing, based on Tikhon's November 1920 decree, with Platon to remain as head. In short, Tikhon compromised under the pressure from the Soviet government to remove Metropolitan Platon, but in such a way that the decision remained unimplementable.[39]

Introducing Calendrical Reform

Reform of the church calendar figured prominently among the demands that Yaroslavsky formulated as a condition for Patriarch Tikhon's release.[40] All the Orthodox Churches had continued to follow the Julian calendar, inherited from the Roman Empire, as did the Russian Empire, long after Western Christians and nations had adopted the reformed Gregorian calendar. At the same time, it was broadly understood that the Julian calendar was astronomically inaccurate, and therefore Orthodox leaders began, in the early twentieth century, to discuss prospects for calendrical reform. After the Bolsheviks adopted the Julian calendar in early 1918, the issue became more acute because Russian ecclesiastical leaders acknowledged that it did not make sense for civil time and church time to be out of sync. The Church Council of 1917–1918 found that while there were no pressing dogmatic or canonical issues that should prevent the calendrical reform (except for some considerations of the timing of Easter), it was a question of such importance to worldwide Orthodoxy that the Church in Russia needed to act in concert with other Orthodox Churches.[41] Before 1923, Patriarch Tikhon was not an advocate of calendrical reform per se, but at the same time, he did not regard it as a fundamentally dogmatic or canonical issue and expressed a degree of flexibility in finding a solution. This can be seen in his letter to the ecumenical patriarch of Constantinople on January 21, 1919, in which he laid out a range of possibilities and clearly was trying to initiate a pan-Orthodox discussion on the matter.[42]

The Soviets pushed hard for the Orthodox Church to adopt the Gregorian calendar, which was part of their modernizing efforts. They evidently also hoped that transforming the ecclesiastical calendar would be the first step to replace religious holidays altogether with revolutionary ones. Pressure was put first on the Renovationists, who approved the new calendar at their council in May 1923 and then adopted it in June. Believers, who were lukewarm about the Renovationists already, vehemently opposed the calendrical change.[43] Because the common people were still deeply religious, Soviet calendars included ten days off for religious holidays, but after the Renovationists adopted the new calendar, these holidays were given according to the Gregorian rather than the Julian calendar.

Tikhon, in a letter to the government, explained that the Renovationists presented themselves as innovators not bound by the canons and traditions of the Orthodox Church. For the mass of believers, the new calendar symbolized and became synonymous with the whole movement. The new calendar was deeply opposed by believers because it was so central to the lived experience of their faith and their rhythm of life. "Our people," the patriarch wrote, "highly value ritual and its traditional invariability." Moreover, "the church year is closely intertwined with the daily life (*byt*) of the people and agricultural year of the peasant."[44] In the village, peasants still marked the seasons (including times for planting and harvesting) by the Church calendar, so that shifting the celebration of key feasts by thirteen days would be a profound disruption to their lives.[45]

The Soviet leadership pressured Tikhon also to adopt the new calendar so that he, too, would be seen as an innovator in the eyes of the conservative Orthodox and his authority would be undermined.[46] Indeed, as one believer declared, "We love Tikhon and respect him because he did not change anything in the church and left the church in its previous form, but if Tikhon introduces innovations into the church, then we will turn away from him, despite the respect and love we have for him."[47]

Because Tikhon did not regard the calendar reform as a canonical issue, he was willing to compromise on it when negotiating his release from prison. Tuchkov evidently misinformed him that a pan-Orthodox Congress in May–June 1923 in Constantinople approved the calendrical reform.[48] The patriarch felt he could legitimately implement the calendrical reform if it was being adopted in concert by all Orthodox Churches. He therefore convened a conference of bishops on September 24, 1923, which decreed that the new calendar would be introduced beginning October 15. He composed an encyclical to the faithful explaining that there were no dogmatic obstacles to reforming the calendar in accordance with scientific evidence.[49] The calendrical change was only announced in Moscow, and there many churches adopted (often reluctantly) the new calendar. Tikhon was waiting for his encyclical explaining the reform to be printed so he could distribute the explanation at the same time as announcing the reform itself for the rest of the country. There was a delay in printing the encyclical for an entire month, however, so that the opportune time to introduce the change without interfering with the Orthodox liturgical cycle was missed. Especially after he learned that other Orthodox Churches had in fact not adopted the new calendar, the patriarch announced on November 8 that the calendrical change was postponed. This caused tremendous confusion, especially after the encyclical was finally published and distributed by the Soviet authorities. On the night of November 15, moreover, the patriarch's closest coworker, Archbishop Ilarion (Troitsky), was arrested as a way of applying maximum pressure on the patriarch. On December 10, 1923, Tikhon issued new instructions that the calendrical reform was to remain in force, though exceptions could be made locally.[50]

The patriarch faced mass opposition to the calendrical reform from ordinary believers. On February 5, 1924, therefore, he met with Dmitry Kursky (1874–1932), the head of the Commissariat of Justice, to plead that the government reverse its position. Kursky agreed and the pressure on the Church to reform the calendar ceased, despite ARK's outrage.[51] When pressures to reform the calendar resumed in September 1924, Patriarch Tikhon sent a strong protest to the Central Executive Committee, which is reminiscent of the addresses to the Soviet government from before his arrest. He asserted that the demand for calendrical reform constituted state interference in the life of Church and thus a contravention of the law of separation of the Church from the state. All the same, he agreed to cooperate because he was not opposed in principle to a reform which did not violate Orthodox dogma or canons. However, his initial effort at implementation had been based on misinformation about the adoption of the new calendar by the pan-Orthodox Congress. The laity not only opposed the calendrical reform because of its disruption to their religious life, but they also understood that it was being introduced as a result of government pressure and resented government interference in their religious lives. Successful calendrical reform, the patriarch concluded, depended on the government allowing the Church to work independently. It would succeed in Russia if it were part of a pan-Orthodox calendrical reform, but for that to happen, Tikhon would need to be able to communicate freely with other Orthodox leaders. In short, the patriarch was arguing to the government that the only way to see the results it wanted was to grant the Church and the patriarch more freedom to work it out.[52]

Some of the patriarch's biographers argue that, contrary to his statements, Tikhon was actually opposed to calendar reform and therefore set it up to fail.[53] Tikhon's statements since 1919, however, consistently indicate that he did not oppose the calendar reform on principle. His guiding principle in such matters was that compromise was possible so long as doing so did not go against Orthodox doctrines or canons. The attempt to introduce it failed because he had empowered the laity since 1918 and, according to his own principle of sobornost (conciliarity), he was obliged to listen to the voice and will of the people, especially when it expressed itself in such a concerted way. The Russian patriarch, he explained to the government (see the chapter's epigraph), was not the pope who had unlimited power, but had to lead the Church in agreement with believers. Tikhon had received delegations and letters from believers across the Soviet Union asking him not to introduce the new calendar because everywhere it aroused anxiety, discontent, and resistance. In view of this, Tikhon considered it his pastoral duty to "take into account the voice of believers so as not to commit violence against the conscience of the people."[54] Ultimately, the believers won, and even the Politburo conceded defeat.[55] The Soviets never succeeded in forcing the Russian Orthodox Church to adopt the new calendar, which remains tainted in the Russian Church precisely by its association with the Renovationists and Soviet efforts to impose it.

Case Closed

On January 21, 1924, Vladimir Lenin died. On January 26, *Izvestiia* published the following statement by Patriarch Tikhon: "I ask you through your newspaper to express my condolences to the government of the Union of Soviet Republics regarding the grave loss they suffered in the person of the unexpectedly deceased chairman of the Soviet of People's Commissars V. I. Ul'ianov-Lenin."[56] Such a statement by the head of the Church regarding the death of the head of state is hardly surprising, and Tikhon did not express his personal sorrow, but rather condolences to the government. According to GPU reports, the statement was well received by believers.[57] The patriarch received questions about whether churches could serve memorials for Lenin. The newspaper *Evening Moscow (Vecherniaia Moskva)* published a statement according to which the patriarch said that it was not forbidden to pray for Lenin, since he had not been excommunicated from the Church. But he considered that it would be an offence to Lenin's memory and to his family for clergy to participate in the funeral, since Lenin never expressed any desire to have them do so. The patriarch's response was entirely different than the obsequious statements made by the Renovationist leaders.[58]

After Tikhon's release, ARK and Tuchkov continued to use the fact that Tikhon's case was never formally closed as a mechanism to pressure the patriarch if they felt he was being uncooperative. In early 1924, ARK intended to reopen the investigation to increase pressure on the patriarch to make further compromises, especially the calendar reform.[59] But this intention was nipped in the bud when, on March 13, 1924, the Politburo resolved that Tikhon's case be closed at the same time as the release and exile of Catholic Archbishop Ciepliak from the Soviet Union.[60] A last minute addition to the Politburo's agenda by Stalin, the reconsideration of the two cases may have been prompted by the Commissariat for Foreign Affairs as a result of continuing international pressure.[61] The Politburo's secret decision was handed down to the Presidium of the Central Executive Committee, the official state legislative organ, to pass a formal public resolution. Its resolution of March 21 stated that, since the hold of religion over the laboring classes in Russia was weakening, and the patriarch had publicly repented of his counter-revolutionary statements, he was no longer considered "socially dangerous to the Soviet government."[62] The news was published in *Izvestiia* the following day.[63]

On March 23, *Izvestiia* published an interview with the patriarch, who evidently learned about the termination of his case from the correspondent. Expressing his gratitude, Tikhon stated that the Soviet government would find him to be a loyal citizen. As for his future plans, he stated that he was occupied with the "organizational side of his church, considering that the framework of Soviet legislation gives a wide scope for this." He added that reconciliation with the Renovationists was ongoing, but his position that the Renovationists must repent of their activities remained unchanged.[64] ARK was infuriated that the press had published this article without its approval and tasked Tuchkov with finding out who had allowed the interview to be published in such a form.[65] Evidently, ARK was not pleased with the patriarch's assertion that Soviet law allowed "wide scope" for building up the ecclesiastical administration.

In an April 5, 1924, report to the head of the Secret Department of the OGPU (Joint State Political Administration, as the GPU was renamed in November 1923), Tuchkov made it clear how unanticipated—and unwanted—the Politburo decision was for both ARK and the OGPU. "The unexpected termination of Tikhon's case," he wrote, "brought some difficulties into our work with the churchmen." So long as the case against him was ongoing, the patriarch had been "under our influence," and the patriarch's status as a potential criminal gave the Renovationists their main argument against the patriarch's authority. "The amnestied Tikhon has become significantly bolder and our advice is no longer compulsory for him, and also the renovationist current has significantly lost heart, having in the person of Tikhon an opponent who is very strong."[66] That Tuchkov would make such an observation so briefly after the case against the patriarch was closed indicates what a major impact it had.

No longer under investigation, Tikhon actively pursued the legalization of the ecclesiastical administration. The Renovationist ecclesiastical administration was registered by the Soviet government and therefore considered legal. By contrast, the Soviet authorities refused to register Tikhon's administration. The trials of 1922 declared the very existence of the Church administration as illegal, and without receiving any legal recognition its members could be arrested any time the authorities chose to do so, which they frequently did when they were not pliant enough (such as Archbishop Ilarion Troitsky). ARK unofficially permitted a rump Holy Synod consisting of Serafim (Aleksandrov, 1867–1937), Tikhon (Obolensky, 1856–1926), both of whom were sufficiently pliant, and the recently appointed Petr (Poliansky, 1862–1937).[67]

After the Politburo's decision to end the case, Tikhon was able to go around Tuchkov and appeal directly to Mikhail Kalinin as head of Central Executive Committee, the supreme governing body. After meeting with Kalinin on April 9, the patriarch submitted an appeal which asserted that believers recognized his leadership, not that of the Renovationists, to be the legitimate head of the Church. Soviet laws guaranteeing freedom of conscience should protect the believers' choice and permit him, now as a free citizen, to organize a legal church administration.[68] The patriarch pointed out that although Soviet state bodies officially declared that they did not show preference for one religious body over another, in practice they allowed renovationist bishops to operate freely. But whenever the patriarch appointed a bishop to a diocese, that bishop was either sent back to Moscow, arrested, or sent into exile by the local authorities on arriving at his destination—all because he was a "Tikhonite." Besides asking for legal recognition of his authority and those under him, Tikhon also requested that the cases of bishops (which he listed by name) who had been sent into administrative exile be reexamined. Finally, since believers recognized him as the legitimate patriarch, he and they found it offensive that the Soviet government and press continued to refer to him exclusively as the "former patriarch."[69]

A month later the patriarch met with Aleksei Rykov, who had succeeded Lenin as chairman of the Council of People's Commissars and therefore was formally head of the Soviet government. Tikhon gave a virtually identical petition to Rykov as he had given to Kalinin.[70] Tikhon then submitted a protest to Rykov against the repression of two of his closest coworkers just the day after they met: Metropolitan Petr (Poliansky) had been administratively exiled, and Serafim (Aleksandrov) was arrested.[71] On May 16, Rykov forwarded the patriarch's petitions to the head of the Commissariat of Justice, Dmitry Kursky. In informing him of the patriarch's complaint about the preferential treatment of the Renovationist church, Rykov appeared sensitive to the charge of hypocrisy by noting the contradiction between the decrees and the practices of various organs of government.[72] Kursky agreed and concluded that "there are no hindrances for the so-called Tikhonite church to follow the path of legalization of its organization along with the renovationists." He stated categorically: "I consider it the more correct position to allow a free competition between the Tikhonite and renovationist churches."[73] The patriarch had thus convinced leading government officials that the Church administration be granted legal recognition—but that legal recognition did not follow, and Tikhon was still struggling for it in the last months of his life.

Patriarch Tikhon and the Renovationists

The control that the Renovationists extended over the structures of the Church at the time Tikhon was released from prison should not be underestimated. The Renovationists controlled virtually all the diocesan administrations and most of the parishes. Those who remained loyal to the patriarch were fragmented and driven to the margins. It was not without reason Patriarch Tikhon felt compelled to make the compromises he did in exchange for being able to resume leadership of the Church, gaining the possibility of winning it back from the Renovationists.

Archbishop Evdokim (Meshchersky) became the head of the Renovationist administration after he arrived in Moscow on July 20, 1923, replacing such unpopular leading figures as Antonin (Granovsky) and Fr. Krasnitsky. Evdokim had been archbishop of a major diocese before the Renovationist schism and therefore could present himself as a more traditional bishop; his administration also renamed itself to the more traditional Holy Synod in an effort to be more acceptable to believers.[74] Its main task became its struggle against the Tikhonite Church, and its primary means of distinguishing itself was through its unswerving loyalty to the Soviet government and denouncing Tikhon as "counter-revolutionary." The Soviet authorities allowed the two factions to battle each other in the hopes that the struggle would cause a general popular disaffection with Orthodoxy altogether, but they supported the Renovationists, especially outside of Moscow, if the Tikhonite Church threatened it with collapse.[75]

Over the summer of 1923, Patriarch Tikhon received a steady stream of clergy and parish representatives asking to be brought under his omophorion (the distinguishing vestment of a bishop that is a symbol of his authority). As one observer in Moscow wrote in August 1923, "When the Patriarch came to power, a popular movement wave arose which, in three weeks, completely wiped out the 'Living Church' in Moscow."[76] Intent on deepening the schism, ARK also resolved that the Tikhonite administration not be permitted to reestablish itself in dioceses outside Moscow except in those places where the Renovationists were firmly entrenched.[77]

Clergy came to Tikhon from Moscow and all over Russia to be received back to his administration. Clergy came to repent for having joined the Renovationists and to ask that they be received back under the patriarchate. Many had sided with Renovationism not out of conviction in its platform, but because of confusion over what constituted the proper ecclesiastical authority, GPU pressure, or the fact that their fellow parish clergy had already done so. The patriarch also met with others who professed that they had refused to recognize the Renovationist ecclesiastical administration and its reforms, that they had continued to commemorate the patriarch in the liturgy, and that they had remained faithful to Orthodoxy and the patriarch.[78]

The most dramatic episode of repentance and return to the patriarchal Church involved Metropolitan Sergy (Stragorodsky), who would be Tikhon's controversial successor. Tikhon at first refused to receive him back, but Sergy managed to convince Tikhon to receive him without a public repentance. That exemption proved unacceptable to other bishops. Those bishops who had remained true to Tikhon during his imprisonment and categorically rejected the Renovationists were particularly scandalized by Metropolitan Sergy's recognition of them. As the most senior bishop to have done so and one who commanded respect, they blamed Sergy for leading others astray. Given that other bishops would not serve with Sergy unless he publicly repented, the patriarch changed his decision.[79] On August 27, 1923, Sergy came to the Donskoi Monastery dressed as a simple monk with none of his episcopal regalia. During the service in Church, he prostrated himself before the patriarch, voiced his repentance, and prostrated himself again. Approaching the patriarch, Tikhon endowed him again with the symbols of his episcopal rank: the panagia, the cross, and the white hood and staff, after which the patriarch greeted Sergy back into communion and they exchanged the kiss of peace.[80] But he never chose Sergy to serve on the Holy Synod. Tikhon welcomed back those clergy who had accepted the Renovationist administration out of pressure or confusion, but since Sergy had rendered substantial support to them by signing the "Memorandum of Three," a more serious public repentance was necessary. The same would follow for the other bishop who signed the "Memorandum," Serafim (Meshcheriakov), a year later (who was then arrested and exiled).

Amid the intense competition between the Renovationists and the Tikhonites after Tikhon's reinstatement, there were also attempts at reconciliation. Initial negotiations occurred on August 26, 1923, between Evdokim (Meshchersky) and three of Patriarch Tikhon's close assistants. Evdokim agreed to reconciliation on the condition that Tikhon abdicate. Evdokim's proposal was discussed at a meeting of twenty-seven bishops on August 29, but it was rejected. This was a pivotal moment confirming of the legitimacy of Tikhon's leadership: Not only had the faithful flocked to him after his release, but now also the bishops expressed their desire for him to resume the Church's leadership.[81] Reconciliation with Evdokim having failed, the patriarch defrocked him, together with Antonin (Granovsky), and summoned them to appear before an ecclesiastical court in April 1924.[82]

The Krasnitsky Affair

The Politburo's closure of the case against Patriarch Tikhon significantly reduced the control that ARK and the political police (OGPU) could exert over him. ARK sought a way to control the patriarchal church from the inside, as it already did with the Renovationists. This scheme involved reconciling Tikhon with the priest Vladimir Krasnitsky, one of the foremost—and most reviled—of Renovationist leaders, a decision that they arrived at on April 8, 1924, shortly after the case was closed. ARK instructed Evgeny Tuchkov to accomplish this through "verbal influence," and if that alone did not work, then he should "discreetly take other measures that are able to have the appropriate effect on Tikhon and the bishops around him."[83]

According to a later account by Father Vasily Vinogradov (1868–1968), one of the patriarch's assistants, Tuchkov came to them with a "friendly proposal" according to which the Soviet authorities would be willing to legalize the Tikhonite Church. Tuchkov explained that the main obstacle to legalization was that the Soviet government did not have confidence that it could trust everyone that the patriarch might appoint. If they could but include one person in his administration whom they trusted, that would open the possibility of the government legalizing the entire ecclesiastical structure as stipulated by the Church Council of 1917–1918, namely a Holy Synod and a Higher Church Council, each with twelve members.[84] Tuchkov proposed Krasnitsky, assuring the patriarch that Krasnitsky was ready to repent and recognize the patriarch's leadership.[85]

Two attempts at negotiation in April and May 1924 both ended in failure because of opposition among Tikhon's supporters and Krasnitsky's own "insolence" on coming to meet the patriarch. Both instances were met with repression—the arrest or exile of bishops, which constituted the "other measures" designed to have the appropriate effect on Tikhon—forcing him back to negotiations.[86] The influential layman Aleksandr Samarin wrote after the arrests that "I am afraid that Krasnitsky will be ordered to sign any sort of penitential form, and the Patriarch, completely isolated, will not be able to resist the new onslaught. This is his situation: remaining firm, he not only becomes the reason for arrests and exiles of bishops, but he also loses the people who are in some way capable and resistant."[87]

The situation followed as Samarin predicted. Krasnitsky submitted a request to the patriarch in which he asked him to "cover with his archpastoral love everything in which I transgressed in the period of the ecclesiastical-renovation movement."[88] Based on Krasnitsky's repentance, Tikhon agreed to receive him back into the patriarchal Church and discuss with the Holy Synod the possibility of including Krasnitsky on the Higher Church Council. There was, however, no Synod to discuss the matter, since all but one of its members had been arrested or exiled. Because Tikhon was willing to negotiate, the OGPU allowed members to return.[89] At the same time as Tikhon expressed his willingness, Krasnitsky was submitting secret reports to the OGPU that Tikhon and his administration should neither be trusted, negotiated with, nor legalized. He also proposed that the authorities allow the Church to hold a Council under Tikhon's auspices—so it would be considered legitimate—and that Krasnitsky would orchestra a coup from within to overthrow Tikhon "*by strictly canonical means*."[90]

Poised to make a serious compromise, the patriarch expected significant returns—namely the legalization of his Church and permission to convene a Church Council—and acted quickly to secure them. Tikhon drafted an encyclical for diocesan bishops to hold local congresses to prepare for the council.[91] The Holy Synod sent an appeal to the Central Executive Committee requesting its legal registration. Tuchkov and Tikhon both drew up alternate lists of people to serve on the Synod and Higher Church Council. Anticipating legalization of his Church, the patriarch also submitted a petition on May 24 asking Tuchkov to instruct local Soviet officials that those bishops the patriarch sent to provincial dioceses were not to be arrested or exiled, as was routinely the case, but allowed to conduct their work freely, and also that those bishops in prison or exile be released.[92] Just when it seemed that an agreement had finally been reached, Krasnitsky undermined the whole process with statements to the press in late May in which he asserted that the patriarch admitted he had chosen the wrong course and that the Living Church had been correct all along.[93]

The patriarch immediately (May 24) issued a resolution that the Holy Synod consider his earlier decision on receiving Krasnitsky and appointing him to the Higher Church Council annulled, given the insincerity of Krasnitsky's repentance. Tikhon broke off negotiations with Krasnitsky before he had been received into communion.[94] At the same time, the patriarch did not make this break in negotiations public so that he could continue pressing Tuchkov with his requests for the legal recognition of the patriarchal and diocesan administrations as well as the amnesty of 115 people, over half of whom were bishops.[95] ARK was indeed prepared to grant these concessions.[96] Tikhon was evidently also trying to buy time in the hopes that his parallel negotiations with Kalinin and Rykov would bear fruit and he would not have to accept Tuchkov's conditions. As seen in the exchange between Rykov and Kursky (May 16–21), that in fact nearly happened.[97]

Bishops were released from prison and exile. Metropolitan Kirill (Smirnov), for example, returned to Moscow from exile in June. On meeting with the patriarch, he asked Tikhon what had prompted his release. "My heart aches," Tikhon replied, "that there are so many archpastors in prisons, and they promised me to release them if I accept Krasnitsky." Kirill responded: "Your holiness, do not think about us, the hierarchs. We are fit now only for prisons."[98]

There were some in the Church who welcomed the possibility of reconciliation between the Tikhonite and Renovationist Churches to end the schism.[99] Krasnitsky's provocative statements in the press, however, caused extreme alarm among Orthodox clergy and believers. Samarin stated that if members of the Living Church were accepted en masse, without proper penance, a new schism would unfold, this time with those who had been faithful to the patriarch. The Renovationist church was nothing but a "clergy without a flock," most of whom were already compromised and could be easily manipulated by the OGPU. Bringing the control of the political police into the heart of the Church, he concluded, made no sense.[100] The acceptance of Krasnitsky into the Church threatened to undermine people's trust in Tikhon.[101] The patriarch responded to one such query with the following reassurance: "I ask you to believe that I will not make any agreements or concessions that could threaten the integrity of Orthodoxy." If the negotiations with Krasnitsky and the latter's unrepentant statements were causing such anxiety—as the patriarch understood they were— "then I find it timely to completely cut off negotiations with Fr. Krasnitsky about reconciliation."[102]

Given the increasing alarm among believers, the patriarch decided to announce publicly his break with the unrepentant Renovationist. Now he could do so in a way that responsibility fell not on the Church leadership—which would suffer repression as a result—but on the mass of believers who rejected Krasnitsky. If there was mass popular resistance, the Soviet authorites could hardly force the issue. On June 28, 1924, Tikhon wrote to Tuchkov that, because of the "innumerable petitions from pastors and especially from lay believers about the undesirability of any sort of communion with Fr. Krasnitsky, I am informing you that I consider it timely to terminate all negotiations on reconciliation with Fr. Krasnitsky." He therefore annulled the agreement he signed on May 21 on organizing a Higher Church Administration.[103]

ARK and Tuchkov responded by ending concessions regarding the establishment of the Church administration. Bishops such as Kirill (Smirnov) were exiled again. Both Tuchkov and Krasnitsky sowed confusion by publishing false statements in the press, for example that the agreement was still in place and that Krasnitsky was already serving in the Church administration.[104] On July 10, *Izvestiia* published an interview ostensibly with the patriarch and Metropolitan Petr, in which the patriarch asserted he had indeed signed the reconciliation agreement with Krasnitsky and had no intention of renouncing it. It is not clear whether the patriarch's words were taken out of context or had been said earlier, or the interview was a complete fabrication—which would have been the first, and likely only, such instance of fabricating the patriarch's words (something that the Soviets would do in later years).[105] Only in September 1924 did the Soviet newspapers report that negotiations between Patriarch Tikhon and Krasnitsky had fallen apart.[106] Knowing about the popular opposition to a reconciliation with Krasnitsky, Tuchkov used that to sow discord between Tikhon and his supporters by spreading falsehoods. In sum, Tikhon was willing to negotiate and compromise with the Soviet authorities, especially when they put enormous pressure on him and he expected significant returns, but was skillfully able to rely on the popular opposition—and his conciliar model of leadership—to resist excessive compromise in the end.

The Right Opposition

ARK's efforts to pressure Tikhon into making compromises were motivated in part by the intention to drive a wedge between the patriarch and his loyal supporters. From his faraway prison cell in Central Asia, the bishop of Ufa, Andrei (Ukhtomsky, 1873–1937), wrote a letter to Patriarch Tikhon in April 1924 criticizing his leadership since his release. During that time, Andrei asserted, the patriarch had accomplished nothing to heal the Church after the divisions that ensued from the Renovationist schism. He criticized the patriarch for having no program for rebuilding Church life, for being consumed only with serving grand liturgies that did little for those outside of Moscow. While the Soviet government and the Renovationists were spreading their falsehoods, Tikhon remained silent. Andrei laid out some proposals which, however, were hardly realistic given the very limited room for maneuver that the patriarch had.[107]

An opposition emerged among conservative bishops and others who criticized the patriarch for being too weak and too willing to compromise. The main opposition was concentrated at the Danilov Monastery, which had become a refuge for bishops returning from prison or exile. Because of their refusals to compromise, the Danilov group was highly respected among believers and Tikhon had to reckon with them. This opposition sometimes criticized Tikhon for his "friendship" with the GPU and considered him a "Soviet" patriarch.[108] Observing this opposition, ARK attempted to magnify it into a new schism.[109]

The Danilov Monastery was headed by Bishop Feodor (Pozdeevsky, 1876–1937). After the patriarch's release, Feodor met with him, but it was clear they did not see eye to eye. A strict monk, Feodor was appalled by the patriarch's easy manner and his humor. "It's all hee-hee and ha-ha, while he's petting a cat."[110] When, however, the bishops met and heard the proposal of Evdokim (Meshchersky) that the patriarch abdicate, Feodor and the other bishops from the Danilov Monastery rejected it. Feodor apparently believed that if Tikhon were not the patriarch, the Soviet government would allow no patriarch (as indeed happened for nearly twenty years after Tikhon's death), which could lead to the collapse of the Church. When Tikhon decreed the adoption of the new calendar in October–November 1923, the Danilov Monastery refused to make the change—and stopped commemorating the patriarch's name during the liturgy until he abandoned the reform. The Danilov opposition to Patriarch Tikhon remained steadfast, disobeying any of his instructions they decided resulted from Soviet pressure. The patriarch related to the opposition with some ambivalence: Some evidence indicates he referred to them as the "Danilov Synod" or "Conspiratorial Synod," and as rebels who threatened Church unity. But other witnesses suggested that he respected the firm line that they took, even using their opposition to his attempts at compromise as justification for ultimately abandoning those compromises.[111] Contrary to ARK's hopes, the criticisms against the patriarch by the "right opposition" did not result in a schism. Their staunch opposition to reconciliation with Krasnitsky led to the arrest of Feodor and many others from the Danilov Monastery in April 1924.[112]

One of those who sided with the Danilov opposition was Aleksandr Samarin. In May 1924, Samarin wrote a letter to Metropolitan Antony (Khrapovitsky) harshly criticizing Tikhon's postprison activities as patriarch. "It is known that anyone who makes the slightest agreement with the GPU in time becomes its complete slave. The Patriarch," Samarin claimed, "did not take this into account when, believing the promises of complete freedom and independence in church affairs, he agreed to make a public repentance and declaration of loyalty to the Soviet government."[113] According to Tuchkov's report discussed above, Tikhon himself was concerned about that possibility. But Samarin also understood how difficult the secret police were making life for the patriarch. He explained that Tuchkov only allowed those that he felt he could control to help Tikhon administer the Church; he controlled them by regularly summoning them to Lubianka, threatening them into submission, and then giving them instructions. If the patriarch attempted to appoint anyone to his administration who did not enjoy Tuchkov's approval, that person would be arrested. According to Samarin, Tuchkov controlled the affairs of the Church like the pre-Revolutionary chief procurators.

Samarin nevertheless believed that "only the Patriarch can resist the GPU, because some force is clearly guarding him, and despite ... their desire they do not commit explicit violence against him." At the same time, the GPU knew how to exert control over him. "I have no doubt that he is not guided by a cowardly fear for his personal safety," but when Tikhon refused to cooperate, "revenge strikes not the patriarch, but someone among his close co-workers." By threatening "arrests, exile, and shootings" of other clergy, the GPU was able to manipulate the patriarch. Indeed, this was the GPU's main tactic in exerting pressure on Tikhon, as can be seen in the Krasnitsky affair, because Tikhon felt responsible when those around him suffered repression. Samarin also observed that Tikhon's vacillations on issues such as introducing the calendar reform undermined his authority. "Nevertheless, everyone felt that they must not break with the Patriarch. In the end, a kind of tacit agreement formed: relations with the Patriarch must in no case be broken," but those directives that he was compelled by the government to issue need not be obeyed.[114]

Attempting to Legalize the Church

After Tikhon was released from prison, the Politburo ceased issuing orders related to the patriarch. After the Krasnitsky affair, ARK directed its focus away from the Orthodox Church toward other religious groups, rarely even discussing the patriarch. These circumstances granted Tikhon a bit more room to maneuver.[115] At the same time, Tikhon's health was declining. In May 1924, Samarin observed that although the patriarch was fifty-nine, "he gives the impression of an old man. Continual worries and anxieties, as well as illness, undermine his strength" (Figure 9). Between July 1923 and May

Figure 9. Patriarch Tikhon in 1924

1924, the patriarch had three episodes during which he fell unconscious for some twenty-thirty minutes, and he experienced some kind of medical emergency in June 1924 as well. The doctors diagnosed the patriarch with liver disease (nephritis).[116] Given the more tolerant atmosphere combined with his own declining health, Tikhon's main efforts were directed to legalizing his Church in the latter part of 1924.[117]

Tuchkov submitted a brief memorandum to Patriarch Tikhon on November 27, 1924, in which he laid out a series of requirements for the negotiations on the Church's legalization to proceed, which was no doubt elaborated during their meetings: "1) Declaration. 2) Dismiss 3 bishops. 3) A judgment over the actions of the bishops abroad. 4) Adoption of the new calendar. 5) Declaration about the council."[118] By the first point ("declaration"), Tuchkov meant for the patriarch to prepare a statement expressing the Church's relationship to the Soviet government; this became the main precondition for Tuchkov's approval of the ecclesiastical administration and became paramount in the negotiations in the coming months—and was the impetus for what would become known as Tikhon's "deathbed testament." Soviet leaders had also been trying to secure from Tikhon a forceful condemnation of the bishops of the Church Abroad—to the point of suspending or defrocking them—since 1923. The declaration concerning the Council may refer to the proposal for a future council that was subsequently prepared by Metropolitan Sergy (Stragorodsky) in December, which was very explicit about the church's loyalty to the Soviet government.[119] The Soviet authorities also made one last (unsuccessful) attempt to force the patriarch to adopt the new calendar in November 1924.[120]

In response to Tuchkov's requirements, Tikhon requested the summoning of a council of bishops that would have brought together the thirty-six bishops residing in Moscow; an unusually large number of bishops resided in Moscow because they were prevented from going to their dioceses by the OGPU. When Tuchkov crossed some names off the list the patriarch had provided him, Tikhon protested, noting that a truncated council of bishops would "not have the desired authority in the eyes of the believers."[121] The patriarch understood that a council from which some bishops were excluded for ideological reasons would not be considered conciliar by the laity, just as the selective nature of the Renovationist Council had undermined its legitimacy.

As his health steadily declined, Tikhon must have felt a sense of urgency to secure a legal and legitimate Church administration, especially if a Council could not be convened to choose a new patriarch after his death. At the end of February 1925, he submitted a request to the Soviet of People's Commissars and the Commissariat of Internal Affairs to register the Synod, asking Tuchkov for assistance. Once the Synod was in place, Tikhon explained, then it could issue a declaration about the Church's relationship to the Soviet government.[122] On the one hand, as Metropolitan Sergy had pointed out in his note regarding the proposed church Council, such a declaration would have greater authority if issued by a higher church body than just by the patriarch himself. On the other hand, Tikhon likely wanted to have the Synod formed and registered before issuing any declaration to ensure that Tuchkov kept his end of the bargain. It is unclear why nothing came of this. The OGPU observed that, after the sharp decline of the patriarch's health at the end of 1924 and "fearing the collapse of the church in case of his death, prominent Tikhonites were at present taking all measures to establish a Synod," for if they succeeded in legalizing it, that would be a clear authority to succeed the patriarch.[123] Tikhon's file contains a draft of a reply from Tuchkov in which he stated that he "saw no obstacles" to the Synod's registration.[124] Perhaps once the patriarch's health took the turn for the worse, Tuchkov preferred to see the patriarchal Church plunge into disarray.

Last Months

On the evening of December 9, 1924, two armed men stormed into Patriarch Tikhon's apartments. Yakov Polozov, who had been the patriarch's attendant, bodyguard, and devoted assistant for over twenty years, rushed to the door. One of the gunmen shot Polozov twice, once in the head and once in the heart, and then the men turned around and fled, grabbing two of the patriarch's fur coats on the way out. Polozov, who was like a son to the patriarch, died in his arms. It was a shocking blow for Tikhon, whose health declined steeply in the aftermath.[125] The murder was never solved. People speculated at the time (and since) that the political police were behind it, and that perhaps Tikhon was the intended target, but nothing in the available evidence confirms that. Internal OGPU reports focused on the incident as a robbery.[126] Believers were struck with grief over Polozov's murder as well as with sympathy for the patriarch. Many people converged on Donskoi Monastery from all ends of Moscow to attend Polozov's funeral on December 12, 1924.[127]

Polozov's murder took its toll on the patriarch's health. On December 30, 1924, after serving a long liturgy, the patriarch collapsed and was unconscious. This episode was far more serious than previous ones, and he was not recovering. On January 7, 1925, the patriarch drew up a Testament regarding succession in case of his death. In it, he appointed a locum tenens to fill the patriarchal throne until a legitimate Church Council could hold elections. He appointed Metropolitan Kirill (Smirnov), and if Kirill were unable to assume the office, Metropolitan Agafangel, followed by Metropolitan Petr (Poliansky).[128]

The patriarch had the best doctors, including professors Maksim Konchalovsky (1875–1942), Vasily Shervinsky (1850–1941), and Dmitry Pletnev (1871–1941), who concluded that the latest episode was caused by angina, a sign that he was also suffering from heart disease.[129] Concerned for his safety, some of his doctors were afraid to send him to the hospital. In the end, on January 13, 1925, Tikhon was admitted to the Bakunin private clinic, where he would remain until the end of his life. The main doctor, Aleksei Bakunin (1874–1945), was the nephew of the famous anarchist. Both he and his wife, Emilia Bakunina (1875–1960), also a doctor, left accounts of the patriarch's illness and death.[130]

Because Tikhon was no ordinary patient, the doctors were extra scrupulous regarding his medical care. According to Bakunina, when Tikhon was admitted, he looked "much older than his age" (he turned sixty during his stay in the hospital), and he was very nervous and agitated. When he wore his patriarchal vestments, he looked grand, but when he was by himself in the hospital in comfortable clothes, he became a "pitiable old man." For two weeks he enjoyed relative peace and quiet and began to recover. As he was feeling better, he relaxed by reading Russian classics by Ivan Turgenev and Ivan Goncharov, as well as Pobedonostsev's letters. But during the first week of March, which was also the first week of Great Lent, he went to the Donskoi Monastery every day and served the Great Canon of St. Andrew of Crete. By the end of the week, he was extremely fatigued. After that, he continued to serve, but only on the weekends, but each time he did so he suffered from exhaustion.[131]

From the day he moved into the clinic, and especially after he began to feel a bit better, the patriarch never ceased to have visitors. Polozov's widow came frequently. Metropolitan Petr visited daily to discuss issues of church business, often against the recommendation of his doctors. Sometimes Tikhon also attended meetings of the Synod, after which he would return late and in particularly bad shape. The patriarch felt alone because all the people with whom he had been close had been sent away. Tuchkov questioned the Bakunins about the patriarch's condition and care. He visited several times during the months the patriarch was in the clinic. Tikhon did not say anything about their conversations, except that Tuchkov had suggested to the patriarch that he retire and move to the south of Russia; the patriarch replied that he would have time for rest—but until then "it was necessary to work." Bakunina observed that Tikhon was anxious before Tuchkov's visits, but in his way, tried to joke about it, saying that "tomorrow, 'someone in gray' will visit me."[132]

Tuchkov commented on the situation of the Church during the winter of 1924–1925 after Tikhon's health took a turn for the worse. He admitted that they were unable to control the patriarch, but at least could exert enough influence to ensure he remained loyal to the government. He further conceded that the patriarchal Church had fully rebuilt itself after its clash with the government in 1922. The patriarch had succeeded in restoring the hierarchical apparatus and placing bishops in almost every diocese who, for their part, were laboring to create a normal administrative apparatus locally, even though these did not have legal registration. One of the things that distinguished the Tikhonite Church from the Renovationists was that the former declared their political "neutrality," while the latter declared their "loyalty" to the Soviet government. Though Tikhon had succeeded in consolidating the Church since his release, according to Tuchkov, "in connection with the sufficiently serious illness of patriarch Tikhon and his possible death, the situation of the Tikhonites could abruptly change for the worse" because, without a single authoritative person to lead the Church, it could fragment into different groups.[133]

The patriarch was interrogated by one of Tuchkov's assistants on March 21, 1925, with the intent to implicate him in a case involving a group of people who had been arrested in December 1924. These individuals were accused of gathering information on clergy who had been repressed by the Soviet regime that they were going to send to a pan-Orthodox Council that the 1923 Congress in Constantinople planned for 1925 (though it never took place). After the interrogation, Tuchkov's assistant drew up a resolution on opening a case against the patriarch on the grounds that he had the information on repressed clergy compiled to discredit the Soviet government, which violated article 73 of the criminal code. This resolution, however, did not get approval and remained an undated draft in the archive.[134] Opening a new case against the patriarch, which was evidently an OGPU initiative, was not discussed by ARK. Most likely the main intent was to create another mechanism to pressure the patriarch to be more cooperative.

Final Days

In the first week of April, the patriarch had a dental operation to remove some teeth and was administered Novocain. Subsequently, his gums swelled and his throat became painful, so that it was even hard for him to swallow or talk. Nevertheless, on April 5, he went to serve liturgy in one of Moscow's churches, which would turn out to be his last. When the pain did not subside, specialists were called in on the evening of April 7. Before the consultation, Metropolitan Petr arrived and engaged in a long, intense discussion with Tikhon. The patriarch's attendant fetched the doctor, telling her that the patriarch was agitated and "dreadfully exhausted by the conversation, and feels very bad." On entering the room, Dr. Bakunina met Metropolitan Petr on his way out "with some sort of papers."[135] Metropolitan Serafim (Aleksandrov), the other remaining member of the Synod alongside Petr, later reported that on the day he died, Patriarch Tikhon gave to Petr his testament regarding succession and the document known as the "deathbed testament."[136]

After the medical consultation, the patriarch felt another seizure coming on and was given some morphine. When his attendant asked him to lay down, the patriarch replied: "I'll have time, Kostia, to lay down. The night will be long, the night will be dark." He calmed down and appeared to be feeling better when the doctor left, but as soon as she returned to her apartment, she was called back. She found Tikhon in the midst of an attack of angina pectoris, pointing to his heart and complaining of pain, while his pulse was dropping. The medicines administered did not help, and at 11:45 in the evening of April 7, 1925, Patriarch Tikhon died.[137]

There was immediate speculation in Moscow and rumors about the cause of the patriarch's death, even though it was generally known that he was gravely ill. Some surmised that the suffering resulting from the division in the Church had hastened his death; rumors that he was poisoned circulated, especially abroad.[138] According to a report from the Latvian embassy, there were rumors that the dose of morphine he was given caused his death.[139] The morphine dose, however, was administered with the oversight of his regular doctor. Patriarch Tikhon's death did not, moreover, come as a surprise to his doctors and others close to him.[140] There is currently no available evidence to support the rumors of foul play. The Bakunin doctors, who enjoyed the complete trust of the patriarch, asserted unequivocally that he died of natural causes—one in the Soviet press after the patriarch's death, the other years later while in emigration. They pointed out that his declining health could have been slowed with complete rest but was exacerbated by the patriarch's exhausting schedule of Church service. There is no evidence that has come to light thus far that either the Politburo or ARK was even preoccupied with the patriarch, let alone planning his demise, and the OGPU would not have acted on its own initiative in such a high-profile case. As the patriarch himself anticipated on the very day that he was chosen for the patriarchate, "from now on the care for all the churches of Russia are laid upon me and there stands before me a dying for them each day."[141] The prolonged imprisonments, with the constant threat of death or further arrest to himself and everyone around him, combined with the constant anxiety about how to lead the Church under such pressures, took a heavy toll on his health.[142]

Upon Patriarch Tikhon's death, the doctors immediately called Metropolitan Petr to inform him. Tuchkov also came and wanted to know all the details, even inspecting the patriarch's body to ensure there was no foul play. Tuchkov ordered that the patriarch's body be transferred that night by ambulance to the Donskoi Monastery.[143] The following day, the head of the Secret Department of the OGPU sent a secret memorandum to the Party Central Committee, informing them of the patriarch's death that relayed the basic facts of time, place, and cause of death.[144] In its final resolution relating to Patriarch Tikhon, on April 8 the Politburo directed that the press should wait to announce his death until the following day in the normal order, though in a prominent place, and that only the basic facts were to be included in the notice.[145]

The next day, Tikhon's body was clothed in his patriarchal vestments and moved into the center of the church. The news of the patriarch's death spread immediately throughout Moscow. According to a Latvian diplomat, people had to wait in line six to ten hours to pay their respects, the line was a mile or more, and there were far more people for Tikhon's funeral than for Lenin's.[146] The OGPU report that approximately 5,000 people came on the first day and an estimated 50,000 people came each day, often late into the night, on April 9, 10, and 11. The OGPU informants paid careful attention to rumors and conversations, and while they assessed the crowd as being "anti-Soviet," they observed that, overall, there were no suspicious political conversations.[147]

On the day of the patriarch's funeral, April 12, OGPU informants estimated that 30,000–40,000 people were gathered inside the monastery grounds, with an added 15,000 outside the monastery walls. A priest who came from Leningrad described how he made his way to the Donskoi Monastery on the morning of the funeral with difficulty because there were so many people cramming onto trams; those who could not find one walked together as an unbroken mass of people heading to the funeral. The service, which began in the church and included a procession around it, lasted for seven hours. Some two hundred clergy served, and delegates from the American and English missions were present as well. The entire courtyard was packed with people. OGPU informants observed that good order was kept despite the large crowds and absence of police. The funeral procession went through the courtyard with the coffin and made their way into the monastery's small church, where Patriarch Tikhon's body was laid to rest.[148]

Conclusions

On April 9, 1925, two days after Patriarch Tikhon died, Metropolitan Petr (Poliansky) wrote to Mikhail Kalinin to inform him that he was taking up the administration of the Russian Orthodox Church and forwarded to him Patriarch Tikhon's testament regarding succession of January 7, 1925. On April 12, when bishops were gathered for the patriarch's funeral, the patriarch's succession testament was read aloud. Given that Metropolitans Kirill and Agafangel were both in exile, the only person able to assume the position was Metropolitan Petr. All the bishops present signed an act to that effect.[1]

Tikhon's "Deathbed Testament"

One of the most disputed issues in Patriarch Tikhon's biography is the authenticity of the text known as his "deathbed testament," which Metropolitans Petr and Tikhon (Obolensky) delivered to the Soviet press agency on April 14 and was published in *Izvestiia* and *Pravda* on April 15, 1925. The papers included a facsimile of the patriarch's signature dated the day he died, April 7, 1925.[2] Because of its statements regarding acceptance of the Soviet government and criticism of the Church Abroad, many—especially among the Church Abroad—believed that the text was a forgery or that Tikhon was forced to sign it. Metropolitan Antony (Khrapovitsky), making such arguments immediately after the text appeared, implied that the patriarch's instructions, especially as directed at the Church Abroad, could be ignored.[3]

The purpose of the "testament" was to explicate the Church's proper relationship to the Soviet state. The text declared: "Without allowing any sort of compromises or concessions in the sphere of faith, as citizens we should be sincere towards the Soviet government and the work of the USSR for the common good." The Church should not engage in politicking and should not harbor hopes or designs of a return of the monarchist order. It also celebrated that Soviet law and the constitution should guarantee freedom of conscience and religion.[4]

The text focused particularly on the Church Abroad, criticizing its leaders who "use Our name and Our ecclesiastical authority" to engage in harmful anti-Soviet activities. "They are free to [have] their convictions," but they had disobeyed the patriarch by conducting political activities in the name of the Church. If the leaders of the Church Abroad did not cease their political activities, they would face possible suspension and judgment by a future Church Council, even in absentia. The patriarch also countered the Church Abroad's attempts to undermine his authority when they claimed that his statements were not issued freely and therefore did not have to be obeyed. "We declare as a lie and temptation all fabrications about Our lack of freedom, for there is not a power on earth that could bind Our episcopal conscience and Our patriarchal word."[5]

The declaration ended by placing obedience to the government in a religious framework, telling believers that they could obey the Soviet government without fear they were going against the Church; moreover, they should do so "not out of fear, but out of conscience," since St. Paul himself stated that there was no power that was not permitted by God (Romans 13:1). If believers show themselves to be good citizens, the "testament" concluded, the government would come to trust them and reciprocate by allowing them to engage in religious instruction for the faithful (which was especially important to ordinary believers), to have theological schools for training clergy, and to publish books and journals.[6]

Although the text does not say anything substantially new from his earlier declarations, it became the subject of controversy because it appeared as the patriarch's final word, his final instructions to the Church, and therefore carried a special weight. The intensity of contrary viewpoints can be seen in the commentary of two émigré churchmen who knew Patriarch Tikhon personally and had information from witnesses to the events: Metropolitan Elevfery (Bogoiavlensky) and Father Vasily Vinogradov. Elevfery, who was metropolitan of Vilnius and visited Moscow in 1928, asserted that, according to its content, the document "would not have aroused either dispute or suspicion that it authentically belonged to the patriarch had his life continued." What allowed room for doubt was precisely that it was published after his death. But Serafim (Aleksandrov), who served on the Synod in those years, assured Elevfery that the text was authentic.[7] Father Vinogradov, by contrast, considered the text a profound reversal of Tikhon's earlier positions. Having left Russia and joined the Church Abroad, Vinogradov published an influential argument that the patriarch and the Synod drafted a text on the day Tikhon died, which was then edited by Tuchkov, and when the final version with Tuchkov's edits was taken to Tikhon, the patriarch did not approve the changes and refused to sign it.[8] Vinogradov may not be an entirely trustworthy witness, however, since years earlier he claimed in a private letter that he had firsthand knowledge that the patriarch had signed the text a few hours before his death.[9]

The original copy signed by the patriarch has not (yet) been found in the archives, which means the authenticity of the text remains an open question. Since the publication of documents from the Politburo (in 1997) and the patriarch's political police file (in 2000), we now have access to three substantively different versions which show a clear progression from a first draft to the final version that was published in the papers. Father Dimitry Safonov has made the only substantive analysis of the textual evolution of the "deathbed testament," which is frequently cited by other scholars as conclusive. Safonov builds his argument on Vinogradov's testimony, presupposing a hypothetical first draft composed by the patriarch and the Synod and later modified by Tuchkov, enabling Safonov to come to an apparently a priori conclusion that the patriarch did not sign the version which was published.[10]

It is clear from the extant drafts that the evolution was in fact the opposite from what Safonov argued: The first draft is the most Soviet of all, containing expressions and declarations that the patriarch rejected on earlier occasions and were removed in the final text (such as condemning the archbishop of Canterbury and suspending the leaders of the Church Abroad). In other words, the first draft laid out what the Soviets wanted the patriarch to say, while the second draft, evidently worked on by intermediaries from both sides (possibly Tuchkov and Metropolitan Petr) to reach a compromise text, modified some elements in a more churchly direction. The third and final draft is the most substantively changed, omitting what Tikhon repeatedly refused to say and including language and ideas that the Soviets did not include, emphasizing how the Constitution should guarantee freedom of religion and the last lines about the Soviet government reciprocating by granting religious education.[11]

The final text was therefore clearly a composite which multiple people worked on, with parts composed by a Soviet actor—imparting a Soviet flavor to some ideas and language that many readers detected and aroused suspicions. Although extant copies with minor editorial differences suggest that the text was still being negotiated up until the patriarch's death, nothing in the textual evidence leads to the conclusion that the patriarch refused to sign the version that Metropolitans Petr and Serafim sent to the press agency.[12] Moreover, Metropolitan Petr (Poliansky) insisted on the document's authenticity. In an interview with *Izvestiia* a month after its publication, he stated categorically that rumors of the text being a forgery "had no basis," and in fact among believers there were no doubts.[13]

The proclamation was not originally intended to be a "deathbed testament" and was in the works for months before Tikhon's death. The text itself mentions Tikhon's return to health and resumption of Church leadership,[14] suggesting it was first drafted at a time (such as the end of February) when his health appeared to be improving. Early drafts bore the title of "appeal" (*vozzvanie*) and "epistle" (*poslanie*), and it was the press agency that changed to the name to "deathbed testament" after Tikhon's death. In November 1924, Tuchkov first made Tikhon's issuing a new declaration clarifying church's relationship to the state a precondition for legalizing the patriarchal administration, which was Tikhon's foremost goal at the end of his life. At the end of February 1925, the patriarch asserted to Tuchkov that the declaration would be issued by the Synod once the latter was officially registered.[15] As that did not happen, perhaps Tikhon signed the final version based on a promise from Tuchkov that it would lead to the Church's legalization.

Although many Church commentators interpreted the text as embodying what the Soviets wanted Tikhon to say, in fact one Soviet actor intimately involved in the process was intensely dissatisfied with the changes that were made to the final text. An unsigned internal memo in the patriarch's secret police file objected to the notion that the Soviet government was to be tolerated by believers "only because it was allowed by God" and not out of sincere conviction in the absolute rightness of the Soviet cause. The author was also displeased with the discussion of the freedom of conscience (which was not in the first draft) as well as the "casuistic reservations and limitations" that clergy could only be judged by a Church Council, which meant the Soviet government would have to allow a Council before any clergy could be judged. The testament's final paragraph, which obliged the Soviet government to respond in a reciprocal way, particularly irked the memo writer. He asserted that the patriarch justified making his concessions to the Soviet government in a way that set up a "new Golgotha for Tikhon"—a reference to the fact that believers understood the patriarch's earlier compromises to be a sacrifice for the sake of the Church—to receive permission for religious education. The memo's author also felt that the declaration's ending pointed to the "firm intractability" of the Tikhonite Church, which had reasserted its strength—placing the Soviet government in the weak position of also granting concessions. Although this author understood the patriarch's testament to be "revolutionary" in its acceptance of the Soviet government, he concluded overall that the "testament" had the effect of subverting what the Soviets intended to gain from having Tikhon make such a statement in the first place.[16]

In short, it is clear that the text published as his "deathbed testament" was not solely authored by Tikhon, but rather was a composite text showing multiple hands, including, likely, the patriarch himself. We cannot yet know for certain whether Patriarch Tikhon signed the text that was published, but the testimony of those close to him indicates he did so on the day he died. What is certain is that he was intending to produce a declaration that articulated in a fuller form the Church's relationship to the Soviet state that was supposed to be part of a deal to ensure the Church's legalization along the lines of the text published. Because of the circumstances in which it appeared, "deathbed testament" did not have the effect on believers that the Soviet authorities hoped, nor did it lead to the Church's legalization as the patriarch wanted.

The Russian Orthodox Church After Patriarch Tikhon's Death

Patriarch Tikhon had been close to securing some sort of normalization of relations between the Orthodox Church and the Soviet state. To do so, he was willing to make certain concessions, but within limits that did not compromise the integrity of the Church. The patriarch reportedly said before his death that he needed to live "three more years"—and indeed, had he, he might have been able to normalize and legalize the Church's situation. With his death, however, the Anti-Religious Commission and the political police seized on the patriarch's absence to sow confusion and disarray.

Without question the choices the patriarch faced were unclear. Russian émigré sources repeat a story of the catacomb bishop Maksim (Zhizhilenko, 1885–1931), who claimed that the patriarch, late in life, expressed to him his "tormenting doubts" about the path of compromise with the Soviet government he had chosen and became convinced that the government's political demands came into conflict with maintaining one's loyalty to Christ. Shortly before his death, the patriarch supposedly told Zhizhilenko that the only way for the Church to remain faithful to Christ would be to go into the catacombs.[17] Such a story served to legitimate the catacomb church and cast doubt on the compromises made by Tikhon's successor, Sergy (Stragorodsky), by suggesting that any compromise with the Soviets was a betrayal, and the only option was to go underground as the catacomb church did.

Although Tikhon likely did have "tormenting doubts" about the limits of compromise, the evidence demonstrates that until his death the patriarch continued to negotiate with the Soviet government in the attempt to secure a legal existence for the Church. The Russian Orthodox Church had no choice but to coexist within the Soviet Union; Tikhon sought to find a way for it to be neither "pro-Soviet" nor "anti-Soviet," but "non-Soviet," maintaining its independent existence to offer a sphere for Orthodox Christians to maintain their own private beliefs and values. Given Bolshevik ambitions to eliminate any sphere distinct from communist ideology, this was a nearly impossible struggle—but Tikhon showed the path for some who succeeded.

Patriarch Tikhon enjoyed a unique authority in the Church both among ordinary believers and among clergy. None of the other bishops that remained in Russia enjoyed his reputation, and those who could have commanded respect had all been arrested or exiled. As a consequence, the Church leadership was in disarray. On December 6, 1925, Metropolitan Petr appointed Metropolitan Sergy (Stragorodsky) as his deputy should anything happen to him—and days later Petr was arrested. Sergy assumed the office of the deputy patriarchal *locum tenens* and then was himself arrested in 1926 and subject to intense pressure until he agreed to compromises.

Sergy issued a declaration of loyalty to the Soviet Union on June 29, 1927, which caused division both within the Soviet Union and with the Church Abroad. Even more than the declaration itself, Sergy allowed the interference of the OGPU in internal matters of the Church, including the appointment of bishops and suspension of clergy who disagreed with his policy. Sergy also demanded that Russian Orthodox clergy abroad declare their loyalty to the Soviet government, a step too far for clergy living in other countries to tolerate. Within the Soviet Union, some authoritative Church leaders also broke relations with Sergy. Soviet authorities were content with both its control over Sergy and with the confusion and division among different Church factions that his compromises caused.[18]

Although there was turmoil in the Church's leadership, Tikhon, by empowering the laity, ensured that religion remained vibrant among the people, especially in the countryside. This became intolerable to Stalin, which resulted in an intense assault on lived religion that accompanied the campaign to collectivize agriculture beginning in 1929, when village churches were closed and clergy "de-kulakized" and exiled along with peasants who resisted collectivization.[19] Repression reached a fever pitch during the Great Terror of 1937–1938, when the political police targeted clergy and active believers. The Terror, which was sparked off by the Secret Order No. 447 of July 30, 1937, listed "church people" (*tserkovniki*) as one category of "anti-Soviet elements" to be targeted in the operation. By November, the head of the political police (NKVD) reported to Stalin that over 31,000 "church people and sectarians" had been arrested, including 166 bishops, over 9,000 priests and 2,000 monks, and nearly 20,000 laity. The NKVD executed half those clergy and a third of the lay believers, sending the rest to the Gulag. The Orthodox episcopate was decimated, and half of the priests had already been repressed just in these first months of the operation—which continued for another year.[20] By 1939, only four Orthodox bishops remained alive and free to serve.

Soviet policy subsequently alternated between more restrictive and more relaxed. After the Nazis invaded the Soviet Union in 1941, Stalin dramatically reversed policy toward the Church, ending antireligious propaganda and persecution and allowing churches to reopen to strengthen support for the Soviet Union. In 1943, Church leaders even met with Stalin in the Kremlin, as a consequence of which they were permitted to hold a council of bishops and elect Metropolitan Sergy (Stragorodsky) to the patriarchate. The Orthodox Church finally received legal status, and a new government body, the Council for Russian Orthodox Affairs (later the Council for Religious Affairs) was formed to manage the Church. Yet Nikita Khrushchev's program of "de-Stalinization" entailed a reversal of the late Stalin policy of religious tolerance and reinvigorated the antireligious campaign. For the last decades of the Soviet Union, the government exercised tight control over the Orthodox Church, such that its leadership was accustomed to state control and the institutional culture of the Church itself was thoroughly "sovietized." The state also found means to dissuade believers' religious participation, so that the population was thoroughly "unchurched."

In 1988, the young reformer Mikhail Gorbachev (1931–2022) permitted a massive public celebration of the millennium of the Christianization of Rus. In the new atmosphere of tolerance, when communist ideology was crumbling, people began returning to church on a mass scale. Both the Orthodox Church and Russia itself experienced a period of freedom in the 1990s, much as it did in 1917, though it was an unstable and disorienting period for many. Indeed, there was renewed public interest in the Church Council of 1917–1918 and hopes that the promise of that Council could finally come to fruition. As in 1917, a different direction was possible for the Russian Orthodox Church as it was for Russia itself.

Since 2009, when Kirill (Gundiaev) became patriarch, the Russian Orthodox Church has returned to an imperial-hierarchal model which seeks its support less through deepening its cooperation with believers at the grassroots level, and more through greater cooperation with the state under President Putin and aligning with the state's agenda as the means of securing political and financial support. Many mechanisms of rule and propaganda remain the same in Putin's Russia as they were in the Soviet Union; only the ideological content has changed. Now, instead of a state ideology hostile to Russian Orthodoxy, a particular expression of Russian Orthodoxy is bolstering the state's ideology with an anti-Western construction of "traditional Christian values," Russian patriotism, and imperialistic militarism. Patriarch Kirill's leadership style could hardly be more different from that of Patriarch Tikhon. As a mirror to Putin's presidency, Kirill has established a "vertical of power" that has undercut the authority of the Church Council, which is now called only to elect new patriarchs, and concentrated the power in the council of bishops, the Holy Synod, and above all the patriarchate. Rather than resisting and remaining independent in the face of unjust political power, as Patriarch Tikhon had done, Patriarch Kirill has made the Orthodox Church complicit with it.

Canonization

Because of Tikhon's resistance to the Soviet persecution of the Orthodox Church, he was long regarded in Church circles in Russia and abroad as an exemplary figure. The Church Abroad canonized Patriarch Tikhon as a "confessor," someone who suffers for defending the faith, on November 1, 1981, along with other "new martyrs and confessors," including the royal family. The possibility of canonizing the new martyrs was raised in the Church Abroad a decade earlier—though some doubted whether the Church Abroad, as not representing the fullness of the Russian Church, had the authority and right to canonize saints. Among the participants of the Bishops' Council in 1981, there was clearly ambivalence toward Patriarch Tikhon, both because of his attempt to adopt the new calendar—something the Church Abroad rejected as a fundamental point of canonical importance—and his concessions to the Soviet government and calls for a complete cessation of the political struggle against it. The council nevertheless ascribed particular importance to the fact that the patriarch had, in their interpretation, anathematized the "satanic and anti-Christian essence" of the Soviet government and ostensibly never retracted that anathema. There was also controversy over whether the council would canonize Tsar Nicholas II and the royal family along with and "heading" the new martyrs of the Church, or whether it was more correct to speak of the new martyrs "headed by Patriarch Tikhon." In the end, the act of canonization mentioned the "special place" occupied by the tsar and the royal family—who were listed in the prayers before Patriarch Tikhon and other clergy leaders.[21]

Even before the Soviet Union collapsed, Patriarch Tikhon was canonized a saint by the Moscow Patriarchate at a Bishops' Council on October 9, 1989. Paradoxically, the initiative, or at least decisive support, came from the head of the Soviet Council for Religious Affairs (1984–1989), Konstantin Kharchev, who had initiated the reversal of Soviet policy toward religion under Perestroika. Kharchev, in learning about Tikhon, concluded that the patriarch had in fact been a wise leader who had followed the "only correct path." Kharchev therefore expended considerable energy to "restore his good name and remove the stigma of an 'enemy of the people.'" The Church leadership would have been unable to canonize Tikhon then without Kharchev's cooperation.[22]

The Acts of the October 1989 Council canonized Tikhon together with Patriarch Iov (d. 1607) as part of a celebration of the four-hundredth anniversary of the foundation of the Moscow Patriarchate. The justification for canonization sounded very different than that of the Church Abroad and glossed over the patriarch's conflict with the Soviet regime, avoiding any political references. Tikhon was canonized because of the "purity of his life" and the way he submitted himself to God's will; his service to the Church and to people in general; his "courageous standing up for the faith" in the face of mortal danger (without explicit reference to his conflict with the Soviet government); his resistance of the "schismatics" (i.e., the Renovationists), the abuse he endured from them, and his struggle to reunify the Church; and his missionary activity.[23] Tikhon was canonized as a *sviatitel*—the standard title for a sainted bishop who was a great church leader—rather than confessor (*ispovednik*), someone who suffered for the truth, because the Church was still concerned about a negative reaction from the Soviet government.[24]

The act of Tikhon's canonization mentioned that his remains in the small cathedral of the Donskoi Monastery were to be regarded as holy relics. At his death in 1925, Tikhon was buried near the southern wall inside that church, but at the time of canonization the exact location was unknown. There had been persistent rumors that his body was no longer there, that it had been removed at some point in the Soviet period—either by the Soviets, who reburied or destroyed his remains to prevent them from being venerated, or by someone within the Church to prevent that from happening—but where, no one knew. The mystery was solved a few years later when, during reconstruction after a fire in November 1992, a crew excavated behind a nineteenth-century air duct for the heating and found a secret crypt with an oak coffin topped by a marble plaque with the inscription "His Holiness Tikhon, Patriarch of Moscow and all Russia," which contained Tikhon's body. Patriarch Aleksy II came on the night of November 17–18, 1992, when the coffin was brought out. On November 22, there was a solemn public ceremony in which the coffin was opened.[25] His remains, considered as relics by the Orthodox faithful, have since resided in a reliquary inside the main cathedral at Donskoi Monastery. Today, icons of St. Tikhon adorn Orthodox Churches both in Russia and the Church Abroad, which reconciled with the Moscow Patriarchate in 2007, and the differences between them recede into the past. The Orthodox Church in America venerates him as "confessor" and "enlightener of North America" (Figure 10).

Figure 10. Icon of St. Tikhon the Confessor, Patriarch of Moscow and Enlightener of North America

Patriarch Tikhon as Conciliar Leader

Patriarch Tikhon was canonized as an exemplary leader of the Orthodox Church at a time of its greatest challenges, yet his legacy has been interpreted differently depending upon the political context. To this day, Western scholars are caught in a binary interpretation: Either religious leaders were dissidents and rejected any compromise with communist governments or they became "collaborationists." They routinely depict Patriarch Tikhon as having rejected any compromise in the beginning but making compromises by the end.[26] In fact, the patriarch attempted to negotiate with the Soviet authorities even before his arrest in 1922. Tikhon called on believers to oppose actions of the Soviet government in attempts to defend the Church and in the hope that the government, seeing the popular opposition to particular measures, would compromise and modify their policies. As he stated, the Soviet government was not infallible—just as he, as head of the Church, was not infallible—and therefore he, and believers, had the right to protest its decisions to correct its mistakes or missteps. Some leaders of the Soviet state, such as Bonch-Bruevich and Kalinin, were likewise open to dialogue. At the most critical junctures compromise was possible. And as Patriarch Tikhon never tired of pointing out, if the Soviets had been willing to adhere to their own laws of separation of Church and state and freedom of conscience, the Church and the Soviet state could have coexisted. But for Lenin, the Bolshevik Party under his leadership was indeed infallible ("the Party is always right," Trotsky declared), and any criticism was inherently counter-revolutionary. Ultimately it was Lenin's views that shaped hardline policies implemented by Krasikov, Trotsky, and the secret police. Patriarch Tikhon's numerous efforts at reasoning with the Soviet leadership were repeatedly rejected and only became possible after Lenin's death. The situation that emerged with Tikhon's release entailed not only a compromise and change of course for the patriarch, but also for the Soviet leadership, at least until Stalin's "great turn."

Émigré Churchmen, as well as some recent interpreters, attempted to discern which of Tikhon's declarations and actions resulted from Soviet pressure, suggesting that his instructions were not obligatory because they did not express his will. Such an approach is too simplistic, however. It is now possible to discern how the Soviet authorities pressured Tikhon: First, to be released, Tuchkov "worked over" Tikhon in ways we do not know but also promised to allow Tikhon to return to Church leadership—a promise which was kept, and which made a profound difference. Subsequently the Soviets pressured him with the threat of reopening the case against him, until the Politburo put an end to that in March 1924; of arrest of those closest to the patriarch; but also with promises to legalize the Church and grant it room for greater operation. In other words, the pressure consisted not only of threats of repression but also of reciprocal concessions.

Even more important, it is also possible to know what compromises the Soviet government pressured Tikhon to make—and how he responded to them. The Soviet government pressured Tikhon to adopt the new calendar, to accept the reviled Renovationist Krasnitsky, to issue statements criticizing the archbishop of Canterbury and Ecumenical Patriarch Meletius, to both censure and defrock the leaders of the Church Abroad. Tikhon was willing to adopt the new calendar because he did not consider it a dogmatic or canonical issue but also thought initially he was doing it in concert with other Orthodox Churches; he abandoned it because of the popular resistance. He was willing to accept Krasnitsky on the condition that Krasnitsky sincerely repented of his past actions, and when it became clear that was not the case, he cut off negotiations despite the consequences. At the same time, for the last two years of his life, he consistently refused to criticize the archbishop of Canterbury and Patriarch Meletius; this was something he simply would not compromise on. He was willing to censure Church Abroad leaders for their political statements because they were disobeying his 1919 encyclical on political neutrality and continued to engage in anti-Soviet agitation despite his repeated instructions to the contrary—and because such statements were harmful to the Church in Russia. He was also willing to dissolve their ecclesiastical administration because he believed its existence unnecessary. But he consistently refused to issue any harsher judgment against them (such as suspension or defrocking), deferring such judgment to a Church Council whenever such might happen. In short, Tikhon was willing to make certain compromises—but which ones were still a matter of his choice, and he was willing to do so on some issues but not others based on his principles.

With the polarizing passions aroused by the Soviet experiment behind us, what kind of Church leader Tikhon was can best be understood in the broad perspective of his entire life. In his very first sermon at his new cathedral in San Francisco in 1898, when he called on the clergy and believers to cooperate with him in building up the diocese, Tikhon sounded a leitmotif that would be one of the consistent features of his leadership. Tikhon administered his diocese in a collaborative way that granted initiative, voice, and autonomy to the clergy and the laity. Tikhon embodied the principle of sobornost (conciliarity) in his leadership years before it had become the central concept for renewing the Church. Although the practice resonated with the ethos of American Christianity—where churches had to depend on the support and activism of the laity—Tikhon announced this before he even had any experience in America. Moreover, he repeated the same invitation for cooperation in his first sermons in Yaroslavl, Vilna, and Moscow. It was this trait above all that resulted in Tikhon's election to the see of Moscow in summer 1917. On being chosen patriarch by the Church Council in 1917, when the principle of sobornost had become the cornerstone of the Council itself, Tikhon allayed the fears of those who thought the authority of the patriarch might undermine the hard-won achievement of conciliarity. Rather, he promised to lead the Church as a facilitator of sobornost.

Empowering the laity was one area where, paradoxically, the efforts of the Council and the patriarch converged with those of the Bolsheviks. Parish autonomy was a political issue for the Soviets who intended to eliminate the authority of the ecclesiastical hierarchy altogether by transferring control over the local church to the parishioners. The Church Council, with the patriarch, confirmed that the laity should take control of their churches. Had they not done so, the consequences would have been devastating. As it was, the laity took control of their parishes—but against the expectations of the Soviets, mostly stayed loyal to the patriarch.

This loyalty proved decisive after Patriarch Tikhon's arrest and the Soviet-supported takeover of the Church by the Renovationists. The faithful mostly rejected the Renovationists' efforts to carry out a Reformation of Orthodox Christianity that violated their age-old faith so intimately tied to the lifeways of peasants and even workers. But while the people voluntarily gathered around Tikhon after his release, they also provided limits to his concessions to government pressure. Sometimes it proved difficult for Tikhon to resist pressures from the Soviet government to make certain compromises, such as adopting the new calendar or reconciling with Krasnitsky, because his resistance resulted in the repression visited upon those closest to him. Believers, however, resisted compromises they felt unacceptable. As Tikhon wrote to the Central Executive Committee, the Russian Patriarch does not enjoy "unlimited and boundless power" to govern the Church tyrannically without the agreement of the people. Such an argument was in keeping with the way he had always led the Church, but it was also convincing to Soviet leaders such as Kalinin. The patriarch's empowerment of the laity, which they reciprocated with loyalty, was one of the most decisive factors in the Orthodox Church's ability to adapt and survive during the Soviet era.

For Patriarch Tikhon, sobornost also guided how he approached thorny problems facing the Orthodox Christian communion in the early twentieth century. Even before the Soviets attempted to impose the new calendar on the Orthodox Church, Patriarch Tikhon approached the issue as one needing to be decided by the entire Orthodox communion rather than just the Russian Church. Tikhon did not authorize the Church Abroad's administration until he understood that the Ecumenical Patriarch had already done so, given that the Church Abroad was initially centered in Constantinople. In response to pressures from newly independent states to have their Orthodox Churches granted autocephaly, Tikhon consistently responded that it was not his to grant, but rather the prerogative of a Church Council. Patriarch Meletius of Constantinople similarly spoke of the need of autocephaly to be resolved by a pan-Orthodox Council, though his successor acted on autocephaly and the calendar unilaterally. The subsequent inability of Orthodox leaders to act in conciliar consensus created divisions that continue to contribute to problems and divisions a century later.

In a context of the most profound social and political divisions, Patriarch Tikhon consistently offered one pathway forward: repentance and reconciliation. Repentance followed an authentic self-examination in humility, acknowledging one's own faults and contribution to the problems at hand rather than blaming others, whether those others were other individuals, categories of people, or political parties and ideologies. Only from that basis could reconciliation follow—seeing one's own faults and responsibility should generate forgiveness for the failings of others, rather than judgment against them. Perhaps in this message of repentance and reconciliation is Patriarch Tikhon's most enduring legacy in an ever-divided world.

A Note on Historiography and Sources

There is very little scholarly research on Patriarch Tikhon in languages other than Russian. Aside from the 1960s biographies by Swan, Chrysostomus, and Rössler, only Edward Roslof contributed a short article on him. More has been written in English on Tikhon's American period, including an article by Fr. Leonid Kishkovsky, a special issue of *St. Tikhon's Theological Journal*, and a recent dissertation by Monica Cognolato.[1] As I have been researching and writing this book, Francesca Silano completed a doctoral dissertation focused on Patriarch Tikhon and the Soviet State at the University of Toronto and has contributed several important articles. I have benefited greatly from her research. Her monograph, when complete, will deepen considerably what I have presented and provide many fresh insights.[2]

Research on the Orthodox Church in imperial Russia has flowered in recent decades. Gregory Freeze pioneered the study; since the collapse of the Soviet Union, a new generation of scholars produced a rich array of studies.[3] Until very recently, there was less scholarship on the period of the Revolution and Civil War outside of Russia, and, as a consequence, scholars relied on the outdated and inadequate work of John Shelton Curtiss. Two important recent articles by Vera Shevzov and Gregory Freeze have sketched new directions for research.[4] Several important works focused on Soviet antireligious policy in the 1920s (Luukkanen, Husband, Smolkin). Other scholars have focused on specific themes: Stephen Smith and Robert Greene on the antirelic campaign, Edward Roslof on the Renovationist movement, my research on monasticism, Catriona Kelly on the fate of churches, and Glennys Young on religion in the village in the 1920s. Catherine Evtuhov studied the diocesan congresses of clergy and laity in 1917, and Evtuhov and Simon Dixon have both reexamined the restoration of the patriarchate. Gregory Freeze has analyzed the resistance to the adoption of the Gregorian calendar, the ways in which the

Revolution had an impact on marriage and divorce, and the revival of the parish in the 1920s. The scholarship on the Church Council of 1917–1918 is growing (Kravetskii and Kenworthy, Schulz, Destivelle, Cunningham) (see Bibliography for full references).

Russian Language Historiography

In the Soviet Union, research on religion and the Church was driven by an ideological agenda and served propaganda purposes. With few exceptions, it is not reliable for academic research—though they are not without interest as primary sources to understand how Soviet propaganda portrayed religion. Works by leaders of the Renovationist movement—leftist churchmen who sided with the Bolsheviks in 1922, and whose books were published by the Soviet government at the time—had a profound impact on both Western and Russian historiography.[5] As Church insiders, their writings had an air of plausibility and were not usually marred by the same extremes as Soviet antireligious propaganda. Nevertheless, their writings served an agenda to legitimize their takeover of the Church and justify the condemnation of Patriarch Tikhon, and they were published by the Soviets precisely for that reason; they are, therefore, hardly neutral sources. Since the collapse of the Soviet Union, there has been a burgeoning of interest in and scholarship on the Orthodox Church during the Revolution that has resulted in very important studies (Firsov, Kashevarov, Krapivin, Krivova, Kurliandskii, Rogoznyi, and others).

There has also been tremendous interest in Russia in Patriarch Tikhon since his canonization.[6] Paradoxically, however, there is still no adequate biography even in Russian. The standard is Mikhail Vostryshev (*Patriarkh Tikhon*, 4th ed., 2009), which is published in the series "Zhizn' zamechatel'nykh liudei" [The life of remarkable people]. It is a popular rather than scholarly, critical biography, and is devoid of footnotes. Another biography is Archimandrite Tikhon (Zatekhin), *Sviatitel' Tikhon, Patriarkh Moskovskii i Vseia Rossii: Zhizni i podvigi* [St. Tikhon, patriarch of Moscow and all Russia: Life and feats] (2018). This massive volume reads more like a chronicle than a modern biography, proceeding in a strict chronological fashion by stringing together lengthy quotations from the primary sources, with little interpretation or analysis. It is useful precisely in that it gathers those sources and is richly illustrated with rare photographs.

The only other substantive biography is Mikhail Odintsov, *Zhrebii Pastyria* [The pastor's lot] (2021). Odintsov's publication of primary sources stemming back to the time of Perestroika has been very valuable. Many of Odintsov's interpretations are still very Soviet, which shapes how he presents the evidence. Most problematic, he makes up fictional thoughts and dialogues between historical figures (ostensibly to make the book more "readable," he explains in the preface), which is bizarre for something published by one of the leading publishers of scholarly historical work (Rosspen). Because he frequently does not provide citations to quotations, the reader does not know whether they are from primary sources or his imagination, rendering the book unreliable for historians.[7]

In addition to the biographies which cover the patriarch's entire life, there have been a vast number of valuable specialized studies that focus on particular periods or aspects of his life. Andrei Efimov and Oksana Lasaeva have published a monumental study of the Orthodox Church in North America under Tikhon, while Irina Aref'eva and German Shlevis's book tells the story of the Lithuanian diocese during his time there.

Three important books on the Soviet period are V. V. Lobanov, *Patriarkh Tikhon i Sovetskaia vlast' (1917–1925 gg.)* [Patriarch Tikhon and the Soviet State (1917–1925)] (2008), S. G. Petrov, *Russkaia Pravoslavnaia Tserkov' vremeni Patriarkha Tikhona* [The Russian Orthodox Church in the age of Patriarch Tikhon] (2013), and Father Sergii Ivanov, *Sviatoi Patriarkh Tikhon i iz"iatie tserkovnky tsennostei v 1922 godu* [St. Tikhon and the confiscation of church valuables in 1922] (2024). Lobanov and Petrov focus on selected moments during the Soviet period, rather than attempting to be comprehensive as a biography would. Ivanov's monograph is a rich analysis of the critical period between the famine and the confiscation of church valuables based on a meticulous examination of previously untapped sources, many of which are published in the volume. All three are systematic in basing their arguments on evidence from the sources, judicious in their judgments, and insightful in their conclusions.

The final work of note is Father Dimitrii Safonov, *Sviatitel' Tikhon, Patriarkh Moskovskii i vseia Rossii, i ego vremia* [St. Tikhon, patriarch of Moscow and all Russia and his age] (2nd ed., 2019). This book is focused on the last years of the patriarch's life (1921–1925). Safonov had access to documents in the political police archives that no other researchers have seen; this is very illuminating and makes the book indispensable. Though the work is mostly solidly researched, there are several moments where Safonov is at pains to interpret Patriarch Tikhon's relationship to the Soviet government in a way that results in unconvincing arguments. He repeatedly resorts to conspiratorial explanations, for example hypothesizing that one or another document was not actually authored by the patriarch without any evidence to substantiate his suppositions or even contrary to the evidence.

Primary Sources

Although I have utilized the research of other scholars, the argument of this book is based primarily upon extensive use of printed and archival primary sources. One source that touches on all phases of his life are various remembrances or diaries by people who knew Tikhon. Many of these were collected by Mikhail Gubonin (1907–1971), who as a young man knew the patriarch and collected everything he could about him—remembrances about him as well as his encyclicals, letters, and decisions as patriarch. Some of these circulated as samizdat in the Soviet period and were published in the post-Soviet period (abbr. *Akty* and *Sovremenniki*). Later memoir accounts are used sparingly and with caution.

Although Tikhon corresponded with a whole range of people, not many of his personal letters have been found; there is no personal file for him in any archive as there are for many other bishops. Tikhon evidently had boxes of personal materials that, as he was evacuating Vilna in 1915, he sent to the town of Velikie Luki, near Toropets, where a friend was abbot of a monastery. It may be that those materials were lost when the monastery was closed, though there is a mysterious note in Tikhon's political police file referring to the Supreme Court receiving a box of personal letters and various unsystematized papers. I have never seen any further evidence regarding what was in that box or what became of it.[8] The exception among Tikhon's correspondence are letters to Metropolitan Flavian (Gorodetsky), who was a mentor figure for Tikhon from the time he served in Poland, and their correspondence lasted until Flavian's death in 1915.[9] These letters provide a unique glimpse into Tikhon's personality that is hard to access from any other source.

Before becoming patriarch, Tikhon was a student in Pskov and St. Petersburg and seminary professor in Pskov, dean of the seminary in

Kholm and later bishop of Lublin for the same region, then bishop in North America and archbishop of Yaroslavl, Vilna, and Moscow. For each of those places, I have consulted published reports, diocesan journals, and pertinent documents in the archive of the Holy Synod and Chief Procurator in the Russian State Historical Archive (RGIA) in St. Petersburg, as well as local archives. This is the first biography that has utilized the local archives in each place that Tikhon served: in Pskov, Lublin, America, Yaroslavl, and Vilnius (listed in the Bibliography); the archives of the Church in North America are currently held partially by the Library of Congress and partially by the Archives of the Orthodox Church in America. Father Aleksandr Popov edited a series of books compiling primary sources on Tikhon in North America, containing in separate volumes Tikhon's letters, sermons and articles, extracts from the diocese's periodical on Tikhon's travels, and archival documents (see Bibliography).

The Church Council of 1917–1918 is richly documented. In 2012, a new project was initiated to publish all the materials of the Council, including the reports and discussions from the various commissions as well as a complete publication of the stenographs of the General Assembly.[10] In addition, diaries and recollections of participants provide an important witness, including the recently published diaries of Father Leonid Turkevich, one of the Council's representatives from North America who later came to head the American Church as Metropolitan Leonty.[11]

For a complete picture of the relationship between Patriarch Tikhon and the Bolsheviks, I have drawn on documents stemming from the patriarch and the Church administration, from the Bolshevik Party leadership and organs, and from the Soviet state and its organs, especially the political police (Cheka/GPU/OGPU). Of key importance is a collection of Patriarch Tikhon's encyclicals, sermons, and letters to the Soviet authorities (abbr. *Poslanie*). The most important documents are kept in the political police file on Patriarch Tikhon—a massive multivolume collection of everything the political police thought relevant to building a case against him. The archive is currently held by the successor body, the Russian Security Service (FSB), but I was denied access when I requested to work there in 2016. Fortunately, St. Tikhon's Orthodox University in Moscow was granted access and in 2000 published the *Sledstvennoe delo Patriarkha Tikhona: Sbornik dokumentov po materialam Tsentral'nogo arkhiva FSB RF* [Investigative file of Patriarch Tikhon: A collection of documents from the Central Archive of the FSB], a thousand-page collection of documents; though it is far from the entire file, it is nonetheless the single most important source for anyone researching Patriarch Tikhon (abbr. SD).

Collections of the Patriarch's Chancellery are held in two archives, in the State Archive of the Russian Federation (GARF fond 4652) in Moscow and the Russian State Historical Archive (RGIA f. 831). The former consists of five large files closely connected to the patriarch; the latter is a much larger collection of three hundred files of ecclesiastical administrative business as well as reports to Tikhon from diocesan bishops up until 1924. Historians have barely begun to tap this second collection.[12]

Documents from Soviet state bodies, such as the Liquidation Department, are held in GARF; those of the Communist Party are in the Russian State Archive of Socio-Political History (RGASPI) among other repositories. Fortunately for the researcher, the most important documents from the archives pertaining to Party and state policy toward the Orthodox Church have been recently published in numerous collections. The collections of archival documents that have been utilized for this research include documents related to the passage and implementation of the January 1918 Decree of Separation of Church and State (abbr *Otdelenie*), Bonch-Bruevich's collection in the archive of the Museum of the History of Religion in St. Petersburg (abbr. SGiR), and the minutes from the sessions of the Anti-Religious Commission (abbr. *ARK*).

A crucially important collection is *Arkhivy Kremlia: Politbiuro i tserkov' 1922–1925 gg.* [Kremlin Archives: Politburo and Church, 1922–1925, abbr. AK], edited by N. N. Pokrovskii and S. G. Petrov (1997–1998), which contains materials from the Politburo together with internal correspondence between its members (Lenin, Trotsky, Stalin, and others) regarding religious policy. The second volume contains supplemental material from diverse archives, such as reports from the political police and the Anti-Religious Commission.

The final collection is *Konfessional'naia politika Sovetskogo Gosudarstva, 1917–1991 gg.: Dokumenty i materialy, tom 1: 1917–1924 gg.* [Confessional policy of the Soviet government, 1917–1991, vol. 1: 1917–1924, abbr. KPSG] (2018). It is a synthetic collection that includes much of the material from previous publications but also contains unique documents. It consists of four books: documents from the Bolshevik Party, central organs of the Soviet state, the People's Commissariats, and religious groups and civil organizations. In addition to these collections, various journals routinely publish primary sources, which are cited when relevant in this book.

In addition to Russian archives from Church, Party, and state, I have utilized archives in the United States and Britain: the Hoover Institution Archive (Stanford University), the Bakhmeteff Archive (Columbia University), documents from Americans who were in Russia at the time of the Revolution in the Kautz Family YMCA Archive (University of Minnesota), and materials of the British Foreign Office in the National Archives (London).

Based upon this rich array of sources, the story of Patriarch Tikhon's life can now be told far more completely than ever before.

Abbreviations

AK	N. N. Pokrovskii and S. G. Petrov (eds.), *Arkhivy Kremlia: Politbiuro i Tserkov' 1922–1925 gg.*, 2 vols. (Moscow: ROSSPEN, 1997)
Akty	M. E. Gubonin (ed.), *Akty Sviateishego Tikohna, Patriarkha Moskovskogo i vseia Rossii, 1917–1943* (Moscow: PSTGU, 1994)
APV	*Amerikanskii Pravoslavnyi Vestnik (Russian Orthodox American Messenger)*
APZh	A.V. Popov (ed.), *Amerikanskii period zhizni i deiatel'nosti sviatitelia Tikhona Moskovskogo 1898–1907 gg.* (St Petersburg: Satis, 2013)
ARA	American Relief Administration
ARCA	Alaska Russian Church Archives, Library of Congress
ARK	Anti-religious Commission, 1922–1928
ARK	*Protokoly Komissii po provedeniiu otdelenie tserkvi ot gosudarstva pri TsK RKP(b)-VKP(b) (Antireligioznaia komissii): 1922–1929 gg.*, ed. V. V. Lobanov (Moscow: PSTGU, 2014)
Arsenii	Arsenii (Stadnitskii), *Dnevnik na Pomestnyi Sobor 1917–1918 gg.* (Moscow: PSTU, 2018)
BogSb 6	*Bogoslovskii sbornik: K 75-letiiu so dnia konchiny sviatogo Patriarkha Tikhona* No. 6 (2000)
Delo	N. A. Krivosheeva (ed.), *Delo velikogo stroitel'stva tserkovnogo: Vospominaniia chlenov Sviashchennogo Sobora Pravoslavnoi Rossiiskoi Tserkvi 1917–1918 godov* (Moscow: PSTGU, 2009)
Dokumenty	A.V. Popov (ed.), *Amerikanskii period zhizni i deiatel'nosti sviatitelia Tikhona Moskovskogo: Dokumenty* (St. Petersburg: Satis, 2014)
Dokumenty Sobora	A. I. Mramornov (ed.), *Dokumenty Sviashchennogo Sobora Pravoslavnoi Rossiiskoi Tserkvi 1917–1918 gg.*, 20 vols. (Moscow: Izdatel'stvo Novospasskogo monastyria, 2012–)
Evlogy	Evlogy (Georgievskii). *My Life's Journey: The Memoirs of Metropolitan Evlogy*, trans. Alexander Lisenko (Yonkers, NY: St. Vladimir's Seminary Press, 2014)
GAIaO	Gosudarstvennyi arkhiv Iaroslavskoi oblasti
GAPO	Gosudarstvennyi arkhiv Pskovskoi oblasti

338 ABBREVIATIONS

GARF	Gosudarstvennyi arkhiv Rossiiskoi Federatsii
GPU	Gosudarstvennoe politicheskoe upravlenie (Secret Police, 1922–1923)
IaEV	*Iaroslavskie eparkhial'nye vedomosti*
Instructions	Tikhon of Moscow. *Instructions and Teachings for the American Orthodox Faithful (1898–1907)*, ed. and trans. Alex Maximov and David C. Ford (Waymart, PA: St. Tikhon's Monastery Press, 2016)
Ivanov, *Tikhon*.	Sergii Ivanov, *Sviatoi Patriarkh Tikhon i iz"iatie tserkovnykh tsennostei v 1922 godu* (Moscow: PSTGU, 2024)
KPSG	M. I. Odintsov (ed.), *Konfessional'naia politika sovetskogo gosudarstva, 1917–1991 gg.: Dokumenty i materialy* (Moscow: Rosspen, 2017), vol. 1 (in four books)
LEV	*Litovskie eparkhial'nye vedomosti*
LVIA	Lietuvos centrinis valstybės archyvas (Lithuanian State Historical Archive)
OGPU	Ob"edinennoe Gosudarstvennoe politicheskoe upravlenie (Secret Police, 1923–1934)
OR RGB	Otdel rukopisei. Rossiisskaia gosudarstvennaia biblioteka
Otdelenie	Vladimir Vorob'ev, and L. B. Miliakova, (eds.), *Otdelenie tserkvi ot gosudarstva i shkoly ot tserkvi v Sovetskoi Rossii. Oktiabr' 1917–1918 g. Sbornik dokumentov* (Moscow: Izdatel'stvo PSTGU, 2016)
PE	*Pravoslavnaia Entsiklopediia* (Moscow, 2000–)
Petrov, *RPTs*	S. G. Petrov, *Russkaia pravoslavnaia tserkov' vremeni Patriarkha Tikhona (istochnikovedcheskoe issledovanie)* (Novosibirsk: Russian Academy of Sciences, 2013)
Pis'ma	A. V. Popov (ed.), *Pis'ma sviatitelia Tikhona* (St. Petersburg: Satis, 2010)
Poslaniia	N.A. Krivosheeva (ed.), *"V godinu gneva Bozhia…": Poslaniia, slova i rechi sv. Patriarkha Tikhona* (Moscow, 2009)
PSTGU	St. Tikhon's Orthodox Humanities University
RGASPI	Rossiiskii gosudarstvennyi arkhiv sotsial'no-politicheskii istorii
RGIA	Rossiiskii gosudarstvennyi istoricheskii arkhiv
Safonov	Dimitrii Safonov, *Sviatitel' Tikhon, Patriarkh Moskovskii i vseia Rossii, i ego vremia* (Moscow: Izdatel'skii dom Poznanie, 2019)
SD	Vladimir Vorob'ev (ed.), *Sledstvennoe delo Patriarkha Tikhona: Sbornik dokumentov* (Moscow, 2000)
SGiR	E. M. Luchshev (ed.), *Sovetskoe gosudarstvo i religiia 1918–1938: Dokumenty iz Arkhiva Gosudarstvennogo muzeia istorii religii* (St Petersburg, 2012).
Sovremenniki	M. E. Gubonin (ed.), *Sovremenniki o Patriarkhe Tikhone*, 2 vols. (Moscow, 2007)

TsGIAM	Tsentral'nyi gosudarstvennyi arkhiv g. Moskvy
Vestnik PSTGU 19	*Vestnik Pravoslavnogo sviato-Tikhonovskogo Gumanitarnogo Universiteta. Istoriia Russkoi pravoslavnoi tserkvi* II: 2 (19) (2006). *Posviashchaetsia 80-letiiu so dnia konchiny sviatogo Patriarkha Tikhona*
VVPSDB	*Vestnik Vilenskogo Pravoslavnogo Sv.-Dukhovskogo Bratstva*
ZhMP	*Zhurnal Moskovskoi Patriarkhii*

Archival notation follows the standard form of abbreviation for Russian archives: f. (fond), op. (opis'), d. (delo), l. (list').
For Lithuanian Archives: f. (fondas), ap. (apyrašas), b. (byla), l. (lapas).

Notes

Introduction

1. Greeting speech to the Lithuanian diocesan congress, May 16, 1917, in I. N. Zhiianova (ed.), "'Da budem soiuzom liubve sviazuemi': Neizvestnye obrashcheniia Sviatitelia Tikhona, Patriarkha Moskovskogo i Vseia Rusi," *Bogoslovskii sbornik* No. 11 (2003): 409–12.
2. Editorial, *Moskovskii Tserkovnyi golos* No. 16 (1917): 1–2.
3. "Pervyi moskovskii arkhipastyr' po svobodnomu izbraniiu tserkovnogo klira i naroda," *Bogoslovskii vestnik* No. 6–7 (1917): 135–39, 141.
4. "Izbranie moskovskogo mitropolita," *Moskovskie vedomosti* No. 193 (1917), in *Sovremenniki* 2: 46–48.
5. See S. L. Firsov, "Lichnost' i obraz sviatogo Patriarkha Tikhona (Bellavina) v Sovietskoi pechati (K istoriografii voprosa)," *Tserkov' i vremia* 75 (2016): 208–52.
6. Gregory Freeze, "Religion and Revolution: The Russian Orthodox Church Transformed," in *A Companion to the Russian Revolution*, ed. Daniel Orlovsky (Malden, MA: Wiley-Blackwell, 2020), 277.
7. Felix Corley, "Believers' Responses to the 1937 and 1939 Soviet Censuses," *Religion, State and Society* 22, no. 4 (1994): 403–17.
8. E.g., Laura Engelstein, *Russia in Flames: War, Revolution, Civil War, 1914–1921* (New York: Oxford University Press, 2018), Mark Steinberg, *The Russian Revolution, 1905–1921* (Oxford: Oxford University Press, 2017), and Yuri Slezkine, *The House of Government: A Saga of the Russian Revolution* (Princeton: Princeton University Press, 2017); none of these works discuss the fate of Russian Orthodoxy during the Revolution. Astonishingly, the international team of editors who put together *The Bloomsbury Handbook of the Russian Revolution*, ed. Geoffrey Swain, Charlotte Alston, Michael Hickey, Boris Kolonitsky, and Franziska Schedewie (London: Bloomsbury, 2023) did not include anything on religion or the Orthodox Church at all. S. A. Smith, *Russia in Revolution: An Empire in Crisis, 1890 to 1928* (Oxford: Oxford University Press, 2017), and Robert Service, *Blood on the Snow: The Russian Revolution, 1914–1924* (New York: Picador, 2023), are exceptions in that they devote some attention to religion during the revolution; and the Wiley-Blackwell *Companion to the Russian Revolution*, ed. Daniel Ostrovsky, contains an important article by Gregory Freeze cited above.
9. For a fresh reassessment of religion in Revolutionary Russia, see Alexander Agadjanian, Scott Kenworthy, Nadieszda Kizenko, and Francesca Silano, *Religion and the Russian Revolution of 1917: Conflicts, Encounters, and Transformations* (Bloomington: Indiana University Press, forthcoming).
10. Curiously, the other book on the Church in the Soviet period, Dimitry Pospielovsky's *The Russian Church Under the Soviet Regime 1917–1982* (Crestwood, NY: St. Vladimir's Seminary Press, 1984), has had little impact on the general historical scholarship—perhaps in part because its bias was clearly in favor of the Church.
11. See my article "Rethinking the Orthodox Church and the Bolshevik Revolution," *Revolutionary Russia* 31, no. 1 (2018): 1–23.
12. John Shelton Curtiss, *The Russian Church and the Soviet State, 1917–1950*, 1st ed. (Boston: Little, Brown, 1953), 71–105
13. Smith, *Russia in Revolution*, 215.
14. A notable exception is Francesca Silano, "'In the Language of the Patriarch': Patriarch Tikhon, the Russian Orthodox Church, and the Soviet State (1865–1925)," PhD diss. (University of Toronto, 2017); also see Edward E. Roslof, "Russian Orthodoxy and the Tragic Fate of Patriarch

Tikhon (Bellavin)," in *The Human Tradition in Modern Russia*, ed. William B. Husband (Wilmington: SR Books, 2000), 77–91.
15. Jane Ballard Swan, "A Biography of Patriarch Tikhon," PhD diss. (University of Pennsylvania, 1955); *The Biography of Patriarch Tikhon* (Jordanville, NY: Holy Trinity Monastery, 1964); recently republished as *Chosen for His People: A Biography of Patriarch Tikhon*, preface by Scott Kenworthy (Jordanville, NY: Holy Trinity Seminary Press, 2015). Two studies about him in German were also published in the 1960s: Johannes Chrysostomus, *Kirchengeschichte Rußlands der neuesten Zeit: Patriarch Tichon 1917–1925* (München: Anton Pustet, 1965); Roman Rössler, *Kirche und Revolution in Russland: Patriarch Tichon und der Sowjetstaat* (Köln: Böchlau Verlag, 1969).
16. M. V. Kail, "Patriarkh Tikhon: Lichnost', istoricheskii obraz i bor'ba mifologem," *Novyi istoricheskii vestnik* 50 (2016): 165–78.

Chapter 1

1. The family name Bellavin was not uncommon in northwestern Russia at the time. See *Sovremenniki* 1: 153. Soviet documents and the press generally referred to him as "Patriarch Tikhon" until spring 1922. In March, summons from the secret police interrogations were addressed to "citizen Bellavin" (spelled correctly) (SD 117). The name began to be misspelled in Soviet sources in 1922: e.g., see "'Russkii papa' pered sudom Revoliutsionnogo Tribunala," *Izvestiia* No. 99 (May 6, 1922): 1; see also SD 129, 162. The secret police and official government documents used both spellings interchangeably throughout 1922–1923. It is not clear when or why the incorrect spelling took over.
2. For a general introduction to the features and history of Russian Orthodoxy, see Alexander Agadjanian and Scott Kenworthy, *Understanding World Christianity: Russia* (Minneapolis: Fortress Press, 2021).
3. Timothy Snyder, *The Reconstruction of Nations: Poland, Ukraine, Lithuania, Belarus, 1569–1999* (New Haven, CT: Yale University Press, 2003), 3, 17–24.
4. Barbara Skinner, *The Western Front of the Eastern Church: Uniate and Orthodox Conflict in Eighteenth-Century Poland, Ukraine, Belarus, and Russia* (DeKalb: Northern Illinois University Press, 2009).
5. G. L. Freeze, "Handmaiden of the State? The Church in Imperial Russia Reconsidered," *Journal of Ecclesiastical History* 36 (1985): 82–102.
6. Paul W. Werth, *The Tsar's Foreign Faiths: Toleration and the Fate of Religious Freedom in Russia* (New York: Oxford University Press, 2014); Randall A. Poole and Paul W. Werth (eds.), *Religious Freedom in Modern Russia* (Pittsburgh: University of Pittsburgh Press, 2018).
7. For an overview of the new scholarship, see the introduction to Poole and Werth (eds.), *Religious Freedom*, 1-43; the introduction to Heather Coleman (ed.), *Orthodox Christianity in Imperial Russia: A Source Book on Lived Religion* (Bloomington: Indiana University Press, 2014), 1–20; Nadieszda Kizenko, "The Orthodox Church and Religious Life in Imperial Russia," in *The Oxford Handbook of Russian Religious Thought*, ed. C. Emerson et al. (Oxford: Oxford University Press, 2020), 21–37; on atheism, see Victoria Frede, *Doubt, Atheism, and the Nineteenth-Century Russian Intelligentsia* (Madison: University of Wisconsin Press, 2011).
8. Vera Shevzov, "The Orthodox Church and Religion in Revolutionary Russia," in *The Oxford Handbook of Russian Religious Thought*, ed. C. Emerson et al., 38–59 (Oxford: Oxford University Press, 2020).
9. Swan, *Chosen*, 2; M. Pol'skii, *Novye mucheniki Rossiiskie* (Jordanville: Holy Trinity Monastery, 1949), 1: 85; Mikhail Vostryshev, *Patriarkh Tikhon*, 4th ed. (Moscow: Molodaia Gvardiia, 2009), 9; Tikhon (Zatekin), *Sviatitel' Tikhon, Patriarkh Moskovskii i vseia Rossii: Zhizn' i podvig* (Nizhnii Novgorod: Voznesenskii Pecherskii Monastery, 2018) leaves the story out. According to the version told in émigré sources, Tikhon's father took the three boys into the hayloft, and in the dream Tikhon's grandmother predicted his father's immanent death; but Vasilii had three brothers, and by the time Fr. Ioann Bellavin died, two of his sons had already passed away. The version told by Archimandrite Kronid (Liubimov) is OR RGB f. 766, k. 2, d. 5, ll. 1–3, published

in *BogSb* 6: 90 and *Sovremenniki* 2: 470. In this account, Tikhon was a young boy and his father's death is not mentioned, but details about the identity of the brothers are confused. Tikhon's point to telling the story, according to Kronid, was to explain the impact of the dream on his father, who stopped drinking afterward.
10. On the Bellavin family, see Nikolai Novikov, *Kolybel' opal'nogo patriarkha*, 2nd ed. (Velikie Luki: Izd. Sergeia Markelova, 2010). A *pogost* in nineteenth-century Pskov province was a village that served as the center of a parish community surrounded by other small villages (*derevni*), where the church was located together with the homes of the clergy and a cemetery.
11. Clerical statement for the churches of the Toropets district for 1870, GAPO f. 39, op. 1, d. 1302, l. 80ob.
12. Fr. Ioann Bellavin's report on the conditions of the clergy for Klin, GAPO f. 39, op. 2, d. 839, ll. 110–110ob; for details on the land, see GAPO f. 39, op. 1, d. 1302, l. 181.
13. Iu. G. Popov, *Toropets patriarkha Tikhona* (Toropets: Izd. Uchebnogo informatsionno-komp'iuternogo tsentra, 2000), 18–20; Vostryshev, 8; *Entsiklopedicheskii slovar' Brokgauza i Efron* (St. Petersburg, 1901), vol. XXXIIIa: 641–62.
14. *Sovremenniki*, 1: 128.
15. Report on the Spaso-Preobrazhenskaia Church (Toropets) for 1870, GAPO f. 39, op. 1, d. 1302, ll. 79–84.
16. V. V. Bovkalo, "K istorii sem'i Bellavinykh," *Vestnik PSTGU* 19: 11–16; Tikhon (Zatekin), *Sviatitel' Tikhon*, 16–17.
17. Archimandrite Tikhon, "Rech' v den' godichnogo akta v Kholmskoi dukhovnoi seminarii 9 sentiabria 1897 g.," *Kholmsko-Varshavskii Eparkhial'nyi Vestnik* No. 20 (October 15/27, 1897): 367–68.
18. Gregory Freeze, "Russian Orthodoxy: Church, People and Politics in Imperial Russia," in *The Cambridge History of Russia*, vol. 2, *Imperial Russia, 1689–1917*, ed. Dominic Lieven (Cambridge: Cambridge University Press, 2015), 295.
19. I. K. Smolitsch, *Istoriia russkoi tserkvi, 1700–1917* (Moscow: Izd-vo Spaso-Preobrazhenskogo Valamskogo monastyria, 1996), 1: 452–62; A. V. Sushko, "Religious Seminaries in Russia (to 1917)," *Russian Studies in History* 44 (2006): 47–61; Sushko, *Dukhovnye seminarii v poreformennoi Rossii (1861–1884 gg.)* (St. Petersburg: SPbGMA im. I. I. Mechnikova, 2010).
20. Evlogy 1: 83–88.
21. See Popov, *Toropets* 35–38; V. D. Shchukin, *Istoricheskii ocherk Toropetskogo dukhovnogo uchilishcha* (Saint Petersburg, 1899).
22. See M. Grigorevskii, *Otchet o revizii Pskovskoi Dukhovnoi seminarii i uchilishcha (1873 god)* (Saint Petersburg, 1874), 27; Shchukin, *Istoricheskii ocherk*, 43.
23. The typikon is the instructions for the order of the Byzantine liturgical rite.
24. See the *Ustavy i shtaty dukhovnykh seminarii i uchilishch, vysochaishe utverzhdennye 14 maia 1867 goda* (St. Petersburg, 1871), 72 and 81–82; for the curriculum of the Toropets school in the 1850s and 1860s, see Shchukin, *Istoricheskii ocherk*, 45–47.
25. A list of pupils who finished the ecclesiastical schools in the Pskov diocese in 1878 is found in GAPO f. 291, op. 1, d. 27. Vasilii Bellavin is listed on l. 3.
26. N. M. Medvedeva, "Soslovnaia struktura naseleniia gorodov Pskovskoi gubernii vo vtoroi polovine XIX v.," *Pskov* 25 (2006): 162–70 at 163.
27. E. P. Ivanov, *Pskovskii krai v istorii Rossii* (Pskov: POIUU, 1996), 120.
28. *PE* 11: 184–85; Derek Hopwood, *Russian Presence in Syria and Palestine: Church and Politics in the Near East* (Oxford: Clarendon Press, 1969), 164–71.
29. Gerasimos was metropolitan of Zahle. After his death, Raphael (Hawaweeny) was elected to replace him, though he declined the position.
30. Alphabetical list of students in the seminary for the 1879–1880 academic year, GAPO f. 291, op. 1, d. 28, ll. 1–6ob; Vasilii Bellavin is listed on l. 1.
31. Report on the condition of the Pskov Seminary for the 1882–1883 academic year, GAPO f. 291, op. 1, d. 29, ll. 1–12. His teacher of French was the Swiss Alfred Anspach, who published a book about the Russian economy in 1904.
32. GAPO f. 291, op. 1, d. 29, l. 5ob.
33. GAPO f. 291, op. 1, d. 29, ll. 4–6.
34. *Sovremenniki*, 1: 128, translation mine. After the Revolution, Fr. Rozhdestvenskii emigrated abroad, where he published this memoir in 1922. An English translation was published: A. Roshestvensky, *His Holiness Tikhon, Patriarch of Moscow and of All the Russians: A Memoir*, trans. H. P. (London: SPCK, 1923).

35. Alexander Polunov, "Church, Regime, and Society in Russia (1880–1895)," *Russian Studies in History* 39, no. 4 (2001): 33–53.
36. I. A. Chistovich, *S.-Peterburgskaia Dukhovnaia Akademiia za poslednie 30 let* (St. Petersburg, 1889); Polunov, "Church, Regime, and Society," 44–46; Igor Smolitsch, *Istoriia Russkoi Tserkvi, 1700–1917* 1: 465–473; N. Iu. Sukhova, *Vysshaia dukhovnaia shkola: problem i reform (vtoraia polovina XIX veka)* (Moscow: PSTGU, 2006).
37. *Instruktsiia S.-Peterburgskoi Dukhovnoi Akademii dlia studentov, zhivushchik v zdanii Akademii* (St. Petersburg, 1894).
38. Evlogy, 50; "Patriarshii kurs," *Vestnik PSTGU* 19: 61–62.
39. *Sovremenniki* 1: 154–70.
40. Evlogy, 1: 49; I modified the translation because the reference is not to saving the Church from "public prosecutors," but from the intrusion of the procurators into Church affairs.
41. Petr Bulgakov, "Patriarshii kurs," written after the patriarch's death and published in *Vestnik PSTGU* 19: 44–67; citation, *Vestnik PSTGU* 19: 50.
42. *Vestnik PSTGU* 19: 51–52.
43. *Vestnik PSTGU* 19: 52.
44. *Vestnik PSTGU* 19: 54–55.
45. *Vestnik PSTGU* 19: 56–57.
46. *Vestnik PSTGU* 19: 55–56; cp. Rozhdestvenskii in *Sovremenniki* 1: 129.
47. *Sovremenniki* 2: 43.
48. Silano, "In the Language," 43–53.
49. According to Antony (Khrapovitsky) on Tikhon's election as patriarch: *Sovremenniki* 2: 109; 1: 448.
50. A protodeacon is a rank of deacon who serves with a bishop (or patriarch), usually distinguished by deep and booming voices.
51. *Vestnik PSTGU* 19: 57–58.
52. Tikhon to Bulgakov, January 5, 1914, *Vestnik PSTGU* 19: 80.
53. *Vestnik PSTGU* 19: 32.
54. List of students who graduated in 1888, RGIA f. 797, op. 58, otd. 1, st. 2, d. 36, ll. 25ob–26.
55. N. Iu. Sukhova (ed.), "Neopublikovannaia stat'ia sviatitelia Tikhona (Bellavina)," *Vestnik PSTGU* 67 (2015): 97–122; Sukhova, "Iansenizm v otsenke vypusknikov Sankt-Peterburgskoi dukhovnoi Akademii: ot I. E. Troitskogo k sviatiteliu Tikhonu (Bellavinu)," *Vestnik PSTGU* 72 (2016): 31–47.
56. *Zhurnal Soveta S.-Peterburgskoi Dukhovnoi Akademii za 1887–88 uchebnyi god* (SPb, 1892), 292–93.
57. List of students who completed the Academy course of studies in 1888, RGIA f. 797, op. 58, otd. 1, st. 2, d. 36, ll. 25ob–26.
58. Popov, *Toropets*, 7.
59. Service record of instructor of the Pskov Seminary hieromonk Tikhon, RGIA f. 796, op. 173, d. 318, l. 2ob.
60. Letter of Bishop Germogen Dobronravin to A. V. Dobriakov, administrator of the Synodal Education Committee, 22.6.1888, RGIA f. 802, op. 9, d. 36, l. 108.
61. Letter of Candidate Vasilii Bellavin to Chief Procurator K. P. Pobedonovtsev, 18.6.1888, RGIA f. 797, op. 58, otd. 1, st. 2, d. 40, l. 10. This is the first known document found in the archives from Tikhon's own hand.
62. Report of the Synodal Educational Committee, 6.7.1888, RGIA f. 797, op. 58, otd. 1, st. 2, d. 40, ll. 4–6; on ll. 11, 12, and 22, the Educational Committee informs the Synod's Economic administration, the Council of the St Petersburg Theological Academy, and Bishop Germogen of the appointment.
63. Popov, *Toropets*, 5.
64. Report on the condition of the Pskov seminary for 1889–1890 academic year, RGIA f. 802, op. 9, razdel VIII, god 1890, d. 3, ll. 4ob–5, 16ob–17; for the 1890–1891 academic year, l. 43ob.
65. RGIA f. 802, op. 9, razdel VIII, god 1890, d. 3, l. 5.
66. RGIA f. 802, op. 9, razdel VIII, god 1890, d. 3, ll. 5, 16ob–17, 43ob–44.
67. Levitin-Krasnov and Shavrov, *Ocherki po istorii Russkoi Tserkovnoi Smuty* (Moscow: Krutitskoe podvor'e, 1996), 45.
68. Service record of instructor of the Pskov Seminary hieromonk Tikhon, RGIA f. 796, op. 173, d. 318, ll. 2–4; also RGIA f. 802, op. 9, razdel VIII, god 1890, d. 3, ll. 10–12.
69. *Sovremenniki* 1: 129.

70. *Sovremenniki* 1: 129.
71. Evlogy, 37–46, 55–70.
72. Novikov, *Kolybel'*, 70.
73. Levitin-Krasnov and Shavrov, *Ocherki po istorii Russkoi Tserkovnoi Smuty*, 43.
74. *Pskovskii gorodskoi listok* for 18.12.1891, as quoted in Popov, *Toropets*, 6.
75. *Sovremenniki* 1: 130.
76. Letter of Hieromonk Tikhon to Petr Bulgakov, 23.1.1892, *Vestnik PSTGU* 19: 70.
77. *Vestnik PSTGU* 19: 70.
78. Tikhon's service records, GAIO f. 230, op. 2, d. 4991, ll. 2ob–3; RGIA f. 796, op. 439, d. 833, l. 3ob.
79. Holy Synod, ukaz to Bishop Flavian, March 18, 1892, RGIA f. 796, op. 173, d. 318, l. 8.
80. Evlogy, 1: 112.
81. Synodal ukaz, July 15, 1892, RGIA f. 796, op. 173, d. 448, l. 5ob; *Kholmsko-Varshavskii Eparkhial'nyi Vestnik* No. 16 (August 15/27, 1892): 285.
82. Evlogy, 1: 112.
83. Witold Bobryk, "Rite Changes in the Uniate Diocese of Chełm in the 18th Century," in *On the Border of the Worlds: Essays About the Orthodox and Uniate Churches in Eastern Europe in the Middle Ages and the Modern Period*, ed. Andrzej Gil and Witold Bobryk (Siedlce-Lublin: Akademia Podlaska and Instytut Europy Srodkowo-Wschodniej, 2010), 171–86.
84. On the region, see Matteo Piccin, *Nazionalismi di frontiera. Russi, polacchi e ucraini a Cholm (1830–1918)* (Firenze: Firenze University Press, 2025); Andrej Szabaciuk, *"Rosyjski Ulster": Kwestia Chełmska w polityce imperialnej Rosji w latach 1863–1915* (Lublin: Wydawnictwo KUL, 2013).
85. John-Paul Himka, *Religion and Nationality in Western Ukraine: The Greek Catholic Church and the Ruthenian National Movement in Galicia, 1867–1900* (Montreal: McGill-Queen's University Press, 1999), 32–41.
86. Himka, 57–58. See also A. S. Mel'kov, "Vliianie russkogo Pravoslaviia na politiku rusifikatsii Kholmshchiny v XIX–XX vv.," *Studia Humanitatis* No. 1 (2016). DOI: 10.24411/2308-8079-2016-00003.
87. Theodore R. Weeks, "The 'End' of the Uniate Church in Russia: The 'Vozsoedinenie' of 1875," *Jahrbücher für Geschichte Osteuropas* 44, no. 1 (1996): 28–40; Weeks, *Nation and State in late Imperial Russia: Nationalism and Russification on the Western Frontier, 1863–1914* (DeKalb: Northern Illinois University Press, 1996), 172–74.
88. See, for example, files in the archive of the ecclesiastical administration on the "Orthodox" way to conduct religious processions, measures to dissuade Orthodox believers from visiting Catholic churches, and efforts struggling with the "stubborn" ones: Archiwa Panstwow w Lublinie, fond 97, files 2002 and 2027.
89. *PE* 40: 50–57.
90. In addition to Tikhon, the list included Antonii (Khrapovitskii), who taught at the seminary in 1886; Evlogii (Georgievskii), who replaced Tikhon as dean (1896–1902) and then bishop of Lublin (1903–1912); Anastasii (Gribanovskii) was bishop of Lublin in 1914; Elevferii (Bogoiavlenskii) was seminary inspector from 1906 to 1909.
91. *Instructions*, 157–58.
92. See, for example, the discussion of his speeches to students by Nataliia Krivosheeva, "Sviateishii Patriarkh Tikhon ob obrazovanii i vospitanii," *Pokrov* (October 10, 2019); Evlogy's memoir is full of his discussion of his efforts to "strengthen Russian self-consciousness" (1: 151–91).
93. Evlogy 1: 117–18. "Ruthenian" was the term used to describe eastern Slavs in the Polish-Lithuanian Commonwealth before they diverged into distinct identities of Belarusian, Ukrainian, and Rusyn.
94. Privy Councillor Chistovich, review of educational institutions in the Kholm-Warsaw Diocese in May–June 1892, RGIA f. 802, op. 9, d. 18, l. 13.
95. Journal of the Synodal Education Committee, August 5, 1892, RGIA f. 802, op. 9, d. 18, l. 28–28ob.
96. *Kholmsko-Varshavskii Eparkhial'nyi Vestnik* No. 20 (October 15/27, 1892): 364; *Kholmsko-Varshavskii Eparkhial'nyi Vestnik* No. 20 (October 15/27 1897): 373.
97. RGIA f. 802, op. 9, razdel X, unnumbered file, "Kholmsko-Varshavskaia eparkhiia, Kholmskaia dukhovnaia seminaria 1895–1896 god," l. 23ob. See also Evlogy, 1: 118–19.
98. See *Sbornik statei po istorii Kholmskoi Dukhovnoi Seminarii (1760–1910 gg.)* (Kholm, 1910), 173–81.

99. RGIA f. 802, op. 9, razdel X, "Kholmsko-Varshavskaia eparkhiia, Kholmskaia dukhovnaia seminariia 1895–1896 god," ll. 22–23; Evlogy, 1: 119.
100. "Godichnyi akt v Kholmskoi dukhovnoi seminarii v 1897 g.," *Kholmsko-Varshavskii Eparkhial'nyi Vestnik* No. 20 (October 15/27, 1897): 369–74, esp. 371.
101. See T. V. Shabanova, "Kholmskii period zhizni i deiatel'nosti Patriarkha Tikhona (Bellavina), 1892–1898 gg.," *Vestnik Voennogo universiteta* No. 2 (26) (2011): 132–36; and Shabanova, "Deiatel'nost' Arkhimandrita Tikhona na postu rektora Kholmskoi Dukhovnoi Seminarii po materialam Kholmsko-Varshavskogo eparkhial'nogo vestnika 1892–1897 gg.," *Izvestiia Tomskogo politekhnicheskogo universiteta* No. 6 (2012): 167–72. On the activities of the educational council, see *Tsirkuliarnye ukazaniia, raz"iasneniia i rasporiazheniia kholmsko-varshavskogo eparkhial'nogo uchilishchnogo soveta s 1895 do 1902 goda* (Kholm, 1902), and Archiwa Panstwow w Lublinie, fond 101.
102. Archimandrite Tikhon, "Rech' pred nachalom uchebnykh zaniatii v Kholmskoi dukhovnoi seminarii, skazannaia 4 sentiabria 1892 g.," *Kholmsko-Varshavskii Eparkhial'nyi Vestnik* No. 19 (October 1/13, 1892): 343–45.
103. Archimandrite Tikhon, "Rech' k okanchivaiushchim kurs ucheniia v Kholmskoi Dukhovnoi Seminarii v 1893 g.," *Kholmsko-Varshavskii Eparkhial'nyi Vestnik* No. 17 (September 1/13, 1893): 284–86.
104. "Rech' k okanchivaiushchim kurs v Kholmskoi dukhovnoi seminarii v 1897 g.," *Kholmsko-Varshavskii Eparkhial'nyi Vestnik* No. 14 (July 15/27, 1897): 265–66.
105. V. Bellavin, "Vzgliad sv. Tserkvi na brak (po povodu lozhnykh vozzrenii gr. L. Tolstogo)," *Strannik* No. 12 (1893): 640–52; Archimandrite Tikhon (Bellavin), "Vegeterianstvo i ego otlichie ot khristianskogo posta," *Strannik* No. 3 (1895): 487–99.
106. For an analysis of Tikhon's writings, see Silano, "In the Language," chapter 2.
107. Evlogy, 1: 119.
108. Copy of Pobedonostsev's report to Nicholas II, October 10, 1897, with Nicholas's resolution, RGIA f. 797, op. 67, d. 131, ll. 4–5. See also Archiwa Panstwow w Lublinie, fond 97, d. 2381.
109. "Rech' arkhimandrita Tikhona pri narechenii ego vo episkopa Liublinskogo," *Kholmsko-Varshavskii eparkhial'nyi vestnik* No. 22 (1897): 413; also in *Pribavlenie k Tserkovnym Vedomostiam* No. 43 (October 25, 1897): 1559–62.
110. "Rech' arkhimandrita Tikhona pri narechenii ego vo episkopa Liublinskogo."
111. Evlogy, 169.
112. Evlogy, 119; "Proshchanie Episkopa Liublinskogo Tikhona so vsoeiu pastvoiu," *Kholmsko-Varshavskii eparkhial'nyi vestnik* No. 24 (1898): 512.; see also No. 22 (1898): 453–57, No. 23 (1898): 480–84, and No. 24 (1898): 509–13.

Chapter 2

1. The literature on the American period of Tikhon's life is substantial. On sources, see Alexis Liberovsky, "The Archival Legacy of Saint Tikhon in North America," *St Tikhon's Theological Journal* 4 (2008–2009): 18–40. Of particular importance are the documentary collections edited by A. V. Popov, especially *Pis'ma, Dokumenty*, and APZh (see Abbreviations). For studies, see A. B. Efimov and O. V. Lasaeva, *Aleutskaia i Severo-Amerikanskaia eparkhiia pri sviatitele Tikhone* (Moscow: PSTGU, 2012); Monica Cognolato, "'The Orthodox Church Does Not Build on Other People's Foundations': The Orthodox Church in America During Bishop Tikhon's Years (1898–1907)," PhD diss., University of Padua, 2014; Leonid Kishkovsky, "Archbishop Tikhon in America," *St. Vladimir's Theological Quarterly* 19 (1975): 9–31.
2. Tikhon to Flavian, September 9, 1898, *Pis'ma*, 8.
3. Tikhon to Flavian, September 23, 1898, *Pis'ma*, 9.
4. Tikhon to Flavian, October 31, 1898, *Pis'ma*, 11.
5. Tikhon to Flavian, December 3, 1898, *Pis'ma*, 15; "Pribytie Preosviashchennogo Tikhona, episkopa Aleutskogo i Aliaskinskogo, vo vverennuiu emu Eparkhiiu," *APV* 3, no. 1 (January 13, 1899): 9–21. The narrative in North America follows the Gregorian calendar, although the sources (Tikhon's letters, sermons, reports, etc.) are usually dated according to the Julian (unfortunately, *Instructions* is not always consistent).

6. The following sketch of the development of Orthodoxy in North America is based on the following: John Erickson, *Orthodox Christians in America: A Short History* (New York: Oxford University Press, 2008); Mark Stokoe and Leonid Kishkovsky, *Orthodox Christians in North America, 1794–1994* (Syosset, NY: Orthodox Christian Publication Center, 1995); Constance J. Tarasar and John H. Erickson (eds.), *Orthodox America, 1794–1976: Development of the Orthodox Church in America* (Syosset, NY: Orthodox Church in America, 1975); Michael Oleksa, *Orthodox Alaska: A Theology of Mission* (Crestwood, NY: St. Vladimir's Seminary Press, 1998); Metropolitan Kliment (Kapalin), *Russkaia pravoslavnaia tserkov' na Aliaske do 1917 goda* (Moscow: OLMA Media Group, 2009) and his *Pravoslavie na Aliaske: retrospektiva razvitiia v 1741–1917 gg.* (Tver, 2014).
7. Sergei Kan, "Russian Orthodox Missionaries at Home and Abroad: The Case of Siberian and Alaskan Indigenous Peoples," in *Of Religion and Empire: Missions, Conversion, and Tolerance in Tsarist Russia*, ed. Robert P. Geraci and Michael Khodarkovsky (Ithaca, NY: Cornell University Press, 2001), 173–200; Jesse D. Murray, "Together and Apart: The Russian Orthodox Church, the Russian Empire, and Orthodox Missionaries in Alaska, 1794–1917," *Russian History* 40 (2013): 91–110.
8. See Alexander Krivonosov, "Where East Meets West: A Landscape of Familiar Strangers—Missionary Alaska, 1794–1898," PhD diss., Pennsylvania State University, 2008.
9. Terence Emmonds, *Alleged Sex and Threatened Violence: Doctor Russel, Bishop Vladimir, and the Russians in San Francisco, 1887–1892* (Stanford, CA: Stanford University Press, 1997); V. V. Pechatnov and V. O. Pechatnov, "Amerikanskaia epopeia episkopa Nestora (Zassa)," *Vestnik Viatskogo gosudarstvennogo universiteta* No. 2 (144) (2022): 41–56.
10. Joel Brady, "Transnational Conversions: Greek Catholic Migrants and Russky Orthodox Conversion Movements in Austria-Hungary, Russia, and the Americas (1890–1914)," PhD diss., University of Pittsburgh, 2012.
11. See V. V. Pechatnov and V. O. Pechatnov, "Russkii episkop v Amerike 'pozolochennogo veka,'" *Vestnik MGIMO-Universiteta* 14, no. 1 (2021): 7–30.
12. "Pribytie Preosviashchennogo Tikhona," 14.
13. "Head of the Russian Church Here," *New York Herald* (December 14, 1898); Tikhon's letter to Flavian, December 3, 1898, *Pis'ma*, 15.
14. "Pribytie Preosviashchennogo Tikhona," 14–21; F. Pashkovskii, "Pribytie Preosviashchennogo Tikhona v S.-Frantsisko i ot"ezd Preosviashchennogo Nikolaia," *APV* 3, no. 2 (January 27, 1899): 57–59; Tikhon (Zatekin), *Sviatitel' Tikhon*, 86–87.
15. "Rech' Ego Preosviashchenstva, Preosviashchenneishago Tikhona, Episkopa Aleutskago i Aliaskinskago, pri vstuplenii na Arkhiereiskuiu kafedru/Inaugural Address by the Right Rev. Tikhon, Bishop of Alaska and the Aleutian Islands," *APV* 3, no. 2 (1899): 50, 52; the original Russian and an English translation are side-by-side; I have used this English translation.
16. "Rech' Ego Preosviashchenstva, Preosviashchenneishago Tikhona, Episkopa Aleutskago i Aliaskinskago, pri vstuplenii na Arkhiereiskuiu kafedru," *APV* 3, no. 2 (1899): 50–53.
17. "Rech'/Inaugural Address," 53.
18. Tikhon to Flavian, December 22, 1898, *Pis'ma*, 17–18.
19. Short Report on the Condition of the Aleut diocese for 1898, April 12, 1899, RGIA f. 796, op. 442, d. 1707, ll. 1–6.
20. *Pis'ma*, 35.
21. *APZh*, 25–30; *Pis'ma*, 31–34. For Tikhon's sermon in Minneapolis, see *Instructions*, 19–22.
22. P. P[opov], "Puteshestvie ego Preosviashchenstva, Preosviashchenneishego Tikhona, Episkopa Aleutskogo i Aliaskinskogo, po vostochnym shtatam Ameriki," *APV* 3, no. 13 (July 13, 1899): 356–59; *Pis'ma*, 40–41; *Dokumenty*, 101.
23. Report on the state of the diocese in 1899, April 19, 1900. OCA Archive, Series I.C.
24. Tikhon's report to the Synod, November 4, 1899, RGIA f. 796, op. 180, d. 3686, ll. 1–2; *APV* 4, no. 4 (February 27, 1900): 87–88; the Synod's ukaz of December 31, 1899, OCA Archive, Series I.A.
25. "Iz perepiski Ego Preosviashchenstva, Preosviashchenneishego Tikhona, Episkopa Aleutskogo i Aliaskinskogo, s General'nym Agentom po narodnomu obrazovaniiu v Aliaske," *APV* 4, no. 4 (February 27, 1900): 81–85.
26. Chronicles for the first trip to Alaska can be found in *APZh*, 39–52; the sermon he delivered in Sitka is in *Instructions*, 23–25.
27. *APZh*, 45–52.
28. I. [Korchinskii], "Puteshestvie ego Preosviashchenstva, Preosviashchenneishego Tikhona, Episkopa Aleutskogo i S.-Amerikanskogo na krainii sever Severnoi Ameriki," *APV* 4, no. 20 (October 28, 1900): 409–14 and *APV* 4, no. 21 (November 15, 1900): 429–32.

29. Tikhon to Flavian, August 17, 1900, *Pis'ma*, 67–68. The picture is in *APV* 4, no. 21 (1900): 431.
30. I. [Korchinskii], "Puteshestvie ego Preosviashchenstva, Preosviashchenneishego Tikhona, Episkopa Aleutskogo i S.-Amerikanskogo na krainii sever Severnoi Ameriki," *APV* 4, no. 22 (November 28, 1900): 447–50; see the later recollections: Ioann Orlov, "Iz vospominanii o sviat. Patriarkhe Tikhone," in *Iubileinyi sbornik v pamiat' 150-letiia Russkoi pravoslavnoi tserkvi na severnoi Amerike* (New York: Izd. Izdatel'skoi iubileinoi kommissii, 1944), vol. 1: 168.
31. I. [Korchinskii], "Puteshestvie ego Preosviashchenstva, Preosviashchenneishego Tikhona, Episkopa Aleutskogo i S.-Amerikanskogo na krainii sever Severnoi Ameriki," *APV* 4, no. 23 (December 14, 1900): 465–69, citation at 466.
32. Robert J. Wolfe, "Alaska's Great Sickness, 1900: An Epidemic of Measles and Influenza in a Virgin Soil Population," *Proceedings of the American Philosophical Society* 126, no. 2 (1982): 91–121.
33. I. [Korchinskii], "Puteshestvie," 467, 469.
34. "Pravoslavnaia Missiia v Aliaske (Sev Amerika) v 1900–1901 gg.," *Pravoslavnyi blagovestnik* 1: no. 3 (1902): 103–7, citation, 105.
35. Report on the diocesan inspection to the Synod, November 3, 1899, RGIA f. 799, op. 14, d. 1052, l. 13 (published in *Dokumenty*, 109).
36. Sermon preached in San Francisco, June 10/23, 1900, *Instructions*, 45–46.
37. *Instructions*, 46–47.
38. Tikhon's report on the state of the diocese in 1899, April 19, 1900, OCA Archive, Series I.C.
39. Report to the Synod, November 3, 1899, RGIA f. 799, op. 14, d. 1052, ll. 13ob–14.
40. *Instructions*, 57–58; citation, 131; "Pravoslavnaia Missiia v Aliaske (Sev Amerika) v 1900–1901 gg.," 107.
41. *Dokumenty*, 109–10; 121.
42. Letter to Flavian, August 4/17, 1900, *Pis'ma*, 67–68.
43. D. Oliver Herbel, *Turning to Tradition: Converts and the Making of an American Orthodox Church* (New York: Oxford University Press, 2013), 25–60; Konstantin Simon, "Alexis Toth and the Beginnings of the Orthodox Movement among the Ruthenians in America (1891)," *Orientalia Christiana Periodica* 54 (1988): 387–428; James Jorgenson, "Father Alexis Toth and the Transition of the Greek Catholic Community in Minneapolis to the Russian Orthodox Church," *St. Vladimir's Theological Quarterly* 32, no. 2 (1988): 119–37; Iu. G. Akimov and K. V. Minkova, "Perekhod v pravoslavie emigrantov-uniatov v SShA v 1891–1892 gg. i Sviateishii Sinod RPTs," *Voprosii istorii* No. 1 (2018): 160–70.
44. Report for November 3, 1899, RGIA f. 799, op. 14, d. 1052, ll. 3–5; on the transnational dimension of conversions, see Brady, "Transnational Conversions."
45. Tikhon's report for November 3, 1899, RGIA f. 799, op. 14, d. 1052, l. 5; Tikhon's report on the state of the diocese for 1903, June 28, 1904, RGIA f. 796, op. 185, d. 5851, ll. 8–9; "Aleutskaia eparkhiia v 1903 godu," *Pribavleniia k Tserkovnym vedomostiam* No. 47 (November 20, 1904): 1887–91, esp. 1889; see also Joel Brady, "Becoming What We Always Were: 'Conversion' of U.S. Greek Catholics to Russian Orthodoxy, 1890–1914," *U.S. Catholic Historian* 32, no. 1 (2014): 23–48.
46. Brady, "Transnational," 223–38.
47. *Pis'ma*, 21.
48. *Pis'ma*, 47.
49. See Keith S. Russin, "Father Alexis G. Toth and the Wilkes-Barre Litigations," *St. Vladimir's Theological Quarterly* 16 (1972): 128–49; *Pis'ma*, 42–43; *Instructions*, 82–84; *Dokumenty*, 117.
50. Brady, "Transnational," 489–94.
51. Tikhon's report to the Holy Synod, February 19, 1901, RGIA f. 796, op. 177, d. 3339, ll. 7–9; Synodal Ukaz of January 23, 1901, OCA Archive, Series I.A.
52. Report on the condition of the diocese for 1902, June 9, 1903. OCA Archive, Series I.C.
53. *Instructions*, 152; Tikhon to Pobedonostsev, October 22, 1902, *Pis'ma*, 118–19; report to the Synod, October 22, 1902, RGIA f. 796, op. 183, d. 4643, l. 1.
54. See Frances Swyripa, *Storied Landscapes: Ethno-Religious Identity and the Canadian Prairies* (Winnipeg: University of Manitoba Press, 2010). For Orthodoxy in Canada, see Efimov and Lasaeva, chapter 9; V. E. Kukushkin, "U istokov kanadskogo pravoslaviia: ukrainskaia immigratsiia kontsa XIX-nachala XX v. i vozniknovenie pervykh pravoslavnykh prikhodov v zapadnoi Kanade," *St. Petersburg Historical Journal* No. 1 (2016): 83–96.
55. Report on the Diocese for 1900, March 21, 1901, in *Dokumenty*, 121.
56. Priest I. K[orchin]skii, "Puteshestvie Ego Preosviashchenstva Preosviashchennneishego Tikhona, Episkopa Aleutskogo i S.-Amerikanskogo, po Eparkhii," *APV* 5, no. 18 (September 28, 1901): 383–88. The dates in the article are given according to the old calendar.

57. Letter to Flavian, September 6, 1901, *Pis'ma*, 90.
58. "Mnogostradal'noe puteshestvie," *APV* 5, no. 18 (September 28, 1901): 387–88.
59. For his sermon on the occasion, see *Instructions*, 88–92.
60. I. K[orchin]skii, "Puteshestvie Ego Preosviashchenstva Preosviashchenneishego Tikhona, Episkopa Aleutskogo i S.-Amerikanskogo, po Eparkhii," *APV* 5, no. 19 (October 14, 1901): 403–7.
61. Tikhon to Flavian, September 6, 1901, *Pis'ma*, 90; see also 86–87.
62. Efimov and Lasaeva, 305.
63. Tikhon to Sabler, September 5, 1901, *Pis'ma*, 88–89; Tikhon's report to the Holy Synod, November 26, 1901, RGIA f. 796, op. 182, d. 4165, l. 2; sermon at the ordination of Skibinskii, *Instructions*, 117–19.
64. Report to the Holy Synod, December 2/15, 1902, RGIA f. 796, op. 182, d. 4122, l. 35; see Cognolato, "The Orthodox Church," 165–70; an entire Synodal file on him is here: RGIA f. 796, op. 182, d. 4122.
65. Tikhon's report on the Canadian situation, August 1903, RGIA f. 796, op. 182, d. 4122, ll. 55–58; "Otnoshenie Rossiiskogo imperatorskogo posol'stva v Konstantinopole," *Iubileinyi sbornik*, 172–73.
66. Letter of March 12, 1903, *Pis'ma*, 130; "Puteshestvie Ego Preosviashchenstva Preosviashchenneishego Tikhona, Episkopa Aleutskogo i S.-Amerikanskogo," *APV* 7, no. 7 (April 1/14, 1903): 99–101.
67. "Puteshestvie Ego Preosviashchenstva Preosviashchenneishego Tikhona, Episkopa Aleutskogo i S.-Amerikanskogo," *APV* 7, no. 8 (April 15/28, 1903): 122–26; while there, Tikhon also visited and had an interesting encounter with Dukhobors (see also *Pis'ma*, 130).
68. RGIA f. 796, op. 182, d. 4122, ll. 55–58. On appointing the priest, see l. 71. See also his report on the state of the diocese for 1903, RGIA f. 796, op. 185, d. 5851, ll. 6–8; *Pis'ma*, 200–203.
69. APZh, 241–51; *Dokumenty*, 144–45.
70. Report to the Holy Synod, September 21/October 4, 1904, RGIA f. 796, op. 182, d. 4122, ll. 91; report to the Holy Synod, September 26/October 9, 1905, op. 186, d. 5946, l. 4; memorandum of February 1/14, 1906, f. 182, d. 4122, l. 153; APZh, 363.
71. V. V. Pechatnov and V. O. Pechatnov, "Amerikanskoe sluzhenie sviashchennomuchenika Aleksandra Khotovitskogo," *Vestnik Viatskogo gosudarstvennogo universiteta* No. 3 (145) (2022): 56–70; V. V. Pechatnov and V. O. Pechatnov, "Sviashchennomuchenik Ioann Kochurov: gody sluzheniia v Amerike," *Izvestiia Irkutskogo gosudarstvennogo universiteta* 44 (2023): 62–79.
72. Short Report on the Condition of the Aleut diocese for 1898, April 12, 1899, RGIA f. 796, op. 442, d. 1707, ll. 1–6.
73. Tikhon to P. I. Ostroumov February 28, 1899, RGIA f. 799, op. 25, d. 226, ll. 29–30; to Pobedonostsev, l. 31.
74. Memorandum to Pobedonostsev, September 9, 1899, RGIA f. 799, op. 25, d. 226, l. 41–43. On the challenge of the high costs, see "Puteshestvie ego Preosviashchenstva, Preosviashchenneishego Tikhona, Episkopa Aleutskogo i Aliaskinskogo," *APV* 4, no. 3 (February 13, 1900): 48–51.
75. *Pis'ma*, 44–46.
76. *Vsepoddanneishii otchet ober-prokurora sviateishego Sinoda K. Pobedonostseva po vedomstvu pravoslavnogo ispovedaniia za 1899 god* (St. Petersburg, 1902), 154–55.
77. *Pis'ma*, 51; APZh, 56
78. "Puteshestvie ego Preosviashchenstva, Preosviashchenneishego Tikhona, Episkopa Aleutskogo i Aliaskinskogo," *APV* 3, no. 3 (February 13, 1900): 49; M. Pokrovsky (ed.), *St. Nicholas Cathedral of New York: History and Legacy* (New York: St. Nicholas Cathedral Study Group, 1968), 13–14; on the building of the church, see also V. O. Pechatnov and V. V. Pechatnov, "'Glavnyi russkii khram Ameriki': iz istorii Sviato-Nikolaevskogo kafedral'nogo sobora v N'iu-Iorke," *Istoriia* 11, no. 109 (2021), https://history.jes.su/s207987840017595-3-1/.
79. Tikhon to Flavian, January 24, 1900, *Pis'ma*, 56.
80. "Puteshestvie ego Preosviashchenstva, Preosviashchenneishego Tikhona, Episkopa Aleutskogo i Aliaskinskogo," *APV* 3, no. 3 (February 13, 1900): 48–51; memorandum to Pobedonostsev, January 6/18, 1900, RGIA f. 799, op. 14, d. 1052, l. 18; *Pis'ma*, 54–55.
81. Tikhon's report to the Holy Synod, February 1, 1900, RGIA f. 799, op. 25, d. 226, l. 86; report to the Holy Synod, August 10/23, 1900, RGIA f. 796, op. 178, d. 3672, l. 23; Efimov and Lasaeva, 101–2.
82. "The New Russian Church," *New York Times* (May 23, 1901), 5.
83. Letter to Flavian, November 19, 1902, *Pis'ma*, 121.
84. "New Russian Orthodox Church Consecrated," *New York Times* (November 24, 1902).
85. *Instructions*, 124–26.

86. Tikhon's memoranda to Pobedonostsev, June 15, 1899, RGIA f. 799, op. 25, d. 226, l. 36, and January 25, 1901, RGIA f. 799, op. 31, d. 263, ll. 11, 52 (page out of order in the file); Popov APZh, 57, 99 fn. 152; *Pis'ma*, 29, 31–33. On building the church in Chicago, see O. V. Lasaeva, "K istorii vozniknoveniia russkogo pravoslavnogo prikhoda i vozvedeniia Sviato-Troitskogo sobora v g. Chikago pri svt. Tikhone (Bellavine)," *Vestnik PSTGU* 44 (2011): 41–49; Elizabeth Gassin, "Precious Jewels in Chicago's Crown: St. Tikhon, St. John Kochurov, and Holy Trinity Orthodox Cathedral," *St. Tikhon's Theological Journal* 4 (2008-2009): 1–17.
87. Norman E. Saul, *Life and Times of Charles R. Crane, 1858-1939: American Businessman, Philanthropist, and a Founder of Russian Studies in America* (Lanham, MD: Lexington Books, 2013), 64–66; Tikhon's report to the Synod, July 22, 1902, RGIA f. 796, op. 183, d. 4590, l. 2.
88. RGIA f. 799, op. 31, d. 263, ll. 11, 52; letters from Sullivan to Tikhon in January 1901 are ll. 20–22; the contract signed by Sullivan is ll. 24–51.
89. Letter to Sabler, September 5, 1901, *Pis'ma*, 88; APZh, 157, 164–66, 203–5; "Russians Begin a Church: Lay Corner-Stone for New St. Trinity Edifice," *Chicago Daily Tribune* (April 14, 1902): 7; *Instructions*, 147–50; *Vsepoddanneishii otchet ober-prokurora sviateishego Sinoda po vedomstvu pravoslavnogo ispovedaniia za 1903–1904 gody* (St. Petersburg, 1909), 181. See also Anatoly Bezkorovainy (ed.), *A History of Holy Trinity Russian Orthodox Cathedral of Chicago, 1892–1992* (Chicago: Holy Trinity Russian Orthodox Cathedral, 1992), 19; "Church Aided by Czar Opened by the Bishop," *Chicago Tribune* (March 30, 1903), 11.
90. Letter of November 2, 1899, *Pis'ma*, 47; letter to Flavian, November 30, 1899, *Pis'ma*, 51.
91. See John H. Erickson, "Slavophile Thought and Conceptions of Mission in the Russian North American Archdiocese, Late 19th–Early 20th Century," *St Vladimir's Theological Quarterly* 55, no. 3 (2012): 245–68.
92. Sermon at the ordination of Fr. Alexandrov, March 19, 1900: *Instructions*, 40–41.
93. Sermon on the Sunday of Orthodoxy, February 23, 1903, *Instructions*, 140–46 (quote p. 141).
94. Sermon in New York, January 18, 1904: *Instructions*, 165–68.
95. *Instructions*, 33.
96. Open letter to *Svit*, July 9, 1902: *Instructions*, 120–21. On the experiences of Orthodox immigrants and the clergy, see Aram Sarkisian, *Orthodoxy on the Line: Russian Orthodox Christians and Labor Migration in the Progressive Era* (New York: NYU Press, 2025).
97. *Dokumenty*, 109–10; 121.
98. See V. V. Pechatnov and V. O. Pechatnov, "Russkoe dukhovenstvo v Amerike kontsa XIX–nachala XX vv.: Problemy rekrutirovaniia i motivatsii," *Kontsept: filiosofiia, religiia, kul'tura* 8, no. 2 (2024): 50–68; Cognolato, "The Orthodox Church," 145–64.
99. *Pis'ma*, 86.
100. *Pis'ma*, 99, 88.
101. *Dokumenty*, 113. Emphasis in the original.
102. *Pis'ma*, 92.
103. *Pis'ma*, 80.
104. *Pis'ma*, 97; see 99.
105. *Pis'ma*, 121.
106. Ilia Klopotovskii, "Dumy nad Amerikanskoi letopis'iu," *Iubileinyi sbornik*, 187–88.
107. *Pis'ma*, 123.
108. Tikhon's request to the Holy Synod, January 19, 1903, RGIA 796, op. 184, d. 5216, l. 1.
109. *Pis'ma*, 127.
110. *Pis'ma*, 127.
111. Arsenii (Stadnitskii), dean of the Moscow Theological Academy, was one candidate—but Arsenii did not want to go: see his *Dnevnik 1902-1903* (Moscow: PSTGU, 2012), vol. 2: 119, 129; Bishop Nikolai (Ziorov) also considered returning (*Pis'ma*, 135).
112. "Na piatiletiiu sviatitel'skogo sluzheniia Preosviashchenneishego Vladyki Tikhona v Severnoi Amerike," *APV* 7, no. 22 (November 28, 1903): 393–94.
113. "Adres podneseenyi Ego Preosviashchenstvu, Preosviashchenneishemu Tikhonu, Episkopu Aleutskomu i Sever-Amerikanskomu," *APV* 7, no. 11 (June 14, 1903): 169–70.
114. "Nashe delo—Bozh'e delo (Po povodu proshchal'noi besedy Preosviashchenneishego Vladyka Tikhon s missionerami Vost. Shtatov)," *APV* 7, no. 13 (July 14, 1903): 213–14.
115. Fr. V. Belogostitskii, "Soobshcheniia iz zagranitsy: Iz Berlina," *Pribavlenie k Tserkovnym vedomostiam* No. 23 (1903): 890–91; Fr. M. Riurikov, "Poseshchenie g. Toroptsa Preosviashchennym Tikhonom, Episkop Aleutskim i Severo-Amerikanskim," *APV* 7, no. 15 (August 1, 1903): 249–50.

116. *Pis'ma*, 138.
117. *Pis'ma*, 140.
118. Report on the condition of the diocese for 1903, June 15/28, 1904, RGIA f. 796, op. 185, d. 5851, l. 4.
119. See *Pis'ma*, 142-54, 161.
120. *Pis'ma*, 148.
121. Tikhon's memorandum to the Holy Synod on restoring the Sitka vicariate, August 16, 1903, RGIA f. 796, op. 184 d. 5332, ll. 2-3.
122. RGIA f. 796, op. 184 d. 5332, ll. 3ob-5.
123. RGIA f. 796, op. 184 d. 5332, ll. 5-6.
124. *Pis'ma*, 155.
125. *Pis'ma*, 156-59.
126. "Ukaz (No. 11598) iz Sviateishego Pravitel'stvuiushchego Sinoda," *APV* 8, no. 2 (January 28, 1904): 39.
127. *Instructions*, 163, citing Romans 15:20.
128. APZh, 219-21.

Chapter 3

1. "Pribytie Ego Preosviashchenstva, Preosviashchenneishego Tikhona, Episkopa Aleutskogo i S.-Amerikanskogo v svoiu eparkhiiu," *APV* 8, no. 3 (February 14, 1904): 51-52; *Instructions*, 165-68.
2. "Vozvrashchenie Preosviashchenneishego Tikhona Episkopa Aleutskogo i Severo-Amerikanskogo, v San-Frantsisko," *APV* 8, no. 9 (May 1, 1904): 161-63.
3. *Pis'ma*, 169.
4. "Anna Bellavina," *APV* 8, no. 10 (May 15, 1904): 201. Tikhon's mother died on April 30/May 13, 1904. The obituary states that she died on April 29 (o.s.). Tikhon told Flavian that he received a telegram in the night of April 29-30 (*Pis'ma*, 169), but it was already April 30 in Russia. See Novikov, *Kolybel'*, 56-57.
5. *Pis'ma*, 170-71.
6. See *Pis'ma*, 172-75; 186-92; 215-17.
7. *Tserkovnye vedomosti* No. 19 (May 1905): 144; "Radostnaia vest'" and "'Posledniaia Paskha' (Iz letopisi Kafedral'nogo grada)," *APV* 9, no. 10 (May 28, 1905): 183 and 200-201.
8. *Pis'ma*, 173; APZh, 241-51.
9. A. Khotovitskii, "Puteshestvie Ego Preosviashchenstva, Preosviashcheneishego Tikhona v S. Luis, Poseshchenie Vsemirnoi Vystavki, osviashchenie tserkvi v Madisone," *APV* 8, no. 23 (December 14, 1904): 453-58. The Grunwaldt collection never made it back to Russia.
10. Tikhon's report on the state of the diocese for 1905 (August 25, 1906), RGIA f. 796, op. 187, d. 7376, ll. 3-21, published in *BogSb* 6: 180-205.
11. APZh, 64-66, 115, 122, 162; *Instructions*, 112-13.
12. Letter to Nicholas II, May 12, 1904, *Instructions*, 186-87; Nicholas's reply, *APV* 8, no. 13 (July 14, 1904): 246. See also APZh, 224.
13. Letter to Flavian, February 3, 1904, *Pis'ma*, 164; see also 166.
14. *Instructions*, 181; Reflection on the Nativity, December 25, 1900: *Instructions*, 60-63.
15. On the origins of the Russo-Japanese War, see David Schimmelpenninck van der Oye, *Toward the Rising Sun: Russian Ideologies of Empire and the Path to War with Japan* (DeKalb: Northern Illinois University Press, 2001).
16. *Instructions*, 182.
17. Letter to Petr Bulgakov, April 5, 1905, *Pis'ma*, 184; see also 179.
18. Letter to Hegumen Arkadii, November 15, 1905, GAPC f. 499, op. 1, d. 67, l. 5-6.
19. *Instructions*, 204-5. The sermon was also published in English at the time: *Russian Orthodox American Messenger*, May 1905 Supplement, 149-58.
20. *APV* 9, no. 10 (May 28, 1905): 184. This note was not included in *Instructions* (or the collection the translation was made from). On this sermon in the broader context, see Monica Cognolato, "The Tsar's Power Explained to America: Notes from a 1905 Homily," in *New Perspectives on Russian-American Relations*, ed. William Benton Whisenhunt and Norman E. Saul (New York: Routledge, 2016), 99-111.

21. James Cunningham, *A Vanquished Hope: The Movement for Church Renewal in Russia, 1905–1906* (Crestwood, NY: St. Vladimir's Seminary Press, 1981).
22. *Pis'ma*, 187, 191.
23. Letter to Flavian, April 25, 1905, *Pis'ma*, 186.
24. Letter to Bulgakov, July 7, 1905, *Pis'ma*, 191.
25. *Instructions*, 214–16.
26. *Instructions*, 218–21. See Gregory L. Freeze, "Profane Narratives About a Holy Sacrament: Marriage and Divorce in Late Imperial Russia," in *Sacred Stories: Religion and Spirituality in Modern Russia*, ed. Mark Steinberg and Heather Coleman (Bloomington: Indiana University Press, 2007), 146–78.
27. *Instructions*, 224–26.
28. *Instructions*, 227.
29. *Instructions*, 228. The central prayer of the liturgy, the eucharistic prayer, was generally said silently by the priest during the liturgy.
30. "Pribytie Preosviashchennogo Tikhona, episkopa Aleutskogo i Aliaskinskogo, vo vverennuiu emu Eparkhiiu," *APV* 3, no. 1 (January 13, 1899): 14–15.
31. Alexander Doumouras, "Greek Orthodox Communities in America Before World War I," *St. Vladimir's Seminary Quarterly* 11, no. 4 (1967): 172–92.
32. *Instructions*, 208–9.
33. Matthew Namee, "The Myth of Past Unity and the Origins of Jurisdictional Pluralism in American Orthodoxy," *Journal of American Orthodox Church History* 1 (2011): 2–34.
34. *Instructions*, 216–17.
35. See N. Iu. Sukhova, "'Arabskaia koloniia' v Kieve: Stipendiaty imperatorskogo pravoslavnogo palestinskogo obshchestva v Kievskoi dukhovnoi akademii (1887–1918)," *Trudy Kyivskoi dukhovnoi akadenii* No. 17 (2012): 181–92.
36. Sukhova, "Arabskaia koloniia," 185–86; Paul D. Garrett, "The Life and Legacy of Bishop Raphael Hawaweeny," in *The First One Hundred Years: A Centennial Anthology Celebrating Antiochian Orthodoxy in North America*, ed. George S. Corey et al. (Englewood, NJ: Antakya Press, 1995), 3–30; Patrick Viscuso's introduction to Raphael Hawaweeny, *The True Significance of Sacred Tradition and Its Great Worth* (Ithaca: Cornell University Press, 2017), 3–39; Basil Essey, "Saint Raphael Hawaweeny, Bishop of Brooklyn," in *The Orthodox Christian World*, ed. Augustine Casiday (London: Routledge, 2021), 338–44; Andre Issa, *Our Father Among the Saints Raphael, Bishop of Brooklyn* (Englewood, NJ: Antakya Press, 2000).
37. See APZh, 33, 61–63, 67–68, 160–61.
38. Patriarch Meletius II to the Russian Holy Synod, July 12, 1900 (Arabic original and Russian translation), RGIA 796, op. 181, d. 3157, ll. 6–7; Tikhon to Pobedonostsev, December 11, 1900, l. 17; Tikhon's report to the Holy Synod, December 11, 1900, l. 18; Raphael to Tikhon, December 5, 1900, l. 19; Synodal ukaz, March 6, 1901, ll. 22–23; Syrian Orthodox Parish of New York to the Russian Holy Synod, l. 31; their letter to Tikhon, June 21, 1902, ARCA Box B9, Reel 12; see also *Pis'ma*, 78.
39. Tikhon, memorandum to Pobedonostsev, December 2/14, 1899, RGIA f. 799, op. 25, d. 226, l. 81; see also *Pis'ma*, 53, 55; "Torzhestvo osviashcheniia pravoslavnogo Siro-Arabskaia khrama v Brukline," *APV* 6, no. 22 (December 14, 1902): 469–76.
40. *Instructions*, 127–28.
41. Tikhon's submission to the Synod, December 15/28, 1903, RGIA f. 796, op. 184, d. 5434, ll. 1–2; the Synod's order, February 4, 1904, l. 13.
42. *Instructions*, 176–78; "Torzhestvo narecheniia i khirotonii Arkhimandrita Rafaila vo Episkopa Bruklinskogo, vtorogo vikariia Aleutskoi Eparkhii," *APV* 8, no. 6 (March 28, 1904): 102–7.
43. Translation made by John Meyendorff, "The Patriarch of Antioch and North America in 1904," *SVTQ* 31 (1989): 84.
44. *Instructions*, 183–84.
45. Tikhon's report on the state of the diocese for 1903, June 28, 1904, RGIA f. 796, op. 185, d. 5851, l. 26.
46. On Sebastian and the Serbian mission, see *PE* 62: 228–29; A. B. Efimov and O. V. Lasaeva, *Aleutskaia i Severo-Amerikanskaia eparkhiia pri sviatitele Tikhone* (Moscow: PSTGU, 2012), 364–432, 540–44 (some of Sebastian's letters are incorrectly transcribed); Bishop Sava of Šumidija, *History of the Serbian Orthodox Church in American and Canada, 1891–1941*, trans. Karin Pieck-Radovanovic (Kragujevac: Kalenić, 1998), 21–60; *"To the Glory of God the Father": The Lives of St. Mardarije of Libertyville and St. Sebastian of Jackson* (Alhambra: Sebastian Press, 2015).

47. He was tonsured on December 30, 1888, and ordained deacon January 6, 1889. RGIA f. 796, op. 183, d. 4568, ll. 6–8, 16–17.
48. *Pis'ma*, 227–28; APZh, 392; letters from Sebastian to Tikhon, November 19 and 28 and December 8, 1906, ARCA, Reel 359.
49. Tikhon's report on the state of the diocese for 1903, RGIA f. 796, op. 185, d. 5851, l. 26.
50. Tikhon's report to the Holy Synod, June 2, 1905, RGIA f. 796, op. 186, d. 5906, ll. 1–2; *APV* 9, no. 18 (September 28, 1905): 370.
51. *Instructions*, 210; APZh, 320.
52. Sava, 24–25.
53. Sebastian, letters to Tikhon, dated 1904, and December 22, 1905, ARCA, Reel 359; Sava, 25–31, 49.
54. Sebastian's letter to Tikhon, December 27, 1905, ARCA H1, Reel 359; Sava, 32–33.
55. Sebastian's letter to Tikhon, no date (third from last in the file). The letter must be late 1906 or 1907 after Fr. Krajnović arrived.
56. Sebastian's letter to Tikhon, March 22, 1907, ARCA, Reel 359.
57. Tikhon's proposal to the Holy Synod, June 22,1904, RGIA f. 796, op. 185, d. 5862, ll. 2–5 (*Dokumenty*, 128–31).
58. *Pis'ma*, 189; see also 167, 174.
59. Synodal ukaz of June 10, 1905, OCA Archive, Series I.A; Tikhon's report to the Synod, July 19, 1905, RGIA f. 796, op. 185, d. 5862, l. 16.
60. Tikhon to Flavian, August 17, 1905, *Pis'ma*, 194.
61. *Instructions*, 212–13; "Puteshestvie Ego Vysokopreosviashchenstva, Vysokopreosviashchenneishego Tikhona, Arkhiepiskopa Aleutskogo i Sev.-Amerikanskogo, po eparkhii," *APV* 9, no. 19 (October 14, 1905): 376–78.
62. On the sale of the property in San Francisco, see RGIA f. 796, op. 185, d. 5862, ll. 18–34; Tikhon's report to the Synod on the fire, April 17/30, 1906, is op. 187, d. 7217, ll. 1–2; see Tikhon to Flavian, May 19, 1906, *Pis'ma*, 222.
63. Report for 1898, RGIA f. 796, op. 442, d. 1707, ll. 1–6; report for 1905, *BogSb* 6: 196.
64. Efimov and Lasaeva, 231–38.
65. Tikhon's report to the Synod on education, RGIA f. 796, op. 178, d. 3625, ll. 42–44 (the whole document is in *Dokumenty*, 132–39).
66. RGIA f. 796, op. 178, d. 3625, ll. 44ob–46; also *Dokumenty*, 110–12, *Instructions*, 154–55.
67. RGIA f. 796, op. 178, d. 3625, l. 47.
68. RGIA f. 796, op. 178, d. 3625, ll. 47ob–48ob; see also Tikhon's report to the Synod, March 24, 1906, RGIA f. 796, op. 187, d. 7303, ll. 2–3.
69. Scott M. Kenworthy, "Metropolitan Leonty, Saint Tikhon, and the Establishment of America's First Orthodox Seminary," in *The Life and Work of Metropolitan Leonty*, ed. David C. Ford (Waymart, PA: Saint Tikhon's Monastery Press, 2019), 37–50.
70. *Instructions*, 240.
71. See Scott M. Kenworthy, "Russian Orthodox Monasticism from 988 to 1917," in *Oxford Handbook of Christian Monasticism*, ed. Bernice Kaczynski (Oxford: Oxford University Press, 2020), 478–94; "Monasticism in Modern Russia," in *Monasticism in Eastern Europe and the Former Soviet Republics*, ed. Ines A. Murzaku (London: Routledge, 2015), 265–84; *The Heart of Russia: Trinity-Sergius, Monasticism and Society After 1825* (Oxford: Oxford University Press and Washington, DC: Wilson Center Press, 2010).
72. *Dokumenty*, 110; *Instructions*, 136, 236–37.
73. *Pis'ma*, 116–17; on establishing St. Tikhon's monastery, see N. V. Soldatova, *Otrazhenie: Istoriia pravoslaviia v Amerike v istorii sviato-Tikhonovskoi obiteli* (Moscow: Otdel religioznogo obrazovaniia i katekhizatsii Russkoi Pravoslavnoi tserkvi, 2006).
74. Efimov and Lasaeva, 139.
75. Hieromonk Arsenii, "Prebyvanie Ego Vysokopreosviashchenstva, Vysokopreosviashchenneishego Tikhona, Arkhiepiskopa Aleutskogo i S.-Amerikanskogo, v Vostochnykh Shtatakh," *APV* 9, no. 13 (July 14, 1905): 248–51; Hieromonk Arsenii, "Poseshchenie Ego Vysokopreosviashchenstvom, Vysokopreosviashchenneishim Tikhona, sv. Tikhonovskoi obiteli i Sirotskogo Priiuta," *APV* 9, no. 21 (November 14, 1905): 411–15; APZh, 337; *Pis'ma*, 193.
76. Report to the Holy Synod, November 14, 1905, *Dokumenty*, 154–56. Tikhon would substantially repeat the same arguments in his report on the state of the diocese for 1905, *BogSb* 6: 184–86.
77. Tikhon to Flavian, January 20 and March 20, 1906 *Pis'ma*, 217, 220.
78. A. Hotovitzky, "V Sviato-Tikhonovskoi obiteli," *APV* 10, no. 11 (June 14, 1906): 214–29.
79. *Instructions*, 240–43.

80. Ukaz of the Holy Synod to Archbishop Tikhon, June 26, 1906, OCA Archive, Series I.A.
81. "Pervyi den' prebyvaniia Ego Vysokoprosviashchenstva, Vysokopreosviashchenneishego Tikhona, Arkhiepiskopa Aleutskogo i Severo-Amerikanskogo v Sviato-Tikhonovskogo Obiteli," *APV* 10, no. 14 (July 28, 1906): 273–74.
82. "The Founding of St. Tikhon's Monastery in South Canaan, Pennsylvania, 1905–1906: Part VII," *Alive in Christ: The Magazine of the Diocese of Eastern Pennsylvania, Orthodox Church in America* 22, no. 2 (Summer 2006): 10–22, at 22; also Hegumen Arsenii, "Prebyvanie Ego Vysokopreosviashchenstva, Vysokopreosviashchenneishego Tikhona Sviato-Tikhonovskoi obiteli i poseshchenie sosednikh prikhodov," *APV* 10, no. 15 (August 14, 1906): 292–94; *APV* 10, no. 17 (September 14, 1906): 337–43; and *APV* 10, no. 18 (September 28, 1906): 355–59.
83. Thomas C. Reeves, "The Anglo-Catholic Movement in Wisconsin," *The Wisconsin Magazine of History* 68, no. 3 (1985): 188–98; for Anglican-Orthodox relations more broadly, see *PE* 2: 311–22.
84. "K istorii vzaimnykh otnoshenii pravoslavnoi i episkopal'noi tserkvi v Amerike," *APV* 5, no. 21 (November 15, 1901): 452–53; Peter Carl Haskell, "Archbishop Tikhon and Bishop Grafton: An Early Chapter in Anglo-Orthodox Relations in the New World," *St. Vladimir's Seminary Quarterly* Part One, 11, no. 4 (1967): 193–206; and Part Two, 12, no. 1 (1968): 2–16. E. C. Miller, *Toward a Fuller Vision: Orthodoxy and the Anglican Experience* (Wilton: Morehouse Barlow, 1984), 103–16.
85. *Instructions*, 54.
86. John M. Kinney, "'The Fond du Lac Circus': The Consecration of Reginald Heber Weller," *Historical Magazine of the Protestant Episcopal Church* 38, no. 1 (1969): 3–24; Mikhail Taganov, "Anglo-katoliki v Viskonsine i sviatitel' Tikhon: istoriia odnoi fotografii," *Vestnik PSTGU* 19 (2006): 17–26.
87. Kinney, 6; Efimov and Lasaeva, 402–4.
88. Tikhon to Grafton, November 20, 1900, in the Diocese of Fond du Lac Archive.
89. Tikhon's report to the Holy Synod, July 2, 1903, RGIA f. 796, op. 445, d. 39, ll. 39–40; Grafton's letter is in the same file; see Iaroslav (Ochkanov), "Vzaimootnosheniia mezhdu russkoi pravoslavnkoi i anglikanskoi tserkvami v pervoe desliatiletie XX v.," *Bogoslovskii vestnik* No. 2 (41) (2021): 88–100.
90. Tikhon to Pobedonostsev, August 7, 1903, *Pis'ma*, 146–47; Tikhon to Grafton, August 26, 1903, written from St. Petersburg, in Diocese of Fond du Lac Archive; Haskell, "Archbishop Tikhon," 10–13.
91. Synodal resolution from August 10–October 16, 1904, RGIA f. 796, op. 209, d. 2219, ll. 384–85; Synodal ukaz to Bishop Tikhon, October 19, 1904, OCA Archive, Series I.A.
92. Ex., APZh, 226, 234, 256–57.
93. A. Hotovitzky, "Pravoslavnoe torzhestvo v N'iu-Iorke 10 i 22 Oktiabria," *APV* 8, no. 21 (November 14, 1904): 413–20, esp. 419–20.
94. Peter Carl Haskell, "Bishop Grafton and the Orthodox Church, 1900–1905" (MA thesis, University of Minnesota, 1970), 57.
95. Oliver Herbel, "American Restorationism, the Public Sphere, and Anglican-Orthodox Relations: The Case of Ingram Nathaniel Washington Irvine (1849–1921)," *Anglican and Episcopal History* 83, no. 1 (2014): 42–66.
96. *Pis'ma*, 201.
97. *Pis'ma*, 204–5.
98. The telegrams of Grafton and Tikhon are in the Diocese of Fond du Lac Archive.
99. "Extract from letter dated Fond du Lac, November, 1905," in Diocese of Fond du Lac Archive.
100. Tikhon to Grafton, November 13, 1905 (?), *Russian Orthodox American Messenger*, November Supplement (1905): 370–74 (and *Pis'ma*, 207–10).
101. Tikhon to Grafton, November 23, 1905, Fond du Lac Archive; Haskell, "Bishop Grafton," 63–70.
102. "Excerpt from letter dated Fond du Lac, February 1, 1906," in the Diocese of Fond du Lac Archive.
103. "Russian Church favors Union," *San Francisco Call* (December 30, 1905), 9. The materials from the commission as well as material relating to the Irvine affair were published in the English-language supplements of the *Russian Orthodox American Messenger* in 1905.
104. A series of letters from Hapgood to Tikhon are preserved in the OCA Archive. Unfortunately, Tikhon's replies are not among Hapgood's papers which are held at the New York Public Library Manuscript Division.
105. Report on the state of the diocese in 1902, June 9, 1903, OCA Archive, Series I.C. On Hapgood, see Stuart H. Hoke, "A Generally Obscure Calling: A Character Sketch of Isabel Florence

Hapgood," *St. Vladimir's Theological Quarterly* 45, no. 1 (2001): 55–93; Marina Ledkovsky, "A Linguistic Bridge to Orthodoxy: In Memoriam Isabel Florence Hapgood," https://anglicanhistory.org/women/hapgood/ledkovsky.pdf.
106. Letter to Pobedonovtsev, *Pis'ma*, 200–203; report to the Holy Synod, February 7, 1907, RGIA f. 796, op. 184, d. 5355, l. 4; see APZh, 400.
107. An English translation of Tikhon's message, November 3, 1921, Kauz Family YMCA Archive, University of Minnesota, y.usa.9-2-1, box 21, folder 5.
108. *Instructions*, 223.
109. E. Iu. Litvinenko and Iu. V. Balakshina, "'Dela Tserkvi reshaiutsia soborne . . .': arkhiepiskop Tikhon (Bellavin) i pravoslavnye bratstva Severnoi Ameriki," *Vestnik Sviato-Filaretovskogo instituta* 16, no. 2 (2024): 52–76; *Dokumenty*, 119–20, 150–51; on temperance societies, *Instructions*, 86–87; Constance J. Tarasar and John H. Erickson (eds.), *Orthodox America, 1794–1976: Development of the Orthodox Church in America* (Syosset, NY: Orthodox Church in America, 1975), 113–18.
110. "Rech' skazannaia Preosviashchenneishim Tikhonom, Episkopom Aleutskim i S.-Amerikanskim pri vruchenii zhezla Preosviashchennomu Innokentiiu, Episkopu Aliaskinskomu," *APV* 8, no. 2 (January 28, 1904): 23.
111. *Instructions*, 176–77.
112. A. Hotovitzky, "Poezdka na konventsiiu," *APV* 9, no. 11 (June 14, 1905): 204–19, esp. 217–18. On conciliarism in the American Church and the Council, see Cognolato, "The Orthodox Church," 214–18; Tarasar and Erickson, 97–99.
113. "Protokol sobraniia dukhovenstva Severo-Amerikanskoi eparkhii, sostoiashchagosia v g. Klevelande, Sht. Ogio, 20 Maia–2 iunia 1905 goda," *APV* 9, no. 12 (June 28, 1905): 245–46.
114. Hotovitzky, "Poezdka," 218.
115. "Pis'mo Vysokopreosviashchenneishego Nikolaia, Arkhiepiskopa Iaponskogo, na imia Vysokopreosviashchenneishego Arkhiepiskopa Tikhona," *APV* 10, no. 10 (May 28, 1906): 191–95.
116. "Protokol sobraniia dukhovenstva Severo-Amerikanskoi eparkhii, sostoiashagosia v g. Klevelande, Sht. Ogaio, 20 Maia–2 iunia 1905 goda," *APV* 9, no. 13 (July 14, 1905): 255–56.
117. "Po povodu predpolagaemykh reguliarnykh soborov dukhovenstva S. Amerikanskaia eparkhii," *APV* 9, no. 13 (July 14, 1905): 256–58. The author signed with the abbreviation Nem-skii (presumably Nemolovskii).
118. "Nuzhen li nam sobor?" *APV* 10, no. 3 (February 14, 1906): 49–50.
119. "K predstoiashchemu Soboru," *APV* 10, no. 23 (December 14, 1906): 458–60.
120. Innokentii to Arsenii, October 3, 1906, in Efimov and Lasaeva, 555–56.
121. Innokentii to Arsenii, April 9, 1907, in Efimov and Lasaeva, 559.
122. Tikhon wrote to Flavian on December 12/25, 1906, asking when the Council in Russia would take place (*Pis'ma*, 227); in his letter to Flavian of February 4/17, 1907, he noted the timing of the American Council in conjunction with that of the Russian Council—but also acknowledged that he had since heard it may not happen, though clearly he had not yet heard of his transfer (*Pis'ma*, 232).
123. The meeting in the Riga diocese was also called a Sobor: Irina Paert, "Conciliarity in the Borderlands: The Riga Orthodox Council (Sobor) of 1905 and the Church Reform Movement in Imperial Russia," *Journal of Ecclesiastical History* 73, no. 3 (2022): 572–94.
124. Synodal ukaz to Archbishop Tikhon, January 29, 1907 (o.s.), OCA Archive, Series I.A.
125. *Pis'ma*, 234.
126. "Otzvuki Sobora," *APV* 11, no. 7 (August 14, 1907): 121.
127. OCA Archives, Series II.B. #14, contains a series of proposals by various leading clergy of the diocese (fathers Hotovitzky, Turkevich, Toth, and others) in 1902–1903, culminating in a report by Bishop Tikhon of February 11, 1903.
128. On the Council, see "Pervyi Sobor Severo-Amerikanskii Pravoslavnoi Tserkvi," *APV* 11, no. 5 (March 14, 1907): 80–82; A. Hotovitzky, "Khod soveshchanii na pervom Sobore Severo-Amerikanskoi Pravoslavnoi Tserkvi," *APV* 11, no. 5 (March 14, 1907), 82–86.
129. "Otzvuki Sobora," 121.
130. "Proshchal'naia beseda," *APV* 11, no. 5 (March 14, 1907): 87–88.
131. *BogSb* 6: 193.
132. "Proshchal'naia voskresen'e 1907 g. v Niu-Iorke," *APV* 11, no. 5 (March 14, 1907): 89–94.
133. *Instructions*, 258–59.
134. "Ot"ezd Vysokopreosviashcheneishego Vladyki Tikhona v Rossiiu," *APV* 11, no. 6 (March 28, 1907): 98–100.

Chapter 4

1. There is less literature on the Yaroslavl period of Tikhon's life than any other. See Tikhon (Zatekin), *Sviatitel' Tikhon*, 178–242; N. S. Borisov, "Sviatitel' Tikhon vo glave Iaroslavskoi eparkhii," *Zhurnal Moskovskoi Patriarkhii* No. 6 (2005): 75–79; Oleg Nepospekhov, "Sviatitel' Tikhon (Bellavin) na Rostovskoi zemle," in *Rostov Velikii: imena, sobytiia, sud'by*, ed. M. Rubtsov, 76–102 (Moscow: Palomnik, 2012).
2. See John D. Morison, "The Church Schools and Seminaries in the Russian Revolution of 1905–06," in *Church, Nation and State in Russia and Ukraine*, ed. Geoffrey A. Hosking, 193–209 (Alberta: Canadian Institute of Ukrainian Studies Press, 1990).
3. See Simon Dixon, "The 'Mad Monk' Iliodor in Tsaritsyn," *Slavonic and East European Review* 88, no. 1 (2010): 377–415.
4. Dixon, "Mad Monk," 380–82; N. E. Gerasimova, "Srednee dukhovnoe obrazovanie v Iaroslavskoi i Kostromskoi guberniiakh vo vtoroi polovine XIX–nachale XX vv." (Kandidat diss., Iaroslavskii gosudarstvenyi universitet, 2001), 172–80; Ia. A. Sedova, *Iliodor: Misticheskii drug Rasputina* (Moscow: Rodina, 2022), Vol. 1: 59–87.
5. "Pribytie Vysokopreosviashchennogo Tikhona Arkhiepiskopa Iaroslavskogo i Rostovskogo v Iaroslavl," *IaEV* 48, no. 18 (Unofficial Part) (May 6, 1907): 259.
6. Tikhon shares some aspects in common with the "Orthodox patriots" discussed in John Strickland, *The Making of Holy Russia: The Orthodox Church and Russian Nationalism Before the Revolution* (Jordanville, NY: Holy Trinity Publications, 2013), though Tikhon's sense of Russia as especially devoted to Orthodoxy never overshadowed his universalism.
7. "Pribytie," 259.
8. These figures come from Tikhon's report on the diocese for 1908: RGIA f. 796, op. 442, d. 2315, ll. 4, 10ob.
9. Popov, *Pis'ma*, 237.
10. Tikhon's report on Yaroslavl diocese in 1907, RGIA, f. 796, op. 442, d. 2254, l. 9, 9ob.
11. *IaEV* 48, no. 20 (Official Part) (May 20, 1907): 278.
12. "Izvestiia," *IaEV* 48, no. 18 (Official Part) (May 6, 1907): 245.
13. O. N. Kopylova (ed.), "Vospominaniia protoiereia Nikolaia Kniazeva (1947 g.)," *Vestnik tserkovnoi istorii* No. 2 (2006): 111.
14. RGIA f. 796, op. 442, d. 2371, l. 3ob; d. 2434, l. 6; d. 2499, l. 3ob.
15. For one such instance, see Priest I. Alferov, "Poseshchenie Krestobogorodskogo khrama i obozrenie ego Vysokopreosviashchenneishim Tikhonom, Arkhiepiskop Iaroslavskim i Rostovskim," *IaEV* 48, no. 45 (Unofficial Part) (November 11, 1907): 697–99.
16. See the "journals" of the diocesan consistory, GAIaO, f. 203, op. 2, d. 5728 (for 1907–1908); d. 5088 (for 1909); and d. 5168 (for 1910–1911).
17. His salary is listed in his CV; see GAIaO f. 230, op. 2, d. 4991, l. 2ob; see also RGIA f. 796, op. 439, d. 833, which contains CVs from throughout his career until 1916: As dean of the Kholm seminary, he made 2,000 rubles a year (l. 1ob), but received extra income for extra classes as well as dean of monasteries, so in 1896 he received 2,300 rubles (l. 32ob); as archbishop of Vilna and Lithuania, he received 4,000 rubles plus an extra 500 rubles as abbot of the Holy Spirit Monastery (l. 53–54). His donations exceeded his income while he was in Yaroslavl. The largest single donation of 10,000 rubles was made in 1910 for the support of the St. Tikhon's Monastery in Pennsylvania: *Sovremenniki* 1: 195–97; GARF f. 4652, op. 1, d. 1, l. 217.
18. *Sovremenniki* 1: 195–97; he donated 10,400 rubles between 1907 and 1913 (his income was 10,500 rubles for the same period), and in addition he donated another 1,000 rubles for the education of impoverished girls of the clerical estate in 1908.
19. "Osviashchenie novogo korpusa v Eparkhial'nom ioanafanovskom uchilishche," *IaEV* 51, no. 45 (Unofficial Part) (November 7, 1910): 898–901.
20. Report for 1908, RGIA f. 796, op. 442, d. 2315, ll. 13ob–14.
21. E.g., the dean's reports for 1908: GAIaO f. 203 op. 3, d. 3017. Someone—evidently Tikhon—read through the reports carefully and marked them up with blue pencil, which served as the basis for Tikhon's annual report to the Synod.
22. Report for 1912, RGIA f. 796, op. 442, d. 2561, l. 15–15ob.
23. Report for 1911, RGIA f. 796, op. 442, d. 2499, l. 15ob. On shifting concerns toward the urban intelligentsia, see Gregory Freeze, "'Going to the Intelligentsia': The Church and Its Urban Mission in Post-Reform Russia," in *Between Tsar and People: Educated Society and the Quest*

for Public Identity in Late Imperial Russia, ed. Edith Clowes, Samuel Kassow, and James West, 215–32 (Princeton, NJ: Princeton University Press, 1991).
24. Report for 1910, RGIA f. 796, op. 442, d. 2434, l. 23.
25. RGIA f. 796, op. 442, d. 2315, l. 14–15; d. 2371, l. 22; d. 2499, l. 10; d. 2561, l. 13ob–14.
26. RGIA f. 796, op. 442, d. 2254, ll. 9–10 (for 1907), 28ob–29; d. 2315, ll. 12–15 (for 1908).
27. Tikhon to Bulgakov, January 1, 1910, *Vestnik PSTGU* 19: 78; Tikhon's CV, RGIA f. 796, op. 439, d. 833, ll. 46–47.
28. Daniil Toropov, "Dialog Rossiiskoi Pravoslavnoi tserkvi so starokatolicheskim dvizheniem vo vtoroi polovine XIX–nachale XX veka" (kand. diss., Obshchetserkovnaia aspirantura i doktorantura im. Sv. Kirilla i Mefodiia, 2015), 211–13 (also 193–99); Andrei Psarev, "'They Have Neither Laymen Nor Money': Overview of the Correspondence (1907–1911) Between Archbishop Tikhon Bellavin and Archpriest Evgenii Smirnov," *Sobornost* 37, no. 2 (2015): 16–28.
29. "Pervyi moskovskii arkhipastyr' po svobodnomu izbraniiu tserkovnogo klira i naroda," *Bogoslovskii vestnik* No. 6–7 (June–July 1917): 136.
30. *Bol'shaia Sovetskaia entsiklopediia*, 3rd ed., vol. 25; "Soiuz Russkogo Naroda," *Kratkaia evreiskaia entsiklopediia*, vol. 8, 518–24; O. A. Platonov (ed.), *Chernaia Sotnia: Istoricheskaia entsiklopediia* (Moscow: Institut russkoi tsivilizatsii, 2008), 547.
31. Argyrios K. Pisiotis, "Between State and Estate: The Political Motivations of the Russian Orthodox Episcopate in the Crisis of Tsarist Monarchy, 1905–1917," *Canadian-American Slavic Studies* 46 (2012): 337–38. For an analysis of Tikhon's position, see Silano, "In the Language," 140–48.
32. SD 227–28.
33. Pisiotis, "Between," 340.
34. Katsaurov, brief information about the Yaroslavl branch of the URP, July 31, 1907, GARF f. 116, op. 1, d. 595, l.9–10ob.
35. Katsaurov's letter of January 9, 1911, GARF f. 116, op. 1, d. 595, l. 54ob.
36. Letter to Flavian, April 20, 1907, *Pis'ma*, 237.
37. Historians long assumed that the Church, or the episcopate at least, universally supported the radical right. Such views were inherited from Soviet propaganda, and the actual picture is far more complex. See Argyrios K. Pisiotis, "Russian Orthodoxy and the Politics of National Identity in Early Twentieth Century," *Balkan Studies* 42, no. 2 (2001): 225–43; Pisiotis, "Russian Orthodox Clergy and Populism in the Twilight of the Romanovs," in *Metropolitan Antonii (Khrapovitskii): Archpastor of the Russian Diaspora*, ed. Vladimir Tsurikov, 143–94 (Jordanville, NY: Foundation of Russian History, 2014).
38. GARF f. 116, op. 2, d. 98.
39. "Sobranie Iaroslavskogo Soiuza 'Russkogo naroda,'" *IaEV* (Unofficial Part) 53, no. 52 (December 23, 1912): 1042–44.
40. "Otchet o vedenennykh v 1910 i 1911 godakh Iaroslavskim Otdelom Soiuza Russkogo Naroda religiozno-nravstvennykh i istoricheskikh chteniiakh v g. Iaroslavle, za r. Kotorosl'iu," *IaEV* 52, no. 38 (Unofficial Part) (September 18, 1911): 761–64.
41. O. V. Volobuev (ed.), *Pravye partii: Dokumenty i materialy* (Moscow: Rosspen, 1998), vol. 1: 464, and vol. 2: 304.
42. M. L. Razmolodin, *Chernosotennoe dvizhenie v Iaroslavle i guberniiakh verkhnego povolzh'ia v 1905–1915 gg.* (Iaroslavl': Aleksandr Rutman, 2001), 79–80.
43. Letter to Flavian, November 15, 1908, RGIA f. 796, op. 205, d. 752, l. 178–78ob.
44. See Tikhon's letters to Bulgakov, May 17 and July 17, 1908, in *Vestnik PSTGU* 19: 76; and letter to Flavian, June 24, 1908, RGIA f. 796, op. 205, d. 752, ll. 172–73; this letter (along with all of Tikhon's letters to Flavian) was transcribed in N. A. Muralev, "Epistoliarnoe nasledie sviateishego Patriarkha Tikhona (pis'ma k mitropolitu Kievskomu i Galitskomu Flavianu)" (Diploma thesis, St. Petersburg Theological Academy, 1995), 86–87, but he has incorrectly dated this and several other letters. See also letters to Flavian, December 23, 1908, and February 21, 1909: RGIA f. 796, op. 205, d. 752, l. 180–81.
45. *IaEV* No. 11 (Official Part) (March 15, 1909): 81–82; Tikhon's letter to Bulgakov, July 29, 1909: *Vestnik PSTGU* 19: 77. The person chosen, Iosif (Petrovykh), though he bore the title of bishop of Uglich, though resided in Rostov.
46. Letter to Flavian, October 29, 1908, RGIA f. 796, op. 205, d. 752, l. 174.
47. *IaEV* No. 48 (Unofficial Part) (November 29, 1909).
48. Letter to Flavian, in Muralev, "Epistoliarnoe nasledie," 93. Muralev dates the letter December 28, 1909, but it must be 1908.

49. Letters to Flavian, April 7 and 15, 1911, Muralev, "Epistoliarnoe nasledie," 97; on the whole episode, see Dixon, "Mad Monk," 398–402.
50. The correspondence from the governor's office to Tikhon or the consistory is GAIaO f. 230, op. 4, d. 1806, ll. 12–40.
51. For various correspondence to Tikhon in preparation for the event, see GAIaO f. 230, op.3, d. 3199.
52. "Izvestiia," *IaEV* 54, no. 22 (Official Part) (June 2, 1913): 162–64; "Poseshchenie Iaroslavlia Ikh Imperatorskim Velichestvami," *IaEV* 54, no. 23 (Unofficial Part) (June 9, 1913): 455–59.
53. See Beliaev's diary, *BogSb* 6: 99.
54. "Vysochaishaia gramota Preosviashchennomu Tikhonu, arkhiepiskopu Iaroslavskomu i Rostovskomu," *IaEV* 54, no. 24 (Official Part) (June 16, 1913): 169.
55. "Telegramma Ego Imperatorskogo Velichestva," *IaEV* 54, no. 34 (Official Part) (August 25, 1913): 249.
56. Tikhon to Flavian, May 31, 1913, Muralev, "Epistoliarnoe nasledie," 103.
57. Letter to Flavian, Muralev, "Epistoliarnoe nasledie," 101–2; Muralev gives the date as December 21, 1912, but it must be 1913, the day before the Synod met to make the decision.
58. Synodal ukaz, January 2, 1914, GARF f. 4652, op. 1, d. 1, l. 224; a copy is GAIaO f. 203, op. 3, d. 3268, l. 1.
59. Tikhon to Bulgakov, January 5, 1914, *Vestnik PSTGU* 19: 80.
60. Silvester to the Consistory, January 14, 1914, GAIaO f. 230, op. 3., d. 3268, l. 10; also l. 6.
61. "Provody arkhiepiskopa Tikhona," *IaEV* 55, no. 6 (Unofficial Part) (February 9, 1914): 118.
62. "Provody arkhiepiskopa Tikhona," *IaEV* 55, no. 10 (Unofficial Part) (March 9, 1914): 203–5.
63. "Provody arkhiepiskopa Tikhona," *IaEV* 55, no. 6 (Unofficial Part) (February 9, 1914): 119–20.
64. Session of the Yaroslavl City Duma, January 23, 1914, GAIaO f. 509, op. 3, d. 273, l. 2. This proposal received the approval of Governor Tatishchev and, by December, the tsar (see ll. 3–5). The telegram of December 19, 1914, is informing Tikhon is LVIA, f. 605, ap. 9, b. 1739, l. 55; Tikhon's reply, December 20, 1914, is GAIaO f. 509, op. 3, d. 273, l. 8.
65. "Pribytie v Vil'nu Vysokopreosviashchenneishego Tikhona, Arkhiepiskopa Litovskogo i Vilenskogo," *VVPSDB* No. 4 (1914): 56.
66. RGIA f. 797, opis' 84, l. 126ob (for d. 284). The Synodal file (f. 796, op. 196, 5 st., I otd., d. 603) is also missing.
67. Irina Aref'eva and German Shlevis, "*Primite menia v svoiu liubov'. . ."* (Vilnius: SAVO, 2008), 56–58; I. G. Men'kova (ed.), *Radi Mira Tserkovnogo: Zhiznennyi put' i arhipastorskoe sluzhenie sviatitelia Agafangela, mitropolita Iaroslavskogo i Rostovskogo, ispovednika*, 2 vols. (Moscow: PSTGU, 2005), 1: 489–91.
68. From the newspaper Golos, February 1, 1914, in Men'kova (ed.), *Radi Mira*, 1: 521.
69. From Arsenii's diary for January 28, 1914, in Men'kova (ed.), *Radi Mira*, 1: 520, quoting Psalm 119: 126; the rest of the verse is "for Thy law has been broken."
70. Aref'eva and Shlevis, *Primite menia*, 54. A *khorugv'* is the kind of banners with icons that are carried in Orthodox religious processions, whereas a *stiag* is the type of banner carried in a political demonstration.
71. Aref'eva and Shlevis, *Primite menia*, 54–56.
72. SD 231, 249–50, 335.
73. "Pribytie v Vil'nu," 55.
74. "Pribytie v Vil'nu," 55–56.
75. *PE* 8: 465–75.
76. On Russian imperial Lithuania, see Theodore R. Weeks, "Russification and the Lithuanians, 1863–1905," *Slavic Review* 60 (2001): 96–114. On attempts to "Orthodoxize" imperial spaces, see Irina Paert and James White, "Reimagining the Diocese: Administrative, Sacred, and Imperial Space in the Russian Empire," *Canadian Slavonic Papers* 62, no. 3–4 (2020): 234–44.
77. Darius Staliunas, *Making Russians: Meaning and Practice of Russification in Lithuania and Belarus After 1863* (Amsterdam: Rodopi, 2007), 131–59; Vilma Žaltauskaitė, "Interconfessional Rivalry in Lithuania After the Decree of Tolerance," in *The Tsar, the Empire, and the Nation: Dilemmas of Nationalization in Russia's Western Borderlands, 1905–1915*, ed. Darius Staliunas and Yoko Aoshima, 113–39 (Budapest: CEU Press, 2021).
78. Selections from Zhirkevich's diary have been published in *BogSb* 6: 216–29; citation, 220.
79. *BogSb* 6: 221–22.
80. *BogSb* 6: 223–24; see also letter to Flavian, February 16, 1914: Muralev, "Epistoliarnoe nasledie," 105–6.
81. Tikhon's report on Lithuanian diocese in 1914, RGIA f. 796, op. 442, d. 2647, ll. 5ob–6.

82. RGIA f. 796, op. 442. d. 2647, ll. 14ob–15.
83. The Minutes from the Congress are in *LEV* 53, no. 7–8 (April 1, 1914): 68–77.
84. *BogSb* 6: 224.
85. Vytaytas Petronis, "Right-Wing Russian Organizations in the City of Vil'na and the Northwestern Provinces, 1905–1915," in *The Tsar, the Empire, and the Nation*, ed. Darius Staliunas and Yoko Aoshima (Budapest: CEU Press, 2021), 287–325.
86. "Khronika tserkovno-obshchestvennoi zhizni," *VVPSDB* 8, no. 6 (March 15, 1914): 129.
87. Appeal of Nikanor Razumovskii in 1924, SD 769.
88. "Vysochaishee poseshchenie gor. Vil'ny," *VVPSDB* 8, no. 19 (October 1, 1914): 399–402; Tikhon's report on Lithuanian diocese in 1914, RGIA f. 796, op. 442, d. 2647, l. 19ob–20.
89. Letter to Flavian, October 20, 1914, Muralev, "Epistoliarnoe nasledie," 108–9.
90. "Khronika tserkovno-obshchestvennoi zhizni," *VVPSDB* 8, no. 15–16 (August 1914): 349–51.
91. "Khronika tserkovno-obshchestvennoi zhizni," VVPSDB 8, no. 17 (September 1, 1914): 371. See also RGIA f. 796, op. 442, d. 2647, l. 18; Muralev, "Epistoliarnoe nasledie," 108–10. On the Orthodox Church and World War I, see Gregory Freeze, "'Churching' Russian History: Orthodoxy in the Great War and Revolution,' in *Religion in the Russian Revolution*, ed. A. Agadjanian et al. (Bloomington: Indiana University Press, forthcoming).
92. RGIA f. 796, op. 442. d. 2647, l. 15–15ob.
93. Tikhon's report on Lithuanian diocese in 1915, RGIA f. 796, op. 442, d. 2709, l. 7ob.
94. "Arkhipastyrskoe obozrenie eparkhii s 1 po 6 maia 1915 g.," *VVPSDB* 9, no. 12 (June 15, 1915): 195–99; "Eparkhial'nye khronika," *VVPSDB* 10, no. 2 (May 1, 1916): 15–23.
95. RGIA f. 796, op. 442. d. 2647, l. 17ob.
96. "Pastyrskaia rabota dukhovenstva Litovskoi eparkhii v obsluzhivanii dukhovnykh i material'nykh nuzhd voinov destvuiushchei armii," *VVPSDB* 9, no. 11 (June 1, 1915): 178–79.
97. "Pastyrskaia rabota," 179; "Khronika tserkovno-obshchestvennoi zhizni," *VVPSDB* 9, no. 7 (April 1, 1915): 112.
98. Aref'eva and Shlevis, *Primite menia*, 206–12; even Tikhon believed that the Kovno fortress would stop the Germans: letter to Flavian, June 1, 1915, in Muralev, "Epistoliarnoe nasledie," 111.
99. Borzenskii, "Patriarkh Tikhon: po lichnym vospominaniiam," *Vozrozhdenie* (Paris) No. 310 (April 8, 1926): 2.
100. RGIA f. 796, op. 442, d 2709, l. 10.
101. Zhirkevich, diary, August 9, 1915, *BogSb* 6: 227–28; diary from 1923, 229–29.
102. Letter to Flavian, September 16, 1915, in Muralev, "Epistoliarnoe nasledie," 112 (Flavian died on November 4); "Eparkhial'nye khronika," *VVPSDB* 10, no. 1 (April 10, 1916): 9; see also Tikhon's letter to Governor Verevkin, Aref'eva and Shlevis, *Primite menia*, 223.
103. Synodal ukazes of October 29, 1915 and June 6, 1916: LVIA, f. 605, ap. 9, b. 2070, l. 1, 5.
104. Letter to Flavian, November 5, 1913: Muralev, "Epistoliarnoe nasledie," 103. Tikhon sarcastically uses the term *pervobytnoe sostoianie*, which referred to a monk who, when defrocked, was removed from the clerical estate and returned to the estate they were born into. Sabler was assistant to chief procurator Pobedonostsev from 1892 to 1905 and chief procurator from 1911 to 1915.
105. Sabler's memorandum to Varnava, RGIA f. 797, op. 84, d. 372, l. 18, and GARF f. 4652, op. 1, d. 1, l. 229 (copy). On the episode, see also Gregory L. Freeze, "Subversive Piety: Religion and the Political Crisis in Late Imperial Russia," *Journal of Modern History* 68, no. 2 (1996): 342–48; Douglas Smith, *Rasputin: Faith, Power, and the Twilight of the Romanovs* (New York: Picador, 2017), 444–51.
106. Quoted in Smith, *Rasputin*, 450; Shavel'skii also observed that the tsar's removal of Samarin turned the aristocracy against him: Georgii Shavel'skii, *Vospominaniia poslednego protopresvitera russkoi armii i flota* (Moscow: Krutitskcto podvor'e, 2010), 324.
107. Chief Procurator, report to the Synod, December 10, 1915, and other correspondence, RGIA f. 797, op. 84, d. 372, ll. 90–95; Synodal ukaz to Tikhon, December 11, 1915, GARF f. 4652, op. 1, d. 1, l. 227.
108. RGIA f. 796, op. 199, d. 189: Tikhon's report is ll. 253–56; the appendices he sent, including the investigation of miracles, ll. 257–66.
109. "Eparkhial'naia khronika," *VVPSDB* 10, no. 2 (May 1, 1916): 15–23.
110. Letter from the chief procurator to Tikhon, April 29, 1916, LVIA f. 605, ap. 9, b. 1739, l. 56; "Nagrady k 6 maiu," *LEV* 55, no. 2 (May 1, 1916): 5.
111. Letter to Verevkin, October 11, 1916, in Aref'eva and Shlevis, *Primite menia*, 292.

112. There is a large archival file devoted to this question which demonstrates the extensive degree of Tikhon's personal involvement: LVIA, f. 605, ap. 9, b. 2052; see also b. 2331 for 1917; Aref'eva and Shlevis, *Primite menia*, 242–48.
113. "13 avgusta v g. Disne," *VVPSDB* 10, no. 11 (September 15, 1916): 108.
114. "S. Prozorki, Disn. u.," *VVPSDB* 10, no. 11 (September 15, 1916): 110; for a similar encounter in another village, see "Obozrenie Vysokopreosviashchenneishim Tikhonom, Arkhiepiskopom Litovskim i Vilenskim, khramov i prikhodov Litovskoi eparkhii," *VVPSDB* 10, no. 11 (September 15, 1916): 112.
115. "Arkhipastyr' Litovskii na fronte," *VVPSDB* 10, no. 13 (October 15, 1916): 136–43, esp. 142.
116. Priest Mirinovich, "Osviashchenie obnovlennoi Ugorsko-Boginskoi prikhodskoi tserkvi," *VVPSDB* 10, no. 16–17 (December 31, 1916): 167.
117. "Vysochaishaia gramota Ego Vysokopreosviashchenstvu," *LEV* 55, no. 3 (May 15, 1916): 9; "Nagrady," *LEV* 55, no. 14–15 (November 15, 1916): 51; LVIA, f. 605, ap. 9, b. 1739, l. 64–65.
118. LVIA, f. 605, ap. 9, b. 2103, l. 1 (Synodal ukaz appointing him to the Synod), l. 2–3 (ukaz appointing him to the preconciliar commission), and l. 4 (ukaz from the Synod sending him to Astrakhan, February 20, 1917).
119. R. G. Rogoznyi, *Pravoslavnaia Tserkov' i Russkaia Revoliutsiia: Ocherki istorii* (Moscow: Izdatel'stvo 'Ves' Mir', 2018), 26.
120. M. A. Babkin, *Sviashchenstvo i Tsarstvo (Rossiia, nachalo XX v.–1918 g.): Issledovaniia i materialy* (Moscow: Indrik, 2011), blames the Church; Odintsov, *Zhrebii*, 135.
121. Rogoznyi, *Pravoslavnaia Tserkov'*, 27–28.
122. M. A. Babkin (ed.), *Rossiiskoe dukhovenstvo i sverzhenie monarkhii v 1917 godu (Materialy i arkhivnye dokumenty po istorii Russkoi pravoslavnoi tserkvi)*, 2nd ed. (Moscow: Indrik, 2008), 23, 29, 32.
123. Copies of Synodal ukazes with Tikhon's instructions, LVIA, f. 605, ap. 9, b. 2190, ll. 8, 11, 14.
124. Babkin, *Rossiiskoe dukhovenstvo*, 29–30; Odintsov, *Zhrebii*, 148–49.
125. These events were discussed at the Council: *Dokumenty Sobora* 5: 360–92; Tikhon's account of events is 371–72.
126. Arsenii, *Dnevnik*, 361–63; see *Dokumenty Sobora*, 5: 392–411.
127. On the "church revolution" generally, see Rogoznyi, *Tserkovnaia revoliutsiia*; on the contentious case of the Tver diocese, see Daniel Scarborough, *Russia's Social Gospel: The Orthodox Pastoral Movement in Famine, War, and Revolution* (Madison: University of Wisconsin Press, 2022), 167–78.
128. See Kenworthy, "Monasticism in War and Revolution," 230–35. Shevzov, "The Orthodox Church and Religion," cautions that not all those who were baptized Orthodox were actually believers, which likely played a role in these conflicts at the parish level.
129. Materials from the congress are in LVIA, f. 605, ap. 9, b. 2197.
130. Greeting speech to the Lithuanian diocesan congress, May 16, 1917, in I. N. Zhiianova (ed.), "'Da budem soiuzom liubve sviazuemi': Neizvestnye obrashcheniia Sviatitelia Tikhona, Patriarkha Moskovskogo i Vseia Rusi," *Bogoslovskii sbornik* No. 11 (2003): 410–12.
131. "Vybory mitropolitov," *Vserossiiskii Tserkvno-obshchestvennyi vestnik* No. 2 (April 4, 1917): 1–2.
132. *PE* 42: 390–401.
133. Makarii's letter, March 31, 1917, RGIA f. 796, op. 204, d. 72, ll. 5–8. I am immensely grateful to Daniel Scarborough for sharing his notes on this file with me. See his treatment of the subject: Scarborough, *Russia's Social Gospel*, 179–80; see also Sergii Golubtsov, *Moskovskoe dukhovenstvo v preddverii i nachale gonenii 1917–1922 gg.* (Moscow: Izd-vo Pravoslavnogo bratstva Sporuchnitsy greshnykh, 1999), 32–33; Rogoznyi, *Tserkovnaia revoliutsiia*, 64–69.
134. Rogoznyi, *Tserkovnaia revoliutsiia*, 154–55; Scarborough, *Russia's Social Gospel*, 181, 184–85.
135. "Vybory moskovskogo arkhiereia," *Vserosiiskii Tserkvno-obshchestvennyi vestnik* No. 54 (June 23, 1917): 3; "Pervyi moskovskii arkhipastyr' po svobodnomu izbraniiu tserkovnogo klira i naroda," *Bogoslovskii vestnik* No. 6/7 (1917): 135–42, especially 139; S. Friazinov, "Preds"ezdnye dumy," *Moskovskii tserkovnyi golos* No. 20 (1917): 2–5, esp. 3; "Izbranie Moskovskogo mitropolita," *Moskovskie vedomosti* No. 193 (1917), reprinted in *Sovremenniki* 2: 46–47.
136. Friazinov, "Preds"ezdnye dumy," 3.
137. "Pervyi moskovskii arkhipastyr'," 141.
138. "Izbranie mitropolita. Izbran arkhiepiskop Vilenskii Tikhon," *Moskovskii listok* No. 139 (June 22, 1917), reprinted in *Sovremenniki* 2: 190.

139. "Izbranie pervosviat telia tserkvi Moskvoi," 4; a separate account from the secular newspaper *Moskovskii listok* gives a similar account (*Sovremenniki* 2: 189-91). See Professor Beliaev's diaries: *BogSb* 6: 95-105. See also A. N. Kazakevich (ed.), *Pravoslavnaia Moskva v 1917-1921 godakh: sbornik dokumentov i materialov* (Moscow: Izd. Glavarkhiva Moskvy, 2004), 66-76; N. A. Krivosheeva, "Sviatitel' Tikhon—mitropolit Moskovskii i Kolomenskii. Khrolonologiia sobytii (21 iunia-26 noiabria 1917 goda)," *Kadashevskie chteniia* No. 11 (2012): 136-53.
140. Synodal ukaz, June 23, 1917, TsIAM f. 203, op. 744, d. 1453, l. 50.
141. Matthew Lee Miller (ed.), *John R. Mott, the American YMCA, and Revolutionary Russia* (Bloomington, IN: Slavica, 2020), 20.
142. "Pervyi moskovskii arkhipastyr," 135-39, 141.
143. "Izbranie moskovskogo mitropolita," *Moskovskie vedomosti* No. 193 (1917), in *Sovremenniki* 2: 46-48.
144. Simon Dixon, "Orthodoxy and Revolution: The Restoration of the Russian Patriarchate in 1917," *Transactions of the Royal Historical Society* 28 (2018): 166-67.
145. See "Izbranie pervosviatitelia tserkvi Moskvoi," *Moskovskii tserkovnyi golos* NN 17-18 (1917): 3-5.
146. *Dokumenty sobora* 1/1: 428, 479.
147. Borzenskii, "Patriarkh Tikhon: po lichnym vospominaniiam," *Vozrozhdenie* (Paris) No. 310 (April 8, 1926): 2.
148. *Sovremenniki* 2: 192-95.
149. From *Moskovskii listok* (July 26, 1917) in Kazakevich (ed.), *Pravoslavnaia Moskva*, 82.
150. Krivosheeva, "Sviatitel' Tikhon—mitropolit Moskovskii," 147-53.

Chapter 5

1. "Opredelenie Sviate shego Sinoda," *Tserkovnye Vedomosti* No. 35 (September 2, 1917): 295; the Synodal decree sent to Tikhon is TsGAM f. 203, op. 744, d. 1453, l. 78.
2. Evlogy, 341-42; Rudnev in *Delo*, 395-96. On the Church Council, see Aleksandr Kravetskii and Scott Kenworthy, "The Council of the Orthodox Church in Russia, 1917-1918," in *Wiley-Blackwell Companion to Conciliarity in Modern Orthodox Christianity*, ed. Irina Paert, Alison Kolosova, and Andrei Shishkov (Oxford: Wiley, 2026), 141-54; Hyacinthe Destivelle, *The Moscow Council (1917-1918): The Creation of the Conciliar Institutions of the Russian Orthodox Church*, trans. Jerry Ryan, ed. Michael Plekon and Vitaly Permiakov (Notre Dame, IN: University of Notre Dame Press, 2015); James W. Cunningham, *The Gates of Hell: The Great Sobor of the Russian Orthodox Church, 1917-1918* (Minneapolis: University of Minnesota, 2002); Gregory L. Freeze, "The 'Long' Church Council of 1917-1918: Institutional Crisis, Intellectual Capital," *Ostkirchliche Studien* 67 (2018): 187-211; Günther Schulz, Gisela-A. Schröder, and Timm C. Richter, *Bolschewistische Herrschaft und Orthodoxe Kirche in Russland: Das Landeskonzil 1917-1918. Quellen und Analysen* (Münster: Lit, 2005).
3. On the composition of the Council, see *Dokumenty Sobora* 27.
4. *Dokumenty Sobora* 5: 39-40.
5. See Francesca Silano, "(Re)Constructing an Orthodox 'Scenario of Power': The Restoration of the Russian Orthodox Patriarchate in Revolutionary Russian (1917-1918)," *Revolutionary Russia* 32 (2019): 5-30.
6. *Dokumenty Sobora* 5: 70; Arsenii, 61; *Delo*, 83, 92f, 398, 503.
7. Arsenii, 24, 70; for other instances, see 65, 80-82, 103, 143.
8. *Dokumenty Sobora* 5: 334; see Francesca Silano, "'A Dishonor to You and to the Church': Patriarch Tikhon, Pogroms, and the Russian Revolution, 1917-19," *Kritika* 23, no. 1 (2022): 9-12.
9. V. M. Lavrov, V. V. Lobanov, I. V. Lobanova, and A. V. Mazyrin, *Ierarkhiia russkoi pravoslavnoi tserkvi, patriarshestvo i gosudarstvo v revoliutsionnuiu epokhu* (Moscow: Russkaia Panorama, 2008), 119-32.
10. Catherine Evtuhov, "The Church and the Russian Revolution: Arguments for and Against Restoring the Patriarchate at the Church Council of 1917-1918," *Slavic Review* 50: 497-511.
11. *Dokumenty Sobora* 5: 473-74.
12. *Dokumenty Sobora* 5: 440-52.

13. Destivelle, 73–83.
14. Literature on the Russian revolutions of 1917 is vast. For recent overviews, see S. A. Smith, *Russia in Revolution: Empire in Crisis, 1890–1928* (Oxford: Oxford University Press, 2017) and Laura Engelstein, *Russia in Flames: War, Revolution, Civil War 1914–1921* (Oxford: Oxford University Press, 2017); Christopher Read, *War and Revolution, 1914–22: The Collapse of Tsarism and the Establshment of Soviet Power* (Basingstoke: Palgrave Macmillan, 2013). For an excellent recent overview of the Bolshevik seizure of power, see Rabinowitch, *The Bolsheviks in Power: The First Year of Soviet Rule in Petrograd* (Bloomington: Indiana University Press, 2007), 1–13.
15. *Dokumenty Sobora* 5: 689–90.
16. "Vosstanovlenie patriarshestva i izbranie vserossiiskogo patriarkha," *Bogoslovskii vestnik* 2: nn. 10–12 (October–December 1917): 427. When the votes were not close, the numbers were not recorded in the stenographic records; see *Dokumenty Sobora* 5: 698–700. Bishop Pakhomii stated it was a "relatively unanimous decision" (747). Some scholars misleadingly portray this vote as having been close, such as Mikhail Odintsov, *Russkaia pravoslavnaia tserkov' nakanune i v epokhu stalinskogo sotsializma, 1917–1953 gg.* (Moscow: Rosspen, 2014), 40.
17. According to V. Bogdanovich, *Delo*, 461–62.
18. *Dokumenty Sobora* 5: 744.
19. Diary entry for October 30, 1917, Library of Congress, Papers of Metropolitan Leontii, Box 9, Folder 3, knizhka No. 2, p. 64. Turkevich's journals from the Council were recently published: Leonid Turkevich, *Dnevniki i zapisnye knizhki perioda Pomestnogo Sobora 1917–1918 gg.*, ed. A. I. Mramornov (Moscow: Spasskoe delo, 2024), 113.
20. *Dokumenty Sobora* 5: 744–55.
21. *Dokumenty Sobora* 5: 755–56.
22. *Dokumenty Sobora* 5: 758–61.
23. On Antonii, see Dixon, "Orthodoxy and Restoration of the Russian Patriarchate in 1917."
24. Tikhon delivered his report to the Council on November 4, 1917, *Dokumenty Sobora* 5: 790–94; see also the interview with Tikhon for *Utro Rossii*, November 9, 1917 (reprinted in *Delo*, 649–50). On damage to the Kremlin and its churches during the fighting, see *Otdelenie*, 57–74; *Delo*, 130–52.
25. Evlogy, 350 (first published in 1947).
26. *Delo*, 535 (first published in 1948).
27. Entry for November 4, 1917, Arsenii, 129.
28. *Delo*, 422, 466.
29. *Dokumenty Sobora* 5: 811–14; 823–26.
30. On Aleksii, see Kenworthy, *The Heart of Russia*, 241–44, 248–52, 334–48, 434–46; *Delo*, 424; 613–17.
31. *Dokumenty Sobora* 5: 815–16.
32. According to Anastasy in *Delo*, 536, and Bogdanovich, 468.
33. Entry for November 5, Arsenii, 129–30.
34. *Dokumenty Sobora* 5: 827–28.
35. *Dokumenty Sobora* 5: 818–19.
36. *Dokumenty Sobora* 5: 819–20.
37. Entry for November 5, 1917, Arsenii, 130.
38. Arsenii, 130–31, 157; on Antonii's attitude toward the laity and the Council, see 61, 143.
39. N. A. Krivosheeva (ed.), "O prebyvanii v Troitse-Sergievoi Lavre narechennogo Patriarkha Tikhona," *Vestnik PSTGU* 42 (2011): 103–4, which publishes a contemporary report of Tikhon's stay.
40. From an article in *Moskovskii listok* (November 21, 1917), reproduced in Arsenii, 422.
41. Entry for November 19, 1917, Arsenii, 145.
42. Krivosheeva (ed.), "O prebyvanii," 107.
43. *Delo*, 538.
44. Cunningham, *Gates*, chapter 6; A. V. Sokolov, "Deputatsiia Pomestnogo Sobora v Moskovskom voenno-revoliutsionnom komitete 2 noiabria 1917 goda," in *Revoliutsiia 1917 goda v Rossii: novye podkhody i vzgliady*, ed. A. B. Nikolaev (St. Petersburg: Herzen University, 2014), 172–86.
45. Destivelle, 85–93; Cunningham, *Gates*, chapter 10; Günther Schulz, A. G. Kravetskii, and A. A. Pletneva (eds.), *Sviashchennyi Sobor Pravoslavnoi Rossiiskoi tserkvi 1917–1918 gg.: Obzor deianii* (Moscow: Krutitskoe podvor'e, 2000–2002) [hereafter: Schulz et al., *Obzor*], 3 vols., 1: 139–89.
46. *Dokumenty Sobora* 6: 252–57; Silano, "(Re)Constructing."

47. *Dokumenty Sobora* 6: 346–53; entry for November 21, Arsenii, 147.
48. *Delo*, 429; originally published in 1928.
49. *Dokumenty Sobora* 6: 346–53; Arsenii, 149.
50. "Vosstanovlenie patriarshestva i izbranie vserossiiskogo patriarkha," *Bogoslovskii vestnik* 2: nn. 10–12 (October–December 1917): 430.
51. Compare the accounts in *Dokumenty Sobora* 6: 365; Arsenii, 151; *Delo*, 158, 434–35, 547.
52. Diary entry for November 21, 1917, Arsenii, 151; Anastasy in *Delo*, 547.
53. *Dokumenty Sobora* 6: 391–92.
54. *Dokumenty Sobora* 6: 393–94.
55. Tikhon's Epistle on assuming the patriarchal throne, December 18/31, 1917, *Tserkovnye vedomosti* No. 1 (1918): 1–2. On Bulgakov's involvement, see his letter to Florenskii (December 18, 1917), in *Perepiska sviashchennika Pavla Aleksandrovicha Florenskogo so sviashchennikom Sergiem Nikolaevichem Bulgakovym* (Tomsk: Volodei, 2001), 138.
56. *Dokumenty Sobora* 6: 895–97.
57. Rabinowitch, *Bolsheviks*, 19–23, 47; Read, *War and Revolution*, 124–26.
58. See the declaration of November 4, 1917, *Dokumenty Sobora* 6: 84–86; on Bulgakov's authorship, *Delo*, 346, 665.
59. *Otdelenie*, 103–7.
60. For the history, see A. G. Kravetskii, "K istorii poiavlenii 'Dekreta ob otdalenii Tserkvi ot gosudarstva," in Schulz et al., *Obzor*, 1: 424–35; S. A. Sokolov, "Gosudarstvo i pravoslavnaia tserkov' v Rossii, Fevral' 1917-ianvar' 1918 gg," doctoral dissertation, Herzen University (2014), 626–34. Documents can be found in *Otdelenie*, 94–97, 121–22.
61. Rabinowitch, *Bolsheviks*, chapter 4, is an excellent account of the Constituent Assembly and its fate.
62. *Otdelenie*, 123; Sokolov, "Gosudarstvo," 633.
63. Arsenii, 196. See the detailed account in M. V. Sharkovskii, "Aleksandro-Nevskaia Lavra v god revoliutsionnykh potriasenii (1917–1918)," *Khristianskoe chtenie* No. 1 (2010): 6–33.
64. Figes, *People's Tragedy*, 521–22.
65. N. A. Krivosheeva (ed.), *"Prispelo vremia podviga . . .": Dokumenty sviashchennogo sobora Pravoslavnoi Rossiiskoi tserkvi 1917–1918 gg. o nachale gonenii na tserkov'* (Moscow: PSTGU, 2012), 190–217; Arsenii, 194.
66. *Dokumenty Sobora* 7: 30–33.
67. Diary entry for January 18, 1918, Arsenii, 191. For a draft that Arsenii edited, see 235–38; for other drafts, see GARF f. 3431, op. 1, d. 240, ll. 3–9.
68. *Poslaniia*, 45–47.
69. Nadieszda Kizenko, *Good for the Souls: A History of Confession in the Russian Empire* (Oxford: Oxford University Press, 2021), 119.
70. *Poslaniia*, 47–48.
71. *Poslaniia*, 48–49.
72. To add to the confusion, the only translation in English was based on an émigré publication that rearranged the text to make appear that it explicitly anathematized the government: Boleslaw Szczesniak (ed.), *The Russian Revolution and Religion: A Collection of Documents Concerning the Suppression of Religion by the Communists, 1917–1925* (Notre Dame, IN: University of Notre Dame Press, 1959), 36–37.
73. "Delo Patriarkha Tikhona," HIA Frank Golder papers, Box 24, folder 6, p. 14. This anonymous document was written by circles close to the patriarch at the end of February 1923. See also A. Sagarda, "Poslanie Sviateishego Patriarkha," *Pribavlenie k Tserkovnym Vedomostiam* No. 3–4 (January 31, 1918): 149–51.
74. Appeal to the Supreme Court of June 16, 1923: SD 357.
75. Rudnev in *Delo*, 440.
76. *Dokumenty Sobora* 7: 22–24.
77. Arsenii, 197–98. *Dokumenty Sobora* 7: 15–33; also 51–70.
78. *Dokumenty Sobora* 7: 53. This was what one might term a "sense of the Council," a nonbinding resolution—not a decree that carried canonical weight, as some later authors claim.
79. Korovin, "U patriarkha," *ZhMP* No. 6 (2005): 56–60, citation p. 58; originally published in *Fonar'* No. 14 (January 29, 1918).
80. Sokolov, "Gosudarstvo," 687–88.
81. GARF f. 3431, op. 1, d. 240, ll. 11–15.
82. Sokolov, "Gosudarstvo," 670–72; Schulz, Schröder, and Richter, *Bolschewistische Herrschaft*, 158–63.

83. Vladimir Bonch-Bruevich, "Rol' dukhoventstva v pervye dni oktiabria," in *Vospominaniia o Lenine* (Moscow: Nauka, 1969), 202–3; see S. V. Leonov, "VChK i Pravoslavnaia Rossiiskaia Tserkov' v 1918 g.," *Vestnik PSTGU* No. 100 (2021): 67–68.
84. Bonch-Bruevich, "Rol'," 203; see Firsov, "Lichnost' i obraz," 228.
85. Sokolov, "Gosudarstvo," 696.
86. P. G. Rogoznyi, *Pravoslavnaia tserkov' i russkaia revoliutsiia: Ocherki istorii* (Moscow: Izdatel'stvo 'Ves' Mir', 2018), 211.
87. For the draft and Lenin's edits, see *Otdelenie*, 128–29. On the decree, see Shevzov, "The Orthodox Church and Religion," 52–53; A. G. Kravetskii, "K istorii Dekreta ob otdelenii Tserkvi ot gosudarstva," in *1917-i: Tserkov' i sud'by Rossii* (Moscow: PSTGU, 2008), 134–40; S. L. Firsov, *Vlast' i ogon': Tserkov' i sovetskoe gosudarstvo 1918-nachalo 1940-kh gg.* (Moscow: PSTGU, 2014), 13–147; Schulz, Schröder, and Richter, *Bolschewistische Herrschaft*, 53–101.
88. *Otdelenie*, 132.
89. E.g., William B. Husband, *"Godless Communists": Atheism and Society in Soviet Russia, 1917–1932* (DeKalb: Northern Illinois University Press, 2000), 48.
90. James F. McMillan, "Catholic Christianity in France from the Restoration to the Separation of Church and State, 1815–1905," in *The Cambridge History of Christianity: Volume 8. World Christianities c.1815–c.1914*, ed. Sheridan Gilley and Brian Stanley, 175–98 (Cambridge: Cambridge University Press, 2006).
91. Korovin, "U patriarkha," 58–59.
92. Rogoznyi, *Pravoslavnaia*, 210; Sokolov, "Gosudarstvo," 673–74.
93. Schulz et al., *Obzor* 3: 244–45, 251.
94. Rudnev and Bogdanovich in *Delo*, 440–41, 470–78; Sokolov, "Gosudarstvo," 692.
95. "Patriarshii prizyv pastyriam Tserkvi—muzhestvenno snosit' ispytaniia," *Tserkovnye vedomosti* 31, no. 5 (February 7, 1918): 24–26.
96. Christine Worobec, "Lived Religion Gendered: Representations and Practices of Russian Orthodoxy," in *Women and Gender in Russia's Great War and Revolution, 1914–1922*, ed. Adele Lindenmeyr and Melissa K. Stockdale, 105–26 (Bloomington, IN: Slavic Publishers, 2022).
97. See *Otdelenie*, 140–48; A. N. Kashevarov, *Pravoslavnaia tserkov' i sovetskoe gosudarstvo (1917–1922)* (Moscow: Krutitskoe podvor'e, 2005), 132–34.
98. Documents in Kazakevich (ed.), *Pravoslavnaia Moskva*, 313, 318, 322; on a threat to arrest the patriarch and his response, see the diary of Archpriest G. S. Golubtsov, *Delo*, 232–33.
99. N. A. Krivosheeva (ed.), "Zabota o bratskom poseshchenii arestovannykh," *Vestnik PSTGU* 40 (2011): 72–79; Schulz et al., *Obzor* 3: 53; O. V. Rozina, "Sof'ia Dmitrievna Samarina i soiuz pravoslavnykh zhenshchin v 1918 godu," *Vestnik Moskovskogo gosudarstvennogo oblastnogo universiteta* No. 5 (2017): 145–53.
100. The Soviet government adopted the Gregorian calendar so that January 31 was followed by February 14. The narrative follows the new calendar from this point forward.
101. *Poslaniia*, 54–62.
102. "Delo Patriarkha Tikhona," HIA Frank Golder papers, Box 24, folder 6, 13–14.
103. See *Pravoslavnye bratstva v istorii Rossii: K 100-letiiu vozzvaniia patriarkha Tikhona ob obrazovanii dukhovnykh soiuzov* (Moscow: Preobrazhenie, 2018), 2 vols.
104. See Schulz et al., *Obzor* 2: 169. On Tikhon's weakness, see *Delo*, 294, 385.
105. "U Patriarkha: Ot nashego spetsial'nogo korrespondenta," signed "Moskvich," *ZhMP* No. 6 (2005): 60–61. Originally published in *Zhizn'* (Khar'kov), March 2, 1918.
106. For letters from believers to Tikhon, see Silano, "(Re)Constructing," 16–18.
107. *Delo*, 234–35, 253. See also Rogoznyi, *Pravoslavnaia*, 217ff.
108. See the manuscript *Bogosluzhebnyi dnevnik Sviateishego Tikhona, Patirarkha Moskovskogo i vseia Rossii, 1917–1925*, held in the Library of the St. Petersburg Theological Academy, 5–10, for details about the patriarch's services. Also the regular articles "Sluzhenie Sviateishego Patriarkha," *Moskovskie tserkovnye vedomosti*, No. 2 (1918): 4; No. 3 (1918): 3–4; No. 4 (1918): 4; No. 5 (1918): 4; No. 6 (1918): 5.
109. "Nikolin den' v Moskve," *ZhMP* No. 6 (2005): 65–73; Kazakevich (ed.), *Pravoslavnaia Moskva*, 422.
110. Appeal to Moscow believers, May 21, 1918, *BogSb* 6: 238.
111. V. Murav'ev, "Preobrazhenie dushi narodnoi," *Zaria Rossiii* (May 23, 1918), reprinted in *ZhMP* No. 6 (2005): 69–70; "Beseda s Patriarkhom Tikhonom," *Svoboda Rossii* (May 22, 1918), in *ZhMP* No. 6 (2005): 66–67; see also Silano, "(Re)Constructing," 18–20.

112. "Pervoe slovo Sviateishego Patriarkha Moskovskogo i vseia Rossii Tikhona k Petrogradskoi pastve," *Petrogradskii Tserkovno-eparkhial'nyi vestnik*, No. 16 (June 20, 1918): 1; *Sovremenniki* 1: 139.
113. "Patriarshie dni v Petrograde," *Petrogradskii Tserkovno-eparkhial'nyi vestnik*, No. 16 (June 20, 1918): 2–4, at p. 3. See also "Prebyvanie Sviateishego Patriarkha v Petrograde," *Pribavlenie k Tserkovnym Vedomostiam* No. 23–24 (July 1/14, 1918): 687ff.
114. "Patriarkh Tikhon v Petrograde: Beseda s Patriarkhom Tikhonom," ZhMP No. 6 (2005): 61–63. This is an interview originally published in *Vechernii chas* (June 14, 1918).
115. "Svet vechernii: Beseda s Patriarkhom Tikhonom—Moskovskim i vseia Rossii," ZhMP No. 6 (2005): 63–63, originally published in *Moskovskaia malen'kaia gazeta* (June 29, 1918).
116. *Poslaniia*, 49–53; Beliaev comments on it on February 16/March 2, that is, right before the Brest-Litovsk treaty (*BogSb* 6: 133).
117. *Poslaniia*, 63–67; see *Delo*, 243; Kizenko, *Good for the Souls*, 265.
118. SD 357.
119. Schulz et al., *Obzor* 3: 15–18; documents from the Council are GARF f. 3431, op. 1, d. 239, ll. 2–8.
120. *Poslaniia*, 208–10; Schulz et al., *Obzor* 3: 32–33. Because it was an extemporaneous sermon, Fr. Lakhostskii wrote it down as the patriarch delivered it, which the patriarch later corrected. See GARF f. 3431, op. 1, d. 239, ll. 10–11.
121. Resolution of the Sobornyi Soviet, *Otdelenie*, 153; see *Obzor* 2: 248–49.
122. See especially Kashevarov, *Pravoslavnaia*, 138–53; for documents, see KPSG 2: 286–89; KPSG 3: 6, 136–42, 339ff; *Otdelenie*, 156–59. Curtiss, typically, blames the Church for breaking off the negotiations (59–60).
123. Minutes of the commission on the implementation of the separation of church and state, May 19, 1918, KPSG 3: 145.
124. The Instructions are in *Otdelenie*, 173–78, with a model agreement with believers for the use of a church, 178–79; see Kashevarov, *Pravoslavnaia*, 153–68.
125. See *Otdelenie*, 267–490; Scott Kenworthy, "Monasticism in War and Revolution," in *Russia's Home Front, Book 2: The Experience of War and Revolution*, ed. Adele Lindenmeyr, Christopher Read, and Peter Waldron (Bloomington, IN: Slavica Publishers, 2016), 238ff.
126. The draft statement to Sovnarkom and the practical instructions for believers are *Otdelenie*, 189–96; see especially p. 195, which has two contrary variations on the point in question (VIII); the Council's instructions of September 12, 1918, are 196–197 (translation in Destivelle, 311–13).
127. The Council's resolution is in Destivelle, 327; see E. V. Beliakova, N. A. Beliakova, and E. B. Emchenko, *Zhenshchina v pravoslavie: Tserkovnoe pravo i rossiiskaia praktika* (Moscow: Kuchkovo pole, 2011), 353–66, 537–608; I. G. Eferov (ed.), *Sviashchennyi Sobor Pravoslavnoi rossiiskoi tserkvi 1917–1918 gg. o roliakh zhenshchin v tserkvi* (Moscow: Spasskoe delo, 2020).
128. *Poslaniia*, 211–13.

Chapter 6

1. Paul Dukes, *Red Dusk and the Morrow: Adventures and Investigations in Red Russia* (London: Williams and Norgate, 1923), 307.
2. See Tikhon's speech at the Council after Vladimir's murder, February 28, 1918, *Poslaniia*, 199–201; on Vladimir's murder, see *Sovremenniki* 2: 481–509. On the early repression against the Church, see S. V. Leontov, "Nachalo antitserkovnogo terrora v period Oktiabr'skoi revoliutsii," *Vestnik PSTGU* No. 73 (2016): 69–90.
3. Lenin, telegram to Penza provincial Executive Committee, August 9, 1918; *Polnoe sobranie sochinenie* 50: 144.
4. James Ryan, "Bolshevik Justifications for Violence and Terror During the Civil War," *Slavic Review* 74, no. 4 (2015): 808–31.

5. Jonathan Smele (ed.), *Historical Dictionary of the Russian Civil Wars* (Lanham, MD: Rowman & Littlefield, 2015), 2: 932–33; on estimates of victims, see 253; Smele, *The "Russian" Civil Wars, 1916–1926: Ten Years That Shook the World* (New York: Oxford University Press, 2015), 192–94; James Ryan, *Lenin's Terror: Ideological Origins of Early Soviet State Violence* (London: Routledge, 2012), 2, 114, and chapter 5. On terror against the clergy, see Alexander Yakovlev, *A Century of Violence in Soviet Russia* (New Haven: Yale University Press, 2002), 155–62; on the number of clergy and believers, see N. E. Emel'ianov and O. I. Khailova, "Goneniia na Russkuiu Pravoslavnuiu tserkov' (1917–1950-e gody)," *Rossiia i sovremennyi mir* No. 4 (61) (2008): 120.
6. M. Iu. Krapivin, "Arkhiepiskop Varnava (Nakropin) i religioznaia politika VChK: 1918–1922 gody," *Vestnik Tserkovnoi istorii* No. 3/4 (23/24) (2011): 114–16; for documents on the Vostorgov case, see Kazakevich (ed.), *Pravoslavnaia Moskva*, 231–308.
7. For instances, see KPSG 2: 380–82.
8. Tikhon's appeal to Sovnarkom, September 5, 1919, SGiR 37–38; on the Polish clergy, see KPSG 2: 450–59.
9. "Patriarkh Tikhon i soiuznykh diplomaty," *Izvestiia VTsIK* No. 190 (September 4, 1918): 4; see S. V. Leonov, "VChK i Pravoslavnaia Rossiiskaia Tserkov' v 1918 g.," *Vestnik PSTGU* No. 100 (2021): 75.
10. Jonathan Schneer, *The Lockhart Plot: Love, Betrayal, Assassination and Counter-Revolution in Lenin's Russia* (Oxford: Oxford University Press, 2020), 105–6; Evgeny Sergeev, *The Bolsheviks and Britain During the Russian Revolution and Civil War, 1917–1924* (London: Bloomsbury, 2022), 46.
11. Schulz et al., *Obzor* 3: 273–74; *Vestnik PSTGU* 19 (2006): 143; KPSG 2: 357–58.
12. Sermon on March 2, 1919, *Poslaniia*, 225.
13. Richard Pipes, *Russia under the Bolshevik Regime* (New York: A. A. Knopf, 1994), 345.
14. Tikhon told Latsis during the interrogation that it did not intend it for distribution (SD, 96). On its distribution, see the Aleksei Filippov, report to the Cheka (discussed below), KPSG 4: 199–200.
15. Appeal to Sovnarkom in connection with the first anniversary of the October Revolution, November 7 (October 25 o.s.), 1918: *Poslaniia*, 241–43.
16. *Poslaniia*, 243–44.
17. *Poslaniia*, 244–46.
18. *Poslaniia*, 247.
19. See, for example, Maxim Gorky, *Untimely Thoughts: Essays on Revolution, Culture, and the Bolsheviks, 1917–1918* (New Haven, CT: Yale University Press, 1995), 85–87.
20. SD 69–71; *Vestnik PSTGU* 19: 150–52.
21. SD 73.
22. Declaration of the Higher Church Administraiton to Sovnarkom, November 29, 1918, GARF f. 550, op. 1, d. 130, l. 1–2 (published in *Vestnik PSTGU* 19: 153–54); SD 72.
23. SD 74.
24. SD 75.
25. *Vestnik PSTGU* 19: 155.
26. See the petitions and subsequent correspondence in *Vestnik PSTGU* 19: 156–57; SD 77–79.
27. Sermon for the Nativity of Christ, January 7, 1919: *Poslaniia*, 216–19.
28. See T. G. Leont'eva, "'Vlast', pravoslavnaia tserkov', obshchestvo v gody Grazhdanskoi voiny," in *Rossiia v gody Grazhdanskoi voiny, 1917–1922 gg.: ocherki istorii i istoriografii* (Moscow: Tsentr gumanitarnykh initsiativ, 2018), 183–211; S. L. Firsov, *'Vremia voine i vremia miru': Pravoslavnaia Rossiiskaia tserkov' i grazhdanskaia voina v Rossii. Ocherki istorii i istoriografii* (St. Petersburg: Izdatel'stvo RGPU im. A. I. Gertsena, 2018); A. N. Kashevarov, *Pravoslavnaia Rossiiskaia Tserkov'* (Moscow: Krutitskoe podvor'e, 2005), 319–45; Iu. A. Biriukova and E. A. Ageeva (eds.), *Tserkov' na Donu v gody grazhdanskoi voiny 1918–1919 gg.: Rassledovaniia Osoboi kommissii* (Volgograd: PrinTerra Dizain, 2022).
29. A. A. Valentinov, *Assault of Heaven: The Black Book Containing Official and Other Information Illustrating the Struggle Against All Religion Carried by the Communist (Soviet) Government of Russia* (London: Boswell, 1925), 176–77.
30. G. Trubetskoi, "Pamiati sv. Patriarkha Tikhona," *Put'* No. 1 (September 1925): 116–20, at p. 117.
31. Veniamin (Fedchenkov), *Na rubezhe dvukh epokh* (Moscow: Otchii Dom, 2016), 419–20. There is contrary testimony from Kolchak's aide-de-camp V. V. Kniazev, but the details and the language of Tikhon's purported letter are inconsistent with other evidence. V. V. Kniazev, *Zhizn' dlia vsekh i smert' dlia vsekh: zapiski lichnogo adiutanta Verkhnovogo Pravitelia Admirala A. V. Kolchaka, rotmistra V. V. Kniazeva* (Jordanville, NY: Holy Trinity Monastery, 1971), 20–21.

32. A. V. Kartashev, "Vremennoe pravitel'stvo i Russkaia tserkov'," in *Iz istorii khristianskoi tserkvi na rodine i za rubezhom v XX stoletii* (Moscow: Krutitskoe podvor'e, 1995), 26; V. V. Lobanov, *Patriarkh Tikhon i Sovetskaia vlast' (1917-1925 gg.)* (Moscow: Russkaia Panorama, 2008), 68-69. On this conspiratorial group, see Stuart Finkel, *On the Ideological Front: The Russian Intelligentsia and the Making of the Soviet Public Sphere* (New Haven, CT: Yale University Press, 2007), 15-17.
33. *Akty*, 238.
34. I. Zhiianova (ed.), "'Da budem soiuzom liubve sviazuemi': Neizvestnye obrashcheniia Sviatitelia Tikhona, Patriarkha Moskovskogo i Vseia Rusi," *Bogoslovskii sbornik* No. 11 (2003): 408-25. The sermons in question were also included in *Poslaniia*.
35. Sermon during Holy Week, March 2, 1919: *Poslaniia*, 224.
36. *Poslaniia*, 225-26.
37. *Poslaniia*, 226-29.
38. Sermon during Holy Week, April 17, 1919: *Poslaniia*, 229-31.
39. I. Sh., "Delo o pokushenii na patriarkha Tikhona," *Revoliutsiia i Tserkov'* No. 3-5 (1919): 45-46. See *Sovremenniki* 1: 218-26; *BogSb* 6: 147. Most biographers assume she was the same woman that attacked Rasputin: *Sovremenniki*, 1: 223; Tikhon (Zatekin), *Sviatitel' Tikhon*, 537; Odintsov, *Zhrebii pastyria*, 347. Khionia Guseva, who attacked Rasputin, was thirty-three years old and single in 1914 (Smith, *Rasputin*, 332); Pelageia Guseva was forty-six in 1919, a widow with three children, two grown sons fighting in the Red Army (*Sovremenniki*, 1: 225). That Khionia had a sister Pelageia, see Smith, *Rasputin*, 345, 348.
40. Sermon at Christ the Savior Cathedral, July 27, 1919: *Poslaniia*, 234-37.
41. See Elissa Bemporad, *Legacy of Blood: Jews, Pogroms, and Ritual Murder in the Lands of the Soviets* (New York: Oxford University Press, 2019); Jeffrey Veidlinger, *In the Midst of Civilized Europe: The Pogroms of 1918-1921 and the Onset of the Holocaust* (New York: Metropolitan Books, Henry Holt and Company, 2021); Oleg Budnitskii, *Russian Jews Between the Reds and the Whites, 1917-1920*, trans. Timothy Portice (Philadelphia: University of Pennsylvania Press, 2012).
42. Francesca Silano, "'A Dishonor to You and to the Church': Patriarch Tikhon, Pogroms, and the Russian Revolution, 1917-19," *Kritika* 23, no. 1 (2022): 5-27; S. L. Firsov, "'Evreiskii vopros' i sviatoi Patriarkh Tikhon," *Kontinent* No. 111 (2002): 367-79, esp. 372.
43. Encyclical with a warning against revenge, July 21, 1919: *Poslaniia*, 103-7.
44. *Poslaniia*, 107.
45. *Poslaniia*, 108-9.
46. Filippov, report to the Cheka, KPSG 4: 201.
47. Karin, "Riasofornye pogromshchiki," *Izvestiia VTsIK* No. 166 (July 30, 1919): 1; Tikhon's appeal to Sovnarkom, August 1, 1919, SGiR 77-78; for a discussion of this episode, see Lobanov, *Patriarkh*, 70-76.
48. The institutional history is given in M. Iu. Krapivin, "Arkadii Antonov i nachal'nyi period formirovaniia politiki VChK v otnoshenii Pravoslavnoi Rossiiskoi Tserkvi (vesna-leto 1918 g.)," *Vestnik Tserkovnoi istorii* No. 35-16 (2014): 304-6; M. Iu. Krapivin and Iu. N. Makarov, "6-e otdelenie Sekretnogo otdela VChK (rabota po tserkovnikam i sektantam): voprosy organizatsionno-kadrovoi politiki," *Bylye Gody* 73, no. 3 (2015): 742-49.
49. M. V. Medovarov, *Natsional-monarkhist, natsional-demokrat, natsional-Bol'shevik: Aleksei Frolovich Filippov* (St. Petersburg: Vladimir Dal', 2021). M. Iu. Krapivin has also written extensively about Filippov in various articles, including those devoted to other figures such as Varnava (Nakropin).
50. On Ispolkomdukh, see Medovarov, 581-614; Krapivin, "A. F. Filippov i 'Ispolinitel'nyi komitet po delam dukhovenstva vseia Rossii' (1919-1920)," in *Istoricheskie chteniia na Lubianke: 15 let* (Moscow: Kuchkovo pole, 2012), 62-73; N. A. Krivosheeva, "'Vsetselo prisposoblenie k dukhu vremeni': Pervyi sovetskii razvedchik A. F. Filippov," *Vestnik PSTGU* vyp. II: 3 (32) (2009): 70-98. On the tasks of the Committee, see Aleksei Filippov, *Poslanie Patriarkha Tikhona k Dukhovenstvu ot 25 sentiabria/8 oktiabria 1919 g.* (Moscow: Komitet po delam dukhovenstva vseia Rossii, 1920), 4-5 (also reprinted by Krivosheeva).
51. Minutes of the Ispolkomdukh meeting, October 1, 1919, in Krivosheeva, "Vsetselo," 86.
52. Filippov to Fr. Nikolai Liubimov, October 5, 1919, SD 654-57 (the editors of SD are unaware of Filippov's authorship and confuse old/new style calendars).
53. *Poslaniia*, 109-12; on the reasons for clergy conducting such services, see Veniamin, *Na rubezhe*, 420.

54. SD 228; see 225.
55. Liubimov to Filippov, October 8, 1919, *Vestnik PSTGU* 19: 162; SD 228.
56. SD 226.
57. Filippov, report to Ispolkumdukh, August 1920, SGiR 27; see also the documents published by I. N. Smoliakova, "Novye dokumenty o poslanii Sviateishego Patriarkha Tikhona ot 25 sentiabria (8 oktiabria) 1919 goda," *Vestnik PSTGU* 19: 161–68.
58. Filippov's report, October 7, 1919, in the Russian State Archive of Social-Political History (RGASPI), f. 5, op. 1, d. 120, is published in Ia. N. Shchapov and O. Iu. Vasil'eva (eds.), *Russkaia pravoslavnaia tserkov' i kommunisticheskoe gosudarstvo, 1917–1940: Dokumenty i fotomaterialy* (Moscow: Izd. Bibleisko-Bogoslovskogo Instituta sv. Apostola Andreia), 47–55; a copy from RGASPI f. 274, op. 1, d. 29, is KPSG 4: 195–203.
59. Quoted in Krapivin, "Arkhiepiskop Varnava (Nakropin)," 124.
60. Document in Krivosheeva, "Vsetselo prisposoblenie k dukhu vremeni," 87–88.
61. Minutes of the Politburo meeting, October 26, 1919, KPSG 1: 223; Krapivin, "Arkhiepiskop Varnava (Nakropin)," 126.
62. SD 81–83.
63. Krapivin, "Arkhiepiskop Varnava (Nakropin)," 127.
64. Filippov, *Poslanie Patriarkha Tikhona*, 6–7, 10–12.
65. In Valentinov, *The Assault on Heaven*, 177; originally published in the newspaper *Rul'*, July 12, 1923.
66. Veniamin (Fedchenkov), *Na rubezhe*, 418–20.
67. See the appeals and correspondence in *Vestnik PSTGU* 19: 176–78, and SD 84–85, 92–93.
68. Cheka report "on the bases and causes for detaining Patriarch Tikhon under house arrest," no date, SD 93–98; KPSG 2: 103–8. The report is without date or authorship; the editors of SD attribute it incorrectly (to the Liquidation Commission rather than the Cheka), and the editors of KPSG date it incorrectly.
69. SD 93–94.
70. SD 94–95.
71. The Cheka's account is not the transcript of the interrogation but rather a summary as part of the secret report on the reasons the patriarch was arrested (SD 95–98). A transcript clearly was prepared (Liubimov mentions the patriarch checking and approving it), but it has never been published, if it still exists in the security services archive. Liubimov's account is contained in the Resolution of the Higher Church Administration, December 26, 1919, RGIA f. 831, op. 1, d. 25, ll. 129–31. It has been published: A. N. Kashevarov (ed.), "Arest i dopros patriarkha Tikhona v dekabre 1919 g.," *Russkoe Proshloe* 8 (1998): 215–27, and *BogSb* 6: 165–70. The main studies rely only on Liubimov's account: A. N. Kashevarov, *Pravoslavnaia Rossiiskaia Tserkov'*, 316–17; Lobanov, *Patriarkh*, 86–87; Safonov, 35.
72. SD 96–97.
73. RGIA f. 831, op. 1, d. 25, l. 130.
74. RGIA f. 831, op. 1, d. 25, l. 130–130ob.
75. SD 97.
76. RGIA f. 831, op. 1, d. 25, l. 131.
77. RGIA f. 831, op. 1, d. 25, l. 131.
78. RGIA f. 831, op. 1, d. 25, l. 131ob.
79. According to Archbishop Janis (Pommers), who was interrogated by Latsis after Tikhon: *Vestnik PSTGU* 19: 172–73.
80. Tikhon (Zatekin), *Sviatitel' Tikhon*, 561. Zatekin mistakenly states that Tikhon was released on Christmas Eve, 1920, as with his previous arrest (558).
81. SD 96–98.
82. SGiR 120–21.
83. Tikhon (Zatekin), *Sviatitel' Tikhon*, 575.
84. SD 98–99.
85. My calculation based on Mikhail Vostryshev, *Patriarkh Tikhon*, 4th ed. (Moscow, 2009), 320–28.
86. See Daniel Peris, "Commissars in Red Cassocks: Former Priests in the League of the Militant Godless," *Slavic Review* 54 (1995): 340–64.
87. Scott M. Kenworthy, "Monasticism in War and Revolution," in *Russia's Home Front, Book 2: The Experience of War and Revolution*, ed. Adele Lindenmeyr, Christopher Read, and Peter Waldron, 221–249 (Bloomington: Slavica Publishers, 2016); Kenworthy, *Heart of Russia* (Oxford: Oxford University Press and Washington, DC: Wilson Center Press, 2010), chapter 8.

88. Lenin, speech at the first all-Russian Congress of Working Women, November 19, 1918, *Collected Works* 28: 181.
89. Edward E. Roslof. *Red Priests* (Bloomington: Indiana University Press, 2002), 27–28; Catriona Kelly, "The 'Bolshevik Reformation,'" in *Was Revolution Inevitable? Turning Points of the Russian Revolution*, ed. Tony Brenton (New York: Oxford University Press, 2017), 230.
90. Rex A. Wade (ed.) *Documents of Soviet History* (Gulf Breeze, FL: Academic International Press, 1991), 1: 332.
91. For documents, see *Otdelenie*, 454–65, especially the bizarre logic of the Cheka justifying, in their language, the "fable of the wax doll" (459–60). See also S. A. Smith, "Bones of Contention: Bolsheviks and the Struggle Against Relics, 1918–1930," *Past and Present* 204 (2009): 157; R. H. Greene, *Bodies Like Bright Stars Saints and Relics in Orthodox Russia* (DeKalb, IL: Northern Illinois University Press, 2010), 123–26; P. G. Rogoznyi, "Bol'sheviki i sviatye moshchi," *Noveishaia istoriia Rossii* 10, no. 4 (2020): 991–92. Characteristically, Western historians, including Greene (but not Smith), repeat the falsehood of the "wax doll," assuming the reliability of Soviet propaganda.
92. Smith, "Bones," 161; Greene, 138–41.
93. Kashevarov, *Pravoslavnaia Rossiiskaia Tserkov'*, 175.
94. *Poslaniia*, 101–3.
95. SD 235; Akty, 247.
96. I explore this episode at length in *The Heart of Russia*, chapter 9; see also Andronik (Trubachev), *Zakrytie Troitse-Sergievoi Lavry i sud'ba moshchei prepodobnogo Sergiia Radonezhskogo v 1918–1946 gg.* (Moscow: Izdatel'skii Soviet Russkoi Pravoslavnoi tserkvi, 2008).
97. SD 536–37. There exists an earlier letter from March, but it is unclear exactly what it is (an unsent draft perhaps?): SD 534–35.
98. John MacKay, "Built on a Lie: Propaganda, Pedagogy, and the Origins of the Kuleshov Effect," in *The Oxford Handbook of Propaganda Studies*, ed. Jonathan Auerbach and Russ Castronovo (Oxford: Oxford University Press, 2013).
99. Kenworthy, *Heart of Russia*, 312–19. For documents, see *Pravoslavnaia Moskva*, 497–511; Andronik (Trubachev), *Zakrytie*, 124–53; KPSG 2: 398–407.
100. Tikhon's appeal to Lenin, November 7, 1919, SGiR 39; Tikhon's declaration to Lenin, March 24, 1920, SD 587–88; another copy is SGiR, 78–80, where the editors dated it to February 27, 1920.
101. Sovnarkom discussions and resolutions, KPSG 2: 317–19; Sovnkarkom decree, April 20, 1920, SD 591; Tikhon to Bonch-Bruevich (pleading with him to immediately give his letter to Lenin), SGiR 80; Tikhon to Lenin, May 10, 1920, SGiR80–82; see also Andronik, *Zakrytie*, 228–30; Kenworthy, *Heart of Russia*, 324.
102. Some documents indicate that Tikhon himself submitted the complaint; others that Bonch-Bruevich did: see Andronik, *Zakrytie*, 230, 235; Molver's report is SD 605–12 (also Andronik, *Zakrytie*, 235–45).
103. Small Sovnarkom minutes, August 27, 1920, KPSG 2: 323–24.
104. SD 613–47; Andronik, *Zakrytie*, chapter 10.
105. Small Sovnarkom minutes, September 2, 1920, KPSG 2: 324–25.
106. *Poslaniia*, 113–15; *Heart of Russia*, 325–26.
107. *Poslaniia*, 115–16.
108. KPSG 3: 55.
109. Smith, "Bones of Contention," 165.
110. Irina Aref'eva and German Shlevis, *Primite menia v svoiu liubov'*. . . (Vilnius: SAVO, 2008), 327.
111. "Delo 'vilenskikh ugodnikov,'" *Revoliutsiia i tserkov'* No. 9–12 (1920): 92–96; Kashevarov, *Pravoslavnaia Rossiiskaia Tserkov'*, 215; Vostryshev, 138–52; Aref'eva and Shlevis, 324–35.
112. SD 502–9 (interrogation of Tikhon is 509).
113. SGiR 24.
114. "Delo 'vilenskikh ugodnikov,'" 95; SD 509.
115. SGiR 15.
116. SD 100.
117. SD 102–7.
118. "Postanovlenie Sviateishego Patriarkha, Sviashchennogo Sinoda i Vysshego Tserkovnogo Soveta Pravoslavnoi Rossiiskoi Tserkvi ot 7/20 noiabria 1920 goda No. 362," *Tserkovnye vedomosti* No. 17–18 (September 1926): 6–7.

119. Petition for Tikhon's release from the parish of St. Nicholas in Drachakh, December 29, 1920, SD 108; Kalinin to Dzerzhinsky, January 13, 1921, SD 108–9.
120. Copies of the letter can be found in SD 600–604; Akty, 170–73; KPSG 2: 131–36; SGiR 82–86.
121. SGiR 87.
122. SGiR 87–89.
123. SGiR 90.
124. KPSG 2: 141.
125. KPSG 2: 142.
126. *Poslaniia*, 116–19.
127. P. N. Okunev, *Dnevnik Moskvicha*, vol. 2: 1920–1924 (Moscow: Voennoe izdatel'stvo, 1997), 102.

Chapter 7

1. John Shelton Curtiss, *The Russian Church and the Soviet State, 1917–1950*, 1st ed. (Boston: Little, Brown, 1953), 106–28; Catriona Kelly, "The 'Bolshevik Reformation': February 1922," in *Was Revolution Inevitable? Turning Points of the Russian Revolution*, ed. Tony Brenton (New York: Oxford University Press, 2017), 244–61.
2. The first monograph that utilized the new archives was N. A. Krivova, *Vlast' i tserkov' v 1922–1925 gg.* (Moscow: AIRO-XX, 1997). The most comprehensive treatment is Sergii Ivanov, *Sviatoi Patriarkh Tikhon i iz"iatie tserkovnykh tsennostei v 1922 godu* (Moscow: PSTGU, 2024) [hereafter: Ivanov, *Tikhon*].
3. Lenin to Molotov, April, 1921, in Lenin, *Pol'noe sobranie sochinenie* 52: 140.
4. Resolution of the Plenum of the Central Committee of the Bolshevik Party, July 26, 1921, KPSG 1:152.
5. Stuart Finkel, "An Intensification of Vigilance: Recent Perspectives on the Institutional History of the Soviet Security Apparatus in the 1920s," *Kritika* 5, no. 2 (2004): 303.
6. Safonov, 55–75; S. G. Petrov, *Dokumenty deloproizvodstva Politbiuro TsK RKP(b) kak istochnik po istorii Russkoi tserkvi (1921–1925)* (Moscow: Rosspen, 2004), 34–38; M. Iu. Krapivin, "Vsevolod Putiata v kontekste religioznoi politiki organov VChK (1918–1919 gg)," *Vestnik Tserkovnoi Istorii* 1/2, no. 29–30 (2013): 247–311; Krapivin, "Diskussiia o sozdanii 'sovetskoi' Pravoslavnoi tserkvi"; Krapivin, "'Neobkhodimo sdelat' vse, chtoby unizit' tserkov' v glazakh naroda': Dokladnaia zapiska M. I. Latsisa, 1920 g.," *Istoricheskii arkhiv* No. 2 (2011).
7. Ivanov, *Tikhon*, 83; M. Krapivin, *Nepridumannaia tserkovnaia istoriia: Vlast' i tserkov' v Sovetskoi Rossii (oktiabr' 1917-go-konets 1930-kh godov* (Volgograd: Peremena, 1997), 60–90.
8. See the account by N. A. Bezpalov, a Cheka informant who later defected, originally published in Harbin in 1924, reprinted in *Vestnik PTSGU* 19: 252–55.
9. N. A. Krivosheeva, "'Kto dushu svoiu polozhit za drugi svoia': Keleinik sviatogo Patriarkha Tikhona Iakov Anisimovich Polozov (23 oktiabria 1879 g.–9 dekabria 1924 g.)," *Vestnik PSTGU* 22 (2007): 52–74.
10. Krivosheeva, "'Kto dushu," 60.
11. According to Bezpalov: *Vestnik PTSGU* 19: 255–57.
12. According to Bezpalov: *Vestnik PTSGU* 19: 254.
13. SD 112–13.
14. "O sovremennom polozhenii pravoslavnoi tserkvi v Rossii," Hoover Institution Archives (HIA), Frank Golder papers, Box 24, folder 6, p. 3. This anonymous document was published: E. V. Ivanova (ed.), "Patriarkh Tikhon v 1920–1923 godakh: Analitcheskaia zapiska iz Guverskogo arkhiva," *ZhMP* No. 11 (2007): 62–85. Robert Hodgson, the British representative in Moscow, received a copy and sent it to Curzon on August 21, 1922: "The Present Position of the Orthodox Church in Russia," in *British Documents on Foreign Affairs: Reports and Papers from the Foreign Office Confidential Print*, Part II, Series A, vol. 6, ed. Dominic Lieven, 245–64 (here, p. 247). Hodgson stated that it "was drawn up by a small group of priests and laymen." Given that Hodgson received a copy, and a copy ended up in Frank Golder's papers (presumably through an ARA link), and the Irish journalist Francis McCullagh also had a copy, it is clear that the authors sought to inform an international audience about what the

Soviets were doing to the Russian Church. Hodgson (whose wife's name was Olga Bellavina), however, thought the text "biased," although in fact all its assertions are substantiated by new archival revelations The document provides a unique firsthand account from circles close to the patriarch. Citations are to the original document and the British publication.

15. There is a fairly extensive literature on the history of the Russian Orthodox Church Outside Russia (ROCOR), though much of it is polemical. For the history of the Higher Church Administration Outside Russia, see *PE* 10: 106–9; a balanced study is A. Kostriukov, *Russkaia Zarubezhnaia Tserkov' v pervoi polovine 1920-kh godov: Organizatsiia tserkovnogo upravleniia v emigratsii* (Moscow: PSTGU, 2007).
16. Kostriukov, *Russkaia Zarubezhnaia*, 47–48.
17. Antonii's report to Tikhon, July 1921, SD 691–92; Antonii to Tikhon, October 11, 1921, SD 694; report from Archbishop Anastasii to Tikhon, SD 597–99.
18. Nikolai Artemov, "Postanovlenie No. 362 ot 7/20 noiabria 1920 g. i zakrytie zarubezhnogo VVTsU v mae 1922 g.: Istoricheskoe i kanonicheskoe znachenie," in *Istoriiia Russkoi Pravoslavnoi Tserkvi v XX veke (1917–1933 gg.)* (Munich: Izd. Obiteli Prep. Iova Pochaevskogo, 2002), 145; S. N. Bakonina, *Tserkovnaia zhizn' russkoi emigratsii na Dal'nem Vostoke v 1920–1931 gg.: Na materialakh Kharbinskoi eparkhii* (Moscow: PSTGU, 2014), 78.
19. SD 674–75.
20. Resolution of March 21, 1921: SD 679. Normally the parishes of Europe were administered by the metropolitan of St. Petersburg.
21. SD 200.
22. Request of the Higher Church Administration Abroad to Patriarch Tikhon, July 22, 1921: SD 688–91; Antonii to Tikhon, July (?) 1921: SD 691–92.
23. Antonii to Tikhon, October 11, 1921: SD 694.
24. SD 695. The decree uses both the term *sobranie* and *sobcr* with reference to the planned meeting.
25. Tikhon to Georgii (Iaroshevskii), September 27, 1921, published in A. A. Chibisova, "Patriarkh Tikhon i avtokefaliia Pol'skoi Pravoslavnoi Tserkvi 1924 goda," *Vestnik PSTGU* 95 (2020): 139.
26. On Asia, see Bakonina, *Tserkovnaia zhizn' russkoi emigratsii*, 72; on the Baltics and Finland, see Chapter 9.
27. The patriarch discussed passing the decree and sending under interrogation: SD 192, 196. The decree is not mentioned in Church Abroad documents or by its historians prior to 2000; it was apparently unknown even to Gubonin, who collected every scrap of information on every decree and decision made by the patriarch, because it is not in *Akty*. Kostriukov does not give it due attention (*Russkaia Zarubezhnaia*, 53).
28. Kostriukov, *Russkaia Zarubezhnaia*, 55, 67–68.
29. *PE* 31: 177–86; Kostriukov, *Russkaia Zarubezhnaia Tserkov'*, 54–69. The encyclical was published in the émigré newspaper *Novoe vremia* in December 1921; also "Poslanie zagranichnogo Russkogo Tserkovnogo Sobora: Chadam Russkoi Pravoslavnoi Tserkvi v rasseianii i izgnanii sushchim," *Tserkovnye vedomosti* No. 1 (March 15/28. 1922): 1–2.
30. Metropolitan Evsevii's letter, addressed to someone in Vladivostok, was published in *Golos Rodiny* (Vladivostok) (October 5, 1921) and reprinted in S. N. Bakonina, *Tserkovnaia zhizn' russkoi emigratsii*, 250–51.
31. Tikhon to Evlogy, December 24, 1921, in N. Iu. Lazareva (ed.), "Perepiska sviatitelia Tikhona, patriarkha vserosiiskogo i mitropolita Evlogiia (Georgievskogo) 1921-1922 gg.," *Uchenye zapiski* No. 6 (2000): 107–9; see Tikhon's and Nikandr's statements under interrogation, SD 192, 196; Evlogy's letter to Tikhon, March 20, 1922: SD 707.
32. According to Nikandr's testimony given on January 24, 1923: SD 196–97.
33. The patriarch's appeal to the Bishop of New York was published in "Soviet Accepts Hoover's Terms for Famine Relief," *New York Times* (July 31, 1921): 1.
34. Charles M. Edmondson, "The Politics of Hunger: The Soviet Response to Famine, 1921," *Soviet Studies* 29, no. 4 (1977): 506–18; E. V. Ivanova, "Sviateishii Patriarkh Tikhon i golod 1921–1922 gg. v Rossii," *Bogoslovskie Trudy* No. 41 (2007): 504–29; Gorky's common-law wife, Maria Andreeva, stated that Lenin suggested Tikhon write a letter: see Ivanov, *Tikhon*, 96.
35. From the remembrances of Ilarion (Troitskii): S. A. Volkov, "Arkhiepiskop Ilarion (Troitskii)," *Vestnik Russkogo Khristianskogo dvizheniia* No. 134 (1981): 233–34; according to Gorky's assistant E. I. Kirakozova, Gorky was confused about how to address the patriarch in writing: Ivanova, "Sviateishii Patriarkh Tikhon i golod," 506.
36. N. P. Okunev, diary for July 12, 1921, in *Dnevnik moskvicha* 2: 158.

37. Gorky to V. G. Korolenko, July 13, 1921, in Gorky *Polnoe sobranie sochinenie* (Moscow: Nauka, 2007), vol. 13: 207.
38. Minutes of the Politburo meeting, July 6–7, 1921, KPSG 1: 229–30; see also Petrov, *Dokumenty*, 41–46.
39. "Davno by tak," *Izvestiia* No. 149 (July 10, 1921): 3. See the reaction in Okunev, *Dnevnik moskvicha* 2: 158.
40. Gorky to M. I. Budberg, July 13, 1921, *Pol'noe sobranie sochinenie* 13: 205.
41. "Says Soviet Didn't Appeal to America," *New York Times* (July 17, 1921): 10.
42. Cyril Brown, "Russians Plead for Famine Relief," *New York Times* (July 19, 1921): 2; "Soviet Accepts Hoover's Terms for Famine Relief," *New York Times* (July 31, 1921): 1.
43. Tikhon's letter, July 5, 1921, to Pope Benedict XV: *The Vatican Secret Archives* (Brussels: VdH, 2009), 92; Ovanes Akopian, "Pis'mo patriarkha Tikhona pape rimskomu Benediktu XV i drugie dokumenty iz istorii otnoshenii Sviatogo Prestola s SSSR (1920-e gody)," *Novoe literaturnoe obozrenie* 154 (2018): 141–60.
44. Ivanov, *Tikhon*, 111.
45. Ivanova, "Sviateishii Patriarkh Tikhon i golod," 509.
46. Charles M. Edmondson and R. Barry Levis, "Archbishop Randall Davidson, Russian Famine Relief, and the Fate of the Orthodox Clergy, 1917–1923," *Journal of Church & State* 40, no. 3 (1998): 624–31.
47. Ivanov, *Tikhon*, 112–13; Richard Gribble, "Cooperation and Conflict Between Church and State: The Russian Famine of 1921–1923," *Journal of Church and State* 51 (2009): 634–62; Marisa Patulli Trythall, "'Russia's Misfortune Offers Humanitarians a Splendid Opportunity': Jesuits, Communism, and the Russian Famine," *Journal of Jesuit Studies* 5 (2018): 71–96; James T. Zatko, "The Vatican and Famine Relief in Russia," *The Slavonic and East European Review* 42 (1963): 54–63.
48. Douglas Smith, *The Russian Job: The Forgotten Story of How America Saved the Soviet Union from Ruin* (New York: Farrar, Straus and Giroux, 2019); Bertrand M. Patenaude, *The Big Show in Bololand: The American Relief Expedition to Soviet Russia in the Famine of 1921* (Palo Alto, CA: Stanford University Press, 2002); Charles M. Edmondson, "The Politics of Hunger: The Soviet Response to Famine, 1921," *Soviet Studies* 29, no. 4 (1977): 506–18.
49. E. Kuskova, "Mesiats 'soglashatel'stva," *Volia Rossii* No. 4 (Prague, 1928): 48–49.
50. Kuskova, "Mesiats," 48–49.
51. Kuskova, "Mesiats," 49–51.
52. Tikhon, letter to the Presidium of the All-Russian Committee for Famine Relief, August 5, 1921. In *Iz"iatie tserkovnykh tsennostei v Moskve v 1922 godu: Sbornik dokumentov iz fonda Revvoensoveta Respubliki*, ed. A. V. Mazyrin, A. Goncharov, and I. V. Uspenskii [hereafter: Mazyrin, *Iz"iatie*] (Moscow: PSTGU, 2006), 135–37.
53. Minutes of the session of the Presidium of Pomgol, August 17, 1921; Tikhon's letter to VTsIK, August 17, 1921: Mazyrin, *Iz"iatie*, 137–40.
54. Kuskova, "Mesiats," 52–53.
55. "O sovremennom polozhenii," 4 ("The Present Position," 248).
56. On the civic Committee and its fate, see Finkel, *On the Ideological Front*, 19–39.
57. Kuskova, "Mesiats," 51.
58. Tikhon to VTsIK, August 31, 1921: Mazyrin, *Iz"iatie*, 142.
59. Petrov, *Dokumenty*, 48 n. 27. It is possible that Patriarch Tikhon visited Gorky in connection with getting the Church relief committee recognized by the government, because a visiting card from the patriarch was written to Gorky on September 8, 1921: Ivanova, "Sviateishii Patriarkh Tikhon i golod," 507.
60. "O sovremennom polozhenii," 5 ("The Present Position," 248); contributions came in all the same (Ivanov, *Tikhon*, 126).
61. Petrov, *Dokumenty*, 48–57; I. A. Kurliandskii, *Stalin, Vlast', Religiia* (Moscow: Kuchkovo Pole, 2011), 91–93; KPSG 1: 233–34.
62. KPSG 2: 41; see SD 340; Mazyrin, *Iz"iatie*, 143.
63. AK 2: 8–10.
64. Ivanova, "Sviateishii Patriarkh Tikhon i golod," 515–20, 527–28.
65. Ethan Colton, "Contacts with the Russian Church. January to April 1922," in the Kautz Family YMCA Archive, y.usa.9-2-1, Box 21, folder "Russia—Church—Interpretations—YMCA Relationships 1920-1925," p. 7.
66. Ivanova, "Sviateishii Patriarkh Tikhon i golod," 515. There was also an invitation for Tikhon to visit England: V. A. Goncharova (ed.), "Perepiska narkoma inostrannykh del G. V. Chicherina

s Sekretariatom TsK RKP(b) po povodu poezdki Sviateishego Patriarkha Tikhona v Angliiu," *Vestnik PSTGU* 27 (2008): 110–16.
67. Jonathan W. Daly, "'Storming the Last Citadel': The Bolshevik Assault on the Church, 1922," in *The Bolsheviks in Russian Society: Revolution and Civil Wars*, ed. Vladimir N. Brovkin (New Haven, CT: Yale University Press, 1997), 235–68.
68. Ivanov, *Tikhon*, 410–25; Petrov, *RPTs*, 45–57.
69. See the minutes of the sessions on the Commission for the concentration of valuables on January 2 and 23, 1922, in Ivanov, *Tikhon*, 487, 491; see also Ivanov's discussion, 126–29.
70. "Bor'ba s golodom: O bogatsvakh tservi," *Izvestiia VTsIK* No. 24 (February 1, 1922): 3; Ivanov, *Tikhon*, 171–82.
71. "O sovremennom polozhenii," 6 ("The Present Position," 249); SD 130; AK 2: 12–14.
72. Tikhon's appeal for famine relief, February 6, 1922, AK 2: 10–11; see also "O sovremennom polozhenii," 8–9 ("The Present Position," 250).
73. Politburo resolution, February 9, 1922, AK 2: 15; Ivanov, *Tikhon*, 125–126.
74. "Vozvanie patriarkha Tikhona," *Izvestiia VTsIK* No. 36 (February 15, 1922).
75. Francis McCullagh, *The Bolshevik Persecution of Christianity* (New York: E. P. Dutton and Company, 1924), 14–15; though McCullagh does not say more about his source, it is almost verbatim the same as "O sovremennom polozhenii pravoslavnoi tserkvi v Rossii," 8–9 ("The Present Position," 250), although McCullagh seems not to have used the British diplomat's translation.
76. Pomgol instructions to provincial executive committees, SD 346–47.
77. The decree of February 23, 1922, as published is in *Iz″iatie*, 149–50; the history is laid out in Ivanov, *Tikhon*, 129–31.
78. Quoted in Mazyrin, *Iz″iatie*, 242.
79. Tikhon to Kalinin, February 25, 1922: KPSG 2: 145–47. Both Gorky and Korolenko felt they had been deceived and made to be "provocateurs" after the members of the civic famine relief committee were arrested: Ivanov, *Tikhon*, 131.
80. Vinokurov's undated assessment of Tikhon's letter to Kalinin, KPSG 2: 148–49. Kalinin only sent it to Vinokurov the same day as the patriarch's encyclical, February 28.
81. Nikandr's testimony given on December 21, 1922, in SD 183; Safonov, 149–50.
82. Encyclical of February 28 in *Poslaniia* 130–32, quote 132. The canons cited were the Apostolic canon 73 and the Council of Constantinople (861), canon 10.
83. See Francesca Silano, "Canon Law in the Bolshevik Courtroom: The Russian Revolution as an Orthodox Legal Revolution," in *Religion in the Russian Revolution*, ed. A. Agadjanian et al. (Bloomington: Indiana University Press, forthcoming); Ivanov, *Tikhon*, 137–70.
84. SD 115–16.
85. Nikandr's testimony, December 21, 1922, in SD 183.
86. E.g., SD 181, 184, 187; Nikandr testified the same: SD 185.
87. James Ryan, "Cleansing NEP Russia: State Violence Against the Russian Orthodox Church in 1922," *Europe-Asia Studies* 65, no. 9 (2013): 1807–26. The scholarship on this period is rich and well developed. See especially Daly, "Storming"; Krivova, *Vlast'*, 42–93; Pokrovskii's introduction to *Arkhivy Kremlia* in AK 1: 24–37; Kurliandskii, *Stalin*, 94–118; Petrov, *RPTs*, 57–81; Safonov, 150–70; Ivanov, *Tikhon*; Francesca Silano, *The Battle for Russia's Souls: Patriarch Tikhon, the Russian Orthodox Church, and the Soviet State* (forthcoming).
88. Pipes, *Russia Under the Bolshevik Regime*, 348; Krivova, *Vlast'*, 41.
89. KPSG 2: 149; see Ivanov, *Tikhon*, 128–30.
90. Trotsky to the Politburo, March 17, 1922: KPSG 1: 249. See also AK 1: 23–24; Petrov, *Dokumenty*, 70 and *RPTs*, 55–57.
91. AK 1: 119–22, 129.
92. AK 1: 115–17, 123–27; AK 2: 52.
93. This point was first discussed by Trotsky's commission on January 23, 1922: in Ivanov, *Tikhon*, 492.
94. AK 2: 51.
95. Trotsky to Politburo, March 17–20, 1922, AK 1: 134–35.
96. Colton, "Contacts with the Russian Church," 5.
97. GPU svodka, March 13, 1922: AK 2: 56–57.
98. Telegram from Presidium of VTsIK and the Central Committee to provincial authorities, March 30, 1922: AK 1: 166.
99. "Tserkovnye tsennosti dlia pomoshchi golodaiushchim (Beseda s patriarkhom Tikhonom)," *Izvestiia VTsIK* No. 60 (March 15, 1922): 5.

100. "Tserkovnye tsennosti golodaiushchim: Golodaiushchie u Tikhona," *Izvestiia* No. 69 (March 26, 1922): 2.
101. E. E. Young, US Commissioner in Riga, "Memorandum of Conversation with Mr. Colton of the American YMCA," in Boleslaw Szczesniak (ed.), *The Russian Revolution and Religion: A Collection of Documents Concerning the Suppression of Religion by the Communists, 1917–1925* (Notre Dame, IN: University of Notre Dame Press, 1959), 72.
102. Galkin to Trotskii, March 25, 1922, in Ivanov, *Tikhon*, 581.
103. See N. A. Krivova, "The Events in Shuia: A Turning Point in the Assault on the Church," *Russian Studies in History* 46, no. 2 (Fall 2007): 8–38.
104. Central Committee cipher telegram, March 19, 1922: AK 1: 139; minutes of the confiscation commission, March 20, 1922, KPSG 1: 400–2; Petrov, *RPTs*, 70.
105. Quotes here are from Richard Pipes's translation: Lenin et al., *The Unknown Lenin: From the Secret Archive* (New Haven, CT: Yale University Press, 1996), 152–55; the original is AK 1: 140–44.
106. Pipes, *Unknown Lenin*, 152–53.
107. Pipes, *Unknown Lenin*, 153–55.
108. GPU report to the Politburo, March 20, 1922: AK 1: 149–50.
109. Trotsky's letter to the Politburo, March 22, 1922: AK 1: 151–52; see AK 1: 153–55, 159–60, 251–52.
110. Some historians wonder why there was not more resistance, as if people did not care: Pipes, *Russia Under the Bolshevik Regime*, 356; Daly, 258.
111. Ivanov, *Tikhon*, 475; Patenaude, *Big Show*, 662. On the repressions, see N. E. Emel'ianov and O. I. Khailova, "Goneniia na Russkuiu Pravoslavnuiu tserkov' (1917–1950-e gody)," *Rossiia i sovremennyi mir* No. 4 (61) (2008): 122; they estimate 20,000 arrests and 1,000 deaths for 1922–1923. On the Politburo and executions, see AK 1: 197–200, 213–24, 235–45.
112. Safonov, 160–69; introduction to Mazyrin, *Iz"iatie*, 15; Sergii Golubtsov, *Moskovskoe dukhovenstvo v preddverii i nachale gonenii 1917–1922 gg.* (Moscow: Izd. Pravoslavnogo bratstva Sporuchinitsy greshnykh, 1999). The list of those to be charged with opposing the confiscations in Moscow was prepared by the 6th section of the Secret Department of the Moscow GPU on April 9: AK 2: 175–77.
113. SD 117–18.
114. Daly, "Storming," argues that the fact that the Church Abroad was not mentioned earlier, for example, in Lenin's March 19 letter, indicates that Bolshevik leaders did not see it as a real threat (244–45). But the timing is crucial.
115. "Poslanie mirovoi konferentsii ot imenii Russkogo Vsegranichnogo Tserkovnogo Sobora," *Tserkovnye Vedomosti* (April 28, 1922): 2–4.
116. Interrogation record, March 28, 1922: SD 119–20.
117. GPU Ultimatum to Tikhon, March 28, 1922: SD 118–19.
118. SD 121–22.
119. This important letter, which was previously unknown, is published in Ivanov, *Tikhon*, 588–89.
120. SD 128–29. The record is in a fragmentary draft form. On the date, see Ivanov, *Tikhon*, 166–67, 729–30; Safonov, 172–73; Krivova, *Vlast'*, 131–32.
121. Tikhon's letter to Kalinin and the text of the encyclical sent to him, April 4, 1922: Mazyrin, *Iz"iatie*, 159–60.
122. Draft appeal of patriarch Tikhon to diocesan bishops, April 9, 1922: SD 124–25. See Safonov 174–76; Ivanov, *Tikhon*, 167–68. "O sovremennom polozhenii, 11 ("The Present Position," 252); see McCullagh, *Bolshevik Persecution*, 17 (which draws from the same source).
123. Statement to the GPU, April 5, 1922: SD 122–23.
124. Colton's letter to Bouimistrow, May 4, 1922. Exhibit 23, *Court of Appeals of the State of NY-Kedrovsky v Rojdestvensky and Turkevich* (1924), 568–69. RBWP UW Box 7, Folder 5. I am grateful to Aram Sarkisian for providing me with a scan of this trial record. See also 567, 622–23, 633. Colton's meeting with the patriarch has frequently been cited by Church Abroad historians with an incorrect date to argue that Patriarch Tikhon was affirming the Church Abroad administration later than he actually did: Grigorii (Grabbe), *Zavet sviatogo Patriarkha* (Moscow, 1996), 163, confused the date of the meeting with that of Colton's letter, which is of crucial importance. All other scholars simply follow Grabbe: Safonov, 186; Artemov, "Postanovlenie No. 362," 165–66; Kostriukov, *Russkaia Zarubezhnaia*, 70–71.
125. Akty, 193; the document was also reprinted with the final resolution of the patriarchal Higher Church Administration in *Tserkovnye vedomosti* NN. 12–13 (September 1–15, 1922): 6. The patriarch informed the GPU of his proposal to the Synod already on April 9 (KPSG 3: 443).

126. Letter to Mikhail (Ermakov) in A. N. Sukhorukov (ed.), "Maloizvestnye stranitsy tserkovnogo sluzheniia Ekzarkha Ukrainy mitropolita Mikhaila (Ermakova) v 1922–1923 godakh," *Vestnik PSTGU* No. 30 (2009): 83.
127. Pashkovsky's deposition, October 31, 1922, *Court of Appeals of the State of NY—Kedrovsky v Rojdestvensky and Turkevich*, 632–35; this document was later translated into Russian by the Cheka and appears in the patriarch's file (SD 710–12).
128. Pashkovsky's testimony at the trial, *Court of Appeals of the State of NY—Kedrovsky v Rojdestvensky and Turkevich*, 322.
129. SD 192; Ivanov, *Tikhon*, 285.

Chapter 8

1. See Francesca Silano, "'I Am a Sincere Believer': Rethinking Religiosity and Identity in the Early Soviet Union," *Slavic Review* 82 (2023): 714–36 and Francesca Silano, "Canon Law in the Bolshevik Courtroom: The Russian Revolution as an Orthodox Legal Revolution," in *Religion in the Russian Revolution*, ed. A. Agadjanian et al. (Bloomington: Indiana University Press, forthcoming).
2. AK 1: 199. Trotsky's secret note to the editorial of *Izvestiia, Pravda*, and *Rabochaia Moskva*: AK 1: 254–55.
3. "O sovremennom polozhenii pravoslavnoi tserkvi v Rossii," Hoover Institution Archives (HIA), Frank Golder papers, Box 24, folder 6, p. 16; the English translation of the same, sent by Hodgson to Curzon, August 21, 1922, is "The Present Position of the Orthodox Church in Russia," in *British Documents on Foreign Affairs: Reports and Papers from the Foreign Office Confidential Print*, Part II, Series A, vol. 6, ed. Dominic Lieven, 255.
4. Petr Ashevskii, "I 'sviateishii' i 'pravitel'stvuiushchii'...," and Mark Krinitskii, "'Russkii papa' pered sudom Revoliutsionnogo Tribunala," *Izvestiia VTsIK* No. 99 (May 6, 1922): 1.
5. "O sovremennom polozhenii," 16 ("The Present Position," 255).
6. SD 130–33, 150.
7. SD 143.
8. SD 142.
9. SD 150. For a fascinating analysis of the trial and Tikhon's testimony, see Francesco Silano, *The Battle for Russia's Souls: Patriarch Tikhon, the Russian Orthodox Church, and the Soviet State* (Ithaca, NY: Cornell University Press, forthcoming).
10. AK 1: 212; the entire judgment of the Tribunal is 200–212.
11. "O sovremennom polozhenii," 18–19 ("The Present Position," 256).
12. SD 155–56.
13. Akty, 193–94 (where it is numbered 347); *Tserkovnye vedomosti* NN. 12–13 (September 1–15, 1922): 6.
14. SD 154–55. On the timing of the interrogations, see Safonov, 188–91.
15. Artemov, "Postanovlenie No. 362," 177–82; Safonov, 186–89; for an overview of the debate, see Dionisii Khmyrov, *Spornye voprosy istorii RPTsZ (1920–1945)* (St. Petersburg: St. Petersburg State University, 2014), 247–335.
16. SD 153.
17. SD 159–60.
18. The historiography on Renovationism is extensive. See *PE* 52: 257–63. The most comprehensive study in English is Edward E. Roslof, *Red Priests: Renovationism, Russian Orthodoxy, and Revolution, 1905–1946* (Bloomington: Indiana University Press, 2002); see also V. V. Lobanov, "*Obnovlencheskii*" *raskol v Russkoi Pravoslavnoi Tserkvi (1922–1946 gg.)* (SPb: Petroglif, 2019); on the Renovationist take-over of the ecclesiastical leadership, see Ivanov, *Tikhon*, 259–92.
19. Trotsky's memorandum to the Politburo, March 30, 1922: AK 1: 161–64.
20. AK 1: 307–9; compare the earlier GPU proposal, AK 2: 185–86.
21. Commission on the concentration of valuables, May 11, 1922, Ivanov, *Tikhon*, 505–7; see other documents, 609–15; S. N. Ivanov, "Khronologiia obnovlencheskogo 'perevorota' v Russkoi Tserkvi po novym arkhivnym dokumentam," *Vestnik PSTGU* 3, no. 58 (2014): 24–60, esp. 31–36.
22. "O sovremennom polozhenii," 21–22 ("The Present Position," 258).

23. A. Levitin-Krasnov and V. Shavrov, *Ocherki po istorii russkoi tserkovnoi smuty* (Moscow: Krutitskoe podvor'e, 1996), 69.
24. SD 162.
25. Ivanov, *Tikhon*, 272–74; Roslof, following Vvedenskii, incorrectly refers to the patriarch's decision as an "abdication" (Roslof, *Red Priests*, 55).
26. Bishop Antonin et al., "Veruiushchim synam pravoslavnoi tserkvi Rossii," *Izvestiia* No. 106 (May 14, 1922): 2.
27. Record of Agafangel's interrogation, May 20, 1922, in I. G. Men'kova (ed.), *Radi Mira Tserkovnogo: Zhiznennyi put' i arhipastorskoe sluzhenie sviatitelia Agafangela, mitropolita Iaroslavskogo i Rostovskogo, ispovednika*, 2 vols. (Moscow: PSTGU, 2005), 2: 164–65; "O sovremennom polozhenii," 24 ("The Present Position," 259).
28. SD 165–66.
29. Ivanov, *Tikhon*, 278–83, and S. N. Ivanov, "O prichinakh peredachi sv. Patriarkhom Tikhonom kantseliarskikh del gruppe sviashchennikov v mae 1922," *Vestnik PSTGU* No. 40 (2011): 17–35. The Renovationists later falsified their request to the patriarch: Compare the original in SD 165 with the later redaction in Akty, 216.
30. SD 168–70; see V. V. Lobanov, "Ob obstoiatel'stvakh domashnego aresta Patriarkha Tikhona v mae 1923 g.," *Tserkov' v istorii Rossii* No. 7 (2007): 268–77.
31. SD 166.
32. Safonov, 203.
33. "K ukhodu patriarkha Tikhona," *Izvestiia* 111 (May 20, 1922): 3; Ivanov, "Khronologiia," 47.
34. Men'kova (ed.), *Radi mira tserkovnogo*, 2: 165; "O sovremennom polozhenii," 24 ("The Present Position," 260).
35. *PE* 7: 617–23; AK 1: 52–54.
36. See the analysis in Safonov, 218–24; Odintsov, *Zhrebii*, 474–80; Ivanov, *Tikhon*, 299–304.
37. Akty, 219–21; *PE* 1: 235–37; Men'kova (ed.), *Radi mira tserkovnogo*, 2: 174–206.
38. For an examination of the Renovationist reform program, see my article, "Russian Reformation? The Program for Religious Renovation in the Orthodox Church, 1922–1925," *Modern Greek Studies Yearbook* 16/17 (2000/2001): 89–130.
39. November 1921 appeal, *BogSb* 6: 289–98. On his position in 1905, see *Instructions*, 228.
40. Ivanov, *Tikhon*, 80–81.
41. Safonov, 204–5.
42. "O sovremennom polozhenii," 32–33 ("The Present Position," 264).
43. "Delo Patriarkha Tikhona," HIA Frank Golder papers, Box 24, folder 6, p. 3; this document was evidently written by the same author as "O sovremennom polozhenii." It was published in E. V. Ivanova (ed.), "Patriarkh Tikhon v 1920–1923 godakh: Analitcheskaia zapiska iz Guverskogo arkhiva," *ZhMP* No. 11 (2007): 86–95 (citations are to the original).
44. Tuchkov's report to Samsonov, July 18, 1922, SD 177–78; Safonov, 211; Lobanov, "Ob obstoiatel'stvakh."
45. Mariia Veshneva, "'Eto pamiat' o dniakh v Donskom …' (Osen' 1922–vesna 1923)," *Iunost'* No. 9 (1990): 77 (the text was published under Semenova's married name).
46. Veshneva, "Eto pamiat," 77–78.
47. Veshneva, "Eto pamiat," 78; "Delo Patriarkha Tikhona," 2–3.
48. Veshneva, "Eto pamiat," 79.
49. "Delo Patriarkha Tikhona," 3.
50. Veshneva, "Eto pamiat," 79.
51. Veshneva, "Eto pamiat," 81.
52. S. N. Ivanov, "'Sovershenno sekretno. Khranit' konspirativno': Protokoly neizvestnoi komissii L. D. Trotskogo po raskolu Russkoi Pravoslavnoi Tserkvi (mai-oktiabr' 1922 g.)," *Vestnik PSTGU* No. 107 (2022): 134–66; V. V. Lobanov, "'Podtverdit' k neuklonnomu ispolneniiu …': Protokoly zasedanii Biuro Tsentral'noi Komissii po iz"iatiiu tserkovnykh tsennostei," *Tserkov' v istorii Rossii* 6 (2005): 208–17; documents can be found in KPSG 1: 559–602; Ivanov, *Tikhon*, 479–630.
53. The minutes of ARK sessions, an extremely important source for this period, are held in the Russian State Archive of Social-Political History, fond 17 (Central Committee of the Communist Party), op. 112, dd. 443a, 565a, and 775; copies are also in Yaroslavsky's collection (f. 89), op. 4, d. 115. They were published by V. V. Lobanov (ed.), *Protokoly Komissii po provedeniiu otdelenie tserkvi ot gosudarstva pri TsK RKP(b)-VKP(b) (Antireligioznaia komissii): 1922–1929 gg.* (Moscow: PSTGU, 2014) (abbr. *ARK*); German translation by Ludwig Steindorff,

Partei und Kirchen im frühen Sowjetstaat: die Protokolle der Antireligiösen Kommission beim Zentralkomitee der Russischen Kommunistischen Partei (Münster: LIT, 2007). On Stalin's role: I. A. Kurliandskii, "Stalin i religioznyi vopros v politike Bol'shevistskoi vlasti (1917–1923 gg.)," *Vestnik PSTGU* No. 48 (2012): 72–84. On ARK, see *PE* 36: 533–34; Kurliandskii, *Stalin*, 168–70; Petrov, *Dokumenty*, 246–60; Lobanov's introduction in *ARK*, 5–13; Arto Luukkanen, *The Party of Unbelief: The Religious Policy of the Bolshevik Party, 1917–1929* (Helsinki: SHS, 1994), 123–28; and Ludwig Steindorff, "Zwischen Bürokratie und Ideologie: Die Antireligiöse Kommission beim Zentralkomitee als Koordinator bolshchewistischer Religionspolitik in den zwanziger Jahren," *Kirchliche Zeitgeschichte* 12 (1999): 106–42.
54. Roslof, *Red Priests*, 86–96 and Lobanov, *Obnovlencheskii*, 97–104.
55. Interrogation record, August 31, 1922, and other documents SD 178–182.
56. Interrogation record, February 16, 1923, SD 201–2.
57. Veshneva, "Eto pamiat," 79.
58. The records of Tikhon's interrogations between December 1922 and Apri 1923, as well as his co-defendants, are in SD 184–260. For further analysis of these interrogations see Ivanov, *Tikhon*, 251–59.
59. For an overview of the process of building the case against Tikhon, see Roslof, *Red Priests*, 96–103.
60. AK 1: 258–60. On March 27, ARK requested that Krasikov, Yaroslavskii and Popov be added to the commission overseeing the patriarch's case, which did not include any members of ARK on it (*ARK*, 66). The Politburo added the first two (but not Popov) on April 5: AK 1: 243–44, though evidently only Yaroslavskii participated.
61. *ARK*, 57, 61; AK 1: 363. "Delo Patriarkha Tikhona," 8–9; this document was written in spring 1923, for the author notes the press only began to write about the patriarch's trial "recently." *Pravda* reported on the patriarch's trial, e.g., on March 11: "Sud k protsessu Patriarkha Tikhona," *Pravda* No. 55 (March 11, 1923): 8. Brochures published by the end of March included two by Vvedenskii, *Tserkov' patriarkha Tikhona* and *Tserkov' i revoliutsiia*, I. Brikhnichev's *O patriarkhe Tikhone*, and Ia. Shipov, *Tikhonovskaia tserkov' i Vrangel'*.
62. *ARK*, 61.
63. AK 1: 368.
64. SD 229–30.
65. SD 234–38.
66. SD 248–51; KPSG 3: 477.
67. Roslof, *Red Priests*, 96, 101.
68. House of Lords debate, March 20, 1923, *Hansard Debates* 53, no. 15: 454–56.
69. The Commissariat for Foreign Affairs followed the international reaction; see KPSG 3: 526–36.
70. SD 253–55.
71. SD 231, 252–56; AK 1: 261–62, 265; see also AK 2: 347–49; KSPG 1: 603–5; *ARK*, 69–70.
72. Report to Evlogy (Georgievsky), June 2, 1923, by an anonymous author in Moscow under the pseudonym "Sillogizm," HIA Grigorii N. Trubetskoi papers, https://digitalcollections.hoover.org/objects/62186/doklad-metropolitu-evlogiu-ot-sillogizma, 2–3. The author, writing from Moscow, told Evlogy that his identity had to be kept secret. See "Sudebnyi otdel: Protsess kniazei tserkvi," *Izvestiia* No. 76 (April 6, 1923): 4.
73. *Obvinitel'noe zakliuchenie po delu grazdan: Bellavina Vasiliia Ivanovicha, Fenomenova Nikandra Grigor'evicha, Stadnitskogo Arseniia Georgievicha i Gur'eva Petra Viktorovicha po 62 i 119 st. st. Ugolovnogo Kodeksa* (Moscow: GPU tipografiia, 1923), which was published in 5,000 copies. It is included in SD 262–333 and *Akty*, 225–80.
74. *Obvinitel'noe zakliuchenie*, 14, 30–31.
75. *Obvinitel'noe zakliuchenie*, 41–42, 45–46, 53, 83.
76. John Shelton Curtiss, *The Russian Church and the Soviet State, 1917–1950*, 1st ed. (Boston: Little, Brown, 1953), 91–93.
77. AK 1: 262–63.
78. The *New York Times* reported on the trial of the Catholic clergy and Patriarch Tikhon, on March 28 and 30, April 1, 5, 6, 7, 1923. Multiple articles were published on April 8, Orthodox Easter, including a lengthy expose, "The Soviet War on Religion," and one by Tikhon's former collaborator Isabel Hapgood: "Life of Russia's Patriarch Now Hangs in Soviet Balance," both in *New York Times* (April 8, 1923): XX3. Coverage continued to appear almost every day in April.
79. KPSG 3: 538–46.

80. AK 1: 263–64.
81. AK 1: 265–66.
82. AK 1: 267.
83. AK 1: 267–69.
84. "The Patriarch Tikhon," *Russian Information and Review*, vol. 2 (October 1922–June 1923) (London: Information Department of the Russian Trade Delegation, 1923), 444.
85. E.g., Stephen White, *Britain and the Bolshevik Revolution: A Study in the Politics of Diplomacy, 1920–1924* (New York: Holmes and Meier, 1979), 153–54.
86. F. A. MacKenzie, "Second Thoughts in Russia," *New York Times* (April 10, 1923): 20.
87. E.g., "Soviet Threatens Wrath on Tikhon: Kursky Says Foreign Press Campaign Can't Affect Russian Supreme Court," *New York Times* (April 16, 1923): 19.
88. The text of the protest, the comment, and some contemporary reactions are in G. K. A. Bell, *Randall Davidson: Archbishop of Canterbury* (Oxford: Oxford University Press, 1935), 2: 1079–81.
89. Karl Radek, "A History Lesson for the Archbishop of Canterbury—And a History Lesson on the Archbishops of Canterbury," *International Press Correspondence* 3, no. 35 (May 3, 1923): 303–5; *Pravda* No. 32 (April 15, 1923): 2.
90. AK 1: 270–72.
91. See AK 1: 266 and AK 2: 348 for the approval to place Tikhon in the GPU prison; SD 334–38.
92. "Sillogizm," report to Evlogy (Georgievsky), June 2, 1923, 4.
93. AK 1: 273.
94. Safonov notes that one entire volume of the file on Patriarch Tikhon (no. 24) was devoted to reporting about the patriarch in the domestic and foreign press (257); Trotsky also received the reports: Ivanov, *Tikhon*, 333–36.
95. AK 1: 273–74; see Petrov, *Dokumenty*, 287ff.
96. AK 1: 277–79. Other governments also protested the trial.
97. AK 1: 275–76.
98. AK 1: 371; Lobanov, *Obnovlencheskii*, 104–6.
99. On the Renovationist council, see Roslof, *Red Priests*, 103–09; Lobanov, *Obnovlencheskii*, 97–108; Petrov, *RPTs*, 191–214.
100. SD 349–50. His family name was misspelled.
101. SD 348, 350–51; Roslof, *Red Priests*, 105.
102. *ARK*, 71; AK 1: 280; SD 351–53.
103. SD 353–54.
104. SD 354–55.
105. "Sillogizm," report to Evlogy (Georgievsky), June 2, 1923, 5.
106. KPSG 3: 547. See also Roslof, *Red Priests*, 107.
107. "Sillogizm," report to Evlogy (Georgievsky), June 2, 1923, 5.
108. "Call the Soviet Evangelical," *New York Times* (May 4, 1923): 1, 6.
109. "Bolshevism Swallows the Church," *New York Times* (May 5, 1923): 10; see also "Russia's 'Living Church,'" *New York Times* (May 1, 1923): 20.
110. Walter Duranty, "Red Mystic Is Made a Bishop in Russia," *New York Times* (May 6, 1923): 3.
111. See *Russia No. 2 (1923). Correspondence Between His Majesty's Government and the Soviet Government Respecting the Relations Between the Two Governments* (London: H. M. Stationary Office, 1923), 3–5.
112. W. M. Medlicott, Douglas Dakin, and Gillian Bennett, eds., *Documents on British Foreign Policy 1919–1939*, First Series (London: Her Majesty's Stationary Office, 1984), vol. 25: 74 (n. 7). The quote comes from Ronald Lindsay, assistant undersecretary of state for the Foreign Office, in mid-April.
113. *Documents on British Foreign Policy* 25: 96.
114. See Evgeny Sergeev, *The Bolsheviks and Britain During the Russian Revolution and Civil War, 1917–24* (London: Bloomsbury, 2022), 139–50.
115. See the Renovationist letter to the archbishop of Canterbury: Walter Duranty, "Russian Church Heads Champion the Soviet," *New York Times* (May 15, 1923): 3.
116. AK 1: 280–82.
117. "Sillogizm," report to Evlogy (Georgievsky), June 2, 1923, 4.
118. *ARK*, 73, 76, 78.
119. Hodgson to Curzon, June 18 1923: National Archives, FO 371/9493, f. 46.

120. Safonov, 271–72, 278. One contemporary wrote that Tikhon was taken to a Kremlin hospital: "Svet Rossii: Moskovskie vospominaniia, 1923–1927," *Tserkovno-istoricheskii vestnik* No. 9 (2002): 6–7.
121. The proposal was confirmed after the fact on June 12 by ARK: *ARK*, 79–80.
122. Yaroslavsky's memorandum to the Politburo, June 11, 1923, AK 1: 282–83. On Pope Pius's efforts, see AK 1: 258–61; KPSG 3: 524–25. On Patriarch Meletius, see Chapter 9.
123. AK 1: 283–84; both documents are also translated in Roslof, *Red Priests*, 113–15.
124. AK 1: 284–85.
125. The original copy in Tikhon's hand is SD 357; Tuchkov's copy to Stalin is AK 1: 285–86.
126. Tikhon did write a commentary on the indictment, challenging particular elements: Akty, 225–80.
127. *ARK*, 81–82.
128. AK 1: 375–76.
129. AK 1: 244–45.
130. *ARK*, 83.
131. AK 1: 283.
132. AK 2: 401–2.
133. AK 2: 408. See also Safonov, 268–69.
134. See Lobanov, *Patriarkh*, 135–46, and Kurlianskii, *Stalin*, 191–202. Safonov makes an unconvincing attempt to dismiss the significance of the international pressure (253–56).
135. See the letter from the archbishop of Malines (Brussels) to King George V and Curzon's reply on his behalf, National Archives, FO 371/9493, ff. 18–22.
136. Hodgson to Curzon, June 29, 1923, National Archives, FO 371/9493, f. 43.
137. See Lobanov, *Patriarkh*, 118–35; Ivanov, *Tikhon*, 333–48.
138. Letter of "Sillogizm" to unnamed bishop (Evlogy?), August 2, 1923, HIA Grigorii N. Trubetskoi papers, folder "Razlichnye pis'ma k G. N. Tribetskomu (podpisannye), 1920–1929," 50, https://digitalcollections.hoover.org/internal/media/dispatcher/308664/full.
139. Grigorii Trubetskoi, "Pamiati sv. Patriarkha Tikhona," *Put'* No. 1 (September 1925): 118.
140. Letter of "Sillogizm," August 2, 1923, p. 50; see also Trubetskoi, "Pamiati," 118.
141. Hodgson to Curzon, June 29, 1923, National Archives, FO 371/9493, f. 43.
142. Foreign Office to G. K. A. Bell, July 17, 1923, National Archives, FO 371/9493, ff. 40–41.
143. Metropolitan Antonii (Khrapovitskii), "Ne nado smushchast'sia," *Tserkovnye vedomosti* NN 13–14 (July 1923): 9–10.

Chapter 9

1. O. V. Kosik, *Golosa iz Rossii: Ocherki istorii sbora i peredachi za granitsu informatsii o polozhenii Tserkvi v SSSR (1920-e-nachalo 1930-kh godov)* (Moscow: PSTGU, 2013), 51–60.
2. Letter to Patriarch Dimitry, March 16, 1922, *BogSb* 6: 262.
3. Greeting of Archimandrite Iakov (Dimopoulos) on Tikhon's enthronement, *Dokumenty Sobora*, 6: 369–73; "Obshchitel'naia (intronizatsionnaia) gramota Ego Sviateishestva, Sviateishego Tikhona, Patriarkha Moskovskogo i vseia Rossii, Ego Sviateshestvu, Sviateishemu Germanu piatomu, Arkhiepiskopu Konstantinopolia, Novogo Rima, i Vselenskomu Patriarkhu," *Tserkovnye vedomisti* No. 21–22 (June 15/28, 1918): 144–49, citation 148.
4. A. V. Mazyrin and A. A. Kostriukov, *Iz istorii vzaimootnoshenii Russkoi i Konstantinopol'skoi Tserkvi v XX veke* (Moscow: PSTGU, 2017), 17–18.
5. *Poslaniia*, 68–77.
6. Paschalis M. Kitromilides, *Religion and Politics in the Orthodox World: The Ecumenical Patriarchate and the Challenges of Modernity* (London: Routledge, 2019), 64–69.
7. Patrick Viscuso, *A Quest for Reform of the Orthodox Church: The 1923 Pan-Orthodox Congress: An Analysis and Translation of Its Acts and Decisions* (Berkeley, CA: InterOrthodox Press, 2006). See A. V. Mazyrin, "K voprosu o prichinakh podderzhki sviatogo patriarkha Tikhona (Bellavina) Patriarkhom Meletiiem (Metaksakisom) vesnoi 1923 g," *Khristianskoe chtenie* No. 3 (2023): 327–42.

8. Extracts from the minutes of the Constantinople Holy Synod session, May 6, 1924 (in Russian), *Russkaia pravoslavnaia tserkov' i kommunisticheskoe gosudarstvo, 1917–1940: Dokumenty i fotomaterialy*, ed. Ia. N. Shchapov and O. Iu. Vasil'eva (Moscow: Izd. Bibleisko-Bogoslovskogo Instituta sv. Apostola Andreia, 1996), 193–94; see Ivanov, *Tikhon*, 382–84.
9. *Poslaniia*, 170.
10. Daniela Kalkandjieva, *The Russian Orthodox Church, 1917–1948: From Decline to Resurrection* (London: Routledge, 2015), 21, and Edward E. Roslof, *Red Priests: Renovationism, Russian Orthodoxy, and Revolution, 1905–1946* (Bloomington: Indiana University Press, 2002), 135, both mistakenly state that Constantinople recognized the Renovationists as the legitimate Church in Russia; but see the analysis in Mazyrin and Kostriukov, *Iz Istorii*, 63–68; Ivanov, *Tikhon*, 384–88.
11. "Polozhenie Sv. Patriarkha Tikhona i Pravoslavnoi Tserkvi v sovetskoi Rossii," *Tserkovnye vedomosti* NN 19–20 (October 14–28, 1924): 17.
12. Most studies about the relationship between Tikhon and the patriarchate of Constantinople have been conducted by Russians. See A. V. Mazyrin, "Patriarkh Tikhon i Konstantinopol'skaia Patriarkhiia: k voprosu o prichinakh fakticheskogo razryva otnoshenii," *Vestnik PSTGU* 67 (2015): 9–37; Mazyrin and Kostriukov, *Iz istorii*; and Mikhail Shkarovskii, *Konstantinopol'skii Patriarkhat i Russkaia pravoslavnaia tserkov' v pervoi polovine XX veka* (Moscow: Indrik, 2014), 15–52. Unfortunately, these works are not free of polemics.
13. Report of representatives of Eastern Orthodox Churches, July 23, 1924, Shchapov and Vasil'eva (eds.), *Russkaia pravoslavnaia*, 195–96; though see Ivanov, *Tikhon*, 388, 756.
14. For an overview, though with inaccuracies in the details, see Kalkandjieva, *Russian Orthodox Church*, 12–64; Kalkandjieva, "The Soviet Authorities and the Orthodox Churches: The Role in Promoting New Autocephalies (1917–1991)," in *Autocephaly: Coming of Age in Communion. Historical, Canonical, Liturgical Studies*, ed. Edward G. Farrugia and Željko Paša (Rome: Oriental Pontifical Institute, 2023), 1: 785–821.
15. Paul Werth, "Georgian Autocephaly and the Ethnic Fragmentation of Orthodoxy," *Acta Slavica Iaponica* 23 (2006): 74–100.
16. Letter to Flavian, June 24, 1908, RGIA f. 796, op. 205, d. 752, ll. 172–73ob.
17. A. V. Shchelkachev and I. E. Mel'nikova, "Vosstanovlenie avtokefal'nogo statusa Gruzinskoi Pravoslavnoi Tserkvi v XX v.," *XXX Ezhegodnaia bogoslovskaia konferentsiia PSTGU* (2020): 51–57.
18. *Poslaniia*, 34–44.
19. Werth, "Georgian Autocephaly"; Shchelkachev and Mel'nikova, "Vosstanovlenie"; *Poslanie Sviateishego Leonida, Katolikosa-Patriarkha vseia Gruzii, k Sviateishemu Tikhonu, Patriarkhu Moskovskomu i vseia Rossii* (Tiflis, 1920); A. V. Mazyrin, "K istorii obnovlencheskogo raskola v Zakavkaz'e i neudachnykh proektov primireniia Russkoi i Gruzinskoi pravoslavnykh tserkvei (1922–1923 gg.)," *Vestnik Ekaterinburgskoi dukhovnoi seminarii* 46 (2024): 121–57.
20. Nicholas Denysenko, *The Orthodox Church in Ukraine: A Century of Separation* (DeKalb: Northern Illinois University Press, 2018), chapter 1; Bohdan R. Bociurkiw, "The Politics of Religion in the Ukraine: The Orthodox Church and the Ukrainian Revolution, 1917–1919" (Kennan Institute Occasional Paper, 1985); Ricarda Vulpius, *Nationalisierung der Religion: Russifizierungspolitik und ukrainische Nationsbildung (1860–1920)* (Wiesbaden: Harrasowitz Verlag, 2005).
21. Bociurkiw, "Politics," 7–17.
22. *Dokumenty Sobora* 5: 577–78, 586, 694.
23. *Dokumenty Sobora* 2: 203.
24. *Dokumenty Sobora* 6: 895–97.
25. Tikhon's letter was published in *Vira ta derzhava* No. 2 (1918): 12–13, as quoted in Feodosii (Protsiuk), *Obosoblencheskie dvizheniia v Pravoslavnoi Tserkvi na Ukraine (1917–1943)* (Moscow: Krutitskoe podvor'e, 2004), 92; see also Tikhon to Metropolitan Antony, May 23 and June 19, 1918, SD 660–61.
26. Letters from the Hetmanate to Tikhon and Tikhon to Antonii, September 26, 1918, in R. G. Iferov, *Sviashchennyi Sobor Pravoslavnoi Rossiiskoi Tserkvi 1917–1918 gg. i Vseukrainskii Sobor 1918 g. ob ukrainskom tserkovnom voprose* (Moscow: Spasskoe delo, 2019), 268–73.
27. Hyacinthe Destivelle, *The Moscow Council (1917–1918): The Creation of the Conciliar Institutions of the Russian Orthodox Church*, trans. Jerry Ryan and ed. Michael Plekon and Vitaly Permiakov (Notre Dame, IN: University of Notre Dame Press, 2015), 117–19, 302–6.

28. Denysenko, *The Orthodox Church*, 17-23; Bociurkiw, "Politics," 17-36; Igor' Kamennyi, "Patriarkh Tikhon: Vzgliad na ukrainskii tserkovnyi vopros," *Trudy Kyivskoi Dukhovnoi Akademii* No. 24 (2016): 249-51; on the 1918 All-Ukrainian Council as a whole, see Andrii Starodub, *Vseukraïns'kyi pravoslavnyi tserkovnyi Sobor 1918 roku: Ohliad dzherel* (Kyiv: Instytut ukraïns'koï arkhehrafiï ta dzhereloznavstva im M. S. Hrushevs'koho, 2010).
29. Kamennyi, 252-53; Bohdan R. Bociurkiw, "The Rise of the Ukrainian Autocephalous Orthodox Church, 1919-1922," in *Church, Nation and State in Russia and Ukraine*, ed. Geoffrey A. Hosking (Edmonton: Unversity of Alberta, 1990), 228-49; Vulpius, *Nationalisierung*, 382-89, 402-7.
30. Andrii Starodub, "Borot'ba za tserkovnu samostiinist' 1917-1921 rokiv ta uchast' v nii epyskopiv-ukraïntsiv," in *Naukovi zapyski: Zbirnyk prats' molodykh vchenykh ta aspirantiv* (Kyiv: Instytut ukraïns'koï arkhehrafiï ta dzhereloznavstva im M. S. Hrushevs'koho, 1999), vol. 3: 338.
31. Parfenii's letter to Tikhon, December 31, 1920, in *Pershyi Vseukraïnskyi Pravoslavnyi Tserkovnyi Sobor UAPTs 14-30 zhovtnia 1921 r.: Dokumenty i materialy*, ed. S. M. Plokhii, P. S. Sokhran, and L. V. Iakovleva (Kyiv: NAN Ukraïny, 1999), 437-39
32. T. M. Yevseeva, *Rosiis'ka Pravoslavna Tserkva v Ukraïni 1917-1921 rr.: konflikt natsional'nykh identychnostei u pravoslavnomu poli* (Kyiv: In-t Istoriï Ukraïny NAN Ukraïny, 2005), 234-36; *Pershyi Vseukraïns'kyi*, 76-77.
33. Tikhon's encyclical to believers in Ukraine, July 23, 1921, in *Pershyi Vseukraïnskyi*, 503-4.
34. Andrii Starodub, "Problema statusu Rosiis'kï Pravoslavnoï tserkvy v Ukraïni v 1918-1921 rr.," in *Proseminarii: Medievistyka, Istoriia Tserkvy, nauky i kul'tury* (Kyiv: Instytut ukraïns'koï arkhehrafiï ta dzhereloznavstva im M. S. Hrushevs'kohc, 1998), vyp. 2: 209.
35. Bociurkiw, "Ukrainian Autocephalous," 237-38.
36. *Pershyi Vseukraïns'kyi*, 503-4.
37. *PE* 45: 631-34.
38. Bociurkiw, "Ukrainian Autocephalous," 237-40.
39. Yevseeva, *Rosiis'ka*, 239-40.
40. Bohdan R. Bociurkiw, "The Russian Orthodox Church in Ukraine: The Exarchate and the Renovationists, and the 'Conciliar-Episcopal' Church, 1920-1939," *Harvard Ukrainian Studies* 26 (2002-2003): 63-91; SD 783.
41. Tikhon's letter to the chair of the Council of Ministers of the Belarusian People's Republic, February 14, 1922, Lietuvos centrinis valstybės archyvas f. 582, AP. 1, B. 40. I am grateful to Aliksandr Gorny for sharing a copy of this file with me; he published it: A. S. Gorny, "Belarusizatsyia Pravaslaunai Tsarkvy u mizhvaenny peryiad: dakumenty i materyialy, Chastka 1," *KhRONOS Tserkovno-istoricheskii al'manakh* No. 5 (2017): 142-61 (Tikhon's letter is 149-50); see also T. S. Prot'ko, ed., "Obrashchenie ('Memorial') pravitel'stva Belarusskoi Narodnoi Respubliki k Patriarkhu Tikhonu i ego otvet na eto obrashchenie," *Vestnik PSTGU* 40 (2011): 80-98.
42. G. E. Shcheglov, "Avtonomiia Belarusskoi Pravoslavnoi Tserkvi 1922 g.," *Vestnik PSTGU* 40 (2011): 99-116; Feodor Krivonos, *U Boga mertvykh net: Neizvestnye strainitsy iz istorii Minskoi eparkhii (1917-1939 gody)* (Minsk: MFTsP, 2007).
43. There is extensive literature about the Orthodox Church in interwar Poland (especially in Polish but also in Russian and Ukrainian), sometimes very polemical. Two recent studies utilize new sources from Polish archives: Andrii Starodub, "Perehovori mizh Pol'skym diplomatychnym predstavnytstvom u Moskvi ta patriarkhom Tykhonom (Bellavinym) u spravi statusu ta iurisdiktsii pravoslavnoï tserkvy v Pol'shchi (veresen' 1921 - kviten' 1922 rokiv)," *Ukraïnskii arkheografichnyy shchorichnyk* 18 (2013): 514-46; and A. A. Chibisova, "Patriarkh Tikhon i avtokefaliia Pol'skoi Pravoslavnoi Tserkvi 1924 goda," *Vestnik PSTGU* 95 (2020): 118-41. See also Chibisova's dissertation: "Bor'ba za avtokefaliiu pravoslavnoi Tserkvi v Pol'she v 1918-1925 godakh," Kand. Diss., Moscow State University, 2023. There are also documents in the file "'Avtokefaliia' of the Orthodox Church in Poland, 1922-36," in the Aleksandr K. Svitich Papers, Bakhmeteff Archive.
44. Kalkandjieva, *Russian Orthodox*, 30-32.
45. Starodub, "Perehovori," 518, 522-26; Chibisova, "Patriarkh Tikhon," 125.
46. Tikhon's letter to T. Filipovich, September 22, 1921, in Chibisova, "Patriarkh Tikhon," 135-38 and Starodub, "Perehovori," 538-40.
47. Starodub, "Perehovori," 516-22.

48. Tikhon's letter to Georgii Iaroshevskii, September 27, 1921, in Chibisova, "Patriarkh Tikhon," 138–39 (emphasis in the original); Georgii's letter to Tikhon, September 6, 1921, in Chibisova, "Patriarkh Tikhon," 134–35, also in Starodub, "Perehovori," 535–37. See also Chibisova, "Bor'ba," 90.
49. Chibisova, "Patriarkh Tikhon," 124.
50. Starodub, "Perehovori," 524; Chibisova, "Patriarkh Tikhon," 119–25. Tikhon evidently suggested that Serafim would be appointed metropolitan of Krutitsky (administrator of the Moscow diocese) in exchange, and then when that was given to Nikandr in February, Serafim complained that he's been "thrown out on the street like a dog by the patriarch" (Safonov, 142).
51. For Tikhon (Sharapov)'s dramatic account, see "Otrykvok iz vospominanii episkopa Tikhona (Sharapova) o ego poezdke v SSSR v 1922 godu," *ZhMP* No. 4 (1998): 82–88. See also A. V. Slesarev, "Protivodeistvie arkhimandrita Tikhona (Sharapova) vvedeniiu novogo stilia i provozglasheniiu avtokefalii Pravoslavnoi Tserkvi v Pol'she (1922–1924 gg.)," *KhRONOS Tserkovno-istoricheskii al'manakh* No. 2 (2015): 138–84.
52. Tikhon to Georgii, January 30, 1922, in Starodub, "Perehovori," 542.
53. *Akty*, 181. Gubonin's dating (1921) is incorrect; it is clear from a document evidently stemming from Tikhon (Sharapov) that it was in response to the statutes passed in Warsaw in January 1922: see the document in Slesarev, "Protivodeistvie," 154–57. See also Chibisova, "Bor'ba," 113–17.
54. See the comment in Slesarev, "Protivodeistvie," 157. On the attitude of the clergy and laity in Poland, see 160.
55. Andrzej Borkowski, *Między Konstantynopolem a Moskwą: Źdódła Greckie do autokefali kościoła Prawosławnego w Rzecypospolitej (1919–1927)* (Białystok: Wydawnictwo Uniwersytetu w Białymstoku, 2015), 65–75; Meletius's letters, 151–55.
56. Minutes of ARK January 12, and March 21, 1924 sessions, *ARK*, 115, 121.
57. *Akty*, 320–21.
58. Chibisova, "Patriarkh Tikhon," 132–33; Borowski, 49, 101ff; Slesarev, "Protivodeistvie," 149–50; *Akty*, 352–61, 752–57.
59. This section draws on the following studies: Sebastian Rimestad, *The Challenges of Modernity to the Orthodox Church in Estonia and Latvia (1917–1940)* (Frankfurt am Main: Peter Lang, 2012); see also balticorthodoxy.com; Kalkandjieva, *Russian Orthodox*, 23–30. On Estonia: Irina Paert, "A Family Affair? Post-Imperial Estonian Orthodoxy and Its Relationship with the Russian Mother Church, 1917–1923," *Canadian Slavonic Papers* 62 (2020): 1–26; Priit Rohtmets and Toomas Schvak, "The Establishment of the Estonian Apostolic Orthodox Church: History and Interpretations," *Usuteaduslik Ajakiri* 84 (2023): 1–35. On Latvia and Lithuania: Sebastian Rimestad, "From Empire to Nation State: The Consolidation of the Relationship Between the Orthodox Church and Independent Lithuania and Latvia after the First World War," *Studia Podlaskie* 20 (2012): 211–23. On Finland: T. I. Shevchenko, "K voprosu o iurisdiktsii Finliandskoi Pravoslavnoi Tserkvi," *Vestnik PSTGU* 26 (2008): 42–69; Shevchenko, *Valaamskii monastyr' i stanovlenie Finliandskoi Pravoslavnoi Tserkvi (1917–1957)* (Moscow: PSTGU, 2013); Shevchenko's publications: "Pervyi Sobor avtonomnoi Finliandskoi Pravoslavnoi Tserkvi i politicheskaia atmosfera na Karel'skom peresheike v 1920-e gg.," *Vestnik PSTGU* 35 (2010): 93–114 and 36 (2010): 122–32, and "N. N. Glubokovskii. 'Voina i mir' v Finliandskoi Pravoslavnoi Tserkvi," *Vestnik PSTGU* 31 (2009): 99–119; V. I. Musaev, "Pravoslavnaia Tserkov' v nezavisimoi Finliandii (1918–1930 gg.)," *Vestnik Tserkovnoi Istorii* No. 2 (6) (2007): 194–212.
60. Patriarchal ukaz, December 9, 1919, in Nikolai Balashov and S. L. Kravets (eds.), *Pravoslavie v Estonii: Issledovaniia i dokumenty* (Moscow: Pravoslavnaia Entsiklopediia, 2010), vol. 2: *Dokumenty*, 26–27.
61. Paert, "Family Affair," 17.
62. Balashov and Kravets (eds.), *Pravoslavie*, 1: 119–23, 2: 30–31, 35–37.
63. Rimestad, *Challenges*, 113–21; Iu. L. Sidiakova (ed.), *Istoriia v pis'makh: iz arkhiva sviashchennomuchenika arkhiepiskopa Rizhskogo Ioanna (Pommera)*, 2 vols. (Tver': Bulat, 2015), vol. 1: 100–142.
64. T. I. Shevchenko, "K voprosu," 51–53, 61; Shevchenko, *Valaamskii*, 126–80, 367–71; Musaev, "Pravoslavnaia Tserkov'," 200–203; S. G. Petrov, "Perekhod Valaamskogo monastyria na novyi kalendarnyi stil' v osveshchenii ieromonakha Pamvy (Ignat'eva), *Istoricheskii kur'er* No. 2 (10) (2020): 84–112, contains Tikhon's letter to Valaam of October 6, 1923 (as well as a falsified letter ostensibly written while Tikhon was imprisoned in Donskoi monastery), 100 (on the fake letter, see *Akty*, 221–22, 731–32). See also *Poslaniia*, 92–93.

65. Balashov and Kravets (eds.), *Pravoslavie*, 2: 32.
66. Rohtmets and Schvak, 'Establishment," 20–30.
67. Aleksandr (Paulus) to Metropolitan Sergii (Stragorodskii), November 10, 1940, in Balashov and Kravets (eds.), *Pravoslavie*, 2: 117–18.
68. Tikhon's resolution, November 27, 1923, *Akty*, 304; Musaev, "Pravoslavnaia Tserkov."
69. Balashov and Kravets (eds.), *Pravoslavie*, 2: 118–19.
70. Rimestad, *Challenges*, 121–31, 141–42.
71. Sebastian Rimestad, "From Empire," 215.
72. Arsenii, 152; see also 144–45, 170, 190.
73. "Tri neizdannykh chastnykh pis'ma patriarkha Tikhona Arkhiepiskopu Serafimu Finliandskomu," *Vestnik RKhD* No. 1 (115) (1975): 88.
74. Janis (Pommers) to Elevferii (Bogoiavlenskii), November 1, 1927, in Sidiakova (ed.), *Istoriia*, 1: 360–63; see also 2: 452–64.

Chapter 10

1. Tikhon's declaration to VTsIK, September 30, 1924, *Poslaniia*, 274.
2. A. Levitin-Krasnov and V. Shavrov, *Ocherki po istorii russkoi tserkovnoi smuty* (Moscow: Krutitskoe podvor'e, 1996), 306–8. The authors claim that these events were described to them by the patriarch's staff-bearer. A different account can be found in V. P. Vinogradov, *Nekotorykh vazhneishikh momentakh poslednego perioda zhizni i deiatel'nosti sv. Patriarkha Tikhona (1923-1925 gg.) po lichnym vospominaniiam* (Munich, 1959), 5–8. Neither book is completely reliable; other evidence indicates that the patriarch was in fact released from Lubianka, contrary to Vinogradov's claims. The picture is in *Ogonek* No. 15 (1923): 9.
3. Safonov, 285.
4. *ARK*, 83; AK 2: 352; "Sredi tserkovnikov," *Izvestiia* No. 147 (July 4, 1923).
5. Encyclical to clergy and believers, June 28, 1923, AK 2: 349–52. On Tikhon's "repentance" texts and Yaroslavsky's demands, see Petrov, *RPTs*, 112–36.
6. *ARK*, 81–82.
7. On this, see Edward D. Wynot, Jr., *The Polish Orthodox Church in the Twentieth Century and Beyond: Prisoner of History* (Lanham, MD: Lexington Books, 2015), 38. Yaroslavsky's original demand about criticizing the pope is AK 1: 282. See also Walter Duranty, "Tikhon accuses pope of proselytizing," *New York Times* (July 7, 1923): 2.
8. AK 2: 353–54. This message was also printed in the Soviet newspapers: "Novoe vozzvanie Tikhona," *Izvestiia* No. 149 (1886) (July 6, 1923): 6.
9. "Konets gnusnoi komedii," *Pravda* No. 141 (June 27, 1923): 1.
10. These words were recorded by Gubonin from V. M. Mironova in Moscow, 1957. In "Vospominaniia sovremennikov," *BogSb* 6: 308–9.
11. *BogSb* 6: 309.
12. "Beseda s b. patriarkhom Tikhonom," *Izvestiia* No. 143 (1880) (June 29, 1923): 5.
13. "B. patriarkh Tikhon," *Izvestiia* No. 146 (1883) (July 3, 1923): 7; *Akty*, 285–86.
14. Safonov, 291.
15. Safonov, 298–300, 330.
16. Safonov, 304–19.
17. Levitin-Krasnov and Shavrov, 320; "Tikhon na ekrane," *Pravda* No. 160 (July 19, 1923): 6; *ARK*, 90.
18. Levitin-Krasnov and Shavrov, 315; *Akty*, 295.
19. Serafim (Luk'ianov) to Antonii (Khrapovitskii), February 17, 1925, in M. I. Odintsov, *Russkie patriarkhi XX veka: Sud'by otechestva i tserkvi na stranitsakh arkhivnykh dokumentov* (Moscow: RAGS, 1999), 215; Safonov, 309–13, 330.
20. *Poslaniia*, 149–55 (quotes: 150, 52).
21. *ARK*, 90.
22. The letter is printed by S. G. Petrov, "Sovetskaia tsenzura i vozzvaniia patriarkha Tikhona 1923 g.," *Gumanitarnye nauki v Sibirii* 2 (2008): 26–27.
23. *ARK*, 94.

24. Letter of "Sillogizm," August 2, 1923, HIA Grigorii N. Trubetskoi papers, folder "Razlichnye pis'ma k G. N. Tribetskomu (podpisannye), 1920-1929," 51, https://digitalcollections.hoover.org/internal/media/dispatcher/308664/full.
25. Petrov, *RPTs*, 164-68.
26. *ARK*, 93-94.
27. AK 1: 289; *ARK*, 86, 94.
28. AK 2: 350.
29. AK 2: 354-55.
30. A. A. Kostriukov, *Russkaia Zarubezhnaia Tserkov' v pervoi polovine 1920-kh godov: Organizatsiia tserkovnogo upravleniia v emigratsii* (Moscow: PSTGU, 2007), 73-133; key documents are on 242-353.
31. Kostriukov, *Russkaia Zarubezhnaia*, 191.
32. The resolution and other materials are in A. A. Kostriukov (ed.), "Novye dokumenty po istorii vzaimootnoshenii mezhdu Patriarkhom Tikhonom i Karlovatskim Sinodom," *Vestnik PSTGU* 28 (2008): 119-25.
33. The Minutes of the Constantinople Synod session on April 30, 1924, in I. a. N. Snchapov and O. Iu. Vasil'eva, eds., *Russkaia pravoslavnaia tserkov' i kommunisticheskoe gosudarstvo, 1917-1940: Dokumenty i fotomaterialy* (Moscow: Izd. Bibleisko-Bogoslovskogo Instituta sv. Apostola Andreia, 1996), 192.
34. A. V. Mazyrin and A. A. Kostriukov, *Iz istorii vzaimootnoshenii Russkoi i Konstantinopol'skoi Tserkvi v XX veke* (Moscow: PSTGU, 2017), 278-79.
35. Serafim (Luk'ianov) to Antonii (Khrapovitskii), February 17, 1925, in Odintsov, *Russkie patriarkhi*, 217.
36. Kostriukov, *Russkaia Zarubezhnaia*, 201; for the period between the patriarch's release and death, see 186-208.
37. "Opredeleniia Arikhiereiskogo Sinoda Russkoi Pravoslavnoi Tserkvi zagranitsei," *Tserkovnye vedomosti* NN 15-16 (August 14-28, 1925): 3-4.
38. Tikhon to Patriarch Gregory of Antioch, January 30, 1922, *Tserkovnye Vedomosti* No. 5 (May 28, 1922): 1-2 (also *BogSb* 6: 244-47); see also SD 696, 707.
39. ARK minutes, December 12, 1923, *ARK*, 112; "Sredi tserkovnikov: Ukaz byvsh. Patriarkha Tikhona," *Izvestiia* No. 18 (January 22, 1924), 5 (*Akty*, 309). See also SD 401, 673, 687, 693, 696, 707, 713-14, 721-25; AK 2: 512-16; *PE* 56: 658-63; Ivanov, *Tikhon*, 394-96.
40. An excellent study of the calendar question is S. G. Petrov, "Patriarch Tikhon and the Preservation of the Old Calendar Style in the Russian Orthodox Church," *Herald of the Russian Academy of Sciences* 93 (Supplement 1) (2023): 66-74; also Petrov, *RPTs*, 136-61; V. V. Lobanov, *Patriarkh Tikhon i Sovetskaia vlast' (1917-1925 gg.)* (Moscow: Russkaia Panorama, 2008), 163-68.
41. *Dokumenty Sobora* 7: 238ff.
42. *Poslaniia*, 90-101.
43. Gregory L. Freeze, "Counter-Reformation in Russian Orthodoxy: Popular Response to Religious Innovation," 1922-1925," *Slavic Review* 54, no. 2 (1995): 305-39; Lobanov, *Tikhon*, 163-68.
44. *Poslaniia*, 282.
45. On the calendar and daily life, see Freeze, "Counter-Reformation," 320-21; Vera Shevzov, *Russian Orthodoxy on the Eve of Revolution* (Oxford: Oxford University Press, 2004), chapter 4.
46. Yaroslavsky's original proposal, AK 1: 284; ARK report, September 1923 AK 1: 424.
47. Freeze, "Counter-Reformation," 323.
48. The Congress discussed the calendrical reform, but some Churches opposed it; see Patrick Viscuso, *A Quest for Reform in the Orthodox Church*; and Dimitrios Stamatopoulos's review article in *Journal of Modern Greek Studies* 26, no. 2 (2008): 518-21.
49. *Akty*, 299; SD 360-62.
50. Tikhon's order, November 8, 1923, SD 362-63; ARK minutes, November 13, 20, and December 12, 1923, ARK 104, 107, 112; on the December 10 letter, see Petrov, *RPTs*, 151-52; Vinogradov, 26-30. On the confusion, see Freeze, "Counter-Reformation," 324-27. See also Tikhon's poslanie to the Serbian Patriarch (*Poslaniia*, 158-62); Tikhon to Archbishop Serafim (Lukianov), August 13 and November 9, 1923, *Vestnik russkogo khristianskogo dvizheniia* 1, no. 115 (1975): 89-90.
51. Tikhon's letter to Kurskii was published by S. G. Petrov (from GARF f. A353, op. 7, d. 16, l. 32), together with an introductory article: "Neizvestnoe pis'mo Patriarkha Tikhona o novom kalendarnom stile," *Obshchestvennaia mysl' i traditsii russkoi dukhovnoi kul'tury v istoricheskikh i literaturnykh pamiatnikakh XVI-XX bb.*, ed. L. G. Panin and S. A. Krasil'nikov (Novosibirsk: Izd. SO RAN, 2005), 487-508; see ARK minutes, February 13, 1924, *ARK*, 117.

52. Tikhon's appeal to VTsIK, September 30, 1924, *Poslaniia*, 272–89; for ARK's reaction, see *ARK* 141.
53. Safonov, 362.
54. *Poslaniia*, 281.
55. Petrov, "Patriarch Tikhon," 74.
56. Patriarch Tikhon, "Pis'mo v redaktsiiiu," *Izvestiia* No. 21 (January 26, 1924): 5. In *Akty* (311–12), and subsequently some scholars, cite the text as having been sent by the entire Holy Synod, but that is not how it was published in *Izvestiia*. As to whether the letter was actually written by Tikhon, compare Safonov, 399 and Odintsov, *Zhrebii*, 557; Safonov apparently confuses the *Izvestiia* article with the one in *Vecherniaia Moskva*, neither of which are cited.
57. Safonov, 399.
58. "Pravoslavnoe dukhovenstvo o pokhoronakh Il'icha," *Vecherniaia Moskva* No. 20 (January 25, 1924): 3. See also "Dukhovenstvo o konchine V. I. Lenina," *Izvestiia* No. 20 (January 25, 1924): 6; M. I. Odintsov and A. S. Kochetova, "'Pust' mogila eta rodit eshche million novykh Leninov . . .': Obrashcheniia, zaiavleniia, telegrammy religioznykh organizatsii v sviazi so smert'iu V. I. Lenina," *Rodina* No. 1 (2018): 114–19.
59. ARK minutes, January 12 and February 13, 1924, *ARK*, 115, 117.
60. Politburo resolution, March 13, 1924, AK 1: 290.
61. S. G. Petrov, *Dokumenty deloproizvodstva Politbiuro TsK RKP(b) kak istochnik po istorii Russkoi tserkvi (1921–1925)* (Moscow: Rosspen, 2004), 366–69.
62. Presidium TsIK SSSR resolution, March 21, 1924, AK 2: 414 (SD 364). On the concept of "socially dangerous," see James Ryan, "'They Know Not What They Do'? Bolshevik Understandings of Agency of Perpetrators, 1918–1930," *Historical Research* 90 (2017): 151–71.
63. "Prekrashchenie dela patriarkha Tikhona i drugikh," *Izvestiia* No. 67 (March 22, 1924).
64. "Sredi Tserkovnikov: U byvsh. Patriarkha Tikhona," *Izvestiia* No. 68 (March 23, 1924): 4; *Akty*, 313–14.
65. ARK minutes, March 25, 1924, *ARK*, 123.
66. AK 2: 420.
67. Safonov, 391–92.
68. AK 2: 420–23.
69. AK 2: 423–26. A list of twenty-five bishops still in exile sent at the same time is AK 2: 426–27; see also SD 365–66. The patriarch also sent to Kalinin a protest of taxes levied against both churches and clergy (AK 2: 427–29).
70. KPSG 2: 530–35.
71. KPSG 2: 535.
72. AK 2: 430.
73. AK 2: 431–32.
74. Edward E. Roslof, *Red Priests: Renovationism, Russian Orthodoxy, and Revolution, 1905–1946* (Bloomington: Indiana University Press, 2002), 130. On the period broadly, see V. V. Lobanov, "Patriarkh Tikhon i bor'ba patriarshei Tserkvi s obnovlencheskim raskolom (1923–1925 gg.)," *Tserkov' v istorii Rossii* 12 (2021): 19–58.
75. See AK 1: 421–22; AK 2: 403–6.
76. Letter of "Sillogizm," August 2, 1923, 50.
77. ARK minutes, July 17, 1923, *ARK*, 88.
78. Lobanov, "Patriarch Tikhon i bor'ba," provides a survey of many such petitions, 23–29; also Vasilii Alekseev, "Moskovskie Protodiakony: O. Mikh. Kholmogorov," *Novyi Zhurnal/The New Review* No. 117 (1974): 157–64.
79. Serafim (Lukianov)'s letter to Antonii (Khrapovitskii), February 17, 1925, in Odintsov, *Russkie patriarkhii*, 216. On Sergii and the renovationists, see A. V. Mazyrin, "Evoliutsiia otnosheniia mitropolita (Patriarkha) Sergiia (Stragorodskogo) k obnovlencheskomu raskolu v 1920–1940-e gody," *Vestnik PSTGU* 90 (2019): 55–78.
80. Maniul (Lemeshevskii), *Die Russischen Orthodoxen Bischöfe von 1893–1965* (Erlangen, 1989), part VI: 177.
81. *Poslaniia*, 170; Yaroslavskii's different account is AK 1: 423; also letter from Serafim (Aleksandrov), Ilarion (Troitskii), and Tikhon (Obolenskii) to Evdokim, November 10, 1923, has been published in N. A. Krivosheeva, "Kto zhe iavliaetsia rasprostranitelem 'lozhnykh slukhov'?," *Uchenye zapiski* No. 6 (2000): 116–18. On the whole episode, see A. V. Mazyrin, "Na kakoi kompromiss s obnovlentsami soglashalsia Patriarkh Tikhon v 1923–1924 gg., chast' 1: Peregovory so 'Sviashchennym Sinodom' Evdokima (Meshcherskogo) 1923 g.," *Vestnik Ekaterinburgskoi dukhovnoi seminarii* 36 (2021): 379–98.

82. Tikhon's encyclical, April 15, 1924, *Akty*, 315-16.
83. ARK minutes, April 8, 1924, *ARK*, 125. On Krasnitskii affair, see A. V. Mazyrin, "Na kakoi kompromiss s obnovlentsami soglashalsia Patriarkh Tikhon v 1923-1924 gg., chast' 2: Peregovory s 'Zhivoi Tserkov'iu' Vladimira Krasnitskogo, 1924 g.," *Vestnik Ekaterinburgskoi dukhovnoi seminarii* No. 37 (2022): 161-98; Safonov, 418-42, 450-55; Lobanov, "Patriarch Tikhon i bor'ba," 31-36.
84. See the evolving discussions in the ARK sessions from December 1923 to April 1924 concerning this scheme: *ARK*, 110, 119, 123, 125.
85. Vinogradov, 33-34.
86. Safonov, 421-22; Mazyrin, "Na kakoi kompromiss," part 2, 165; SD 731-32; Vinogradov, 36-38.
87. Samarin's letter was published by O. V. Kosik (ed.), "Patriarshee upravlenie i OGPU (1923-1924 gg.): Vyderzhka iz pis'ma A. D. Samarina deiateliam Zarubezhnoi Tserkvi s izlozheniem sobytii tserkovnoi zhizni v Rossii," *Vestnik PSTGU* No. 37 (2010): 65.
88. SD 737.
89. Mazyrin, "Na kakoi kompromiss," part 2, 171.
90. SD 736, emphasis in the original.
91. SD 366.
92. SD 369-73; see also SD 367-68, 741-42, for drafts that were not enacted.
93. SD 737-38; "Sredi tserkovnikov: Tikhon i Krasnitskii," *Izvestiia* No. 117 (May 24, 1924): 4; "Sredi tserkovnikov: K ob"edineniiu zhivotserkovnikov s Tikhonom," *Izvestiia* No. 120 (May 28, 1924): 6.
94. SD 777-78.
95. SD 373-74, 776.
96. ARK minutes, June 17, 1924, *ARK*, 130.
97. AK 2: 431. It is not clear why nothing came of the exchange between Rykov and Kurskii.
98. Mazyrin, "Na kakoi kompromiss," part 2, 178-79; see Vinogradov, 39.
99. SD 755-58; Mazyrin, "Na kakoi kompromiss," part 2, 185.
100. Samarain's letter, May 1924, in Kosik (ed.), "Patriarshee upravlenie," 64.
101. Mazyrin, "Na kakoi kompromiss," part 2, 175-83.
102. Tikhon's reply to clergy from Elisavetgrad, July 9, 1924, *Akty*, 325-26.
103. SD 379.
104. "Sredi tserkovnikov," *Izvestiia* No. 147 (July 1, 1924); "Sredi tserkovnikov. K primireniiu Tikhona s Krasnitskim (Beseda s Krasnitskim)," *Izvestiia* No. 151 (July 5, 1924): 6; Vinogradov, 39.
105. "Sredi tserkovnikov: K primireniiu Tikhona s Krasnitskim (Beseda s Tikhonom)," *Izvestiia* No. 155 (July 10, 1924): 6; SD 778; Mazyrin, "Na kakoi kompromiss," part 2, 188.
106. "Sredi tserkovnikov: Na dispute," *Izvestiia* No. 216 (September 21, 1924).
107. Andrei (Ukhtomskii), letter to Tikhon, April 17, 1924, KPSG 4: 500-501.
108. AK 2: 418; see also 407.
109. AK 1: 424.
110. Levitin-Krasnov and Shavrov, 315.
111. T. V. Petrova, "K voprosu o 'Danilovskoi oppozitsii' Patriarkhu Tikhonu," *Ezhegodnaia bogoslovskaia konferentsiia Pravoslavnogo Sviato-Tikhonovskogo gumanitarnogo universiteta* 25 (2015): 149-54; Mitrofan (Shkurin), "'Antireligioznye mudretsy' protiv Patriarkha Tikhona. Statia II," *Al'fa i Omega* No. 46 (2006): 88-95; N. A. Krivosheeva, "Novye materialy iz arkhiva M. E. Gubonina," *Vestnik PSTGU* 2, no. 19: 121-24; Safonov, 354-58; Ivanov, *Tikhon*, 401-5.
112. Kosik, "Patriarshee upravlenie," 65; Safonov, 421-22.
113. Kosik, "Patriarshee upravlenie," 60.
114. Kosik, "Patriarshee upravlenie," 63; see also Serafim (Lukianov), letter to Antonii (Khrapovitskii), February 17, 1925, in Odintsov, *Russkie patriarkhii*, 215-16.
115. See Central Committee circular, August 16, 1923, AK 1: 414-18, and Tuchkov's summary report, July 4, 1924, 446-48; Presidium VTsIK circular, August 21, 1924, KPSG 2: 57-61; ARK minutes, July 2, 1924, *ARK*, 132-35.
116. Samarin's letter, May 1924, Kosik (ed.), "Patriarshee upravlenie," 62; GPU report, June 13, 1924, in Vladimir Markovchin (ed.), "'Politicheskikh razgovorov ne zamecheno': Delo 'Donskoi monastyr'. Raporty agentov naruzhnogo nabliudeniia," *Istochnik* 5 (1996): 59.

117. His request to the Moscow Soviet to register the Church's "hierarchical organization" in September 1924 is SD 381–83.
118. SD 387.
119. Sergy (Stragorodsky), "Orthodox Russian Church and the Soviet Government" (for the convocation of a Church Council), December 20, 1924, SD 784–804; ARK minutes, February 14, 1925, *ARK*, 158.
120. Petrov, "Patriarch Tikhon," 74.
121. SD 386; the list is 384–86.
122. SD 396–98.
123. OGPU overview of the political situation in the USSR, March 3, 1925, *"Sovershenno skekretno": Lubianka-Stalinu o polozhenii v strane (1922–1934 gg.)* (Moscow, 2002), v. 3, part 1: 109.
124. SD 398–99.
125. The impact was observed by the OGPU: *Sovershenno sekretno* vol. 3, part 1: 109.
126. See SD 390–95; see also the collection of documents from the OGPU archive: Markovchin (ed.), "Politicheskikh razgovorov ne zamecheno," 60. On Polozov, see N. A. Krivosheeva, "Kto dushu svoiu polozhit za drugi svoia."
127. Markovchin (ed.), "Politicheskikh razgovorov ne zamecheno," 59.
128. AK 2: 441. This replaced an earlier such text, dated November 23, 1923, appointing first Agafangel and second Kirill (AK 2: 357).
129. SD 392–94, 398; *ARK*, 159.
130. "Bolezn' i smert' Tikhona," *Vecherniaia Moskva* No. 91 (April 23, 1925): 2; E. Bakunina, "Poslednie dni Patriarkha Tikhona (Vospominaniia vracha)," *Vestnik Russkogo Khristianskogo Dvizheniia* No. 115 (1975): 97–107. The first was published in a Soviet paper and was brief and more technical; the second was published abroad (originally in 1930) and discussed far more details of the patriarch's life. Both, however, say the same about the patriarch's illness.
131. Bakunina, "Poslednie dni," 97–100.
132. Bakunina, "Poslednie dni," 100–103.
133. Tuchkov's report, February 1 (?), 1925, AK 2: 444–45; see also OGPU overview of the political situation in the USSR, March 3 and April 7, 1925, *Sovershenno sekretno* vol. 3, part 1: 47, 106–10, 134–35.
134. SD 399–402.
135. Bakunina, "Poslednie dni," 104.
136. Elevferii, "Nedelia v Patriarkhii" (originally written in 1930), in *Iz istorii Khristianskoi tserkvi na Rodine i za rubezhom v XX stoletii* (Moscow: Krutitskoe podvor'e, 1995), 230–31; see also Vinogradov, 44ff.
137. Bakunina, "Poslednie dni," 104–5; "Bolezn' i smert' Tikhona"; Bakunin refers to his wife by her maiden name Lopatina. For another account from a Leningrad priest who was present at the funeral and reported what he heard from witnesses, which coincides in most respects, see *Akty*, 368–69; according to this account, Tikhon's last words were "Glory to you, O Lord" and he crossed himself as he died (369).
138. Markovchin (ed.), "Politicheskikh razgovorov ne zamecheno," 61–62.
139. Report from counselor of the Latvian embassy Aleksandrs Birznieks to the General Secretary of the Latvian Ministry of Foreign Affairs, April 15, 1925, Latvian State Historical Archive, 1313.3.46. I extremely grateful to Aleksandr Gavrilin for sharing this with me.
140. Tuchkov refers to his illness as serious and potentially leading to his death already in early February (AK 2: 445).
141. *Dokumenty Sobora* 5: 827–28.
142. See Lobanov, *Patriarkh*, 182–92; Lobanov, "Konchina Patriarkha Tikhona: fakty i mneniia," *Tserkov' v istorii Rossii* 8 (2009): 199–212.
143. Bakunina, "Poslednie dni," 105–6.
144. AK 1: 296.
145. AK 1: 297–99.
146. Birznieks's report.
147. OGPU agent reports to Tuchkov, April 8–12, 1925, in Markovchin (ed.), "Politicheskikh razgovorov," 61–66. Church sources estimated three times as many people: *Akty*, 365.
148. OGPU agent report, April 13, 1925, in Markovchin (ed.), "Politicheskikh razgovorov," 65–68; *Akty*, 370–78.

Conclusions

1. Petr to Kalinin, April 9, 1924, AK 2: 454; for the copy of Tikhon's testamentary instructions sent to the government, see AK 2: 441. Act appointing Petr to the administration and Petr's encyclical announcing his appointment, April 12, 1925, SD 414–16.
2. "Predsmertnoe zaveshchanie Tikhona," *Izvestiia* 86 (April 15, 1925): 1 and *Pravda* 86 (April 15, 1925): 3.
3. Metropolitan Antonii, "Poslanie predsedatelia Arkhiereiskogo Sinoda Russkoi Pravoslavnoi Tserkvi zagranitsei Vysokopreosviashchennogo Mitropolita Antoniia k russkoi pravoslavnoi pastve zagranitsei," *Tserkovnye Vedomosti* 9–10 (May 14–28, 1925): 3–4.
4. The text of the "deathbed testament" is SD 410–12; citation, 410.
5. SD 411–12.
6. SD 412.
7. Elevferii, "Nedelia v Patriarkhii" (originally written in 1930), in *Iz istorii Khristianskoi tserkvi na Rodine i za rubezhom v XX stoletii* (Moscow: Krutitskoe podvor'e, 1995), 230–31. Elevferii's account of how Metropolitan Petr "forgot" about the sealed envelope for the week after the patriarch's death is, however, an odd one.
8. Vinogradov, *Nekotorykh vazhneishikh momentakh*, 40–46.
9. Vinogradov, letter to Bishop Ioann (Shakhovskoi) [1947], in *Tserkovno-istoricheskii vestnik* No. 1 (1998): 42.
10. D. V. Safonov, "K voprosu o podlinnosti 'Zaveshchatel'nogo poslaniia' sv. Patriarkha Tikhona," *Bogoslovskii Vestnik* No. 4 (2004): 265–311; the article contains a useful side-by-side synopsis of the three variants in an appendix (299–311), which will be cited below. For a more convincing analysis, see V. V. Lobanov, *Patriarkh Tikhon i Sovetskaia vlast' (1917–1925 gg.)* (Moscow: Russkaia Panorama, 2008), 173–82.
11. The three successive drafts are in SD 402–13.
12. A copy sent by the Russian press agency to the Politburo was published in AK 1: 291–96, with differences from the copy sent to Yaroslavsky indicated in the notes. There is yet another copy with minor editorial changes in two hands, one of which is evidently Tuchkov's (see notes, SD 412); the changes were not included in the text published by the newspapers. None of these copies is substantively different from the published version.
13. "Sredi tserkovnikov: Posle smerti Tikhona," *Izvestiia* No. 108 (May 14, 1925): 6.
14. SD 411.
15. SD 387, 397.
16. SD 413. The memo has no date, attribution, or addressee, but it was clearly for internal communication by someone who knew what was in the first draft. It would not be from Tuchkov, since he was involved in the compromise texts, but perhaps Galkin, Krasikov, or Yaroslavsky.
17. M. Pol'skii, *Novye mucheniki rossiiskie* (Jordanville: Holy Trinity Monastery, 1957), 2: 21.
18. For an overview of the Orthodox Church in the Soviet Union, see Alexander Agadjanian and Scott M. Kenworthy, *Understanding World Christianity: Russia* (Minneapolis: Fortress Press, 2021), 133–201.
19. Gregory L. Freeze, "Subversive Atheism: Soviet Antireligious Campaigns and the Religious Revival in Ukraine in the 1920s," in *State Secularism and Lived Religion in Soviet Russia and Ukraine*, ed. Catherine Wanner (New York: Oxford University Press, 2012), 27–62.
20. I. A. Kurliandskii, *Stalin, Vlast', Religiia* (Moscow: Kuchkovo Pole, 2011), 516–18.
21. https://sinod.ruschurchabroad.org/Arh%20Sobor%201981%20Prot.htm.
22. 2024 interview with Kharchev, https://kremlinhill.com/2024/11/14/константин-харчев-я-сделал-для-церкви/. See also Fr. Nikolai Sokolov, "On byl molitvennikom pred litsom Bozhiim za nashu zemliu," https://monasterium.ru/novosti/28-rch/on-byl-molitvennikom-pred-lit som-bozhiim-za-nashu-zemlyu/.
23. "Deianie osviashchennogo Arkhiereiskogo Sobora Russkoi Pravoslavnoi Tserkvi o kanonizatsii sviatitelei Iova i Tikhona, Patriarkhov Moskovskikh i vseia Rusi," *ZhMP* No. 1 (1990): 6. See also "Zhitie sviatitelia Tikhona, Patriarkha Moskovskogo i vseia Rusi," *ZhMP* No. 2 (1990): 56–68; see also *ZhMP* No. 4 (1990): 63–72.
24. Damaskin (Orlovskii), *Slava i tragediia russkoi agiografii: Prichislenie k liku sviatykh v Russkoi Pravoslavnoi Tserkvi, istoriia i sovremennost'* (Moscow: Regional'nyi obshchestvennyi fond 'Pamiat' muchenikov i ispovednikov Russkoi Pravoslavnoi Tserkvi', 2018), 226. On Tikhon's canonization, see Per-Arne Bodin, "From Biography to Hymnography: On the Canonization

of Patriarch Tikhon," in *Spiritual and Ecclesiastical Biographies: Research, Results, Reading*, ed. Anders Jarlet (Stockholm: Kungl. Vitterhets Historie och Antikvitetsakademien, 2017), 149–65.

25. Elena Dorofeeva, "Kanonizatsiia patriarkha Tikhona proizvela oshelomlenie—sotrudnik instituta vseobshchei istorii RAN Sergei Beliaev," February 24, 2012, https://pravoslavie.ru/51767.html; Tikhon (Shevkunov), *Everyday Saints and Other Stories* (Moscow: Pokrov Publications, 2012); "Finding the Relics of Saint Tikhon of Moscow," https://www.oca.org/saints/lives/2014/02/22/100253-finding-of-the-relics-of-saint-tikhon-of-moscow.

26. For a recent example, see Geraldine Fagan, "'These Are Things in History That Should Be Called by Their Proper Names': Evaluating Russian Orthodox Collaboration with the Soviet State," in *The Dangerous God: Christianity and the Soviet Experiment*, ed. Dominic Erdozain (DeKalb: Northern Illinois University Press, 2017), 187–209.

A Note on Historiography and Sources

1. Jane Swan, *The Biography of Patriarch Tikhon* (Jordanville, NY: Holy Trinity Monastery, 1964); Roman Rössler, *Kirche und Revolution in Russland: Patriarch Tichon und der Sowjetstaat* (Köln: Böchlau Verlag, 1969); Johannes Chrysostomus, *Kirchengesichthe Rußlands der neuesten Zeit: Patriarch Tichon 1917–1925* (München: Anton Pustet, 1965); Edward E. Roslof, "Russian Orthodoxy and the Tragic Fate of Patriarch Tikhon (Bellavin)," in *The Human Tradition in Modern Russia*, ed. William B. Husband (Wilmington: SR Books, 2000), 77–91; Leonid Kishkovsky, "Archbishop Tikhon in America," *St. Vladimir's Theological Quarterly* 19 (1975): 9–31; "Patriarch Tikhon: The American Years, 1898–1907—Our Common Legacy," *St. Tikhon's Theological Journal* 4 (2006); Monica Cognolato, "'The Orthodox Church Does Not Build on Other People's Foundations': The Orthodox Church in America During Bishop Tikhon's Years (1898–1907)," PhD diss. (University of Padua, 2014) and articles. On the archives, see Alexis Liberovsky, "The Archival Legacy of Saint Tikhon in North America," *St Tikhon's Theological Journal* 4 (2008–2009): 18–40.

2. Francesca Silano, "'In the Language of the Patriarch': Patriarch Tikhon, the Russian Orthodox Church, and the Soviet State (1865–1925)," PhD diss. (University of Toronto, 2017), *The Battle for Russia's Souls: Patriarch Tikhon, the Russian Orthodox Church, and the Soviet State* (Ithaca, NY: Cornell University Press, forthcoming), and articles (see Bibliography).

3. See Scott Kenworthy, "Gregory L. Freeze: Historian of the Orthodox Church in Modern Russia," in *Church and Society in Modern Russia: Essays in Honor of Gregory L. Freeze*, ed. Manfred Hildermeier and Elise Kimerling Wirtschafter (Wiesbaden: Harrassowitz Verlag, 2015), 211–29. For an overview of the new scholarship, see the introduction to Poole and Werth (eds.), *Religious Freedom*, 1-43; the introduction to Heather Coleman (ed.), *Orthodox Christianity in Imperial Russia: A Source Book on Lived Religion* (Bloomington: Indiana University Press, 2014), 1–20; Nadieszda Kizenko, "The Orthodox Church and Religious Life in Imperial Russia," in *The Oxford Handbook of Russian Religious Thought*, ed. C. Emerson et al. (Oxford: Oxford University Press, 2020), 21–37.

4. For an overview, see my article "Rethinking the Orthodox Church and the Bolshevik Revolution," *Revolutionary Russia* 31, no. 1 (2018): 1–23; two of the most important recent essays are Vera Shevzov, "The Orthodox Church and Religion in Revolutionary Russia," in *The Oxford Handbook of Russian Religious Thought*, ed. C. Emerson et al. (Oxford: Oxford University Press, 2020), 38–59, and Gregory Freeze, "Religion and Revolution: The Russian Orthodox Church Transformed," in *A Companion to the Russian Revolution*, ed. Daniel Orlovsky (Malden, MA: Wiley-Blackwell, 2020), 277–85.

5. A. I. Vvedenskii, *Tserkov' i gosudarstvo: ocherk vziamootnoshenii tserkvi i gosudarstva v Rossii 1918—1922 g.* (Moscow, 1923); B. V. Titlinov, *Tserkov' vo vremia revoliutsii* (Petrograd: Byloe, 1924).

6. For the historiography, see the articles by Serafim (Nikolin): "Zhizn' i deiatel'nost' sviatogo Patriarkha v otechestvennoi istoriografii: imperatorskii period," *Khristianskoe chtenie* 4 (2020): 247–59; "Zhizn' i deiatel'nost' sviatogo Patriarkha Tikhona: arkheograficheskii aspekt," *Elektronnyi zhurnal studentov i aspirantov bogoslovskogo fakul'teta PSTGU*. https://pstgu.ru/

upload/iblock/241/2413af79770d43c3ba03575197599a27.pdf; "Diskussiia ob otnoshenii sviatogo patriarkha Tikhona k sovetskoi vlasti v sovremennoi otechestvennoi istoriografii v 2000–2018 gg.," *Khristianskoe chtenie* 3 (2022): 305–13.
7. Odintsov's fictionalizing of Tikhon's biography stems all the way back to his earliest articles ("Zhrebii pastyria") published in *Nauka i religiia* in 1989, much of which is reproduced in the latest book. A new biography appeared too late for me to see a copy: M. V. Artiushenko, *Sviatitel' Tikhon Patriarkh Moskovskii i vseia Rossii: Arkhipastyr', Ispovednik, Chelovek* (Moscow: Donskoi Monastery, 2024).
8. Receipt by assistant V. F. Yakovlev of the Prosecutor of the Judicial Collegium on criminal cases of the Supreme Court on receiving the archive of Patriarch Tikhon from Velikie Luki, May 28, 1923, SD 356; see also Aref'eva and Shlevis, *Primite*, 230–40, and Novikov, *Kolybel'*, 97–104.
9. The letters are contained in RGIA f. 796, op. 205, d. 752. The letters written while he was in America have been published in *Pis'ma*. All of the letters were transcribed by N. A. Muralev, "Epistoliarnoe nasledie sviateishego Patriarkha Tikhona (pis'ma k mitropolitu Kievskomu i Galitskomu Flavianu)" (Diploma thesis, St. Petersburg Theological Academy, 1995); however, there are numerous mistakes, so this text must be used with caution.
10. A. I. Mramornov (ed.), *Dokumenty Sviashchennogo Sobora Pravoslavnoi Rossiiskoi Tserkvi 1917–1918 gg.* (Moscow: Izdatel'stvo Novospasskogo monastyria, 2012–), 20 vols. to date. The first post-Soviet publication was *Deiianiia Sviashchennogo sobora pravoslavnoi rossiiskoi tserkvi 1917–1918 gg.*, 10 vols. (Moscow: Izdatel'stvo Novospasskogo monastyria, 1994–2000). See also the helpful summaries in Günther Schulz, A. G. Kravetskii, and A. A. Pletneva (eds.), *Sviashchennyi Sobor Pravoslavnoi Rossiiskoi tserkvi 1917–-1918 gg.: Obzor deianii*, 3 vols. (Moscow: Krutitskoe podvor'e, 2000–2002).
11. Arsenii, *Dnevnik*; *Delo*; Leonid Turkevich, *Dnevniki i zapisnye knizhki perioda Pomestnogo Sobora 1917—1918 gg.*, ed. A. I. Mramornov (Moscow: Spasskoe delo, 2024).
12. See Damaskin (Orlovskii), "Dokumenty kantseliarii patriarkha Tikhona v Rossiiskom gosudarstevennom istoricheskom archive," *Otechestvennye arkhivy* 4 (2013): 67–73.

Bibliography

Archival Sources

Archives in Russia

Gosudarstvennyi arkhiv Iaroslavskoi oblasti
(State Archive of the Iaroslavl Region)
    f. 230. Iaroslavl Ecclesiastical consistory
    f. 509. Iaroslavl City Government

Gosudarstvennyi arkhiv Pskovskoi oblasti
(State Archive of the Pskov Region)
    f. 39. Pskov Ecclesiastical Consistory
    f. 291. Pskov Seminary
    f. 499. Pskov-Caves Monastery

Gosudarstvennyi arkhiv Rossiiskoi Federatsii
(State Archive of the Russian Federation)
    f. 3431. Local Council of the Russian Orthodox Church, 1917–1918
    f. A-353. People's Commissariat of Justice

Otdel rukopisei. Rossiisskaia gosudarstvennaia biblioteka
(Manuscript Division. Russian State Library)
    f. 766. Kronid (Liubimov)

Rossiiskii gosudarstvennyi arkhiv sotsial'no-politicheskii istorii
(Russian State Archive of Social-Political History)
    f. 17. Central Committee of the Communist Party of the Soviet Union
    f. 89. Iaroslavskii Emel'ian Mikhailovich

Rossiiskii gosudarstvennyi istoricheskii arkhiv
(Russian State Historical Archive, St. Petersburg)
    f. 796. Chancellery of the Holy Synod
    f. 797. Chancellery of the Chief Procurator
    f. 802. Educational Committee of the Holy Synod
    f. 831. Chancellery of Patriarch Tikhon and the Holy Synod, 1916–1924
    f. 833. Local Council of the Russian Orthodox Church, 1917–1918
    f. 1574. K. P. Pobedonostsev

Tsentral'nyi gosudarstvennyi arkhiv g. Moskvy
(Russian State Historical Archive of the City of Moscow)
    f. 203. Moscow Ecclesiastical Consistory

Archives in the United States

Archives of the Orthodox Church in America
Hoover Institution Archives
    Frank Golder Papers
Kautz Family YMCA Archives (University of Minnesota)
    Ethan Colton Papers
    Records of YMCA International Work in Russia and the Soviet Union (Y.USA.9-2-1)
Library of Congress
    Alaska Russian Church Archive
    Leontii Turkevich Papers
New York Public Library Manuscript Division
    Isabel Hapgood Papers

Other Archives:

Archiwum Panstwowe w Lublinie (State Archives in Lublin)
    Fond 97. Chelmski Zarzad Duchowny, 1874–1905
    Fond 98. Chelmsko Warszawski Duchowny Konsystorz Prawoslawny (1875–1905)
    Fond 101. Chelmska Diecezi Rada Szkolna
    Fond 102. Seminarium Duchowne w Chelmie
Lietuvos centrinis valstybės archyvas (Lithuanian State Historical Archive)
    Fond 605. Lithuanian Orthodox Ecclesiastical Consistory
    Fond 607. Chancellery of the Archbishop of Lithuania and Vilnius
National Archives (London, UK)
    Foreign Office 371. Political Departments: General Correspondence 1906–1966

Books and Articles

Agadjanian, Alexander, and Scott M. Kenworthy. *Understanding World Christianity: Russia.* Minneapolis: Fortress Press, 2021.

Agadjanian, Alexander, Scott Kenworthy, Nadieszda Kizenko, and Francesca Silano, eds. *Religion in the Russian Revolution: Conflicts, Encounters, and Transformations.* Bloomington: Indiana University Press, forthcoming.

Alekseev, Vasilii. "Moskovskie Protodiakony: O. Mikh. Kholmogorov." *Novyi Zhurnal/The New Review* No. 117 (1974): 157–64.

Aref'eva, Irina, and German Shlevis. *Primite menia v svoiu liubov'...* Vilnius: SAVO, 2008.

Arsenii (Stadnitskii). *Dnevnik na Pomestnyi Sobor 1917–1918 gg.* Moscow: PSTGU, 2018.

Arsenii (Stadnitskii). *Dnevnik 1902–1903.* Vol. 2. Moscow: PSTGU, 2012.

Artemov, Nikolai. "Postanovlenie No. 362 ot 7/20 noiabria 1920 g. i zakrytie zarubezhnogo VVTsU v mae 1922 g.: Istoricheskoe i kanonicheskoe znachenie." In *Istoriiia Russkoi Pravoslavnoi Tserkvi v XX veke (1917–1933 gg.)*, 93–212. Munich: Izd. Obiteli Prep. Iova Pochaevskogo, 2002.

Babkin M. A., ed. *Rossiiskoe dukhovenstvo i sverzhenie monarkhii v 1917 godu (Materialy i arkhivnye dokumenty po istorii Russkoi pravoslavnoi tserkvi).* 2nd ed. Moscow: Indrik, 2008.

Babkin, M. A. *Sviashchenstvo i Tsarstvo (Rossiia, nachalo XX v.–1918 g.): Issledovaniia i materialy.* Moscow: Indrik, 2011.

Bakonina, S. N. *Tserkovnaia zhizn' russkoi emigratsii na Dal'nem Vostoke v 1920–1931 gg.: Na materialakh Kharbinskoi eparkhii.* Moscow: PSTGU, 2014.

Balashov, Nikolai, and S. L. Kravets, eds. *Pravoslavie v Estonii: Issledovaniia i dokumenty.* 2 vols. Moscow: Pravoslavnaia Entsiklopediia, 2010.

Beliaev, S. "O vospominaniiakh episkopa Tikhona (Sharapova) i ikh avtora." *ZhMP* No. 4 (1998): 80–88.

Beliakova, E. V., N. A. Beliakova, and E. B. Emchenko. *Zhenshchina v pravoslavie: Tserkovnoe pravo i rossiiskaia praktika*. Moscow: Kuchkovo pole, 2011.
Bell, G. K. A. *Randall Davidson: Archbishop of Canterbury*. Oxford: Oxford University Press, 1935.
Bemporad, Elissa. *Legacy of Blood: Jews, Pogroms, and Ritual Murder in the Lands of the Soviets*. New York: Oxford University Press, 2019.
Bezkorovainy, Anatoly, ed. *A History of Holy Trinity Russian Orthodox Cathedral of Chicago, 1892-1992*. Chicago: Holy Trinity Russian Orthodox Cathedral, 1992.
Biriukova, Iu. A. "Dokumenty Osoboi komisii po rassledovaniiu zlodeianii bol'shevikov pri Glavnokomanduiushchem Vooruzhennym silami na Iuge Rossii kak istochnik po istorii Russkoi Pravoslavnoi tserkvi." *Vestnik PSTGU* 79 (2017): 55-67.
Biriukova, Iu. A., and E. A. Ageeva, eds. *Tserkov' na Donu v gody grazhdanskoi voiny 1918-1919 gg.: Rassledovaniia Osoboi kommissii*. Volgograd: PrinTerra Dizain, 2022.
Bishop Gregory (Afonsky). *A History of the Orthodox Church in Alaska (1794-1917)*. Kodiak, AK: St. Herman's Theological Seminary, 1977.
Bobryk, Witold. "Rite Changes in the Uniate Diocese of Chełm in the 18th Century." In *On the Border of the Worlds: Essays About the Orthodox and Uniate Churches in Eastern Europe in the Middle Ages and the Modern Period*, edited by Andrzej Gil and Witold Bobryk. Siedlce-Lublin: Akademia Podlaska and Instytut Europy Srodkowo-Wschodniej, 2010.
Bociurkiw, Bohdan R. "The Politics of Religion in the Ukraine: The Orthodox Church and the Ukrainian Revolution, 1917-1919." Kennan Institute Occasional Paper, 1985.
Bociurkiw, Bohdan R. "The Rise of the Ukrainian Autocephalous Orthodox Church, 1919-1922." In *Church, Nation and State in Russia and Ukraine*, ed. Geoffrey A. Hosking, 228-49. Edmonton: Unversity of Alberta, 1990.
Bociurkiw, Bohdan R. "The Russian Orthodox Church in Ukraine: The Exarchate and the Renovationists, and the 'Conciliar-Episcopal' Church, 1920-1939." *Harvard Ukrainian Studies* 26 (2002-2003): 63-91.
Bodin, Per-Arne. "From Biography to Hymnography: On the Canonization of Patriarch Tikhon." In *Spiritual and Ecclesiastical Biographies: Research, Results, Reading*, ed. Anders Jarlet, 149-65. Stockholm: Kungl. Vitterhets Historie och Antikvitetsakademien, 2017.
Bonch-Bruevich, Vladimir. *Vospominaniia o Lenine*. Moscow: Nauka, 1969.
Borisov, N. S. "Sviatitel' Tikhon vo glave Iaroslavskoi eparkhii." *Zhurnal Moskovskoi Patriarkhii* no. 6 (2005): 75-79.
Borkowski, Andrzej. *Między Konstantynopolem a Moskwą: Źdódła Greckie do autokefali kościoła Prawosławnego w Rzecypospolitej (1919-1927)*. Białystok: Wydawnictwo Uniwersytetu w Białymstoku, 2015.
Brady, Joel. "Becoming What We Always Were: 'Conversion' of U.S. Greek Catholics to Russian Orthodoxy, 1890-1914." *U.S. Catholic Historian* 32, no. 1 (2014): 23-48.
Brady, Joel. "Transnational Conversions: Greek Catholic Migrants and Russky Orthodox Conversion Movements in Austria-Hungary, Russia, and the Americas (1890-1914)." PhD diss., University of Pittsburgh, 2012.
Budnitskii, Oleg. *Russian Jews Between the Reds and the Whites, 1917-1920*. Translated by Timothy Portice. Philadelphia: University of Pennsylvania Press, 2012.
Chaplin, Valentin, ed. *Iz Istorii Khristianskoi Tserkvi Na Rodine i Za Rubezhom v XX Stoleti: Sbornik*. Moscow: Krutitskoe patriarshee podvor'e, 1995.
Chibisova, A. A. "Bor'ba za avtokefaliiu pravoslavnoi Tserkvi v Pol'she v 1918-1925 godakh." Kand. diss., Moscow State University, 2023.
Chibisova, A. A. "Patriarkh Tikhon i avtokefaliia Pol'skoi Pravoslavnoi Tserkvi 1924 goda." *Vestnik PSTGU* 95 (2020): 118-41.
Chistovich, I. A. *S.-Peterburgskaia Dukhovnaia Akademiia za poslednie 30 let*. St. Petersburg, 1889.
Chrysostomus, Johannes. *Kirchengeschicthe Rußlands der neuesten Zeit: Patriarch Tichon 1917-1925*. München: Anton Pustet, 1965.

Cognolato, Monica. "'The Orthodox Church Does Not Build on Other People's Foundations': The Orthodox Church in America During Bishop Tikhon's Years (1898–1907)." PhD diss., University of Padua, 2014.

Cognolato, Monica. "The Tsar's Power Explained to America: Notes from a 1905 Homily." In *New Perspectives on Russian-American Relations*, edited by William Benton Whisenhunt and Norman E. Saul, 99–111. New York: Routledge, 2016.

Cunningham, James. *A Vanquished Hope: The Movement for Church Renewal in Russia, 1905–1906*. Crestwood, NY: St. Vladimir's Seminary Press, 1981.

Cunningham, James W., Keith P. Dyrud, and Grace Dyrud. *The Gates of Hell: The Great Sobor of the Russian Orthodox Church, 1917–1918*. Minneapolis: University of Minnesota, 2002.

Curtiss, John Shelton. *The Russian Church and the Soviet State, 1917–1950*. 1st ed. Boston: Little, Brown, 1953.

Daly, Jonathan. "Storming the Last Citadel: The Bolshevik Assault on the Church, 1922." In *The Bolsheviks in Russian Society: Revolution and Civil Wars*, edited by Vladimir N. Brovkin, 235–68. New Haven, CT: Yale University Press, 1997.

Denysenko, Nicholas. *The Orthodox Church in Ukraine: A Century of Separation*. DeKalb: Northern Illinois University Press, 2018.

Destivelle, Hyacinthe. *The Moscow Council (1917–1918): The Creation of the Conciliar Institutions of the Russian Orthodox Church*. Translated by Jerry Ryan and edited by Michael Plekon and Vitaly Permiakov. Notre Dame, IN: University of Notre Dame Press, 2015.

Dixon, Simon. "The 'Mad Monk' Iliodor in Tsaritsyn." *Slavonic and East European Review* 88, no. 1 (2010): 377–415.

Dixon, Simon. "Orthodoxy and Restoration of the Russian Patriarchate in 1917." *Transactions of the Royal Historical Society* 28 (2018): 149–74.

Edmondson, Charles M. "The Politics of Hunger: The Soviet Response to Famine, 1921." *Soviet Studies* 29, no. 4 (1977): 506–518.

Edmondson, Charles M., and R. Barry Levis. "Archbishop Randall Davidson, Russian Famine Relief, and the Fate of the Orthodox Clergy, 1917–1923." *Journal of Church & State* 40, no. 3 (1998): 624–31.

Eferov, I. G., ed. *Sviashchennyi Sobor Pravoslavnoi rossiiskoi tserkvi 1917–1918 gg. o roliakh zhenshchin v tserkvi*. Moscow: Spasskoe delo, 2020.

Efimov, A. B., and O. V. Lasaeva. *Aleutskaia i Severo-Amerikanskaia eparkhiia pri sviatitele Tikhone*. Moscow: PSTGU, 2012.

Emel'ianov and O. I. Khailova, "Goneniia na Russkuiu Pravoslavnuiu tserkov' (1917–1950-e gody)," *Rossiia i sovremennyi mir* No. 4 (61) (2008): 114–32.

Emmonds, Terence. *Alleged Sex and Threatened Violence: Doctor Russel, Bishop Vladimir, and the Russians in San Francisco, 1887–1892*. Palo Alto, CA: Stanford University Press, 1997.

Engelstein, Laura. *Russia in Flames: War, Revolution, Civil War, 1914–1921*. New York: Oxford University Press, 2018.

Erdozain, Dominic. *The Dangerous God: Christianity and the Soviet Experiment*. DeKalb: Northern Illinois University Press, 2017.

Erickson, John. *Orthodox Christians in America: A Short History*. New York: Oxford University Press, 2008.

Erickson, John H. "Slavophile Thought and Conceptions of Mission in the Russian North American Archdiocese, Late 19th–Early 20th Century." *St Vladimir's Theological Quarterly* 55, no. 3 (2012): 245–68.

Essey, Basil. "Saint Raphael Hawaweeny, Bishop of Brooklyn." In *The Orthodox Christian World*, edited by Augustine Casiday, 338–44. London: Routledge, 2021.

Evlogy (Georgievskii). *My Life's Journey: The Memoirs of Metropolitan Evlogy*. Translated by Alexander Lisenko. Yonkers, NY: St. Vladimir's Seminary Press, 2014.

Evtuhov, Catherine. "The Church's Revolutionary Moment: Diocesan Congresses and Grassroots Politics in 1917." In *Cultural History of Russia in the Great War and Revolution*, Book 1, edited by Murray Frame et al., 377–402. Bloomington, IN: Slavica Publishers, 2014.

Evtuhov, Catherine. "The Church in the Russian Revolution: Arguments for and Against Restoring the Patriarchate at the Church Council of 1917–1918." *Slavic Review* 50 (1991): 497–511.

Feodosii (Protsiuk). *Obosoblencheskie dvizheniia v Pravoslavnoi Tserkvi na Ukraine (1917–1943)*. Moscow: Krutitskoe podvor'e, 2004.

Finkel, Stuart. "An Intensification of Vigilance: Recent Perspectives on the Institutional History of the Soviet Security Apparatus in the 1920s." *Kritika* 5, no. 2 (2004): 299–320.

Finkel, Stuart. *On the Ideological Front: The Russian Intelligentsia and the Making of the Soviet Public Sphere*. New Haven, CT: Yale University Press, 2007.

Firsov, S. L. "'Evreiskii vopros' i sviatoi Patriarkh Tikhon." *Kontinent* 111 (2002).

Firsov, S. L. "Lichnost' i obraz sviatogo Patriarkha Tikhona (Bellavina) v Sovietskoi pechati (K istoriografii voprosa)." *Tserkov' i vremia* 75 (2016): 208–52.

Firsov, S. L. *Vlast' i ogon': Tserkov' i sovetskoe gosudarstvo 1918-nachalo 1940-kh gg*. Moscow: PSTGU, 2014.

Firsov, S. L. "'Vremia voine i vremia miru': Pravoslavnaia Rossiiskaia tserkov' i grazhdanskaia voina v Rossii. Ocherki istorii i istoriografii." St. Petersburg: Izdatel'stvo RGPU im. A. I. Gertsena, 2018.

Freeze, Gregory L. "Counter-Reformation in Russian Orthodoxy: Popular Response to Religious Innovation 1922–1925." *Slavic Review* 54, no. 2 (1995): 305–39.

Freeze, Gregory L. "Handmaiden of the State? The Church in Imperial Russia Reconsidered." *Journal of Ecclesiastical History* 36 (1985): 82–102.

Freeze, Gregory L. "The 'Long' Church Council of 1917–1918: Institutional Crisis, Intellectual Capital." *Ostkirchliche Studien* 67 (2018): 187–211.

Freeze, Gregory. "Religion and Revolution: The Russian Orthodox Church Transformed." In *A Companion to the Russian Revolution*, edited by Daniel Orlovsky, 277–85. Malden, MA: Wiley-Blackwell, 2020.

Freeze, Gregory. "Russian Orthodoxy: Church, People and Politics in Imperial Russia." In *The Cambridge History of Russia*, vol. 2, *Imperial Russia, 1689–1917*, edited by Dominic Lieven, 284–305, Cambridge Cambridge University Press, 2015.

Freeze, Gregory L. "Subversive Atheism: Soviet Antireligious Campaigns and the Religious Revival in Ukraine in the 1920s." In *State Secularism and Lived Religion in Soviet Russia and Ukraine*, edited by Catherine Wanner, 27–62. New York: Oxford University Press, 2012.

Garrett, Paul D. "The Life and Legacy of Bishop Raphael Hawaweeny." In *The First One Hundred Years: A Centennial Anthology Celebrating Antiochian Orthodoxy in North America*, edited by George S. Corey et al., 3–30. Englewood, NJ: Antakya Press, 1995.

Garrett, Paul D. *St. Innocent: Apostle to America*. Crestwood, NY: St. Vladimir's Seminary Press, 1979.

Gerasimova, N. E. "Srednee dukhovnoe obrazovanie v Iaroslavskoi i Kostromskoi guberniiakh vo vtoroi polovine XIX–nachale XX vv." Kandidat diss., Iaroslavskii gosudarstvenyi universitet, 2001.

Golovushkin, D. A. "Fenomen obnovlenchestva v Russkom pravoslavii pervoi poloviny xx veka." PhD diss., Herzen University, 2019.

Golubtsov, Sergii. *Moskovskoe dukhovenstvo v preddverii i nachale gonenii 1917–1922 gg*. Moscow: Izd. Pravoslavnogo bratstva Sporuchinitsy greshnykh, 1999.

Goncharova, V. A., ed. "Perepiska narcoma inostrannykh del G. V. Chicherina s Sekretariatom TsK RKP(b) po povodu poezdki Sviateishego Patriarkha Tikhona v Angliiu." *Vestnik PSTGU* 27 (2008): 110–16.

Gorky, Maxim. *Untimely Thoughts: Essays on Revolution, Culture, and the Bolsheviks, 1917–1918*. New Haven, CT: Yale University Press, 1995.

Gorny, A. S. "Belarusizatsyia Pravaslaunai Tsarkvy u mizhvaenny peryiad: dakumenty i materyialy, Chastka 1." *KhRONOS Tserkovno-istoricheskii al'manakh* No. 5 (2017): 142–61.

Grabbe, Grigorii. *Zavet sviatogo Patriarkha*. Moscow: AO Astra-sem, 1996.

Greene, R. H. *Bodies Like Bright Stars: Saints and Relics in Orthodox Russia*. DeKalb, IL: Northern Illinois University Press, 2010.

Gribble, Richard. "Cooperation and Conflict Between Church and State: The Russian Famine of 1921–1923." *Journal of Church and State* 51 (2009): 634–62.

Grigorevskii, M. *Otchet o revizii Pskovskoi Dukhovnoi seminarii i uchilishcha (1873 god)*. Saint Petersburg, 1874.

Gubonin, M. E., ed. *Akty Sviateishego Tikohna, Patriarkha Moskovskogo i vseia Rossii, pozdneishie dokumenty i perepiska o kanonicheskom preemstve vysshei tserkovnoi vlasti, 1917–1943.* Moscow: PSTGU, 1994.

Gubonin, M. E., ed. *Sovremenniki o Patriarkhe Tikhone*. 2 vols. Moscow: PSTGU, 2007.

Haskell, Peter Carl. "Archbishop Tikhon and Bishop Grafton: An Early Chapter in Anglo-Orthodox Relations in the New World." *St. Vladimir's Seminary Quarterly* 11, no. 4 (1967): 193–206 and Part Two, 12, no. 1 (1968): 2–16.

Haskell, Peter Carl. "Bishop Grafton and the Orthodox Church, 1900–1905." MA thesis, University of Minnesota, 1970.

Hawaweeny, Raphael M. *The True Significance of Sacred Tradition and Its Great Worth*, edited and translated by Patrick Viscuso. Ithaca: Cornell University Press, 2017.

Herbel, Oliver. "American Restorationism, the Public Sphere, and Anglican-Orthodox Relations: The Case of Ingram Nathaniel Washington Irvine (1849–1921)." *Anglican and Episcopal History* 83, no. 1 (2014): 42–66.

Herbel, D. Oliver. *Turning to Tradition: Converts and the Making of an American Orthodox Church*. New York: Oxford University Press, 2013.

Himka, John-Paul. *Religion and Nationality in Western Ukraine: The Greek Catholic Church and the Ruthenian National Movement in Galicia, 1867–1900*. Montreal: McGill-Queen's University Press, 1999.

Hoke, Stuart H. "A Generally Obscure Calling: A Character Sketch of Isabel Florence Hapgood." *St. Vladimir's Theological Quarterly* 45, no. 1 (2001): 55–93.

Hopwood, Derek. *The Russian Presence in Syria and Palestine, 1843–1914: Church and Politics in the Near East*. Oxford: Clarendon Press, 1969.

Husband, William B. *'Godless Communists': Atheism and Society in Soviet Russia, 1917–1932*. DeKalb: Northern Illinois University Press, 2000.

Iakushev, M. I. "Pervyi patriarkh-arab na antiokhiiskom prestole." *Vostochnyi arkhiv* No. 14–15 (2006): 99–106.

Iferov, R. G. *Sviashchennyi Sobor Pravoslavnoi Rossiiskoi Tserkvi 1917–1918 gg. i Vseukrainskii Sobor 1918 g. ob ukrainskom tserkovnom voprose*. Moscow: Spasskoe delo, 2019.

Instruktsiia S.-Peterburgskoi Dukhovnoi Akademii dlia studentov, zhivushchik v zdanii Akademii. St. Petersburg, 1894.

Issa, Andre. *Our Father Among the Saints Raphael, Bishop of Brooklyn*. Englewood, NJ: Antakya Press, 2000.

Iubileinyi sbornik v pamiat' 150-letiia Russkoi pravoslavnoi tserkvi na severnoi Amerike, 2 volumes. New York: Izd. Iubileinoi komissii, 1944–1945.

Ivanov, S. N. "Khronologiia obnovlencheskogo 'pereverota' v Russkoi Tserkvi po novym arkhivnym dokumentam." *Vestnik PSTGU* 58 (2014): 24–60.

Ivanov, S. N. "O prichinakh peredachi sv. Patriarkhom Tikhonom kantseliarskikh del gruppe sviashchennkov v mae 1922 g." *Vestnik PSTGU* 40 (2011): 17–35.

Ivanov, S. N. "Pozitsiia Sviateishego Patriarkha Tikhona v voprose ob iz"iatii sviashchennykh predmetov iz khramov v 1922." *Tserkovno-istoricheskii vestnik* No. 18–19 (2011/2012): 89–135.

Ivanov, Sergii. "'Sovershenno sekretno. Khranit' konspirativno': Protokoly neizvestnoi komissii L. D. Trotskogo po raskolu Russkoi Pravoslavnoi Tserkvi (mai-oktiabr' 1922 g.)." *Vestnik PSTGU* 107 (2022): 134–66.

Ivanov, Sergii. *Sviatoi Patriarkh Tikhon i iz"iatie tserkovnykh tsennostei v 1922 godu*. Moscow: PSTGU, 2024.

Ivanova, E. V., ed. "Patriarkh Tikhon v 1920–1923 godakh: Analitcheskaia zapiska iz Guverskogo arkhiva." *Zhurnal Moskovskoi Patriarkhii* No. 11 (2007): 60–95.

Jorgenson, James. "Father Alexis Toth and the Transition of the Greek Catholic Community in Minneapolis to the Russian Orthodox Church." *St. Vladimir's Theological Quarterly* 32, no. 2 (1988): 119–37.
Kalkandjieva, Daniela *The Russian Orthodox Church, 1917–1948: From Decline to Resurrection.* London: Routledge, 2015.
Kalkandjieva, Daniela. "The Soviet Authorities and the Orthodox Churches: The Role in Promoting New Autocephalies (1917–1991)." In *Autocephaly: Coming of Age in Communion. Historical, Canonical, Liturgical Studies*, edited by Edward G. Farrugia and Željko Paša, vol. 1: 785–821. Rome: Oriental Pontifical Institute, 2023.
Kamennyi, Igor. "Patriarkh Tikhon: Vzgliad na ukrainskii tserkovnyi vopros." *Trudy Kyivskoi Dukhovnoi Akademii* No. 24 (2016): 244–56.
Kashevarov, A. N. "Arest i dopros patriarkha Tikhona v dekabre 1919 g." *Russkoe Proshloe* 8 (1998): 215–27.
Kashevarov, A. N. *Pravoslavnaia rossiiskaia tserkov' i sovetskoe gosudarstvo (1917–1922).* Moscow: Krutitskoe podvor'e, 2005.
Kazakevich, A. N., ed. *Pravoslavnaia Moskva v 1917–1921 godakh: sbornik dokumentov i materialov.* Moscow: Izd. Glavarkhiva Moskvy, 2004.
Kelly, Catriona. "The 'Bolshevik Reformation': February 1922." In *Was Revolution Inevitable? Turning Points of the Russian Revolution*, edited by Tony Brenton, 244–61. New York: Oxford University Press, 2017.
Kelly, Catriona. *Socialist Churches: Radical Secularization and the Preservation of the Past in Petrograd and Leningrad, 1918–1988.* DeKalb: Northern Illinois University Press, 2016.
Kenworthy, Scott M. *The Heart of Russia: Trinity-Sergius, Monasticism and Society After 1825.* Oxford: Oxford University Press and Washington, DC: Wilson Center Press, 2010.
Kenworthy, Scott M. "Metropolitan Leonty, Saint Tikhon, and the Establishment of America's First Orthodox Seminary." In *The Life and Work of Metropolitan Leonty*, edited by David C. Ford, 37–50. Waymart, PA: Saint Tikhon's Monastery Press, 2019.
Kenworthy, Scott M. "Monasticism in Modern Russia." In *Monasticism in Eastern Europe and the Former Soviet Republics*, edited by Ines A. Murzaku, 265–284. London: Routledge, 2015.
Kenworthy, Scott M. "Monasticism in War and Revolution." In *Russia's Home Front, Book 2: The Experience of War and Revolution*, edited by Adele Lindenmeyr, Christopher Read, and Peter Waldron, 221–249. Bloomington, IN: Slavica Publishers, 2016.
Kenworthy, Scott M. 'Rethinking the Russian Orthodox Church and the Bolshevik Revolution." *Revolutionary Russia* 31, no. 1 (2018): 1–23.
Kenworthy, Scott M. "Russian Orthodox Monasticism from 988 to 1917." In *Oxford Handbook of Christian Monasticism*, edited by Bernice Kaczynski, 478–494. Oxford: Oxford University Press, 2020.
Kenworthy, Scott M. "Russian Reformation? The Program for Religious Renovation in the Orthodox Church, 1922–1925." *Modern Greek Studies Yearbook* 16/17 (2000/2001): 89–130.
Khairulina, P. A. "Missionerskaia poezdka v Kvikhpakhskuiu i Kuskokvimskuiu missii (Aliaska) episkopa Tikhona (Bellavina)." *Vestnik Cheliabinskogo gosudarstvennogo universiteta. Istoriia* No. 17 (2005): 84–92.
Khmyrov, Dionisii. *Spornye voprosy istorii RPTsZ (1920–1945).* St. Petersburg: St. Petersburg State University, 2014.
Kinney, John M. "'The Fond du Lac Circus': The Consecration of Reginald Heber Weller." *Historical Magazine of the Protestant Episcopal Church* 38, no. 1 (1969): 3–24.
Kishkovsky, Leonid. "Archbishop Tikhon in America." *St. Vladimir's Theological Quarterly* 19 (1975): 9–31.
Kitromilides, Paschalis M. *Religion and Politics in the Orthodox World: The Ecumenical Patriarchate and the Challenges of Modernity.* London: Routledge, 2019.
Kizenko, Nadieszda. *A Prodigal Saint: Father John of Kronstadt and the Russian People.* University Park: Penn State University Press, 2000.
Kliment (Kapalin). *Pravoslavie na Aliaske: retrospektiva razvitiia v 1741–1917 gg.* Tver, 2014.

Kliment (Kapalin). *Russkaia pravoslavnaia tserkov' na Aliaske do 1917 goda*. Moscow: OLMA Media Group, 2009.
Kopylova, O. N., ed. "Vospominaniia protoiereia Nikolaia Kniazeva (1947 g.)." *Vestnik tserkovnoi istorii* no. 2 (2006): 109–30.
Kosik, O. V. *Golosa iz Rossii: Ocherki istorii sbora i peredachi za granitsu informatsii o polozhenii Tserkvi v SSSR (1920-e-nachalo 1930-kh godov)*. Moscow: PSTGU, 2013.
Kosik, O. V., ed. "Patriarshee upravlenie i OGPU (1923–1924 gg.): Vyderzhka iz pis'ma A. D. Samarina deiateliam Zarubezhnoi Tserkvi s izlozheniem sobytii tserkovnoi zhizni v Rossii." *Vestnik PSTGU* No. 37 (2010): 57–69.
Kostriukov, A. A., ed. "Novye dokumenty po istorii vzaimootnoshenii mezhdu Patriarkhom Tikhonom i Karlovatskim Sinodom." *Vestnik PSTGU* 28 (2008): 119–25.
Kostriukov, A. A. *Russkaia Zarubezhnaia Tserkov' v pervoi polovine 1920-kh godov: Organizatsiia tserkovnogo upravleniia v emigratsii*. Moscow: PSTGU, 2007.
Krapivin, M. Iu. "A. F. Filippov i 'Ispolnitel'nyi komitet po delam dukhovenstva vseia Rossii' (1919–1920)." In *Istoricheskie chteniia na Lubianke: 15 let*, 62–73. Moscow: Kuchkovo pole, 2012.
Krapivin, M. Iu. "Arkadii Antonov i nachal'nyi period formirovaniia politiki VChK v otnoshenii Pravoslavnoi Rossiiskoi Tserkvi (vesna-leto 1918 g)." *Vestnik Tserkovnoi istorii* 35–36 (2014): 304–16.
Krapivin, M. Iu. "Arkhiepiskop Varnava (Nakropin) i religioznaia politika VChK: 1918–1922 gody." *Vestnik Tserkovnoi istorii* 23/24 (2011): 113–56.
Krapivin, M. Iu. "Deiatel'nost S. M. Trufanova (byvshego ieromonakha Iliodora) v Sovetskoi Rossii (1918–1922 gg.) v sviazi s formirovaniem gosudarstvennoi politiki v otnoshenii pravoslavnoi Tserkvi." *Vestnik Tserkovnoi istorii* No. 21–22 (2011): 137–59.
Krapivin, M. Iu. "Diskussiia o sozdanii 'sovetskii' Pravoslavnoi tserkvi v rukovodiashchikh krugakh bol'shevistskoi partii i sovetskoe gosudarstvo (1919–1921 gg)." *Modern History of Russia* 2 (2016): 277–98.
Krapivin, M. Iu. "Glavmuzei i komissiia L. D. Trotskogo 'Po uchetu i sosredotocheniiu tsennostei' (noiabr' 1921 g.–oktiabr' 1922 g.)." *Voprosy muzeologii* 1, no. 13 (2016): 11–33.
Krapivin, M. Iu. "'Neobkhodimo sdelat' vse, chtoby unizit' tserkov' v glazakh naroda': Dokladnaia zapiska M. I. Latsisa, 1920 g." *Istoricheskii arkhiv* No. 2 (2011): 91–102.
Krapivin, M. Iu. *Nepridumannaia tserkovnaia istoriia: Vlast' i tserkov' v Sovetskoi Rossii (oktiabr' 1917-go-konets 1930-kh godov)*. Volgograd: Peremena, 1997.
Krapivin, M. Iu. "'S religiei nado schitat'sia kak s faktom . . .': iz stenogrammy vystupleniia zaveduiushchego Sekretno-operativnym otdelom VChK M. I. Latsisa na 4-i Vserossiiskoi konferentsii chrezvychainykh komissii (3 fevralia 1920 g)." *Noveishaia istoriia Rossii* 8, no. 4 (2018): 1051–57.
Krapivin, M. Iu. "Vsevolod Putiata v kontekste religioznoi politiki organov VChK (1918–1919 gg)." *Vestnik Tserkovnoi Istorii* 29–30 (2013): 247–311.
Kravetskii, A. G. "K istorii Dekreta ob otdelenii Tserkvi ot gosudarstva." In *1917-i: Tserkov' i sud'by Rossii: K 90-letiiu Pomestnogo Sobora i izbraniia Patriarkha Tikhona*, edited by Vladimir Vorob'ev, 134–40. Moscow: PSTGU, 2008.
Kravetskii, Aleksandr and Scott Kenworthy, "The Council of the Orthodox Church in Russia, 1917–1918." In *Wiley-Blackwell Companion to Conciliarity in Modern Orthodox Christianity*, ed. Irina Paert, Alison Kolosova, and Andrei Shishkov, 141–54. Oxford: Wiley, 2026.
Krivonos, Feodor. *U Boga mertvykh net: Neizvestnye strainitsy iz istorii Minskoi eparkhii (1917–1939 gody)*. Minsk: MFTsP, 2007.
Krivonosov, Alexander. "Where East Meets West: A Landscape of Familiar Strangers—Missionary Alaska, 1794–1898." PhD diss., Pennsylvania State University, 2008.
Krivosheeva, N. A., ed. *Delo velikogo stroitel'stva tserkovnogo: Vospominaniia chlenov Sviashchennogo Sobora Pravoslavnoi Rossiiskoi Tserkvi 1917–1918 godov*. Moscow: PSTGU, 2009.
Krivosheeva, N. A. "'Kto dushu svoiu polozhit za drugi svoiia': Keleinik sviatogo Patriarkha Tikhona Iakov Anisimovich Polozov (23 oktiabria 1879 g.–9 dekabria 1924 g.)." *Vestnik PSTGU* 22 (2007): 52–73.

Krivosheeva, N. A. "Kto zhe iavliaetsia rasprostranitelem 'lozhnykh slukhov'?" *Uchenye zapiski* No. 6 (2000): 112-19.
Krivosheeva, N. A. "Novye materialy iz arkhiva M. E. Gubonina." *Vestnik PSTGU* No. 19 (2006): 121-24.
Krivosheeva, N. A. "O prebyvanii v Troitse-Sergievoi Lavre narechennogo Patriarkha Tikhona." *Vestnik PSTGU* 42 (2011): 99-110.
Krivosheeva, N. A., ed. *"Prispelo vremia podviga . . .":* Dokumenty sviashchennogo sobora Pravoslavnoi Rossiiskoi tserkvi 1917-1918 gg. o nachale gonenii na tserkov'. Moscow: PSTGU, 2012.
Krivosheeva, N. A. "Sviatitel' Tikhon—mitropolit Moskovskii i Kolomenskii. Khrolonologiia sobytii (21 iunia–26 noiabria 1917 goda)." *Kadashevskie chteniia* No. 11 (2012): 136-153.
Krivosheeva, N. A. "'Vsetselo prisposoblenie k dukhu vremeni': Pervyi sovetskii razvedchik A. F. Filippov." *Vestnik PSTGU* 32 (2009): 70-98.
Krivosheeva, N. A., ed. "Zabota o bratskom poseshchenii arestovannykh." *Vestnik PSTGU* 40 (2011): 72-79.
Krivova, N. A. "The Events in Shuia: A Turning Point in the Assault on the Church." *Russian Studies in History* 46, no. 2 (Fall 2007): 8-38.
Krivova, N. A. *Vlast' i tserkov' v 1922-1925 gg.* Moscow: AIRO-XX, 1997.
Kukushkin, V. E. "U istokov kanadskogo pravoslaviia: ukrainskaia immigratsiia kontsa XIX-nachala XX v. i vozniknovenie pervykh pravoslavnykh prikhodov v zapadnoi Kanade." *St. Petersburg Historical Journal* No. 1 (2016): 83-96.
Kurliandskii, I. A. "'Aleksei Maksimovich! Esli by vy tol'ko videli ves' etot uzhas!' (A. M. Gork'kii i golod 1932-1933 gg.)." *Russkii istoricheskii sbornik* Vyp II. Moscow: Evrolints-Kimmeriiskii tsentr, 2010.
Kurliandskii, I. A. "Stalin: religioznyi vopros v politike Bol'shevistskoi vlasti (1917-1923 gg.)." *Vestnik PSTGU* 48 (2012): 72-84.
Kurliandskii, I. A. *Stalin, Vlast', Religiia.* Moscow: Kuchkovo Pole, 2011.
Kuskova, E. D. "Mesiats 'soglashatel'stva'." *Volia Rossii* No. 4 (Prague, 1928): 43-61.
Lasaeva, O. V. "K istorii vozniknoveniia russkogo pravoslavnogo prikhoda i vozvedeniia Sviato-Troitskogo sobora v g. Chikago pri svt. Tikhone (Bellavine)." *Vestnik PSTGU* 44 (2011): 41-49.
Lavrov, V. M., V. V. Lobanov, I. V. Lobanova, and A. V. Mazyrin. *Ierarkhiia russkoi pravoslavnoi tserkvi, patriarshestvo i gosudarstvo v revoliutsionnuiu epokhu.* Moscow: Russkaia Panorama, 2008.
Lazareva, N. Iu, ed. "Perepiska sviatitelia Tikhona, patriarkha vserosiiskogo i mitropolita Evlogiia (Georgievskogo) 1921-1922 gg." *Uchenye zapiski* No. 6 (2000): 93-111.
Ledkovsky, Marina. "A Linguistic Bridge to Orthodox: In Memoriam Isabel Florence Hapgood." https://anglicanhistory.org/women/hapgood/ledkovsky.pdf.
Lemeshevskii, Maniul. *Die Russischen Orthodoxen Bischöfe von 1893-1965.* Six vols. Erlangen: Lehrstuhl für Geschichte und Theologie des Christlichen Ostens, 1989.
Lenin, Vladimir Il'ich, Richard Pipes, David Brandenberger, and Catherine A. Fitzpatrick. *The Unknown Lenin: From the Secret Archive.* New Haven, CT: Yale University Press, 1996.
Leont'eva, T. G. "Vlast', pravoslavnaia tserkov', obshchestvo v gody Grazhdanskoi voiny." In *Rossiia v gody Grazhdanskoi voiny, 1917-1922 gg.: ocherki istorii i istoriografii,* 183-211. Moscow: Tsentr gumanitarnykh initsiativ, 2018.
Levitin-Krasnov, A., and V. Shavrov. *Ocherki po istorii russkoi tserkovnoi smuty.* Moscow: Krutitskoe podvor'e, 1996.
Liberovsky, Alexis. "The Archival Legacy of Saint Tikhon in North America." *St Tikhon's Theological Journal* 4 (2008-2009): 18-40.
Lobanov, V. V. "Konchina Patriarkha Tikhona: fakty i mneniia." *Tserkov' v istorii Rossii* 8 (2009): 199-212.
Lobanov, V. V. *"Obnovlencheskii" raskol v Russkoi Pravoslavnoi Tserkvi (1922-1946 gg.).* SPb: Petroglif, 2019.

Lobanov, V. V. "Patriarkh Tikhon i bor'ba patriarshei Tserkvi s obnovlencheskim raskolom (1923–1925 gg.)." *Tserkov' v istorii Rossii* 12 (2021): 19–58.
Lobanov, V. V. *Patriarkh Tikhon i Sovetskaia vlast' (1917–1925 gg.)* Moscow: Russkaia Panorama, 2008.
Lobanov, V. V. "'Podtverdit' k neuklonnomu ispolneniiu . . .': Protokoly zasedanii Biuro Tsentral'noi Komissii po iz"iatiiu tserkovnykh tsennostei." *Tserkov' v istorii Rossii* 6 (2005): 208–17.
Lobanov, V. V., ed. *Protokoly Komissii po provedeniiu otdelenie tserkvi ot gosudarstva pri TsK RKP(b)-VKP(b) (Antireligioznaia komissii): 1922–1929 gg.* Moscow: PSTGU, 2014.
Lopukhin, A.P. *Nastoiashchee i budushche Pravoslaviia v S. Amerike.* St. Petersburg, 1897.
Luukkanen, Arto. *The Party of Unbelief: The Religious Policy of the Bolshevik Party, 1917–1929.* Helsinki: SHS, 1994.
MacKay, John. "Built on a Lie: Propaganda, Pedagogy, and the Origins of the Kuleshov Effect." In *The Oxford Handbook of Propaganda Studies*, edited by Jonathan Auerbach and Russ Castronovo. Oxford: Oxford University Press, 2013.
Maffly-Kipp, Laurie F. "Eastward Ho! American Religion from the Perspective of the Pacific Rim." In *Retelling U.S. Religious History*, edited by Thomas A. Tweed, 127–148. Berkely: University of California Press, 1997.
Marić, Ružica, and Fr. Damascene Christenson. *To the Glory of God the Father: Lives of Saints Mardarije of Chicago and Libertyville and Sebastian of San Francisco and Jackson.* Los Angeles: Sebastian Press, 2015.
Markovchin, Vladimir, ed. "'Politicheskikh razgovorov ne zamecheno'. Delo 'Donskoi monastyr'": raporty agentov naruzhnogo nabliudeniia." *Istochnik* 5 (1996): 58–68.
Mazyrin, A. V., and A. A. Kostriukov, *Iz istorii vzaimootnoshenii Russkoi i Konstantinopol'skoi Tserkvi v XX veke.* Moscow: PSTGU, 2017.
Mazyrin, A. V. "K voprosu o prichinakh podderzhki sviatogo patriarkha Tikhona (Bellavina) Patriarkhom Meletiiem (Metaksakisom) vesnoi 1923 g." *Khristianskoe chtenie* 3 (2023): 327–42.
Mazyrin, A. V., A. Goncharov, and I. V. Uspenskii, eds. *Iz"iatie tserkovnykh tsennostei v Moskve v 1922 godu: Sbornik dokumentov iz fonda Revvoensoveta Respubliki.* Moscow: PSTGU, 2006.
Mazyrin, A. V. "K istorii obnovlencheskogo raskola v Zakavkaz'e i neudachnykh proektov primireniia Russkoi i Gruzinskoi pravoslavnykh tserkvei (1922–1923 gg.)." *Vestnik Ekaterinburgskoi dukhovnoi seminarii* 46 (2024): 121–57.
Mazyrin, A. V. "Na kakoi kompromiss s obnovlentsami soglashalsia Patriarkh Tikhon v 1923–1924 gg., chast' 1: Peregovory so 'Sviashchennym Sinodom' Evdokima (Meshcherskogo) 1923 g." *Vestnik Ekaterinburgskoi dukhovnoi seminarii* No. 36 (2021): 379–98.
Mazyrin, A. V. "Na kakoi kompromiss s obnovlentsami soglashalsia Patriarkh Tikhon v 1923–1924 gg., chast' 2: Peregovory s 'Zhivoi Tserkov'iu' Vladimira Krasnitskogo, 1924 g." *Vestnik Ekaterinburgskoi dukhovnoi seminarii* No. 37 (2022): 161–98.
McCullagh, Francis. *The Bolshevik Persecution of Christianity.* New York: E. P. Dutton and Company, 1924.
McMillan, James F. "Catholic Christianity in France from the Restoration to the Separation of Church and State, 1815–1905." In *The Cambridge History of Christianity: Volume 8. World Christianities c.1815–c.1914*, edited by Sheridan Gilley and Brian Stanley, 175–98. Cambridge: Cambridge University Press, 2006.
Medovarov, M. V. *Natsional-monarkhist, natsional-demokrat, natsional-Bol'shevik: Aleksei Frolovich Filippov.* St. Petersburg: Vladimir Dal', 2021.
Medvedeva, N. M. "Soslovnaia struktura naseleniia gorodov Pskovskoi gubernii vo vtoroi polovine XIX v." *Pskov* 25 (2006): 162–70.
Meijer, Jan M., ed. *The Trotsky Papers 1917–1922.* 2 vols. The Hague: Mouton, 1971.
Mel'kov, A. S. "Vliianie russkogo Pravoslaviia na politiku rusifikatsii Kholmshchiny v XIX–XX vv." *Studia Humanitatis* No. 1 (2016). DOI: 10.24411/2308-8079-2016-00003.

Men'kova, I. G., ed. *Radi mira tserkovnogo: Zhiznennyi put' i arkhipastyrskoe sluzhenie Sviatitelia Agafangela, Mitropolita Iaroslavskogo, ispovednika*. 2 vols. Moscow: PSTGU, 2006.
Meyendorff, John. "The Patriarch of Antioch and North America in 1904." *St. Vladimir's Theological Quarterly* 31 (1989): 80–86.
Miller, Charles. *Toward a Fuller Vision: Orthodoxy and Anglican Experience*. Wilton: Morehouse Barlow, 1984.
Miller, Matthew Lee, ed. *John R. Mott, the American YMCA, and Revolutionary Russia*. Bloomington, IN: Slavica, 2020.
Mitrofan (Shkurin). "'Antireligioznye mudretsy' protiv Patriarkha Tikhona." *Al'fa i Omega* no. 45 (2006): 115–137, No. 46 (2006): 88–95.
Morison, John D. "The Church Schools and Seminaries in the Russian Revolution of 1905–06." In *Church, Nation and State in Russia and Ukraine*, edited by Geoffrey A. Hosking, 193–209. Alberta: Canadian Institute of Ukrainian Studies Press, 1990.
Mramornov, A. I., ed. *Dokumenty Sviashchennogo Sobora Pravoslavnoi Rossiiskoi Tserkvi 1917–1918 gg.*, 20 vols. Moscow: Izdatel'stvo Novospasskogo monastyria, 2012–.
Murray, Jesse D. "Together and Apart: The Russian Orthodox Church, the Russian Empire, and Orthodox Missionaries in Alaska, 1794–1917." *Russian History* 40 (2013): 91–110.
Musaev, V. I. "Pravoslavnaia Tserkov' v nezavisimoi Finliandii (1918–1930 gg.)." *Vestnik Tserkovnoi Istorii* No. 6 (2007): 194–212.
Namee, Matthew. "The Myth of Past Unity and the Origins of Jurisdictional Pluralism in American Orthodoxy." *Journal of American Orthodox Church History* 1 (2011): 2–34.
Nepospekhov, Oleg. "Sviatitel' Tikhon (Bellavin) na Rostovskoi zemle." In *Rostov Velikii: imena, sobytiia, sud'by*, edited by M. Rubtsov, 76–102. Moscow: Palomnik, 2012.
Nikon (Rklitskii). *Mitropolit Antonii (Khrapovitskii) i ego Vremia 1863–1936*. Nizhnii Novgorod: Izdanie Bratstva vo imia sviatogo kniazia Aleksandra Nevskogo, 2003–.
Novikov, Nikolai. *Kolybel' opal'nogo patriarkha*. 2nd ed. Velikie Luki: Izd. Sergeia Markelova, 2010.
Ochkanov, Iaroslav. "Vzaimootnosheniia mezhdu russkoi pravosnavkoi i anglikanskoi tserkvami v pervoe desliatiletie XX v." *Bogoslovskii vestnik* No. 41 (2021): 88–100.
Odintsov, M. I. *Russkie patriarkhi XX veka: Sud'by otechestva i tserkvi na stranitsakh arkhivnykh dokumentov*. Moscow: RAGS, 1999.
Okunev, P. N. *Dnevnik Moskvicha*, 2 volumes. Moscow: Voennoe izdatel'stvo, 1997.
Oleksa, Michael. *Orthodox Alaska: A Theology of Mission*. Crestwood, NY: St. Vladimir's Seminary Press, 1998.
Paert, Irina. "Conciliarity in the Borderlands: The Riga Orthodox Council (Sobor) of 1905 and the Church Reform Movement in Imperial Russia." *Journal of Ecclesiastical History* 73, no. 3 (2022).
Paert, Irina. "A Family Affair? Post-Imperial Estonian Orthodoxy and Its Relationship with the Russian Mother Church, 1917–1923." *Canadian Slavonic Papers* 62 (2020): 1–26.
Paert, Irina, and James White. "Reimagining the Diocese: Administrative, Sacred, and Imperial Space in the Russian Empire." *Canadian Slavonic Papers* 62, no. 3–4 (2020): 234–44.
Patenaude, Bertrand M. *The Big Show in Bololand: The American Relief expedition to Soviet Russia in the Famine of 1921*. Palo Alto, CA: Stanford University Press, 2002.
Pechatnov, V. V., and V. O. Pechatnov. "Amerikanskoe sluzhenie sviashchennomuchenika Aleksandra Khotovitskogo." *Vestnik Viatskogo gosudarstvennogo universiteta* 3, no. 145 (2022): 56–70.
Pechatnov, V. O., and V. V. Pechatnov. "'Glavnyi russkii khram Ameriki': iz istorii Sviato-Nikolaevskogo kafedral'nogo sobora v N'iu-Iorke." *Istoriia* No. 11 (109) (2021). https://history.jes.su/s207987840017595-3-1/. DOI: 10.18254/S207987840017595-3.
Pechatnov, V. V., and V. O. Pechatnov. "Russkii episkop v Amerike 'pozolochennogo veka.'" *Vestnik MGIMO-Universiteta* 14, no. 1 (2021): 7–30.
Pechatnov, V. V., and V. O. Pechatnov. "Sviashchennomuchenik Ioann Kochurov: gody sluzheniia v Amerike." *Izvestiia Irkutskogo gosudarstvennogo universiteta* 44 (2023): 62–79.

Peris, Daniel. "Commissars in Red Cassocks: Former Priests in the League of the Militant Godless." *Slavic Review* 54 (1995): 340–64.
Petrov, S. G. *Dokumenty deloproizvodstva Politbiuro TsK RKP(b) kak istochnik po istorii Russkoi tserkvi (1921–1925)*. Moscow: Rosspen, 2004.
Petrov, S. G. "Patriarch Tikhon and the Preservation of the Old Calendar Style in the Russian Orthodox Church." *Herald of the Russian Academy of Sciences* 93 (Suppl. 1) (2023): 66–74.
Petrov, S. G. *Russkaia pravoslavnaia tserkov' vremeni Patriarkha Tikhona (istochnikovedcheskoe issledovanie)*. Novosibirsk: Russian Academy of Sciences, 2013.
Petrov, S. G. "Sovetskaia tsenzura i vozzvaniia patriarkha Tikhona 1923 g." *Gumanitarnye nauki v Sibirii* No. 2 (2008): 24–27.
Petrov, S. G. "Sviateishii Patriarkh Tikhon i sokhranenie starogo kalendarnogo stilia v tserkovnom letoschislenii." *Bogoslovskii sbornik Novosibirskoi pravoslavnoi dukhovnoi seminarii* No. 12 (2018): 61–77
Petrova, V. V. "K voprosu o 'Danilovskoi oppozitsii' Patriarkhu Tikhonu." *Ezhegodnaia bogoslovskaia konferentsiia Pravoslavnogo Sviato-Tikhonovskogo gumanitarnogo universiteta* 25 (2015): 149–54.
Piccin, Matteo. *Nazionalismi di frontiera. Russi, polacchi e ucraini a Cholm (1830–1918)*. Firenze: Firenze University Press, 2025.
Pipes, Richard. *Russia Under the Bolshevik Regime*. New York: A. A. Knopf, 1994.
Pisiotis, Argyrios K. "Between State and Estate: The Political Motivations of the Russian Orthodox Episcopate in the Crisis of Tsarist Monarchy, 1905–1917." *Canadian-American Slavic Studies* 46 (2012): 335–63.
Pisiotis, Argyrios K. "Russian Orthodox Clergy and Populism in the Twilight of the Romanovs." In *Metropolitan Antonii (Khrapovitskii): Archpastor of the Russian Diaspora*, edited by Vladimir Tsurikov, 143–94. Jordanville, NY: Foundation of Russian History, 2014.
Pisiotis, Argyrios K. "Russian Orthodoxy and the Politics of National Identity in Early Twentieth Century." *Balkan Studies* 42, no. 2 (2001): 225–43.
Plokhii, S. M., P.S. Sokhran, L.V. Iakovleva, ed. *Pershyi Vseukraïns'kyi Pravoslavnyi Tserkovnyi Sobor UAPTs 14–30 zhovtnia 1921 r.: Dokumenty i materialy*. Kyiv: NAN Ukraïny, 1999.
Pokrovsky, M., ed. *St. Nicholas Cathedral of New York: History and Legacy*. New York: St. Nicholas Cathedral Study Group, 1968.
Pol'skii, M. *Novye mucheniki Rossiiskie*, 2 vols. Jordanville: Holy Trinity Monastery, 1949–1957.
Polunov, Alexander. "Church, Regime, and Society in Russia (1880–1895)." *Russian Studies in History* 39, no. 4 (2001): 33–53.
Poole, Randall A., and Paul W. Werth, eds. *Religious Freedom in Modern Russia*. Pittsburgh: University of Pittsburgh Press, 2018.
Popov, A.V., ed. *Amerikanskii period zhizni i deiatel'nosti sviatitelia Tikhona Moskovskogo 1898–1907 gg.* St Petersburg: Satis, 2013.
Popov, A.V., ed. *Amerikanskii period zhizni i deiatel'nosti sviatitelia Tikhona Moskovskogo: Dokumenty*. St. Petersburg: Satis, 2014.
Popov, A.V., ed. *Amerikanskii period zhizni i deiatel'nosti sviatitelia Tikhona Moskovskogo: Propovedi, stat'i*. St Petersburg: Satis, 2011.
Popov, A. V., ed. *Pis'ma sviatitelia Tikhona: Amerikanskii period zhizni i deiatel'nosti sviatitelia Tikhona Moskovskogo*. St. Petersburg: Satis, 2010.
Popov, Iu. G. *Toropets patriarkha Tikhona*. Toropets: Izd. Uchebnogo informatsionno-komp'iuternogo tsentra, 2000.
Pospelovskii, Dmitrii. "Professor Protoierei Vasilii Vinogradov o Patriarkhe Tikhone." *Tserkovno-istoricheskii vestnik* No. 1 (1998): 6–7.
Pravye partii: Dokumenty i materialy. 2 vols. Moscow: Rosspen, 1998.
Prot'ko, T. S., ed. "Obrashchenie ('Memorial') pravitel'stva Belarusskoi Narodnoi Respubliki k Patriarkhu Tikhonu i ego otvet na eto obrashchenie." *Vestnik PSTGU* 40 (2011): 80–98.
Psarev, Andrei. "'They Have Neither Laymen nor Money': Overview of the Correspondence (1907–1911) Between Archbishop Tikhon Bellavin and Archpriest Evgenii Smirnov." *Sobornost* 37, no. 2 (2015): 16–28.

Rabinowitch, Alexander. *The Bolsheviks in Power: The First Year of Soviet Rule in Petrograd.* Bloomington: Indiana University Press, 2007.
Razmolodin, M. L. *Chernosotennoe dvizhenie v Iaroslavle i guberniiakh verkhnego povolzh'ia v 1905–1915 gg.* Iaroslavl': Aleksandr Rutman, 2001.
Read, Christopher. *War and Revolution in Russia, 1914–22: The Collapse of Tsarism and the Establishment of Soviet Power.* Houndmills, Basingstoke, Hampshire: Palgrave Macmillan, 2013.
Reeves, Thomas C. "The Anglo-Catholic Movement in Wisconsin." *The Wisconsin Magazine of History* 68, no. 3 (1985): 188–98.
Rimestad, Sebastian. *The Challenges of Modernity to the Orthodox Church in Estonia and Latvia (1917–1940).* Frankfurt am Main: Peter Lang, 2012.
Rimestad, Sebastian. "From Empire to Nation State: The Consolidation of the Relationship Between the Orthodox Church and Independent Lithuania and Latvia after the First World War." *Studia Podlaskie* 20 (2012): 211–23.
Rogoznyi, P. G. "Bol'sheviki i sviatye moshchi." *Noveishaia istoriia Rossii* 10, no. 4 (2020): 989–1004.
Rogoznyi, P. G. *Pravoslavnaia tserkov' i russkaia revoliutsiia: Ocherki istorii.* Moscow: Izdatel'stvo 'Ves' Mir', 2018.
Rogoznyi, P. G. *Tserkovnaia Revoliutsiia 1917 goda: Vysshee Dukhovenstvo Rossiiskoi Tserkvi v bor'be za vlast' v eparkhiiakh posle fevralskoi revoliutsii.* Saint Peterburg: "Liki Rossii," 2008.
Rohtmets, Priit, and Toomas Schvak. "The Establishment of the Estonian Apostolic Orthodox Church: History and Interpretations." *Usuteaduslik Ajakiri* 84 (2023): 1–35.
Roslof, Edward E. *Red Priests: Renovationism, Russian Orthodoxy, and Revolution, 1905–1946.* Bloomington: Indiana University Press, 2002.
Roslof, Edward E. "Russian Orthodoxy and the Tragic Fate of Patriarch Tikhon (Bellavin)." In *The Human Tradition in Modern Russia*, ed. William B. Husband, 77–91. Wilmington: SR Books, 2000.
Rössler, Roman. *Kirche und Revolution in Russland: Patriarch Tichon und der Sowjetstaat.* Köln: Böchlau Verlag, 1969.
Rozina, O. V. "Sof'ia Dmitrievna Samarina i soiuz pravoslavnykh zhenshchin v 1918 godu." *Vestnik Moskovskogo gosudarstvennogo oblastnogo universiteta* No. 5 (2017): 145–53.
Russin, Keith S. "Father Alexis G. Toth and the Wilkes-Barre Litigations." *St. Vladimir's Theological Quarterly* 16 (1972): 128–49.
Ryan, James. "Cleansing NEP Russia: State Violence Against the Russian Orthodox Church in 1922." *Europe-Asia Studies* 65, no. 9 (2013): 1807–26.
Ryan, James. *Lenin's Terror: The Ideological Origins of Early Soviet State Violence.* Hoboken, NJ: Taylor and Francis, 2012.
Ryan, James. "The Sacralization of Violence: Bolshevik Justifications for Violence and Terror during the Civil War." *Slavic Review* 74, no. 4 (2015): 808–31.
Ryan, James. "'They Know Not What They Do'? Bolshevik Understandings of Agency of Perpetrators, 1918–1930." *Historical Research* 90 (2017): 151–71.
Safonov, Dimitrii. *Sviatitel' Tikhon, Patriarkh Moskovskii i vseia Rossii, i ego vremia.* Moscow: Izdatel'skii dom Poznanie, 2019.
Safonov, D. V. "K voprosu o podlinnosti 'Zaveshchatel'nogo poslaniia' sv. Patriarkha Tikhona." *Bogoslovskii Vestnik* No. 4 (2004): 265–311.
Sarkisian, Aram. *Orthodoxy on the Line: Russian Orthodox Christians and Labor Migration in the Progressive Era.* New York: NYU Press, 2025.
Saul, Norman E. *The Life and Times of Charles R. Crane, 1858–1939: American Businessman, Philanthropist, and a Founder of Russian Studies in America.* Lanham, MD: Lexington Books, 2013.
Sava, Bishop of Šumadija. *History of the Serbian Orthodox Church in America and Canada, 1891–1941.* Translated by Karin Pieck-Radovanovic. Kragujevac: Kalenić, 1998.

Scarborough, Daniel. *Russia's Social Gospel: The Orthodox Pastoral Movement in Famine, War, and Revolution.* Madison: University of Wisconsin Press, 2022.
Schimmelpenninck van der Oye, David. *Toward the Rising Sun: Russian Ideologies of Empire and the Path to War with Japan.* DeKalb: Northern Illinois University Press, 2001.
Schneer, Jonathan. *The Lockhart Plot: Love, Betrayal, Assassination and Counter-Revolution in Lenin's Russia.* Oxford: Oxford University Press, 2020.
Schulz, Günther, Gisela-A. Schröder, and Timm C. Richter, *Bolschewistische Herrschaft und Orthodoxe Kirche in Russland: Das Landeskonzil 1917–1918. Quellen und Analysen.* Münster: Lit, 2005.
Schulz, Günther, A. G. Kravetskii, and A. A. Pletneva, eds. *Sviashchennyi Sobor Pravoslavnoi Rossiiskoi tserkvi 1917–1918 gg.: Obzor deianii,* 3 vols. Moscow: Krutitskoe podvor'e, 2000–2002.
Sedova, Ia. A. *Iliodor: Misticheskii drug Rasputina.* Moscow: Rodina, 2022.
Serafim (Nikolin). "Diskussia ob otnoshenii sviatogo patriarkha Tikhona k sovetskoi vlasti v sovremennoi otechestvennoi istoriografii v 2000-2018 gg.." *Khristianskoe chtenie* No. 3 (2022): 305–13.
Serafim (Nikolin). "Sviatitel' Tikhon, Patriarkh Vserosiiskii, i ego otnoshenie k gosudarstvennoi vlasti 1917–1918 gg.." *Vestnik Omskoi Pravoslavnoi dukhovnoi seminarii* No. 1 (2017): 46–59.
Serafim (Nikolin). "Zhizn' i deiatel'nost' sviatogo Patriarkha Tikhona: arkheograficheskii aspekt." *Elektronnyi zhurnal studentov i aspirantov bogoslovskogo fakul'teta PSTGU.* https://pstgu.ru/upload/iblock/241/2413af79770d43c3ba03575197599a27.pdf.
Serafim (Nikolin). "Zhizn' i deiatel'nost' sviatogo Patriarkha Tikhona v otechestvennoi istoriografii: imperatorskii period." *Khristianskoe chtenie* No. 4 (2020): 247–59.
Sergeev, Evgeny. *The Bolsheviks and Britain during the Russian Revolution and Civil War, 1917–1924.* London: Bloomsbury Academic, 2022.
Service, Robert. *Blood on the Snow: The Russian Revolution 1914–1924.* New York: Picador, 2023.
Sevostianov, G. N. et al., eds. *"Sovershenno skekretno": Lubianka-Stalinu o polozhenii v strane (1922–1934 gg.).* 10 vols. Moscow: Institut Rossiyskoy Istorii Rossiyskoy Akademii Nauk, 2001.
Shabanova, T. V. "Deiatel'nost' Arkhimandrita Tikhona na postu rektora Kholmskoi Dukhovnoi Seminarii po materialam Kholmsko-Varshavskogo eparkhial'nogo vestnika 1892–1897 gg." *Izvestiia Tomskogo politekhnicheskogo universiteta* No. 6 (2012): 167–72.
Shabanova, T. V. "Kholmskii period zhizni i deiatel'nosti Patriarkha Tikhona (Bellavina), 1892–1898 gg." *Vestnik Voennogo universiteta* No. 26 (2011): 132–36.
Sharkovskii, M. V. "Aleksandro-Nevskaia Lavra v god revoliutsionnykh potriasenii (1917–1918)." *Khristianskoe chtenie* 1 (2010): 6–33.
Shavel'skii, Georgii. *Vospominaniia poslednego protopresvitera russkoi armii i flota.* Moscow: Krutitskoto podvor'e, 2010.
Shchapov, Ia. N., and O. Iu. Vasil'eva, eds. *Russkaia pravoslavnaia tserkov' i kommunisticheskoe gosudarstvo, 1917–1940: Dokumenty i fotomaterialy.* Moscow: Izd. Bibleisko-Bogoslovskogo Instituta sv. Apostola Andreia, 1996.
Shcheglov, G. E. "Avtonomiia Belarusskoi Pravoslavnoi Tserkvi 1922 g.." *Vestnik PSTGU* 40 (2011): 99–116.
Shchelkachev, A. V., and I. E. Mel'nikova. "Vosstanovlenie avtokefal'nogo statusa Gruzinskoi Pravoslavnoi Tserkvi v XX v.." *XXX Ezhegodnaia bogoslovskaia konferentsiia PSTGU* (2020): 51–57.
Shchukin, V. D. *Istoricheskii ocherk Toropetskogo dukhovnogo uchilishcha.* Saint Petersburg, 1899.
Shevchenko, T. I. "K voprosu o iurisdiktsii Finliandskoi Pravoslavnoi Tserkvi." *Vestnik PSTGU* 26 (2008): 42–69.
Shevchenko, T. I. *Valaamskii monastyr' i stanovlenie Finliandskoi Pravoslavnoi Tserkvi (1917–1957).* Moscow: PSTGU, 2013.
Shevzov, Vera. *Russian Orthodoxy on the Eve of Revolution.* Oxford: Oxford University Press, 2004.

Shevzov, Vera. "The Orthodox Church and Religion in Revolutionary Russia." In *The Oxford Handbook of Russian Religious Thought*, ed. C. Emerson et al., 38–59. Oxford: Oxford University Press, 2020.

Shipov, Ia. *Tikhonovskaia tserkov' i Vrangel'*. Moscow, 1923.

Sidiakova, Iu. L., ed. *Istoriia v pis'makh: iz arkhiva sviashchennomuchenika arkhiepiskopa Rizhskogo Ioanna (Pommera)*, 2 vols. Tver': Bulat, 2015.

Silano, Francesca. *The Battle for Russia's Souls: Patriarch Tikhon, the Russian Orthodox Church, and the Soviet State*. Ithaca, NY: Cornell University Press, forthcoming.

Silano, Francesca. "'A Dishonor to You and to the Church': Patriarch Tikhon, Pogroms, and the Russian Revolution, 1917–19." *Kritika* 23, no. 1 (2022): 5–27.

Silano, Francesca. "Canon Law in the Bolshevik Courtroom: The Russian Revolution as an Orthodox Legal Revolution," in *Religion in the Russian Revolution*, ed. A. Agadjanian et al. Bloomington: Indiana University Press, forthcoming.

Silano, Francesca. "'I Am a Sincere Believer': Rethinking Religiosity and Identity in the Early Soviet Union," *Slavic Review* 82 (2023): 714–36.

Silano, Francesca. "'In the Language of the Patriarch': Patriarch Tikhon, the Russian Orthodox Church, and the Soviet State (1865–1925)." PhD diss., University of Toronto, 2017.

Silano, Francesca. "(Re)Constructing an Orthodox 'Scenario of Power': The Restoration of the Russian Orthodox Patriarchate in Revolutionary Russian (1917–1918)." *Revolutionary Russia* 32 (2019): 5–30.

Simon, Konstantin. "Alexis Toth and the Beginnings of the Orthodox Movement Among the Ruthenians in America (1891)." *Orientalia Christiana Periodica* 54 (1988): 387–428.

Skinner, Barbara. *The Western Front of the Eastern Church: Uniate and Orthodox Conflict in Eighteenth-Century Poland, Ukraine, Belarus, and Russia*. DeKalb: Northern Illinois University Press, 2009.

Slesarev, A. V. "Protivodeistvie arkhimandrita Tikhona (Sharapova) vvedeniiu novogo stilia i provozglasheniiu avtokefalii Pravoslavnoi Tserkvi v Pol'she (1922–1924 gg.)." *KhRONOS Tserkovno-istoricheskii al'manakh* No. 2 (2015): 138–84.

Slezkine, Yuri. *The House of Government: A Saga of the Russian Revolution*. Princeton, NJ: Princeton University Press, 2017.

Smele, Jonathan. *The "Russian" Civil Wars, 1916–1926: Ten Years That Shook the World*. New York: Oxford University Press, 2015.

Smith, Douglas. *Rasputin: Faith, Power, and the Twilight of the Romanovs*. New York: Picador, 2017.

Smith, Douglas. *The Russian Job: The Forgotten Story of how America Saved the Soviet Union from Ruin*. New York: Farrar, Straus and Giroux, 2019.

Smith, S. A. "Bones of Contention: Bolsheviks and the Struggle Against Relics, 1918–1930." *Past and Present* 204 (2009): 155–94.

Smith, S. A. *Russia in Revolution: An Empire in Crisis, 1890 to 1928*. 1st ed. Oxford: Oxford University Press, 2017.

Smith, Scott B. *Captives of Revolution: The Socialist Revolutionaries and the Bolshevik Dictatorship, 1918–1923*. Pittsburgh: University of Pittsburgh Press, 2011.

Smolitsch, K. *Istoriia russkoi tserkvi, 1700–1917*. 2 vols. Moscow: Izd-vo Spaso-Preobrazhenskogo Valamskogo monastyria, 1996.

Smolkin, Victoria. *A Sacred Space Is Never Empty: A History of Soviet Atheism*. Princeton, NJ: Princeton University Press, 2018.

Snyder, Timothy. *The Reconstruction of Nations: Poland, Ukraine, Lithuania, Belarus, 1569–1999*. New Haven, CT: Yale University Press, 2003.

Sokolov, A.V. "Deputatsiia Pomestnogo Sobora v Moskovskom voenno-revoliutsionnom komitete 2 noiabria 1917 goda." In *Revoliutsiia 1917 goda v Rossii: novye podhody i vzgliady*, edited by A.B. Nikolaev, 172–86. St. Petersburg: Herzen University, 2014.

Soldatova, N. V. *Otrazhenie: Istoriia pravoslaviia v Amerike v istorii sviato-Tikhonovskoi obiteli*. Moscow: Otdel religioznogo obrazovaniia i katekhizatsii Russkoi Pravoslavnoi tserkvi, 2006.

Soliakova, I. N. "Novye dokumenty o poslanii Sviateishego Patriarkha Tikhona ot 25 sentiabria (8 oktiabria) 1919 goda." *Vestnik PSTGU* 19 (2006): 161–68.

Staliunas, Darius. *Making Russians: Meaning and Practice of Russification in Lithuania and Belarus After 1863*. Amsterdam: Rodopi, 2007.

Starodub, Andrii. "Perehovori mizh Pol'skym diplomatychnym predstavnytstvom u Moskvi ta patriarkhom Tykhonom (Bellavinym) u spravi statusu ta iurisdiktsii pravoslavnoï tserkvy v Pol'shchi (veresen' 1921–kviten' 1922 rokiv)." *Ukraïnskii arkheografichnyy shchorichnyk* 18 (2013): 514–46.

Starodub, Andrii. "Problema statusu Rosiis'kï Pravoslavnoï tserkvy v Ukraïni v 1918–1921 rr." In *Proseminarii: Medievistyka, Istoriia Tserkvy, nauky i kul'tury*, vyp. 2, 202–12. Kyiv: Instytut ukraïns'koï arkhehrafiï ta dzhereloznavstva im M. S. Hrushevs'koho, 1998.

Starodub, Andrii. *Vseukraïns'kyi pravoslavnyi tserkovnyi Sobor 1918 roku: Ohliad dzherel*. Kyiv: Instytut ukraïns'koï arkhehrafiï ta dzhereloznavstva im M. S. Hrushevs'koho, 2010.

Starodub, Andriy. "Borot'ba za tserkovnu samostiinist' 1917–1921 rokiv ta uchast' v nii epyskopiv-ukraïntsiv." In *Naukovi zapyski: Zbirnyk prats' molodykh vchenykh ta aspirantiv*, vol. 3, 325–43. Kyiv: Instytut ukraïns'koï arkhehrafiï ta dzhereloznavstva im M. S. Hrushevs'koho, 1999.

Steinberg, Mark D. *The Russian Revolution, 1905–1921*. 1st ed. Oxford: Oxford University Press, 2017.

Steindorff, Ludwig. "Zwischen Bürokratie und Ideologie: Die Antireligiöse Kommission beim Zentralkomitee als Koordinator bolshchewistischer Religionspolitik in den zwanziger Jahren." *Kirchliche Zeitgeschichte* 12 (1999): 106–42.

Stokoe, Mark, and Leonid Kishkovsky. *Orthodox Christians in North America, 1794–1994*. Syosset, NY: Orthodox Christian Publication Center, 1995.

Strickland, John. *The Making of Holy Russia: The Orthodox Church and Russian Nationalism before the Revolution*. Jordanville, NY: Holy Trinity Publications, 2013.

Sukhorukov, A. N., ed. "Maloizvestnye stranitsy tserkovnogo sluzheniia Ekzarkha Ukrainy mitropolita Mikhaila (Ermakova) v 1922–1923 godakh." *Vestnik PSTGU* 30 (2009): 79–122.

Sukhova, N. Iu. "'Arabskaia koloniia' v Kieve: Stipendiaty imperatorskogo pravoslavnogo palestinskogo obshchestva v Kievskoi dukhovnoi akademii (1887–1918)." *Trudy Kyivskoi dukhovnoi akademii* 17 (2012): 181–92.

Sukhova, N. Iu., ed. "Neopublikovannaia stat'ia sviatitelia Tikhona (Bellavina)." *Vestnik PSTGU* 67 (2015): 97–122.

Sukhova, N. Iu. *Vysshaia dukhovnaia shkola: problemy i reform (vtoraia polovina XIX veka)*. Moscow: PSTGU, 2006.

Sushko, A. V. *Dukhovnye seminarii v poreformennoi Rossii (1861–1884 gg.)*. St. Petersburg: SPbGMA im. I. I. Mechnikova, 2010.

Swain, Geoffrey, Charlotte Alston, Michael C. Hickey, Boris Kolonitsky, and Franziska Schedewie, eds. *The Bloomsbury Handbook of the Russian Revolution*. London: Bloomsbury, 2023.

Swan, Jane Ballard. "A Biography of Patriarch Tikhon." PhD diss., University of Pennsylvania, 1955.

Swan, Jane Ballard. *The Biography of Patriarch Tikhon*. Jordanville, NY: Holy Trinity Monastery, 1964.

Swan, Jane Ballard. *Chosen for His People: A Biography of Patriarch Tikhon*. Preface by Scott Kenworthy. Jordanville, NY: Holy Trinity Seminary Press, 2015.

Swyripa, Frances. *Storied Landscapes: Ethno-Religious Identity and the Canadian Prairies*. Winnipeg: University of Manitoba Press, 2010.

Szabaciuk, Andrzej. *"Rosyjski Ulster": Kwestia Chełmska w polityce imperialnej Rosji w latach 1863–1915*. Lublin: Wydawnictwo KUL, 2013.

Szczesniak, Boleslaw. *The Russian Revolution and Religion: A Collection of Documents Concerning the Suppression of Religion by the Communists, 1917–1925*. Notre Dame, IN: University of Notre Dame Press, 1959.
Tarasar, Constance J., and John H. Erickson, eds. *Orthodox America, 1794–1976: Development of the Orthodox Church in America*. Syosset, NY: Orthodox Church in America, 1975.
Tikhon (Bellavin). "Vegeterianstvo i ego otlichie ot khristianskogo posta." *Strannik* No. 3 (1895): 487–99.
Tikhon of Moscow. *Instructions and Teachings for the American Orthodox Faithful (1898–1907)*. Edited and translated by Alex Maximov and David C. Ford. Waymart, PA: St. Tikhon's Monastery Press, 2016.
Tikhon (Zatekin). *Sviatitel' Tikhon, Patriarkh Moskovskii i vseia Rossii: Zhizn' i podvig*. Nizhnii Novgorod: Voznesenskii Pecherskii Monastery, 2018.
Titlinov, B. V. *Tserkov' vo vremia revoliutsii*. Petrograd: Byloe, 1924.
Toropov, Daniil. "Dialog Rossiiskoi Pravoslavnoi tserkvi so starokatolicheskim dvizheniem vo vtoroi polovine XIX–nachale XX veka." Kandidat diss., Obshchetserkovnaia aspirantura i doktorantura im. Sv. Kirilla i Mefodiia, 2015.
Trubachev, Andronik. *Zakrytie Troitse-Sergievoi Lavry i sud'ba moshchei prepodobnogo Sergiia Radonezhskogo v 1918–1946 gg*. Moscow: Izdatel'skii Soviet Russkoi Pravoslavnoi tserkvi, 2008.
Trubetskoi, Grigorii. "Pamiati sv. Patriarkha Tikhona." *Put'* No. 1 (September 1925): 116–20.
Trythall, Marisa Patulli. "'Russia's Misfortunate Offers Humanitarians a Splendid Opportunity': Jesuits, Communism, and the Russian Famine." *Journal of Jesuit Studies* 5 (2018): 71–96.
Valentinov, A. A. *Assault of Heaven: The Black Book Containing Official and Other Information Illustrating the Struggle Against All Religion Carried by the Communist (Soviet) Government of Russia*. London: Boswell Print. & Publishing Co., 1925.
The Vatican Secret Archives. Brussels: VdH, 2009.
Vedeneeva, A. E. "Tseremonial prebyvaniia v Rostove imperatorskoi sem'i v mae 1913 goda." In *Istoriia i kul'tura Rostovskoi zemli*, 135–46. Rostov: GMZ Rostovskii kreml', 2014.
Veidlinger, Jeffrey. *In the Midst of Civilized Europe: The Pogroms of 1918–1921 and the Onset of the Holocaust*. New York: Metropolitan Books, Henry Holt and Company, 2021.
Veniamin (Fedchenkov). *Na rubezhe dvukh epokh*. Moscow: Otchii Dom, 2016.
Veshneva, Mariia. "'Eto pamiat' o dniakh v Donskom ...' (Osen' 1922–vesna 1923)." *Iunost'* 9 (1990): 77–83.
Vinogradov, V., et al., eds. *Arkhiv VChK: Sbornik dokumentov*. Moscow: Kuchkovo Pole, 2007.
Vinogradov, V. P. *Nekotorykh vazhneishikh momentakh poslednego perioda zhizni i deiatel'nosti sv. Patriarkha Tikhona (1923–1925 gg.) po lichnym vospominaniiam*. Munich, 1959.
Viscuso, Patrick. *A Quest for Reform of the Orthodox Church: The 1923 Pan-Orthodox Congress: An Analysis and Translation of Its Acts and Decisions*. Berkeley, CA: InterOrthodox Press, 2006.
Volkov, A. "Arkhiepiskop Ilarion (Troitskii)." *Vestnik Russkogo Khristianskogo dvizheniia* No. 134 (1981): 227–34.
Vorob'ev, V. M. and S. E. Gorshkova, eds. *Patriarkh Moskovskii i vseia Rusi Sviateishii Tikhon: Izbrannye doklady Toropetskikh mezhdunarodnykh konferentsii 1997–2013 godov*. Tver': Sed'maia bukva, 2015.
Vorob'ev, Vladimir, ed. *1917-i: Tserkov' i sud'by Rossii: K 90-letiiu Pomestnogo Sobora i izbraniia Patriarkha Tikhona*. Moscow: PSTGU, 2008.
Vorob'ev, Vladimir, and L. B. Miliakova, eds. *Otdelenie tserkvi ot gosudarstva i shkoly ot tserkvi v Sovetskoi Rossii. Oktiabr' 1917–1918 g. Sbornik dokumentov*. Moscow: Izdatel'stvo PSTGU, 2016.
Vostryshev, Mikhail. *Patriarkh Tikhon*. 4th ed. Moscow: Molodaia Gvardiia, 2009.
Vulpius, Ricarda. *Nationalisierung der Religion: Russifizierungspolitik und ukrainische Nationsbildung (1860–1920)*. Wiesbaden: Harrasowitz Verlag, 2005.

Vvedenskii, A. I. *Tserkov' i gosudarstvo: ocherk vziamootnoshenii tserkvi i gosudarstva v Rossii 1918–1922 g.* Moscow: Krasnyi preletarii, 1923.

Vvedenskii, A. I. *Tserkov' patriarkha Tikhona.* Moscow, 1923.

Weeks, Theodore R. "The 'End' of the Uniate Church in Russia: The 'Vozsoedinenie' of 1875." *Jahrbücher für Geschichte Osteuropas* 44, no. 1 (1996): 28–40.

Weeks, Theodore R. *Nation and State in late Imperial Russia: Nationalism and Russification on the Western Frontier, 1863–1914.* DeKalb: Northern Illinois University Press, 1996.

Weeks, Theodore R. "Russification and the Lithuanians, 1863–1905." *Slavic Review* 60 (2001): 96–114.

Werth, Paul. W. "Georgian Autocephaly and the Ethnic Fragmentation of Orthodoxy." *Acta Slavica Iaponica* 23 (2006): 74–100.

Werth, Paul W. *The Tsar's Foreign Faiths: Toleration and the Fate of Religious Freedom in Russia.* New York: Oxford University Press, 2014.

Whisenhunt, William Benton, and Norman E. Saul, eds. *New Perspectives on Russian-American Relations.* New York: Routledge, 2016.

White, Stephen. *Britain and the Bolshevik Revolution: A Study in the Politics of Diplomacy, 1920–1924.* New York: Holmes and Meier, 1979.

Wolfe, Robert J. "Alaska's Great Sickness, 1900: An Epidemic of Measles and Influenza in a Virgin Soil Population." *Proceedings of the American Philosophical Society* 126, no. 2 (1982): 91–121.

Worobec, Christine. "Lived Religion Gendered: Representations and Practices of Russian Orthodoxy." In *Women and Gender in Russia's Great War and Revolution, 1914–1922,* edited by Adele Lindenmeyr and Melissa K. Stockdale, 105–26. Bloomington, IN: Slavic Publishers, 2022.

Wynot, Edward D. Jr., *The Polish Orthodox Church in the Twentieth Century and Beyond: Prisoner of History.* Lanham, MD: Lexington Books, 2015.

Yevseeva, T. M. *Rosiis'ka Pravoslavna Tserkva v Ukraïni 1917–1921 rr.: konflikt natsional'nykh identychnostei u pravoslavnomu poli.* Kyiv: In-t Istoriï Ukraïny NAN Ukraïny, 2005.

Young, Glennys. *Power and the Sacred in Revolutionary Russia: Religious Activists in the Village.* University Park, PA: Pennsylvania State University Press, 1997.

Žaltauskaitė, Vilma. "Interconfessional Rivalry in Lithuania after the Decree of Tolerance." In *The Tsar, the Empire, and the Nation: Dilemmas of Nationalization in Russia's Western Borderlands, 1905–1915,* ed. Darius Staliunas and Yoko Aoshima, 113–39. Budapest: CEU Press, 2021.

Zatko, James T. "The Vatican and Famine Relief in Russia." *The Slavonic and East European Review* 42 (1963): 54–63.

Zhiianova, I., ed. "'Da budem soiuzom liubve sviazuemi': Neizvestnye obrashcheniia Sviatitelia Tikhona, Patriarkha Moskovskogo i Vseia Rusi." *Bogoslovskii sbornik* No. 11 (2003): 408–25.

Index

For the benefit of digital users, indexed terms that span two pages (e.g., 52–53) may, on occasion, appear on only one of those pages.

Agafangel (Preobrazhensky), Metropolitan, 113–15, 117–19, 131
   and Renovationist takeover, 232–34, 235–37, 286–87, 309
Agranov, Iakov (Yankel Sorenson), 240, 241–42, 243
Alaska, 43–44, 47–48, 49, 65, 66, 72–73, 85–86, 87, 90–91, 99–100, 102–3
   Alaska vicariate, 68–71, 81, 83
   Tikhon's travels to, 49–54
Alexander (Nemolovsky), Bishop, 99–100, 262–63, 291
America, Church in after 1917, 290–91
American Relief Administration (ARA), 208, 211, 212, 219, 220, 236–37
Anastasy (Gribanovsky), Archbishop, 137, 139–40, 141, 144, 146, 262–63, 289–90
Anti-Religious Commission (ARK), 248, 249, 274, 286–88, 293–94, 295–97, 298, 300, 302, 303, 304, 305–7, 310–11, 318, 334
   and case against Tikhon 241, 242–43, 247–48, 252
   establishment of, 239–40
   and Tikhon's release, 255–56, 280–82, 283–84
antirelic campaign, 186–90, 194
antisemitism, 104, 107, 136, 175–76, 177
Antonin (Granovsky), Bishop, 232–33, 268–69, 298, 299–300
Antony (Khrapovitsky), 29, 32–33, 254, 259–60, 267–68, 269, 283, 305, 314
   and Church Abroad, 201–5, 288–90
   elections to patriarchate, 139–43
   at St. Petersburg Theological Academy, 24–27
Antony (Vadkovsky), 27, 29–30, 69, 92, 111
Arab Orthodox Christians, 77–82
Arseny (Chagovtsov), Hegumen, 87–90, 99–100
Arseny (Stadnitsky), Metropolitan, 114–15, 136, 150, 167, 175, 182, 278
   and patriarchate, 139–44, 146

Austro-Hungarian Empire, 8, 44–45, 54–55, 57–58, 79–80, 82, 83–84
autocephaly, 264–70, 271–79

Bakunina, Emilia, doctor, 309–13
Belarus, 270–71
Bellavin, Mikhail, 18, 34, 42–43, 67
Bonch-Bruevich, Vladimir, 154, 155, 170, 182, 183, 188–89, 325, 334
Britain, 208, 244–46, 251–53, 257
brotherhoods, 38–39, 48, 65, 77, 82, 96–97, 103, 123–24, 158–59, 161
Budkiewicz, Constantine (Butkevich), 242, 244, 245–46, 252
Bulgakov, Petr, Archpriest, 25–28, 32–34, 74, 76, 113
Bulgakov, Sergei, 129–30, 146–47

calendar and calendrical reform, 77, 249, 253–54, 262–63, 276, 280–83
   Soviets pressure to introduce, 291–94, 295, 304, 305, 307, 321–22, 326, 327–28
Canada, 57–60, 72–73
Canterbury, Archbishop of, 8–9, 207, 247, 253–54, 259, 283–84, 316, 326. *See also* Davidson, Randall
Catholic, Roman, Church, 11–12, 13, 29, 36, 37, 38–39, 156, 163–64, 283
   in America, 53–54, 55, 76, 85, 88, 90–91, 246
   and Poland-Lithuania, 116–17, 118, 120, 124
   and the Soviets, 167, 208, 242, 251–52, 253–54
Central Committee of the Communist Party, 180–81, 199, 221, 312
Central Executive Committee, 185, 209–10, 211–12, 215–16, 241, 293–94, 295, 297, 301, 327–28

Cheka (All-Russian Extraordinary
    Commission, 1917–1922), 166–67,
    169–70, 174–75, 178, 179–80, 191–94, 219,
    226–27, 270–71, 275–76, 333–34. *See also*
    GPU; OGPU
  attempts to spy on Tikhon, 199–201
  Tikhon's second arrest and interrogation,
    182–85
Chełm. *See* Kholm
Chicago, 44, 46, 48–49, 83
  building Holy Trinity Church, 60–63
Chicherin, Georgy, 207, 244–45, 250–51, 253
Christ the Savior cathedral, 131, 140, 153, 174–
    75, 210–11, 214–15 ·
Church Abroad, 193, 243–44, 262–63, 272,
    280–82, 307, 314, 315, 319–20, 321–22,
    326, 328
  as factor in GPU interrogations, 223–27
  formation and Karlovci Council, 201–5
  relations with Tikhon after release, 288–91
  Tikhon abolishes administration (May 5,
    1922), 230–31
Church reform, 75–77, 98–99, 126–27, 136,
    137, 231–32, 236, 258
church valuables, confiscation of, 213–24, 225–
    26, 227, 241
Civil War, 168, 171–77, 179, 180–81, 182, 196–
    97, 198, 245, 269
Cleveland, 48–49, 86–87, 98
Colton, Ethan, 212, 219, 226
Commissariat of Justice, 162–63, 170, 182, 186,
    190, 191–92, 195, 293–94, 297–98. *See also*
    Liquidation Department
conciliarity. *See* sobornost
Constituent Assembly, 126, 128, 134, 135,
    147–49
Council, All-Ukrainian (1918), 266–68
Council, North America (1907), 96–102
Council, Karlovci (1921), 202–3, 204–5, 223–
    24, 226, 227, 230, 240–41, 290
Council, Renovationist (1923), 247–52, 262–64,
    282–83, 292
Council of 1917-1918, 2, 126, 128, 133, 134,
    135–47, 148–49, 153–54, 156, 157–58,
    159–60, 161, 162–64, 167, 236, 291–92
Council of People's Commissars (Sovnarkom),
    147–48, 149, 162–63, 168, 170, 177, 181,
    182, 185, 297–98, 307–8
  and relics of St. Sergius, 188–90
  small Sovnarkom, 188–89, 195
Councils, Church, 271–72, 276–77, 307–8, 328
Crane, Charles, 63, 72–73
Curtiss, John Shelton, 6–7, 198–99, 243–44

Curzon, George, Marquess of Kedleston, 252,
    257, 259
Curzon Ultimatum, 250–53, 257, 283–84

Dabovich, Sebastian. *See* Sebastian (Dabovich)
Danilov Monastery, 121, 304–5
Davidson, Randall, Archbishop of Canterbury,
    208, 242, 246, 247, 253, 259, 263–64, 283–
    84. *See also* Canterbury, Archbishop of
Decree on Confiscation of Church Valuables
    (1922), 215–16, 217–18, 219–20, 225,
    228–29
Decree of Separation of Church and State
    (1918), 148–49, 155–59, 162–64, 186,
    229–30, 249
  Tikhon's appeals to, 189, 194–95, 293–94
democracy, Tikhon's attitudes toward, 74–75,
    128–29, 131–32, 133, 184
Donskoi Monastery, 190, 234, 260, 280, 284,
    285, 286, 299, 308, 309, 312, 313, 323
  Tikhon imprisoned in, 236–39, 240, 242,
    246–47, 249–50, 253
Dzerzhinsky, Felix, 191–92, 193–94, 200–1,
    222, 247, 253

Ecumenical Patriarchate of Constantinople,
    201–2, 261–64, 276–77, 289–90, 291–92,
    293, 328. *See also* Gregory VII, Patriarch;
    Meletius (Metaxakis), Patriarch
education, Tikhon and, 85–86, 107, 112–13,
    157, 159, 163, 316, 317–18
Elevfery (Bogoiavlensky), Bishop, 115–16, 273,
    275, 277–78, 279, 315–16
Episcopal Church, 90–95, 108, 212
Estonia, 264–65, 275–79
ethnic diversity among Orthodox, 77–80
Evdokim (Meshchersky), Archbishop, 235–36,
    298, 299–300, 304
Evlogy (Georgievsky), Metropolitan, 19, 32–33,
    34, 37, 39–41, 202, 203–5, 226–27, 230,
    231, 288–90
Executive Committee of Clergy Affairs
    (Ispolkomdukh), 178–81, 185

famine and famine relief, 1921–1922, 198–99,
    205–12, 213–18
famine relief, committee for, 208–12, 225
February Revolution, 1917, 125–29, 130–31,
    132–33, 136, 147–48, 184, 235, 251
Filippov, Aleksei, 178–81, 185, 190–91
Finland, 264–65, 275–79
Flavian (Gorodetsky), Metropolitan, 34, 36, 40,
    122–23, 332

INDEX 411

Tikhon writes to, 42, 48–49, 51, 54, 55–56, 58, 59, 60, 66–67, 74, 76, 106, 109–11, 113, 121, 122
freedom of conscience, 155–56, 168–69, 186, 188–89, 194–97, 249, 297, 317–18, 325

Galkin, Mikhail (Gorev), 186, 188–89, 220, 234
Georgian Orthodox Church, 264–66
Georgy (Yaroshevsky), Metropolitan, 203–4, 272–74
Gorky, Maxim, 169, 206–7, 208, 211, 215–16, 235–36
GPU (State Political Administration, 1922–1923), 220–22, 241–42, 246, 247, 287, 304, 305
 and ARK, 239–40
 informants after Tikhon's release, 280, 286
 interrogations of Tikhon (1922), 223–27, 230–31
 and Renovationists, 232–33, 234, 235, 248, 249–50, 299
 and Tikhon's incarceration (1922–1923), 236–39, 242, 246–47
 and Tikhon's release, 253, 254, 255–57, 260
Grafton, Charles Chapman, Bishop, 62, 90–95
Greek Catholics, 11–12, 43, 44–45, 54–58, 59–60, 63–64, 73, 84, 86, 90–91, 101, 116. *See also* Uniates
Gregory VII, Patriarch of Constantinople, 263–64, 274, 289–90

Hapgood, Elizabeth, 95
Hawaweeny, Raphael: *see* Raphael (Hawaweeny)
Higher Church Administration Abroad. *See* Church Abroad
Hodgson, Robert, 249, 251–52, 257, 259
Holy Synod, 12–13, 14–15, 24, 34, 40, 42, 49, 54, 61, 63, 65, 67, 69, 70–71, 76–77, 81, 83, 84–85, 88–89, 92–93, 94–95, 100–1, 104–5, 111, 113, 115, 122, 131, 132–33, 135
 and February Revolution, 125–27
 under Patriarch Tikhon, 144–45, 159, 162–63, 169–70, 182, 201, 203–4, 226, 230–31, 264, 265, 269, 276, 297, 300, 301, 307–8, 311, 317
 tensions with the tsar, 111, 122–23
 Tikhon serving on, 108, 121–22, 123–24
Holy Trinity church in Chicago. *See* Chicago
Hotovitzky, Alexander, priest, 45–46, 60–61, 62, 68, 93, 98–100, 153

Ilarion (Troitsky), Archbishop, 137, 223, 274, 285, 293, 296–97

Iliodor (Trufanov), 104–5, 111
immigrants, immigration, 8, 44–45, 57–58, 59, 63–65, 79, 96
Innocent (Veniaminov), Metropolitan, 43, 46, 68, 69, 70–71
Innokenty (Pustynsky), Bishop of Alaska, 70–71, 81, 97–98, 99–100
international reaction to Tikhon's impending trial, 244–48, 250–53
Irvine, Ingram N. W., 93–94
Ispolkomdukh. *See* Executive Committee of Clergy Affairs
Izvestiia, 14, 167, 207, 215, 233
 misinformation, 177, 235, 303
 publishing statements and interviews of Tikhon, 214, 219–20, 285, 291, 295–96, 314

Jackson, Sheldon, 43–44, 49
Janis (Pommers), Archbishop, 276, 277, 279
Jews, 13, 36, 116–17, 118, 136, 175–77, 246. *See also* antisemitism, pogroms
John of Kronstadt (Ioann Sergiev), priest, 14, 62, 63

Kalinin, Mikhail, 186, 219, 241, 247, 302, 314, 325
 permission for Tikhon to serve liturgies, 185, 191–94
 Tikhon writes to, 195, 196, 215–17, 225–26, 232–33, 297
Kamenev, Lev, 179–80, 208, 209, 247, 257
Karlovci Council. *See* Council, Karlovci
Katsaurov, Ivan, 104–5, 109–10
Kholm, 34–41, 42, 54–55, 59, 66–67, 76, 96, 283
Khrapovitsky, Antony. *See* Antony (Khrapovitsky)
Kirill (Smirnov), Metropolitan, 182, 302, 303, 309
Klin, Tikhon's birthplace, 11, 16–18
Kochurov, John, priest, 45, 60–61, 63, 91, 165–66
Kolchak, Alexander, admiral, 171–72, 182–83, 245
Korchinsky, Jacob, priest, 50–51, 58–59
Krasikov, Petr, 131–32, 162–63, 174–75, 180–81, 186, 188–89, 192–93, 196, 199, 215, 225, 325
Krasin, Leonid, 244, 252
Krasnitsky, Vladimir, Renovationist priest, 232–33, 298, 300–3, 304, 305, 326, 327–28
Kremlin (Moscow), 133, 135, 138, 139, 144, 145, 146, 151–52, 160–61, 162, 167

Krylenko, Nikolai, 241, 243
Kursky, Dmitry, 293–94, 297–98, 302
Kuskova, Ekaterina, 208, 210–11

laity, role in church, 14–15, 96–102, 107, 129–30, 135, 136, 156, 161, 292–94, 302–3
    empowerment of by Tikhon, 1–2, 7–8, 46–47, 105, 116, 128–29, 133, 134, 163–64, 294, 320, 326–28
    loyal to Tikhon, 39–40, 170, 182, 185, 192, 238, 240, 258, 263, 285, 297, 327–28
    role in defending the Church, 152, 157–59, 217–18, 220–21, 240–41, 243–44, 262
Latsis, Martin, 178, 179–81, 182–85
Latvia, 264–65, 275–79
legalization of ecclesiastical administration, 229–30, 280–82, 296–98, 300, 301, 305–8, 310, 317, 318, 326
Lenin, Vladimir (Ulianov), 2, 7, 10, 14, 25, 147–48, 155, 165–66, 181, 194, 198–99, 206, 295
    and antireligious policies, 155–56, 162–63, 186, 187, 188–89, 199, 218, 232, 257, 325
    letter of March 19, 1922, 221–22, 228
    Tikhon writes to, 187–88, 189
Liquidation Department, 162–63, 180–81, 186–87, 191–92, 193–94, 199
Lithuania, 9, 11–12, 116–17, 123–24, 264–65, 275–79
    Tikhon as Archbishop of, 113–21
Lithuanian martyrs, relics of, 115–16, 121, 190–91, 194
liturgy, 18, 28, 38, 77, 106, 236, 268–69
Living Church. *See* Renovationists
Lockhart Plot, 167
Lubianka, 183, 223, 230, 246–47, 249–50, 253, 280, 305
Lublin, 36, 40–41
Lvov, Vladimir, chief procurator, 125–29, 132–33

Makary (Nevsky), Metropolitan, 126–27, 129
Markell (Popel), Bishop, 35–36, 37
Mayfield, PA, 57, 68, 87–88, 101
Meletius (Metaxakis), Patriarch of Constantinople, 253–54, 262–63, 274, 276–77, 283–84, 326, 328. *See also* Ecumenical Patriarchate
Mikhail (Ermakov), Metropolitan, 226–27, 269
Minneapolis, 48–49, 60, 86–87
monarchy, Tikhon's attitudes toward, 3, 74–75, 109–10, 118–19, 126, 128–29, 172, 174, 184, 226, 243, 254–55, 314

Mott, John, 131, 212
Mutual Aid Society, Orthodox Catholic, 65, 87–88, 96–97, 100, 101

Nansen, Fritjof, 247
New York, 42–43, 44, 45–46, 47, 48–49, 64–65, 68, 72, 73, 80, 81, 93, 103
    Building church in, 60–63
    transferring cathedral to, 84–85
New York Times, 62, 207, 244
Nicholas II, Tsar, 14, 75–76, 104, 110–11, 125–26
    execution of, 162
    interference in Church affairs, 102, 111, 122–23, 129, 134
    and Tikhon, 40, 61, 71, 73, 74, 81, 112–13, 119–20, 123
Nikandr (Fenomenov), Archbishop, 216–18, 223
Nikolai (Ziorov), Bishop, 42, 44, 45, 46, 47, 70, 80, 82, 99–100
Novorussky, Mikhail, 25, 26–27

OGPU (Joint State Political Administration, 1923–1934), 287, 296, 300, 301, 302, 307–8, 310–13
orphanages, 42, 53–54, 87–88, 209–10

patriarch, authority of, 144–45, 280
patriarchate, restoration of, 24, 75–76, 136–38, 142–43, 147, 249, 261–62, 266–67
Petr (Poliansky), Metropolitan, 297–98, 303, 309, 311, 312, 314, 316–17, 319
Petrograd, 121–22, 123, 124, 127, 129, 133, 137, 144, 149, 154, 155, 157, 161, 162–63, 232. *See also* St. Petersburg
Platon (Rozhdestvensky), Metropolitan, 130, 145, 226–27, 291
Pobedonostsev, Konstantin, 22–24, 35, 40, 69, 74–76, 94, 309
    Tikhon writes to, 29–30, 61, 66, 67, 93
Pogroms, Tikhon's condemnation of, 136, 175–77
Poland, 11–12, 34–41, 203–4, 271–74
Politburo, 211, 215, 219, 221, 222, 228–29, 232, 235–36, 239–40, 294, 305–7, 311–12, 316
    and case against Tikhon, 241, 244–45, 246–49, 252–54, 255–56, 287–88, 295–98
    permission to publish Tikhon's encyclicals, 180–81, 207, 214, 287
Polozov, Iakov, 200–1, 223, 280, 308–10

Pomgol (Soviet famine relief committee under VTsIK), 211–12, 213–16, 218–19
Pommer, Ioann. *See* Janis (Pommers)
Pravda, 233, 235, 283–84, 286, 314
processions, religious, 88–89, 114–15, 144, 146, 157–61, 163, 167
property, church, 2–3, 10, 120–21, 148–49, 155–57, 159, 163, 215, 216, 224–25, 230–31
Protestant missionaries, 8–9, 43–44, 53–54, 90–91
Pskov seminary, 19–22, 29–34

Raphael (Hawaweeny), Bishop, 20, 45–46, 77, 78, 80–82, 85, 92, 97–98
Rasputin, Grigory, 104–5, 122–23, 125–27, 129, 130–31, 132–33, 174–75
Red Terror, 165–67, 168, 169, 177
registration, of Tikhonite church. *See* legalization
relics of saints. *See* antirelic campaign
religious tolerance, Soviets and. *See* freedom of conscience
Renovationists, 254, 258, 259–60, 270, 280–88, 291, 292, 294, 296–98, 303–4, 310, 327–28. *See also* Council, Renovationists; Krasnitsky, Vladimir
  reconciling with the Renovationists, 298–303
  takeover of Church administration, 231–34, 235–36, 240
Revolution of 1905, 73–77, 98, 104, 265
right opposition to Tikhon, 303–5
Rozhdestvensky, Aleksandr, archpriest, 22, 32–33
Russo-Japanese War, 73–77
Rusyns, Ruthenians, 35–36, 37, 44–45, 47–48, 54–55, 56, 58, 86, 88, 100
Rykov, Aleksei, 241, 247, 297–98, 302

Sabler, Vladimir, 35, 42–43, 65–66, 114–15, 122–23
Saint Petersburg, 25, 26–27, 37, 40, 42–43, 57–58, 69, 70–71. *See also* Petrograd
Samarin, Aleksandr, 122–23, 129–31, 158–59, 300–1, 302, 305–7
San Francisco, 44, 46, 47, 48–52, 66, 69, 72–73, 82, 84, 85, 96
Sebastian (Dabovich), archimandrite, 82–84, 91, 93
secret police. *See* Cheka, GPU, and OGPU
Semenova, Maria (Veshneva), 236–39, 240
seminary, establishing in America, 85–87
Serafim (Aleksandrov), Archbishop, 296–98, 311, 314, 315–17

Serafim (Chichagov), Metropolitan, 272–73
Serafim (Lukianov), Archbishop, 275, 276, 277, 278–79, 290
Serbian Orthodox Christians, 78, 79, 82–84
Sergy (Stragorodsky), 127, 130, 235–36, 279, 299, 307–8, 318–21
Shpitsberg, Ivan, 148–49, 186, 190–91, 195, 196, 200–1
Shuia, disorders in, 220–22, 224–25, 227
sobornost, 14–15, 45–46, 96–102, 105, 136, 137, 143, 164, 269, 276–77, 307. *See also* laity, role; Tikhon, sobornost
Sovnarkom. *See* Council of People's Commissars
St. Nicholas church in New York. *See* New York
St. Sergius of Radonezh, relics of, 187–90
Sullivan, Louis, architect, 63
Synod. *See* Holy Synod
Syrian, Syro-Arab Orthodox Christians. *See* Arab Orthodox Christians

Tikhon (Bellavin), Patriarch
  accused of "speculation," 190–95
  anathema against the Bolsheviks. *See* Tikhon, encyclical, anathema, January 19, 1918
  appeals for famine relief, 205–12, 214–15
  arrest (1922), 231, 234, 237, 240
  arrest, first (1918), 169–70
  arrest, second (1919) 182–85
  attempted murder, 174–75
  canonization, 321–23
  case against, 240–44, 246–48
  case closed, 295–96
  contested legacy, 6–7
  dean of Kholm seminary, 34–41
  death, 311–12
  deathbed testament, 314–18
  Decree No. 348, patriarchal, May 5, 1922, on Church Abroad, 226–27, 230, 231, 288–89
  Decree No. 362, November 20, 1920, on Church autonomy, 193, 202, 271, 291
  defrocking, by Renovationist Council, 248–50
  ecumenical relations, 8–9, 90–95
  education, 18–22
  election as Moscow Archbishop, 1–2, 129–33
  election, to the patriarchate, 138–47
  encyclical against confiscation of valuables, February 28, 1922, 216–18, 223, 224, 228–29, 240–41, 254–55
  encyclical, anathema, January 19, 1918, 147–55, 254–55
  encyclical, condemning pogroms, July 21, 1919, 175–77

Tikhon (Bellavin), Patriarch (*cont.*)
  encyclical, on political neutrality, October 8, 1919, 178–81, 204–5, 226, 231, 288–89, 326
  encyclical, on relics of St Sergius, September 10, 1920, 189–90
  encyclical, on Treaty of Brest-Litovsk, March 18, 1918, 162, 254–55
  encyclicals after release, 282–84, 286–87, 288, 289–90
  enthronement, as patriarch, 145–46
  episcopate, view of, 40, 70–71, 78, 83
  family, 11, 15–18, 19, 72
  film about, 286
  health, 305–8, 311–13
  incarceration in Donskoi Monastery, 1922–1923, 236–39
  indictment against, 243–44
  interrogation by Latsis (1919), 182–85
  interrogations, spring 1922, 223–27, 228–31
  interviews with, 153–54, 157, 159–60, 219–20, 285, 296, 303
  letter on Lenin's death, 295
  letter to Soviet leaders, November 7, 1918, 168–69
  letters to Soviet officials (*see* Kalinin, Mikhail; Lenin, Vladimir)
  Lithuania, Archbishop of (*see* Tikhon, Vilna, Archbishop of)
  Lublin, Bishop of, 40–41
  monastic tonsure, 33
  patriarchal authority, 139–40, 202–4, 208, 229–30, 282–83, 285, 286–87, 296, 297, 315
  petition to the Supreme Court, 254–55
  political views after October Revolution, 151–52, 154, 159–60, 161–62, 171–74, 183–84, 205, 224, 230, 280–82, 283, 289–90, 314–15
  political views, 2, 9, 26–27, 74–75, 77, 108–13, 114–15, 119, 128–29, 131–32
  release from prison, 260, 280
  sermons, 37, 120, 326–27
  sermons after 1917, 162, 167, 172–74, 285
  sermons in America, 46–47, 52–53, 57, 62, 64–65, 70–71, 74–75, 78, 81, 85, 88–89, 96, 97–98, 103
  sobornost, 7–8, 96–102, 128–29, 130–31, 132–33, 134, 135–36, 146–47, 325–28 (*see also* sobornost)
  sobornost, under the Soviets, 164, 280–82, 285, 294, 303
  Soviet attempts to undermine Tikhon's authority, 169–70, 179–80, 196, 199, 248, 250, 256, 292–93
  teacher at Pskov seminary, 29–32
  trial, preparation for, 240–44
  views of patriarchal authority, 76–77, 229, 267–68, 271–72, 280, 294
  Vilna, Archbishop of 113–21
  Yaroslavl, Archbishop of, 105–15
Tikhon (Sharapov), Bishop, 273, 274
Tikhonite Church, 240, 248, 250–51, 255–56, 258, 287–88, 297–98, 299–300, 302, 307–8, 310, 317–18
Tolstoy, Leo, 25, 26, 27, 38–39, 95
Toropets, 17–20, 42, 59, 68, 71
Toth, Alexis, priest, 54, 55–56
Trial of 54 Moscow clergy and laity, 228–31
Trinity-St. Sergius Lavra, 143–44, 178–79, 187–88
Trotsky, Lev, 147–49, 228, 239–40, 247, 257, 325
  and the Renovationist schism, 222, 231–32, 234
  and seizure of church valuables, 213, 215, 218–19, 220–21, 222
Trubetskoi, Grigory, 171–72, 181
Tuchkov, Evgeny, 232–33, 237, 239–40, 249–50, 295–97, 307–8, 309–11, 312, 315–17, 325–26
  pressure on Tikhon to compromise, 291, 293, 300–3, 305
  and Tikhon's "repentance," 253, 256–57, 280–82, 283
Turkevich, Benedict, Priest, 42–43, 86–87, 99–100
Turkevich, Leonid, Priest, 101–2, 138, 333

Ukraine, 11–12, 13, 35, 44–45, 57–58, 60, 162, 175–76
  autocephaly, 264–65, 266–70
Uniates, 11–12, 35–36, 44–45, 54–55, 58, 96, 101. *See also* Greek Catholics
Union of Russian People (URP), 104–5, 108–13, 114–15, 118–19, 245
United Kingdom. *See* Britain
Ustvolsky, Serafim (Stefan), 59–60

Varnava (Nakropin), Bishop, 122–23
Veniamin (Fedchenkov), Metropolitan, 171–72, 181, 204–5, 289

Veniamin (Kazansky), Metropolitan, 129, 149, 155, 232–33, 235–36, 252
Vilna (Vilnius), 113, 114–19, 133, 242–43, 332
Vilnius martyrs, relics of, 190–91
Vinogradov, Vasily, priest, 300, 315–16
Vinokurov, Aleksandr, 213–16
Vladimir (Bogoiavlensky), Metropolitan, 122–23, 125–26, 140, 141–42, 145–46, 165–66
Vostorgov, Ioann, Archpriest, 167
Vvedensky, Aleksandr, Renovationist priest, 232–34, 248–49, 251
Vyshinsky, Andrei, 243

Warsaw, 34, 36, 272–73
White Army, 6, 147–48, 169, 171–75, 178–81, 193, 198, 201–2, 240–41
  Soviet allegations, 182–83, 185, 243–44
  Tikhon and, 172, 173, 174, 175–76, 177
Women, 107, 129–30, 135, 158–59, 164, 236–39, 284
World War I, 119–21, 161–62

Yaroslavl, 9, 104–7, 108–10, 112–15, 235–36, 245
Yaroslavsky, Emilian, 242–43, 247–48, 252
  and Tikhon's "repentance," 253–57, 282–83, 291–92

Zhirkevich, Aleksandr, 117–19, 121